JOHN THE THEOLOGIAN AND HIS PASCHAL GOSPEL

This study brings three different kinds of readers of the Gospel of John together with the theological goal of understanding what is meant by Incarnation and how it relates to Pascha, the Passion of Christ, how this is conceived of as revelation, and how we speak of it. The first group of readers are the Christian writers from the early centuries, some of whom (such as Irenaeus of Lyons) stood in direct continuity, through Polycarp of Smyrna, with John himself. In exploring these writers, John Behr offers a glimpse of the figure of John and the celebration of Pascha, which held to have started with him.

The second group of readers are modern scriptural scholars, from whom we learn of the apocalyptic dimensions of John's Gospel and the way in which it presents the life of Christ in terms of the Temple and its feasts. With Chris's own body, finally erected on the Cross, being the true Temple in an offering of love rather than a sacrifice for sin. An offering in which Jesus becomes the flesh he offers for consumption, the bread which descends from heaven, so that 'incarnation' is not an event now in the past, but the embodiment of God in those who follow Christ in the present.

The third reader is Michel Henry, a French Phenomenologist, whose reading of John opens up further surprising dimensions of this Gospel, which yet align with those uncovered in the first parts of this work. This thought-provoking work brings these threads together to reflect on the nature and task of Christian theology.

John Behr is the Regius Chair in Humanity at the University of Aberdeen. He previously served as Fr George's Florovsky Distinguished Professor of Patristics at St Vladimir's Seminary, where he acted as Dean from 2007–17, and the Metropolitan Kallistos Chair of Orthodox Theology at the Vrije Universiteit of Amsterdam. His publications include critical editions and translations of the fragments of Diodore of Tarsus and Theodore of Mopuestia (2011) and *Origen's On First Principles* (2017). He is also the author of *Irenaeus of Lyons: Identifying Christianity* (2013), *Becoming Human: Theological Anthropology in Word and Image* (2013), and *Asceticism and Anthropology in Irenaeus and Clement* (2000).

John the Theologian and his Paschal Gospel

A Prologue to Theology

JOHN BEHR

OXFORD
UNIVERSITY PRESS

Great Clarendon Street, Oxford, OX2 6DP,
United Kingdom

Oxford University Press is a department of the University of Oxford. It furthers the University's objective of excellence in research, scholarship, and education by publishing worldwide. Oxford is a registered trade mark of Oxford University Press in the UK and in certain other countries

First published 2019
First published in paperback 2021

Published in the United States of America by Oxford University Press
198 Madison Avenue, New York, NY 10016, United States of America

British Library Cataloguing in Publication Data
Data available

Library of Congress Cataloging in Publication Data
Data available

Printed and bound by
CPI Group (UK) Ltd, Croydon, CR0 4YY

ISBN 978–0–19–883753–4 (Hbk.)
ISBN 978–0–19–284491–0 (Pbk.)

For Leon Lysaght and John Barnet

Preface

After I let it be known a few years ago that I was writing a book on John, I was often asked how my commentary is coming on. To avoid disappointment or confusion, I should make it clear up-front: this is not a commentary on John! It is rather an attempt to put into dialogue various readers of John, ancient and modern—Fathers, especially from the second and third centuries but also later figures, and modern scriptural scholars, theologians, and philosophers—with, ultimately, a theological goal: that of understanding what is meant by Incarnation and how it relates to the Passion, how this is conceived of as revelation, and how we speak of it, that is, the relationship between scriptural exegesis and theological discourse.

The genesis of this volume lies primarily in the work in which I have been engaged over the past decades on the Fathers of the first centuries, especially Irenaeus and Origen. Having made my way in a series of publications through to the controversies of the sixth century, I realized that to go further meant returning backwards, to reconsider Origen's *On First Principles*. During the preparation of a new edition of that work, I was also asked to write a new volume on Irenaeus, taking me back even earlier. This immersion in the literature of early Christianity persuaded me that they were not reading John, and especially the Prologue to his Gospel, in the way that we often presume today. That is, they did not read the Prologue as a narrative of a 'pre-Incarnate Word' (a phrase I have yet to encounter in the Fathers) who subsequently becomes incarnate by being born in the world to return later on through the Passion to the Father, such that 'Incarnation' is 'an episode in the biography of the Word', as Rowan Williams (negatively) characterized it. Indeed, so much is this not the case, that the classic work devoted to the topic, *On the Incarnation* by Athanasius, speaks of creation as having been effected by 'our Lord Jesus Christ' and barely even mentions the birth of Jesus!

Persuaded that something more is going on, I began reading through modern scriptural scholarship on John, and found that, even while such a picture is often presumed, fresh avenues of reflection have opened up in recent decades, especially with the work of John Ashton and those whom he has inspired, seeing the Gospel of John in terms of the apocalyptic literature of the late first century. At the same time, Russ Hittinger recommended that I read *I Am the Truth* by Michel Henry; fascinated by this work, I found myself going even further back, this time to my initial studies in continental philosophy, to retrace the path that led to Henry and his work. It is these threads that are brought together in this present volume. Its central argument is that Incarnation should be understood not as a past event, but as the ongoing embodiment of God in those who follow Christ.

The work begins with various methodological considerations in the Introduction, in particular Quentin Skinner's caution regarding the 'mythology of doctrines' and Hans-Georg Gadamer's notion of the 'effective-history' always at work in the process of understanding. It also considers briefly ways in which early Fathers understood the identity of Jesus as the Word of God other than as 'an episode in a biography', the notion of 'pre-existence' and 'incarnation' as analysed by Hebert McCabe, and concludes with a section on the readers we have invited to this theological symposium. Part I is devoted to the question of the identity of John and the particular character of his Gospel. It begins in Chapter 1, building upon the work of Richard Bauckham and Charles Hill, by considering the identity of John, as he is remembered in the second century, especially by those who trace their lineage to him. Of particular interest here is that they look back to him not only as the author of the Gospel (and the Apocalypse), but as the one whose observance of Pascha, Easter, they claim to follow, and indeed it seems that initially they were the only ones to keep this feast. Chapter 2 picks up Ashton's suggestion that the Gospel should be understood as 'an apocalypse—in reverse, upside down, inside out' in the light of more recent work on the subject of apocalyptic literature and apocalypticism ('the mother of all Christian theology', as Ernst Käsemann put it), the relationship between the Apocalypse attributed to John and the Gospel, the particular character of his Gospel as a 'paschal gospel', and what is entailed by all this for the discipline of reading Scripture *as Scripture*. Part II turns to the Gospel of John, considering it under two different facets of embodiment that are 'finished' at the cross: the Temple and the living human being, the Son of Man, this last category being one of the more significant places (alongside the treatment of John 6) where insights from Irenaeus and others are brought to bear upon the texts from John. The final chapter of Part II suggests that if the Gospel can be considered as a paschal gospel, the Prologue is best understood as a 'paschal hymn', and offers a way of reading this text very different to those usually given today, despite all their variety. Part III explores Michel Henry's reading of John, bringing the work so far developed into dialogue with his own phenomenological reading, giving further clarity to the life that the Word offers and the flesh that the Word becomes and in turn clarifying some aspects of Henry's phenomenological presentation of Christianity. The Conclusion draws our findings together and offers some suggestions regarding the nature and task of theology. The three parts of this work are thus each engaged with a different body of scholarship—respectively: historical investigation, scriptural exegesis, and philosophical reflection—though there is of course overlap, especially between the first two parts. These three different disciplines are brought together with, ultimately, a constructive theological purpose. As such, this work is understood as itself a prologue to theology.

It should be noted that I use the terms the 'Passion' and 'Pascha' ('Easter') to refer to the singular event embracing the Crucifixion, Resurrection, Ascension, and Pentecost. I do this for two reasons. First, because this is, as we will see, how the writers of the early centuries speak, and continue to do so even when, from the fourth century onwards, this singular feast of Pascha is refracted, as it were, into a spectrum of particular feasts. The 'Passion' does not refer, at least for these writers, to the suffering in Gesthsemane and on the cross *in distinction to* the resurrection and the joy it brings: the cross is the sign of victory, the means of life, and the source of joy. The second reason is that even when refracted into different commemorations, the crucifixion and resurrection still hold together in the unity of the single event; they are, indeed, aspects of it. This is particularly important in regard to the question of that most notable theme coming from the Gospel of John, the Incarnation. It was many centuries before a feast of the nativity was added to the liturgical calendar, and when it is, it is celebrated as seen through the prism of the Passion, as an aspect of Pascha. Skinner's caution regarding the mythology of doctrines holds with regard to liturgy as well: now that we have a full cycle of liturgical celebrations from the Annunciation to Pentecost (and before and after this, for the Marian feasts), it is very hard to think otherwise than in terms of a series of discrete events leading from conception and birth (this being taken as the moment of 'Incarnation') to death and resurrection. Yet, as scriptural scholars have long pointed out, the Gospels are told from the perspective of the end. Likewise, the liturgical year opens out from Pascha, the first feast to be celebrated (in particular, if not uniquely, by those following John), extending both backwards and forwards. Pascha, both historically and theologically, this work argues, is the starting point and register in which to hear the Gospel of John and also its Prologue. It is only more recently that the Prologue has come to be read as the Christmas reading, reinforcing the idea that 'Incarnation' can be separated from the Passion: in the Western tradition, from around the thirteenth century, it was the reading, the 'second gospel', that concluded the celebration of the Mass, the Word becoming flesh in the bread of the eucharistic celebration and in the communicant; in the Eastern tradition (in which I stand), it is the Paschal reading, read at the midnight liturgy, the transition from darkness to light—a Paschal hymn and a prologue to theology.

This work has been many years in preparation, and so there are a great many people to thank. The seed for the ideas were developed in a seminar I gave at St Vladimir's Seminary on the Paschal Christ; the questions asked by the students and the ensuing discussion were instrumental in helping shape the work in its initial stages. As the work developed, I benefitted considerably from many colleagues, especially: Bishop Suriel, Conor Cunningham, Crina Gschwandtner, Philip Kariatlis, Andrew Louth, George Parsenios, Paul Saieg, and Richard Schneider. I had the opportunity to present a key part of my work as my inaugural lecture as the Metropolitan Kallistos (Ware) Chair of

Orthodox Theology at the Vrije Universiteit in Amsterdam, and I thank my colleagues there for the honour of appointing me to this Chair and for the feedback they gave me during a wonderful seminar. I also had the opportunity to present the work as a whole to members of the University of Divinity in Sydney and, in Moscow, to members of the Saints Cyril and Methodius Postgraduate School and the St Philaret's Institute, and to the Community of the Servants of the Will of God in Crawley Down, and benefitted considerably from the wide-ranging discussions these opportunities generated. No work of this scale, of course, could be completed without the support of librarians; I thank Eleana Silk for all the materials that she tracked down for me. My gratitude is also owed to Tom Perridge, at Oxford University Press, for his encouragement regarding this work over the past years, and to all those at the Press who have helped see this work into print. This work, furthermore, has benefitted immensely from the various readers' reports: their input, especially when the work was still in process, was vital in helping focus and sharpen the arguments developed therein. Lastly, this book is dedicated to two colleagues, in different capacities, and friends—John Barnet and Liam Lysaght—without whose support and encouragement over the past years this work would never have been written.

Contents

List of Abbreviations

Abbreviations for classical and Patristic texts are those found in the following:

The SBL Handbook of Style for Ancient Near Eastern, Biblical and Early Christian Studies, ed. P. H. Alexander et al. (Peabody, MA: Hendrickson, 1999).

For texts not listed in this handbook, the following have been used:

H. G. Liddell and R. Scott, *A Greek-English Lexicon*, rev. H. S. Jones with R. McKenzie, 9th edn, with revised supplement (Oxford: Clarendon Press, 1996).

G. W. Lampe, *A Patristic Greek Lexicon* (Oxford: Clarendon Press, 1961).

Scriptural references have been given according to the LXX; this principally affects the numeration of the Psalms and the naming of 1 and 2 Samuel and 1 and 2 Kings as 1–4 Kingdoms.

ACW	Ancient Christian Writers
ANF	Ante-Nicene Fathers
ATANT	Abhandlung zur Theologie des Alten und Neuen Testaments
BBET	Beiträge zur biblischen Exegese und Theologie
BET	Bibical Exegesis and Theology
BETL	Biblioteca Ephemeridum Theologicarum Lovaniensum
BIS	Biblical Interpretation Series
BJS	Brown Judaic Studies
BZ	*Biblische Zeitschrift*
BZNW	*Beihefte zur Zeitschrift für die neutestamentliche Wissenschaft*
CBQ	*Catholic Biblical Quarterly*
CBR	*Currents in Biblical Research*
CCSG	Corpus Christianorum: Series Graeca
CCSL	Corpus Christianorum: Series Latina
CH	*Church History*
CRINT	Compendia Rerum Iudaicarum ad Novum Testamentum
CSCO	Corpus Scriptorum Christianorum Orientalum
CSEL	Corpus Scriptorum Ecclesiasticorum Latinorum
CSHB	Corpus Scriptorum Historiae Byzantinae
ET	English translation
ExpTim	*Expository Times*
FC	Fathers of the Church

FRLANT	Forschungen zur Religion und Literatur des Alten und Neuen Testaments
GCS	Die griechischen christlichen Schriftsteller der ersten [drei] Jarhunderte
GNO	Gregorii Nysseni Opera
GOTR	*Greek Orthodox Theological Review*
HSS	Harvard Semitic Studies
HTR	*Harvard Theological Review*
JBL	*Journal of Biblical Literature*
JECS	*Journal of Early Christian Studies*
JETS	*Journal of the Evangelical Theological Society*
JSJ	*Journal for the Study of Judaism*
JSNT	*Journal for the Study of the New Testament*
JSNTSup	Journal for the Study of the New Testament Supplement Series
JSOT	*Journal for the Study of the Old Testament*
JSOTSup	Journal for the Study of the Old Testament Supplement Series
JTS	*Journal of Theological Studies*
LCL	Loeb Classical Library
LNTS	Library of New Testament Studies
LSJ	Henry George Liddell and Robert Scott, revised by Henry Stuart Jones, *A Greek-English Lexicon* (Oxford: Clarendon Press, 1996)
LXX	Septuagint
Mansi	J. D. Mansi, ed., *Sacrorum conciliorum nova et amplissima collectio* (Florence, 1759–98)
MT	Masoretic Text
NF	Neue Folge
NovT	*Novum Testamentum*
NPNF	Nicene and Post Nicene Fathers
NTS	*New Testament Studies*
OCA	Orientalia Christiana Analecta
OCP	*Orientalia Christiana Periodica*
OECS	Oxford Early Christian Studies
OECT	Oxford Early Christian Texts
PG	Patrologia Graeca
PL	Patrologia Latina
PO	Patrologia Orientalis
PPS	Popular Patristic Series
PTS	Patristische Texte und Studien
RB	*Revue biblique*

RevistB	*Revista bíblica*
RSR	*Recherches des science religieuse*
SBL	Society of Biblical Literature
SBLMS	Society of Biblical Literature Monograph Series
SBLSP	Society of Biblical Literature Seminar Papers
SBLDS	Society of Biblical Literature Dissertation Series
SC	Sources chrétiennes
SJLA	Studies in Judaism in Late Antiquity
SJT	*Scottish Journal of Theology*
SNTSMS	Society for New Testament Studies Monograph Series
SPCK	Society for the Promotion of Christian Knowledge
STI	Studies in Theological Interpretation
SupNovT	Supplements to Novum Testamentum
SupVC	Supplements to Vigiliae Christianae
SVTQ	*St Vladimir's Theological Quarterly*
TDNT	*Theological Dictionary of the New Testament*. Ed. G. Kittel and G. Friedrich; ET G. W. Bromiley, 10 vols. (Grand Rapids, MI: Eerdmans, 1964–76)
TU	Texte und Untersuchungen
VC	*Vigiliae Christianae*
WGRW	Writings from the Greco-Roman World
WMANT	Wissenschaftliche Monographien zum Alten and Neuen Testament
WTJ	*Westminster Theological Journal*
WUNT	Wissenschaftliche Untersuchungen zum Neuen Testament
ZAC	*Zeitschrift für Antikes Christentum*
ZKT	*Zeitschrift für katholische Theologie*
ZNW	*Zeitschrift für die neutestamentliche Wissenschaft und die Kunde der älteren Kirche*

ὁδὸς ἄνω κάτω μία καὶ ὡυτή
The way up and down is one and the same

Heraclitus, 61 [F38]

Ἐπεὶ γὰρ οὖν ἐγίγνετ᾽ ἄνθρωπος θεὸς
θεὸς τελεῖτ᾽ ἄνθρωπος εἰς τιμὴν ἐμήν·

Since then God became human
the human ends up as God to my honour.

Gregory the Theologian, *Carmina Dogmatica* 1.1.10,
De incarnatione, adversus Apollinarium (PG 37.465a)

Ἀλλὰ μυστικῶς τῷ ῥητῷ τῆς ἱστορίας τὸ τῆς θεωρίας ἄρρητον
ὁ μέγας ἐξέδωκε διὰ τοῦ Πνεύματος εὐαγγελιστὴς Ἰωάννης,
ἵνα τὸν ἡμέτερον νοῦν διὰ τῶν ἱστορουμένων
ἐπὶ τὴν ἀλήθειαν ὁδηγήσῃ τῶν νοουμένων.

To be sure, the great Evangelist John, through the Spirit, mystically gave
the literal word of the narrative the wordless character of a contemplation,
so that through it he might guide our intellect to the truth of its intelligible meaning.

Maximus the Confessor, *Ad. Thal.* 4.2

Introduction

The Gospel of John and Christian Theology

Christian theology, as we know it, is inconceivable without the Gospel of John and especially its Prologue. Within a century or so after its composition, it was described as 'the spiritual gospel' and in the following centuries its author was referred to simply as 'the theologian'. Its opening lines present the basic lineaments of Christian theology thereafter, in striking and beguilingly simple words. It begins with the Word in the beginning, with God, and as God. All things were made by him, we are told, the one who is the life and light of all human beings, shining in the darkness of this world, but not overcome by it. After a few lines about John the Baptist, which many scholars think are later additions to an original poem or hymn about the Word, we hear that the Word became flesh, enabling us to see his glory, full of grace and truth, by which we are given the possibility of being born of God. After further words about the Baptist, also possibly added later, this short text concludes that, while the Law was given through Moses, grace and truth have come through Jesus Christ (now mentioned by name for the first time), and so, although no one has ever seen God, the only-begotten God, resting in the bosom of the Father, has now, nevertheless, made him known. The Word, with God and as God, and the becoming flesh of this Word, stated here in simple and beautiful prose, are the key points that theology would grapple with in subsequent centuries, in controversies that resulted in imperially convoked world-wide councils which defined, dogmatically, the chief articles of the Christian faith: Trinity and Incarnation.

This dramatic opening to the Fourth Gospel, beginning in the divine realm rather than on earth, is quite unlike that of the other three canonical Gospels, and its uniqueness continues in the narrative that follows. For, unlike the Synoptics, the Christ who appears on the pages of John manifests the glory of God at every point, such that Ernst Käsemann would notoriously describe him as 'a God striding over the earth'.[1] He further asserts that the Passion is but 'a mere postscript [to the Gospel] which had to be included because John could not ignore this tradition nor yet could he fit it organically into his work', and so decries the Gospel as little more than 'naïve Docetism'.[2] And yet, in this Gospel, as Luke Timothy Johnson points out, Jesus often appears more human than in the others: here alone he has friends and even cries at the death of one of them.[3] Writing over half a century before Käsemann, Harnack, in words echoed by Käsemann, stated the paradox, and problem, forcefully:

> Looking at it from a literary- and systematic-historical standpoint, the formation of John's Gospel is incidentally the greatest riddle that Christianity's most ancient history offers: It depicts a Christ who puts the indescribable into words and proclaims as his own witness what is the very basis of this witness and what his disciples sensed of him: a Pauline Christ walking upon the earth, speaking and acting, far more human than that one and yet far more divine, [with] an abundance of connections to the historical Jesus, yet at the same time the most sovereign treatment and displacement of history.[4]

The Gospel, Harnack continues, reaches it apogee in the seventeenth chapter, the chapter that Käsemann focused upon in his study: here 'one feels that it is Christ who awoke in the disciple what he has returned to him in words. But word and deed, history and doctrine are enveloped in the light mist of what is ecclesial-historical, trans-historical, but also un-historical and spectral, while embedded in a hard and unreal contrast'. Over a century later than Harnack, Bart Ehrman came to a similar conclusion, describing his shock at his realization, after reading only the Synoptics for three years and then turning to the Gospel of John ('In Greek. In one sitting', no less!), that here Jesus himself has been elided, for his words 'are not Jesus's words; they are John's words placed on Jesus's lips'. It is this rewriting of history, and of Jesus himself, that enables John, Ehrman asserts, to make 'bald statements that equate Jesus with God and say that he was a pre-existent divine being who came into the world . . . [that] Jesus was equal with God and even shared his name and his glory in his preincarnate state'.[5] The Gospel, its origins, presentation of the

[1] Ernst Käsemann, *The Testament of Jesus: A Study of the Gospel in the Light of Chapter 17*, trans. Gerhard Krodel (Philadelphia: Fortress, 1968 [German 1966]), 9 ('schreitend', translated by Krodel, as 'going about'). In an earlier article Käsemann had spoken of Christ, in John, as 'walking' (wandelnd): 'Aufbau und Anliegen des johanneischen Prolog', in Walter Matthias and Ernest Wolf, eds, *Libertas Christiana: Friedrich Delekat zum 65. Geburtstag*, Beiträge zur evangelischen Theologie 26 (Munich: Kaiser, 1957), 75–99.

[2] Käsemann, *Testament*, 7, 26.

[3] Luke Timothy Johnson, *The Real Jesus: The Misguided Quest for the Historical Jesus and the Truth of the Traditional Gospels* (San Francisco: Harper Collins, 1997), 156.

[4] Adolf von Harnack, *Lehrbuch der Dogmengeschichte*, 4th edn (Darmstadt: Wissenschaftliche Buchgesellschaft, 1964 [Tübingen 1909]), 1.108 (Prolegomena, §5, Zusatz 4).

[5] Bart D. Ehrman, *How Jesus Became God: The Exaltation of a Jewish Preacher from Galilee* (San Francisco: HarperCollins, 2014), 270–1.

humanity of Christ, and indeed what it is to be human, and also its handling of history and theology, time and eternity, remain very much a riddle, 'the greatest riddle' of early Christianity.

And yet, there is unanimous agreement that the Gospel of John is the prime example of a 'high Christology': it begins 'from above', with a divine pre-existent figure, the Word, who then becomes a human being in our own time, though now in times past. During the last century this was often viewed as a betrayal of the actual human figure of Jesus and the 'low Christology' of primitive Christianity. More recent scholarship, however, has become increasingly aware of the complex world, or worlds, of ancient Judaism, and the background of early Christianity in Second Temple Judaism, its liturgy, and its, often apocalyptic, mysticism, and it has become more accustomed to living in (or at least thinking in terms of) a world in which divine heavenly figures might descend from above or visionaries and mystics might ascend from below. It is certainly the case that some of the earliest Christian proclamations spoke of the crucified Jesus being 'made Lord and Christ' (Acts 2:36) or being appointed to divine sonship at his resurrection (Rom. 1:3–4). But it is now generally accepted that it is not the case that an originally 'low Christology' developed over time into a 'high Christology', for some kind of divine pre-existence was ascribed to Christ, if not from the very beginning, then at least from the earliest Christian writings we have, the letters of Paul: whether as one who, while being 'in the form of God', 'lowered himself' by taking on the form of a servant and undergoing crucifixion, to then being exalted, or hyperexalted, to bear the very divine name itself (Phil. 2:5–11), or as the agent of creation (1 Cor. 8:6), or as the spiritual rock, providing spiritual waters to the Israelites in the wilderness (1 Cor. 10:4), or the human being who came 'from heaven', rather than from the earth as did Adam (1 Cor. 15:47), one who is perhaps an 'angel of God' (Gal. 4:14).[6] Moreover, this pre-existent divine being did not simply appear among us, but was affirmed to have been 'born of a woman' (Gal. 4:4). And yet, even acknowledging that the pre-existence of Christ was affirmed earlier than had earlier been thought, it is clear that John has taken a further step: this pre-existent divine being is himself no less than God with God, and becomes incarnate to dwell among us on earth, as, in Rowan Williams' arresting phrase, 'an episode in the biography of the Word',[7] before

[6] The literature just from recent decades is immense. For a comprehensive and compelling presentation, and references to an abundance of secondary literature, see Larry Hurtado, *Lord Jesus Christ: Devotion to Jesus in Earliest Christianity* (Grand Rapids, MI: Eerdmans, 2003) and Larry Hurtado, *Ancient Jewish Monotheism and Early Christian Jesus-Devotion: The Context and Character of Christological Faith*, Library of Early Christianity (Waco, TX: Baylor University Press, 2017); and Richard Bauckham, *Jesus and the God of Israel: God Crucified and Other Studies on the New Testament's Christology of Divine Identity* (Grand Rapids, MI: Eerdmans, 2008).

[7] Rowan Williams, *Arius: Heresy and Tradition*, 2nd edn (London: SCM Press, 2001 [1987]), 244; the context of this phrase is negative, for reasons we will consider in the second section of this chapter.

returning to heaven, taking his human nature with him. 'Incarnational Christology' begins with the Prologue of John, and, it is held, quickly comes to predominate, replacing an exaltation model as too low a view of the Son and Word of God.

So fertile is the Gospel of John that it was the first Gospel to receive a commentary, already in the second century, and of course innumerable times thereafter throughout the ages. So what more can be said? As it turns out, there is much more to be said. Johannine scholarship, as we will see, has developed remarkably over the last couple of decades, in what constitutes nothing less than a complete paradigm shift. Foremost here is John Ashton, whose book *Understanding the Fourth Gospel* has become a landmark and the author himself characterized as 'one of the juggernauts of Johannine scholarship'.[8] In the first edition of his work, the first part of the book was devoted to reviewing the previous century of Johannine scholarship, a span that Ashton divides around the figure of Rudolf Bultmann—'Before Bultmann' and 'After Bultmann'—the most important of all twentieth-century Johannine scholars.[9] It is perhaps not too far-fetched to say that Ashton's own work is also such a turning point, so that work hereafter will be described as 'After Ashton'. Building upon recent scholarship, in particular that of J. Louis Martyn, and drawing upon the revival of interest in apocalypticism, Ashton concluded that 'the fourth evangelist conceives of his own work as an apocalypse—in reverse, upside down, inside out'.[10] This is indeed a fascinating suggestion, and one that we will explore further in subsequent chapters. And yet, while taking back some of his previous claims about the Gospel as an apocalypse, Ashton concludes the more recent, popular version of his work, by asserting that 'despite what seems to be a general consensus among Johannine scholars the fourth evangelist was not a theologian', not, at least, if by that one means someone rationally reflecting about God or working out 'a consistent and satisfactory Christology'.[11]

And here's the rub. What are we to make of this Gospel and its author: is he, or is he not, a theologian? How do we read this apparently most simple, and yet most perplexing of Gospels? What are we to make of his 'incarnational' theology? What is meant by 'Incarnation' anyway, despite it being such a beguilingly easy concept to use? Who is this Word and what is the 'flesh' that the Word becomes? Is it really the case that the Passion is uneasily appended to the Gospel as a mere nod to tradition, and does an 'incarnational'

[8] The words are those of Tom Thatcher, quoted by John Ashton in, 'Second Thoughts on the Fourth Gospel', in Tom Thatcher, ed., *What We Have Heard from the Beginning: The Past, Present, and Future of Johannine Scholarship* (Waco TX: Baylor University Press, 2007), 1–18, at 1.

[9] John Ashton, *Understanding the Fourth Gospel* (Oxford: Oxford University Press, 1991).

[10] John Ashton, *Understanding the Fourth Gospel*, new edn. (Oxford: Oxford University Press, 2007), 328–9. Hereafter I will be referring to this edition.

[11] John Ashton, *The Gospel of John and Christian Origins* (Fortress, 2014), 201.

Christology really replace one focused on the Passion and exaltation? And if he is to be recognized as 'a theologian', or more correctly '*the* theologian', what does this mean for our understanding of Christian theology and the nature of its discourse? These are the questions that this book addresses, and its argument is that the Gospel, together with its Prologue, in fact pivots upon the Passion—it is a 'paschal gospel'—such that the becoming flesh of the Word speaks not of the birth of a 'pre-incarnate Word', but of Jesus' ascending the cross to the Father to be identified as the apocalyptic Son of Man whose flesh is in turn brought down from heaven to be eaten, so that he dwells in those who see his glory and who themselves take up the cross to become his witnesses, born of God in their own martyrdom and born into life as living human beings, the glory of God, the completion of the Temple, and perfection of God's stated purpose in the opening chapter of Scripture, that is, to make human beings in his image. The Incarnation, in brief, is not 'an episode in a biography', an event now in the past, but the ongoing embodiment of God in those who follow Christ. This is a bold argument and it further entails, as we will see, careful attention to how Scripture is read *as Scripture* and what we understand to be the nature of the discourse of theology.

But, before we can turn to John and his Gospel, we need first to consider carefully where we stand in such an investigation, and in particular how our own presuppositions for reading him, and indeed his early readers, have been shaped by the centuries of theological reflection that followed. We will begin this task with some methodological considerations, drawing especially from Quentin Skinner and his caution about 'the mythology of doctrines', and Hans-Georg Gadamer and the role of tradition in understanding, and look at some examples of how neglect of this has adversely affected studies of early Christian theology and its relation to scriptural exegesis. We will then turn, in section two, to consider how the 'mythology of doctrines' has led to a rather mythological understanding of 'Incarnation' by way of a provocative essay written by Herbert McCabe and some further examples from the early centuries of how the identity of Jesus as the Word of God was thought otherwise than as an 'episode in a biography'. This chapter concludes with a third section considering the different kind of readers of John who are brought into dialogue in this volume and the constructive theological project to be accomplished.

METHODOLOGY AND MYTHOLOGY

The picture described in the opening paragraph of this chapter is readily recognizable to all with even only a passing acquaintance with the Christian faith. The Word of God, who is with God from all eternity, at a certain moment in time became flesh, becoming incarnate as a human being (presumably by being born of the Virgin Mary, although the Prologue does not in fact mention a birth any more than the infancy narratives in Matthew and Luke, recounting the birth of the Son of God, mention the Word of God) and, after fulfilling his work upon earth, then returns to the Father by ascending, with his humanity, to the divine realm, so that the Incarnation is 'an episode in the biography of the Word'. Put this way, the 'Incarnation', along with the Trinity—for it is the second person of the Trinity who becomes incarnate—is presupposed as a standard article of Christian doctrine. So strong is this presupposition that it is almost inconceivable to think of Christian theology without it.

But precisely for this reason due caution is needed when reading the Gospel of John, and indeed other early Christian texts contributing to the history of Christian theology. Particularly helpful here is Quentin Skinner's analysis of the various mythologies, especially 'the mythology of doctrine', that operate when due care is not taken.[12] Although his concern is primarily with early modern social and political thought, his comments are also salutary for theological investigation. By 'the mythology of doctrines', Skinner means 'the expectation that each classic writer . . . will be found to enunciate some doctrine on each of the topics regarded as constitutive of the subject'.[13] It is impossible to study any text without bringing our own expectations and prejudgements about what is being said in the text, for, as Skinner acknowledges, 'the models and preconceptions in terms of which we unavoidably organise and adjust our perceptions and thoughts will themselves tend to act as determinants of what we think and perceive'.[14] However, the problem this raises for intellectual history is that 'our expectations about what someone must be saying or doing will themselves determine that we understand the agent to be doing something which they would not—or even could not—have accepted as an account of what they *were* doing'.[15] Presuming that our way of organizing or classifying our understanding of a discipline and its component elements, our 'paradigm' to use Kuhn's word, is essential to the discipline itself, as some kind of eternally fixed constellation of themes in which every previous writer has also worked, is to labour under a 'mythology of doctrines'.

Doing so leads into various historical absurdities. There is, for instance, 'the danger of converting some scattered or incidental remarks by classic theorists into their "doctrine" on one of the expected themes', often resulting in the claim that writers held a view about something which, in principle, they cannot have

[12] Quentin Skinner, 'Meaning and Understanding in the History of Ideas', *History and Theory* 8 (1969), 3–53; reprinted in a much abbreviated and extensively revised version in Quentin Skinner, *Visions of Politics*, vol. 1, *Regarding Method* (Cambridge: Cambridge University Press, 2002), 57–89; it is to this latter version that I will refer.

[13] Skinner, 'Meaning', 59. [14] Ibid. 58. [15] Ibid. 59, italics original.

possibly meant, or alternatively, having assumed that they did indeed mean to give an account of a certain doctrine, the historian is left to explain why they failed to do so and to reconstruct their understanding of the doctrine 'from guesses and hints'.[16] Ideas and doctrines have been 'hypostasised into an entity' so that 'it becomes all too easy to speak as if the developed form of the doctrine has always in some sense been imminent in history', while the actual thinking agent drops out of sight 'as ideas get to do battle on their own behalf'.[17] When investigation of a classic text proceeds by elaborating the author's doctrines of each of the themes assumed to be proper to the subject, the 'mythology of coherence' arises, in which the historian supplies the texts with a coherence that is presupposed but which the texts in fact lack. Such investigations, Skinner notes, are habitually phrased in terms of effort and quest: 'The ambition is always to "arrive" at "a unified interpretation", to "gain" a "coherent view of an author's system"', but which they may never even have had in view.[18] In its most extreme form, it leads to 'the assumption that it may be quite proper, in the interests of extracting a message of maximum coherence, to discount statements of intention that the authors themselves make about what they are doing, or even to discount whole works that may seem to impair the coherence of their systems of thought'.[19] We will see later in this section just such an example and one pertaining to the classic work on our topic, Athanasius' *On the Incarnation*.

Taking his argument further, Skinner rehabilitates a nuanced notion of authorial intent or meaning. Unless such meaning is taken into account, Skinner argues, a further mythology arises, that of prolepsis or anticipation. This is generated, as Skinner puts it, 'when we are more interested in the retrospective significance of a given episode than its meaning for the agent at the time'.[20] Skinner gives the example of Petrarch's ascent of Mount Ventoux, which is routinely described as the dawning of the age of the Renaissance; we could easily substitute the equally routine assertion that some pre-Nicene writer anticipated the creed of Nicaea, as if that is what they were aiming at all along. It is certainly true that an author may have penned something that later comes to have greater significance than was known at the time of writing, but that cannot be used to understand what the author intended by so writing, for, as Skinner points out, 'any plausible account of what the agent meant must necessarily fall under, and make use of, the range of descriptions that the agent could in principle have applied to describe and classify what he or she was saying or doing'.[21] To strengthen this appeal to authorial intent or intended meaning, Skinner draws upon Wittgenstein and J. L. Austin, to focus the appeal not on inaccessible mental acts (as is often caricatured in the fashionable rejection of 'authorial intent') but on texts as intentional and meaningful

[16] Ibid. 62. [17] Ibid. [18] Ibid. 68. [19] Ibid. 69.
[20] Ibid. 73. [21] Ibid.

acts of communication.[22] Any adequate account of such texts must include not only an exposition of the text within the historical context of meaning in which the author wrote, what 'they may have meant by saying what was said',[23] but also the rhetorical strategies employed by the author, what they are *doing* by writing, and the questions to which they are responding.[24]

Having dismantled the idea that there are 'ideas' or 'doctrines', as quasi-hypostasized metaphysical (and mythological) entities, to which individual writers have 'contributed' (and are thereby elided as thinking agents in their own right), Skinner comments:

> as soon as we see that there *is* no determinate idea to which various writers contributed, but only a variety of statements made by a variety of different agents with a variety of different intentions, what we are seeing is that there is no history of the idea to be written. There is only a history of its various uses, and of the varying intentions with which it was used.[25]

In concluding his essay, Skinner offers two positive results. First, regarding method: 'To understand a text must at least be to understand both the intention to be understood and the intention that this intention be understood, which the text as an intended act of communication must have embodied'.[26] The second is the possibility of the dialogue with ancient texts that this opens up. Only once we accept that there are no 'perennial problems' that are being addressed by classical texts, but that they are concerned with their own questions and not ours, are we able to have our predetermined set of prejudices and presuppositions prised open. The commonplace that 'our own society places unrecognized constraints upon our imagination' needs to be matched, Skinner asserts, by what should also be a commonplace: 'that the historical study of the beliefs of other societies should be undertaken as one of the indispensible and irreplaceable means of placing limits on those constraints'.[27] Classical texts, then, should be studied not to find answers to our own questions, but to hear other voices in an open dialogue, and so to grow in our own understanding. The root problem of a 'history of ideas', then, is not simply a methodological fallacy but 'something like a moral error': 'to learn from the past—and we cannot otherwise learn at all—the distinction between what is necessary and what is contingently the product of our own local arrangements is to learn one of the keys to self-awareness itself'.[28] It is just such a dialogue, bringing different readers of John together, that this work aims to hold.

[22] This is more fully developed in chapters 5 and 6 of *Regarding Method*, 'Motives, Intentions and Interpretation' and 'Interpretation and the Understanding of Speech Acts' respectively, which also revise and expand earlier essays.

[23] Skinner, 'Meaning', 79. [24] Cf. Ibid. 82. [25] Ibid. [26] Ibid. 86.

[27] Ibid. 89. [28] Ibid.

The strong position taken by Skinner has, of course, come in for criticism. Elizabeth Clark highlights three areas of concern.[29] First is his understanding of written texts on the basis of speech-acts, drawing from J. L. Austin, but not engaging with Derridean claims for the priority of writing. The second is his emphasis on the importance of context for understanding texts, taking their context as primarily linguistic and theoretical rather than social or economic. And, third, his appeal to authorial intent, even if not in terms of accessing an inner psychological act of the author, but an intent nevertheless, one that is embodied in the text itself. Responding to such criticism, Skinner acknowledges that there is always a surplus of meaning to a text, and that a meaning may well be found in the text which the author never intended.[30] Yet Skinner maintains the point that authors were nevertheless still doing something meaningful in composing their texts, a 'linguistic action' that is discernible on the basis of our knowledge of how words were used in particular epochs. This, I take it, is indeed a meaningful task, without which no serious historical or exegetical work could be undertaken, or, for that matter, any kind of conversation. It does not mean, however, that the goal is simply to uncover the 'original' (and thus supposedly 'correct') meaning of the author, in this case John and his Gospel, but, by allowing our own presuppositions to be exposed and thereby growing in self-awareness in dialogue with ancient readers (whose horizon was closer to that of the author than our own) as well as modern readers, to hear more adequately a foundational text of Christian theology as far as possible and perhaps even to (continue to) draw new wine out of old skins, as indeed every reading does, though some more adequately than others.

The most thorough and influential analysis of the hermeneutic issues involved in such reading, as a dialogue between ancient voices and our own, is that of Hans-Georg Gadamer in his work *Truth and Method*.[31] He emphasizes the importance of recognizing the *Wirkungsgeschichte*, the 'history of effect' or 'effective history', always at work in the task of interpreting texts and attaining understanding. We cannot, indeed, totally detach ourselves from our own historical context to reach back, without any presuppositions, to a different period to understand it solely within the original context and with

[29] Elizabeth A. Clark, *History, Theory, Text: Historians and the Linguistic Turn* (Cambridge MA: Harvard University Press, 2004), 138–9, and 130–55 more generally, and the references given there for further discussion.

[30] Cf. Quentin Skinner, 'A Reply to My Critics', in James Tully, ed., *Meaning and Context: Quentin Skinner and His Critics* (Cambridge: Cambridge University Press, 1988), 231–88, at 269–72.

[31] Hans-Georg Gadamer, *Wahrheit und Methode: Grundzüge einer philosophischen Hermeneutik*, 6th edn (Tübingen: Mohr Siebeck, 1990); *Truth and Method*, 2nd rev. edn, with revised ET Joel Weinsheimer and Donald G. Marshall (London: Continuum, 2004). For a short, but excellent, study of the importance of Gadamer's hermeneutics for theology, see Andrew Louth, *Discerning the Mystery: An Essay on the Nature of Theology* (Oxford: Clarendon Press, 1983).

the meaning of any given author. Texts, he points out, are always mediated to us through the historical process of reception, that is, tradition. But far from tradition being a hindrance to understanding, it is in fact what makes understanding possible at all. The hermeneutic circle, as Gadamer explains,

> is neither subjective nor objective, but describes understanding as the interplay of the movement of tradition and the movement of the interpreter. The anticipation of meaning that governs our understanding of a text is not an act of subjectivity, but proceeds from the commonality that binds us to the tradition. But this commonality is constantly being formed in our relation to tradition. Tradition is not simply a permanent precondition; rather, we produce it ourselves inasmuch as we understand, participate in the evolution of tradition, and hence further determine it ourselves. Thus the circle of understanding is not a 'methodological' circle, but describes an element of the ontological structure of understanding.[32]

Understanding, in Gadamer's account, takes place through the mediation of different horizons, the always changing perspectives upon the world. It begins when something addresses us, as happens when we encounter 'a traditionary text'.[33] When this occurs, our own presuppositions or prejudices are brought to light and can thereby be put in suspension. As such, 'the hermeneutically trained mind will also include historical consciousness'.[34] But this does not mean that our presuppositions are 'simply set aside and the text or other person accepted as valid in its place. Historical objectivism shows its naivete in accepting this disregarding of ourselves as what actually happens. In fact our own prejudice is properly brought into play by being put at risk. Only by being given full play is it able to experience the other's claim to truth and make it possible for him to have full play himself'.[35] Yet, it is also the case that our own horizon in the present is itself formed on the basis of the past. As such, Gadamer argues '[t]here is no more an isolated horizon of the present in itself than there are historical horizons which have to be acquired. *Rather, understanding is always the fusion of these horizons supposedly existing by themselves*'.[36] Thus the task of understanding when reading a text such as the Gospel of John, in a historically effected (*wirkungsgeschichtlichen*) manner, involves several steps.

> Projecting a historical horizon, then, is only one phase in the process of understanding; it does not become solidified into the self-alienation of a past consciousness, but is overtaken by our own present horizon of understanding. In the process of understanding, a real fusing of horizons occurs—which means that as the historical horizon is projected, it's sublation is simultaneously accomplished.

[32] Gadamer, *Truth and Method*, 293–4. [33] Ibid. 298. [34] Ibid.
[35] Ibid. 298–9. [36] Ibid. 305, italics original.

> To bring about this fusion in a regulated way is the task of what we call historically effected consciousness.[37]

The task of 'projecting a historical horizon' is necessary, and one which requires us to take Skinner's cautions seriously. But the task does not, and cannot, stop at that, for understanding is always in the present, in the melding together of the different horizons in our own understanding, yet always open to further revision and deeper insight. Moreover, in this melding of horizons we will always find a surplus of meaning in a text, as Skinner also accepts. 'Not just occasionally but always, the meaning of a text goes beyond its author. That is why understanding is not merely a reproductive but always a productive activity as well. Perhaps it is not correct to refer to this productive element in understanding as "better understanding".... It is enough to say that we understand in a *different* way, *if we understand at all*'.[38]

Our purpose in this Introduction is not to resolve, or even explore further, all the philosophical complexities of texts and their meanings, but to remind ourselves of the pitfalls that arise when a 'mythology of doctrines' holds sway unexamined and to orient ourselves towards the task of understanding the Gospel of John and what it speaks to us about, which is neither simply the projection of a historical horizon (though that must be carefully done) nor simply a reading in the present oblivious of the past. Hearing other ancient voices alongside and after John helps expose our own presuppositions, and in particular the 'mythology' (in Skinner's sense) of 'incarnation', that is, the assumption that the author of the Fourth Gospel (or at least the author of its Prologue) has a notion or doctrine of 'Incarnation' (for the word is not used in the Gospel) similar to that typically assumed today, that is, as referring to an event in which the 'pre-incarnate Word' was born in the flesh to dwell in the world, an 'episode in the biography of the Word'. The argument of this book, as already stated, is that he and his early readers did not. Yet such is the powerful hold that a particular understanding of 'Incarnation' (as an 'episode

[37] *Wahrheit und Methode*, 312; *Truth and Method*, 305–6, modified. Weinsheimer and Marshall have 'it is simultaneously superseded'. The term 'Aufhebung' implies 'taking up', a 'sublation', as it is regularly translated when used by Hegel, which is clearly in the background for Gadamer, rather than a making-redundant, as is implied by 'superseded'. The term 'fusion of horizons' is also a somewhat misleading translation for 'Horizontverschmelzung', though is now the customary translation: 'fusion' implies a much more integrated and unified union than does 'Verschmelzung', which is more 'melding together', always messy and not a total fusion, resulting in a union that can't be separated, but not necessarily monolithic or evenly mixed.

[38] *Truth and Method*, 296, italics original. See also Mikhail M. Bakhtin, 'Response to a Question from the *Novy Mir* Editorial Staff, in Bakhtin, *Speech Genres and Other Late Essays*, translated by Vern W. McGee (Austin: University of Texas Press, 2013), 1–9, at 4: 'Works break through the boundaries of their own time, they live in centuries, that is, in *great time* and frequently (with great works, always) their lives there are more intense and fuller than are their lives within their own time.... It seems paradoxical that... great works continue to live in the distant future. In the process of their posthumous life they are enriched with new meanings, new significance: it is as though these works outgrow what they were in the epoch of their creation'.

in a biography') has in our theological imagination, combined with an equally deeply ingrained idea about how Scripture is to be read, that to prepare the ground more fully for our subsequent examination it is necessary to explore just how extensively the 'mythology of doctrines' has dominated theological scholarship over the past century and how this is bound up with different ways of reading Scripture.

Labouring under the shadow of Harnack, historical theology has worked in the framework of the 'history of dogma', examining the Trinitarian debates of the fourth century, followed by the Christological debates of the subsequent centuries, a periodization which owes more to our handbooks of dogma (where Christology follows the Trinity) than it does to the texts and creeds from the periods themselves. Summaries of such histories, for example that staple of all students of the early Church in the second half of the last century, J. N. D. Kelly's *Early Christian Doctrine*, gather together, thematically, what different writers have to say about any given topics—Trinity, Christology, creation and salvation, ecclesiology, exegetical practices—with the result that the reader is not introduced to any particular figure, nor how these different aspects fit together in the thought of any one writer, if that is, they would even have considered them to be separate ideas.[39] One cannot, of course, indeed treat everything at once. But dividing up their work in this manner presupposes that the theology of those being presented is amenable to being dissected in this way, without considering how any given writer in fact conceives of his or her task, that is, how *they* understand the discipline of theology. Even when this 'history of dogma' approach has been abandoned in recent decades, to consider particular writers in their social, political, and polemical contexts, investigations habitually still have recourse to particular themes (the Incarnation, the Trinity) as fixed elements of Christian theology for which an account needs to be given for any particular writer.

A glaring example of Skinner's 'mythology of doctrines' is provided by Richard Hanson, in his mammoth tome, *The Search for the Christian Doctrine of God*; indeed the very title—'the search for . . . '—is one of the problematic indicators that Skinner highlighted. As Hanson put it in an article written shortly after completing the work, the 'trinitarian doctrine' elaborated in the fourth century was 'a solution, *the* solution, to the intellectual problem which had for so long vexed the church'.[40] The problem perplexing the Church was, thus, an intellectual one: that of establishing the doctrine of the Trinity. Moreover, this is, for Hanson at least, a task separable from the exegetical

[39] J. N. D. Kelly, *Early Christian Doctrines*, 5th edn (San Francisco: Harper, 1978 [1958]).

[40] Richard P.C. Hanson, 'The Achievement of Orthodoxy in the Fourth Century AD', in R. Williams, ed., *The Making of Orthodoxy: Essays in Honour of Henry Chadwick* (Cambridge: Cambridge University Press, 1989), 142–56, at 156, italics original.

practices of those whom he studied, for, as he puts it, in the conclusion to his volume:

> the expounders of the text of the Bible are incompetent and ill-prepared to expound it. This applies as much to the wooden and unimaginative approach of the Arians as it does to the fixed determination of their opponents to read their doctrine into the Bible by hook or crook.[41]

He then continues with this even more perplexing statement:

> It was much more the presuppositions with which they approach the Biblical text that clouded their perceptions, the tendency to treat the Bible in an 'atomic' way as if each verse or set of verses was capable of giving direct information about Christian doctrine apart from its context, the 'oracular' concept of the nature of the Bible, the incapacity with a few exceptions to take serious account of the background and circumstances of the writers. *The very reverence with which they honoured the Bible as a sacred book stood in the way of their understanding it.* In this matter they were of course only reproducing the presuppositions of all Christians before them, of the writers of the New Testament itself, of the tradition of Jewish rabbinic piety and scholarship.[42]

That is, their exegetical practice is simply wrong, even if it is a practice going back to the apostles themselves and their proclamation of the Gospel, a manner of exegesis moreover shared with the rabbis, and which was, in fact, the common approach to sacred texts in antiquity.[43] And yet, more perplexingly, this was the exegetical practice within which the doctrine of the Trinity was elaborated and had its meaning. Hanson clearly has no time for the exegetical practices of the theologians of this period by which they reached their conclusions, that is, reading the Scriptures—the Law, the Psalms, and the Prophets—as speaking of Christ. For Hanson, the doctrine of the Trinity was an 'intellectual problem' that was resolved in the fourth century, and which can now simply be called upon as a given item of Christian theology, leaving the following centuries to establish Christological doctrine, the next chapter of modern dogmatic textbooks.

Hanson never, as far as I am aware, addressed the question of what happens when one takes these supposed core theological elements (Trinity and Incarnation) out of the context in which they were composed—the particular practice of reading Scripture and the celebration of liturgy within which they had meaning, both leading to a *praxis* of piety, practices of identity formation shaping the believer in the image of Christ, to be his body—and

[41] Richard P. C. Hanson, *The Search for the Christian Doctrine of God: The Arian Controversy, 318–381* (Edinburgh: T & T Clark, 1988), 848.

[42] Ibid. 848–9, italics mine.

[43] Cf. James L. Kugel, *Traditions of the Bible: A Guide to the Bible as it was at the Start of the Common Era* (Cambridge, MA: Harvard University Press, 1998), 14–19.

places them in another context, in this case that of systematic theology and a reading of Scripture that focuses on the historical context of each verse, rather than seeing Scripture as the book of Christ. This transition in exegetical practices may well lie behind the narratival understanding of incarnation that we will consider further in the next section of this chapter.

Similarly problematic is Hanson's treatment of the 'Incarnation', especially when he discusses the first work to be specifically devoted to the topic, Athanasius' *On the Incarnation*. Assuming that 'Incarnation' refers solely to the birth of the divine Word from Mary, has led to an approach which holds that the proper task of 'Christology' is to analyse the composition of the being of Jesus Christ—to determine whether he has the requisite elements of a true human being, or whether the divine Word has replaced the soul (as Hanson supposes is the case for Athanasius, whose Christology he ridicules as a 'space-suit Christology')—and then trace in a historical manner his life and activity. Separating Athanasius' understanding of who Christ is from what Christ has done, specifically the Passion, also results in ascribing to Athanasius what is often referred to as a 'physical theory of redemption'. It is in this context that Hanson makes one of his most perplexing statements, that 'one of the curious results of this theology of the incarnation is that it almost does away with a doctrine of the atonement. Of course Athanasius believes in the atonement, in Christ's death as saving, but he cannot really explain why Christ should have died'.[44] Hanson continues by referring to Athanasius' discussion, beginning in chapter 19 of *On the Incarnation*, which presents, he says, 'a series of puerile reasons unworthy of the rest of the treatise', to conclude that 'the fact is that his doctrine of the incarnation has almost swallowed up any doctrine of the atonement, has rendered it unnecessary'. Hanson overlooks the fact that in chapter 26 Athanasius signals that the preceding chapters are not his final word. Indeed, they are not even his own proper word: 'These remarks are for those outside the church, who pile argument on argument for themselves'. Only after having toyed with such spurious reasons, perhaps for the rhetorical effect that allowing his readers, ancient and modern, to identify with them would have, does Athanasius then undermine such speculation and provide instead a reflection on why Christ died, not by some other means, but on the cross, for those who inquire about this 'not in a contentious spirit, but as a lover of truth'. Hanson's analysis fails the most basic demand, emphasized by Skinner, of attending to what an author tells us that he or she is doing in the text that he or she is writing.

As we have seen emphasized by Skinner, the first task of understanding texts—especially ancient ones, the perspectives and presuppositions of which will certainly differ even more considerably from our own than that of a

44 Hanson, *Search*, 450.

contemporary—is to pay attention to what the authors say about their texts, even if we then determine not to take them at their word. It is indeed necessary to do so, because, quite simply, a work such as *On the Incarnation* might not be about what we have become conditioned to expect when hearing the term 'Incarnation'. The work is the second part of a two-part treatise, the first part being *Against the Gentiles*. This work opens with the stated intention that the purpose of this work is to demonstrate that we should 'confess that he who ascended the cross is the Word of God and the Saviour of the universe'.[45] The order of identification is important: he does not say that he will show how the Word of God, presumably having become 'incarnate' (in the 'space-suit' of an inanimate human body) then ascends the cross, but rather that *the one on the cross* is the Word of God. The work is, thus, intended as an 'apology for the cross'.[46] Likewise when opening the second part, *On the Incarnation* itself, Athanasius begins by saying that, having laid out, in the first part of his treatise, the problems to which the work of God in Christ responds, he will now turn to 'the incarnation of the Word and . . . his divine manifestation to us, which the Jews slander and the Greeks mock'.[47] It is not that Athanasius has substituted the scandal of the cross for a scandal of incarnation, as we might understand that term, but rather understands the incarnation already in terms of the cross, as the allusion to 1 Cor. 1:23 makes clear. Far from 'the doctrine of incarnation' rendering the atoning death of Christ unnecessary, it is in fact the death of Christ that Athanasius is expounding in a work entitled *On the Incarnation*! And for this reason, contrary to our set expectations, Athanasius' classic text on the subject of Incarnation does not at all focus on the birth of the Word, in the sense of a biographical 'episode', conflating the infancy narratives of Matthew and Luke (who do not mention the Word of God) with John 1:14 (which doesn't speak of a birth); indeed, it barely even mentions the birth of Jesus (and never Mary by name). Rather, the work demonstrates how the one on the cross is in fact the Word of God, who through the Passion demonstrates his resurrection in those who follow him, as his body, in taking up the cross.[48]

Something *very* serious has happened in all this: the very subject of Christian theology has changed, from Jesus Christ, the crucified and risen Lord proclaimed by the Gospel, to the narrative of the Word of God, treated first as 'pre-incarnate' (a term I have yet to find in patristic literature) or as '*asarkos*', 'fleshless' (a term which is found, but used, as we will see, quite differently to

[45] *C. Gent.* 1: *ὁμολογεῖν Θεοῦ Λόγον καὶ Σωτῆρα εἶναι τοῦ παντὸς τὸν ἐπὶ τοῦ σταυροῦ ἀναβάντα.*

[46] Cf. Khaled Anatolios, *Athanasius: The Coherence of His Thought* (London and New York: Routledge, 1998), 28: the work is 'first and foremost an *apologia crucis*'.

[47] Athanasius, *Inc.* 1, cf. 1 Cor. 1:22–5.

[48] Cf. John Behr, *Introduction to St Athanasius: On the Incarnation*, ed. and trans. John Behr PPS 44a (Crestwood, NY: St Vladimir's Seminary Press, 2011), 36–40.

how we might expect), who then, later, becomes enfleshed, for the next phase of his biography. And in so doing, the paradigm within which 'Incarnation' is understood has also changed. So ingrained is this approach in modern theology, historical as well as systematic reflection and scriptural exegesis, that it is rather startling to note that it is not inscribed in any of the creeds or conciliar definitions: the creeds of Nicaea and Constantinople do not even use the term 'Word', and the Chalcedonian definition only employs the term 'Word' as one of the titles ascribed to the one subject, our Lord Jesus Christ. Noting this fact, John Meyendorff comments that the Chalcedonian definition:

> certainly insisted very strongly on Christ's unity and used in passing the term 'union' (of the natures); but strictly speaking, the term *ὑπόστασις* designated there, in a way parallel to *πρόσωπον*, the 'point where the particularities of the two natures meet'. Therefore, the council did not say that the *hypostasis of the union was the pre-existent hypostasis of the Logos*. In order to acquire a fully orthodox sense, the definition had to be read in a Cyrillian context, and this was certainly the way in which the majority of the council had conceived it.[49]

Meyendorff is indeed correct in his comment on the Chalcedonian definition. But the definition then does not fit into his set expectations of 'orthodox' Christology, as he holds this to have been formulated by Cyril, that is, a 'pre-existent hypostasis of the Logos' who (after a pre-incarnate phase) becomes flesh.[50] But is this in fact the way that even Cyril of Alexandria, the Father held by all as the touchstone of Christology, spoke? In his work *That Christ is One*, Cyril makes it clear that, for him, the term 'Word' is rather a title which is *attributed to* Jesus Christ: 'We say that there is one and the same Jesus Christ, from the God and Father, on the one hand, as the God Word, and, on the other hand, from the seed of the divinely-inspired David according to the flesh'.[51] There is one subject, and this is emphatically Jesus Christ, who, as from the God and Father, is the Word of God. So much is this the case that Cyril can state, rather jarringly to our modern ears: 'One is the Son, one Lord,

[49] John Meyendorff, *Christ in Eastern Christian Thought* (Crestwood, NY: St Vladimir's Seminary Press, 1975), 44, his emphasis.

[50] The problem is compounded when investigation turns to the later use of the word 'enhypostasis', taken in a localizing sense (the human nature of Jesus Christ is 'enhypostasized' *in* the pre-existing hypostasis of the Word), a twentieth-century reading, going back to Friedrich Loofs. See the introduction to Brian Daley, ed. and trans. *Leontius of Byzantium: Complete Works*, OECT (Oxford: Oxford University Press, 2017), 73–4, and the material cited therein, and F. LeRon Shults, 'A Dubious Christological Formula: From Leontius of Byzantium to Karl Barth', *Theological Studies* 57 (1996), 431–46; John Behr, 'Severus of Antioch: Eastern and Oriental Orthodox Perspectives', *St Nersess Theological Review*, 3.1–2 (1998), 23–35.

[51] Cyril of Alexandria, *That Christ is One* (ed. Pusey, 371.12–14): *ἕνα καὶ τὸν αὐτὸν εἶναί φαμεν Χριστὸν Ἰησοὺν, ἐκ Θεοῦ μὲν Πατρὸς ὡς Θεὸν Λόγον, ἐκ σπέρματος δὲ κατὰ σάρκα τοῦ θεσπεσίου Δαυείδ.*

Jesus Christ, both before the incarnation and after the incarnation'.[52] It is none other than Jesus Christ who is the one subject, both before and after the Incarnation!

Our tendency to begin with the Word of God, who then becomes Jesus Christ, rather than Jesus Christ, who is the Word, stems in large measure from modifications in the approach to theological reflection arising from the systematizing of early theological debates in later centuries. Karl Rahner, as is well known, lamented the development in the Middle Ages of a separation between treatises on the one God and on the triune God.[53] But a more fundamental transition occurred when the Trinity began to be treated before turning to the Incarnation, separating the Word, as a divine person, from the historical figure, or perhaps better, the apocalyptic figure of Jesus Christ.[54] This transition, moreover, significantly modifies what is meant by the term 'Incarnation', especially when combined with the historicizing approach to scriptural exegesis over the last few centuries.

Regarding the Prologue of John, Irenaeus of Lyons, in opposition to Ptolemy's reading of the text, is emphatic that each noun—Word, Life, Light, etc.—should not be reified or hypostasized into different figures, with a narrative describing the derivation of one from the other, but should instead all be taken as referring to the one Jesus Christ: he is the Word in the beginning, he is the one by whom all things happen, he is the one who became flesh, and so on.[55] One of the few, and certainly the most notable, theologians in modern times who dared to make such a radical, and apparently paradoxical, statement—paradoxical because of our narratival approach to theology—is Karl Barth. Working through the theme of election, Barth asserts: 'In Jn. 1[1] the reference is very clear: *ὁ λόγος* is unmistakably substituted for Jesus. His is the place which the predicates attributed to the Logos are meant at once to mark off, to clear and to reserve. It is He, Jesus, who is in the beginning with God. It is He who by nature is God. This is what is guaranteed in Jn. 1[1]'.[56] This order of predication is made more explicitly in that other Johannine writing, the Apocalypse, and done so even more paradoxically, or rather, apocalyptically: speaking of the rider on the white horse, 'clad in a robe dipped in blood', the author asserts that 'the name by which he is called is the Word of God' (Apoc. 19:13). It is specifically as the crucified one that Christ—the slain lamb enthroned with the Father, able to open the books, which turn out to speak

[52] Cyril of Alexandria, *First Letter to Succensus*, 4: *εἷς οὖν ἐστιν υἱός, εἷς κύριος, Ἰησοῦς Χριστὸς καὶ πρὸ τῆς σαρκώσεως καὶ μετὰ τὴν σάρκωσιν.*

[53] Karl Rahner, *The Trinity* (Tunbridge Wells: Burns and Oates, 1970 [German edn 1967]), 15–21.

[54] Cf. Karl-Josef Kuschel, *Born Before All Time? The Dispute over Christ's Origin* (New York: Crossroad, 1992), 25–7.

[55] Irenaeus of Lyons, *haer.* 1.9.2.

[56] Karl Barth, *Church Dogmatics* 2.2, *The Doctrine of God* (Edinburgh: T & T Clark, 1957), 96.

of him—is called the Word of God. Rather than looking for the background to the Prologue's utilization of the term 'Logos' in ancient philosophy or the figure of Wisdom in Scripture (though these are not, of course, to be excluded), we should perhaps heed Edwyn Hoskyn's suggestion that the choice of the term 'Word' in the Prologue was determined by the fact that by that time 'the Word' had become synonymous for the Gospel itself, so that in using the term 'the Word' the Prologue already contains a reference to the death and resurrection of Jesus; the Gospel, the apostolic preaching of the crucifixion and resurrection, 'the word of the cross' (1 Cor. 1:18), has become identified with the content of the Gospel, Jesus Christ.[57]

Regarding the use of the phrase *asarkos logos*, and the enfleshing of this Word, the following passage from a work attributed to Hippolytus indicates that, again, something more is going on:

> For the Word of God, being fleshless [ἄσαρκος ὤν], put on the holy flesh from the holy virgin, as a bridegroom a garment, *having woven it for himself in the sufferings of the cross*, so that having mixed our mortal body with his own power, and having mingled the corruptible into the incorruptible, and the weak with the strong, he might save the perishing human being.[58]

The flesh of the Word, received from the Virgin and 'woven in the sufferings of the cross', is, Hippolytus continues, by using an extended metaphor of a loom, woven by the patriarchs and prophets, whose actions and words proclaim the manner in which the Word became present and manifest. It is in the preaching of Jesus Christ, the proclamation of the one who died on the cross, interpreted and understood in the matrix, the womb, of Scripture, that the Word receives flesh from the Virgin. The Virgin in this case, Hippolytus later affirms following Revelation 12, is the Church, who will never cease 'bearing from her heart the Word that is persecuted by the unbelieving in the world', while the male child she bears is Christ, God and human, announced by the prophets, 'whom the Church continually bears as she teaches all nations'.[59]

The writers we have briefly considered clearly understood the becoming flesh of the Word in other and richer ways than simply as a new episode in the life of the Word, as we might have supposed when labouring under the methodological fallacy of the 'mythology of doctrines', and this is combined with a very different way of reading Scripture than is typically presupposed, as

[57] E. C. Hoskyns, *The Fourth Gospel*, 2nd rev. edn, ed. F. N. Davey (London: Faber and Faber, 1947), 159–63.

[58] Hippolytus, *Antichr.* 4, italics mine. Cf. J. A. Cerrato, *Hippolytus between East and West: The Commentaries and the Provenance of the Corpus*, OTM (Oxford: Oxford University Press, 2002), 128–37; John Behr, *The Way to Nicaea*, Formation of Christian Theology, 1 (Crestwood, NY: St Vladimir's Seminary Press, 2001), 141–62.

[59] Hippolytus, *Antichr.* 61, . . . ὃν ἀεὶ τίκουσα ἡ ἐκκλησία διδάσκει πάντα τὰ ἔθνη.

we have seen in the case of Hanson. But before we turn to the various readers of John and the conversation to be achieved in this volume, it will be useful also to consider systematically the coherence of the idea of pre-existence and Incarnation.

'PRE-EXISTENCE' AND 'INCARNATION'

I have used Rowan Williams' striking characterization of the way in which 'Incarnation' is typically understood as 'an episode in the biography of the Word'. The phrase appears in a discussion about the significance of the affirmation at the Council of Nicaea regarding the eternal generation of the Son of God. This affirmation, Williams points out, is simultaneously a denial of temporality in God: there was no period when the Son was not begotten and God was only God and not also Father. Here are the words in their full context:

> Rather paradoxically, the denial of a 'history' of transactions in God focuses attention on the history of God with us in the world: God has no *story* but that of Jesus of Nazareth and the covenant of which he is the seal. It is a matter of historical fact at least that the Nicene *verus Deus* was the stimulus to a clarification of the *verus homo* in the century and a half after the council: the Word of God is the condition of there being a human identity which is the ministering, crucified and risen saviour, Jesus Christ; but the existence of Jesus is not an episode in the biography of the Word. It remains obstinately—and crucially—a fact of our world and our world's limits.[60]

That 'God has no *story* but that of Jesus of Nazareth' is a conclusion that Herbert McCabe came to, a few years earlier, in his insightful and provocative essay 'The Involvement of God'.[61]

'It is part of my thesis', McCabe states boldly, 'that there is no such thing as the pre-existent Christ'. It was 'invented', he suggests, 'in the nineteenth century, as a way of distinguishing the eternal procession of the Son from the incarnation of the Son', that is, to affirm that 'Jesus did not become Son of God in virtue of the incarnation. He was already Son of God before that'.[62] McCabe further suggests that the affirmation of Christ's 'pre-existence' marks the development from a 'low' to a 'high' Christology, as was traced by Raymond Brown's discussion, in both his *Community of the Beloved Disciple* and his Anchor Bible commentaries, about which McCabe laments that '[it] is, I am afraid, conducted throughout in terms of the pre-existent Christ', though

[60] Williams, *Arius*, 244.

[61] Herbert McCabe, 'The Involvement of God', in McCabe, *God Matters* (London: Continuum, 2012), 39–51 (first appeared in *New Blackfriars*, November 1985).

[62] Ibid. 49. See also Karl-Josef Kuschel, *Born Before All Time?*

the same could be said for most other scriptural and 'history of dogma' scholarship.[63]

McCabe rejects the notion of 'the pre-existent Christ' from two points of view. First, 'to speak of the pre-existent Christ is to imply that God has a life-story, a divine story, other than the story of the incarnation . . . *First* the Son of God pre-existed as just the Son of God and *then* later he was the Son of God made man'. This is, he argues, not only incoherent, but 'incompatible at least with the traditional doctrine of God', for as he points out: 'There can be no succession in the eternal God, no change. Eternity is not, of course, a very long time; it is not time at all. Eternity is not timeless in the sense that an instant is timeless [. . .] No: eternity is timeless because it totally transcends time'.[64] Speaking of the Son of God 'becoming man' or 'coming down from heaven', McCabe writes, 'makes a perfectly good metaphor, but could not literally be true', for God is outside space and time; up and down, before and after, are determinants of created reality. 'From the point of view of God, then, *sub specie eternitatis* [*sic*], no sense can be given to the idea that at some point in God's life-story, the Son became incarnate'.[65]

Yet, from our point of view, in history, McCabe continues, 'there was certainly a time when Jesus had not yet been born'. And so, as McCabe puts it: 'Moses could have said with perfect truth "Jesus of Nazareth is not yet" or "Jesus does not exist" because, of course, the future does not exist; this is what makes it future'.[66] Yet while saying 'Jesus does not exist', Moses could also have simultaneously said truthfully: 'The Son of God does exist'. This, McCabe concedes, might be called the 'pre-existence of Christ',

> meaning that at an earlier time in our history (and there isn't any time except in history) these propositions would both have been true: 'Jesus does not exist', 'The Son of God does exist', thus apparently making a distinction between the existence of Jesus and the existence of the Son of God. But the phrase 'pre-existent Christ' seems to imply not just that in the time of Moses 'The Son of God exists' would be true, but also that the proposition 'The Son of God exists *now*' would be true. And this would be a mistake. Moses could certainly have said, 'It is true now that the Son of God exists' but he could not have truly said 'The Son of God exists now'. *That* proposition, which attributes *temporal* existence ('now') to the Son of God, is the one that became true when Jesus was conceived in the womb of Mary. The simple truth is that apart from incarnation the Son of God exists at no time at all, at no 'now', but in eternity, in which he acts upon all time but is not himself 'measured by it', as Aquinas would say. 'Before Abraham was, I am'.[67]

[63] McCabe, 'Involvement', 49.

[64] Ibid., italics original. See now Ilaria Ramelli and David Konstan, *Terms for Eternity: Aiônios and Aïdios in Classical and Christian Texts* (Piscataway, NJ: Gorgias Press, 2011).

[65] McCabe, 'Involvement', 50. [66] Ibid. [67] Ibid., italics original.

Grappling with the intersection of time and eternity does indeed, and necessarily, stretch the limits of human thought, acting as it must do within time. The intersection between time and eternity is naturally correlated to the relationship between 'theology' and 'economy': in the first we speak of Christ as divine, in the second we speak of the same Christ as the mediator; but this distinction between theology and economy does not provide a narrative that begins with a divine subject who then subsequently becomes human.[68]

Nevertheless, McCabe wants to maintain a 'high' Christology, every bit as 'high' as that attributed to John, but in so doing understands 'Incarnation' differently than is usually done. Rather than Incarnation as an 'episode' (to use William's phrase once more), McCabe wants to maintain that 'the doctrine of the incarnation is such that the story of Jesus is not just the story of God's involvement with his creatures, but that it is actually the "story" of God'.[69] Certainly God, in one sense, has no 'story', no temporal narrative, but, he asserts, 'there is also a sense, the only sense, in which God has or is a life-story, and this is the story revealed in the incarnation and it is the story we also call the Trinity'. McCabe continues: 'The story of Jesus is nothing other than the triune life of God projected onto our history, or enacted sacramentally in our history, so that it becomes story'.[70] When a film is projected onto a screen, McCabe points out, if that screen is smooth and flat, the film can be seen clearly; but as soon as the screen is distorted or twisted in any way, it distorts the image being projected. In this sense: 'The story of Jesus—which in its full extent is the entire bible—is the projection of the Trinitarian life of God on the rubbish dump that we have made of the world'.[71] Rather than distinguishing the missions of the Son and the Spirit in time from their eternal relations within the Trinity, or even to allow that the former reflect the latter, as is commonly done, McCabe would argue for their strict identity:

> The historical mission of Jesus is nothing other than the eternal mission of the Son from the Father; the historical outpouring of the Spirit in virtue of the passion, death, and ascension of Jesus is nothing but the eternal outpouring from the Father through the Son. Watching, so to say, the story of Jesus, we are watching the processions of the Trinity. [...] they are not just reflection but sacrament—they contain the reality they signify. The mission of Jesus is *nothing other* than the eternal generation of the Son. That the Trinity looks like a story of (*is* a story of) rejection, torture and murder, but also of reconciliation is because it is being projected on, lived out on, our rubbish tip; it is because of the sin of the world.[72]

[68] As Frances M. Young puts it: 'There is no possibility of "narrative" in *theologia*, but narrative constitutes *oikonomia*; one is in time, the other beyond time'. *Biblical Exegesis and the Formation of Christian Culture* (Cambridge: Cambridge University Press, 1997), 143.

[69] McCabe, 'Involvement', 48. [70] Ibid. [71] Ibid.

[72] Ibid. 48–9, italics original.

McCabe concludes his essay by saying that 'I would be much happier in an odd way with the notion of a "pre-existent Jesus" in the innocuous sense that, as I said, the entire Bible, spanning all history, is, all of it, the story of Jesus of Nazareth ("Moses wrote of me"). But that merely tells us how to read the Bible, it does not make any claims about the relationship of divine and human in Jesus'.[73]

We are back, as we were with Hanson, to the question of how we read Scripture. As Hanson correctly noted, though with disdain, the Fathers of the fourth century, following a practice going back to the apostles themselves, read Scripture 'atomically', that is, they did not pay attention to the historical context of the writing, nor, primarily at least, did they read Scripture (what we now call the Old Testament) as an ongoing narrative leading up to Christ, but rather read it as speaking about Christ and his Passion; although increasingly called 'the Old Testament' it was still primarily *the Scriptures*, read as speaking about Christ himself. As we will see in Chapter 2, it is through the medium of the Scriptures that, after the Passion, the apostles understood Christ and proclaimed him in its terms, images, and poetry. In this way, the Gospels were not understood as 'what happened next', after the Old Testament. Apart from Marcion, the first writers to separate out the two testaments, to claim that the Scriptures (i.e. the Old Testament) did not speak about Christ but about their own times, were Diodore of Tarsus and Theodore of Mopsuestia.[74] They were accused of being Marcionites for this, but more importantly it led them to a 'dyoprosopic' Christology, separating the Word of God, spoken of in the Old Testament, from Jesus Christ, whose 'biography' the Gospels narrate. Reading Scripture as a historical narrative, from the Old Testament to the New Testament, seems to entail a parallel narrative of the Word of God, from his existence with God to, at a later time, his Incarnation as 'an episode' in his biography. This is not, however, what McCabe is suggesting: he appeals to a reading of 'the entire Bible' as 'the story of Jesus of Nazareth', for Moses was already writing of Christ. What is the force of the 'story' that McCabe and Williams want to focus on? How is that story told? Are we to understand the Gospels, and especially the Gospel of John, as some form of biography, or, as Ashton suggested, an inverse apocalypse? Quite what this might mean is something we will have to consider fully in Chapter 2.

McCabe has helpfully highlighted the problem of the phrase 'the pre-existent Christ' and the incoherence of the approach which takes 'Incarnation' as part of a temporal narrative of the Word. His points might perhaps have been clearer if he had spoken instead of 'the pre-incarnate Word', a phrase which abounds in secondary scholarship but which I have yet to find in

[73] Ibid. 51.

[74] Cf. John Behr, *The Case Against Diodore and Theodore: Texts and Their Contexts*, OECT (Oxford: Oxford University Press, 2011).

patristic literature. It is hard even to understand what 'pre-existent' might mean, apart from the ascription of some kind of timeless eternality to the one so described; the phrase 'pre-incarnate' makes clearer the point of McCabe's critique, that is, the problematic ascription of temporality to a divine subject, with the consequence of treating the 'Incarnation' as but an episode. For McCabe 'Incarnation' seems not to be understood as a single event—the birth from the Virgin—but rather the enfleshing of the reality of God in the whole 'story of Jesus'. In this way, McCabe avoids the problematic change of subject (from Christ to Word) that we noted in the previous section of this introduction: although the creeds do speak of how the Son 'came down from heaven and was incarnate', which as McCabe suggests is a good metaphor, the subject of the second article of the Creeds of Nicaea and Constantinople, the one who came down from heaven to be incarnate, is not a 'pre-incarnate Word' (the term 'Word' does not even appear in the creeds), but rather the one subject, the one Lord Jesus Christ.

We will look at the motif of ascent and descent in the Gospel of John in Chapter 4, but for now, regarding the term 'Incarnation', it is clear that when Cyril of Alexandria says, as we saw earlier, 'One is the Son, one Lord, Jesus Christ, both before the incarnation and after the incarnation', he has something else in mind by 'incarnation' than a new episode in the life of the Word. His words seems to fly in the face of what we think we know about the 'Logos Christology' and the 'Incarnational theology' of the early Church. But it is also something that we have seen in Irenaeus, for whom Jesus Christ is the one subject throughout the Prologue, and in Athanasius, whose work *On the Incarnation* is written to demonstrate that the one ascended upon the cross is the Word of God. We even find it, perhaps most surprisingly, in Origen, with whom above all we might have expected to find a place for a disembodied Logos, who takes flesh as a temporary accommodation before returning to his original state through the Passion.[75] However, that he does not think along these lines but in a very different manner, one that might strike us as even shocking, is made abundantly clear in the last chapters of his *Commentary on John*, which, as it survives in Greek, are undisputedly his own words. Here he treats the words of Christ, 'Now is the Son of Man glorified and God is glorified in him' (John 13:31), which, he points out, were spoken by the one who previously said 'you seek to kill me, a man who has spoken the truth to

[75] It is indeed easy to read Origen in this way, as when he says, for instance, that 'we ought to share with them [that is, those "established in the Spirit"] the Word who was restored from being made flesh to what "he was in the beginning with God"' (*Comm. Jo.* 1.43; John 1:2); however, his point here is that we must advance from seeing Christ simply as a human being to seeing him, the same one, as the eternal Word of God. Cf. Behr, *Way to Nicaea*, 163–206, and also the introduction to John Behr, ed. and trans., *Origen: On First Principles*, OECT (Oxford: Oxford University Press, 2017), vol. 1, lxvi–lxxxviii.

you' (John 8:40), and explains this by by reference to Paul's analogy of how we are united to the Lord:

> Now I think God also highly exalted this one when he 'became obedient unto death, and the death of a cross' [Phil. 2:8]. For the Word in the beginning with God, the God Word, was not capable of being highly exalted. But the high exaltation of the Son of Man which occurred when he glorified God in his own death consisted in the fact that he was no longer different from the Word but was the same with him [*τὸ μηκέτι ἕτερον αὐτὸν εἶναι τοῦ λόγου ἀλλὰ τὸν αὐτὸν αὐτῷ*]. For if 'he who is joined to the Lord is one spirit' [1 Cor. 6:17], so that it is no longer said that 'they are two' [Matt. 19:6], even in the case of this one and the Spirit, might we not much more say that the humanity of Jesus became one with the Word [*τὸ ἀνθρώπινον τοῦ Ἰησοῦ μετὰ τοῦ λόγου λέγοιμεν γεγονέναι ἕν*] when he 'who did not consider equality with God something to be grasped' was 'highly exalted'? [Phil. 2:6, 9] The Word, however, remained in his own grandeur, or was even restored to it, when he was again with God, the God Word being human [*ὅτε πάλιν ἦν πρὸς τὸν θεόν, θεὸς λόγος ὢν ἄνθρωπος*].[76]

The identity of Jesus and, or rather as, the Word of God is revealed, or rather wrought, upon the cross. The abasement of the cross is not, therefore, a kenotic concealment of his divinity in a state of dereliction abandoned by God, but is instead the fullest revelation of his divinity. As Origen put it earlier in the same *Commentary*: 'We must dare say that the goodness of Christ appeared greater and more divine and truly in accordance with the image of the Father "when he humbled himself and became obedient unto death, even death on a cross", than had he "considered being equal to God robbery" and had not been willing to become a servant for the salvation of the world'.[77] The kenosis, the self-emptying, on the cross, as the supreme moment of weakness, is also the supreme manifestation of the power of God (cf. 2 Cor. 12:9) and thus the revelation of the true divinity of Christ.

Gregory of Nyssa elaborates this point in a helpful manner. Gregory is often held to be one of the most 'Origenist' of the Cappadocian Fathers, yet he was also recognized by the Seventh Ecumenical Council as 'being called by all the father of the fathers'.[78] In *Contra Eunomium* 3.3, Gregory provides an account of Peter's statement in Acts, that 'God made [*ἐποίησεν*] him both Lord and Christ, this Jesus whom you crucified' (Acts 2:36), in terms of the distinction between uncreated and created.[79] Whereas Eunomius would see the Son's suffering upon the cross as a mark of distinction between him and the impassible Father, for Gregory it instead reveals 'the supreme exercise of his power' rather than 'an indication of weakness', showing that 'the God made

[76] Origen, *Comm. Jo.* 32.324–6. [77] Origen, *Comm. Jo.* 1.231, citing Phil. 2:8, 6.

[78] *Acta*, sixth session (Mansi, 13.293e).

[79] For a full exposition of this text, see John Behr, *The Nicene Faith*, 2 vols Formation of Christian Theology, 2 (Crestwood, NY: St Vladimir's Seminary Press, 2004), 2.436–45.

manifest through the cross ought to be honoured just as the Father is honoured'.[80] Moreover, he continues, 'we say that the body also, in which he accepted the passion, being combined with the divine nature, was by that commingling made into that which the assuming nature is'.[81] With regard to Peter's words, that 'God made him both Lord and Christ', Gregory points out that there are not two subjects here, but rather that 'Scripture says two things happened regarding a single person, the passion by the Jews, the honour by God, not as though there was one who suffered and another who was honoured by the exaltation'.[82] This is shown even more clearly, for Gregory, when Peter says he was 'exalted by the Right Hand of God'.[83] So, as Gregory understands this verse, 'the Apostle said that the humanity [*τὸ ἀνθρώπινον*] was exalted, being exalted by becoming Lord and Christ; and this took place after the passion'.[84] He then continues in even stronger terms:

> He who says 'exalted by the Right Hand of God' [Acts 2:33] clearly reveals the unspeakable economy of the mystery, that the Right Hand of God, who made all things that are, who is the Lord by whom all things were made and without whom nothing that is subsists, himself raised to his own height the man [*τὸν . . . ἄνθρωπον*] united to him, making him also, by the commixture, to be what he is by nature: he is Lord and King, and the King is called Christ; these things he made him too. . . . And this we are plainly taught by the voice of the Peter in his mystic discourse, that the lowliness of the one crucified in weakness (and weakness, as we have heard from the Lord, indicates the flesh [cf. Matt. 26:41]), that, by virtue of its mingling with the infinite and boundless [nature] of the Good, remained no longer in its own measures and properties, but by the Right Hand of God was raised up together, and became Lord instead of servant, Christ the King instead of a subject, highest instead of lowly, God instead of man.[85]

For Gregory, the universal extension of this mystery is indicated by the four dimensions mentioned by Paul in his letter to the Ephesians (3:18: the height, breadth, depths, and length): 'this is in order that the great mystery may be revealed thereby, that things in heaven and under the earth and all the furthest of beings are governed and held together by him who demonstrated this ineffable and vast power in the form of the cross'.[86]

Origen and Gregory are clearly not 'adoptionists', though they do indeed seem to anticipate Diodore of Tarsus and Theodore of Mopsuestia.[87] Rather

[80] Gregory of Nyssa, *Eun.* 3.3.30–3.

[81] *Eun.* 3.3.34: *ἡμεῖς μὲν γὰρ καὶ τὸ σῶμα, ᾧ τὸ πάθος ἐδέξατο, τῇ θείᾳ φύσει κατακραθὲν ἐκεῖνο πεποιῆσθαί φαμεν διὰ τῆς ἀνακράσεως, ὅπερ ἡ ἀναλαβοῦσα φύσις ἐστί·.*

[82] *Eun.* 3.3.42: *δύο γὰρ πράγματα περὶ ἓν πρόσωπον ὁ τῆς γραφῆς λόγος γεγενῆσθαί φησι.*

[83] Acts 2:33, reading the dative as expressing agency, rather than 'to the right hand' as most modern translations do.

[84] *Eun.* 3.3.43. [85] *Eun.* 3.3.44. [86] *Eun.* 3.3.40.

[87] Cf. Behr, *The Case against Diodore and Theodore*, 42–7. See especially the passages of Theodore preserved by Leontius (LT 2–6, *Case*, 284–91); that Theodore employs the same

they are simply, or rigorously, following the point made so clearly by Paul: 'even though we once knew Christ according to the flesh, we know him thus no longer' (2 Cor. 5:16). Before the Passion, Jesus could be identified by a set of properties based on how he appeared, physically, in the world, before others, as the son of the carpenter from Nazareth; after the Passion, however, he is no longer known through these properties, but rather is known as the Word of God. This is somewhat akin to the 'Messianic Secret' that has been much debated in scriptural scholarship over the past century, and to which we will return in Chapter 2: the idea that before the Passion, the true identity of Jesus Christ is veiled, a secret to his disciples, though known to some outsiders and those demonically possessed. The approach of Origen and Gregory, however, does not concern the inner 'personal' identity of Jesus Christ, whether always known by him or gradually dawning upon him, as in so much historical reconstruction, but rather focuses on the way in which he is known to others; identity here is understood in terms of identification, as identifying properties, as it is also for Gregory's technical language of 'hypostasis'.[88]

In perhaps his most startling comment, Gregory can even put it this way:

> Christ always [is], both before the economy and after it; [the] human being, however, [is] neither before it nor after it, but only during the time of the economy. Neither [is] the human being before the Virgin, nor, after the ascent into heaven, [is] the flesh still in its own properties.[89]

What he seems to be saying is that although, on one side, 'Moses and all the prophets' had always spoken about how the Son of Man enters his glory by suffering (cf. Luke 24:26–7), and said this because, as Isaiah, they 'saw his glory' (John 12:41), and, on the other side, this is also the content of the apostolic preaching—that is, both before and after the economy, the message about, and identity of, Christ is the same—yet during the time when Jesus walked the earth, seen in the flesh by fleshly eyes, the glory and divinity of Christ was not in fact seen (apart from the Transfiguration, when it was not properly understood), until after the Passion, when he passes out of physical sight. It is, thus, on the cross that we finally see the true form and divinity of

scriptural passages about two becoming one (Matt. 19:6) as Origen, might suggest that not only are the 'Alexandrian' and 'Antiochian' approaches to Christology not so far distinct, as is now increasing recognized, but even that Theodore is continuing an exegetical tradition begun by Origen.

[88] Gregory of Nyssa, *Ep. to Peter* (= Basil. *Ep.* 38) 6: 'the hypostasis is the concurrence of the particular properties of each [*ὑπόστασιν ἀποδεδώκαμεν εἶναι τὴν συνδρομὴν τῶν περὶ ἕκαστον ἰδιωμάτων*] . . . the hypostasis is the individualizing sign of the existence of each [*ἡ ὑπόστασις τὸ ἰδιάζον τῆς ἑκάστου ὑπάρξεως σημεῖόν ἐστι*]'.

[89] Gregory of Nyssa, *Antirrheticus* (GNO 3.1, p.222.25–9): *ἀλλὰ πάντοτε μὲν ὁ Χριστὸς καὶ πρὸ τῆς οἰκονομίας καὶ μετὰ τοῦτο· ἄνθρωπος δὲ οὔτε πρὸ τούτου οὔτε μετὰ ταῦτα, ἀλλ' ἐν μόνῳ τῷ τῆς οἰκονομίας καιρῷ. οὔτε γὰρ πρὸ τῆς παρθένου ὁ ἄνθρωπος οὔτε μετὰ τὴν εἰς οὐρανοὺς ἄνοδον ἔτι ἡ σὰρξ ἐν τοῖς ἑαυτῆς ἰδιώμασιν.*

the Son of God, and from this moment on we no longer 'see' Jesus with our bodily perception, for after it, and in its light, we can no longer differentiate between human and divine properties: we no longer know Christ by a set of fleshly properties, but we now only know him as the Word of God.

Yet, as Gregory points out, it is not a matter of a man being exalted *to* the right hand of God, which would certainly be a form of adoptionism, but instead he is exalted *by* the Right Hand of God, the Right Hand that he in fact is: there is but one subject, though considered in two respects (as with *Eun.* 3.3.42 cited earlier). To paraphrase Gregory's argument in *Against Eunomius* 3.3: through the Passion, Christ, *as human*, becomes that which, *as God*, he always is, the 'Right Hand of God'. The abasement upon the cross is simultaneously an exaltation, two aspects relating to one and the same person. There is, thus, for theology no other 'face' (*πρόσωπον*) at which to look: Christ, reconciling all things to himself and making peace by the blood of the cross, is the 'image of the invisible God'.[90] This means that while we must distinguish between actions which are divine and those which are human, for one cannot say that 'the flesh is pretemporal or that the Word was born recently' as Gregory puts it, yet it is nevertheless one and the same Jesus Christ, known on the cross, who, as God, creates the world and holds it together through the form of the cross, and as human hungers, thirsts, and is weary.[91] However, 'by the bond and conjunction' thus wrought, 'both are common to each, as the Master assumes to himself the bruises of the slave and the slave is glorified with the honour of the Master', so that 'the crucifixion is attributed to the "Lord of glory" and "every tongue confesses that Jesus Christ is Lord to the glory of God the Father."'[92] That is, the principle of *communicatio idiomatum*, the exchange of properties, functions by virtue of the cross.

The cross, then, is the lens for bringing into focus the revelation of God in Christ, 'the God revealed through the cross'. We cannot, for Gregory, begin with an understanding of God, or the Son of God in whom he is revealed, apart from the cross. If we attempt to theologize apart from the cross, to see God revealed in Christ apart from the Passion (after which we no longer know him in the flesh), we will end up defining divinity in human terms. This is Gregory's chief complaint about Apollinarius, who, he claims,

[90] Col. 1:15. Cf. John Behr, 'Colossians 1:13–20: A Chiastic Reading', *St Vladimir's Theological Quarterly*, 40.4 (1996), 247–64. In *Ep. to Peter* 8, Gregory describes the hypostasis of the Son as being 'the shape [*μορφή*] and face [*πρόσωπον*] of the knowledge of the Father', and in *To the Greeks, On Common Notions* (GNO 3.1, p.47), he asserts that: 'All the *prosopa* of the human being[s] [*τὰ τοῦ ἀνθρώπου πρόσωπα*] do not have their being directly from the same person, but some from one and others from another, as regarding the caused, the causes are many and diverse. But with regard to the Holy Trinity, this is not so: for there is one and the same *prosopon* [*ἓν γάρ πρόσωπον καὶ τὸ αὐτό*], that of the Father, from whom the Son is begotten and the Holy Spirit proceeds'.

[91] *Eun.* 3.3.64–5.

[92] *Eun.* 3.3.66, 1 Cor. 2:8, Phil. 2:11.

'defines the divine by perceptible appearance not by what is understood', whereas for Gregory 'the true account' is that Christ 'is human and God, by what is seen human, by what is understood God'.[93] We cannot begin with an understanding of God, or the Son of God in whom he is revealed, apart from the cross. If we were to attempt to theologize apart from the cross, to see God revealed in Christ apart from the Passion, we would end up, as Apollinarius, defining divinity in human terms. If we, for instance, attempt to look *behind* the cross to see the human being Jesus before the Passion, as if the Passion had never happened (rather unhistorical in its attempt to be historical), we will end up seeing Jesus as he appears in his human properties, as the son of the carpenter from Nazareth; we will not 'see', or rather intellectually contemplate, the Word of God, and so will not in fact be theologizing.

If, on the other hand, we look *through* the cross, we see the unchanging identity of the crucified one throughout his life. In *Philokalia* 15, a compilation of Origen's texts made by Basil and Gregory, discussing, in its first part, how Scripture, though apparently poor in style and language, yet contains a divine meaning, and, in the second part, how Christ appeared 'without form or comeliness' [Isa. 53:2] yet also possesses a divine radiance for those who ascend the mountain, Origen concludes by mentioning the different 'forms' in which Christ appeared (cf. Mark 16:12), commenting: 'I refer to the different periods of his life, to anything he did before the Passion, and whatever happened after his resurrection from the dead'.[94] The unchanging identity of Christ is given upon the cross, which, in this sense, is not only a lens but also a prism, refracting the Passion of Christ throughout all aspects of the divine economy, so that we can see the same identity throughout the Gospels, from the birth of Christ and in all aspects of his service and ministry, and, indeed, throughout the whole of creation held together by the form of the cross.[95]

These considerations have significant implications for understanding what is meant by 'Incarnation'. 'This', Gregory claims, 'is the mystery of the Lord in the flesh, that the unchangeable came to be in the changeable, in order that, altering and transforming it from bad to good, he might banish from the race

[93] *Antirrheticus* (GNO 3.1, p.191.24–7): *οὐκοῦν κατὰ τὸν ἀληθῆ λόγον καὶ ἄνθρωπος ἐστι καὶ θεός, τῷ ὁρωμένῳ ἄνθρωπος, τῷ νοουμένῳ θεός. ὁ δὲ οὐ τοῦτό φησιν, ἐν τῷ συμπεράσματι τῷ φαινομένῳ τὸ θεῖον, οὐ τῷ νοητῷ ὁριζόμενος.*

[94] *Philoc.* 15 (= *Cels.* 6.77).

[95] As Gregory of Nazianzus (*Or.* 40.29) points out, late in the fourth century, when the various feasts began to be celebrated in the East, 'Because he had to undergo the Passion for the world's salvation, all things that pertain to the Passion had to converge to the Passion: the manifestation, the baptism, the testimony from above, the proclamation, the crowd coming together, the miracles. And these events became like one body, not dispersed or broken apart by intervals of time' (*ὥσπερ ἓν σῶμα γενέσθαι, μὴ διεσπασμένον μηδὲ ἀπερρηγμένον τοῖς διαστήμασιν*). For the birth of Christ being described this way, see John Behr, *The Mystery of Christ: Life in Death* (Crestwood, NY: St. Vladimir's Seminary Press, 2006), 115–40, 'The Virgin Mother'.

the evil which was involved in the changeable character, using up on himself all that was evil: for our God is a consuming fire, by which all the fuel of evil is consumed'.[96] Origen too had employed the image of a fire in explaining Christ's mediatorial role. When a piece of iron, which is identified by certain properties (e.g. cold and hard), is placed into a fire it is no longer identified by those properties, but rather, while remaining the iron that it is, it is now known solely by the properties of the fire. So also, Origen says, 'that soul which, like iron in the fire, was placed in the Word for ever, in Wisdom for ever, in God for ever, is God in all that it does, feels, and understands'.[97] The Passion is, in effect, the 'assumption' or 'ascension' (for both terms translate the same Greek word: *ἀνάληψις*) of Christ's human nature into the divine reality, so that it is no longer known by the properties of the flesh, but rather is thoroughly permeated by, and only known by, the properties of divinity. While remaining the human flesh that it is, it comes to be beyond space and time, for these are but measurements of this created world, not the divine.[98] The fire remains what it always is, yet when, as Gregory puts it, 'the unchangeable comes to be in the changeable', the changeable, that is the iron, is changed such that it is known by the properties of the fire, and the fire, in turn, while remaining unchanged, is nevertheless now embodied. Instead of thinking of 'incarnation', 'the mystery of the Lord in the flesh', in terms of the assumption of human nature by a divine person, as 'an episode in a biography', such that we can see God in the world in the particular forms or identifying marks of his human body, Origen and Gregory understand 'Incarnation' as referring to the identity wrought upon the cross between the divine and the human, as a transformative act of divine power, whereby the human becomes all that the divine is, and in turn the divine, without change, comes to be embodied, incarnate. In this sense, for Gregory (and Origen and others), as I concluded in *The Nicene Faith*, the Incarnation has less to do with the Word becoming flesh than the flesh becoming Word![99]

We have looked briefly at Irenaeus and Athanasius, and more fully at Origen and especially Gregory of Nyssa, not to predetermine an outcome to be found when we turn to the Gospel of John and his readers, but rather to show that there were indeed other, and perhaps more coherent, ways of

[96] *Eun.* 3.3.52, Deut. 4:24, Heb 12:29. [97] Origen, *Princ.* 2.6.6.

[98] Gregory of Nyssa, *Eun.* 1.25–6. The later tradition would even assert that human beings also become 'uncreated'. Cf. Gregory Palamas, *Triad* 3.1.31: 'But as we have shown above, the saints clearly state that this adoption and deifying gift, actualized by faith, is real.... The divine Maximus has not only taught that it is real, but also that it is unoriginate (and not only uncreated), uncircumscribed and supra-temporal, so that those attaining it are thereby perfected as uncreated, unoriginate, and uncircumscribed, although in their own nature they derive from nothing' (*ὡς καὶ τοὺς αὐτῆς εὐμοιρηκότας δι'αὐτὴν ἀκτίστους, ἀνάρχους, καὶ ἀπεριγράπτους τελέσαι, καὶτοι διὰ τὴ οἰκείαν φύσιν ἐξ οὐκ ὄντων γεγονότας*).

[99] Behr, *Nicene Faith*, 2.443.

conceptualizing the identity of Christ as the Word of God than as 'an episode in a biography', in order that our own presuppositions are brought to light and are not unthinkingly imposed in a 'mythology of doctrines' when reading John. The hermeneutic needed to discern the identity of Christ, as we have seen it in Origen and Gregory, is of course the same that they, and most early Christians, would say is needed to read Scripture and encounter the Word of God. As Origen puts it in the chapter from the *Philocalia* referred to above, the Word of God 'eternally becomes flesh in the Scriptures' so that he might dwell among us, or rather *in* us; but only if we recline on his breast, as did John, do we come to know the Word.[100] We must, Origen exhorts us, ascend the mountain, to see him transfigured, speaking with Moses and Elijah, the Law and the Prophets, about his 'exodus' in Jerusalem.[101] If we stay at the level of the flesh, the letters, we will never come to contemplate the Word; but if we ascend the mountain with him, we 'shall see his transfiguration in every [passage of] Scripture'. And yet, tellingly, the Gospel of John has no event of Transfiguration; Christ appears as the divine Lord on every page, not as a 'naïve docetism', as Käsemann would have it, but as a theological account of the Lord given by the theologian. It is by his intimacy with the Lord, reclining on his breast, and especially by being the only evangelist to witness the Passion, that John leads us to the identity of the Word and his flesh. But before we turn to the identity of John himself, John the Divine, and the theological and paschal tradition that he originated, we must also consider the readers of John we have invited to this symposium.

JOHN AND HIS READERS

There were and are many readers of John. This book does not, and indeed could not, treat them all. Those we have chosen fall into three main categories. In the first category are the early Fathers, especially those from the second and third centuries though occasionally referring to later figures. With the thesis of 'Gnostic Johannophilia' thoroughly demolished by Charles Hill (as we will see at the beginning of Chapter 1), and with a concern for the longer view of the Christian tradition, we have focused on those from the first centuries who were important for the development of the Christian theological tradition thereafter. Of particular interest here are those who traced their lineage back to John himself: they form such a clear and uniform group, that J. B. Lightfoot could designate them as 'the school of John', including, in the first generation, Polycarp of Smyrna and Papias of Hierapolis, and in the next generation

[100] Origen, *Philoc.* 15.19: ἀεὶ γὰρ ἐν ταῖς γραφαῖς ὁ λόγος σάρξ ἐγένετο.
[101] Origen, *Philoc.* 15.19; Luke 9:31; cf. Behr, *Way to Nicaea*, 169–81.

Melito of Sardis, Apollinaris of Hierapolis, Polycrates of Ephesus, and, in a class by himself, Irenaeus of Lyons.[102] Together with these ancient readers, of course, we should also include the modern scholars who work on patristic texts (among whom I have lurked for several decades).

The second category is that of modern scriptural scholarship. It is impossible to give a full review of Johannine scholarship in this context, but it should be noted that with regard to our topic of the Passion and its relationship to the Incarnation and revelation scholars have been divided as to what extent the cross has any soteriological role to play for John, and if so, whether it is primarily a matter of revelation or whether it also includes an expiatory or atoning function.[103] Bultmann and Käsemann, most notably, assert that the cross has no soteriological function at all for John, it has been overshadowed or eclipsed by the Incarnation (as Hanson similarly depicts Athanasius).[104] Others, most forcefully Forestell, take the crucifixion of the Incarnate Word to be the ultimate and paradigmatic means of Christ's saving revelation.[105] Another group of scholars give more weight to the atoning or expiatory role of the Passion in John's Gospel,[106] largely treating the Gospel as a unity,

[102] J. B. Lightfoot, *Essays on the Work Entitled Supernatural Religion* (London: Macmillan, 1889), esp. 217–50, 'The Later School of St John'; 217: 'While St Peter and St Paul converted disciples and organized congregations, St John alone was the founder of a school.... Hence the traditions of St John are more direct, more consistent, and more trustworthy, than those which relate to the other Apostles'. For the relation of Ignatius of Antioch to this 'school', see ibid. 59–88; on Irenaeus, see ibid. 251–71. It should be noted that others use the term 'school' for the 'community' around John, for instance, R. Alan Culpepper, *The Johannine School: An Evaluation of the Johannine-School Hypothesis Based on an Investigation of the Nature of Ancient Schools*, SBLDS, 26 (Missoula, MO: Scholars Press, 1975). Hereafter, when I use the term 'school' it will be in the sense of J. B. Lightfoot.

[103] For a more extensive survey of the literature, Gilbert van Belle, 'The Death of Jesus and the Literary Unity of the Fourth Gospel', in van Belle, ed., *The Death of Jesus in the Fourth Gospel*, BETL 200 (Leuven: University Press, 2007). 3–64, at 43–64, and John Morgan-Wynne, *The Cross in the Johannine Writings* (Eugene, OR: Pickwick Publications, 2011), 4–39.

[104] See Rudolf Bultman, *The Gospel of John*, trans. George R. Beasley-Murray et al. (Oxford: Blackwell, 1971 [1941]); Käsemann, *Testament*; U. B. Müller, 'Die Bedeutung des Kreuzestodes Jesu im Johannesevangelium: Erwägung des Kreuzestheologie im NT', *Kerygma und Dogma* 21 (1975), 31–78; Jürgen Becker, *Das Evangelium des Johannes*, 2 vols (Gütersloh: Mohn, 1979, 1981); William Loader, *The Christology of the Fourth Gospel. Structure and Issues*, 2nd rev. ed., BBET 23 (Frankfurt: Peter Lang, 1992).

[105] J. Terence Forestell, *The Word of the Cross: Salvation and Revelation in the Fourth Gospel, AB 57* (Rome: Biblical Institute, 1974), 19: 'in Jn the incarnation is not simply the necessary condition for Jesus' glorification, nor is it the saving event to which the cross is entirely subordinate. The incarnation of the Logos is rather the beginning of a revelatory process which culminates in the supreme revelation, namely, the glorification of Jesus Christ the Son of God'. See also Hoskyns, *The Fourth Gospel*; C. H. Dodd, *The Interpretation of the Fourth Gospel* (Cambridge: Cambridge University Press, 1953); Günther Bornkamm, 'Towards the Interpretation of John's Gospel: A Discussion of *The Testament of Jesus* by Ernst Käsemann', in John Ashton, ed., *The Interpretation of John*, 2nd edn, Studies in New Testament Interpretation (Edinburgh: T & T Clark, 1997), 97–119.

[106] See Franz Mussner, *ΖΩΗ: Die Anschauung vom 'Leben' im vierten Evangelium unter Berücksichtigung der Johannesbriefe* (Munich: Zink, 1952); Charles Kingsley Barrett, *The Gospel*

though some trace a development within the writing of the Gospel with respect to this theme, with the atoning value of the cross either being there at the beginning, before developing into a more paraenetic style,[107] or only incorporated at a later stage.[108] The cross is regularly seen by scholars in both camps as the means whereby the Word, having entered into the world at the Incarnation, departs from this world to return to the Father,[109] with a related debate as to whether the crucifixion, ascension, and resurrection should be held together as one 'event', and whether doing so constitutes a development within a process by which the Gospel arrived at its final form.[110] Thüsing's proposal that there were two stages to Jesus' glorification, first, that of the cross, and second, the time following the crucifixion,[111] has largely been

according to St. John: An Introduction with Commentary and Notes on the Greek Text (London: SPCK, 1967); Wilhem Thüsing, *Die Erhöhung und Verherrlichung Jesu im Johannesevangelium*, 3rd edn (Munich: Aschendorff, 1979 [1960]); Rudolf Schnackenburg, *The Gospel According to St. John*, vol. 1 ET Kevin Smyth (London: Burns and Oats, 1968), vol. 2 ET Cecily Hastings et al. (London: Burns and Oats, 1980), vol. 3 ET D. Smith and G. A. Korn (New York: Crossroad, 1982), see esp. 1.156–9, 2.39–410; Barnabas Lindars, *The Gospel of John*, New Century Bible (Grand Rapids, MI: Eerdmans 1987 [1972]); Raymond Brown, *The Gospel According to John*, 2 vols, The Anchor Bible, 29, 29A (New York: Doubleday, 1966, 1970); B. H. Rigsby, 'The Cross as an Expiatory Sacrifice in the Fourth Gospel', *JSNT* 15 (1982), 51–80; Max B. Turner, 'Atonement and the Death of Jesus in John—Some Questions to Bultmann and Forestell', *Evangelical Quarterly* 62 (1990), 99–122; Donald A. Carson, *The Gospel According to John* (Leicester: InterVarsity, 1991); Jörg Frey, 'Die "theologia crucifixi" des Johannesevangelium', in Andreas Dettwiler and Jean Zumstein, eds, *Kreuzestheologia im Neuen Testament*, WUNT 151 (Tübingen: Mohr Siebeck, 2002), 169–238; Craig R. Koester, *Symbolism in the Fourth Gospel: Meaning, Mystery, Community*, 2nd edn (Minneapolis: Fortress, 2003); John F. McHugh, *John 1—4: A Critical and Exegetical Commentary* International Critical Commentary (London: Bloomsbury, 2014).

[107] Georg Richter, *Studien zum Johannesevangelium*, ed. Joseph Hainz (Regensburg: Pustet, 1977).

[108] Most fully by Martinus C. de Boer, *Johannine Perspectives on the Death of Jesus, BET 17* (Kampen: Pharos, 1996); see also Wilhelm Wilkens, *Die Entstehungsgeschichte des vierten Evangeliums* (Zollikon: EVZ, 1958) and *Zeichen und Werke: Ein Beitrag zur Theologie des vierten Evangeliums in Erzählungs- und Redestoff*, AThANT 55 (Zürich: TVZ, 1969); Michael Theobald, *Die Fleischwerdung des Logos: Studien zum Verhältnis des Johannesprologs zum Corpus des Evangeliums und zu 1Joh.*, Neutestamentliche Abhandlungen, NF 20 (Münster: Aschendorff, 1988).

[109] See Godfrey C. Nicholson, *Death as Departure: The Johannine Descent-Ascent Schema*, SBLDS 63 (Chico, CA: Scholars Press, 1983); so too in many ways Herbert Kohler, *Kreuz und Menschwerdung im Johannesevangelium: Ein exegetisch-hermeneutischer Versuch zur johanneischen Kreuzestheologie*, ATANT 72 (Zürich: TVZ, 1987) and Thomas Knöppler, *Die theologia crucis des Johannesevangeliums. Das Verständnis des Todes Jesu im Rahmen der johanneischen Inkarnations- und Erhöhungschristologie*, WMANT 69 (Neukirchen: Neukirchener Verlag, 1994).

[110] De Boer, for instance, would see the application of the resurrection/ascension language to the crucifixion as a secondary development in the writing of the Gospel: see *Johannine Perspectives on the Death of Jesus*, 118–44, and 'Jesus' Departure to the Father in John: Death or Resurrection?', in Gilbert van Belle, Jan G. Van der Watt, P. Maritz, eds, *Theology and Christology in the Fourth Gospel* BETL 184 (Leuven: University Press-Peeters, 2005), 1–19.

[111] Thüsing, *Die Erhöhung und Verherrlichung Jesu.*

rejected in preference of seeing the whole life of Jesus upon earth as already a manifestation of his glory, culminating in the ultimate glorification that is the Passion, although as Bornkamm reminds us, 'Christ's life before the Passion can only ever be spoken about *in retrospect*... [for] the faith that lies behind the Johannine picture of Christ is not in the first place grounded in the earthly Jesus but upon him who died on the cross'.[112] One of Thüsing's first critics, Josef Blank, takes this retrospect further, into eternity, to emphasize, much as we would do in this volume, that 'In HIM, as the Exalted One, the cross is abidingly present, because the Exalted One, in all eternity, is the Crucified One and the Crucified One is the Exalted One'.[113]

One other work deserving special mention, as taking a different interest in the death of Christ and the cross, is Hans-Ulrich Weidemann, *Der Tod Jesu im Johannesevangelium*.[114] Noting, as others have done, that the 'flesh' that the Word becomes in John 1:14 already contains an allusion to his later death (for it is in mortal flesh that the Word dies), Weidemann argues that the Prologue functions not as an introduction to the Gospel but as its 'metatext', and so 1:14 does not provide a starting point for narrating what happens next, but is rather the 'Summe', a summary of the whole Gospel.[115] Weidemann pays special attention to the first farewell discourse (13:31–14:31) as the key text for understanding the Passion narrative and appearances of the risen Lord (18–20), taking chapters 15–17 and 21 as being by a later redactor. Weidemann emphasizes what he calls the 'satanological' dimension of the victory of Christ, whose blood acts in an apotropaic manner in warding off and defeating Satan, as the lamb's blood does in Exodus 12,[116] and also the eschatological new creation effected by the Spirit who comes from the crucified one, whose return is now transformed into the coming of the Father and the Son to dwell in those who love Jesus.[117] Our interest in this volume aligns somewhat with Weidemann in seeing, in Part II, what it is that is 'finished' on the cross, in the sense of finally established or constructed, rather than weighing between sacrificial and revelatory interpretations of the Passion, but doing so by seeing this 'finishing' in the light of the 'apocalyptic' reading of John initiated and most fully developed by John Ashton (what is meant by 'apocalyptic' will be explored in Chapter 2). As we do so we will argue that the Incarnation is not the beginning of an episode in the biography of the Word which culminates later with his departure or return via the cross, but a movement that pivots upon the cross itself and the identity of the one hanging upon it. As such we will also give, in Chapter 5, a reading of the Prologue which takes it as a

[112] Bornkamm, 'Towards the Interpretation of John's Gospel', 107–8; italics original.

[113] Josef Blank, *Krisis: Untersuchungen zur johanneischen Christologie und Eschatologie* (Freiburg: Lambertus, 1964), 288; his emphasis.

[114] Hans-Ulrich Weidemann, *Der Tod Jesu im Johannesevangelium: Die erste Abschiedsrede als Schlüsseltext für den Passions- und Osterbericht*, BZNW 122 (Berlin: de Gruyter, 2004).

[115] Ibid. 29. [116] Ibid. 423–44. [117] Ibid. 515–16.

'summary' of the whole Gospel, but in rather different terms than has been done by others.

The third category of readers of John is occupied by a single figure, the French phenomenologist Michel Henry (and those who work on him). There are, of course, many other philosophers whose work could profitably be brought to bear on the themes relating to the study of the Gospel of John. However, Henry's last three books provide a sustained reading of the Gospels and in particular that of John (and also Irenaeus), or, perhaps better, an engagement with the poetics of their texts in reflecting upon the themes that are of central concern for this work, that is, the connection between the Passion, the Incarnation, and revelation. Henry and his work will be introduced fully in Chapter 6.

There are two further categories of readers that are not engaged in this work, although they preoccupy much modern scriptural scholarship. The first is the 'community' for whom the Gospel was written (as distinct to Lightfoot's 'school'), and in the case of the Gospel of John who are also part of its writers. The Gospel of John, unlike the Synoptics, has the community give its own imprimatur to what is written: 'This is the disciple who is bearing witness to these things and who has written these things, and we know that his testimony is true' (21:24). The Gospel of John moreover specifically refers to itself as a 'book' (*βίβλιον* 20:30).[118] There is, therefore, indisputable evidence of authorial layers within this text. In the second edition of his work on John, Ashton argues passionately, against the prevailing trend, for the legitimacy and benefit of reading a work 'diachronically', that is, examining the historical process by which the book came to be composed, working from indications regarding the composition such as 21:24 that directly point to different levels of composition or even different editions. As he points out, the reading of a literary work can be significantly increased by looking at early sketches, the author's notebooks, or relevant correspondence.[119] It is the case, however, that, apart from the episode of the adulterous woman (John 8:1–11) and of course the numerous manuscript variations, the Gospel of John has come down to us from the beginning as we have it today. Nevertheless, there are many *aporias*, difficulties or imponderables, within the text that can be taken as indicators of layers of redaction.[120] These include, most notably, the character of John 21, as an appendix or epilogue given after the stated conclusion of the book (20:30–1),

[118] See now, Christina Petterson, *From Tomb to Text: The Body of Jesus in the Book of John* (London: Bloomsbury T & T Clark, 2017).

[119] Cf. Ashton, *Fourth Gospel*, 13, with some delightful comments from Dr Johnson on Milton's *Paradise Lost*.

[120] The designation of these problematic aspects of the text of the Gospel as *aporia* is that of Eduard Schwartz, 'Aporien in vierten Evangelium', *Nachrichten von der königlichen Gesellschaft der Wissenschaften zu Göttingen: Philologisch-historische Klasse* (1907), 342–72; (1908), 115–88, 497–650.

and indications of a dislocation of an original order, such as the awkward conjunction between chapters 5 and 6, the relation between chapters 9 and 10, and the thoroughly anomalous conclusion to Christ's farewell discourse in 14:31, 'rise, let us go hence', not followed by any movement but rather three more chapters of discourse. As we will see in Chapter 2, ancient readers expected scriptural texts to be enigmatic and cryptic, to have 'stumbling blocks' as Origen describes them. However, for modern readers the only really satisfactory explanation for these *aporias* is an account of how the text came to be as it is. And there have been, of course, many attempts to do just this, most notably the 'ecclesiastical redactor' postulated by Rudolf Bultmann and the histories of the Johannine community written by Raymond Brown and others. Of particular interest for our work are the conclusions of J. Louis Martyn, Martinus C. de Boer, and Paul S. Minear that the context for the Gospel of John, and especially its development of a high Christology, is that of martyrdom, as will be noted in the appropriate places.[121]

This line of inquiry, however, has not been pursued in this work, not because it is deemed unimportant or too speculative, but because our interests lie elsewhere, that is, with understanding the connection between the Incarnation and the Passion, and what kind of revelation this facilitates and for whom. Yet this also turns upon a section of the Gospel which is regularly held to indicate an *aporia*, that is, the Prologue. While the intention of the Gospel is explicitly stated to be 'that you might believe that Jesus is the Christ, the Son of God and that believing you may have life in his name' (20:31), the Prologue, focusing as it does on the Word and becoming flesh of the Word, is regularly considered to be either an adaptation of an earlier Logos hymn or the culmination of a high, incarnational Christology which the author(s) of earlier levels or editions of the Gospel had not yet attained. As with the 'epilogue' (21:24), the Prologue also has a plural authorization (1:14, 'we have seen his glory'). The argument of this book, however, is that the Prologue speaks in a different register, and that this is how it was heard by its earliest (subsequent) readers (the 'school' rather than the 'community'), so that there is no need, at least in the case of the Prologue, to seek a resolution to a perceived *aporia* by referring to the community and its readers and authors. What might seem to us to be an *aporia* might instead be due to the methodological problems associated with the 'mythology of doctrines' discussed earlier. If I have privileged the 'school' of John over his 'community', and treated it in Part I before turning to the Gospel (and modern readers) in Part II, it is not to suggest that the 'school' of John alone gives us access to the proper horizon for reading the

[121] J. Louis Martyn, *History and Theology in the Fourth Gospel*, 3rd edn (Louisville: Westminster John Knox Press, 2003 [1968]); de Boer, *Johannine Perspectives on the Death of Jesus*; Paul S. Minear, *John: The Martyr's Gospel* (Eugene, OR: Wipf and Stock, 1984).

Gospel on its own terms, but to bring to life the figure of John as he was remembered by his 'school' and the further horizons that this opens up for us.

The second category of reader not addressed in this work is the figure often described as the implied reader (and also the implied author) spoken about by those scholars who are primarily, if not exclusively, interested with a synchronic rather than diachronic reading of the finished text, as it has come down to us, focusing on its narrative structures and devices.[122] If the implied reader has not been addressed here (for can one really say 'heard'?),[123] it is not because it is deemed unimportant. Many insights have indeed been gained from approaching the text from such a perspective, paying close attention to the structure of the narrative and its plot. However, it is much weaker when it comes to providing an account of the *aporia* within the text. For instance, Derek Tovey asserts that the 'gaps, lacunae and fissures in the text' should be understood 'as purposively conceived, to be understood and resolved in terms of the rhetorical strategies and ploys of the implied author, or as textual signals inviting the implied reader to actualize the narrative reality or obtain meaning by testing hypotheses and imaginatively filling the gaps'.[124] As Ashton comments: 'this is clearly an invitation to the implied readers of the Gospel (why not the real readers?) to fill in the gaps for themselves. But how? In accordance with "the perceived strategies and ploys", not, be it noted, of the real author, who guards his independence, but of the implied author, always at the beck and call of his inventor, the narrative critic who has designed and constructed him'.[125] Besides the exclusivity of this approach often insisted upon by its practitioners, and rightly protested by Ashton, the character of the implied reader needs to be more fully addressed, for a work such as the Gospel of John certainly, as Markus Bockmuehl notes, 'envisages a certain *kind* of reader', one who has a personal stake in the truthfulness of what is said, who has undergone an intellectual and moral conversion, who is ecclesially situated, and so on.[126] In fact, as Bockmuehl argues, 'the earliest effective

[122] The groundbreaking work for Johannine studies is R. Alan Culpepper's *Anatomy of the Fourth Gospel: A Study in Literary Design*, New Testament: Foundations and Facets (Philadelphia: Fortress Press, 1983).

[123] Cf. M. M. Bakhtin, 'Toward a Methodology for the Human Sciences', in Bakhtin, *Speech Genres*, 159–72, at 165: 'In this understanding the ideal listener is essentially a mirror image of the author who replicates him . . . he cannot be *an-other* or other for the author, he cannot have any *surplus* that is determined by this otherness'.

[124] Derek Tovey, *Narrative Art and Act in the Fourth Gospel*, JSNTSup 151 (Sheffield: Sheffield University Press, 1977), 21.

[125] Ashton, *Fourth Gospel*, 19. See also Petterson, *Tomb to Text*, xxiii, regarding postcolonial, post/structuralist, narratological, or rhetorical approaches, 'such readings, precisely because of their ease and appeal, their unaccountability, and the total oblivion to their historical contexts and ideological framework make me profoundly uncomfortable'.

[126] Markus Bockmuehl, *Seeing the Word: Refocusing New Testament Study*, STI (Grand Rapids, MI: Baker Academic, 2006), 69, italics original; see 68–74 for a full account of the intended reader.

history in the subapostolic period of living memory [i.e. Lightfoot's 'School of John'] might constitute one possible focus for the connection between readers actually addressed by the text and the readings it actually generated'.[127] It is exactly this that we hope to accomplish by bringing in these voices to the conversation, to help us see the text in ways other than we might have assumed, so avoiding assumptions about 'Incarnation' that would otherwise be held, even by narrative critics.

Somewhat related to the postulated community and the implied reader, and a very striking feature of the Gospel of John, is the way in which several of the key passages are written in a manner that blurs the distinction between the time of Jesus as narrated in the Gospel and the present of the narrator now giving his witness. The most startling example of this is Jesus' words to Nicodemus: 'Truly, truly I say to you, we speak of what we know and bear witness to what we have seen; but you do not receive our testimony' (3:11). As Paul Minear comments, 'the present tense of Jesus becomes the present tense (we know) of the narrator and that present tense becomes in turn an inclusive past (we have seen). In saying *we*, the narrator associates himself on the one hand with Jesus and on the other hand with other leaders who have seen and who now join in giving their testimonies'.[128] Similar elisions of time recur frequently throughout the Gospel of John. Perhaps the most graphic is the determination by the Jews that those who believe in Christ should be put out of the synagogue (9:22), which led J. Louis Martyn to suggest that the Gospel be read as a 'two-level drama', as we will see Chapter 2. It also happens more subtly in those places which have an unexpected change of tense, such as 6:51, or those which mention 'the hour' or 'the last day'. As Minear notes, in words which echo those of Ehrman quoted at the beginning of this chapter, 'there is such a complete correlation between the words of the narrator and the words of his major character that they cannot be separated'. For Minear, however, this is a necessary aspect of the task of hermeneutics: 'He interprets past events in such a way as to span the temporal distance between *then* and *now*, and he interprets the events of salvation in such a way as to span the a-temporal distance between the glorified Lord and the worshipping Church'.[129] This merging of times, or melding of horizons in Gadamer's terms, will be a recurring theme as we examine the text of John in Part II.

It should furthermore be noted that the distinction between our first two categories of readers—the 'School of John' and modern scholars—is in fact

[127] Ibid. 68; Bockmuehl devotes chapter 6 to exploring this further.

[128] Minear, *John: The Martyr's Gospel*, 4, italic original. For a full examination of this phenomenon, see Jörg Frey, *Die johanneische Eschatologie*, 3 vols, WUNT 96, 110, 117 (Tübingen: Mohr Siebeck, 1997, 1998, 200), 2.247–68, and more generally Douglas Estes, *The Temporal Mechanics of the Fourth Gospel: A Theory of Hermeneutical Relativity in the Gospel of John, BIS 92* (Leiden: Brill. 2008).

[129] Minear, *John: The Martyr's Gospel*, 12, italics original.

somewhat artificial, for both are reading and interpreting scriptural texts, albeit in different epochs, with different presuppositions, and for different purposes. The primary difference, of course, is that the Fathers (even, usually, when writing commentaries) were not oriented, as modern scriptural scholarship has largely been, towards understanding what the texts meant in their historical context, but rather towards the theological task of thinking though the revelation of God in Christ coherently, in their own context, and for their own (pastoral and polemical) purposes, continuing the merging of times already there in John. Over the last decade increasing attention has been given by New Testament scholars to the reception of scriptural texts through the centuries. A recent example of this is the book by Ben C. Blackwell, *Christosis: Engaging Paul's Soteriology with His Patristic Interpreters*. In his Foreword to the book, John Barclay laments that:

> The last few generations of 'historical-critical scholarship' have made a virtue of attempting to ignore practically the whole history of reception of Paul on the grounds that we, with our superior historical knowledge, know what the text (or the author) is *really* saying, while the history of reception (until perhaps the 19th century) is a catalogue of more or less egregious misreadings of Paul. Thus if one came across a book that paid any attention to the history of reception, one would expect this to be discussed *after* a foundational, 'objective' and 'historical' reading to the text, and as illustration of what later readers did or did not get of what *we* have already determined to be the *real* Paul.[130]

Yet, as we have seen, the attempt to understand a text in its own historical horizon is not only a legitimate task but a necessary one, and, in fact, the same one that must also be carried out whenever we read texts pertaining to the reception of Scripture, for they are also at a historical remove from us. Blackwell himself does not bring together directly the two different readings of Paul, but neither does he treat Patristic readings as a mere postscript. Rather he begins his work by exploring the theme of 'christosis' or deification in Irenaeus and Cyril of Alexandria, a theme which is not an integral part of his own (Western) religious tradition, to open up lines of thought and other ways of thinking to which Paul gave rise in the early (and largely Eastern) tradition, before turning to Paul and his modern readers.[131] It is an attempt, as it were, to break the hold of the 'mythology of doctrine', the unexamined presuppositions which would otherwise direct his reading, and allow him to see in the texts of Paul other possibilities previously neglected within his own scholarly and religious traditions.

[130] John Barclay, 'Foreword', in Ben C. Blackwell, *Christosis: Engaging Paul's Soteriology with His Patristic Interpreters* (Grand Rapids, MI: Eerdmans, 2016), xvi, italics original.

[131] Cf. Blackwell, *Christosis*, 23–4.

My own religious tradition, that of Eastern Orthodoxy, holds the Gospel of John intimately together with the celebration of Pascha or Easter (indeed, the Prologue is the reading for the paschal midnight liturgy), a feast that according to the earliest evidence we have, as we will see, actually originates with John himself. Thus the presuppositions of my own religious tradition are somewhat at odds with those of the Western tradition of historical scholarship (which is nevertheless equally my own) and also much modern (Eastern and Western) theology, which tend to think of John primarily in terms of 'Incarnation', taking this as an episode or event distinct from, and overshadowing, Pascha (or even rendering it redundant as Käsemann on John and Hanson on Athanasius), treating it as an event that occurred only in the past and therefore a proper subject for historical inquiry rather than the ongoing event at the heart of theology. Navigating between both exposes the presuppositions of both, and this has led me to read across the grain of much twentieth-century theology (Western and Eastern) and Johannine scholarship (largely Western), as already indicated, but doing so, as demanded by the tradition of Western scholarship, in a historically and exegetically grounded manner.

Like Blackwell, this work also begins with John's early readers. Unlike Blackwell, however, in Part II I have attempted to bring together the early Fathers and modern scriptural scholars whenever possible, most importantly when treating the Prologue, John 6, and the passages that speak of the Son of Man, for the purpose of this book is not primarily historical—to get to 'the real John', or John as remembered and read by his 'school', or the Gospel as read (and to some extent co-authored) by its original 'community'—but theological. Projecting a historical horizon, however necessary it is, is yet but one step in the process of understanding both the text under consideration and ourselves as its readers, a step needing to be sublated, as Gadamer put it, by a melding of the various historical horizons in the present. This, I would argue, is where the properly theological task emerges, that of thinking through the revelation of God in Christ and ourselves in its light. The apostles and evangelists are, in a unique sense, the historical witnesses to this revelation, and John especially, as the only one present at the crucifixion. Yet they are not only historical witnesses (for our historical investigations), but also theologians, *the* theologian in the case of John, engaged in understanding and communicating the gospel in their own context, their own present, merging the times, and for their own purposes, initiating thereby the tradition of Christian theology.

Scriptural exegesis did, for various reasons, end up, as Barclay laments, in the modern project of focusing on the text only in its historical context. And, as we have seen in the example of Hanson, this way of reading Scripture has become all but normative for theology itself, so splitting apart the way in which the Fathers read Scripture and the supposedly separable task of theological reflection. This has left theology strangely unmoored, with the theology that was developed in the early centuries separated from the exegetical practices in which it was produced and uneasily juxtaposed alongside modern exegesis. Scriptural exegesis, in the way Barclay characterizes it, has also, in turn, become detached from theological reflection and rarely ventures into its domain. Yet this has not been a dead end, for the rigour that modern, historically oriented scholarship has brought to the task of listening to ancient texts (the Fathers as well as Scripture) has allowed them to speak to us in ways that we might not otherwise have heard, breaking the spell of a 'mythology of doctrines', especially when we pay careful attention to the way in which the Fathers reflected theologically through scriptural exegesis, following practices that, as even Hanson concedes, were shared by the apostles and evangelists. These practices of reading Scripture (the 'Old Testament'), and the writings of the New Testament when read *as Scripture*, will be explored in Chapter 2. In one sense, then, this book aims to take the modern historical project further, by taking fuller account of the early readers of John, and, in another sense, by allowing these voices directly into the conversation, to bring historically oriented exegesis (of scriptural and Patristic texts) and theology together again, so melding the horizons in the act of understanding, '*if*', as Gadamer concedes, '*we understand at all*'.

What then of the third category of reader and Part III of this study? The very different nature of Michel Henry's discourse is such that it has not been possible to bring him directly into the conversations in the first two parts; the uneasy relationship between hermeneutics and phenomenology is also at play here. The task of bringing Henry into the discussion is thus left to the penultimate chapter and the conclusion. Yet, inasmuch as our central concern in this volume is the relationship between the Incarnation and the Passion, and how revelation is effected through this, Henry's phenomenology has much to say, both about the theme of revelation (how things appear and in what horizon they do so) and, as it turns out, about flesh itself (is it simply a body or human nature appearing in the world?), such that he too must be invited to address our conversation.

This chapter has already, in an extensive but still preliminary manner, exposed and put into question our own presuppositions about the Incarnation and the Passion by listening to a few ancient and modern writers. We can now begin the work itself by turning to the historical task of situating John as, and for what, he was remembered by his early readers, to open up our own horizons to other ways of thinking about the relationship between the Incarnation and the Passion, the identity of Christ and the cross, and thereby the theme of revelation. We can then explore these themes in the Gospel of John in Part II, bringing together ancient and modern writers, and, in Part III, turn to a philosophical reading, to bring further rigour, or a different kind of rigour, to the task of theological understanding.

Part I

John the Theologian and his Paschal Gospel

1

John the Evangelist

If the publication of Martin Hengel's book *The Johannine Question* delivered, in Charles Hill's words, a 'spanking' to the guild of Johannine scholars for their theories regarding the origins of the Gospel of John and its character, it was only received as a light lashing for they continued their work 'almost unaffected'.[1] Hill's own exhaustive and meticulous study, *The Johannine Corpus in the Early Church*, on the other hand, has surely administered the final flogging of the twin horses that by any academic standard should have been dead at the starting post, that is, the twin theories of 'orthodox Johannophobia' and 'Gnostic Johannophilia'. The idea that the Gospel according to John originated in and was first used by heterodox circles and was initially viewed with suspicion by the orthodox Church, which remained silent about it until Irenaeus appropriated it for use by the Great Church, is not only debunked by Hill, but turned on its head: 'there is no "silence" which needs to be accounted for. On the contrary, instead of a silence one might better speak of a din, a relative tumult, an increasing uproar'.[2] If there was a 'Johannophobia' it was in point of fact among the 'Gnostics', whose relationship to this Gospel was 'critical or adversarial' (as seen especially in *The Acts of John* and the *Apocryphon of James*, and also in the *Trimorphic Protennoia*, the *Second Apocalypse of James*, and the *Gospel of Thomas*), before the Valentians attempted to appropriate the Gospel by a novel interpretation of its Prologue; the Gospel's offence, to them, was its emphasis on the Incarnation of the Word of God and its affirmation of the privileged status of the eyewitnesses, the very points which were already central to the

[1] Charles Hill, *The Johannine Corpus in the Early Church* (Oxford: Oxford University Press, 2004), 58, referring to Martin Hengel, *The Johannine Question* (London: SCM Press, 1989), *Die johanneische Frage: Ein Lösungsversuch*, with a contribution on the Apocalypse by Jörg Frey, WUNT 67 (Tübingen: Mohr Siebeck, 1993). See also Charles E. Hill, 'The "Orthodox Gospel": The Reception of John in the Great Church Prior to Irenaeus', in Tuomas Rasimus, ed., *The Legacy of John*, SupplNovT 132 (Leiden: Brill, 2010), 233–300 and Charles E. Hill, *Who Chose the Gospels? Probing the Great Gospel Conspiracy* (Oxford: Oxford University Press, 2010).

[2] Hill *Johannine Corpus*, 444.

letters of John.[3] Irenaeus did not pull off 'the literary *coup* of the century',[4] but continued the tradition witnessing to what had been known 'from the beginning' (1 John 1:1).

Our purpose here is not to review the details of the case made by Hill; it has been rigorously made. This chapter will rather, first, attempt to clarify one remaining point of contention and to emphasize a few other points regarding the historical witness to the occasion for John having written his Gospel and its connection to the other texts attributed to him, and, second, highlight a specific aspect of the historical witness to John, the significance of which has not yet been fully appreciated for understanding his Gospel. The point of contention concerns a confusion that has existed, if not from the beginning, then at least from Eusebius, regarding the relationship between two Johns—John the Apostle, the son of Zebedee known to us from the Synoptic Gospels, and John the Elder—and the vexed question of which of these Johns was the author of the Gospel. The feature of the historical witness significant for understanding of the Gospel of John concerns the annual celebration of Pascha in the Johannine tradition but likely not initially, as we will see, elsewhere.

JOHN THE ELDER, THE DISCIPLE OF THE LORD

Papias, Irenaeus, and Eusebius

Among the earliest witnesses to the Gospel of John, the most important, and difficult, witness is that of Papias of Hierapolis. Papias, as we will see, had busied himself, early in the second century, collecting information about the apostles and disciples of Christ from any oral tradition that he was able to access. Although Hengel would date Papias' work to between 120 and 135 CE, on the basis of a comment by Philip of Side to the effect

[3] Ibid. 466–7. For the 'Gnostic' reading see ibid., 205–93, concluding: 'All this means that, rather than Irenaeus being the great innovator, as many have thought, pioneering an orthodox interpretation of the gnostic Gospel of John, it appears that Valentinus, or more probably Ptolemy, was the creative genius who engineered a reinterpretation of the abstract nouns of the Johannine Prologue to adapt to a theory of pleromatic aeons and syzygies which had been borrowed from "the Gnostics". Predominantly the earliest appropriation of John on the part of the gnostic writers was adversarial or supersessionary. In this sense it is they who appear to be the first Johannophobes. It was the Valentinians who found a new way of "receiving" this Gospel, used by the mainstream Church, by finding names for its pleromatic aeons in John's "philosophical Prologue"'.

[4] Ibid. 78.

that some of those whom Jesus raised from the dead survived into the reign of Hadrian (117–38 CE), Philip ('a bungler [who] cannot be trusted', as William Schoedel puts it) has probably misattributed to Papias Eusebius' report of a statement made by Quadratus in the pages immediately following his account of Papias.[5] Eusebius is in fact very specific and clear about the dating of Papias. As Vernon Bartlet had earlier pointed out, Eusebius turns to Papias's writings in *h.e.* 3.39, after treating Clement of Rome, whose death he places in the third year of Trajan (i.e. *c.*100 CE).[6] Eusebius notes that it would be impossible to enumerate by name all those who belonged to the first generation after the apostles, and so limits himself to those who preserved the apostolic teaching, mentioning specifically Ignatius and Clement (*h.e.* 3.37.4–38.3). After treating Papias in *h.e.* 3.39, Eusebius ends the third book of his *Ecclesiastical History*, which nowhere goes beyond the times of Trajan, and opens the fourth book with the twelfth year of Trajan (*c.*110 CE, *h.e.* 4.1) before turning to the age of Hadrian (117–38 CE; *h.e.* 4.3.1). As we will see, Eusebius had very mixed feelings about Papias, and, as Bauckham points out, could easily have discredited his witness to the apostolic age by placing him in a later period.[7] The first decade of the second century seems the most secure place to locate Papias' literary activity. However, more significant is the fact that when he began composing his written work, he is recalling information that he had gathered in an earlier period, that is, in the last decades of the first century, the very time when, as most New Testament scholars would hold, the Gospel of John was being written or reached its final form.

Eusebius' account of Papias' writings in *h.e.* 3.39 is a complex, multi-layered chapter, incorporating not only texts from Papias, but a testimony of Irenaeus as well as, of course, Eusebius' own comments. It is necessary to give it in a

[5] Hengel, *Die johanneische Frage*, 77; William Schoedel, *The Apostolic Fathers*, vol. 5, *Polycarp, Martyrdom of Polycarp, Fragments of Papias* (New York: Nelson, 1967), 120. The passage about Quadratus is in Eusebius *h.e.* 4.3. The passage of Philip of Side in question is from his *Hist. Christiana*, in C. de Boor, ed., *Neue Fragmente des Papias, Hegesippus und Pierius. In bisher unbekannten Excerpten aus der Kirchengeschichte des Philippus Sidetes*, TU 5.2b (Leipzig: Hinrich's, 1888), 170, numbered as Papias Fragment 16 by J. Kürzinger, *Papias von Hierapolis und die Evangelien des Neuen Testaments* (Regensburg: Pustet, 1983), 116–17.

[6] Eusebius treats Clement in *h.e.* 3.38, and mentions the date of his death in *h.e.* 3.34. Cf. Vernon Bartlet, 'Papias's "Exposition": Its Date and Contents', in H. G. Wood, ed., *Amicitiae Corolla: A Volume of Essays Presented to James Rendel Harris, D. Litt., on the Occasion of his Eightieth Birthday* (London: University of London Press, 1933), 15–44, at 20–2. See also R. W. Yarbrough, 'The Date of Papias: A Reassessment', *JTS* ns 26 (1983), 181–91; and U. H. J. Körtner, *Papias von Hierapolis: Ein Beitrag zur Geschichte des frühen Christentum*, FRLANT 133 (Göttingen, 1983), 225–6; Hill, *Johannine Corpus*, 383–4.

[7] Richard Bauckham, *Jesus and the Eyewitnesses: The Gospels as Eyewitness Testimony* (Grand Rapids, MI: Eerdmans, 2006), 14.

fairly full form here, so that we can analyse clearly what is being said by whom and how that is heard by the later hands in this text:[8]

> [3.39.1] Of Papias there are five treatises extant, which also have been entitled *Interpretation of the Dominical Oracles* [*λογίων κυριακόν ἐξηγή-σεως*]. Irenaeus mentions these as the only works written by him, saying at any rate as follows [*ὧδέ πως λέγων*]:
>
> > These things Papias also, a hearer of John and a companion of Polycarp, an ancient man [*Παπίας ὁ Ἰωάννου μὲν ἀκουστής, Πολυκάρπου δὲ ἑταῖρος γεγονώς, ἀρχαῖος ἀνήρ*], attests in the fourth of his books. For there are five books composed by him. [= *haer.* 5.33.4]
>
> [2] So, indeed, says Irenaeus. Yet Papias himself in the preface to his discourses makes it plain that he himself had in no way been a hearer and eye-witness of the holy apostles, but declares, through the language he uses, that he had received the things pertaining to the faith from those who were familiar with them:
>
> > [3] I will not hesitate also to set down for you, along with the interpretations,[9] everything that at that time I carefully learnt from the elders and carefully noted down, guaranteeing the truth of them. For I did not take delight, as most do, in those who speak much, but in those who teach the truth, nor in those who recount strange commandments, but in those who recall the commandments given by the Lord to faith and deriving from the truth itself. [4] And if anyone chanced to come by, who had been in attendance on the elders,[10] I inquired about the words of the elders—[that is,] what [according to the elders] Andrew or Peter said [*εἶπεν*], or Philip or Thomas or James or John or Matthew or any other of the disciples of the Lord [*τῶν τοῦ κυρίου μαθητῶν*], and whatever Aristion and John the Elder [*ὁ πρεσβύτερος Ἰωάννης*], disciples of the Lord [*τοῦ κυρίου μαθηταί*], are saying [*λέγουσιν*]. For I did not suppose that things from books would profit me as much as things from a living and abiding voice.

[8] In what follows, I have used the translation of H. J. Lawlor and J. E. L. Oulton, *Eusebius Bishop of Caesarea: The Ecclesiastical History and the Martyrs of Palestine*, 2 vols (London: SPCK, 1927), and that of K. Lake, LCL (Cambridge, MA: Harvard University Press, 1930), also taking into account Kürzinger, *Papias*, and the comments and translation by Bauckham, *Jesus and the Eyewitnesses*, 15–17, 203.

[9] *σοι… συγκατατάξαι ταῖς ἑρμηνείαις*. Bauckham, *Jesus and the Eyewitnesses*, 26, following Kürzinger, *Papias*, 77–82, translates as: 'to put into properly ordered form for you'. Papias, as is clear from the *h.e.* 3.39.14–17, given below, is certainly concerned about the order of events described in the Gospels. At issue here is the relation between 'the interpretations' (*ταῖς ἑρμηνείαις*) and the 'interpretation' (*ἐξηγήσεως*) mentioned in the title of Papias' work. This point, however, does not affect the questions that will be raised below in our discussion of this passage.

[10] *εἰ δέ που καὶ παρηκολουθηκώς τις τοῖς πρεσβυτέροις ἔλθοι*. Following Bauckham I have avoided the usual English translation, 'who had followed the elders', to avoid ambiguity: it is clear Papias means that those he met had personally known the elders, who had in turn known the disciples and apostles, rather than that they belonged to a subsequent generation; the same verb is used likewise in *h.e.* 3.39.15. The editorial insertions in the following clause also follow Bauckham, attempting to clarify any ambiguity.

> [5] Here it is worth noting that the name John is enumerated twice by him [δὶς καθαριθμιοῦντι αὐτῷ τὸ Ἰωάννου ὄνομα]: the first of them he counts with Peter and James and Matthew and the rest of the apostles, clearly indicating the evangelist; but the other John, in a separate clause, he places among the others outside the number of the apostles, putting Aristion before him, [and] he clearly calls him Elder [σαφῶς τε αὐτὸν πρεσβύτερον ὀνομάζει]. [6] This shows that the account of those is true, who say that there were two persons in Asia that bore the same name and that there were two tombs in Ephesus, each of which, to this day, is said to be John's. It is necessary to pay attention to these details, for it is likely that the second, if one is unwilling to admit that it was the first, saw the Apocalypse which bears the name of John. [7] And Papias, of whom we are now speaking, acknowledges that he received the words of the apostles from those who had been in attendance on them, but says that he was himself a hearer of Aristion and John the Elder [Ἀριστίωνος δὲ καὶ τοῦ πρεσβυτέρου Ἰωάννου αὐτήκοον ἑαυτόν φησι γενέσθαι]; indeed, mentioning them frequently by name in his writings, he sets forth their traditions. We have not said these things to no purpose.

After reporting other things mentioned by Papias about Philip the apostle and Justus Barsabbas (*h.e.* 3.39.8–10), Eusebius continues his report by saying that Papias passed on, 'through unwritten tradition, strange parables and teachings of the Saviour and some other more mythical things' pertaining to millenarian teaching, not realizing that the apostolic accounts 'were spoken mystically in figures', for Papias, Eusebius claims, 'appears to have been of very limited understanding, as one can see from his discourses'.[11] That Irenaeus and others followed these teachings of Papias is excused by Eusebius on the grounds that they had relied (mistakenly) on his antiquity (*h.e.* 3.39.11–13). Eusebius concludes his recounting of Papias' account of Aristion and John with these words: 'In the same writing he also hands down other interpretations of the words of the Lord given by Aristion, mentioned above, and the traditions of the Elder John; to which we refer the studious' (*h.e.* 3.39.14).

Eusebius then continues his account of Papias by relating things he had learned about how Mark and Matthew composed their Gospels:

> But now we must add to the words of his already quoted a tradition which he has given in regard to Mark who wrote the Gospel, in these words:
>
> [15] This also the Elder used to say: Mark, having been the interpreter of Peter, wrote down accurately as many things as he recalled, though not in

[11] *H.e.* 3.39.13. John Chapman, 'Papias on the Age of Our Lord', *JTS* 9 (1907), 42–61, at 53 suggests that this comment of Eusebius is based on a self-deprecating statement made by Papias himself, as preserved by Victorinus, *De fabrica mundi*, 9, *tamen ut mens parua poterit conabor ostendere*, 'However, as my small mind is able, I will try to show it', where *mens parua* would correspond to σμικρὸς νοῦς. As Chapman puts it: Eusebius 'seizes upon an expression used by Papias himself in quite commonplace humility, and brutally declares that it is just the epithet which suits him'.

> order [οὐ μέντοι τάξει], of the things either said or done by the Lord. For he [Mark] neither heard the Lord nor accompanied him, but later, as I said, [he heard and accompanied] Peter, who used to give his teaching according to need,[12] but not with a view to making an ordered arrangement of the Dominical oracles [ὥσπερ σύνταξιν τῶν κυριακῶν ποιούμενος λογίων], so that Mark did no wrong in writing down individual items as he recalled them. For he made it his single concern not to omit anything of what he had heard nor to falsify anything in them.

[16] Such, then, is the account given by Papias about Mark. But this is said concerning Matthew:

> So, then, Matthew arranged the oracles in order [τὰ λόγια συνετάξατο] in the Hebrew dialect, but each one interpreted them as he was able.

[17] And the same writer has used testimonies from the former epistle of John and from that of Peter likewise; and he has set forth as well another narrative about a woman accused of many sins before the Lord, which the Gospel according to the Hebrews contains. These things of necessity we have observed, in addition to what has already been set forth.

There are many things in this multi-layered account that are perplexing. Eusebius begins by quoting the testimony of Irenaeus (that Papias was 'a hearer of John and a companion of Polycarp'), yet then accuses Irenaeus of confusion, for according to Eusebius Papias did not claim to be 'a hearer and an eye-witness of the holy apostles', but belonged to a subsequent generation. This, for Eusebius, is the implication of the words of Papias that he then gives: that Papias only hopes to hear from others what Andrew, Peter, James, John, and the others 'said', in distinction to what Aristion and John the Elder 'are saying' (*h.e.* 3.39.3–4). The distinction in tense implies that the former group are deceased while Aristion and John the Elder were very much alive, so that it is only the latter two, and not the former group, the apostles, that Papias would have known. It is possible, of course, that Irenaeus is indeed mistaken. Born around the year 130 CE, Irenaeus is unlikely to have known Papias, but he certainly knew Polycarp and treasured his memory of Polycarp's personal recollections of 'John and others who had seen the

[12] πρὸς τὰς χρείας. Translated by Bauckham, as 'in the form of *chreiai*', that is, 'anecdotes', brief sketches given for the purpose of edification, as outlined in the *Progymnasmata*. Cf. Ronald F. Hock and Edward N. O'Neil, *The Chreia in Ancient Rhetoric*, vol. 1, *The Progymnasmata*, Graeco-Roman Religion Series 9, Texts and Translations 27 (Atlanta, GA: SBL, 1986); Ronald F. Hock and Edward N. O'Neil, *The Chreia and Ancient Rhetoric: Classroom Exercises*, WGRW 2 (Leiden: Brill, 2002); Ronald F. Hock, *The Chreia and Ancient Rhetoric: Commentaries on Aphthonius's Progymnasmata*, WGRW 31 (Atlanta, GA: SBL, 2012). It is true that Papias is here concerned with the question of the lack or order in Mark's arrangement; but the preposition would seem to indicate the primary sense of the word, that of need or necessity. The analysis of these passages by Bauckham and his suggestions are indeed insightful and stimulating, but again do not pertain to the questions that will be raised below.

Lord'.[13] So perhaps, as Bauckham suggests, it was the association of Papias and Polycarp together as the generation of 'elders' intervening between himself and the age of the apostles that led Irenaeus to assume that Papias had also been a 'hearer of John'.[14] Or perhaps it was only later on in his volumes that Papias mentioned having heard John (the apostle) himself. But then, as he is recalling material gathered in previous decades, why would he not mention this in the preface? Either way, Eusebius certainly takes Papias as having said that he was a 'hearer of John the Elder' (*h.e.* 3.39.7). But the addition here of the words 'the Elder' point to the source of the confusion in the opening lines: it is that Eusebius assumes that Irenaeus was speaking about the apostle John, whereas Irenaeus only mentioned the bare name John. We will return to the significance of this point later.

Then again, why does Eusebius conclude his treatment of Papias by quoting his accounts of the circumstances of the composition of the Gospels of Mark and Matthew, but say nothing (at least here) about those of Luke and John? Intriguingly Eusebius notes that Papias did mention the First Epistle of John and the story of the woman accused of many sins. This pericope is, of course, only found in the Gospel of John as we have it, though it is absent in the vast majority of early Greek manuscripts and was not commented on by any Greek writer before Euthymius Zigabenus in the twelfth century and he asserts that the accurate copies of the Gospel do not include it.[15] Eusebius, on the other hand, claims that it is found in the Gospel according to the Hebrews. So, did Papias, as far as Eusebius is aware, or is willing to let on, even know the Gospel of John? Finally, does Eusebius' concluding reference to 'what has already been set forth' refer to the Papian extracts given earlier in *h.e.* 3.39 or to earlier chapters in the *Ecclesiastical History*?

Did Papias know the Gospel of John, and if so, whom did he think was its author? Before we address these questions directly by analysing his words as quoted, and commented on, by Eusebius, it is worth recalling the point made by Lightfoot over a century ago regarding Eusebius' practice when relating information about earlier writers.[16] Lightfoot demonstrated how Eusebius was

[13] See his *Letter to Florinus* (in *h.e.* 5.20.4–8). On the chronology of Irenaeus' life and the reliability of his memory of Polycarp, see Charles E. Hill, *From the Lost Teaching of Polycarp*, WUNT 186 (Tübingen: Mohr Siebeck, 2006) and John Behr, *Irenaeus of Lyons: Identifying Christianity* (Oxford: Oxford University Press, 2013), 57–67.

[14] Cf. Bauckham, *Jesus and the Eyewitnesses*, 19, 457.

[15] Cf. Bruce M. Metzger, *A Textual Commentary on the Greek New Testament*, 2nd edn (Hendrickson, 2005), 187–9. Lightfoot suggests that it might have been Papias himself who was responsible for the recording of this pericope: 'Have we not here one of those illustrative anecdotes which Papias derived from the report of the elders, and to which he "did not scruple to give a place along with his interpretations" of our Lord's sayings?' Lightfoot, *Essays on the Work Entitled Supernatural Religion*, 204–5.

[16] Lightfoot, 'The Silence of Eusebius', chap. 2 in *Essays*, 32–58, esp. 46–7.

not interested in ascertaining which writings of the apostles and evangelists were used as Scripture by earlier Fathers, to provide, as it were, a history of the canon, as he is often read. He does, indeed, provide a 'canon' in the well-known chapter *h.e.* 3.25, where he classifies works as 'accepted', 'disputed', and 'rejected'. This is given after his account of the last days of John, the last of the apostolic figures, who, according to Irenaeus, resided in Ephesus until the times of Trajan (i.e. 98–117 CE; *h.e.* 3.23.1–4; *haer.* 2.33.3, 3.3.4), which is followed by his report, based on an anonymous source, of how Matthew and John came to write their Gospels, a passage to which we will return (*h.e.* 3.24). Having concluded his account of the apostles and evangelists, and detailed which books are 'accepted' and which not, Eusebius takes it for granted that subsequent writers also recognized the scriptural status of those books he knows as canonical. His interest thereafter, as Lightfoot concluded, is in any piece of information that later writers might provide illustrating the circumstances under which the Gospels in particular were written, or any indication as to how they viewed the Letter to the Hebrews and especially the Apocalypse, works whose place in the canon either were or are disputed, and whether they ever treat as Scripture works which altogether lie outside the canon.

Returning now to Papias, there is in fact other evidence that Papias knew the Gospel of John.[17] The Armenian fragments of Papias include his comment that 'there are fifteen kinds of aloe in India' in a discussion about the aloe brought by Nicodemus mentioned in John 19:39.[18] There is also the discussion about the 'many mansions' of John 14:2 reported by Irenaeus as having come from 'the elders, the disciples of the apostles' (*haer.* 5.36.2), which almost certainly comes from Papias (cited by name in *haer.* 5.33.4). And then there is the point noted earlier, that Eusebius records the fact that Papias knew of the account of the adulterous woman, though the connection of this pericope to the Gospel of John, at this point in time, is not clear. This is not much to go on, admittedly, but it does provide background for analysing the perplexing words of Papias given in *h.e.* 3.39, especially when we bear in mind Lightfoot's point, that Eusebius is not interested in whether earlier writers knew and accepted the Gospels (he assumes they did), but what they might know about the circumstances of their composition.

Lightfoot also observed, as have many others since, that there is a strong resemblance between the order of the names given in *h.e.* 3.39.4—Andrew, Peter, Philip, Thomas, James, John, and Matthew—and the order in which the disciples of Christ appear in the Gospel of John (1:40–3 and 21:2), which is very different to any list of disciples or apostles given in the Synoptics: that Andrew should appear before Peter in particular cannot be explained in any

[17] Cf. Hill, *Johannine Corpus*, 385–6.

[18] F. Siegert, 'Unbeachtete Papiaszitate bei armenischen Schriftstellern', *NTS* 27 (1981), 605–14.

other way than by positing the influence of the Gospel of John.[19] The John mentioned in this list along with James clearly refers to the son of Zebedee, known to us from the Synoptic Gospels, but only mentioned once, and then not by name, in the Gospel of John (21:2). Moreover, at the time when Papias was collecting his material (in the last decades of the first century) all these figures, as we saw earlier, are deceased. It is the John mentioned in this list, that is, the son of Zebedee, one of the Twelve, that Eusebius immediately assumes was the evangelist (*h.e.* 3.39.5). But alongside this John Papias mentions another John, together with Aristion, both of whom are very much still alive. Although earlier in this passage Papias had used the term 'elder' in a more general sense to refer to any of those who preceded him, he calls this John 'the Elder' in a distinctive manner, as his own proper title or epithet, as is also done, of course, by the writer of the Second and Third Epistles of John. If one is reluctant, Eusebius says, and as he clearly is, to ascribe the Apocalypse to John the son of Zebedee (and also assuming him to have been the author of the Gospel), it must have been John the Elder that wrote it. That there were indeed two Johns in Ephesus, moreover, is born out by there being, even in Eusebius' day, two tombs in the city bearing the name John.[20]

However, rather than relating any more information that Papias had collected about the Gospel of John and its author, and perhaps even more importantly regarding the Apocalypse, Eusebius turns instead to berating Papias for having passed on mythological nonsense and strange teachings regarding the eschaton, due to his 'very limited understanding'. It is worth noting that Irenaeus' testimony to Papias given by Eusebius at the beginning of the chapter comes, in Irenaeus' own work, immediately after a quotation giving just such millenarian teachings introduced by Irenaeus in this way: 'The elders who saw John, the disciple of the Lord, related that they had heard from him how the Lord used to teach in regard to these times, and say'.[21] Whatever

[19] Cf. Lightfoot, *Essays*, 193; Hengel, *Question*, 17–21; R. Alan Culpepper, *John, the Son of Zebedee: The Life of a Legend* (Columbia, SC: University of South Carolina, 1994), 109–12; Bauckham, *Jesus and the Eyewitnesses*, 417–20; Hill, *Johannine Corpus*, 386.

[20] It is rather implausible to suggest, as do Andreas J. Köstenburger and Stephen O. Stout ('"The Disciple Jesus Loved": Witness, Author, Apostle—A Response to Richard Bauckham's *Jesus and the Eyewitnesses*', *Bulletin for Biblical Research* 18.2 (2008), 209–31, at 219), that 'Papias refers to the same John twice, once as a member of the original Twelve and second as still being alive. In this case, 'Aristion and John the elder' may mean something like 'Aristion and the aforementioned elder John.' This is certainly not the way Eusebius, who had access to the full text of Papias, presents the material.

[21] *Haer.* 5.33.3: The passage quoted states: 'The days will come, in which vines shall grow, each having ten thousand branches, and in each branch ten thousand twigs, and in each true twig ten thousand shoots, and in each one of the shoots ten thousand clusters, and on every one of the clusters ten thousand grapes, and every grape when pressed will give twenty-five metretes of wine. And when any one of the saints shall lay hold of a cluster, another shall cry out, "I am a better cluster, take me; bless the Lord through me." In like manner [the Lord declared] that a grain of wheat would produce ten thousand ears, and that every ear should have ten thousand

Eusebius' hesitation, Papias had no problem handing on such teaching, presumably from John the Elder, and Irenaeus had no problem believing that these were the words of the Lord himself.

Eusebius then concludes his report from Papias with two passages describing the occasion for the composition of the Gospels of Mark and Matthew. Both of these extracts clearly show a concern for the question of proper order in the arrangement of the Dominical Oracles. As such, it is likely, as we will see further below, that Papias' concern for proper order was caused by the appearance of the Gospel of John with its distinctive account of Christ's life.[22] If this is the case, then not only is it a further indication that Papias did know the Gospel of John, but also that it is on the basis of this Gospel that an account has to be given of the lack of proper order in the other Gospels. John is, as it were, the canon.[23]

So, then, if Papias did indeed know of the Gospel of John, did he have anything more to say about it than Eusebius is prepared to report in *h.e.* 3.39? This is the heart of the controversy. Many have argued that not only did Papias know this Gospel, but that he attributed its authorship not to the apostle John, the son of Zebedee, but to John the Elder.[24] Richard Bauckham especially has recently developed the case not only from the historical information we are considering, but also from a compelling reading of the Gospel of John itself.[25] According to Bauckham, the Gospel was written by the Beloved Disciple, an eyewitness of the events of the life of Christ, but an

grains, and every grain would yield ten pounds of clear, pure, fine flour; and that all other fruit-bearing trees, and seeds and grass, would produce in similar proportions; and that all animals feeding [only] on the productions of the earth, should [in those days] become peaceful and harmonious among each other, and be in perfect subjection to man'. Similar ideas, and even identical words, are found in *Second Baruch* 29, which was probably composed in the aftermath of the destruction of the Temple in 70 CE. See Matthias Henze, *Jewish Apocalyptism in Late First Century Israel: Reading Second Baruch in Context*, Texts and Studies in Ancient Judaism, 142 (Tübingen: Mohr Siebeck, 2011). The possible connections here are fascinating, but beyond the scope of this study.

[22] It is important to note the nature of the 'order' expected in ancient works: drawing upon F. H. Colson, '*Τάξει* in Papias (The Gospels and the Rhetorical Schools)', *JTS* 14 (1912), 62–9, and Kürzinger, *Papias*, 49, Bauckham, *Jesus and the Eyewitnesses*, 220, comments: '*taxis* and *syntaxis* in Papias' comments on Mark do not refer to chronological sequence as such, but to the orderly arrangement of material in a literary composition'.

[23] Cf. Bauckham, *Jesus and the Eyewitnesses*, 225–30, stating on 227: 'In summary, then, we find that Papias was contrasting the lack of order in the Gospels of Mark and Matthew with the order to be found in the Gospel of John'.

[24] Cf. C. F. Burney, *The Aramaic Origin of the Fourth Gospel* (Oxford: Clarendon, 1922), 133–49; Hengel, *The Johannine Question*. See now also Dean Furlong, 'John The Evangelist: Revision and Reinterpretation in Early Christian Sources', PhD, Amsterdam: Vrije Universiteit, 2017.

[25] Bauckham, *Jesus and the Eyewitnesses*, esp. 114–54 (chap. 6, 'Eyewitnesses "from the beginning"'), 358–83 (chap. 14, 'The Gospel of John as Eyewitness Testimony') and 384–411 (chap. 15, 'The Witness of the Beloved Disciple').

eyewitness who was not one of the twelve named in the Synoptic Gospels; he is introduced anonymously, with Andrew and before Peter, at the beginning of the Gospel (John 1:35–42); he is identified as 'the disciple whom Jesus loved' as the narrative arrives at the Passion (John 13:23); he is known to the high priest of the Temple (and it is only by him that Peter gains admittance, John 18:15–16); he is the only disciple to remain at the foot of the cross, to provide witness to the blood and water coming from the side of Christ (John 19:35); he is the first disciple, again before Peter, to arrive at the empty tomb, and although Peter enters first, it is he who 'believed' (John 20:4–8); and it is he, not Peter, who recognizes the risen Lord (John 21:7); and finally, while Peter is to lay down his life in service of others, John's mission is to bear witness (John 21:15–25). In this way, Mark's privileging of Peter, the apostle whose witness he is transmitting, by mentioning him first and last (Mark 1:16, 16:7), is subsumed by the *inclusio* given in the Gospel of John, which begins and ends with John, anonymously at first and as the eyewitness whose veracity is confirmed by others at the end.[26] As Bauckham puts it: 'the Beloved Disciple's qualifications to bear witness to Jesus began before Peter became a disciple and his activity of bearing witness will continue into the future even after Peter has completed his discipleship. In a sense it will continue even until the parousia because it is embodied in his Gospel'.[27] For those who hold that the Gospel of John, because of its high literary and interpretative nature compared with the Synoptics, could not have been written by an actual eyewitness of Christ, Bauckham simply replies: 'in fact the high degree of interpretation is appropriate precisely because this is the only one of the canonical Gospels that claims eyewitness authorship',[28] or, to be more precise, the authority of the only evangelist who witnessed the Passion.

Returning now to Papias, as presented by Eusebius, we can readily understand why, if Papias had indeed related information to the effect that the Gospel of John was not written by the son of Zebedee, but by another figure, known as 'the Elder', who had also written the Apocalypse, Eusebius would want to sow confusion regarding Irenaeus' testimony to Papias and to belittle Papias' intellectual ability. Eusebius values Papias' reports about how Mark and Matthew composed their Gospels, but does not, or will not, say why the concern for order was of interest to Papias, a point to which we will return. It does indeed seem that Eusebius is deliberately obfuscating the circumstances of the composition of the Gospel of John.

Charles Hill has mounted a valiant defence against this supposed obfuscation, arguing that the reason why Eusebius does not record what Papias says

[26] Cf. Bauckham, *Jesus and the Eyewitnesses*, 124–9.

[27] Ibid. 392–3. On this point, see now Petterson, *From Tomb to Text.*

[28] Ibid. 411.

about the Gospel of John is that he had already done this back in *h.e.* 3.24. There Eusebius draws upon an account: κατέχει λόγος (*h.e.* 3.24.5). Hill translates this phrase as 'a record preserves', referring to Lawlor's demonstration that this expression 'normally signifies a written source'.[29] This account describes how Matthew and John came to compose their Gospels. In the case of John, the account relates that:

> [*h.e.* 3.24.7] John, they say, who had all the time used unwritten proclamation, at last came also to write for the following reason. After the three [Gospels] which had been previously written had been distributed to all, and also to him, they say that he accepted them, and testified to their truth, but [said] that there was only lacking to the writing an account of what had been done by Christ at first and at the beginning of the preaching.... [11] They say accordingly that for this reason the apostle John was asked to hand down in the Gospel according to himself the time passed over in silence by the first evangelists and the things that had been done by the Saviour at that time (that is, the things before the imprisonment of the Baptist), and that he signalled this when saying 'this beginning of marvels did Jesus'. [cf. John 2:11]

This description of the occasion for the composition of the Gospel of John certainly fits together with the concern for proper order (or lack of it in the Synoptics) mentioned by Papias in *h.e.* 3.39.15–16, and so for this reason, and others, Hill argues that the account related in *h.e.* 3.24 should also be ascribed to Papias. That Eusebius, then, does not mention what Papias had to say about the composition of the Gospel of John in *h.e.* 3.39 is due simply to the fact that he had already given this a few chapters earlier, though anonymously as he was not at that point focusing on Papias himself, but on John.

Hill's argument was contested by Bauckham, which was in turn responded to by Hill himself.[30] It is not necessary for our purposes to enter into the details of that debate. Instead two points must be made. First, it is important to note how Eusebius concludes this section of his work, which had begun with the last days of John and continued with the works attributed to him:

> [*h.e.* 3.24.16] So much for our own account of these things. But in a more suitable time we will endeavour to explain by quotations from the ancients what has been said by others on these points. [17] Of the writings of John in addition to the Gospel, the first of his epistles has been acknowledged as undisputed by those of today and by the ancients also, but the remaining two are disputed, [18] while as to the Apocalypse the opinion of many is still divided either way. This also will similarly receive determination at the proper time by testimonies from the ancients.

[29] Hill, *Johannine Corpus*, 387; referring to H. J. Lawlor, *Eusebiana* (Oxford: Clarendon, 1912), 22.

[30] Bauckham, *Jesus and the Eyewitnesses*, 433–7; Hill, 'The Orthodox Gospel', 288–94.

In other words, Eusebius presents the account he has just been giving as his own; that of the ancients (which would include Papias) is to come later. And Eusebius, once again, is at pains to point out in conclusion the dubious status of the Apocalypse.

Second, even if we accept Hill's argument that the 'record' was in fact written by Papias, this does not, however, resolve the question of the identity of the John who wrote the Gospel: was it the Apostle or the Elder? Eusebius introduces the account in *h.e.* 3.24 by calling John a disciple: 'Yet nevertheless of all the disciples of the Lord, only Matthew and John have left us their recollections' (*h.e.* 3.24.5). In the course of recounting this 'record', John is indeed referred to as 'the apostle': 'Now they say that on account of these things the apostle John was exhorted' (*h.e.* 3.24.11). But it is clear, as Hill acknowledges, that 'Eusebius is here paraphrasing a written account'.[31] The ascription of the Gospel to 'the apostle John', in other words, is not necessarily that of the anonymous writer of the 'record' utilized by Eusebius here, whether or not it was Papias.

Regarding the idea that Papias did indeed indicate that it was the Elder, not the Apostle, who wrote the Gospel, and that Eusebius deliberately obfuscated the point, Hill rightly reminds us that Eusebius exhorts those who are interested to read Papias himself (*h.e.* 3.39.14); the works had been read by others, such as Irenaeus, and were presumably still available for others to check Eusebius' veracity. Hill then comments:

> Moreover, the deception in this case cannot be confined to Eusebius. Other 'interested' people clearly *had* read Papias' books, including Irenaeus and a number of other second- and third-century writers, yet neither they nor anyone else ever reports the opinion that the Gospel according to John had been written by John the Elder. If Papias reported that the true author of the Fourth Gospel was not John the apostle but John the Elder, this would mean that a host of people in different times and places were involved in the same cover-up. In my opinion, this conspiracy theory more than stretches credulity.[32]

But this is, in fact, just what Irenaeus does say, though in slightly different words. Although Eusebius begins his account of Papias by claiming that Irenaeus had mistakenly called Papias a 'hearer and eyewitness of the holy apostles', Irenaeus had done no such thing: he had simply said that Papias was a 'hearer of John'. Eusebius jumped to the conclusion that he must have been referring to the apostle.[33] Irenaeus, however, has his own distinctive and consistent vocabulary for referring to the author of the Fourth Gospel. When he gives us his well-known account of how the four Gospels were composed, after mentioning Matthew, Mark, and Luke, Irenaeus says: 'Afterwards, John,

[31] Hill, *Johannine Corpus* 387. [32] Hill, *Who Chose the Gospels?*, 216, italics original.
[33] This point was already noted by Burney, *Aramaic Origins*, 141.

the disciple of the Lord, who also had leaned upon his breast, did himself publish a Gospel during his residence at Ephesus in Asia'.[34] The two identifying marks of the John who wrote the Gospel bearing his name is that he is 'the disciple of the Lord' and one 'who leaned upon the breast' of the Lord: the first epithet is Irenaeus' habitual description of this John; the second is also found in Polycrates, as we will see in the next section of this chapter.

There are sixty-two occasions when Irenaeus mentions John, the author of the Johannine material, fifty-six times by name and six other times where he is unambiguously referring to this John.[35] Of these sixty-two instances, seventeen describe him as 'John the disciple of the Lord' or 'John his disciple', and he is further referred to, but not mentioned by name, twice as 'the Lord's disciple', three times as 'his disciple', and, finally, Irenaeus once mentions 'Christ, the teacher of John'.[36] This John is associated with 'the apostles' seven times.[37] In one section, where Irenaeus is debating with his opponents about the interpretation of the Prologue, he refers three times to John simply as 'the apostle', in the singular (*haer.* 1.9.2, 3 twice); this is wholly untypical for Irenaeus, and may well derive from the text of his opponents that he has before him, for, as we will see, the designation of the Evangelist as an 'apostle'

[34] *Haer.* 3.1.1: *Ἔπειτα Ἰωάννης, ὁ μαθητὴς τοῦ Κυρίου, ὁ καὶ ἐπὶ τὸ στῆθος αὐτοῦ ἀναπεσών, καὶ αὐτὸς ἐξέδωκεν τὸ εὐαγγέλιον, ἐν Ἐφέσῳ τῆς Ἀσίας διατρίβων.*

[35] *Haer.* 1.8.5 (4×), 1.8.6, 1.9.1, 1.9.2 (4×, once as 'the apostle'), 1.9.3 (3×, twice as 'the apostle'), 1.16.3, 1.26.3, 2.2.5, 2.22.3, 2.22.5 (3×), 3.1.1, 3.3.4 (2×), 3.8.3, 3.11.1 (2×, once as 'the disciple of the Lord'), 3.11.2, 3.11.3 ('the Lord's disciple'), 3.11.7, 3.11.8, 3.11.9, 3.16.2 (2×), 3.16.5, 3.16.8 ('his disciple'), 3.21.3, 3.22.2, 4.2.3., 4.6.1, 4.10.1, 4.14.2, 4.17.6, 4.18.6, 4.20.11 (2×), 4.21.3, 4.30.4, 5.18.2, 5.26.1, 5.28.2, 5.30.1, 5.30.3 ('he who beheld the apocalyptic vision'), 5.33.3, 5.33.4, 5.34.2, 5.35.2 (2×), 5.36.3, *Dem.* 43, *Dem.* 94, *Ep. to Florinus* (*h.e.* 5.20.6), *Ep. to Victor* (*h.e.* 5.24.16). Bauckham counted, but did not provide references for, fifty-nine occurrences. Cf. *Jesus*, 469 for his tabulation, and 458–63.

[36] *Haer.* 1.8.5 (2×), 1.16.3, 2.2.5, 2.22.3, 2.22.5, 3.1.1, 3.3.4, 3.11.1, 3.16.5, 3.22.2 ('John his disciple'), 4.20.11, 4.30.4, 5.18.2, 5.33.3, 5.35.2, *Ep. to Victor* (*h.e.* 5.24.16); 'the Lord's disciple' in 3.11.1 and 3.11.3; 'his disciple' in 3.16.8, *Dem.* 43 and 94; and 'Christ, the teacher of John' in 3.11.3.

[37] *Haer.* 2.22.5, 'John the disciple of the Lord... Some of them [the elders] saw not only John, but the other apostles also'; 3.3.4, twice, 'There are those who heard from him [Polycarp] that John the disciple of the Lord... [ran out of the bath-house at seeing Cerinthus]. Such was the horror which the apostles and their disciples had... [here John is an apostle, Polycarp a disciple]... the Church in Ephesus founded by Paul and having John remaining among them permanently until the time of Trajan, is a true witness of the tradition of the apostles'; 3.5.1, 'the apostles who did write the Gospel'; 3.11.9, 'the Gospels of the apostles' in contrast to the Gospel of Truth; 3.21.3, 'the apostles... agree with this translation [of Isaiah 7:14]... Peter and John and Matthew and Paul, and the rest successively'; *Ep. to Victor* (*h.e.* 5.24.16, 'John the disciple of our Lord and the other apostles'). Lorne Zelyck, 'Irenaeus and the Authorship of the Fourth Gospel', in Stanley Porter and Hughson T. Ong, eds, *The Origins of John's Gospel* (Leiden: Brill, 2016), 239–58, at 242–4, argues, on the basis of *haer.* 2.22.5, 3.3.4, and *h.e.* 5.24.16 that 'Irenaeus considered the Apostle John to be "John, the disciple of the Lord."' Although Irenaeus does indeed associate 'John the disciple of the Lord' with 'the other apostles' in these cases, this is not the same thing as identifying the 'John' clearly intended to be understood as the apostle, the son of Zebedee (*haer.* 2.24.4, 3.12.3–5, and 3.12.15, each accepted by Zelyck, ibid., 241–2) with 'the disciple of the Lord', something never done.

seems to start in 'Gnostic' circles. Irenaeus does use the term 'disciple' in the plural, usually as 'the disciples of Jesus', to refer to those who accompanied Jesus during his ministry; but refers to them as 'apostles' after the resurrection and commissioning. In one place he uses the phrase in the plural, 'the disciples of the Lord', but here the term refers to the rest of the believers in Jerusalem, in contrast to the apostles.[38] No other figure is called by Irenaeus, simply, 'the disciple of the Lord'.

As such the phrase 'the disciple of the Lord' does not classify the John who wrote the Gospel among other disciples, but rather distinguishes him as *the* disciple. The phrase functions as Irenaeus' preferred designation for the Evangelist, much like the later designation of John as 'the Theologian' or the modern convention of referring to him as 'the Beloved Disciple'. In the case of the 'Beloved Disciple', the phrase is drawn from the Gospel itself, though it never appears in that form there (cf. John 13:23; 19:26; 21:20: 'the disciple whom Jesus loved'). The phrase 'the disciple of the Lord', on the other hand, is not as clearly derived from the language of the Gospel. Papias' standard epithet for this John, as we have seen, is 'the Elder', though at one point he does seem to differentiate between, on the one hand, Andrew, Peter, Philip, Thomas, James, John, Matthew, and others, as 'the disciples of the Lord', and, on the other hand, 'in a separate clause' as Eusebius puts it, Aristion and John the Elder as 'disciples of the Lord' (*h.e.* 3.39.4). Perhaps this is an echo of the way in which the latter two were called 'disciples' in a manner distinct to that of the former. That Papias should have preferred the title 'the Elder' is no doubt due to the fact that John was still alive during the time that Papias had been collecting his information and was distinguished by his great old age. If it is not from Papias that Irenaeus' title 'the disciple of the Lord' derives, then it must be from his slightly younger contemporary, Polycarp, in whose circle Irenaeus had received his theological formation. It is interesting to note that when writing to Florinus, to recall him to their common inheritance from Polycarp, who had frequently mentioned his association with John (clearly the writer of the Gospel), Irenaeus simply uses the name 'John' (*h.e.* 5.20.4–8); no further specification is needed, for, as Bauckham notes, Florinus would not have been in any doubt regarding which John is being spoken about.[39] On the other hand, in the one other letter of Irenaeus preserved by Eusebius, that is, his letter to Victor of Rome about paschal practices, Irenaeus instead uses 'John the disciple of our Lord' (*h.e.* 5.24.16). Bauckham's conclusion seems solid: 'For the members of the church of Ephesus and of churches in the

[38] Cf. *haer.* 3.12.5: Peter and John 'returned to the rest of their fellow-apostles and disciples of the Lord, that is, to the Church, and related what had occurred... The whole church, it is then said, "when they had heard that, lifted up the voice to God with one accord, and said... [Acts 4:24–8] These are the voices of the Church... these are the voices of the apostles, these are the voices of the disciples of the Lord'.

[39] Bauckham, *Jesus*, 463, n. 80.

province of Asia generally, *the* disciple of the Lord was their own John, the one who reclined on the Lord's breast and wrote his Gospel in Ephesus'.[40]

This striking usage is paralleled by the way in which Irenaeus refers to Paul, another figure who had lived and worked in Asia Minor. According to Bauckham's reckoning, of the 194 times that Irenaeus refers to Paul (either simply as 'Paul', 'Paul the apostle', or 'the apostle'), seventy-nine times it is simply as 'the apostle'.[41] Just as there is no ambiguity when referring to 'the apostle', so also there is no ambiguity when referring to 'the disciple of the Lord': Paul is *the* apostle, John is *the* disciple. It is also noteworthy that when, in the context of showing how the Scriptures name as God, 'definitely and absolutely', only the true God (*haer.* 3.6.1), Irenaeus treats Paul twice, once as the author of the letters (*haer.* 3.6.5–7.2), and then again as he appears in Acts (*haer.* 3.12.9). His method of proving his point is by way of examining different bodies of scriptural texts, rather than treating particular historical figures as reconstructed from this literature. However, he gives no indication at all that he is speaking of a different character, by means of different ways of speaking of Paul.

In contrast, when Irenaeus refers to the John who appears in the Synoptics and Acts, that is, the apostle, the son of Zebedee, it is never with reference to the Johannine material or its author. Irenaeus twice mentions this John in the company of Peter and James, in reference to the Transfiguration (*haer.* 2.24.4) and as being present with Jesus throughout his ministry, bearing witness to his every action and teaching (*haer.* 3.12.15). And, with reference to Acts, Irenaeus mentions three times John, the son of Zebedee, again with Peter (*haer.* 3.12.3, twice, referring to Acts 3; and 3.12.5, referring to Acts 4). There is only one mention of 'the sons of Zebedee', and that is in an account of how his opponents understood the redemption of the Lord to be bestowed upon them (*haer.* 1.21.2). In none of these cases, however, does Irenaeus use his habitual description of John, the author of the Johannine corpus, 'the disciple of the Lord'. The impression clearly given from all this is that for Irenaeus these are two different figures. Even the fact that, as we have seen, Irenaeus associates John the author with 'the apostles' seven times (and three times refers to him simply as 'the apostle') cannot counter this impression, for in none of these cases does he intimate at all that he is thinking of the son of Zebedee. And, for that matter, the term 'apostle' is much more flexible for Irenaeus, applying not only to the Twelve, but to the Seventy (*haer.* 2.21.1, as does Luke 10:1), and even John the Baptist (*haer.* 3.11.4), even if, strictly speaking, it not only primarily, but distinctively, applies to Paul '*the* apostle'. In this, of course, Irenaeus is following John, who is much less interested in 'the Twelve' than the Synoptics; indeed, in the Gospel of John, 'the Twelve' only appear fleetingly

[40] Bauckham, *Jesus*, 460, italics original.

[41] Ibid. 460–1, and 469.

(6:67–71; 20:24) and their names are never listed. Given all this, Bauckham asserts of the passages where Irenaeus speaks of the John who, by context, is understood to be the son of Zebedee, that there is nothing 'to suggest that this John is the same person as John of Ephesus, the Beloved Disciple and author of the Gospel'.[42] There really is no sense of character given to the son of Zebedee in any of the places where he is mentioned, nothing of the personal affection Irenaeus shows when writing about the teacher of his own beloved teacher Polycarp, and he certainly is never called or given the epithet 'the disciple of the Lord'.

Lorne Zelyck claims that Bauckham has given a 'straw-man argument', for two reasons.[43] The first is that Irenaeus 'never refers to "John, the son of Zebedee," but simply refers to "John."' It is an 'interpretative decision', based on the comparison of what Irenaeus says in each context with the biblical source, to determine that it is the son of Zebedee that is indicated, although Zelyck accepts the identification for the passages in question.[44] The second reason is that

> 'the disciple of the Lord' is an epithet that never refers to one person in the biblical text. Therefore it is impossible to associate 'John, the son of Zebedee' with 'John, the disciple of the Lord' because the former is only found in the biblical text and not in *Against the Heresies*, while the latter only exists in *Against the Heresies* and not in the biblical text.[45]

But this misrepresents the evidence: 'the disciple of the Lord' is indeed an epithet used by Irenaeus to refer specifically and uniquely 'to one person in the biblical text' (even if that epithet does not occur for that figure in the biblical text, which is presumably what Zelyck means), that is, John the disciple whom Jesus loved. As we have seen, Irenaeus uses this epithet abundantly, yet does not do so in any of the cases where he mentions the John who appears with Peter in the Synoptics and Acts. It is not, therefore, as Zelyck asserts, 'a moot argument to claim that Irenaeus distinguishes them because he never associates them. Irenaeus identifies both "John" (the son of Zebedee) and "John, the disciple of the Lord" as an apostle, so the burden of proof is on those who would seek to differentiate the Apostle John'.[46] As we have seen, apart from *haer.* 1.9.2–3, Irenaeus does not 'identify' 'John, the disciple of the Lord' as an apostle; and the abundant, and consistent, use of his epithet 'the disciple of the Lord' for the author of the Gospel (and Apocalypse), but not for the John mentioned in the Synoptics and Acts, demands an account from those who would want to identify the disciple as the apostle, the son of Zebedee; the

[42] Bauckham, *Jesus and the Eyewitnesses*, 459. Bauckham's conclusions have been followed by Paul Trebilco, *The Early Christians in Ephesus from Paul to Ignatius* (Grand Rapids: Eerdmans, 2007), 252–8.

[43] Zelyck, 'Irenaeus and the Authorship of the Fourth Gospel', 244.

[44] Ibid. 241–2.

[45] Ibid. 244.

[46] Ibid. 245.

weight of the evidence is certainly in favour of 'John the disciple of the Lord' being a distinct figure to the John who appears in the Synoptics and Acts, and only fleetingly in the Gospel of John.

Bauckham concludes his treatment of Irenaeus' consistently delineated ways of referring to the disciple and the apostle, both named John, in this way:

> There is therefore no reason to think that either Irenaeus' Asiatic sources or Irenaeus himself thought the author of the Gospel of John to be one of the Twelve. Only those who presuppose without argument, that a John who was a personal disciple of Jesus *must* have been John the son of Zebedee are obliged to read Irenaeus in this way. If we come to Irenaeus instead with the knowledge that the John who resided in Ephesus and was known as the author of the Gospel in local tradition was not John the son of Zebedee, then nothing that Irenaeus says either about John 'the disciple of the Lord' or about John the son of Zebedee even suggests that they might be the same person.[47]

It is with this false assumption that Eusebius introduces his treatment of Papias, leading him to claim that Irenaeus was confused and misleading into confusion many others through the centuries thereafter.

That Irenaeus uses 'the apostle' (in the singular and without the name John) for the author of the Gospel only in *haer.* 1.9.2 and 3, in the context of arguing against Ptolemaeus' reading of the Prologue of John, perhaps gives us an indication of where or in which circles the author of the Gospel of John was spoken of as an apostle.[48] There are three other sources from the second century which purport to give us information about John and which speak of him as an apostle. The first is the so-called 'anti-Marcionite' prologues, found in some manuscripts of the Vulgate, dating from the eighth century onwards, though their composition is reckoned to be anywhere from the mid-second to the fourth century.[49] The preface to the Gospel of Luke asserts that 'Later John the apostle, one of the Twelve, wrote the Apocalypse of the Island of Patmos and after that the Gospel', while the preface to John asserts that Papias wrote down John's words.

The second text is, of course, the *Acts of John*, probably written in Asia Minor in the second quarter of the second century.[50] The *Acts* describe the

[47] Bauckham, *Jesus and the Eyewitnesses*, 462–3.

[48] It should be noted that Origen, when referring to words (which he then quotes) of Heracleon about which words in John 1:15–18 are spoken by the Baptist, refers to John as the 'disciple' (*Comm. Jo.* 6.13–14), but elsewhere, when referring generally to the claim of Heracleon, refers to John as the 'apostle' (*Comm. Jo.* 2.213).

[49] Text in John Wordsworth and Henry J. White, *Novum Testamentum Latine*, 3 vols (Oxford: Oxford University Press, 1889–91): preface to Luke, 1.272; to John, 1:491. Translations in Robert M. Grant, *Second-Century Christianity: A Collection of Fragments* (London: SPCK, 1946), 93.

[50] See P. J. Lalleman, *The Acts of John: A Two-Stage Initiation into Johannine Gnosticism*, Studies on the Apocryphal Acts of the Apostles, 4 (Leuven: Peeters, 1998), 270; Hill, *Johannine Corpus*, 258–63.

activity of the apostle John, the son of Zebedee, in Ephesus and its surroundings. It uses words and descriptions from the Gospel of John, thus identifying the apostle portrayed in the *Acts* with the author of the Gospel.[51] But, on the other hand, several major parts of the work take an aggressively revisionary reading of the Gospel. As Luttikhuizen puts it, in chapters 97–102, 'the relation to the Gospel accounts, especially the Fourth Gospel, is oppositional: in clear contrast to the Gospel, Christ (the descended saviour) reveals to John, who had fled from the crucifixion scene unto the Mount of Olives, that he, Christ, is not the one who is crucified on the wooden cross in Jerusalem. What the ones who believe this say about Christ is "humble" and "unworthy" of him. John is summoned by the saviour to disdain the people who believe that he is crucified. Accordingly, the story concludes with the report that John laughs at the people around the cross in Jerusalem'.[52] According to Lalleman, the *Acts of John* was intended to lead its readers away from the Gospel of John, through a second stage of initiation, into a Johannine form of Gnosticism.

The other document of interest is the *Epistle of the Apostles*. Against the previous tendency to locate the origin of this document in mid-second-century Egypt, Hill argues that it was more likely written in Asia Minor, perhaps even in Smyrna, around 140, or else around 120.[53] The document does not seem to be referenced in any ancient Christian writing, and only survives in a Coptic version, found at the end of the nineteenth century, and a more complete version in Ethiopic, together with a short Latin fragment. The title modern scholars have given to the work is somewhat misleading. It certainly begins by describing itself as a letter: 'What Jesus Christ revealed to his disciples as a letter, and how Jesus Christ revealed the letter of the council of the apostles, the disciples of Jesus Christ, to the Catholics; which was written because of the false apostles Simon and Cerinthus'.[54] However, as even the opening words indicate, and as certainly becomes apparent within a few pages, when the risen Christ gives a series of revelations in reply to questions asked by the disciples, the work really belongs in the category of apocalyptic literature.[55]

[51] *AJ* 89.11; 90.4; Lalleman, *Acts of John*, 40, n. 62 suggests that *AJ* 88.3-5 alludes to John's writing of the Gospel.

[52] G. P. Luttikhuizen, 'The Thought Pattern of Gnostic Mythologizers and their Use of Biblical Traditions', in J. D. Turner and A. McGuire, eds, *The Nag Hammadi Library after Fifty Years: Proceedings of the 1995 Society of Biblical Literature Commemoration*, Nag Hammadi and Manichaean Studies, 44 (Leiden: Brill, 1997), 89–101 at 92–3.

[53] Hill, *Johannine Corpus*, 366–7. See also Charles E. Hill, 'The *Epistula Apostolorum*: An Asian Tract from the Time of Polycarp', *JECS* 7 (1999), 1–53, and Alistair Stewart-Sykes, 'The Asian Context of the New Prophecy and of *Epistula Apostolorum*', *VC* 51 (1997), 416–38.

[54] *Ep. Ap.* 1; in J. K. Elliott, *The Apocryphal New Testament* (Oxford: Clarendon Press, 1993), 558–88.

[55] Cf. Elliot, *Apocryphal New Testament*, 555.

Hill is certainly right to emphasize the interconnections between this document and the Johannine writings, especially the Gospel and the Apocalypse. The *Epistle*, moreover, interweaves many points from the Synoptic Gospels along with John, for instance connecting, for the first time, John 1:14 with the infancy narratives: 'the Word which became flesh through the holy Virgin Mary, was hidden in her birth-pangs by the Holy Spirit and was born not by the lust of the flesh, but by the will of God'.[56] The *Epistle* in addition includes material also found in non-canonical sources, such as the Infancy Gospel of Thomas,[57] indicating again an interest in the early years of Christ, and other ideas which have no parallels, such as that it was Christ himself who came to Mary in the form of Gabriel.[58] There is, however, no sense of hostility towards the Johannine material, such as is found in parts of the *Acts of John*.

After the opening paragraph, the *Epistle* provides a rather unusual list of the apostles: 'John and Thomas and Peter and Andrew and James and Philip and Bartholomew and Matthew and Nathanael, and Judas Zelotes and Cephas' (*Ep. Ap.* 2). In providing this list of the Twelve (or rather eleven; a replacement for Judas has yet to be found), the author has clearly identified John, the son of Zebedee, with the author of the Gospel, although there is no actual mention of 'the son of Zebedee'. However, it is also clear, as Hill and Bauckham note, that this list gives priority to the Johannine account: it places John at the head, privileges Thomas by putting him second, and mentions Nathanael, who is only mentioned in the Gospel of John.[59] As such, this list of apostles echoes the names given by Papias, strongly suggesting that it originated in the same

[56] *Ep. Ap.* 3; it is noteworthy that it takes John 1:13 as referring to Christ. The connection between John 1:14 and the infancy narrative is also made by the *Sybilline Oracles* 8.456–79 (in James H. Charlesworth, *The Old Testament Pseudepigrapha*, 2 vols (Garden City, NY: Doubleday, 185), 2.335–47).

[57] E.g. *Ep. Ap.* 4: 'This is what our Lord Jesus Christ did, who was delivered by Joseph and Mary his mother to where he might learn letters. And he who taught him said to him as he taught him, "Say Alpha." He answered and said to him, "First you tell me what Beta is." And truly [it was] a real thing which was done'. Cf. Infancy Gospel of Thomas 6:3, 14:2 (in Elliot, *Apocryphal New Testament*, 75–83); Pseudo-Matt., Infancy Gospel 38:1 (in Elliot, *Apocryphal New Testament*, 88–99).

[58] *Ep. Ap.* 14: [Christ speaking] '"Do you know that the angel Gabriel came and brought the message to Mary?" And we said to him, "Yes, O Lord." And he answered and said to us, "Do you not remember that I previously said to you that I became like an angel to the angels?' And we said to him, 'Yes, O Lord.' And he said to us, 'At that time I appeared in the form of the archangel Gabriel to Mary and spoke with her, and her heart received [me]; she believed and laughed; and I, the Word, went into her and became flesh; and I myself was servant for myself; and in the likeness of an angel, like him I will do, and after it I will go to my Father.' There is clearly a connection here with the *Ascension of Isaiah*, 10.7–16 (in Charlesworth, *Old Testament Pseudepigrapha*, 2.156–76), in which Christ is said to have taken on the form of an angel as he descends from above in order not to be recognized as he passes through the various heavenly spheres. On Mary's 'laughter', see *Sibylline Oracles* 8.466.

[59] Hill, *Johannine Corpus*, 368–9; Bauckham, *Jesus and the Eyewitnesses*, 464.

milieu, but a generation later, representing a more developed attempt to bring the Synoptic and Johannine material, along with other ideas, all together, in an apocalyptic context.

Whatever we make of the *Epistle of the Apostles*, and its connection with the Johannine circles in Ephesus and its environs, it remains the case that any evidence connecting the Gospel of John with John the apostle, the son of Zebedee, during the second century is sparse. Weighed against the testimony of Irenaeus (and Polycrates, as we will see in the next section of this chapter), and seeing the words of Papias as they are presented by Eusebius in the light of that testimony, the evidence is overwhelming that the John who wrote the Gospel was not the son of Zebedee, one of the twelve known to us from the Synoptics, but another eyewitness of the Lord who resided to a great old age in Ephesus, forming there what Lightfoot described as 'The School of John'.[60]

However, as time went on, the tendency to call all early Christian figures 'apostles' increased. In the next century, Clement of Alexandria calls Clement of Rome 'the apostle Clement', and, when quoting from the *Epistle of Barnabas*, attributes it to 'Barnabas the apostle'.[61] There is also an increasing tendency to refer to the Scriptures, old and new, as 'the prophets' and 'the apostles', encouraging the use of the term 'apostle' for any author of the writings of the New Testament.[62] As Bauckham observes, 'for those who lacked Irenaeus' access to local Ephesian tradition, the idea of a Gospel author for whom the term "the Lord's disciple" was more appropriate than "apostle" must have been highly anomalous'.[63] Once the disciple of the Lord became regularly described as an apostle, the identification with the son of Zebedee would have been irresistible. But that he was not means that his authority did not derive from being part of the twelve, but rested instead upon his own relationship to the Lord. And, as we will now see, it is this authority which is understood as completing, or even authorizing, the witness of others.

The Occasion of the Gospel

The material from Papias with which we began our examination seems to indicate that there was a discussion at the end of the first century about the relationship of the Gospel of John to the other Gospels, especially in terms of the ordering of their material, a concern which, of course, continued to trouble

[60] Lightfoot, 'The Later School of St John', in *Essays*, 217–50.

[61] Clement, *Strom.* 4.17.105.1, for Clement or Rome; 2.6.31.2, 2.7.35.5 for Barnabas, though here he has the precedent of Paul (cf. 1 Cor. 9:1–6).

[62] E.g. Justin *1 Apol.* 67.3: 'the memoirs of the apostles or the writings of the prophets are read' during worship; and *2 Clement* 14: 'the books and the Apostles [τὰ βιβλία καὶ οἱ ἀπόστολοι] declare that...'

[63] Bauckham, *Jesus and the Eyewitnesses*, 468.

others, such as Eusebius, and continues to do so for many more down to the present day. Thus, in the fragments preserved by Eusebius (*h.e.* 3.39.3–4, 15–16), we have two passages where Papias is concerned to account for the ordering of material in Mark and Matthew, or rather, their apparent lack of order. This is most plausibly seen as having been occasioned by the appearance of the Gospel of John in the late first century, or at least that it is in this period that questions began to arise concerning the ordering of their respective narratives. Papias' concern, we have suggested, following Bauckham, is best understood in terms of the authority in which he holds the Gospel of John and, on its basis, then explains, drawing from whatever oral sources he has access to, the reasons why the other Gospels are deficient in their ordering of their material. Likewise, as we have also seen, the anonymous account in *h.e.* 3.24.7 and 11, has John 'accepting' the three other Gospels, and 'testifying to their truth', and, when exhorted so to do, writing his Gospel to complete the account given by the Synoptics.

A similar picture is given in the Muratorian Canon. Although there have been attempts to date this document in the fourth century, most scholars still hold that it was written towards the end of the second century, most likely in Rome.[64] This document begins in midstream, presumably talking about the circumstances in which Matthew wrote his Gospel before turning to Luke, who, as a disciple of Paul, did not see the Lord in the flesh, and so begins his account from the nativity of the Baptist. It then continues with John:

> The fourth [book] of the Gospels is that of John [one] of the disciples [*ex discipulis*]. When his fellow-disciples and bishops urged [him] [*cohortantibus condiscipulis et episcopis suis*], he said: 'Fast together with me for three days and, what shall be revealed to each, let us tell [it] to each other'. On the same night it was revealed to Andrew, [one] of the Apostles [*ex apostolis*], that, with all of them reviewing [it], John should describe all things in his own name. And so, although different beginnings might be taught in the separate books of the Gospels [*et ideo licet varia singulis euangeliorum libris principia doceantur*], nevertheless it makes no difference to the faith of believers, since all things in all [of them] are declared by the one sovereign Spirit—concerning [his] nativity, concerning [his] passion, concerning [his] resurrection, concerning [his] walk with his disciples, and concerning his double advent: the first in humility when he was despised, which has been; the second in royal power, glorious, which is to be. What marvel, therefore, if John so constantly brings forward particular [matters] also in his

[64] For a later date, see A. C. Sundberg, 'Towards a Revised History of the New Testament Canon', *Studia Evangelica*, 4.1 (1968), 42–61; Sundberg, 'Canon Muratori: A Fourth-Century List', *HTR* 66 (1973), 1–41; Geoffrey Martin Hahneman, *The Muratorian Fragment and the Development of the Canon*, Oxford Theological Monographs (Oxford: Clarendon, 1992), and Hahneman, 'The Muratorian Fragment and the Origins of the New Testament Canon', in Lee Martin McDonald and James A. Sanders, eds, *The Canon Debate* (Peabody, MA: Hendrickson, 2002), 405–15. For a review of the arguments, see Hill, *Johannine Corpus*, 129–34.

> Epistles, saying of himself: 'What we have seen with our eyes and have heard with [our] ears and our hands have handled, these things we have written to you' [cf. 1 John 1:1, 4]. For thus he declares that he was not only an eyewitness and hearer, but also a writer of all the wonderful things of the Lord in order [*non solum uisorem sed et auditorem set et scriptorem omnium mirabilium Domini per ordinem profitetur*].[65]

There are many things of note in this report. It is intriguing how the role of Andrew, whom as we saw earlier Papias had listed first among the apostles (*h.e.* 3.39.4), is heightened not only by attributing to him the impulse to ask John to write his Gospel, but saying that this action was 'revealed to him'.[66] It is also noteworthy that the Muratorian Canon classifies John as one 'of the disciples', in contrast to Andrew who is one 'of the apostles'.[67] The document thus confirms, and adds to, the case that we made earlier in this chapter that the title 'apostle' only gradually comes to be attributed to John, the author of the Gospel. If Rome in the late second century was indeed the place where the Canon was written, it would explain why, when writing to Victor of Rome, Irenaeus could mention 'John, the disciple of the Lord' (*h.e.* 5.24.16) and expect that Victor would know to whom he was referring. The Muratorian Canon also echoes what we saw in the anonymous report of *h.e.* 3.24, that is, that John was urged by others to put his own Gospel into a written form, and also indicates an awareness that John's testimony is somewhat different from that of the others.

With regard to the other writings attributed to John, it is noteworthy that the quotation from 1 John 1:1 is given as a testimony not to the authorship of

[65] Muratorian Canon, lines 9–34. The best edition of the Canon is still that of Samuel Prideaux Tregelles, *Canon Muratorianus: The Earliest Catalogue of the Books of the New Testament* (Oxford: Clarendon, 1867), which includes a beautiful facsimile. I have used the restored text and translation given in Daniel J. Theron, *Evidence of Tradition* (Grand Rapids, MI: Baker Book House, 1958), 106–9.

[66] This heightened role of Andrew is taken to a new level by James Patrick, *Andrew of Bethsaida and the Johannine Circle: The Muratorian Tradition and the Gospel Text*, Studies in Biblical Literature, 153 (New York: Peter Lang, 2013) who, on the basis of the Muratorian Canon, the 'anti-Marcionite' prologues, and the texts of Papias, argues that the one who authorizes the witness of the Gospel of John is none other than Andrew of Bethsaida, and that this is an earlier tradition regarding the composition of the Gospel of John other than that preserved by Irenaeus and his predecessors. This is, it has to be said, rather conjectural, and he seems to have misunderstood the words of Irenaeus, blaming him for the confusion between the apostle John and John the disciple of the Lord (see chapter 2: 'Irenaeus: Apologetic Ambiguity'). This heightened role of Andrew may rather indicate that the Muratorian Canon should be placed in the fourth century, as the figure of Andrew, the 'first-called', became ever more important in the growing prestige of Constantinople, something that Patrick notes, but does not recognize the possible implications of this for dating the Muratorian Canon itself (ibid. 71, 123–7).

[67] Cf. Bauckham, *Jesus and the Eyewitnesses*, 429: 'the author of the Muratorian Canon evidently means that John, who was a disciple but not a member of the Twelve, met with his fellow disciples, who the author supposes to have been also bishops'.

the First Epistle of John, but to that of the Gospel. Clearly there is a sense of the unity of the Johannine corpus. Most striking, however, is the way in which the Muratorian Canon speaks about the Apocalypse. Later on, in its recounting of the writings of the disciples and apostles, it asserts that 'we accept only the Apocalypses of John and of Peter, although some of us do not want it to be read in the Church' (lines 71–2). Horbury argued that the fact that this is mentioned late in the list (after the *Wisdom of Solomon* and just before Hermas and his work the *Shepherd*, which is then followed by the rejected books) indicates that the Apocalypse of John had, for the author of the Canon, a dubious status.[68] However, the acceptance of the Apocalypse is assured by an earlier mention, which also strikingly explains, on its basis, why Paul wrote seven letters: 'the blessed Apostle Paul himself, imitating the example of his predecessor, John, wrote to seven churches only by name... For John also, though he wrote in the Apocalypse to seven churches, nevertheless he speaks to them all' (lines 47–50, 57–9).[69] The 'it' which some do not want to be read in the Church must surely, then, refer to the Apocalypse of Peter, not to both together.

Irenaeus provides us with another account of the occasion which prompted John to write down his Gospel. According to Irenaeus, it was not so much a matter of wanting to complete the accounts of the other Gospels, but rather the need to assert the rule of truth that led John to write. It was while residing in Ephesus, Irenaeus reports, that John encountered the heretic Cerinthus, prompting him to run out of the bath-house, crying out 'Let us fly, lest even the bath-house fall down because Cerinthus, the enemy of the truth, is within' (*haer.* 3.3.4). A little later Irenaeus adds that it was specifically to counter Cerinthus that John composed his Gospel:

> John, the disciple of the Lord, preaches this faith, seeking, by the proclamation of the Gospel, to remove that error which by Cerinthus had been disseminated among human beings, and a long time previously by those called the Nicolaitans,... The disciple of the Lord therefore desiring to put an end to all such doctrines, and to establish the rule of truth in the Church, that there is one God, the Almighty, who

[68] William Horbury, 'The Wisdom of Solomon in the Muratorian Fragment', *JTS* ns 45 (1994), 149–59.

[69] Hill, *Johannine Corpus*, 136–7, n. 170, notes three other figures who explain the seven letters to churches written by Paul on the basis of the seven churches of the Apocalypse (cf. Apoc. 1:20): a passage attributed to Hippolytus cited by Dionysius bar Salibi, *In Apocalypsim* 1.4; Cyprian, *Ad Fortunatum* 11; and Victorinus of Pettau, *In Apoc.* 1.7. On the claim that Paul imitated 'his predecessor John' in writing seven letters, see Krister Stendahl, 'The Apocalypse of John and the Epistles of Paul in the Muratorian Fragment', in William Klassen and Graydon F. Snyder, eds, *Current Issues in New Testament Interpretation* (New York: Harper and Brothers, 1962), 239–45. See also John A. T. Robinson, *The Priority of John*, ed. J. F. Coakley (London: SCM 1985), 35 (and *passim*), who argues that, as the only eyewitness to have written a Gospel and the only evangelist to have also written letters, John's 'witness, therefore, alike to the history and the theology, is, I believe, to be accorded a status of *primus inter pares*'.

made all things by his Word, both visible and invisible, showing at the same time that by the Word, through whom God made the creation, he also bestowed salvation on the human beings within creation, thus commenced his teaching in the Gospel: 'In the beginning was the Word'. (*haer.* 3.11.1)

The appeal to the 'rule of truth' here is noteworthy. A similar appeal to the 'rule' or 'canon' occurs in the letter of Polycrates of Ephesus in the context of maintaining the paschal celebration that derived from John, as we will see in the next section of this chapter. The 'canon', of course, holds a central place for Irenaeus, and perhaps goes back to their common teacher, Polycarp.[70] Whether Polycarp himself used the word 'canon' can no longer be determined. But it is certainly the case that it was 'the school of John', culminating, via Polycarp, in Irenaeus that was responsible for what, in the time of Irenaeus, became a clearly and self-consciously articulated 'orthodoxy'.

Also of note in this passage is Irenaeus' specification that the Gospel was written to combat Cerinthus, who was repeating the errors taught by the Nicolaitans 'a long time previously'. The Nicolaitans were also mentioned in the Apocalypse (2:6), and as, according to Eusebius, they were active only for 'a very short time' (*h.e.* 3.29.1), it would seem that Irenaeus would have held that the Apocalypse too was written 'a long time' prior to the Gospel (cf. *haer.* 1.26.3). However, elsewhere Irenaeus seems to assert that the Apocalypse was seen only in the last years of the first century 'towards the end of Domitian's reign', that is, before 96 CE. Yet, once again, things are not necessarily as they might seem at first sight. The statement in question is preserved in Greek by Eusebius, who introduces it this way:

[1] It is recorded that at that time the apostle and evangelist John, being still alive, was condemned to dwell in the island of Patmos for his testimony to the divine word. [2] At any rate [γέ τοι] Irenaeus, writing about the number of the name ascribed to the Antichrist in the so-called Apocalypse of John, states this about John in these very words [αὐταῖς συλλαβαῖς] in the fifth book *Against the Heresies*: [3] 'But if it were necessary that his name should be announced openly at the present time, it would have been declared by that one who also saw [ἑορακότος] the apocalypse, for it/he was seen [ἑωράθη] not long ago, but almost in our own generation, towards the end [πρὸς τῷ τέλει] of the reign of Domitian'.
(*h.e.* 3.18.1–3; cf. *haer.* 5.30.3)

Here Irenaeus' statement is set within the context of a supposed persecution under Domitian (*h.e.* 3.17–20), but when it is repeated later on, Eusebius makes it clear that he intends it to be understood as a testimony to the dating of the Apocalypse itself (*h.e.* 5.8.6–7). However, given the context of the

[70] Though coming from a later date, this is indicated by the postscript to the Moscow manuscript of the *Martyrdom of Polycarp*: Irenaeus 'also handed on the ecclesiastical and universal canon [τὸν ἐκκλησιαστικὸν κανόνα καὶ καθολικόν], as he had received it from the saint' (*M. Polyc.* 22.3). For Irenaeus on the 'canon' see Behr, Irenaeus, 111–16.

quotation in Irenaeus' own work, it is almost certain that the subject of the passive verb 'was seen' is John himself rather than the apocalyptic vision.[71] Irenaeus' words are taken from a passage concerning the significance of the number 666. It opens with the assertion that this number is found in 'all the most approved and ancient copies' of the Apocalypse, and that it was confirmed by 'those bearing witness, who saw John face-to-face' (*haer.* 5.30.1: κατ' ὄψιν . . . ἑορακότων, Greek *apud* Eusebius, *h.e.* 5.8.5). Those who met face to face with John are almost certainly the 'elders', including Papias, whom Irenaeus mentions elsewhere as having 'conferred in Asia with John the disciple of the Lord, . . . who remained with them up to the time of Trajan' (i.e. 98–117 CE; *haer.* 2.22.5: συμβεβληκότες . . . μέχρι τῶν Τραϊανοῦ χρόνων, Greek *apud* Eusebius *h.e.* 3.23.3). Irenaeus' point is that if John, who was seen as late as this period, had meant for the significance of the number and the name of the Antichrist to be known openly, he would have said so when he had met with the elders. In *h.e.* 3.18.3, the use of the aorist (ἑωράθη, 'he was seen') to describe John's appearance, and the preposition πρὸς to specify the time period ('towards the end of the reign of Domitian', i.e. 81–96 CE), indicates a specific period or occasion at which John was seen.[72] The Latin translator of *Against the Heresies* also seems to have had something similar in mind when he translated συμβεβληκότες in *haer.* 2.22.5 with *convenerunt*, implying more 'convened' or 'assembled'. And likewise the translation of ἑωράθη by *visum est* in *haer.* 5.30.3 excludes the apocalyptic vision as the subject of what was seen (for 'apocalypse' is feminine in both Greek and Latin), but is probably an instance known in Latin from this period where an accusative can be used as a subject.[73] Thus, Irenaeus words refer not to the dating of the apocalyptic vision, but to the appearance of John on a specific occasion when he met with the elders to clarify certain matters.

Early in the following century, the Alexandrians Clement and Origen provide further accounts of how John came to write his Gospel. Eusebius preserves an account given by Clement of Alexandria in his lost work the *Hypotyposeis*, which echoes many points that we have already seen, but introduces a new vocabulary for characterizing the Gospel of John:

> And again in the same books, Clement has inserted a tradition of the elders with regard to the order of the Gospels as follows. He said that those Gospels were first

[71] For a review of the literature on this question and a convincing argument that the subject is John, see Furlong, 'John the Evangelist', 104–12. So also Peter Leithart, *Revelation 1–11*, The International Theological Commentary on the Holy Scriptures of the Old and New Testaments (London: Bloomsbury T & T Clark, 2018), 37.

[72] Cf. Furlong, ibid. 108, who points out that it is not 'John was habitually seen (ἑωρᾶτο) up until (μέχρι) the end of Domitian's reign'.

[73] Cf. Furlong, ibid. 110–11, referring to Adam Ledgeway, *From Latin to Romance: Morphosyntactic Typology and Change*, Oxford Studies in Diachronic and Historical Linguistics (Oxford: Oxford University Press, 2012), 329–30.

> written which include the genealogies, but that the Gospel according to Mark had this occasion [οἰκονομίαν]: When Peter had publicly preached the word at Rome and by the Spirit had proclaimed the Gospel, those present, who were many, exhorted Mark, as one who had followed him for a long time and remembered what had been spoken, to make a record of what was said; when he had done this, and distributed the Gospel among those that asked him, the matter became known to Peter, who neither strongly forbade it nor promoted it. But that John, last of all, seeing that the outward facts [τὰ σώματικὰ] had been set forth in the Gospels, was urged on by the disciples, and, divinely moved by the Spirit, composed a spiritual Gospel [πνευματικὸν εὐαγγέλιον]. (*h.e.* 6.14.5–7)

The 'spiritual' nature of the Gospel is something that Clement also perceives in the First Epistle of John.[74] And, finally, Origen also preserves a similar tradition to those that we have seen:

> There is a report which must be noted that John collected the written Gospels in his own lifetime in the reign of Nero, and approved of and received those of which the deceit of the devil had not taken possession; but refused and rejected those which he perceived did not contain the truth.[75]

Throughout the second and early third century, then, John is variously seen as collecting and approving the other Gospels, and being encouraged by others to give written form to his preaching so as to complete the others, to provide a canon against heresy, and to give a spiritual account of what they had reported only bodily or outwardly. That the Asian elders met with John in his latter years, urging him to write his Gospel, is something that is repeated in later centuries by Victorinus, Jerome, and Theodore of Mopsuestia.[76]

Eusebius' presentation of the words of Irenaeus supposedly pertaining to the date of the apocalyptic vision, 'towards the end of the reign of Domitian' (*h.e.* 3.18.3), are connected with the question of the dating of the exile of John. After citing this passage, and giving further words about Domitian's order that 'those who were of family of David should be put to death', prompting accusations from heretics against 'the descendants of Jude, the Saviour's brother after the flesh' (*h.e.* 3.19), Eusebius passes on to Nerva (*r.* 96–8 CE), who annulled the sentences of his predecessor so that, as the ancient Christians (probably Hegesippus) relate, 'the apostle John, after his banishment to the island, took up his abode in Ephesus'.[77] Then, after relating some

[74] Cf. *Frag. Cass.* 3: 'Following the Gospel according to John, and in accordance with it, this Epistle also contains the spiritual principle'. *QDS* 37: 'Divine indeed and inspired [θείως γε καὶ ἐπιπνόως] is the saying of John, "He that loves not his brother is a murderer"' (cf. 1 John 3:15).

[75] Origen, *Hom. Luke*, Frag. 9.

[76] Victorinus, *Comm. Apoc.* 11.1; Jerome, Preface to *Comm. Matt.*; Theodore of Mopsuestia, *Com. John* (ed. Kalantzis, 41–2). For examination of these later witnesses, see Furlong, 'John the Evangelist', 137–40, 155–63.

[77] *H.e.* 3.20.8–9; that he is working from Hegesippus is argued by Lawlor and Oulton, *Eusebius: The Ecclesiastical History*, 2, 90–2.

information from Irenaeus about how John lived on 'to the time of Trajan' (*r.* 98–117 CE; *h.e.* 3.23.3; *haer.* 2.22.5), Eusebius continues by citing a lengthy passage from Clement of Alexandria which describes how 'after the death of the tyrant he passed from the island of Patmos to Ephesus, and used also to go, when asked, in some places to appoint bishops, in others to reconcile whole churches, and in others to ordain some of those pointed out by the Spirit' (*h.e.* 3.23.6; *QDS* 42); Clement doesn't mention the name of the 'tyrant', but the activities described thereafter in the text are implausibly attributed to a nonagenarian, so that the tyrant concerned is extremely unlikely to have been Domitian as Eusebius assumes. Likewise Origen mentions no name when he says that 'the Emperor of the Romans, as tradition teaches, condemned John to the Island of Patmos for testifying to the word of truth'.[78] That it was the emperor himself who exiled John to Patmos might accord with Tertullian's statement, the only witness to this point, that it was from Rome itself that John, after being plunged in boiling oil, was banished to Patmos.[79] Jerome, commenting on this passage, places his sufferings in Rome, like Peter and Paul, under Nero, although elsewhere, when following Eusebius, he places John's exile to the time of Domitian.[80] Epiphanius, on the other hand, places John's return from Patmos to the time of Claudius Caesar (*r.* 41–54 CE)![81] Whatever Epiphanius might have thought about this report, it is probable that, as Robinson suggests, 'his source may have intended Nero, whose other name was Claudius (just as Claudius' other name was Nero)'.[82] Robinson also gives two other later sources identifying Nero as the one who banished John: the Syriac version of the Apocalypse and another Syriac text called *The History of John, the Son of Zebedee.*[83]

Whereas during the course of the nineteenth century it was almost unanimously held that John was exiled to Patmos during the time of Nero, and there saw his vision, the near consensus for most of the twentieth century, at least among New Testament scholars, if not classicists, on the basis of Eusebius' presentation of Irenaeus' words, was that John was exiled under Domitian and that the apocalyptic vision was to be dated to this late period.[84] More recently, the pendulum seems to be swinging back again, realizing that claims about a

[78] Origen, *Com. Matt.* 16.6. [79] Tertullian, *Praescr.* 35.

[80] For Nero, *Contra Jovin.* 1.26 (PL 23, 259; 'Nero' is the reading in the mss and older editions; PL opts for 'sent to Rome' rather than 'sent by Nero'); for Domitian, *vir. ill.* 9.

[81] Epiphanius, *Pan.* 51.12.2.

[82] John A. T. Robinson, *Redating the New Testament* (Philadelphia: Westminster Press, 1976), 224.

[83] Robinson, *Redating*, 224; citing J. Gwynn, ed., *The Apocalypse of St John in a Syriac Version hitherto Unknown* (Dublin, 1897), 1; W. Wright, ed., *Apocryphal Acts of the Apostles* (1871), 2, 55–7. Furlong, 'John the Evangelist', 114–26, also argues for a Neronian date for John's banishment.

[84] The classicists mentioned by Robinson, *Redating*, 225, are G. Henderson, A. D. Momigliano, A. Wiegall, and K. A. Eckhart.

persecution under Domitian have been greatly exaggerated,[85] and, through further analysis of indications internal to the text of the Apocalypse, placing its composition sometime in the late 60s CE, before the destruction of the Temple in Jerusalem in 70 CE.[86] It was Eusebius' attempt to place as much distance as possible between the time of Christ and the Apocalypse that led him, as Furlong puts it, to create 'a *pastiche* of ill-fitting sources, held together by the thread of misinterpreted statements from Clement and Irenaeus, to construct the fiction of the Domitianic banishment of John' so that 'Papias' Elder was consequently transformed into an obscure and unknown figure and Papias was largely dismissed as a fabricator of legends who lacked intelligence; even Irenaeus' testimony concerning Papias' knowledge of John was successfully discounted'.[87]

The dating of the Apocalypse does not, however, enable us to fix that of the Gospel. Attempts to date the composition of the Gospels based on internal indicators depend to a great measure upon presuppositions, such as what one holds about the 'development' of theology and the life and structure of the Church, or the stages involved in the composition of a Gospel, whether by one author alone or by one or more subsequent redactors.[88] Arguments for an early dating of the Gospel have been advanced (Robinson suggests 50–5 CE for the first edition and 65+ for the final form together with the Prologue and Epilogue),[89] though most scholars, basing themselves on the longevity of John and with presuppositions about development (with respect to the Synoptics, theology, and the parting of the ways between Judaism and Christianity), hold to a later dating, sometime towards the end of the first century, that is, at the time when, according to the second- and third-century sources, John met with the elders and was urged by them to compose his Gospel. Securing a date for the Gospel does not really affect this study, although the relation between the Gospel and the Apocalypse will be brought up in Chapter 2, when considering the topic of 'apocalyptic', and again in Chapter 4, when we turn to the title 'Son of Man'.

[85] Eusebius (*h.e.* 3.19–20) does not in fact mention the name of a single Christian put to death under Domitian; it is his connection of events under Domitian to Irenaeus' words about John seeing the vision towards the end of Domitian's reign (though Irenaeus says nothing about a persecution), that has persuaded others to date the Apocalypse late.

[86] Cf. Robert B. Moberly, 'When was Revelation Conceived?', *Biblica* 73.1 (1992), 376–93, who would have an early date for the main vision, but a later date for the letters; J. Christian Wilson, 'The Problem of the Domitianic Date of Revelation', *NTS* 39 (1993), 587–605, who would place it either during the reign of Galba (between June 68 and January 69), or in the latter part of Nero's reign, after the persecution of Christians in 64–5; Thomas B. Slater, 'Dating the Apocalypse to John', *Biblica* 84 (2003), 252–58, during the 60s; Gonzalo Rojas-Flores, 'The *Book of Revelation* and the First Years of Nero's Reign', *Biblica* 85 (2004), 375–92, who would place it as early as 54 to 60; and Mark Wilson, 'The Earliest Christians in Ephesus and the Date of Revelation, Again', *Neotestamenica* 39.1 (2005), 163–93, around the year 69 CE; Leithart, *Revelation 1–11*, 36–40, argues for shortly before the outbreak of Nero's persecutions in 64 CE.

[87] Furlong, 'John the Evangelist', 113.

[88] Cf. Robinson, *Redating*, esp. 336–58.

[89] Robinson, *Redating*, 307.

The Unity of the Johannine Corpus

The swinging of the pendulum of scholarly consensus is not only with regard to the date of the Apocalypse, but also with regard to the question of the common authorship of the Apocalypse and the Gospel, and indeed the two issues are related. Lightfoot, Westcott, and Hort all held that the author of both was John, and dated the Apocalypse early and the Gospel late, so as to allow him time to improve in his mastery of Greek.[90] In the twentieth century, on the other hand, assuming a late date for both works, scholars have uniformly dismissed the idea of the common authorship, primarily on literary grounds. This stands in marked contrast to the century or more following these works themselves, where writers are unanimous in attributing both works to the same figure, and even interweave passages from both works with no awareness at all of any possible discrepancy between them. Justin Martyr is the first to mention the Apocalypse written by John, 'one of the apostles of Christ', explicitly, connecting it with the teaching about the thousand-year reign of Christ in Jerusalem, and Melito of Sardis the first to write a book on it.[91] According to Eusebius, Theophilus of Antioch quoted from the Apocalypse in the work he wrote against Hermogenes.[92] The Apocalypse is also known, and attributed to the same John who wrote the Gospel, by the Muratorian Canon as we have seen. Most striking, though, is the way in which *The Letter of the Churches of Vienne and Lyons to those in Asia and Phrygia*, perhaps written by Irenaeus, interweave quotations from and allusions to the Gospel, the Letters, and the Apocalypse, unquestioningly assuming that they all belong together.[93] Irenaeus, likewise, holds the two works closely together. For instance, after quoting Apoc. 1:12–16, he continues:

> But when John could not endure the sight (for he says, 'I fell at his feet as dead', that what was written might come to pass: 'No human being sees God and lives'), the Word, reviving him and reminding him that it was he upon whose bosom he had leaned at supper, when he put the question as to who should betray him, declared: 'I am the first and the last, and he who lives and was dead, and behold, I am alive for evermore, and have the keys of Death and of Hades'.[94]

The Gospel of John, for Irenaeus, is inextricably bound together with the Apocalypse, with the former providing the background to understanding the latter. Given that there is a connection between the Apocalypse and

[90] Lightfoot, *Essays*, 132–3; B. F. Wesctott, *The Gospel According to St John* (London: John Murray, 1882), lxxxvii; Fenton John Anthony Hort, *The Apocalypse of St John I–III* (London: Macmillan, 1908), x–xii. So also Liethart, *Revelation 1–11*, 74–5.

[91] Justin Martyr, *Dialogue*, 81.4. According to Eusebius (*h.e.* 4.26.2), among many other works written by Melito was one '*On the Devil and the Apocalypse of John*'.

[92] Cf. Eusebius, *h.e.* 4.24.1.

[93] See, for instance, *h.e.* 5.1.10, and Hill's comments, *Johannine Corpus*, 84.

[94] *Haer.* 4.20.11, citing Apoc. 1:17, Exod. 33:20, and Apoc. 1:18, and alluding to John 13:25.

Millenarian teaching regarding the reign of Christ in an earthly generation, as seen at least from Irenaeus (and also in Papias if Eusebius' rhetoric in *h.e.* 3.39.6 and 11–14 is any indication), one might have expected the Alexandrians of the following generations to have been rather more cautious about the Apocalypse. But this is not the case. Clement of Alexandria cites the Apocalypse a number of times, attributes it to John,[95] and interweaves a sentence from the Apocalypse with one from the Prologue to the Gospel: 'Thus the Lord himself is called "Alpha and Omega, the beginning and the end", "by whom all things were made"'.[96] Origen, for his part, opens his great *Commentary on the Gospel according to John* by quoting a passage from 'John in the Apocalypse' to clarify passages from the Old Testament and the New (Num. 27:17; 1 Pet. 3:4; Rom. 2:29) and to provide the key for his commentary thereafter.

When questions about the Apocalypse do begin to emerge, they concern both its teaching and the identity of its author. The first secure evidence we have for this is the account Eusebius gives of two books *On Promises* written by Dionysius of Alexandria in the mid-third century.[97] According to Eusebius, Dionysius was spurred on to write these books because a certain Nepos had been teaching that there would be a millennium reign of Christ on earth, 'devoted to bodily indulgence', and had justified this teaching by interpreting the Scriptures in 'a more Jewish fashion', even writing a book entitled *Refutation of the Allegorists* in support of his case (*h.e.* 7.24.1–3). In his first book, devoted to the refutation of millenarian teaching, Dionysius reports how he had gone to Arsinoë to debate with 'the elders and teachers' there and eventually persuaded Coracion, the leader of this teaching (Nepos has since died), to abandon this approach, a decision which some of the rest of the brethren (but presumably not all) accepted with rejoicing (*h.e.* 7.24.6–9). The second book turns to the question of the Apocalypse. While accepting that 'some deeper meaning underlies the words... [so that] I have come to the conclusion that they are beyond my comprehension', Dionysius affirms that 'for my part I should not dare to reject the book, since many brethren hold it in estimation' (*h.e.* 7.25.4–5). However, he then continues by asserting that, even though 'it cannot be understood in the literal sense' and was certainly written by 'some holy and inspired person', the Apocalypse cannot be attributed to John the apostle, the son of Zebedee, the author of the Gospel according to John and the Catholic Epistle (*h.e.* 7.25.6–7), for two reasons. First, because in the authentic works of John, John never mentions himself by name, whereas the author of the Apocalypse does so in the opening words (*h.e.* 7.25.9–11).

95 *Strom.* 6.13.106.2.

96 *Strom.* 6.16.141.7, citing Apoc. 21:6 and John 1:3.

97 See Eusebius, *h.e.* 7.24–5. Dionysius reports that 'Some, indeed, of those before our time rejected and altogether impugned the book [i.e. the Apocalypse]', attributing its authorship to Cerinthus (*h.e.* 7.25.1–3). On the relation between Dionysius' account and the various, and confused, reports concerning Gaius of Rome and the 'Alogi' (those who reject the Gospel and Apocalypse of John) reported by Epiphanius, Photius, and Dionysius bar Salibi, see Hill, *Johannine Controversy*, 172–204.

The name John, he observes, is extremely common: Acts mentions another John, surnamed Mark (Acts 12:25), and there were two tombs in Ephesus said to be John's (*h.e.* 7.25.12–16). The second reason concerns the textual differences between the Apocalypse and the Gospel together with the (first) Epistle. Not only are their respective vocabularies different (*h.e.* 7.25.17–23), but so also are their style: the Gospel and Epistle 'are not only written in faultless Greek, but also show the greatest literary skill in their diction, their reasonings, and the constructions in which they are expressed', while of the John who wrote the Apocalypse Dionysius points out 'his language and his inaccurate Greek usage, employing as he does, barbarous idioms and in some places committing downright solecisms', although he doesn't deem it necessary to specify in detail any of these points (*h.e.* 7.25.24–7). Dionysius' claims have been repeated, and elaborated, especially over recent centuries. According to Swete's calculations, of the 913 words used in the Apocalypse, 416 are also found in the Gospel, but only eight are distinctive to the Apocalypse and the Gospel alone.[98]

While recognizing the very different literary style between the Gospel and the Apocalypse, it should be pointed out that their respective vocabularies are actually more similar than Dionysius would allow, most notably in the fact that it is only these two texts of the New Testament that call Jesus Christ 'the Word' (John 1:1; Apoc. 1:2, 19:13, though here it is 'the Word of God', an expression not found in John). Staying with the Prologue of John, one might also point to other shared and distinctive vocabulary and imagery: John 1:5, Jesus is 'the Light [that] *shines* in the darkness', and Apoc. 1:16, the face of Jesus '*shines* like the sun', and John 1:14, 'The Word became flesh and *tabernacled* among us', and Apoc. 21:3, 'the *tabernacle* of God is among human beings and he will *tabernacle* among them', and 'we beheld *his glory* as the *Only-begotten* of the Father', and Apoc. 1:5–6, 'Jesus Christ…the *firstborn* from the dead…to *him* be *glory*'. The parallels continue throughout the works, for instance John 7:38, '*rivers* of *living water* will flow' from one

[98] Henry Barclay Swete, *The Apocalypse of St John: The Greek Text with Introduction, Notes, and Indices* (London: Macmillan, 1906), cxxii; the eight words distinctive to the Gospel and Apocalypse are: *ἀρνίον, Ἑβραϊστί, ἐκκεντεῖν, κυκλεύειν, ὄψις, προφύρεος, σκηνοῦν, φοῖνιξ*. Jörg Frey, 'Erwägungen zum Verhältnis der Johannesapokalypse zu den übrigen Schriften des Corpus Johanneum', in Hengel, *Die johanneische Frage*, 326–429, at 341, has *δέκατος* (John 1:39; Apoc. 21:20) instead of *κυκλεύειν* (John 10:24, but only in B). See also, Ian Boxall 'From the Apocalypse of John to the Johannine "Apocalypse in Reverse": Intimations of Apocalyptic and the Quest for a Relationship', in Catrin H. Williams and Christopher Rowland, eds, *John's Gospel and Intimations of Apocalyptic* (London: Bloomsbury, 2013), 58–78, and Jörg Frey, 'Das Corpus Johanneum und die Apokalypse des Johannes: Die Johanneslegende, die Probleme der johanneischen Verfasserschaft, und die Frage der Pseudonymität der Apokalypse', in Stefan Alkier, Thomas Hieke, and Tobias Nicklas, *Poetik und Intertextualität der Johannesapokalypse*, WUNT 346 (Tübingen: Mohr, 2015), 71–134. See also the stylometric analysis of Anthony Kenny, *A Stylometric Analysis of the New Testament* (Oxford: Clarendon Press, 1986), 76–9.

who believes in Christ, and Apoc. 7:17, the lamb 'will guide them to *springs* of *the water of life*', or John 17:24, 'Father, I desire that they also whom have given me may be with me, to behold my glory which you have given me in your love for me before *the foundation of the world*', and Apoc. 17:8, 'the dwellers on earth whose name had not been written in the book of life from *the foundation of the world*'. Finally, the two works end in ways which also parallel each other: John 21:24–5, the disciple bearing witness 'has *written* these things; and we know that his witness is *true*. But there are also many other things which Jesus did; were every one of them to be *written*, I suppose that the world itself could not contain the *books* that would be written', and Apoc. 21:5, 22:19, he who sat on the throne 'said, "*Write* this, for these words are trustworthy and *true*." . . . if anyone takes away from the words of the *book* of this prophecy, God shall take away his share in the tree of life and in the holy city, which are *written* in this *book*'.[99]

The difference in literary style has also been explained in various ways. We have already seen that Lightfoot would explain the difference by positing a period of several decades between the Apocalypse and the Gospel, between the close of the 'Hebraic period' in the life of John, which was followed by his sojourn in Ephesus, a great centre of Greek culture, where, after some twenty or thirty years of a 'Hellenic period' he finally wrote (or dictated) the Gospel. But in addition he points out that another 'very potent influence' must be borne in mind—the difference in subject matter: 'The apocalyptic purport of the one book necessarily tinges its diction and imagery with a very strong Hebraic colouring, which we should not expect to find in a historical narrative'.[100] As such, Lightfoot was prepared to allow for what Luthardt had described as John's 'intentional emancipations from the rules of grammar', for, as he points out, anyone who could write 'from He Who Is' (*ἀπὸ ὁ ὢν*, Apoc. 1:4), as if 'in sheer ignorance that *ἀπὸ* does not take a nominative case, would be incapable of writing any two or three consecutive verses of the Apocalypse', which demonstrates 'a familiarity with the intricacies of the very intricate syntax of this language'.[101] Burney likewise came to the conclusion that the identity of authorship cannot be disproved from a supposed discrepancy of style, though his case rests upon a postulated Aramaic origin for the Gospel of John, subsequently translated into Greek, and parallel Semitisms between the two works.[102]

[99] For further examples, Boxall, 'Johannine "Apocalypse in Reverse,"' 67–74. For a full examination of the cross references between the Gospel and the Apocalypse, and as a two-part, chiastically structured, work see Peter Leithart, *Revelation 1–11*, and *Revelation 12–22*, The International Theological Commentary on the Holy Scriptures of the Old and New Testaments (London: Bloomsbury T & T Clark, 2018).

[100] Lightfoot, *Essays*, 132. [101] Lightfoot, *Essays*, 132–3.

[102] Burney, *Aramaic Origin*, 149–52. Burney would be willing to place the Apocalypse shortly before 96 CE.

The debates about the dates of, and relationship between, the Gospel of John and the Apocalypse of John will no doubt continue. But what cannot be doubted is that the unanimous testimony from the second century is that these two works (along with the Epistles) belong together and that they were written by one and the same person, John the Elder, the disciple of the Lord. Not only that, but there are indications that the unity of the Johannine corpus found material form in the binding of these works into a single codex.[103] The third-century work *Contra Noetum*, attributed to Hippolytus, suggests as much, saying in passing: 'For showing thus this Word of God, being from the beginning and now sent forth, going below he said in the Apocalypse [ὑποβὰς ἐν τῇ Ἀποκαλύψει ἔφη], "And I saw heaven opened, and behold a white horse; and he who sits upon it is faithful and true... and the name by which he is called is the Word of God." [Apoc. 19:11–13]'[104] A manuscript leaf has survived which might well have originally contained the Johannine corpus, that is, P. Antinoopolis 12, from the late third or early fourth century. It contains 2 John 1–9, and at the top of the page it has the numbers 164 and 165. Charles Roberts calculates that the missing 163 pages would not have been filled by the other catholic and pastoral epistles and are not sufficient for the Pauline epistles. But, on the other hand, 'if we were to assume that the codex held a corpus of Johannine writings, with the Gospel, Revelation, and I John all preceding II John, the number of pages required would be only a little short of 160, and the surplus pages might have been accounted for by titles, etc'.[105]

Even if this is not the case, there is no question that for the second century generally, and emphatically for those who traced their theological lineage back to John, the Johannine writings belong together theologically and conceptually, and that they were all held to have been written by the disciple of the Lord. Debate about this, as we have seen, only begins in the mid-third century, prompted by a reaction to millenarian teaching, and then the seeds of confusion were sown in the fourth century by Eusebius. Perhaps we will never know the true identity of the author of the Gospel of John and whether he was the same John who wrote the Apocalypse, but perhaps this is just the point. Modern scholars have often suggested that the reason why the Evangelist has cloaked his identity as 'the beloved disciple' is to invite others also to become beloved disciples.[106] Much more daring, and, it has to be said, accurate in his attention to the words of Christ on the cross, was Origen:

[103] Cf. Hill, *The Johannine Corpus*, 453–9.

[104] Hippolytus, *Contra Noetum* 15.2. As Hill notes (*Johannine Corpus*, 457) 'ὑποβαίνω does not mean "later" in time but refers to a later section in the same book!', confirmed by its use in *Contra Noetum* 12, and contemporary examples.

[105] C. H. Roberts, J. W. B. Barns, and H. Zilliacus, *The Antinoopolis Papyri*, 3 vols (London, 1950–67), 1.24–5.

[106] Cf. James H. Charlesworth, *The Beloved Disciple: Whose Witness Validates the Gospel of John?* (Valley Forge, PA: Trinity Press International, 195), 134–8.

> We might dare say, then, that the Gospels are the firstfruits of all Scriptures, but that the firstfruits of the Gospels is that according to John, whose meaning no one can understand who has not leaned on Jesus' breast nor received Mary from Jesus to be his mother also. But he who would be another John must also become such as John, to be shown to be Jesus, so to speak. For if Mary had no son except Jesus, in accordance with those who hold a sound opinion of her, and Jesus says to his mother, 'Behold your son' [19:26] and not 'Behold, this man also is your son', he has said equally, 'Behold, this is Jesus whom you bore'. For indeed everyone who has been perfected no longer lives, but Christ lives in him [cf. Gal 2:20], and since 'Christ lives' in him, it is said of him to Mary, 'Behold your son', the Christ.[107]

Jeffrey Hamburger has brilliantly explored the ways in which St John the Divine was 'deified' and approximated to the figure of Christ in Western medieval art and theology.[108] A similar point holds for the Eastern iconographic tradition, in which, intriguingly, among all the apostles and evangelists, John is the only one to have two distinct *figurae*: that of a young disciple at the Last Supper or alternatively standing at the foot of the cross, and another as an old man, 'the theologian', who, in Russian iconography from the sixteenth century, is portrayed with his right hand positioned over his mouth, configured in the form used for giving a blessing, that is, spelling IC XC ('Jesus Christ'), not representing a silence but rather bearing witness to Christ, the Word of God. The mystery of the author of the Fourth Gospel is thus a fertile enigma, asking to be explored in every age. Yet there is no doubt, as we have seen, that the second-century writers following in his tradition—Lightfoot's 'School of John'—were convinced that he was indeed John of Ephesus, the disciple of the Lord, and the revered Elder. We will explore further the identity of the Son (on the cross and standing at the foot of the cross) and the Mother when we turn to the Gospel of John itself in Part II and again in Part III from a different perspective.

THE HIGH PRIEST OF THE PASCHAL MYSTERY

In the first section of this chapter, as we began to investigate the identity of John, we started with the earliest testimony to the authorship of the Gospels,

[107] Origen, *Com. John.* 1.23. See also Ephrem the Syrian, *Hymns on Virginity*, 25, esp. 9: 'Your mother saw you in your disciple; and he saw you in your mother. Oh, the seers who at every moment see you, Lord, in a mirror, manifest a type so that we too, in one another, may see you, our Savior'. See now Charles Stang, *Our Divine Double* (Cambridge, MA: Harvard University Press, 2016) for a broader examination of this phenomenon of the 'doubling' of Jesus, as shown especially in the Thomas material from early Christianity, but also picking up on themes going back to Plato and developed in similar ways by Mani and Plotinus as well as other strands in early Christianity.

[108] Jeffrey F. Hamburger, *St. John the Divine: The Deified Evangelist in Medieval Art and Theology* (Berkeley: University of California Press, 2002).

that of Papias, carefully dissecting his words from the construal put on them by Eusebius with his fourth-century presuppositions. We now turn to a particular, and very striking, aspect about John and his 'school' that will give us an insight into the kind of Gospel that it is, which will be further developed in the following chapters. But again, this involves reading through a lengthy passage from Eusebius and disentangling the extracts of Irenaeus and Polycrates of Ephesus that he gives from his own fourth-century perspective and commentary or reconstruction.

According to Eusebius, 'no small controversy arose because all the communities of Asia [*τῆς Ἀσίας ἁπάσης αἱ παροικίαι*] thought it right, as though by a more ancient tradition to observe for the feast of the Saviour's Pascha the fourteenth day of the moon [*σελήνης τὴν τεσσαρεσκαιδεκάτην ᾤοντο δεῖν ἐπὶ τῆς τοῦ σωτηρίου πάσχα ἑορτῆς παραφυλάττειν*], on which the Jews had been commanded to kill the lamb. Thus it was necessary to finish the fast on that day, whatever day of the week it might be [*ὡς δέον ἐκ παντὸς κατὰ ταύτην, ὁποίᾳ δἂν ἡμέρᾳ τῆς ἑβδομάδος περιτυγχάνοι*]' (*h.e.* 5.23.1). Yet such was not the custom, Eusebius claims, 'in the churches throughout the rest of the world, for from apostolic tradition they kept the custom which still exists that it is not right to finish the fast on any day save that of the resurrection of our Saviour [*ἐξ ἀποστολικῆς παραδόσεως τὸ καὶ εἰς δεῦρο κρατῆσαν ἔθος φυλαττούσαις, ὡς μηδ' ἑτέρᾳ προσήκειν παρὰ τὴν τῆς ἀναστάσεως τοῦ σωτῆρος ἡμῶν ἡμέρᾳ τὰς νηστείας ἐπιλύεσθαι*]' (*h.e.* 5.23.1). Eusebius then asserts that 'many meetings and conferences of bishops' were held about this, and 'all unanimously formulated in their letters the ecclesiastical teaching for those of the faithful everywhere that the mystery of the Lord's resurrection from the dead could be celebrated on no day save Sunday, and that on that day alone we should celebrate the end of the paschal fast [*ὡς ἂν μηδ' ἐν ἄλλῃ ποτὲ τῆς κυριακῆς ἡμέρᾳ τὸ τῆς ἐκ νεκρῶν ἀναστάσεως ἐπιτελοῖτο τοῦ κυρίου μυστήριον, καὶ ὅπως ἐν ταύτῃ μόνῃ τῶν κατὰ τὸ πάσχα νηστειῶν φυλλατοίμεθα τὰς ἐπιλύσεις*]' (*h.e.* 5.23.2). He states that still extant are the letters of those who meet in Palestine, in Rome, in Pontus, in Gaul, over which Irenaeus was the bishop, in Osrhoene, and in Corinth, 'and of very many more who expressed one and the same opinion and judgement and gave the same vote' (*h.e.* 5.23.4). Polycrates, however, led the bishops of Asia in their persistence that they should 'keep the custom which they had received from of old' (*h.e.* 5.24.1). Eusebius then reproduces a letter from Polycrates of Ephesus, addressed to Victor and the Church of Rome:

> [2] We, therefore, keep the day without tampering with it, neither adding nor taking away. For indeed in Asia great luminaries have fallen asleep, such as will rise again on the day of the coming of the Lord [*τῇ ἡμέρᾳ τῆς παρουσίας τοῦ κυρίου*], when he comes with glory from heaven to seek out all his saints; [such were] Philip, one of the twelve apostles, who has fallen asleep in Hierapolis, [as

have] also his two daughters who grew old in virginity, and his other daughter who lived in the Holy Spirit and rests at Ephesus; [3] and, moreover, [there is] John also, who lay on the Lord's breast, who was [or 'became'] a priest wearing the petal, both a witness and a teacher [ὁ ἐπὶ τὸ στῆθος τοῦ κυρίου ἀναπεσών, ὃς ἐγενήθη ἱερεὺς τὸ πέταλον πεφορεκὼς καὶ μάρτυς καὶ διδάσκαλος] [4] He has fallen asleep at Ephesus. Moreover, Polycarp too at Smyrna, both bishop and martyr, and Thraseas, both bishop and martyr, of Eumenia, who has fallen asleep at Smryna. [5] And why need I mention Sagaris, bishop and martyr, who has fallen asleep at Laodicea, or the blessed Papirius, or Melito the eunuch who in all things lived in the Holy Spirit, who lies at Sardis, awaiting the visitation [ἐποσκοπήν] from heaven, when he shall rise from the dead? [6] These all observed the fourteenth day for Pascha according to the Gospel, in no way deviating from it, but following the rule of faith [οὗτοι πάντες ἐτήρησαν τὴν ἡμέραν τῆς τεσσαρεσκαιδεκάτης τοῦ πάσχα κατὰ τὸ εὐαγγέλιον, μηδὲν παρεκβαίνοντες, ἀλλὰ κατὰ τὸν κανόνα τῆς πίστεως ἀκολουθοῦντες]. And moreover I also, Polycrates, the least of you all, [do] according to the tradition of my kinsmen, some of whom I was in close attendance on. Seven of my kinsmen were bishops, and I am the eighth. And my kinsmen always kept the day when the people put away the leaven. [7] Therefore I for my part, brethren, who number sixty-five years in the Lord and have conversed with the brethren from all parts of the world and have traversed the entire range of holy Scripture, and am not afraid of threats, for those better than I have said, 'we must obey God rather than men' [Acts 5:29]. [8] He then continues about the bishops who when he wrote were with him and shared his opinion and says thus: But I could mention the bishops present with me, whom I summoned when you yourselves desired that I should summon them. And if I were to write their names, the number would be great. But they who know my littleness approved my letter, knowing that I did not wear my grey hairs in vain, but that I have ever lived in Christ Jesus. (*h.e.* 5.24.2–8)

Upon receiving this letter, 'Victor, who presided over [the church of] the Romans [ὁ μὲν τῆς Ῥωμαίων προεστὼς]', took immediate and drastic action. In Eusebius's words, Victor:

immediately tried to cut off from the common unity [ἀποτέμνειν... τῆς κοινῆς ἑνώσεως] the communities of all Asia [τῆς Ἀσίας πάσης... τὰς παροικίας], together with the adjacent churches, on the ground of heterodoxy, and he denounced them in letters proclaiming that all the brethren there were absolutely excommunicated [ἀκοινωνήτους]. (*h.e.* 5.24.9)

This action, not surprisingly, caused an uproar! Bishops issued counter-requests to Victor, urging him to consider the cause of peace, unity, and love towards his neighbours (πρὸς τὸν πλησίον, *h.e.* 5.24.9). Among these was Irenaeus, who, although he exhorted Victor at length not to 'cut off whole churches of God [μὴ ἀποκόπτοι ὅλας ἐκκλησίας θεοῦ]' for following a tradition of ancient custom, nevertheless recommends that 'the mystery of the Lord's resurrection be observed only on the Lord's day' (*h.e.* 5.24.11). Eusebius then transcribes two extracts from the letter of Irenaeus. The first is as follows:

> [12] For the controversy is not only about the day, but also about the very manner of the fast; for some think that they ought to fast one day, others two, others even more; and in the opinion of others, the 'day' amounts to forty hours, day and night [*οὐδὲ γὰρ μόνον περὶ τῆς ἡμέρας ἐστὶν ἡ ἀμφισβήτησις, ἀλλὰ καὶ περὶ τοῦ εἴδους τῆς νηστείας. οἱ μὲν γὰρ οἴονται μίαν ἡμέραν δεῖν αὐτοὺς νηστεύειν, οἱ μὲν δύο, οἱ δὲ καὶ πλείονας· οἱ δὲ τεσσαράκοντα ὥρας ἡμερινάς τε καὶ νυκτερινὰς συμμετροῦσιν τὴν ἡμέραν αὐτῶν*]. [13] And such variation of observance did not begin in our own time, but much earlier, in the days of our predecessors who, it would appear, disregarding strictness maintained a practice which is simple and yet allows for personal preference, establishing it for the future, and none the less all these lived in peace, and we also live in peace with one another and the disagreement in the fast confirms our agreement in the faith [*ἡ διαφωνία τῆς νυστείας τὴν ὁμόνοιαν τῆς πίστεως συνίστησιν*]. (*h.e.* 5.24.12–13)

The second extract follows immediately, recalling an earlier episode:

> [14] Among these too were the presbyters before Soter, who presided over the church of which you are now the leader, I mean Anicetus and Pius and Telesphorus and Sixtus. They did not observe it themselves, nor did they enjoin it on those who followed them, and though they did not keep it they were nonetheless at peace with those from the communities in which it was observed when they came to them, although to observe it was more objectionable to those who did not do so [*οὔτε αὐτοὶ ἐτήρησαν οὔτε τοῖς μετ' αὐτῶν ἐπέτρεπον, καὶ οὐδὲν ἔλαττον αὐτοὶ μὴ τηροῦντες εἰρήνευον τοῖς ἀπὸ τῶν παροικιῶν ἐν αἷς ἐτηρεῖτο, ἐρχομένοις πρὸς αὐτούς· καίτοι μᾶλλον ἐναντίον ἦν τὸ τυρεῖν τοῖς μὴ τηροῦσιν*]. [15] And no one was ever rejected [*ἀπεβλήθησαν*] for this reason, but the presbyters before you who did not observe [it] sent the Eucharist to those from other communities who did [*ἀλλ' αὐτοὶ μὴ τηροῦντες οἱ πρὸ σοῦ πρεσβύτεροι τοῖς ἀπὸ τῶν παροικιῶν τηροῦσιν ἔπεμπον εὐχαριστίαν*], [16] and when the blessed Polycarp was staying in Rome in the time of Anicetus, though they disagreed a little about some other things as well, they immediately made peace, having no wish for strife between them on this matter. For neither was Anicetus able to persuade Polycarp not to observe [it], inasmuch as he had always done so in company with John the disciple of our Lord and the other apostles with whom he had associated [*οὔτε γὰρ ὁ Ἀνίκητος τὸν Πολύκαρπον πεῖσαι ἐδύνατο μὴ τηρεῖν, ἅτε μετὰ Ἰωάννου τοῦ μαθητοῦ τοῦ κυρίου ἡμῶν καὶ τῶν λοιπῶν ἀποστόλων οἷς συνδιέτριψεν, ἀεὶ τετηρηκότα*]; nor did Polycarp persuade Anicetus to observe [it], for he said that he ought to keep the custom of those who were presbyters before him. [17] And under these circumstances they communed with each other [*ἐκοινώνησαν ἑαυτοῖς*], and in the church Anicetus yielded the celebration of the Eucharist to Polycarp, obviously out of respect, and they parted from each other in peace, for the peace of the whole church was kept both by those who observed and by those who did not [*πάσης τῆς ἐκκλησίας εἰρήνην ἐχόντων, καὶ τῶν τηρούντων καὶ τῶν μὴ τηρούντων*]. (*h.e.* 5.24.14–17)

After describing how Irenaeus lived up to his name by making peace between the churches, Eusebius concludes his account of the controversy with an extract from the letter of the bishops of Palestine, who after treating at length the subject matter of the Pascha as it had come down to them, wrote:

> Try to send copies of our letter to every community, that we may not be guilty towards those who easily deceive their own souls. And we make it plain to you that those in Alexandria also celebrate the same day as we do, for letters have been exchanged between them and us, so that we may observe the holy day harmoniously and together. (*h.e.* 5.25)

Eusebius has presented us with a heavily redacted account of the controversy.[109] That his fourth-century perspective does not match the reality on the ground in the second century is made clear in the discrepancy between, on the one hand, the way Eusebius describes Victor, as a Pope of Rome, breaking communion with churches in far-off Asia, and, on the other hand, the way Irenaeus reports that the different communities had previously exchanged the eucharistic gifts between themselves: 'the presbyters before you who did not observe it sent the Eucharist to those communities who did' (5.24.15). It is surely impossible to conceive of eucharistic gifts being sent from Rome to Asia; the 'communities of Asia' must be communities of Asian Christians living in Rome, distinct communities, that is, from that (or those) of the Romans over which Victor presided. This then was, initially at least, an intra-Roman controversy, between communities of Roman Christians and those of Asian Christians, with the latter having the distinctive paschal practice of celebrating the Lord's Pascha on the fourteenth day of the moon, that is 14 Nissan (for which reason they were called the Quartodecimans, the 'Fourteeners'). This was, moreover, a difference of practice already present earlier in the century: when Polycarp visited Rome in 154 or 155, neither he nor Anicetus could persuade the other to adopt their own practice, yet they remained in peace, for the difference in practice 'confirms [the] unity in faith' (*h.e.* 5.24.16, 13).

Victor did indeed, however, bring about an international dimension to this controversy, by seemingly asking Christian leaders from around the Mediterranean to consult together and give their opinion (or rather adopt his own practice). Eusebius claims that many letters are extant expressing a unanimous consensus that the paschal fast should not conclude on any day save that of Sunday, the day of the resurrection (*h.e.* 5.23.2), including a letter from Irenaeus which, while it exhorts Victor to peace, yet recommends, Eusebius claims, that 'the mystery of the Lord's resurrection be observed only on the Lord's day' (*h.e.* 5.24.11). However, the two main letters from which he cites, those of Polycrates and Irenaeus (no less!), testify to the opposite practice, that the apostolic tradition they knew was to conclude the fast the fourteenth day of

[109] Cf. W. L. Petersen, 'Eusebius and the Paschal Controversy,' in Harold W. Attridge and Gohei Hataeds, *Eusebius, Christianity and Judaism* (Leiden: Brill, 1992), 311–25.

the moon, whatever day of the week it might be. The final extract from the letter of the bishops of Palestine, on the other hand, indicates a concern for a common date and celebration between them and those of Alexandria, though the extract given by Eusebius does not actually say what date this was.

The Celebration of Pascha

Eusebius's interpretation of the controversy is clearly shaped by the practice, near universal in the fourth century, of celebrating the Lord's resurrection on a Sunday, the practice which was endorsed by the decision of the Council of Nicaea in 325 to separate the date of Pascha from the Jewish calendar and to insist that it be celebrated universally on the Sunday following the first full moon after the vernal equinox.[110] What, however, was the state of affairs in the second century? Or more specifically, when Irenaeus repeatedly says that some 'observe [it]' and some do 'not observe [it]' (*h.e.* 5.24.14–16), what is the implied 'it' that they observed or did not? Was it the celebration of the Lord's Pascha on the fourteenth day of the moon, which others, the majority as Eusebius presumes, celebrated instead on a Sunday, or was it the annual celebration of Pascha itself, kept on 14 Nissan, so that the others had no annual commemoration of this feast at all, something which would have been completely unthinkable for Eusebius?

The evidence for all this is sparse, but scholarly opinion has over recent decades come to settle on versions of the latter alternative.[111] Christian paschal practice developed out of the celebration of the Passover in the Temple.[112] But all we know for sure about the celebration of this Passover in the Temple, as opposed to what developed in later centuries, is that the Passover lambs were slain in the afternoon of 14 Nissan, and they were then eaten by the participants within the precincts of the city of Jerusalem, together with unleavened bread, bitter herbs, and perhaps wine, and accompanied by the singing of

[110] For the evidence we have of what was discussed at Nicaea, see Peter L'Huillier, *The Church of the Ancient Councils: The Disciplinary Work of the First Four Ecumenical Councils* (Crestwood: SVS Press, 1996), 19–26, and, more generally, Alden A. Mosshammer, *The Easter Computus and the Origins of the Christian Era*, OECS (Oxford: Oxford University Press, 2008).

[111] Cf. Paul F. Bradshaw and Maxwell E. Johnson, *The Origins of Feasts, Fasts, and Seasons in Early Christianity*, Alcuin Club Collections 86 (Collegeville, MN: SPCK/Liturgical Press, 2011), 39–59. That the Sunday celebration of Pascha was at least as old as the Quartodeciman practice is still defended by Karl Gerlach, *The Antenicene Pascha: A Rhetorical History*, Liturgia condenda 7 (Louvain: Peeters, 1998), 407.

[112] Cf. Baruch M. Bokser, *The Origins of the Seder* (Berkeley: University of California Press, 1984); Clemens Leonhard, *The Jewish Pesach and the Origins of the Christian Easter* (Berlin: de Gruyter, 2006); Gerard Rouwhorst, 'The Quartodeciman Passover and the Jewish Pesach', *Questions Liturgiques* 77 (1996), 152–73.

psalms of praise.[113] After the destruction of the Temple in 70 CE, Passover practice necessarily developed other forms, and, of course, took on significantly different symbolic overtones both for Jews as well as for Christians, developments which were not isolated from, but influenced, each other.[114] Paul identifies Christ as 'our Pascha [who] has been sacrificed' (1 Cor. 5:7: *τὸ πάσχα ἡμῶν ἐτύθη Χριστός*), and the narrative of John's Gospel climaxes in the crucifixion at the very moment the Passover lambs were slain (John 19:14, 31), unlike the other Gospels in which Jesus eats the Passover meal with the disciples and is crucified on the following day.

The earliest indication we have for the Christian observance of Pascha is the *Epistle of the Apostles*, accepting the provenance of this document, as we have earlier, in Asia Minor from either around 140 or around 120. In the Coptic version of the text, Christ says to his disciples:

> 'And you remember my death. If now the Passover takes place, then will one of you be thrown into prison for my name's sake, and he will be in sorrow and care that you celebrate the Passover while he is in prison and far from you; for he will sorrow that he does not celebrate the Passover with you. I will send my power in the form of the angel Gabriel, and the doors of the prison will be opened. He will go out and come to you; he will spend a night of the watch with you, and stay with you until the cock crows. But when you have completed the remembrance that is for me, and the Agape, he will again be thrown into prison for a testimony, until he comes out from there and preaches what I have delivered to you'. And we said to him, 'O Lord, is it perhaps necessary again that we take the cup and drink?' He said to us, 'Yes, it is necessary until the day when I come with those who were killed for my sake'. (*Ep. Ap.* 15)

The Ethiopic version begins: 'And you therefore celebrate the remembrance of my death, which is the Passover', and continues, later on, by saying: 'And when you complete my Agape and my remembrance at the crowing of the cock'. Either way, Bradshaw and Johnson point out that the 'remembrance' and the 'Agape' should not be thought of as a distinct events, and that the celebration concludes, as is clear in the Ethiopic, with the crowing of the cock.[115] They also point to a Syrian text, entitled the *Diataxis* (perhaps related to the *Didascalia Apostolorum*), as cited by Epiphanius, which has the apostles

[113] Cf. Joshua Kulp, 'The Origins of the Seder and Haggadah', *CBR* 4 (2005), 109–34, esp. 112–13.

[114] That the Christian practice influenced the development of the Jewish practices is argued by Joseph Tabory, 'Towards a History of the Paschal Meal', and Israel J. Yuval, 'Easter and Passover as Early Jewish–Christian Dialogue', in Paul F. Bradshaw and Lawrence A. Hoffmann, eds, *Passover and Easter: Origin and History to Modern Times* (Notre Dame: University of Notre Dame Press, 1999), 62–80, 98–124, but note the critical comments by Kulp regarding Yuval's dating of different layers in the Mishnah, 'Origins of the Seder and Haggadah', 118–25. See more generally Daniel Boyarin, *Border Lines: The Partition of Judaeo-Christianity* (Philadelphia: University of Pennsylvannia Press, 2004).

[115] Bradshaw and Johnson, *Origins of Feasts*, 41–2.

saying: 'When they feast, mourn for them by fasting, because on the day of the feast they crucified Christ, and when they mourn by eating the unleavened bread with bitter herbs, you feast'.[116] The switching of feasting/mourning between Jews and Christians is almost certainly a Christian interpretation of the relations between the feasts/fasts kept by Jews and Christians, for there is no indication that the Jews understood the Week of Unleavened Bread, which began after the Passover meal, to be a time of mourning. If the rule of the Mishnah (*Pesahim* 10.1) reflects earlier practice, Jews would have fasted from the time of the evening offering, that is, about 3.00 p.m., until nightfall (which, as Bradshaw and Johnson point out would have, in effect, meant fasting from breakfast), and then continued their celebration of the Passover meal until midnight (*Pesahim* 10.9).[117] As such, Christians would have extended their fast until midnight, at which point they began their celebration of Christ's Pascha, concluding their feast at dawn, when 'the cock crows', as the *Epistle of the Apostles* has it.

It is possible that the oblique reference in Eusebius to 'the great discussion in Laodicea' that arose sometime in the mid-second century and which caused Melito of Sardis to have composed a book *On Pascha*, and Clement of Alexandria to write his own book *On Pascha* 'because of Melito's work', was a debate about whether to extend the time of the fast to midnight or to celebrate Christ's Pascha at the same time as the Jews celebrated Passover.[118] Clement's work is now lost, and it is possible that this work of Melito refers to another text than the one we have bearing the same name, for Eusebius mentions that Melito wrote two works *On Pascha* (*h.e.* 4.26.2), or that, as Alistair Stewart-Sykes suggests, another work has become attached to Melito's *On Pascha*.[119] The extant *On Pascha* by Melito is usually dated to around 160–70 CE, and will be considered again in Chapter 4. For now, it is noteworthy that in expounding the Pascha, Melito develops his theme by etymologizing the word Pascha, which is simply a transliteration of the Hebrew word *pesach*, by deriving it from the Greek word for 'to suffer': 'What is the Pascha [πάσχα]? It is called by its name because of what constitutes it: from "suffer" [παθεῖν] comes "suffering" [πάσχειν]'.[120] Origen, on the other hand, opens his

[116] Epiphanius, *Panarion*, 70.10.1, 11.3. For the evidence given by a possible Quartodeciman substratum to *Didascalia Apostolorum* 5, subsequently overlaid by the practice of a Sunday observance, see Bradshaw and Johnson, *Origins of Feasts*, 43, 54–7.

[117] Ibid. 42.

[118] Cf. Eusebius, *h.e.* 4.26.3–4, see also 6.13.9; Alistair Stewart-Sykes, *The Lamb's High Feast: Melito, Peri Pascha, and the Quartodeciman Paschal Liturgy at Sardis*, SupVC 42 (Leiden: Brill, 1998), 155–60, 169–72.

[119] Alistair Stewart-Sykes, *Melito of Sardis: On Pascha, with Fragments of Melito and Other Material Related to the Quartodecimans*, 2nd edn PPS 55 (Crestwood, NY: St Vladimir's Seminary Press, 2016), 21.

[120] Melito, *Pasch.* 46. See also Irenaeus, *haer*, 4.10.1: Moses 'was not ignorant even of the day of his passion [*passionis*], but figuratively foretold it, calling it Pascha; and on the very day which

work *On Pascha* by acknowledging that 'most of the brethren, if not all, think that the Passover [πάσχα] takes its name from the Passion [πάθος] of the Saviour'. But this is not correct, he asserts, for 'among the Hebrews the real name of this feast is not πάσχα but *fas*—the three letters of *fas* and the rough breathing, which is much stronger with them than it is with us, constituting the name of this feast which means "passage" [διάβασις]' (*Pasch.* 1). We cannot be sure, of course, but perhaps it is this difference in understanding the meaning of 'Pascha' that prompted Clement to write his book 'because of Melito'.[121] While there is clearly a difference of understanding about what the 'Pascha' is all about, there is no indication that the date of its celebration is contested by the Alexandrians.

The next piece of information we have about the Christian paschal celebrations, the two fragments of Apollinarius of Hierapolis preserved in the *Paschal Chronicle*, come from later in the second century, though how much later is uncertain. Although not mentioned as a Quartodeciman by Polycrates (who only named his own relatives), Apollinarius certainly was, as can be seen by this fragment, which is perhaps based upon Melito:

> The fourteenth is the true Pascha of the Lord
> the great sacrifice
> the Son of God standing in place of the lamb.
> The one being bound is the one binding the strong man,
> and the one being judged is the judge of the living and the dead.
> And the one who is betrayed into the hands of sinners to be crucified is
>   raised above the horns of the unicorn.
> And the one whose holy side was pierced
> poured forth from his side the two purifications:
> water and blood
> word and spirit.
> He is buried on the day of Pascha,
> and a stone is put over his tomb.[122]

The other fragment of Apollinarius again indicates a debate about the paschal observance:

> Now there are some who through ignorance love to quarrel about these matters: but what they maintain in this affair is forgivable. For ignorance does not respond well to accusations, but may be amenable to teaching. And they say that on the fourteenth day the Lord ate the sheep with the disciples,

Moses had foretold such a long time before, the Lord suffered, fulfilling the Pascha [*passus est Dominus adimplens Pascha*]'.

[121] In *Strom.* 2.11.51.2, Clement speaks of the Passover as being a passage 'from all trouble and all objects of sense'.

[122] From the *Paschal Chronicle* (ed. Dindorf, CSHB 17, 14); trans. in Stewart-Sykes, *Melito*, 105–6.

> and that on the great day of unleavened bread he suffered, and they say that Matthew speaks thus, according to their interpretation. But their thinking is not in harmony with the Law and the Gospels seem to disagree with them.[123]

The dispute here is reminiscent of the one we saw echoes of in the fragments of Papias, a previous bishop of Hierapolis, regarding the order of the Synoptics and the Gospel of John, although in this case it concerns paschal practice. Some appear to have been arguing that the Pascha should be celebrated in the evening, justifying this by referring to Matthew's account of the Last Supper. It is not specified what the other position was, but almost certainly it was the practice, which we have seen, of celebrating Pascha at night, following the tradition that goes back to John. As such, the justification by appeal to Matthew is in fact 'secondary', as Stewart-Sykes puts it, understanding an evening celebration to be 'a repetition of the Last Supper, whereas those who kept it at night reckoned it to be a commemoration of the Passion and resurrection, as is implied by Melito's work'.[124] In both cases, that is, it is a matter of variation within the Quartodeciman practice, not a debate about a Sunday observance of Pascha.

That a debate about the timing of the paschal celebration should have arisen from the mid-second century onwards, is perhaps best explained, as Bradshaw and Johnson suggest, by an indication in Epiphanius (if he is indeed reliable on this), that such debates began after the bishops of Jerusalem were no longer 'of the circumcision', that is, from around 132 CE.[125] Following the Bar Kochba revolt, and the expulsion of Jews and Jewish Christians from Jerusalem, the leadership of the Jerusalem Church passed into Gentile hands. It is very tempting to suggest, as Bradshaw and Johnson do, that as this happened they 'would no doubt have wanted to distance that church from Judaism', and as such they 'very likely could have been the ones to introduce for the first time then a Sunday Pascha in place of the Quartodeciman observance, a development that was subsequently imitated elsewhere'.[126] If this was indeed the case, there is no trace of this development, for, as we have seen, all the remaining evidence regarding changes in paschal practice points to variations within the timing of the feast celebrated according to the Quartodeciman date. It is also not clear just how much of a Jewish-Christian presence there was in

[123] From the *Paschal Chronicle* (Dindorf ed., CSHB 17, 13–14), trans. in Stewart-Sykes, *Melito*, 105, modifying the translation of the last words, *καὶ στασιάζειν δοκεῖ κατ' αὐτοὺς τὰ εὐαγγέλια* which Stewart-Sykes renders 'and the Gospels conspire to refute them'; R. M. Grant (*Second-Century Christianity* (London: SPCK, 1946), 78) translates these words as: 'according to them the gospels seem to disagree'. Stewart-Sykes is certainly right that the emphasis of this clause is that both the Law and the Gospels stand opposed to their claims, rather than pointing out differences within the Gospels.

[124] Stewart-Sykes, *Melito*, 82. See also Stewart-Sykes, *Lamb's High Feast*, 147–60.

[125] Epiphanius, *Panarion*, 70.9.9; Bradshaw and Johnson, *Origins of Feasts*, 51.

[126] Bradshaw and Johnson, *Origins of Feasts*, 51.

Jerusalem/Aelia at this time. Israel Yuval suggests that it was the adoption in the Haggadah of the Christian interpretation of Pascha by Exodus 12 that prompted the shift of the Quartodeciman dating to Sunday.[127] Undoubtedly a Sunday celebration of Pascha developed at some point in some place, but there is no trace of when or where this occurred, whereas there is evidence, however sparse, of the Quartodeciman practice.

If the evidence for the celebration of Pascha seems sparse, even more so is that for the observance of Sunday and its connection to the celebration of the resurrection.[128] Our purpose here is not to trace the movement from Sabbath to Sunday in early Christianity, a contentious subject with an increasingly vast body of scholarship devoted to it, but simply to note when it was that Sunday became associated with the resurrection, as background for understanding the debate about the proper dating for Pascha at the end of the second century as reported in the text being considered here, that is, Eusebius *h.e.* 5.23–5. There are only three mentions in the New Testament of gathering together on the Sunday and they are all rather short on detail. 1 Cor. 16:2, 'On the first day of every week, each of you is to put something aside and store it up, as he may prosper, so that contributions need not be made when I come'. This certainly implies a regular gathering, but says precious little about what happened or how it was understood. Acts 20:7, 'On the first day of the week, when we were gathered together to break bread, Paul talked with them, intending to depart on the morrow, and he prolonged his speech until midnight'. Were they gathered together to break bread as a regular weekly practice, or because Paul was about to leave the following day? And Apoc. 1:10, 'I was in the Spirit on the Lord's Day': does this mean Sunday, as a regular day of worship, the eschatological Day of the Lord, or Pascha? Most striking is that there is nothing in the accounts of the resurrection in the Gospels to indicate that the event should be commemorated on the day of the week on which it occurred.[129] Even Paul's explicit handing on of what he had received from the Lord makes no mention of a particular day, and ties the practice to Christ's death without mentioning the resurrection: 'For as often as you eat this bread and drink this cup, you proclaim the Lord's death until he comes' (1 Cor. 11:26). In the

[127] Yuval, 'Early Jewish-Christian Dialogue', 114: 'By taking into account Christian interpretations, the Haggadah forced the issue of the Quartodeciman alternative, so that the Christian celebration shifted from Nisan 14 (with an emphasis on crucifixion and sacrifice) to Easter Sunday and an emphasis on resurrection-redemption. A similar process occurred in tannaitic Judaism, as the seder changed from being a celebration emphasizing sacrifice (Rabban Gamaliel) to a celebration of the Exodus event and the redemption it symbolized'.

[128] See now Markus Vinzent, *Christ's Resurrection in Early Christianity and the Making of the New Testament* (Farnham: Ashgate, 2011).

[129] Cf. Harald Riesenfeld, 'The Sabbath and the Lord's Day in Judaism, the Preaching of Jesus and Early Christianity', in Riesenfeld, *The Gospel Tradition* (Oxford: Blackwell, 1970), 111–37, at 124.

Didache the Eucharist is to be offered on 'the Lord's of the Lord',[130] although the section which gives instructions for how to celebrate the Eucharist (*Did.* 9–10) does not mention a particular day, and in neither case is the Lord's resurrection mentioned. Finally, Pliny (*Ep.* 10.96), writing around 112 CE, mentions that Christians gathered together 'on a fixed day', presumably the Sabbath, before daylight and again later on the same day to eat together, but does not specify how this meal was understood.

When the connection between Christian worship on Sunday and the resurrection of Christ begins to appear, it is mentioned almost as if it were an afterthought. The *Epistle of Barnabas*, written perhaps in the first decades of the second century, asserts that 'we also celebrate with gladness the eighth day, in which Jesus also rose from the dead, and was made manifest, and ascended into heaven'.[131] The 'eighth day' is clearly a more embracing concept than that of the day of the resurrection. Similarly, Ignatius of Antioch describes those who have come to the new hope as 'living according to the Lord's [day/life], on which also our life sprang up through him and his death'.[132] Even as late as the middle of the second century, in the most explicit passage we have about the content and understanding of Christian worship in the first two centuries, Justin Martyr can say: 'And it is on Sunday [*τὴν δὲ τοῦ ἡλίου ἡμέραν*] that we all make assembly in common, since it is the first day, on which God changed darkness and matter and made the world, and Jesus Christ our Saviour rose from the dead on the same day'.[133] According to Bradshaw and Johnson, the transition from holding the weekly celebration of the Eucharist from the Sabbath to Sunday 'can only have happened when a congregation finally abandoned an evening eucharistic meal and resorted to a token feeding instead' on Sunday morning, though apart from what can be inferred from Pliny, there is no evidence for this before the third century.[134]

[130] *Did.* 14.1: *Κατὰ κυριακὴν δὲ κυρίου συναχθέντες κλάσατε ἄρτον καὶ εὐχαριστήσατε*. Vinzent, *Christ's Resurrection*, 204–5, notes that this phrase 'must not be translated, as is often done, by "the Lord's day". The context forbids that "the Lord's of the Lord" indicates a particular day; the contrary is intended here: *Didache* claims that Christians can meet any day and time'.

[131] *Barn.* 15.9. For an early dating, see James Carleton Paget, *The Epistle of Barnabas: Outlook and Background* (Tübingen: Mohr, 1994), 9–30 and Stephen G. Wilson, *Related Strangers: Jews and Christians, 70–170 C.E.* (Minneapolis: Fortress Press, 1995), 231–2.

[132] *Magn.* 9.1. As with the similar phrase in the *Didache*, the phrase *κατὰ κυριακὴν*, has no noun. According to Alistair Stewart, 'Although the adjective alone comes to mean "the Lord's Day," it may not have done so at the time of Ignatius. Nonetheless, the context emboldens us to supply the word "day," though one ms [G] supplies the word "life," which is entirely plausible'. Alistair Stewart, *Ignatius of Antioch: The Letters*, PPS 49 (Crestwood, NY: St Vladimir's Seminary Press, 2013), 49, n. 3. Stewart, ibid. 16, would date the letters to 134 CE; see also Alistair Stewart, *Original Bishops: Office and Order in the First Christian Communities* (Grand Rapids, MI: Baker Academic, 2014), 238–41.

[133] *1 Apol.* 67.8. On Justin's adoption of the term 'Sunday' as a possible reaction to, and adoption from, Marcion, see Vinzent, *Christ's Resurrection*, 209.

[134] Bradshaw and Johnson, *Origins of Feasts*, 11.

Regarding the place of the 'Lord's Day' in this early period, they conclude that 'it was understood primarily not as a memorial of Christ's resurrection but as the key weekly expression of the constant eschatological readiness for the *parousia* which was intended to permeate the whole of a Christian's daily prayer and life'.[135]

With this being the only information we have from the first and second centuries regarding both paschal practice and Sunday worship, it seems clear that in the controversy recorded by Eusebius in *h.e.* 5.23–5 the Quartodecimans had a solid claim to be following the original practice for the observance of Pascha. The question remains, however, whether, when Irenaeus says that some do 'not observe [it]', we should read that as meaning that even at that time some still had no annual paschal celebration, or whether some had by that point already transferred this feast to the Sunday. Bradshaw and Johnson give two reasons for holding that the Sunday Pascha derives from the Quartodeciman practice, and, we would add, for supposing that this had already happened before the controversy ignited by Victor of Rome. The second reason they give concerns the various fasting practices.[136] Tertullian is the first to mention that Saturdays are 'never to be kept as a fast except at Pascha'.[137] This discipline is best understood against the background, which we saw earlier, of the Quartodeciman practice of fasting during the day on 14 Nissan in preparation for the celebrations beginning at midnight; when the feast was transferred to the Sunday, the well-established prior practice of fasting beforehand was maintained, now held on the Saturday, thus overriding the prohibition against fasting on that day. That something like this happened before Irenaeus' time is indicated by the otherwise unaccountable words he gives explaining not the date of the day but the fasting practice associated with it:

> For the controversy is not only about the day, but also about the very manner of the fast; for some think that they ought to fast one day, others two, others even more; and in the opinion of others, the 'day' amounts to forty hours, day and night. And such variation of observance did not begin in our own time, but much earlier, in the days of our predecessors. (*h.e.* 5.24.12–13)

Those who fast for one day would be the Quartodecimans; those who fast for two days would be those who celebrate Pascha on Sunday, fasting on both Friday and Saturday; while those who fast for a 'day' of forty hours have combined the Friday and a paschal Saturday fast into one uninterrupted fast. This passage is also the first witness to those who fast for 'even more' than one or two days in preparation for the feast. Tertullian might allude to such a practice and perhaps also the *Gospel of Peter* where, after the disciples have

[135] Ibid. 13. [136] Ibid. 52.
[137] *De Ieiunio*, 14; cf. Bradshaw and Johnson, *Origins of Feasts*, 17–20.

found the empty tomb, they are still said to be fasting 'on the last day of Unleavened Bread': perhaps the Jewish practice of fasting during the Week of Unleavened Bread following Passover was adopted in some Quartodeciman circles and then became a week of fasting before Pascha. The first explicit mention of a week-long fast, however, is not until the third century, with Dionysius of Alexandria and the *Didascalia Apostolorum*.[138] Either way, Irenaeus certainly testifies to variations within the paschal fast as having begun 'much earlier, in the time of our predecessors', most likely referring to a first exchange on these matters between Polycarp and Anicetus in the middle of the 150s (*h.e.* 5.24.16). This construal of the background for Irenaeus' words is the only tangible evidence we would have that some were celebrating Pascha on Sunday from the middle of the second century, as a modified form of the older Quartodeciman practice—the very time when Justin adds that Christians also celebrate the resurrection on Sunday as well as celebrating the first day, God's act of creation.

The first reason given by Bradshaw and Johnson for thinking that the Sunday Pascha derived from the Quartodeciman practice concerns the meaning given to the feast and is more problematic. As they put it, 'not only in Quartodeciman circles but also at first among those who kept the feast on Sunday, the original focus of the celebration was not on the resurrection of Christ, as one might have expected if it had always been associated with the Sunday, but on his death'.[139] However, as we have seen, and as they themselves concluded, even by the middle of the second century, the connection between Sunday and the resurrection is only a secondary one. But, more importantly, the distinction between commemorating the death of Christ and celebrating his resurrection is not so obvious as it might seem today, after 1,500 years or more of liturgical celebrations that appear to divide the crucifixion and resurrection.

When Pascha came to be celebrated on a Sunday the connection between Sunday and the resurrection became clearer, and this in turn, it seems, was the catalyst in the subsequent development of the *triduum*, that is, the idea of the feast as being a three-day (*triduum*, τριήμερον), but still unitary, feast, holding together Christ's crucifixion on the Friday, his burial on the Saturday, and his resurrection on the Sunday.[140] But it is important to recognize that even after this division there was a consciousness of the unitary character of this three-day celebration: the Sunday is still called Pascha, and writers repeatedly thereafter still refer to 'the Passion' as embracing every aspect of this feast.

[138] *De Ieiunio* 13.1; *Gospel of Peter* 58–9 (in Elliott, *Apocryphal New Testament*, 154–8); Bradshaw and Johnson, *Origins of Feast*, 53–7.

[139] Ibid. 51. They begin their chapter on the date of the festival with the surprising assertion that 'Sunday was already the occasion of their regular weekly celebration of the paschal mystery'. Ibid. 48.

[140] On the eventual development of the *triduum*, see ibid. 60–8.

For instance, the Emperor Constantine opens his address *To the Assembly of the Saints* by relating the resurrection directly to the day of the Passion: 'That light which far outshines the day and sun, first pledge of resurrection and renovation of bodies long since dissolved, the divine token of promise, the path which leads to everlasting life—in a word, the day of the Passion—is arrived'.[141] In the following century, Theodoret of Cyrrhus likewise writes of 'the very day of the saving Passion [πάθους], in which we hold vigil to celebrate [πανηγυρίζομεν] the memory both of the Passion [πάθους] and of the Resurrection of the Lord'.[142] The iconographic tradition, the development of which seems to lag behind liturgical innovations, is also a striking witness to this. The earliest depictions of the crucifixion, such as on the doors of the St Sabina Church in Rome, perhaps dating to the early fifth century, and the sixth-century Rabbula Gospels, and the images on the reliquary box in the Lateran Palace consistently depict the crucified Christ with an upright body and eyes wide open, not because of an inability or reluctance to depict him dead, but precisely because the crucified one is the Living One; in the lower register of the image in the Rabbula Gospels, the resurrection is alluded to by the empty tomb and the stunned guards, while the risen Christ greets the myrrh-bearing women.[143] Only much later, perhaps in the ninth century, as images of the resurrection become more prevalent, does an image of the dead Christ on the cross appear: the unitary character of the feast has been refracted, as it were, into two distinct *figurae*. Yet, even then, the image of the resurrection does not actually depict Christ's bodily rising from the tomb (as will appear still later); instead it has Christ with his arms outstretched, in the figure of the cross, standing on the gates of Hades, placed crosswise, raising up Adam and Eve. Although often misleadingly called the 'Descent into Hell' or the 'Harrowing of Hell', it is not: it is consistently called, either written upon the icon itself or in verbal descriptions, the *Anastasis*, and the resurrection it depicts is the raising up of the human race 'in Adam' effected by Christ's Passion. In this it is strikingly reminiscent of the way in which Athanasius treats Christ's resurrection in his work *On the Incarnation*. After having given two rationales for the crucifixion (1–10, 11–20), Athanasius turns to Christ's death itself (20–6) and the resurrection (27–32). In this last section, however, he makes no mention of the resurrectional accounts given in the Gospels; rather, the demonstration of the resurrection of the body is that Christians are now prepared to take up the faith of the cross and themselves trample down death underfoot. That all this is embraced by the title of the work, *On the*

[141] Eusebius of Caesarea, *Laud. Const.* 1.

[142] Theodoret of Cyrrhus, *Affect.* 9.24.

[143] Cod. Plut. 1, 56, fol. 13r, Biblioteca Laurenziana, Florence. Cf. Anna D. Kartsonis, *Anastasis: The Making of an Image* (Princeton: Princeton University Press, 1986), 26; though she takes such images to indicate an inability to depict the dead Christ prior to a full articulation of the two natures of Christ following Chalcedon, ibid. 35–9.

Incarnation, should make us pause before we use the term 'Incarnation' too quickly, as suggested in the Introduction.

Distinguishing too readily and too easily between Christ's crucifixion and his resurrection, and claiming that the Quartodecimans were focused on the former and not the latter, is a misleading presupposition, a 'mythology of doctrines' to use Skinner's designation. This is especially the case when we turn to the source of the Quartodeciman tradition, that is, John, as we will see in Part II. But for now, we may note Ashton's conclusion:

> In the first half of the Gospel John had used the word ὑψοῦν ['to lift up'] to suggest that Jesus' exaltation is conditional upon and contained in his death, so that the passion and resurrection must be viewed as a single happening. Now the expression παραδιδόναι τὸ πνεῦμα ['to hand over the Spirit', cf. John 19:30] allows him to fuse Easter and Pentecost as well, hinting that there is no need to think of the latter as a distinct and separate event.[144]

John holds the crucifixion and resurrection, along with ascension and Pentecost, all together, and does so in the figure of the cross, as indeed does Paul before him, resolving 'to know nothing except Jesus Christ and him crucified' (1 Cor. 2:2) and directing Christians to celebrate the Eucharist to 'proclaim the Lord's death until he comes' (1 Cor. 11:26). The 'School of John' following him did likewise in their annual paschal feast, as we can see it in Melito's *On Pascha*. When Irenaeus and Polycrates claimed to be following the tradition going back to John, we have every reason to accept their claim. This was a tradition that preceded the Sunday paschal observance, and even preceded the commemoration of the resurrection on Sunday, and it would thereafter decisively shape the development of the *triduum* and eventually the full cycle of Holy Week.[145]

If this analysis of Eusebius' account of the paschal controversy (*EH* 5.23–5) and other evidence holds, then Pascha, as an annual feast, originated with John and was only celebrated by those of his 'school' until perhaps the mid-second century, when the resurrection seems to have become associated with Sunday, initially as an afterthought, and then more fully at the end of the second century and thereafter, leading to the eventual refraction of the single feast into a spectrum of commemorations. So far from being a mere nod to a prior tradition, alien to his own Gospel, as Käsemann would have it, John was the origin of the paschal tradition. As such, and because it is only in the Gospel of John that Christ is crucified on the day when the Passover lambs were slain, John's Gospel can rightly be called a 'paschal gospel'.

[144] John Ashton, *Fourth Gospel*, 348.

[145] It is striking, for instance, that in the Eastern Orthodox practice, Holy Week starts with the raising of Lazarus, that the hymnography for Holy Thursday focuses not so much on the 'Last Supper' as on the foot-washing, and that the weekend following Pascha is Thomas Sunday, all of which are only found in John.

John the High Priest

Having begun our analysis of Eusebius' account of the paschal controversy at the end of the second century, and the testimony of Irenaeus to the paschal practice going back to John embedded within it, we can now turn to the other testimony Eusebius cites (*h.e.* 5.24.2–8), that is, the extract from the letter of Polycrates of Ephesus. In this passage, Polycrates gives the names of seven luminaries of Asia, all of whom had held firm to the Quartodeciman tradition: Philip, John, Polycarp, Thraseas, Sagaris, Papirius, and Melito. He then mentions himself as 'the least of all', adding that seven kinsmen of his were bishops, and he is now the eighth. As Bauckham rightly points out, these are not two separate groups of seven witnesses: if the list of names were merely those who had held to the Quartodeciman practice, there are names known to us (Aristion, Papias, and Apollinarius) that are missing. Rather he is tacitly claiming kinship with the seven previously mentioned figures and then adds himself 'as a supernumerary eighth, whose witness is therefore strictly superfluous'.[146] When he names his seven predecessors he only uses the word 'bishop' when he can say 'bishop and martyr' (i.e. for Polycarp, Thraseas, Sagaris), though he clearly regards all seven illustrious figures as bishops.

Polycrates' list begins with Philip, 'one of the twelve apostles', and John, who is not called an apostle. Polycrates seems to have conflated Philip the Evangelist, whose four unmarried daughters prophesied (Acts 21:8–9), with the Philip mentioned as one of the twelve and always listed after John (Mark 3:17–18; Matt. 10:2–3; Luke 6:14; Acts 1:13), thus confirming what we saw earlier in this chapter, that the John Polycrates named after Philip is not the son of Zebedee. Of the John with whom he claims kinship, Polycrates has this to say:

> [there is] John also, who lay on the Lord's breast, who was [or 'became'] a priest wearing the petal, both a witness and a teacher [*ὁ ἐπὶ τὸ στῆθος τοῦ κυρίου ἀναπεσών, ὃς ἐγενήθη ἱερεὺς τὸ πέταλον πεφορεκὼς καὶ μάρτυς καὶ διδάσκαλος*]. He has fallen asleep at Ephesus. (*h.e.* 3.24.3–4)

The identification of John as the one 'who lay on the Lord's breast' clearly goes back to the Gospel of John (13:23, 26; 21:20), and, as we have seen, was used by Irenaeus, together with 'the disciple of the Lord', to identify the author of the Gospel in his name. (*haer.* 3.1.1). Polycrates' use of the description, 'who lay on the Lord's breast', is most likely not derived from Irenaeus, his contemporary, but instead goes back to a common and traditional manner that the school of John had for describing their beloved Elder. Although John has fallen asleep, the description of him as a *μάρτυς* is, as Bauckham points out, surely

[146] Bauckham, *Jesus and the Eyewitnesses*, 440.

meant to be taken in the sense of 'witness', rather than 'martyr': it would be very odd to put 'martyr' before 'teacher' (in the case of the others the word order is reversed: 'bishop and martyr'), and so should be taken as a reference to the 'witness' provided by the author of the Fourth Gospel (cf. John 21:24), and perhaps indicating a different role from that of 'teacher' which he assumes in the letters.[147]

But it is what follows that is most striking and perplexing: this John 'was [or 'became'] a priest wearing the petal', the *petalon*. According to Josephus (*Ant.* 3.172–8), in the fullest description we have of the headdress worn by the high priest in the Jerusalem Temple, this headdress was elaborate and ornate, designed to inspire awe: in addition to the linen headdress worn by other priests, the high priest wore another one on top, embroidered in blue and encircled by a gold crown with three rows, out of which arose a golden embellishment called a *calyx* resembling a crown of petals, which was then itself covered by a golden plate upon which was inscribed the name of God in sacred characters, that is, the tetragrammaton. According to the *Letter of Aristeas*, it 'was an occasion of great amazement to us when we saw Eleazar engaged on his ministry and all the glorious vestments ... [a description which culminates with the *petalon*]. Their appearance makes one awe-struck and dumbfounded: a man would think that he had come out of this world into another one' (96–9).

Josephus does not use the word *petalon*, which simply means 'leaf', but other early Jewish and Christian texts do, as a translation of the Hebrew word *sîs*, meaning 'flower'.[148] This was the distinctive mark of the high priest, and unique: while Solomon had made thousands of other priestly garments, 'the crown upon which Moses wrote [the name of God] was only one, and has remained to this day' (Josephus, *Ant.* 8.93). As Bauckham concludes: 'when Polycrates claims that John "was a priest wearing the *petalon*", his words state, as precisely and unambiguously as it was possible to do, that John officiated as high priest in the Jerusalem Temple'.[149] It is not simply that he was one of the chief priests (ἀρχιερεῖς), as that term is used in the New Testament and by Josephus, for, as Bauckham points out, 'there is no Greek term for "high priest" that unambiguously distinguishes *the* chief priest from the chief priests ... But "a priest wearing the *petalon*" is unambiguous'.[150]

Polycrates' assertion is, by any standard, extraordinary.[151] Various ways of interpreting this claim have been proposed. Some have taken it quite loosely or

[147] Ibid. 443.

[148] Cf. Sirach 45:12; *Letter of Aristeas* 98 (in Charlesworth, *Old Testament Pseudepigrapha*, 2.12–34); *Testament of the Twelve Patriarchs, Levi* 8.2 (in Charlesworth, *Old Testament Pseudepigrapha*, 1.788–95); Bauckham, *Jesus and the Eyewitnesses*, 445–6.

[149] Ibid. 446–7. [150] Ibid. 447.

[151] The *Protoevangelium of James*, 5.1 (in Elliott, *Apocryphal New Testament*, 57–67), and Epiphanius, *Panarion* 29.4, 78.13–14, also describes James as having worn the *petalon*. In the

metaphorically, as no more than an extension of the interest in Christ's high priesthood, evidenced in Hebrews and the Apocalypse, to others, such as the description of Christians as 'a royal priesthood' in the First Epistle of Peter (2:9), or the claim of the *Didache* that the prophets 'are your high priests' (13.3, ἀρχιερεῖς).[152] But this does not, however, do justice to Polycrates' very specific assertion. Others have argued that there is indeed a historical reminiscence behind the words. In the late nineteenth century, Hugo Delff pointed out that there are a number of details in the Gospel of John that indicate that the author had priestly connections.[153] For instance, only he is 'known to the high priest' and it is by his intervention that Peter gains admission to the court of the high priest (John 18:15–16) and he is the only evangelist to mention the name of the high priest's servant, Malchus, whose ear Peter cut off (John 18:10). He alone mentions Joseph of Arimathea and Nicodemus, a member of the Sandhedrin (John 3:1; 7:50; 19:38), and had knowledge of what was happening in the meetings of the Sanhedrin (7:15–52; 11:47–53; 12:10). Delff also takes the step of identifying John the Evangelist with the John mentioned in Acts 4:5–6:

> On the morrow their rulers and elders [πρεσβυτέρους] and scribes were gathered together in Jerusalem [to judge Peter], with Annas the high priest [ἀρχιερεὺς] and Caiaphas and John and Alexander, and all who were of the high-priestly family [ἐκ γένους ἀρχιερατικοῦ].

Delff then draws a picture, not unlike that given by Bauckham in *Jesus and the Eyewitnesses*, of a disciple of Christ called John who was a member of the aristocratic and learned high-priestly family in Jerusalem distinct from the illiterate and unlearned fisherman from Galilee, and suggested that perhaps he officiated in the Temple on occasion.[154] However, as Bauckham points out, this interpretation again falls short of Polycrates' dramatic claim: John was not

case of Epiphanius, he is working from the text of Eusebius, citing Hegesippus (*h.e.* 2.23.6) that James 'used to enter alone into the temple and was found kneeling and praying for forgiveness for the people', which Epiphanius takes as relating to the Day of Atonement and so he would have worn the *petalon*. Cf. Richard Bauckham, 'Papias and Polycrates on the Origin of the Fourth Gospel', *JTS* ns 44 (1993), 24–69, at 37–40.

[152] F.-M. Braun, *Jean le Théologien et son évangile dans l'église ancienne*, 3 vols (Paris: Gabalda: 1959, 64, 72), 1.339–40; F. F. Bruce, 'St John at Ephesus', *Bulletin of the John Rylands Library* 60.2 (1978), 339–61, at 343.

[153] Hugo Delff, *Geschichte des Rabbi Jesu von Nazareth* (Leipzig: Wilhelm Friedrich, 1889), 67ff.; *Das vierte Evangelium, ein authentischer Bericht über Jesus von Nazareth, wiederhergestellt, übersetzt und erklärt* (Husum: C. F. Delff, 1890).

[154] Cf. Delff, *Das vierte Evangelium*, 9–10. William Sanday, *The Criticism of the Fourth Gospel* (Oxford: Clarendon, 1916), 99–108, reviewed Delff's arguments positively, but ultimately did not accept them, while acknowledging that his own position left many things unresolved. Burney, *The Aramaic Origin*, 133–4, is more positive.

simply a member of the high-priestly family who perhaps stepped in on occasion; he was *the* high priest.[155]

Building upon Delff, Robert Eisler took the further step of claiming that John was not simply a member of a high-priestly family, but in fact *the* high priest, mentioned by Josephus, Theophilus the son of Annas, high priest *c.*37 and 41 CE.[156] Eisler makes this connection upon the supposed translation of the Hebrew name Jo-hanan ('God's favour', 'God's grace', or 'God is gracious') into the Greek Theophilus.[157] As Bauckham comments, this is 'quite possible', but 'is achieved only by a series of unverifiable guesses' and does not explain why this reminiscence is only found in Polycrates. More recently, M.-L. Rigato, has also attempted to take Polycrates seriously, identifying Polycrates' John with the John of Acts 4:6 and asserting that at some point he must have indeed served as the high priest.[158] That there is no other record for this other than Polycrates, Rigato explains by three possibilities. First, that Josephus' list is not complete and that John's name would no doubt have been expunged from record and memory. Second, not unlike Eisler, that perhaps John was known by another name. And third, that John substituted for the high priest himself one year on the Day of Atonement, thus meaning that he would have worn the *petalon*. Again, all this is possible, but it doesn't really explain why there is no mention of it other than in Polycrates; there may well have been an attempt to purge the memory of this in Jewish circles, but in the Christian circles, which did indeed preserve memories of John, this would surely have echoed resoundingly. Moreover, as Bauckham points out, there is only one occasion known to us when the high priest was unable to officiate on the Day of Atonement, and both names, Matthias and his replacement Joseph son of Elim, are recalled clearly in both Josephus and the rabbinic tradition, for such a happening was so unusual that it left an abiding impression.[159]

Bauckham's own conclusion regarding Polycrates' words is that they should be understood neither metaphorically nor historically but exegetically. Just as Polycrates had conflated the Philip of the twelve with Philip the Evangelist mentioned in Acts, so too Polycrates has identified the John who wrote the Gospel with the John mentioned in Acts 4:6. Bauckham gives various other examples of such conflation in the early centuries: Judas Paul's host in

[155] Bauckham, *Jesus and the Eyewitnesses*, 448.

[156] Robert Eisler, *The Enigma of the Fourth Gospel: Its Author and its Writer* (London: Methuen, 1938), 36–45. Josephus, *Ant.* 18.123; cf. James C. VanderKam, *From Joshua to Caiaphas: High Priests after the Exile* (Minneapolis: Fortress, 2004), 440–3.

[157] Eisler, *Enigma*, 44.

[158] Maria-Louise Rigato, 'L'"apostolo ed evangelista Giovanni", "sacerdoto" levitico', *RevistB* 38 (1990), 451–83, at 469–81.

[159] Bauckham, *Jesus and the Eyewitnesses*, 449–50. As VanderKam, *From Joshua*, 411, concludes, cited by Bauckham: 'It is understandable that an event so public as the temporary replacement of a high priest on the Day of Atonement would be remembered in the tradition'. Cf. Josephus *Ant.* 17.165–7; *t. Yoma* 1.4; *b. Yoma* 12b; *y. Yoma* 1.1, 38d.

Damascus (Acts 9:11) with Judas the Lord's brother (Mark 6:3) in the *Acts of Paul*; Zechariah the father of the Baptist with the one murdered in the Temple (Matt. 23:35) in the *Protoevangelium of James* (23–4); Clement of Rome with the Clement mentioned in Phil. 4:3 by Eusebius (*h.e.* 3.4.9); Linus of Rome with the Linus of 2 Tim. 4:21 (Irenaeus *haer.* 3.3.3; Eusebius *h.e.* 3.4.8); and Hermas the prophet who wrote the *Shepherd* with the one mentioned in Rom. 16:14 (Origen, *Com. Rom.* 10.31). While Bauckham grants that the last two may be historically plausible, he asserts that the identification was 'doubtless made in the same way as the others—as an *exegetical procedure*'.[160] While there is no doubt that such conflations were made, this still does not explain why Polycrates goes the extra step: he does not simply say that John was 'of the high-priestly family', which would be all that could be derived from Acts 4:6, but that he wore the *petalon*, which is, as Bauckham rightly pointed out, an unambiguous assertion that John was *the* high priest.

While Bauckham styles his interpretation 'exegetical', it is clear that he is working in a historical key, looking for historical information about the author of the Gospel of John. There is another possible approach, equally exegetical but taking its lead from the Gospel of John rather than Acts 4:6, that could properly be called a theological interpretation.[161] The highpoint of the Gospel of John, if not its conclusion ('it is finished', John 19:30), is the crucifixion of Jesus at the moment that the lambs are slain, or rather when the Lamb is slain, interpreting this act by the scriptural injunction that not a bone of it/his shall be broken (John 19:36; Exod. 12:46). Moreover, when Christ invites the Jews to 'destroy this temple, and in three days I will raise it up', he spoke, the Evangelist explains, 'of the temple of his body' (John 2:19–21). It is, finally, of course, only in the Gospel of John that one of the disciples remains at the foot of the cross, along with the mother of Jesus, and that is 'the disciple whom Jesus loved' (John 19:26), who, as the uniquely privileged eyewitness is able not only to bear witness, but be a true witness (John 19:35). Many of the themes that are suggested here will be explored in subsequent chapters, but for now, with regard to Polycrates' words, it is easy to understand how for Polycrates John is *the* high priest ministering at the paschal mystery.[162] The temple in question is not the stone edifice in Jerusalem, but Christ himself, just as the Lamb of God slain in the mystery is also Christ himself. Many different images are brought together by John, who in this way is the high priest of the Christian mystery, the one wearing the *petalon*, initiating the celebration of Pascha.

[160] Bauckham, *Jesus and the Eyewitnesses*, 451, italics original.

[161] This approach was developed in a seminar I held on the Gospel of John; I benefitted immensely from the insights worked out by Will Rettig in his paper for that seminar.

[162] As we will see in Chapter 2, one of the scriptural passages lying behind John's description of the crucifixion scene, Zech. 6:11–13, also speaks of a 'priest' standing by his throne, that is, for John, the cross.

By examining in this chapter the memory of the figure of John, as the disciple of the Lord and the high priest of the paschal mystery, and a particular feature of the tradition observed by his school, that is, the very celebration of Pascha itself, presuppositions we might have held (for instance that the Gospel is focused on 'incarnation', as we have come to understand that term, rather than the Passion) have been challenged and our horizons broadened, so that we can approach the Gospel of John, in the next part of this study, to explore these themes as they are presented and developed therein. But before we do so, we should return to the comment from the *Letter of Aristeas* (99) regarding the awe that seeing the *petalon* inspired: 'a man would think that he had come out of this world into another one'. This is, indeed, the effect that is produced in the reader after turning from the Synoptics to the Gospel of John: everything is not as it seems, everything seems turned upside down, and a new world opens up before us. If this is the case, then it is worth first exploring further the suggestion of Ashton that the Gospel is somehow related to apocalyptic literature, opening out to us if not another world then this world seen from another perspective, or, as it would be put within a few centuries, the 'spiritual' perspective given by the theologian

2

The Paschal Gospel

If, as we concluded in Chapter 1, John, the disciple of the Lord and the high priest of the paschal mystery, in his Gospel opens up another world, or rather this world seen from a different perspective, then we have further reason to return to the intriguing suggestion of John Ashton, mentioned in the Introduction, that the Gospel of John should be thought of as 'an apocalypse—in reverse, upside down, inside out'.[1] Apocalyptic thinking has, perhaps, never been so fashionable. But let us begin, once again, with Ernst Käsemann, whose work stimulated this resurgence of interest, for there are still points to learn from him.

In two articles, published over fifty years ago, Käsemann asserted that 'Apocalyptic was the mother of all Christian theology',[2] and by doing so set off many debates. By 'apocalyptic' he specifically meant the enthusiasm engendered by the possession of the Spirit as a pledge of the imminent Parousia, 'nourished theologically from the tradition of Jewish apocalyptic', and the sense of a corresponding ambassadorial authority for its mission thus kindled.[3] Unlike Albert Schweitzer and his followers, 'who got in their own way by trying to turn the whole question into a problem of research into the life of the historical Jesus and to explain the very early history of dogma in terms of the delay of the Parousia'—landing up in a dead end on both counts—Käsemann suggests that we should take seriously 'post-Easter apocalyptic' as being 'a new theological start', the first chapter, the beginning of dogmatics itself, not the concluding one as has since become the traditional systematic approach.[4] 'The heart of primitive Christian apocalyptic, according to Revelation and the Synoptists alike, is the accession to the throne of heaven by God

[1] Ashton, *Fourth Gospel*, 329.

[2] Ernst Käsemann, 'The Beginnings of Christian Theology', in Käsemann, *New Testament Questions for Today* (Minneapolis: Fortress Press, 1969; first published in *ZKT* 57 [1960], 162–85), 82–107, at 100. See also Ernst Käsemann, 'On the Subject of Primitive Christian Apocalyptic', in Ernst Käsemann, *New Testament Questions*, 108–37 (first published in *ZKT* 59 [1962], 257–84).

[3] Käsemann, 'Beginnings', 92; 'Apocalyptic', 109. n. 1.

[4] Käsemann, 'Beginnings', 101–2.

and by his Christ as the eschatological Son of Man'.[5] Käsemann concludes his essay by tracing how various hopes were dashed, such as those of the 'Petrine party', who, in Matt. 16:18–19, appropriate to their leader what is promised to the whole community in Matt. 18:18, thereby making themselves a sect, thinking they could defy the gates of hell, but 'unable to resist the sands of time which buried them'. Käsemann asks if this episode is an 'archetype of what is always happening in the history of the Church', and 'has there ever been a theological system which has not collapsed? Have we been promised that we should know ourselves to be in possession of a *theologia perennis*?' Clearly not, is the answer his rhetorical question demands. Rather, it is 'only certain theological themes in the proclamation [that] are carried on from one generation to the next and thus preserve the continuity of the history of theology'. And chief among these themes is 'the hope of the manifestation of the Son of Man on his way to enthronement; and we have to ask ourselves whether Christian theology can ever survive in any legitimate form without this theme, which sprang from the Easter experience and determined the Easter faith'.[6]

Käsemann's thesis is provocative and generated much debate, but it is also fairly limited, primarily because he develops his reflections almost exclusively out of the Synoptic Gospels, with an occasional nod to Paul (more attention is given to Paul in his essay 'On the Subject of Primitive Christian Apocalyptic', but even there only to the Corinthian correspondence) and the book of Revelation. This is because he has already determined what is to count as 'Apocalyptic', that is, 'the expectation of an imminent Parousia'.[7] However, his central claims—that 'apocalyptic was the mother of all Christian theology', and that we are not given a system as a *theologia perennis*, but only 'the hope of the manifestation of the Son of Man on his way to enthronement'—are worth bearing in mind, and are, indeed, at the very heart of this study.

'APOCALYPTIC', APOCALYPSES, AND AN 'APOCALYPTIC GOSPEL'

The decades since Käsemann wrote have seen a burgeoning in scholarship on Second Temple Judaism and intertestamental literature, seeing in the period prior to the establishment of rabbinic Judaism many rich and varied seams.

[5] Käsemann, 'Beginnings', 105. [6] Käsemann, 'Beginnings', 107.

[7] As N. T. Wright records, in a letter to Wright, dated 19 January 1983, Ernst Käsemann wrote: 'Apokalyptic ist bei mir stets als Naherwartung verstanden ("for me, apocalyptic always means imminent-expectation")'. *The New Testament and the People of God* (Minneapolis: Fortress, 1992), 286, n. 19.

This has spurred on many to what has been called a 'new *religionsgeschichtliche Schule*', which has as its quest to understand the Jewish roots of Christology by looking to Jewish speculations about a 'second power' in heaven alongside God (most concretely seen in the figure of Metatron in *Third Enoch* or *The Hebrew Apocalypse of Enoch*).[8] More importantly, this scholarship has also given us a greatly enhanced understanding of the role of 'apocalyptic' in the intertestamental period and its significance for understanding Christianity. Although we tend to think of 'apocalyptic' primarily in terms of eschatology (an 'imminent Parousia'), usually described in nightmarish imagery portraying cataclysmic events (as the term is used in popular parlance), modern study of the phenomenon has made it clear that apocalyptic writings are in fact concerned with much more.

However, although new vistas have opened out for modern scholarship, the term 'apocalyptic' has become rather contentious. As N. T. Wright notes, in his survey of Pauline scholarship over the past century, the term 'apocalyptic' is 'slippery and polymorphous' and 'has become the watchword for a whole new family of interpretations', primarily those of Paul but also as something of a catchphrase denoting a particular style of theology.[9] In their Introduction to a collection of essays entitled *Paul and the Apocalyptic Imagination*, the editors helpfully propose a heuristic binary taxonomy for categorizing the different approaches, without intending to imply that these are either mutually exclusive or fixed categories: 'Eschatological Invasion' and 'Unveiled Fulfillment'.[10] These two approaches configure in different ways the three main themes or axes of 'apocalyptic'. The first two concern space and time, that is, the vertical intersection between the heavenly and earthly realms, on the one hand, and the horizontal intersection of the present age with the age to come, with eschatology. The third axis concerns epistemology, that is, how a seer is given to understand previously hidden realities and how this revelation relates to what was previously known, whether history can be viewed *prospectively*, such that what is now revealed is seen to be the fulfilment of what was

[8] Cf. Jarl Fossum, 'The New *Religionsgeschichtliche Schule*: The Quest for Jewish Christology', SBLSP 1991, ed. E. Lovering (Atlanta: Scholars, 1991), 638–46. For material in this vein, among many others, see Alan F. Segal, *Two Powers in Heaven: Early Rabbinic Reports about Christianity and Gnosticism*, SJLA 25 (Leiden: Brill, 1977); Jarl E. Fossum, *The Image of the Invisible God: Essays on the Influence of Jewish Mysticism on Early Christology* (Freiburg: Universitätsverlag Freiburg; Göttingen: Vandenhoeck & Ruprecht, 1995); Christopher Rowland and Christopher R. A. Morray Jones, *The Mystery of God: Early Jewish Mysticism and the New Testament*, CRINT 12 (Leiden: Brill, 2009).

[9] N. T. Wright, *Paul and His Recent Interpreters* (Minneapolis: Fortress, 2015), 135. For examples of 'apocalyptic' theology see the essays in Joshua B. Davis and Douglas Harink, eds, *Apocalyptic and the Future of Theology: With and Beyond J. Louis Martyn* (Eugene, OR: Cascade, 2012).

[10] Ben C. Blackwell, John K. Goodrich, and Jason Maston, 'Paul and the Apocalyptic Imagination', in Blackwell, Goodrich, and Maston, eds, *Paul and the Apocalyptic Imagination* (Minneapolis: Fortress, 2016), 3–21. See also Liethart, *Revelation 1–11*, 55–67 for a broader discussion of 'apocalyptic' in modern thought, from Altizer and Badiou to Derrida and Žižek.

previously promised, or only *retrospectively*, such that it is unanticipated and even perhaps disconnected with what went before. These axes will be explored further in the second section of this chapter. For now we need to look at these two approaches, and how they have influenced the study of the Gospel of John.

Although apocalyptic eschatology had become a strong theme in the work of Johannes Weiss and Albert Schweitzer, in the late nineteenth and early twentieth theology, it was really the emphasis of Karl Barth on divine revelation as a vertical invasion into human history in and through Christ that gave impetus to new ways of seeing Paul in a similar fashion. While Käsemann, as we have seen, and following him J. Christiaan Beker saw the eschatological dimension in terms of 'an imminent end of the world',[11] others, most notably J. Louis Martyn, shifted the focus from the second coming of Christ to the first, specifically to the cross, as the privileged locus where the breakthrough of God into this world is located, true knowledge of God is revealed, the new age is inaugurated, and the world is structured anew.[12] It is only in the light of the solution revealed in Christ that Paul now understands what the human plight is, and has always been, so enabling him to look backwards to reread the Scriptures and see it with the veil now lifted (2 Cor. 3:12–4:6).[13] This dramatic new reading of the Scriptures might seem to imply a discontinuity with what went before, but it need not necessarily be so. Richard Hays notes how 'the eschatological *apokalypsis* of the cross has wrought an inversion in Paul's reading of the text', yet adds that 'when Scripture is refracted through the hermeneutical lens provided by God's action in the crucified Messiah and in forming his eschatological community, it acquires a profound new symbolic coherence'.[14] And such a 'rereading' is precisely that, Hays points out in later work, not a 'repudiation'.[15]

[11] J. Christiaan Beker, *Paul the Apostle: The Triumph of God in Life and Thought* (Philadelphia: Fortress, 1980), 136.

[12] See especially J. Louis Martyn, *Galatians: A New Translation with Introduction and Commentary*, The Anchor Bible 33A (New York: Doubleday, 1997), and, in his collection of essays, *Theological Issues in the Letters of Paul*, Studies of the New Testament and its World (Edinburgh: T & T Clark, 1997), 'Epistemology at the Turn of the Ages', ibid. 89–110; 'Apocalyptic Antinomies', 111–23; 'Christ and the Elements of the Cosmos', 125–40; and 'God's Way of Making Right What Is Wrong', 141–56; 'John and Paul on the Subject of Gospel and Scripture', 209–30.

[13] The classic statement of this point, though not developed in terms of apocalyptic, is E. P. Sanders, *Paul and Palestinian Judaism: A Comparison of Patterns of Religion* (Philadelphia: Fortress Press, 1977), 474: 'for Paul, the conviction of a universal solution preceded the conviction of a universal plight'; see also 442–7.

[14] Richard B. Hays, *Echoes of Scripture in the Letters of Paul* (New Haven and London: Yale University Press, 1989), 169.

[15] 'I contend that Paul's understanding of the new age in Christ leads him not to a rejection of Israel's sacred history but to a retrospective hermeneutical transformation of Israel's story in the light of the story of God's startling redemptive actions.... this requires a dramatic rereading of Israel's story, but what is required is precisely a rereading, not a repudiation'. Richard Hays, 'Apocalyptic *Poesis* in Galatians: Paternity, Passion, and Participation', in Mark W. Elliott et al.,

Martinus de Boer, a student of Martyn, develops many of these themes, focusing especially on Paul's use of the word ἀποκάλυψις and its cognates, and in so doing is led to reflect on how the term 'apocalyptic' is used in modern scholarship, attempting to bring precision to its usage. For de Boer the term 'apocalyptic' is 'an adjective, modifying the noun "eschatology"'.[16] De Boer builds upon the threefold classification given by Paul D. Hanson, wherein 'apocalypse' designates a literary genre (though not unproblematically, as we will see later), 'apocalypticism' a socio-religious movement that has recourse to a particular symbolic universe, and 'apocalyptic eschatology' (often shortened simply to 'apocalyptic') which refers to a particular religious perspective that is not confined to apocalypses, but looks to 'the final saving acts' of God, that is, to eschatology.[17] For de Boer, the adjective 'apocalyptic' used to qualify 'eschatology' derives 'primarily' from the Apocalypse of John, and so 'apocalyptic eschatology' refers 'to the kind of eschatology found in the book of Revelation, and this eschatology is a matter of divine revelation: apocalyptic eschatology is *revealed* eschatology'.[18] But, and this is the crucial difference with Jewish apocalyptic eschatology, 'In Revelation, the eschatological events of the imminent future take their point of departure from an eschatological event of the recent past, the resurrection (and thus ascension) of Jesus Christ to God's heavenly throne'.[19] For Paul (de Boer's primary concern) just as for the John of Revelation, apocalyptic eschatology 'is thus as much a matter of a *past* eschatological event (the resurrection of Jesus, the Messiah) as of an event still to occur (the *parousia*)'.[20] This conviction, de Boer points out, is also reflected in the way in which 'Paul often uses the noun ἀποκάλυψις apocalyptically, that is, to signify God's eschatological activity in and through Christ, as he does the cognate verb ἀποκαλύπτω'.[21] The expectation that the present

eds, *Galatians and Christian Theology: Justification, the Gospel and Ethics in Paul's Letters* (Grand Rapids: Baker, 2004), 200–19, at 204.

[16] Martinus C. de Boer, 'Apocalyptic as God's Eschatological Activity in Paul's Theology', in Blackwell et al., eds, *Paul and the Apocalyptic Imagination*, 45–63, at 45. See also Martinus C. de Boer, *The Defeat of Death: Apocalyptic Eschatology in 1 Corinthians 15 and Romans 5*, JSNTSup 22 (Sheffield: JSOT Press, 1988); 'Paul and Jewish Apocalyptic Eschatology', in Joel Marcus and Marion L. Soards, eds, *Apocalyptic and the New Testament: Essays in Honor of J. Louis Martyn*, JSNTSup 24 (Sheffield: JSOT, 1989), 169–90; 'Paul and Apocalyptic Eschatology', in John J. Collins, ed., *The Encyclopedia of Apocalypticism* (New York: Continuum, 1998), 1.345–83; and 'Paul, Theologian of God's Apocalypse', *Interpretation* 56.1 (2002), 21–33.

[17] Paul D. Hanson, 'Apocalypse, Genre' and 'Apocalypticism', in Keith R. Crim, ed., *The Interpreter's Dictionary of the Bible: Supplementary Volume* (Nashville: Abingdon, 1976), 27–34, and 'Apocalypses and Apocalypticism (Genre, Introductory Overview)', in David Noel Freedman, ed., *Anchor Bible Dictionary* (New York: Doubleday, 1992), 1.279–82.

[18] De Boer, 'Paul and Apocalyptic Eschatology', 351, italics original.

[19] Ibid. 354–5.

[20] Ibid. 355, italics original.

[21] De Boer, 'Apocalyptic as God's Eschatological Activity', 59; see also 'Paul, Theologian of God's Apocalypse', 25–33; and *Galatians: A Commentary*, The New Testament Library (Louisville, KY: Westminster John Knox Press, 2011), 79–82.

order of reality, 'this age', would be replaced with a new transformed order of reality, 'the age to come', has already begun: if God through Isaiah spoke about the future, saying 'For behold, I create new heavens and a new earth; the former things shall not be remembered or come to mind' (Isa. 65:17), John asserts in the present that 'I saw a new heaven and a new earth; for the first heaven and the first earth had passed away... And I saw the holy city, new Jerusalem, coming down out of heaven from God' (Apoc. 21:1–2). As such, for de Boer the 'apocalyptic eschatology' of Paul and John of Revelation is not concerned only with the communication of heavenly mysteries, knowledge revealed to a seer in an ascent to the heavens, but with 'the expectation of God's own visible eschatological activity, what we may, I think, call the Apocalypse of God—where the term "apocalypse" obviously does not denote a literary genre, nor does the term signify only a divine revelation or disclosure of previously hidden information, but also, visible divine movement and activity on a cosmic scale'.[22] And, more specifically, it is this 'Apocalypse of God [that] occurs in the event of Jesus Christ'.[23]

The other approach to understanding Paul as an 'apocalyptic' writer, that of 'Unveiled Fulfilment', is exemplified most extensively by N. T. Wright. Noting that 'the word "apocalyptic" has become so slippery, capable of so many twists and turns of meaning', he argues that 'it would be safest to confine it simply to a literary genre: that of "revelations", which is after all what the word basically means'.[24] And indeed there has in fact been a great deal of reflection on the nature of the genre of 'apocalypse' over the past couple of decades.[25] In particular, the Society of Biblical Literature Genres Project aimed, according to John J. Collins, 'to give precision to the traditional category of "apocalyptic literature" by showing the extent and limits of the conformity among the allegedly apocalyptic texts'.[26] The definition of the genre of 'apocalypse' that they drew up is:

> a genre of revelatory literature with a narrative framework, in which a revelation is mediated by an otherworldly being to a human recipient, disclosing a transcendent reality which is both temporal, insofar as it envisages eschatological salvation, and spatial insofar as it involves another, supernatural world.[27]

[22] De Boer, 'Apocalyptic as God's Eschatological Activity', 51. [23] Ibid.

[24] Wright, *Paul and His Recent Interpreters*, 140.

[25] See especially Christopher Rowland, *The Open Heaven: A Study of Apocalyptic in Judaism and Early Christianity* (New York: Crossroads, 1982); John J. Collins, *The Apocalyptic Imagination: An Introduction to Jewish Apocalyptic Literature*, 2nd edn (Grand Rapids, MI: Eerdmans, 1998 [1987]); James C. VanderKam and William Adler, *The Jewish Apocalyptic Heritage in Early Christianity*, CRINT 4 (Assen: Van Gorcum, 1996); and the part by Christopher Rowland in Rowland and Morray Jones, *The Mystery of God*, 3–201.

[26] Collins, *Apocalyptic Imagination*, 4.

[27] John J. Collins, 'Introduction: Towards the Morphology of a Genre', in Collins, ed., *Apocalypse: The Morphology of a Genre* (*Semeia* 14: Missoula, MT: Scholars Press, 1979), 1–20, at 9; also given in Collins, *Apocalyptic Imagination*, 5.

This definition of the genre of apocalypse has been largely accepted, though it has been subjected to further refinement. John Ashton, for instance, points out that eschatology does not figure in all apocalypses and that one also needs to find a way of differentiating between prophecy and apocalyptic revelation, and, moreover, that attention needs to be given to the milieu of apocalyptic writings and the mode in which the revelations are received.[28] Building upon this, and the work of Adela Yarbro Collins, Benjamin Reynolds has suggested revising the definition as follows:

> a genre of revelatory literature with a narrative framework, in which a revelation is mediated by an otherworldly figure to a human recipient *often, though not always, through visions, dreams, or an ascent to heaven*, disclosing a transcendent reality which is both temporal, insofar as it envisages *personal* eschatological salvation, and spatial insofar as it involves another, supernatural world, '*and an apocalypse is intended to interpret present, earthly circumstances in the light of the supernatural world…, and to influence both the understanding and the behavior of the audience by means of divine authority*'.[29]

Defining the genre of apocalyptic literature and surveying the various themes it contains in this way leads to the foregrounding of other aspects of the 'apocalyptic' Paul, such as his own mystical experiences, his ascent to heaven to receive visions and revelations, hearing things that cannot be told (2 Cor. 12:1–5), and his employment of 'mystery' language in other contexts.[30] On the basis of a full survey of the 'apocalyptic' material of Second Temple Judaism, Paul seems to be more at home in this milieu than he does when seen as an advocate of an 'eschatological invasion', and consequently his reading of Scripture appears to be more continuous than discontinuous. This is the

[28] Ashton, *Fourth Gospel*, 309–10. For a catalogue of items found in apocalypses, see Michael E. Stone, 'Lists of Revealed Things in Apocalyptic Literature', in Frank M. Cross, Werner E. Lemke, and Patrick D. Miller Jr, eds, *Magnalia Dei: The Mighty Acts of God: Essays on the Bible and Archaeology in Memory of G. Ernest Wright* (Garden City, NY: Doubleday, 1976), 414–52.

[29] Benjamin Reynolds, 'John and Jewish Apocalypses: Rethinking the Genre of John's Gospel', in Catrin H. Williams and Christopher Rowland, eds, *John's Gospel and Intimations of Apocalyptic*, 36–57, at 41. The words in italics are additions to the SBL definition, and the last lines, in quotation marks, are adopted from Adela Yarbro Collins, 'Introduction: Early Christian Apocalypticism', *Semeia* 36 (1986), 1–11, at 7, to address the question of apocalyptic milieu; the ellipsis indicates the omission of her phrase 'and of the future', as rendering apocalyptic too exclusively a matter of eschatology. See also Benjamin Reynolds, *The Apocalyptic Son of Man in the Gospel of John*, WUNT 2.249 (Tübingen: Mohr Siebeck, 2008), 16.

[30] See especially Alan F. Segal, *Paul the Convert: The Apostolate and Apostasy of Saul the Pharisee* (New Haven: Yale University Press, 1990); Markus Bockmuehl, *Revelation and Mystery in Ancient Judaism and Pauline Christianity*, WUNT 2.36 (Tübingen: Mohr Siebeck, 1990); and Benjamin L. Gladd, *Revealing the Mysterion: The Use of Mystery in Daniel and Second Temple Judaism with its Bearing on First Corinthians*, BZNW 160 (Berlin: De Gruyter, 2008); G. K. Beale and Benjamin L. Gladd, *Hidden but Now Revealed: A Biblical Theology of Divine Mystery* (Downers Grove, IL: IVP Academic, 2014).

point that N. T. Wright would want to emphasize. Wright accepts, of course, Paul's emphasis on the gospel as an '*apocalyptic event*: that is, something that took place as a free and fresh gift of grace, something through which God's new creation has burst upon a surprised and unready world, winning the victory over the forces of darkness and death'.[31] But, Wright argues, in this 'apocalyptic' there is in fact a greater deal of continuity with what went before than an invasion of something new, for, as he points out, '"apocalypses" regularly concern themselves with *telling the story of Israel and the world* in a way that leads the eye up to the eventual moment of divine rescue'.[32] This, on Wright's telling, is not 'a smooth evolutionary progress, the straw man much beloved of some "apocalyptic" theorists', but it exhibits a continuity nevertheless, both in the practice of 'telling the story of Israel' and as the story that is actually there.[33]

We will return to the issue of continuity and discontinuity in the apostolic and evangelical (re)reading of the Scriptures below. For now, we must make note of a problem inherent in attempting to define 'apocalyptic' in terms of genre. That the word 'apocalypse' might be used as a designation of a genre is based, of course, primarily on the Apocalypse of John, the first word of which is ἀποκάλυψις, specifically 'an apocalypse of Jesus Christ' (Apoc. 1:1) and which was used already in the second century as the title of the work itself.[34] But, as Collins acknowledges, 'the use of the title *apokalypsis* (revelation) as a genre label is not attested in the period before Christianity' and the works held to belong to Jewish apocalyptic literature were not in fact designated as apocalypses in antiquity.[35] Moreover, the definition of the genre of apocalypse, as given by the SBL Genre Project, in fact only applies, as Collins further concedes, 'to various sections' of the books commonly regarded as belonging to apocalyptic literature, *1 Enoch*, *Daniel*, *4 Ezra*, *2 Baruch*, and so on.[36] And so, in turn, 'the literary genre apocalypse is not a self-contained isolated entity', but rather 'the conceptual structure indicated by the genre ... can also be found in works that are not revelation accounts, and so are not technically apocalypses'.[37] As de Boer points out, 'such observations make any clear definition of the genre whereby an apocalypse (as a self-contained book) can be usefully distinguished from

[31] Wright, *Paul and His Recent Interpreters*, 168, italics original.

[32] Ibid. 160, his emphasis.

[33] Ibid. 163. As Wright puts it later on the same page: 'To imagine that such stories are really about an immanent process *within* history, rather than having to do with divine *sovereignty* over history, is to impose a nineteenth-century scheme on first-century material' (italics original). See now also Wright, 'Apocalyptic and the Sudden Fulfillment of Divine Promise', in Blackwell et al., eds, *Paul and the Apocalyptic Imagination*, 111–34.

[34] Irenaeus is the first to use the word 'apocalypse' as the title of the work (*haer.* 5.30.3); it appears as a title in the Codex Sinaiticus and Codex Ephraemi.

[35] Collins, *Apocalyptic Imagination*, 3.

[36] Ibid. 5.

[37] Ibid. 9.

other literary genres (other books) well-nigh impossible'.[38] If the aim was, as Collins puts it, 'to clarify particular works by showing both their typical traits and their distinctive elements', rather than 'to construct a metaphysical entity, "apocalyptic" or *Apocalyptik* in any sense independent of the actual texts',[39] the result has been to construct a genre to which, in fact, no work (apart from perhaps the Apocalypse of John) belongs as a complete whole. De Boer points out that the definition offered in fact corresponds to 'a vision (more accurately, a written report of a vision), a genre designation not applied to whole books', and suggests that it would 'be better to think of an apocalypse as a smaller literary genre (*Form*) akin to prayer, parable, or hymn, and not as a larger literary genre (*Gattung*) for a whole book such as a letter, gospel, or history'.[40] If one can continue to speak of the 'apocalyptic' literature of this period, it can only be in the sense that parts of these works contain elements belonging to this form.

The reason for having explored these developments in the understanding of apocalyptic and/or apocalypse over the past half century, largely centring upon the figure of Paul, is to contextualize its application to John and his Gospel. In developing his reading of the Gospel of John as a 'two-level drama', paralleling the life of Jesus it narrates with the continuing life of John's community, J. Louis Martyn, as we will see later, suggests that this derived from 'the thought-world of Jewish apocalypticism'.[41] Picking up on this, and adopting enthusiastically the work on early Jewish and Christian 'apocalyptic literature' carried out over the last decades, John Ashton has provided a sustained reading of the Gospel of John and its key themes in these terms. Most strikingly he asserts that the SBL Genre Project definition, subject to the modifications mentioned earlier (and incorporated into Reynold's definition), 'fits the Fourth Gospel to a T'.[42] Reynolds helpfully summarizes the elements of 'apocalyptic literature' deployed by the Gospel of John, and they are indeed striking.[43] It is a narrative in which an otherworldly figure descends from heaven (1:1–18; 3:13, 34; 9:33; 17:3–5, etc.) and mediates knowledge about heavenly things (3:12), especially regarding God and his Son (1:18), to a particular human being (19:35; 21:24) and to others (1:14; 2:11). The Son of Man bridges heaven and earth, thus opening the heavens to human beings

[38] De Boer, 'Apocalyptic as God's Eschatological Activity', 47, n. 9; referring to the first edition of Collins work.

[39] Collins, *Apocalyptic Imagination*, 8.

[40] De Boer, 'Apocalyptic as God's Eschatological Activity', 47 n. 9.

[41] Martyn, *History and Theology*, 130. See also his brief discussion of John's reading of Scripture in 'John and Paul on the Subject of Gospel and Scripture'.

[42] Ashton, *Fourth Gospel*, 7. See also Rowland, in Rowland and Morray-Jones, *The Mystery of God*, 123–31, and the various essays collected in Williams and Rowland's, *John's Gospel and Intimations of Apocalyptic.*

[43] Reynolds, 'John and Jewish Apocalypses', 42. See also, more fully, Reynolds, *Apocalyptic Son of Man.*

(1.50–1). This revelation mediates personal eschatological salvation if it finds a response of faith (3:15–16; 14:6), and indeed offers a birth from above, from the Spirit (3:5–8), enabling believers to become children of God (1:12). John also blends together an emphasis on the present reality of judgement and salvation (3:17–18; 9:39; 12:31) with a recognition that the consummation of this still lies in the future (5:28–9; 6:39–40; 14:1–3). The Gospel of John in addition places the events unfolding in its narrative within a heavenly perspective (3:31–2; 6:25–40; 9:39; 13:33; 17:1–5; 20:17), an understanding of which is only available to his disciples after his glorification, when another heavenly figure is sent to remind them of all that he had said and done (12:16; 14:26; 16:12–15). Finally, although it is not specified in the definitions of the genre mentioned above, the Gospel of John has a particular interest in the textuality of this revelation and its own witness (12:16; 21:24–5).[44]

Nevertheless, despite these structural and thematic commonalities, it remains the case that the Gospel of John, as Ashton acknowledges, 'is obviously *not* an apocalypse'.[45] Instead, Ashton suggested that it is an apocalypse, 'in reverse, upside down, inside out'.[46] The reason that led Ashton to this inversion is that: 'There is no divine plan first disclosed to a seer in a vision and then repeated in earthly terms. The divine plan itself—the Logos—is incarnate: fully embodied in the person of Jesus. It is his life that reveals God's grand design of saving the world, a design now being realized, lived out by the community'.[47] However, even this is not quite sufficient, for there are 'apocalypses', such as *4 Ezra* and *2 Baruch*, in which there are no heavenly ascents or visions of God, but which are instead played out fully upon the earth.[48] Reynolds also points out five

[44] Many of the themes here mentioned have clear parallels in Jewish apocalypses. Reynolds ('John and Jewish Apocalypses', 41–2, n. 26) lists the following: the opening of heaven (John 1:51 with *2 Bar.* 22.1; *T. Levi* 2.6; *T. Ab.* A 7.3; *Apoc. Ab.* 19.4; *Apoc. Zeph.* 10.2; Apoc. 4:1–2; 19:11); ascent or descent of an otherworldly figure or human recipient (John 3:13; 6:62, with *1 En.* 14.8; *T. Levi* 2.6–7; *T. Ab.* A 10.1); the revelation of heavenly things (John 1:18, 3:12–13 with *T. Ab.* A 11–14); the vision of God (John 12:41; 14:9, with Apoc. 4–5; *1 En.* 14.8–23; *Apoc. Ab.* 18); the vision of God in the heavenly temple (John 2:21; 12:41 with *1 En.* 14); judgement and the Son of Man (John 5:27; 9:39 with Dan. 7:9–12; *1 En.* 62; *T. Ab.* A 11–13; *Apoc. Ab.* 22.3–5; *3 Bar.* 15–16; cf. *Apoc. Zeph.* 6.17; 10.11); double resurrection of the righteous and the wicked (John 5:28–9 with *1 En.* 51.1–5; *4 Ezra* 7.28–36; *2 Bar.* 50.2–51.4; Apoc. 20:5–6, 11–14); the importance of the written record of revelation (John 20:30–1; 21:24 with *1 En.* 68.1; 81.6; 82.1; 83.8–10; *2 En.* 23.3–6; 40.1–12; *2 En.* J 68.2; Apoc. 1:11; *Jub.* 1.5, 7, 26; 2.1; *4 Ezra* 14.44–6; *2 Bar.* 50.1; cf. 77.12–87.1). For the different dimensions of textuality within apocalypses, see Judith Lieu, 'Text and Authority in John and Apocalyptic', in Williams and Rowland, *John's Gospel and Intimations of Apocalyptic*, 235–53, and for the textuality of the Gospel, see Petterson, *From Tomb to Text.*

[45] Ashton, *Fourth Gospel*, 309, italics original. [46] Ibid. 329.

[47] Ibid. 328. So too Rowland, *Mystery of God*, 131: 'Heavenly visions are not what is on offer in the Fourth Gospel, for claims to see God must be regarded as claims to see Jesus. The Gospel of John is indeed "an apocalypse in reverse"'.

[48] Cf. Reynolds, 'John and Jewish Apocalypses', 51–2. Ashton qualifies his claim in his later *The Gospel of John and Christian Origins*, 114–18, saying on p.114: 'But must I now admit that I was wrong to conclude that "the fourth evangelist conceives his work as an apocalypse—in reverse, upside down, inside out"? No, not wrong, because even though I am now obliged to

specific reasons for concluding that in fact the Gospel of John cannot be counted as an 'apocalypse'.[49] First, in the Gospel the otherworldly mediating figure is not, as it regularly is in Jewish 'apocalypses', an angel, but rather Jesus himself, the Word of God. Second, the mediator is both the content and the centre of the revelation in a manner uncharacteristic of apocalypses, which never focus directly on the angelic mediator figure. 'To describe this as the merging of the Message and the Mediator, or Jesus as Revealer and Revelation captures the sense of the assimilation that moves the Gospel of John beyond the bounds of texts belonging to the genre of "apocalypse"'.[50] Third, Jesus is one with God in a manner that never occurs in Jewish apocalyptic texts, where the angelic mediators are but messengers of God, speaking his words. Fourth, a point 'almost too obvious to mention', is that Jesus is crucified, buried, and raised to life, something that never happens to the mediators of Jewish 'apocalypses'.[51] Finally, while the testimony of the Gospel of John is given by one figure, the disciple whom Jesus loved, it is received by more than one (1:14; 1:51, where the 'you will see' is plural; 2:11; 14:7, again a plural; 21:24). If the Gospel of John is in any sense 'apocalyptic', it is so not simply because of an inversion, but rather because it merges the cast of apocalyptic characters: 'as mediator of the revelation, he is also the centre of the revelation, is one with the source of the revelation, and is a human being, even one who suffers death, like those to whom he discloses the revelation'. As such, Reynolds rightly concludes, this 'bursts the wineskins of the genre of "apocalypse"'.[52]

Reynolds' proposal for how to designate the Gospel of John, which attempts to do justice both to the many structural and thematic commonalities between it and Jewish 'apocalypses', yet recognizes that it is a Gospel and not an apocalypse, even one 'in reverse, upside down, inside out', is to call it an 'apocalyptic Gospel'. Here the word 'apocalyptic' is not an appeal to a theological or ideological presupposition or tendency, but is rather used to indicate the alignment of the Gospel 'with the literary genre and the content of apocalypses': 'The meaning of the adjective "apocalyptic" should be anchored to the genre of "apocalypse", not to any one specific apocalypse'.[53] Although the Gospel of John is clearly different from those of Matthew, Mark, and Luke, they do all, of course, narrate the life and deeds of Jesus and proclaim the good

confess that many of the arguments I used to support my thesis were mistaken, or at best misleading, I still believe that I was right to detect in the Gospel a fundamental affinity with apocalyptic that had not previously been observed'.

[49] 'John and Jewish Apocalypses', 43–50.

[50] Ibid. 45. The merging of Message and Mediator is taken from Robert H. Gundry, *Jesus the Word according to John the Sectarian* (Grand Rapids: Eerdmans, 2001), 14; that of Revealer and Revelation from Bultmann, *Theology of the New Testament*, 2 vols printed in 1, trans. Kendrick Grobel (Waco, TX: Baylor University Press, 2007 [1951]), II, 66. This merging was also noted by Hoskyns, *Fourth Gospel*, 159–63.

[51] Reynolds, 'John and Jewish Apocalypses', 47–8. [52] Ibid. 49. [53] Ibid. 55.

news about him. However one might determine the nature of the genre of Gospel and its origin, it is clear that they do resemble Greco-Roman biography, but also include, and indeed emphasize, the proclamation of the good news, something that is generally absent from Greco-Roman biographies; they are, in this sense, as Hengel calls them, '*kerygmatic* biography'.[54] In the case of John, however, it is not simply a 'kerygmatic biography', but, Reynolds suggests, an 'apocalyptic Gospel': it is a Gospel, in that it is a narrative that proclaims the salvation offered through Christ; but it is apocalyptic, in that it utilizes structural and thematic elements shared with material found in the genre of 'apocalypse'. The Gospel of John, bringing these elements together in a novel manner, Reynolds argues, breaks the moulds of both gospel and apocalypse: 'John's Gospel is not so much an apocalypse reversed, inside out, upside down, but an apocalypse that is shaken, stirred, and inserted into a Gospel'.[55]

While the Gospel of John does undoubtedly employ many of the themes common to 'apocalyptic literature', given the problems we have seen inherent in the attempt to identify a genre 'apocalypse', it is difficult to base the description of the Gospel of John as an 'apocalyptic Gospel' on the basis of genre. The Gospel of John does, however, fit into the category of 'apocalyptic eschatology', as used by de Boer, that is, as 'the Apocalypse of God' revealed and established in Christ and specifically the event of his Passion: portrayed as crucified to the world and elevated above it, this is the judgement of the world (12:31), and, as we will see in Part II, the Temple is finally constructed and the work of God announced at the beginning, to make a human being in his image (Gen. 1:26), is, at the end, 'finished' (19:30), so that, on this basis, Christ is finally and fully, and only in this Gospel, called 'God' (20:28). Exposed in these ways, the mystery of God is unveiled. As such one might indeed call the Gospel of John an 'apocalyptic Gospel', using the term as does de Boer rather than as Reynolds. But as this 'apocalypse' pivots upon the cross, and given that, as we saw in Chapter 1, it is initially only in the 'School of John' that an annual feast was kept celebrating this, on the day when the Passover lambs were slain in the Temple and on which Jesus was crucified (unlike the Synoptics), it is more appropriate, I would suggest, as in Chapter 1, to designate John as a 'paschal gospel'.

[54] Martin Hengel, *The Four Gospels and the One Gospel of Jesus Christ*, trans. John Bowden (Harrisburg, PA: Trinity Press International, 2000), 157; and, summarizing this book, 'The Four Gospels and the One Gospel of Jesus Christ', in C. Horton, ed., *The Earliest Gospels: The Origins and Transmission of the Earliest Christian Gospels: The Contribution of the Chester Beatty Codex P45* (London: T & T Clark, 2004), 13–26, at 22. See also the discussion in Ashton, *Fourth Gospel*, 24–7; and more generally M. Wills, *The Quest of the Historical Gospel: Mark, John, and the Origins of the Gospel Genre* (London: Routledge, 1997) and Richard A. Burridge, *What are the Gospels: A Comparison with Graeco-Roman Biography*, SNTSMS 70 (Cambridge, Cambridge University Press, 1992).

[55] Reynolds, 'John and Jewish Apocalypses', 56.

This discussion about the 'apocalyptic' character of the Gospel of John, in terms of the elements it has in common with works also considered to be 'apocalyptic' and in terms of the final and definitive 'Apocalypse of God', begs for further reflection upon the relationship between the Gospel of John and the Apocalypse also in his name.[56] As we saw in Chapter 1, these two works were almost universally held to be by the same author during the course of the second century. Even if the common authorship of the two works is denied, as is commonly done today, the question about the relation between the two still remains. As noted above, it is problematic to define a genre of 'apocalypse' on the basis of the opening word of John's Apocalypse, and the problem is only further compounded when one then attempts to understand the Apocalypse on the basis of the definition of the genre thus derived. In fact, the Apocalypse of John is distinct from all the other works regularly included in the category of 'apocalyptic literature' for it alone is written in the name of a contemporary and living author, rather than a figure in Israel's distant past. Illuminating as it is to take note of how the Gospel of John deploys various elements found in the 'apocalyptic' literature, one nevertheless risks overlooking the distinctiveness of the Apocalypse, and thereby obscuring the relation between the Gospel and the Apocalypse, claiming to have been written by the same author.

In Chapter 1 we considered the point made by Dionysius of Alexandria in the third century, and discussed repeatedly since, about the apparent difference in vocabulary and style of the two works. Dionysius, however, also raised another point that is pertinent to our present discussion. He notes how some have rejected the Apocalypse, 'declaring it to be unintelligible and illogical, and its title [τὴν ἐπίγραφήν] false. For they say that it is not John's, nor yet an apocalypse since it is veiled [κεκαλυμμένην] by its great and thick curtain of unintelligibility'.[57] Dionysius is here playing on the most basic meaning of the term 'apocalypse', one which must ultimately take priority over our attempt to define a genre or demarcate its elements, that is, that an apocalypse is an 'unveiling'. Yet, if the Apocalypse is an 'unveiling', as is declared by its opening word, why does everything seems so obscure, as if veiled by an impenetrable curtain? If we take the Apocalypse at its word, however, could it be that the Gospel of John in fact is the work which 'veils' that which is unveiled in the Apocalypse, the Gospel veiling the ultimate victory of God in Christ in the form of a narrative of Jesus and his apparent defeat, to all worldly perception, even if that 'veiling' is done in a particular manner, distinct from the Synoptics, by sharing elements found in the 'apocalyptic' literature?[58] Speaking of

[56] Something called for by Martyn, *History and Theology in the Fourth Gospel*, 130, n. 198, on the basis of the 'two levels' that he finds in the Gospel of John, which we will consider in the next section of this chapter.

[57] Eusebius *h.e.* 7.25.2.

[58] Or, as Westcott, *The Gospel according to St John*, lxxxvii, puts it: 'the Gospel is the spiritual interpretation of the Apocalypse'.

the narrative quality of a Gospel as a 'veil' of the gospel is, in a sense, no different than pointing out that the gospel proclaimed by Paul is, historically speaking, only subsequently given narrative form in the Gospels.[59] The hermeneutic movement from the Apocalypse to the Gospel would also be given historical grounding if one were to accept the earlier dating of the Apocalypse as discussed in Chapter 1.

As we will consider further in the third section of this chapter, in their Gospels the evangelists proclaimed Christ by drawing upon the language of the Scriptures, investing or clothing him with these words, as the flesh by which he is made known, seen, and understood. However, these narratives are thus also a veil, which, while essential for communicating the gospel, must also be 'unveiled' for the gospel to be received as a proclamation rather than a report about past events. Origen, in the first sustained reflection on what is meant by the term 'gospel', argues that it does not primarily mean 'the narrative of the deeds, sufferings, and words of Jesus', but rather designates an 'exhortatory address', and as such it includes all the writings which 'present the sojourn [ἐπιδημία] of Christ and prepare for his coming [παρουσία] and produce it in the souls of those who are willing to receive the Word of God, who stands at the door and knocks and wishes to enter their souls'.[60] This definition of 'gospel' is one which thus applies both to the Gospels and the letters of the apostles, and in fact more so to the latter than to the former, for in the Gospels the gospel is veiled under a narrative.[61] And, indeed, for Origen it can also be applied to all the writings of Scripture:

> Before the sojourn of Christ, the Law and the Prophets did not contain the proclamation that belongs to the definition of the gospel, since he who explained the mysteries in them had not yet come. But since the Savior has come, and has caused the gospel to be embodied, he has by the gospel made all things as gospel. (*Com. Jn.* 1.33)

Thus for Origen, the gospel is essentially the proclamation, which is embodied in the Gospels and seen retrospectively throughout the whole of Scripture.[62]

[59] On this, see Willi Marxsen, *Mark the Evangelist: Studies on the Redaction History of the Gospel* (Nashville: Abingdon Press, 1969), 117–51, study 3, 'The Evangelion'.

[60] Origen, *Comm. Jo.* 1.18–26. For this aspect of Origen, see Behr, *Way to Nicaea*, 169–84, and for Origen as an 'apocalyptic' theologian, see my introduction to *Origen: On First Principles*.

[61] As Karen Jo Torjesen, *Hermeneutical Procedure and Theological Method in Origen's Exegesis*, PTS 28 (Berlin: De Gruyter, 1986), 129, puts it: 'Here is the underlying unity between the Gospels and the epistles: Both have the same subject matter, the universal coming of the Logos to the soul through the incarnation, but in the Gospels under the allegorical aspect of the human history of Jesus, the epistles in the direct form of teaching about the divine Logos'.

[62] This is, of course, a point made repeatedly throughout early Christian writings. For instance, Irenaeus, *haer.* 4.2.7: 'The Law never hindered them from believing in the Son of God, but it even exhorted them to do so, saying that human beings can be saved in no other way from the old wound of the serpent than by believing in him who, in the likeness of sinful

The gospel proclaimed in this way is, for Origen, 'the eternal gospel' spoken of in the Apocalypse (14:6), or as he puts it 'the spiritual gospel'. Commenting on the Gospel of John, Origen speaks of his task as being to share with his readers 'the Word who was restored from being made flesh to what he "was in the beginning with God"...to translate the gospel perceptible to the senses into the spiritual gospel. For what is the interpretation of the gospel perceptible to the senses unless it is translated into the spiritual gospel? It is little or nothing, even though the common people believe they receive the things which are revealed from the literal sense'.[63] This is not some kind of 'anti-incarnational' tendency or esoteric elitism, but a necessary hermeneutic move: to be proclaimed as gospel, the Gospels have to be not only read as the narratives they are, but proclaimed, translated into an exhortatory proclamation that effects the 'sojourn' and produces the 'coming', the *parousia*, of the Word in the present. It is not simply that the Gospels are a combination of both narrative and proclamatory passages, as Hengel's description 'kerygmatic biography' might suggest, but rather kerygma is woven into the narratives, needing to be unveiled to become gospel.

In a passage from *Contra Celsum*, preserved also in the *Philokalia*, Origen further develops this imagery of the Word being clothed with the language of Scripture. 'The garments of the Word', he writes, 'are the phrases of the Scripture, the divine thoughts are clothed in these expressions'. These garments can also be considered, he suggests, as the flesh of the Word: 'for always in the Scriptures the Word became flesh that he might tabernacle among us'.[64] Hippolytus speaks similarly of the flesh taken by the Word in a passage we have already seen in the Introduction:

> The Word of God, being fleshless, put on the holy flesh from the holy Virgin, as a bridegroom a garment, having woven it for himself in the sufferings of the cross, so that having mixed our mortal body with his own power, and having mingled the corruptible into the incorruptible, and the weak with the strong, he might save the perishing human being. The web-beam, therefore, is the passion of the Lord upon the cross, and the warp on it is the power of the Holy Spirit, and the woof is the holy flesh woven by the Spirit, and the thread is the grace which by the love of Christ binds and unites the two in one, and the rods are the Word; and the workers are the patriarchs and prophets who weave the fair, long, perfect tunic for Christ; and the Word passing through these, like the combs, completes through them that which his Father wills.[65]

flesh, is lifted up from the earth upon the tree of martyrdom and draws all things to himself and vivifies the dead'.

[63] Origen, *Comm. Jo.* 1.43, 45.

[64] *Cels.* 6.77 (*Philoc.* 15.19): *τὰ ἱμάτια τοῦ λόγου αἱ λέξεις εἰσὶ τῆς γραφῆς· ἔνδυμα τῶν θείων νοημάτων τὰ ῥήματά ἐστι ταῦτα.... ἀεὶ γὰρ ἐν ταῖς γραφαῖς ὁ λόγος σὰρξ ἐγένετο, ἵνα κατασκηνώσῃ ἐν ἡμῖν.*

[65] Hippolytus, *Antichr.* 4.

It is in the preaching of the crucified Lord through the matrix of Scripture that the Word receives flesh, woven by the patriarchs and prophets, whose words and deeds, as recorded in Scripture, foretell and prepare for the coming of the Lord. The Virgin in this case, Hippolytus affirms later on, is the Church, who 'continually bears [Christ] as she teaches all nations'.[66] The cross, the apocalyptic, unveiling event par excellence, is that by which the Word becomes flesh, weaving this flesh from the Scriptures and receiving it from the Virgin, who is thus always giving birth to Christ. As we will explore fully in Part II, Incarnation and the Passion are bound up inseparably together by John in his paschal gospel.

Leaving aside Käsemann's identification of 'apocalyptic' with 'imminent expectation', it is worth returning to his rhetorical questions with which we began this chapter, to the effect that we should not think of ourselves as in possession of a *theologia perennis*, but rather understand that the continuity of theology consists in the preservation of certain themes in the proclamation, especially 'the hope of the manifestation of the Son of Man on his way to enthronement', and that it is this theme 'which sprang from the Easter experience and determined the Easter faith' that ensures the survival of Christian theology, and that this (rather than the 'apocalyptic' as he takes that term) in fact is 'the mother of all Christian theology'. With John and his school being the primary celebrants of the Easter experience and faith, the Gospel of John as a paschal gospel does not a fall into 'naïve doceticism' as Käsemann would have it, but, as we will see in Part II, it speaks of this apocalyptic event and what is established or constructed in it.

THE STRUCTURE AND FRAMEWORK OF APOCALYPTIC

Before we turn to Part II, however, it will be useful to examine more fully the spatio-temporal and epistemological axes of apocalyptic thought. Christopher Rowland suggests that the guidelines laid down in the Mishnah, *Hagigah* 2.1, indicate the broad scope of apocalypse:

> The forbidden degrees [i.e. Lev. 18:6ff.] may not be expounded before three persons, nor the story of creation [i.e. Gen. 1:1ff.] before two, nor [the chapter of] the chariot [i.e. Ezek. 1:4ff.] before one alone, unless he is a sage that understands his own knowledge. Whoever gives his mind to four things it were better for him if he had not come into the world: what is above? what is below? what was beforetime? and what will be hereafter?

[66] Hippolytus, *Antichr.* 61:... ὃν ἀεὶ τίκουσα ἡ ἐκκλησία διδάσκει πάντα τὰ ἔθνη.

Apocalyptic thought (in both the 'Eschatological Invasion' and the 'Unveiled Fulfilment' mode) is concerned with the beginning and the end, and with the realm above and that below, and, specifically, draws out correspondences between these dimensions, as in fact do almost all early Christian writings (Adam and Christ; 'on earth as it is in heaven', etc.). John Ashton helpfully explores the way in which the Gospels and the Fourth Gospel in particular, and, following Martyn and de Boer, we would add, the writings of Paul, deploy these correspondences in four key aspects: two of which are temporal—two ages (mystery) and two stages (dream or vision); and two of which are spatial—insiders/outsides (riddle) and above/below (correspondence). It will be beneficial to review some of Ashton's conclusions, drawing in insights also from J. Louis Martyn and others, before turning to the implications of this for reading the Gospel of John and Scripture more generally.

Mystery

The first aspect is that of 'mystery', a word which occurs extensively in the 'apocalyptic' writings (in Daniel, in the Qumran scrolls, in the Enochic material), and which is the very heart of apocalypse, dividing time into two ages: what was once a mystery, a hidden secret, has now been revealed.[67] And this is, of course, of structural importance for the very self-articulation of Christianity, perhaps nowhere more clearly than the concluding verses to Paul's letter to the Romans:

> Now to him who is able to strengthen you according to my gospel and the preaching of Jesus Christ, according to the apocalypse of the mystery which was kept secret for long ages but is now made manifest and made known through the prophetic writings [*κατὰ ἀποκάλυψιν μυστηρίου χρόνοις αἰωνίοις σεσιγημένου φανερωθέντος δὲ νῦν διά τε γραφῶν προφητικῶν … γνωρισθέντος*], according to the command of the eternal God, to all the nations, to bring about the obedience of faith—to the only wise God be glory for evermore. (Rom. 16:25–7)

The gospel is preached as a mystery, hidden throughout the ages in the writings of Scripture, but now apocalyptically revealed. The revelation of this mystery, this apocalypse, is nothing less than the turn of the ages, marking out two distinct eras, distinct not in content, but in terms of clarity: the revelation of what had been hidden. An essential difference between this mode of apocalypse (shared also by, for instance, the Qumran *Commentary on Habbakuk*), on the one hand, and the Enochic material, on the other hand, is that in the former there is no new revelation, but rather an exposition, or unveiling, of the real meaning of the ancient and authoritative Scriptures.

[67] See the comprehensive study of Benjamin L. Gladd, *Revealing the* Mysterion.

This imagery is developed most extensively in Ephesians: the mystery of the will of God from before the foundations of the world was to unite all things in Christ (cf. Eph. 1:1–10), to bring about one new human being instead of the two, 'reconciling us both to God in one body through the cross' (Eph. 2:15–16). This mystery, made known to Paul 'by an apocalypse', has now been 'apocalypsed' to all those who are fellow heirs, for this is the grace given to the apostle, 'to make all see what is the plan of the mystery hidden for the ages in God who created all things' (Eph. 3:1–10).

Most surprisingly, perhaps, it is equally present in Galatians (an epistle left aside by Käsemann, as not betraying any sense of an imminently impending Parousia). The letter begins with Paul speaking of Christ as having delivered us 'from the present evil age' (Gal. 1:4; a common theme in 'apocalyptic' writings), warning against angels from heaven (cf. Gal. 1:8; again, another common theme), before presenting his own credentials as one who was not taught by men, but 'through an apocalypse of Jesus Christ' (Gal. 1:12; cf. Apoc. 1:1), and who had been set apart before he was born, so that when God 'was pleased to apocalypse his Son to/in me' he might begin preaching among the Gentiles.[68] And the essence of the apostle's message is that he will not boast of anything 'apart from the cross of our Lord Jesus Christ, by which the cosmos has been crucified to me and I to the cosmos; for neither circumcision counts for anything, nor uncircumcision, but a new creation' (Gal. 6:14–15). As J. Louis Martyn has pointed out, in his profound exploration of the apocalyptic dimensions of Paul, the antinomies of the old creation (male/female, slave/free, Jew/Gentile—circumcised/uncircumcised) are now done away with, as belonging to a different era; with the revelation of Christ, the world is structured anew, indeed is a 'new creation', with its own antinomies—the Spirit and the flesh—resolved and brought together in Christ, the Church, and the Israel of God.[69]

Two Stages

This first aspect of apocalypse—the revelation of a hidden mystery—leads naturally into the second aspect, that the revelation itself creates two stages: in the first everything is obscure and in shadows, while in the second everything is now revealed. The classic image used to describe this, from Daniel to the Apocalypse, is the book being shut until the time is ready for it to be opened, to reveal its content, with the specification, in the Apocalypse, that the only one

[68] Gal. 1:16: *ἀποκαλύψαι τὸν υἱὸν ἐν ἐμοὶ*. On this passage, see de Boer, 'Paul, Theologian of God's Apocalypse', 30–2.

[69] J. Louis Martyn, 'Apocalyptic Antinomies'.

who has the authority to do so is the slain lamb (cf. Dan. 12:4; Apoc. 5:1–10). It becomes a matter of paramount importance, therefore, that the 'person' and the 'time' of the scriptural texts becomes clarified. The Ethiopian Eunuch, reading through Isaiah, did not approach Philip asking him to explain the 'meaning' of the text, as we do today, but rather inquired 'about whom does the prophet say this?' (Acts 8:34). Or as the First Epistle of Peter puts it:

> The prophets who prophesied of the grace that was to be yours searched and inquired about this salvation; they inquired what person or time [εἰς τίνα ἢ ποῖον καιρὸν] was indicated by the Spirit of Christ within them when predicting the sufferings of Christ and the subsequent glory. It was apocalypsed [ἀπεκαλύφθη] to them that they were serving not themselves but you, in the things which have now been announced to you [ἃ νῦν ἀνηγγέλη ὑμῖν] by those who preached the good news to you through the Holy Spirit sent from heaven, things into which angels long to look. (1 Pet. 1:10–12)

The Apocalypse is again made through the Scriptures, clarifying the person and time about which their predictions spoke, that is, about the Passion of Christ. Apocalypsed to the prophets, these things are now 'announced' to Christians by those who preach the gospel through the power of the Holy Spirit sent from heaven. As Ashton points out, 'the role assigned in apocalyptic literature to the *angelus interpres* is now assigned to the preachers of the gospel'.[70]

The term ἀναγγέλλειν functions in apocalyptic literature and elsewhere as a technical term meaning 'to expound', 'to explain', 'to interpret'.[71] Nebuchadnezzar's dreams are given an explanation by Daniel (τὴν σύγκρισιν ἀναγγέλλειν, Dan. Θ 2:4, 9, 16, 24). What the prophets spoke in veiled form is given an interpretation by the preachers of the gospel (cf. 1 Pet. 1:10–12). And most strikingly in the Gospel of John it is precisely the role of the Spirit to 'reveal' or 'interpret' the person of Christ himself and that which is to come: 'When the Spirit of truth comes, he will guide you into all the truth; for he will not speak on his own authority, but whatever he hears he will speak, and he will explain (ἀναγγελεῖ) to you the things that are to come. He will glorify me, for he will take what is mine and explain (ἀναγγελεῖ) to you. All that the Father has is mine; therefore I said that he will take what is mine and explain (ἀναγγελεῖ) to you' (John 16:13–15). If the preachers of the gospel seem to take the place of the *angelus interpres* in the usual apocalyptic narrative, it is in fact for John the Holy Spirit who is himself the true *angelus interpres*, the one by whom the evangelists speak.

[70] Ashton, *Fourth Gospel*, 317.

[71] On this term, see Catrin H. Williams, 'Unveiling Revelation: The Spirit-Paraclete and Apocalyptic Discourse in the Gospel of John', in Williams and Rowland, eds, *John's Gospel and Intimations of Apocalyptic*, 104–27, at 115–27.

Riddling Discourse and Messianic Secret

When we turn from the *proclamation* of the gospel, as an apocalyptic revelation of the hidden mystery and the inauguration of a new creation, to the *dramatic depiction* of the gospel in the narratives of the Gospels, we encounter a further utilization of a key element of apocalyptic, that of riddling discourse (*Rätselreden*). While the proclamation of the gospel, as in the concluding doxology of Romans, might seem to imply that the mystery is now clearly known to all (though Paul, of course, recognizes that there are those upon whom the veil of Moses remains; 2 Cor. 3:12–4:6), a common feature of Jewish apocalyptic literature is that the division between the wise and the foolish remains, even when the hidden mystery is revealed (cf. 4 Ezra 12:35–8). This division is reinscribed in the narratives of the Gospels. It is particularly clear in this passage from Mark:

> And he said to them, 'To you [those about him with the twelve] has been given the mystery [τὸ μυστήριον] of the kingdom of God, but for those outside everything is in parables [ἐν παραβολαῖς τὰ πάντα], so that they may indeed see but not perceive, and may indeed hear but not understand, lest they should turn again and be forgiven'. (Mark 4:11–12; cf. Isa. 6:9–10)

The parabolic sayings of Christ, his riddling discourse, divides human beings into two groups: the disciples, the insiders, to whom the 'mystery' of the kingdom has been given, and outsiders, to whom everything, the whole of created reality, is enigmatic. Even when the insiders occasionally fail to understand the parable, an interpretation is immediately given (e.g. Mark 7:14–23); the parable and explanation go together, as with Ezekiel (cf. Ezek. 17:1–21, esp. vv. 2 and 12).

In the Synoptics, nevertheless, the true identity of Christ remains hidden even to the disciples until after the Passion: it is the 'messianic secret' known to the Evangelist himself and also to readers of the Gospel, but not, importantly, to the disciples prior to the Passion.[72] Only through the Passion is the identity of Christ finally revealed: this is the defining, and definitive—'once for all'—event. In Mark, the culminating point is not the disciples' recognition, but the confession of the centurion at the foot of the cross, 'Truly this man was the Son

[72] Peter's confession in Matt. 16:16 is the exception which proves the rule: the identity of Christ is not known to Peter through 'flesh and blood', but 'apocalypsed' by the Father, and misunderstood by Peter, who is called 'Satan' by Christ for attempting to prevent Christ from going to Jerusalem to suffer (Matt. 16:17–23). The epochal study which shifted investigation into the 'messianic secret' from the horizon of Jesus' own psychology and personal development, to the evangelists' account of Christ is W. Wrede, *The Messianic Secret*, trans. J. C. G. Greig (Cambridge and London: James Clarke, 1971 [1901]), though see the insightful comments on Wrede and subsequent scholarship by H. Räisänen, *The 'Messianic Secret' in Mark's Gospel*, trans. C. Tuckett (Edinburgh: T & T Clark, 1990).

of God' (Mark 15:39); in the shorter ending of Mark, the disciples remain perplexed at the empty tomb, while the longer ending concludes with the appearance of the risen Christ to the disciples and his enthronement at the right hand of God. In Matthew and Luke, the disciples' encounter with the risen Lord is presented in a fuller fashion. Of particular importance is the manner in which the disciples come to recognize Christ on the road to Emmaus: he is known specifically as the Christ who must suffer these things to enter into his glory, an identity made known through the opening of the books, preparing their eyes to be opened in the breaking of the bread, to see Christ, who then disappears from physical sight ('no longer known according to the flesh', as Paul puts it) as soon as he is recognized.[73]

When we turn to the Gospel of John, however, things are quite different. As Ashton points out, while only one of Jesus' sayings is actually called a 'parable' (παροιμία rather than παραβολή, John 10:6, the parable of the Good Shepherd), his words continually perplex not only the outsiders but the insiders. In fact, the situation is the inverse of what we see in the Synoptics. In John, Christ asserts that 'I have spoken openly [ἐγὼ παρρησίᾳ λελάκηκα] to the world…I have said nothing in secret [ἐν κρυπτῷ]' (18:20). It is to the disciples, rather, that Christ speaks in figures and cryptically; when he finally says, in 16:25, 'I have said this to you in figures; the hour is coming when I shall no longer speak to you in figures but tell you plainly [οὐκέτι ἐν παροιμίαις…ἀλλὰ παρρησίᾳ] of the Father' (16:25), the disciples respond, 'Ah, now you are speaking plainly not in any figure!' (16:29). Yet they have in fact misunderstood once again: what Christ has just said in 16:28 he has already said in various ways earlier on and, indeed, just beforehand in 16:5; the openness or frankness (παρρησίᾳ) to which he refers in 16:25 still looks forward to 'the coming hour', to 'that day' (16:25, 26), that is, to his final departure and sending of the Spirit, the one who, in the role of the apocalyptic *angelus interpres*, will remind the disciples of Christ's truth and lead them into a full comprehension of this truth, the 'many things I have to tell you, but which you are not yet able to bear' (16:12).

This inversion is heightened by the fact that what is known to the disciples only at the end of the Synoptics, with the opening of the books, is apparently known to the disciples at the very beginning of John: already in the opening chapter, Philip tells Nathanael, 'We have found him of whom Moses in the law and also the prophets wrote, Jesus of Nazareth, the son of Joseph' (1:45). The question, already at the very outset of John, concerns the proper interpretation of the Scriptures which are thus already open; against those who understood the Scriptures to speak of Jesus, but only as the son of Joseph, Christ responds, and does so apocalyptically: 'You shall see greater things than these…you will

[73] Luke 24:13–35; 2 Cor. 5:16. On this see Jean-Luc Marion, 'They Recognized Him And He Became Invisible To Them', *Modern Theology* 18.2 (2002), 145–52.

see the heavens opened and the angels of God ascending and descending upon the Son of Man' (1:51).[74] The importance of correct scriptural interpretation regarding the Christ is reiterated throughout the Gospel of John. When the Spirit is finally bestowed, to 'bring to your remembrance all that I have said to you' (14:26), this is done precisely by remembering *what had been written*: the disciples did not, at the time, understand Jesus' action of entering Jerusalem upon an ass, 'but when Jesus was glorified, then they remembered that this had been written of him and done to him' (12:14–16; citing Zech. 9:9).[75] The coming of the Spirit corresponds with the departure of Christ, and as such his words, and Christ himself, cannot be understood until his glorification: 'for as yet there was no Spirit, because Jesus was not yet glorified'.[76]

Correspondence and Two-Level Drama

The effect of Christ's riddling discourse and the Messianic Secret, whereby the readers of the Gospel know, and therefore see, more than the disciples within the narrative, is to set up a two-level drama in a framework of correspondence. This is the final element of the apocalyptic genre mentioned above. It is found in most 'apocalyptic' literature, especially clearly in the 'Similitudes' of the Enochic material. Although there is some debate about how to translate the Hebrew, Aramaic, and Ethiopic terms, Ashton is probably right to suggest that 'correspondence' is the best rendering, not least because it brings out a further element of the riddling discourse of Christ: παραβολή literally means a 'juxtaposition', with a consequent 'comparison' or 'analogy', so entailing a 'correspondence'.[77] In the Enochic material, the term 'correspondence' is used to compare and liken things on earth and things in heaven, establishing connections between the realm above and the realm below (cf. esp. *1 Enoch* 43:4). Or, as it is put in the *Ascension of Isaiah*: 'as it is on high, so also is it on earth; what happens in the vault of heaven happens similarly here on earth'.[78] It is important to note, as Ashton points out, that 'for Enoch, and for apocalyptic writers generally, there are not two worlds but one: or rather the whole of reality is split into matching pairs (rather like the biological theory of DNA) in which one half, the lower, is the mirror image (albeit in this case a distorting

[74] Cf. Reynolds, *The Apocalyptic Son of Man*, 89–103.

[75] Cf. Birger Olsson, *Structure and Meaning in the Fourth Gospel: A Text-Linguistic Analysis of John 2:1–11 and 4:1–42*, Coniectanea Biblica, New Testament Studies 6 (Lund: Gleerup, 1974), 259–72.

[76] John 7:39: οὔπω γὰρ ἦν πνεῦμα, which, although unambiguous, is consistently mistranslated as 'for as yet the Spirit had not been given'.

[77] Ashton, *Fourth Gospel*, 325.

[78] *Ascension of Isaiah* 7:10, as ET R. H. Charles, rev. by J. M. T. Barton in H. F. D. Sparks, *Apocryphal Old Testament* (Oxford: Clarendon Press, 1984), 797.

mirror) of the higher. That is why a revelation of what is above is not just relevant or related to what happens or is about to happen on earth: rather what happens on earth is a re-enactment in earthly terms of what has happened in heaven: a correspondence!'[79]

In his investigation of the context of the relationship between the community around John and others, both the Jewish community and other Christian communities, J. Louis Martyn came to a very similar insight into the dynamics of what he calls the 'stereoptic vision' of John:

> John did not create the literary form of the two-level drama. It was at home in the thought-world of Jewish apocalypticism: the dicta most basic to the apocalyptic thinker are these: God created both heaven and earth. There are dramas taking place both on the heavenly stage and on the earthly stage. Yet these dramas are not really two, but rather one drama.... One might say that events on the heavenly stage not only correspond to events on the earthly stage, but also slightly precede them in time, leading them into existence, so to speak. What transpires on the heavenly stage is often called 'things to come'. For that reason events seen on the earthly stage are entirely enigmatic to the man who sees only the earthly stage. Stereoptic vision is necessary, and it is precisely stereoptic vision which causes a man to write an apocalypse: 'After this I looked, and lo, in heaven an *open door!* And the first voice, which I had heard... said, "Come up hither and I will show you what must take place after this".'[80]

In his analysis of how this stereoptic vision is enacted in the Gospel of John, Martyn points to three modifications from the correspondence found in apocalyptic literature. First, both levels of the drama are enacted on earth, between the life of Christ and the life of the Johannine community. Second, the temporal extension does not parallel the heavenly with the earthly, but, again, the two stages, or times, of Christ's own life and that of his body, the community. And third, 'John does not in any overt way indicate to his reader a distinction between the two stages'.[81] Although the application of this 'two-level drama' to a postulated parallel between the narrative of the Gospel itself and the development of the Johannine community has been called into question,[82] the characterization of apocalyptic literature in terms of a two-level drama needing 'stereoptic vision' is in fact remarkably helpful, and one to which we will return when discussing the figure of the Son of Man in Chapter 4.

Once we take seriously how an apocalyptic framework is essential to Christianity, as we have discussed above, we are forced to move beyond taking

[79] Ashton, *Fourth Gospel*, 327.

[80] Martyn, *History and Theology in the Fourth Gospel*, 130, quoting Apoc. 4:1, emphasis Martyn's.

[81] Martyn, *History and Theology*, 130–1.

[82] Cf. Tobias Hägerland, 'John's Gospel: A Two-Level Drama?', *JSNT* 25.3 (2003), 309–22.

the Gospels as primarily biographies or even 'kerygmatic biographies'. In the case of John, as we have seen, the Gospel explicitly deploys structural elements and themes from 'apocalyptic' writings. But rather than a human visionary or seer ascending into the heavens to be shown, by an *angelus interpres* who interprets for the mystic what he sees, what is to come, on earth as it is in heaven, in the Gospel of John the Son of Man, known from Daniel (and perhaps Enoch), arrives from the heavens, bringing the heavens down with him, uniting heaven and earth, to show what must be, and so establish the glory of God upon earth, returning to the heavens, with the promise to send the Holy Spirit, who, as the *angelus interpres*, reminds the disciples of what they saw, but did not in fact see, by showing how the formerly closed book speaks of the slain lamb who alone opens the book. And, as Ashton points out, 'when he returns, exalted (*ὑψοθείς*), to heaven—this is surely John's most remarkable conceit—he is stretched out on the cross'.[83]

THE APOCALYPTIC READING OF SCRIPTURE

If 'the apocalypse of the mystery kept secret for long ages is now made manifest and made known through the prophetic writings' (Rom. 16:25–6), then this 'apocalyptic' revelation of Christ in the gospel in turn opens up a new way of reading Scripture, which is, as we will see, taken to greater depths in the Gospel of John than in the Synoptics. In examining how this is so, we can also return to Wright's critique of Martyn noted earlier in this chapter.

Just as the work of Christ, and even Christ himself, was not understood till after the Passion, after which he is not known by the (veil of) flesh, so too Scripture was not and is not understood until it also is unveiled. These points, of course, have long been known and have been emphasized again by Richard Bauckham in his fine study on the nature of eyewitness testimony with an important nuance. As he writes:

> The memories of the passion and death of Jesus must have been the most obstinately meaningless and at the same time most unforgettable of the traditions [of Jesus' life and actions], even in the light of the resurrection. It took scriptural interpretation, which is now woven into the passion narratives, to make these memories even tolerable, but also unexpectedly full of inexhaustible meaning.[84]

It is, however, somewhat misleading to say 'even in the light of the resurrection', for a consistent feature, with one exception, of seeing the empty tomb or

[83] Ashton, *Fourth Gospel*, 328.

[84] Bauckham, *Jesus and the Eyewitnesses*, 353.

encountering the risen Christ is an initial lack of understanding or recognition.[85] Only of John, and only in the Gospel of John, is it said that, upon seeing the empty tomb, 'he saw and believed' (20:8).[86] John's unique status in this regard, as we saw in the last chapter, is tied to his being the only evangelist to have been present at, an eyewitness to, the crucifixion. So, as Bauckham comments, 'whereas scholars have often supposed that this Gospel could not have been written by an eyewitness because of its high degree of interpretation of the events and words of Jesus, by contrast with the Synoptics, in fact the high degree of interpretation is appropriate precisely because this is the only one of the canonical Gospels that claims eyewitness status'.[87] And so, John's unique claim to be an eyewitness of the Passion—the apocalyptic moment par excellence, the 'Apocalypse of God' as de Boer put it—is inseparable from his deeper interpretation of Scripture.

That it is only by the interpretation of Scripture that, from the beginning, the gospel is proclaimed is so important that, in one of the earliest proclamations that we have, Paul appeals to it twice in one sentence: 'I delivered to you, as of first importance, what I also received, that Christ died in accordance with the Scriptures, that he was buried and rose on the third day in accordance with the Scriptures' (1 Cor. 15:3–4). This appeal remains fundamental even in the creeds of later centuries; when the creed of Nicaea specifies that Christ 'rose in accordance with the Scripture', it is to the same 'Old Testament', not the Gospels, that reference is made. The only other occasion where Paul appeals to what he has received and now delivers or 'traditions', is the celebration of the Lord's meal, where he specifies that what he 'traditions' is what he received from the Lord himself (1 Cor. 11:23). Luke, the disciple of Paul, brings these together in his account of the encounter with the risen Lord on the road to Emmaus. It is only when Christ 'interpreted to them in all the

[85] Similar ambiguities occur elsewhere in Bauckham's work. For instance, he rightly notes that: 'Those who deny that "we" in "we have seen his glory" (1:14) are the eyewitnesses correctly point out that to "see his glory" cannot refer merely to the sight of Jesus with the physical eyes that all who came into contact with Jesus had'. But then he immediately continues: 'However, this does not mean that it has no relationship to such empirical contact with Jesus. The preceding context of this statement reads: "The Word became flesh and lived among us..." Whether the "us" in this case are humanity in general or the eyewitnesses in particular, there is undoubted reference here to the physical presence of the Word in the midst of physical humanity. In this context, to "see his glory" must surely be to recognize his divine glory *in his physical presence*'. (Ibid. 404, his emphasis). Likewise for John 2:11: 'The glory was revealed—and therefore seen—then and there, in a named place where something happened' (Ibid. 405). It certainly does have connection with the physical seeing of his physical presence, but it is also inseparably connected, as we will see, with the proper interpretation, through the opening of the Scriptures, of what was, but is no longer, seen.

[86] With regard to encountering the risen Christ, in 21:7, it is certainly the disciple whom Jesus loved, not Peter, who first recognizes him: 'It is the Lord!' But this only occurs after Christ directs them to cast the fishing net into the waters again, for it to be filled with such a quantity that they could not haul it in. Prior to this, 'the disciples did not know that it was Jesus' (21:4).

[87] Ibid. 411.

Scriptures the things concerning himself', specifically that 'Moses and all the prophets' had spoken of how 'it was necessary that the Christ should suffer these things and enter into his glory', that the disciples' hearts were set on fire, so that they were able to recognize him 'in the breaking of bread' (Luke 24:25–35). The books were closed, that is, with a 'veil' lying over them, as Moses had placed it upon himself (2 Cor. 3:12–18), so that their content was not yet known, even if they had been repeatedly read, until Christ himself opens them to show how they had always spoken about him and his Passion. A new way of reading Scripture is now required.

We have already seen something of this new way of reading Scripture in the previous section of this chapter, and in the first section in the case of Origen. It is a practice that is all but ubiquitous in early Christianity, and occasionally, as with Origen, reflected upon directly. Another example of such reflection is given by Irenaeus.[88] Christ, he says, is the treasure hidden in the Scriptures in the field of the world (cf. Matt. 13:38, 44), 'indicated by means of types and parables, which could not be understood by human beings prior to the consummation of those things which had been predicted, that is, the advent of the Lord'. For this reason, he continues, it was said to Daniel the prophet: 'Shut up the words and seal the book, until the time of the consummation, until many learn and knowledge abounds. For, when the dispersion shall be accomplished, they shall know all these things' (Dan. 12:4, 7); and likewise by Jeremiah: 'In the last days they shall understand these things' (Jer. 23:20). So, Irenaeus continues:

> For every prophecy, before its fulfilment, is nothing but an enigma and ambiguity to human beings; but when the time has arrived, and the prediction has come to pass, then it has an exact exposition [ἐξήγησις]. And for this reason, when at this present time the Law is read by the Jews, it is like a myth, for they do not possess the explanation [ἐξήγησις] of all things which pertain to the human advent of the Son of God; but when it is read by Christians, it is a treasure, hidden in a field, but brought to light by the cross of Christ. (*haer.* 4.26.1)

When read in this apocalyptic fashion, with the book being opened at the time of consummation, in the last days, and the treasure it contains, Christ himself, being revealed by the cross, the reading of Scripture 'in this way', Irenaeus concludes, glorifies the reader 'to such an extent, that others will not be able to behold his glorious countenance' (cf. Exod. 34:30–3; 2 Cor. 3:7–18). The books are sealed, and what they speak about, the treasure they contain, cannot be understood until they are opened by the cross; if they are not read in this apocalyptic manner, they will be read as nothing more than myths and fables (even if they are historically true). What the books contain cannot be

[88] *haer.* 4.26.1. For a full exposition of Irenaeus' understanding of the relationship between Scripture and gospel, see Behr, *Irenaeus of Lyons*, 128–40.

understood until the last days, when the time of their accomplishment has arrived and the book is unsealed. And now unveiled, those who read the same Scriptures through a proper exegesis are themselves transfigured, to become like Moses in his descent from the mountain after his encounter with God, themselves shining with the glory of God.

That the Scriptures are unveiled by the cross has significant implications for how early Christians read and understood the Scriptures themselves. Scripture read in this way is, to use Irenaeus' image, like a mosaic depicting the face of the king, which the heretics have rearranged to form the image of a dog or fox (*haer.* 1.8.1). Scripture is a 'thesaurus', a treasury of precious stones, the images and words used to proclaim Christ in the gospel. In recent times, Joel Marcus, drawing from E. Gässer, has used a similar analogy, that of a 'paint-box' used by the evangelists in their depiction of Christ.[89] Richard Hays comes to very much the same conclusion in reflecting on Paul's words in 2 Cor. 3:12–4:6, regarding the unveiling of Moses, now a text, for those who turn to the Lord to see the light of the gospel of the glory of Christ. In Hays' words, this means that 'Scripture becomes—in Paul's reading—a metaphor, a vast trope that signifies and illuminates the gospel of Jesus Christ'.[90] This is not to imply that the gospel itself is, as Ricœur claimed, simply 'the rereading of an ancient Scripture'.[91] The proclamation of the death and resurrection of Christ is not straightforwardly derivable from Scripture; rather, the death and resurrection of Christ acts as a catalyst. Because God has acted in Christ in a definitive, and unexpected, manner, making everything new, Scripture itself must be read anew. The 'word of the cross', the preaching of 'Christ crucified', may be a scandal for the Jews and folly for the Gentiles, but it alone is the 'power of God' making known 'the wisdom of God' (1 Cor. 1:18–25). This preaching, the *kerygma*, provides what we have already seen Hays describe as 'the eschatological *apokalypsis* of the cross', a hermeneutical lens, through which Scripture can now be refracted with 'a profound new symbolic coherence'.[92]

This is a very different way of reading Scripture than has become customary over recent centuries, when theological reflection, both scriptural exegesis and systematic exposition, has worked in a historical key, rather than within an apocalyptic framework. The primary horizon has been that of *Heilsgeschichte*, a 'salvation history' that moves from the narratives of the Old Testament to those of the New Testament, where Gospels are primarily read as biographies

[89] Joel Marcus, *The Way of the Lord: Christological Exegesis of the Old Testament in the Gospel of Mark* (London: T & T Clark, 1992), 2.

[90] Richard Hays, *Echoes of Scripture*, 149.

[91] Paul Ricœur, *Essays on Biblical Interpretation* (Philadelphia: Fortress Press, 1980), 51. See the comments by James Barr, *Holy Scripture: Canon, Authority, Criticism* (Philadelphia: Westminster Press, 1983), 70.

[92] Hays, *Echoes*, 169.

of Jesus followed by the acts of the apostles and their epistles, and perhaps, to conclude, Revelation. In this overarching narrative, one begins with God and his act of creation; the falling away of human beings; and then the long, slow, and patient work of God through the messiness of human history, in a gradually unfolding plan, preparing the way for the advent of Christ, the Incarnation of the Word, whose life is narrated in the Gospels. It is precisely within this kind of continuous narrative, rather than as Martyn's 'vertical invasion', that Wright insists a proper understanding of ('unveiled fulfillment') 'apocalyptic' must be situated. While insisting, as we have seen, that he does not mean some kind of 'smooth evolutionary progress', it is nevertheless a narrative that moves forward. As he writes:

> In one text after another within the broadly 'apocalyptic' world to which Martyn appeals as his history-of-religion matrix there is hardly anything more common than *retellings of the story of Israel.* In fact, one of the central and regular characteristics of actual second-Temple Jewish 'apocalyptic' literature is *a long narrative in search of a resolution, a conclusion.* Often, as with Jubilees and similar writings, this narrative runs from creation to Abraham to Moses, pointing on through the exile to the writer's own day, looking for resolution or conclusion in the immediate future.[93]

The difference, clearly, is that in the proclamation of the gospel the definitive resolution is now seen to be Christ. Wright of course recognizes this:

> Paul really was an 'apocalyptic' theologian, who believed that God had done a radical new thing, a fresh gift of grace, in the sending and the dying and the rising of Jesus the Messiah, and that he had indeed thereby liberated Israel from its plight and the world from the powers of evil.[94]

'But this', Wright adds, 'Paul argues again and again, was the original purpose of the divine covenant with Israel'. That is indeed the claim of the gospel, but it is nevertheless equally true that it is something that no one, not even Paul, was expecting until after the apocalypse itself. And it certainly leads to a 'retelling of the story of Israel', and one so radically different that it led to a parting of the ways.

Martyn's point, however, is not that, as Wright put it, 'everything that has gone before is dust and ashes, a misleading waste of time'.[95] It is rather that the link between the Scriptures and the gospel is *not* understood as a linear movement *from* the Scriptures *to* the gospel, but rather the other way round. As Martyn states:

[93] Wright, *Paul and His Recent Interpreters*, 180, his emphasis. See now, Samuel V. Adams, *The Reality of God and Historical Method: Apocalyptic Conversations in Conversation with N.T. Wright* (Downers Grove, IL: IVP Academic, 2015).

[94] Wright, *Paul and His Recent Interpreters*, 186. [95] Ibid. 180.

> the fundamental arrow in the link joining scripture and gospel points from the gospel story to scripture and not from scripture to the gospel story. In a word, with Jesus' glorification, belief in Scripture *comes into being*, by acquiring an indelible link to belief in Jesus' words and deeds.... we have simply to note in the Gospel of John the absence of a linear sacred history that flows out of Scripture into the gospel story. Indeed the redemptive-historical perspective is more than absent; it is a perspective against which John is waging a battle.[96]

Martyn makes a similar point for Paul: 'Paul did not make his way *from* Isaiah's words about God destroying the discernment of the discerning *to* the foolish word of the crucified Messiah. His hermeneutic worked exactly the other way around, from the previously unknown and foolish gospel of the cross to the previously known and previously misunderstood scripture'.[97] What brought Paul to be a zealous apostle of the gospel was not his former studies of the Scripture, but rather the event in which God revealed (or 'apocalypsed') his Son to Paul, or rather, 'in' him (Gal. 2:16). It is, according to Martyn, Paul's opponents in Galatia, the 'teachers', who, as with John's opponents, moved from the Law to the gospel (in the manner of our 'salvation history') rather than from the gospel to the Scriptures in an apocalyptic unveiling of previously unknown depths.[98]

Moreover, as Martyn puts it, it is with the Passion that that 'belief in Scripture *comes into being*', or, to put it even more forcefully, that these writings are constituted *as Scripture*. James Kugel makes a similar point when he identifies 'four assumptions about Scripture that characterize all ancient biblical interpretation'.[99] The first is that Scripture is 'a fundamentally cryptic text': if it were not cryptic, requiring to be opened or unveiled, it would not be Scripture. The second point is that it is 'a fundamentally *relevant* text'. Scripture is not written simply to inform us about events that happened in the past, but rather written for us, now: as the apostle put it, 'now these things [i.e. what happened in the desert] happened to them as a type [τυπικῶς], but they were written down for our instruction upon whom the end of the ages has come' (1 Cor. 10:11, obscured by the RSV by translating τυπικῶς by 'as a warning'), or as Christ in the Gospel of John says, Moses 'wrote of me' (5:46). The third assumption is that 'Scripture is perfect and perfectly harmonious'. If it is cryptic, but opened in the last times, then it is found to speak of the one who opens the books: 'beginning with Moses and all the prophets [Christ] interpreted to them in all the Scriptures the things concerning himself' (Luke 24:27). Kugel's fourth assumption is that Scripture 'is somehow divinely sanctioned, of divine provenance, or divinely inspired'. Kugel makes the

[96] J. Louis Martyn, 'John and Paul on the Subject of Gospel and Scripture', 216–17, his emphasis.

[97] Ibid. 221, his emphasis.

[98] Martyn, *Galatians*, 117–26, #7, 'The Teachers'.

[99] Kugel, *Traditions of the Bible*, 15, and 15–19 for what follows.

important point that it 'would be a mistake, in my view, to assume that this fourth assumption stands behind the other three', if for no other reason than that the belief in the divine inspiration of the whole of Scripture appears to have developed later than the other three assumptions. More directly to our point would be that, as we have seen, the divinely inspired content of Scripture is not known until the books are opened by the cross of Christ, and so their 'inspiration' cannot be separated from the act of opening nor, for that matter, from the inspired reading: the 'inspired' writing of Scripture cannot be separated from the 'inspired' reading, and both, together, turn upon the act of opening the Scriptures by the one of whom they speak, or, in reverse, the one who speaks in them. It is only when read 'in this way', as Irenaeus puts it, that what we are reading is in fact *Scripture*; if it is not read through the cross, we are only reading 'myths', as Irenaeus put it, even if historically true.

However, Martyn is not quite right when he asserts that: 'When the emerging great church identified Marcion's theology as heretical, it did so, in part, by adopting a view of the relationship between scripture and gospel that, in general terms, looks rather similar to the view of the simple exegetical theologians against whom Paul and John struggled in the first century (see Justin Martyr; Rhodo; Irenaeus)'.[100] Irenaeus did not understand the 'economy' of God as our modern 'salvation history', but, as we have seen, understood the 'economy' more in terms of an 'arrangement', such as the way the tiles in a mosaic are arranged to depict Christ, so that Scripture, from beginning to end, speaks of Christ, whose face is discerned in Scripture when the books are opened at the end by the right key, the cross, to reveal the beginning, Christ. The gospel is not simply the culminating point of a 'salvation history', as Wright would seem to want, but neither is it a proclamation separable from Scripture, as Martyn might seem to imply, in an almost 'Marcionite' fashion.[101] There is indeed a 'vertical invasion': while for Paul the gospel 'came through an apocalypse of Jesus Christ', rather than by teaching or from a human being (Gal. 1:12), for John it is Christ himself who is 'from above' (3:31; 8:23). But both aspects of this 'invasion from above' are inseparable from the apocalyptic unveiling of Scripture, through which Scripture provides the words and images in and by which, from the beginning, the gospel is proclaimed and Christ revealed. In this light, we can indeed read the narrative of Scripture as 'salvation history', but the starting point for that narrative is in fact the end, Christ and his cross.

[100] Martyn, 'John and Paul', 225.

[101] So Wright, *Paul and His Recent Interpreters*, 177: 'What Martyn has done, I think, is to invent a theology for "the Teachers" which includes a significant element in Paul's own theology, forcing him to take a razor-blade to passages which are actually tightly integrated'. Marcion is not mentioned by name, but the allusion is clearly there.

There is one further point to be drawn from this relationship between the cross and Scripture, and that is the third, epistemological, axis of 'apocalyptic' demarcated by Blackwell, Goodrich, and Maston as mentioned earlier. This is, as we have seen in Irenaeus (*haer.* 4.26.1), that it is specifically the cross of Christ that constitutes the focal point for the revelation of the mystery and for the turning of the ages. Martyn further expounds this by reference to the new creation in Christ spoken of in 2 Cor. 5:16–17:

> From now on, therefore, we regard no one from a human point of view [κατὰ σάρκα]; even though we once knew Christ from a human point of view [κατὰ σάρκα], we no longer know him that way. So, if anyone is in Christ, he is a new creation: the old has passed away, behold, the new has come.

To know 'according to the flesh' is to know on the basis of sense perception, in the realm of the old, now passed, age. But, in contrast to this, and especially striking given his words in 1 Cor. 2:6–16, Paul does not appeal instead to a 'spiritual perception': it is his opponents, Martyn concludes, the spiritual enthusiasts in Corinth, who were doing this, claiming to have seen God, perhaps even face to face. Paul had resorted to such an appeal in his first letter to the Corinthians, but now realized that he could not do so again. He appeals to the new creation, yet, as Martyn points out, 'he is careful . . . to imply that the opposite of the old-age way of knowing is not that of the new age—this point must be emphasized—but rather the way of knowing which is granted at the juncture of the ages'.[102] He does not speak of seeing the face of God, nor of knowing by the Spirit, for he, as everyone else, does not yet live in the new age. As Martyn puts it, 'the implied opposite of knowing by the norm of the flesh is not knowing by the norm of the Spirit, but rather knowing *kata stauron* ("by the cross")'.[103] Until we are, in actuality, raised with Christ in the new age, 'knowing by the Spirit can occur only in the form of knowing by the power of the cross. For until the parousia, the cross is and remains the epistemological crisis, and thus the norm by which one knows that the Spirit is none other than the Spirit of the crucified Christ. . . . The cross is the epistemological crisis for the simple reason that while it is in one sense followed by the resurrection, it is not replaced by the resurrection'.[104] The old has indeed passed away, and the new has indeed come, but this is only seen through the faith, the new eyes, of those standing at the juncture of the ages. A new community is being formed, not by knowledge but by active love, as the body of Christ. '*Christ* defines the difference between the two ways of knowing, doing that precisely in his cross'.[105]

[102] J. Louis Martyn, 'Epistemology at the Turn of the Ages', 107.
[103] Martyn, 'Epistemology', 108.
[104] Martyn, 'Epistemology', 108–9.
[105] Martyn, 'Epistemology', 110.

A great deal of excellent scholarly work has been carried out over the past decades regarding the use of Scripture in the Gospels and the interpretation of Scripture in early Christianity. In this a more sophisticated and adequate understanding has been advanced of the various reading strategies or moves deployed, such as allegory, typology, anagogy, and so on.[106] At the most fundamental level, however, these are all variations within what can be called an 'apocalyptic' reading: both Jesus of Nazareth, whom we thought we knew, and the meaning of Scriptures, which we thought we understood, turn out to be other than what we had thought, when the veil is lifted and the glory of Christ shines in Scripture through the cross, so revealing his true and eternal identity. As Gregory of Nyssa put it: 'One may wish to refer to the anagogical interpretation of such sayings as "tropology" or "allegory" or by some other name. We shall not quarrel about the name so long as a firm grasp is kept on thoughts that edify'.[107] What is important is not to define the right method or strategy for reading these texts, but that they are read *as Scripture*, that is, within an apocalyptic framework pivoted upon the cross.

It is exactly at this point that the Gospel of John goes further than the first three Gospels. This progression is captured well by Joel Marcus. He reiterates the point that we have already seen: 'New Testament interpretation of the Old Testament has a Christological starting point. The Old Testament is not read in the New Testament in a straight-line continuum from unambiguous expectation to irrefragable fulfilment. Rather, the entire Old Testament is reread through the lens of the crucified Messiah'. But he then adds the important nuance that this too is not a unidirectional exploitation of Scripture, but a process in which the Evangelist also deepened his understanding of Christ: 'The movement of thought, then, is not *exclusively* from Christ to the Scripture but also from the Scripture christologically construed to a deeper understanding of the events surrounding Christ'.[108] This deepening of the understanding of Scripture and the events concerning Christ is precisely the movement from the Synoptics to the Gospel of the Theologian. Whereas in the Synoptics the disciples are not presented as understanding Christ on the basis of Scripture until after the Passion (the road to Emmaus in Luke 24 being the classic text), the Gospel of John, after the Prologue which we shall examine in Chapter 5, begins at this very point: the Baptist identifies him as 'the Lamb of God' (1:36; cf. Isa. 53:7; Jer. 11:19), and Philip tells Nathanael, 'We have found him of whom Moses in the law and also the prophets wrote, Jesus of Nazareth, the son of Joseph' (1:45). Yet, although it is by reference to the

[106] The literature for this is vast. A good starting place is Young, *Biblical Exegesis and the Formation of Christian Culture.*

[107] Gregory of Nyssa, *Hom. Songs*, Pref. (ed. Norris, 2–5). On this passage of Gregory, and the appeal to what edifies, see Margaret M. Mitchell, *Paul, the Corinthians, and the Birth of Christian Hermeneutics* (Cambridge: Cambridge University Press, 2010), 1–5.

[108] Marcus, *The Way of the Lord*, 108.

Scriptures that Philip identifies Jesus, that he does so as 'the son of Joseph' indicates that he has not yet fully grasped his true identity. After a brief conversation with Jesus, Nathanael then address him, alluding to the title of the crucified one: 'Rabbi, you are the Son of God! You are the King of Israel!'[109] Yet even this is not enough: 'Truly, truly, I say to you, you will see the heaven opened and the angels of God ascending and descending upon the Son of Man' (1:51), though this vision is still located for the disciples in the future when, again, after the Passion and the bestowal of the Spirit they can remember all that had been written about him.

But it is this exalted vision of Christ that John depicts for his readers thereafter on the pages of his Gospel, in a manner indeed very different than the other Gospels. There is no event of transfiguration, for instance, for on every page we see the transfigured Lord: the one 'from above' (3:31; 8:23); the one who is not put to death but rather lays down his life, of his own accord (10:15–18), at the right time (cf. 2:4); the one who does not pray that the cup should pass yet reconciles himself to the Father's will (cf. Matt. 26:39; Mark 14:36; Luke 22:42), but instead asserts: 'What shall I say? "Father save me from this hour"? No, for this purpose I have come to this hour' (12:27). While we hear in the other Gospels that at the crucifixion the curtain of the Temple was rent in two (Matt 27:51; Mark 15:38; Luke 23:45), this is not mentioned in the Gospel of John, for at this point (even if the gospel is still, as a narrative, veiled) we hear the crucified one crying out not, 'My God, my God, why have you forsaken me?' (Matt. 27:46; Mark 15:34), but, rather, with stately majesty, affirming, 'It is finished' and handing over the Spirit (19:30), the one whom he promised to send, to guide his disciples 'into all the truth, ... he will take what is mine and declare it to you' (16:13–14). What it is that is 'finished' when Scripture is read, as Hays put it, with 'the profound new symbolic coherence' as provided by the 'eschatological *apokalypsis* of the cross', is, as we have already indicated, the judgement of the world, the construction of the Temple, and the perfection of the human being in the image of God, and it is to these latter two that we now turn in Part II.

[109] John 1:49; 'The king of the Jews' is inscription upon the cross in all four Gospels (Matt. 27:37; Mark 15:26; Luke 23:38; John 19:19), and 'Son of God' is the words of the centurion at the foot of the cross in Mark (15:39).

Part II

‘It Is Finished’

According to John, Christ's last utterance from the cross was the single word τετέλεσται (19:30). Usually translated as 'it is finished', this might be taken as meaning that the life of Christ has come to an end. This sense is reinforced by the regular mistranslation of the following clause, 'and he bowed his head and gave up his spirit' (RSV), for the second (and the first) 'his' does not occur in the Greek, παρέδωκεν τὸ πνεῦμα, but a definite article, and the Greek word translated as 'gave up' really means to 'hand over'.[1] Christ's final word, τετέλεσται, has more the sense of 'it has been completed' or 'it has been perfected'. In the Gospel of John, Christ has of course come to do the Father's will, all that the Father has 'given' or 'shown' to the Son (cf. 5:20; 13:3; 15:15; 17:7). Yet, as Bultmann argues, τετέλεσται is most closely related not to Luke 18:31, where Christ prospectively tells his disciples that he is going to Jerusalem where 'everything written of the Son of Man by the prophets will be accomplished [τελεσθήσεται]', but to Revelation 10:7, where it is said that in the days when the seventh angel sounds his trumpet, 'the mystery of God as announced to his servants the prophets would be completed [ἐτελέσθη]'.[2] The work of Christ completed upon the cross is not simply a specific or particular task among others (for instance, atonement as distinct to incarnation, or salvation

[1] In modern interpretation, it appears to be Hoskyns (*Fourth Gospel*, 532) who first takes 19:30 as Jesus 'handing over the Spirit' to those at the foot of the cross. See Peter-Ben Smit, 'The Gift of the Spirit in John 19:30? A reconsideration of παρέδωκεν τὸ πνεῦμα', *CBQ* 78.3 (2016), 447–62. The objection is often made that it is only later, in 20:22, that the Spirit is in fact given. However, this is to overlook, first, that in 20:22 the emphasis is on the disciples *receiving* the Spirit, and, second, the unity of the paschal event that we have explored in the preceding chapters, which must nevertheless be narratively told, yet remain a unity even when doing so; as Ashton *Fourth Gospel*, 348, puts it: 'the expression παραδιδόναι τὸ πνεῦμα allows him to fuse Easter and Pentecost as well, hinting that there is no need to think of the latter as a distinct and separate event'.

[2] Rudolf Bultmann, *The Gospel of John: A Commentary*, trans. George R. Beasley-Murra et al. (Philadelphia: Westminster Press, 1971 [1964]), 673–4, n. 6.

as distinct to creation); it is *the very mystery of God* that is now 'completed' or 'perfected', revealed, as we have seen, in the apocalyptic opening of the Scriptures through the Passion, in 'the Apocalypse of God' as de Boer puts it. And at this point Christ hands over the Spirit to 'the mother' (19:26; again, there is no 'his') and the beloved disciple standing at the foot of the cross, the Spirit who 'was not' until Christ is glorified (7:39, which is also regularly mistranslated as 'not yet given'), but now leads his disciples 'into all truth' (16:13).

In Part I our investigation was carried out primarily in a historical key, as we explored the memory of John, as the disciple of the Lord and high priest of the paschal mystery standing at the foot of the cross, the character of his Gospel as a paschal gospel, and its relation to the Apocalypse and apocalyptic literature. In this second part, we turn to an exegetical approach, to explore two key themes relating to incarnation, embodiment, flesh, and revelation, that are 'completed' at the cross as presented by the Gospel of John: the Temple, and the living human being, the glory of God.[3] We will then conclude Part II by examining the Prologue.

[3] Another key theme that is completed at the cross, and which also structures the narrative of the Gospel, is the cosmic trial and judgement. See Andrew Lincoln, *Truth on Trial: The Lawsuite Motif in the Fourth Gospel* (Peabody, MA: Hendrickson, 2000); and more briefly, John Behr, 'John 18:28–19:16: Witnessing Truth', in Chad Raith II, ed., *The Gospel of John: Theological-Ecumenical Readings* (Eugene, OR: Cascade, 2017), 178–91. See also Judith L. Kovacs, '"Now Shall the Ruler of This World be Driven Out": Jesus' Death as Cosmic Battle in John 12:20–36', *JBL* 114.2 (1995), 227–47.

3

'The Temple of His Body'

Unlike the Synoptics, John plots his narrative in a framework measured by the feasts celebrated in the Temple.[1] In contrast to the Synoptic Gospels, which only mention the Passover, as the setting for Christ's Passion (Luke also mentions early on that Jesus' parents went to Jerusalem every year for the Passover),[2] John indicates no less than six different feasts during the course of Christ's life.[3] First, 'the Passover of the Jews' which is 'at hand' so that 'Jesus went up to Jerusalem' (2:13, 23). Second, 'a feast of the Jews', when again 'Jesus went up to Jerusalem' (5:1); this is the only use of the term 'feast' without a definite article and no other indication as to which feast it was, though the healing of the man by the pool with five porticoes took place on the Sabbath (5:9). Third, a second mention of 'the Passover, the feast of the Jews' being 'at hand' (6:4); this time Jesus does not go to Jerusalem but is beside the Sea of Galilee and crosses over to Capernaum in the evening (6:1, 16–17). Fourth, 'the feast of the Jews, the Tabernacles' (7:2), when Jesus went up to Jerusalem 'not publicly but in private' (7:10); there follows references to 'the middle of the feast' (7:14) and 'the last day of the feast, the great day' (7:37). Apart from the healing of the blind man on the Sabbath (9:14), there is no further indication of time till 10:22, 'the feast of the Dedication in Jerusalem', the fifth feast to be mentioned, during which 'Jesus was walking in the Temple, in the portico of Solomon' (10:23). After this feast, Jesus returned to the place where he first began his ministry (10:40; cf. 1:28), never to return to the

[1] On the theme of the Temple and its feasts in the Gospel of John, see esp. Mary L. Coloe, *God Dwells with Us: Temple Symbolism in the Fourth Gospel* (Collegeville, MN: Liturgical Press, 2001); Alan R. Kerr, *The Temple of Jesus' Body: The Temple Theme in the Gospel of John*, JSNTSup 220 (London: Sheffield Academic Press, 2002); Paul M. Hoskins, *Jesus as the Fulfillment of the Temple in the Gospel of John*, Paternoster Biblical Monographs (Eugene, OR: Wipf and Stock, 2006); Michael A. Daise, *Feasts in John: Jewish Festivals and Jesus' 'Hour' in the Fourth Gospel*, WUNT 2.229 (Tübingen: Mohr Siebeck, 2007); Margaret Barker, *King of the Jews: Temple Theology in John's Gospel* (London: SPCK, 2014).

[2] Matt. 26:2, 5, 17–19; 27:15; Mark 14:1, 2, 12–16; 15:6; Luke 2:41, 43; 22:1, 7–15.

[3] Cf. Maarten J. J. Menken, 'Jewish Feasts in the Gospel of John', in Menken, *Studies in John's Gospel and Epistles: Collected Essays*, Contributions to Biblical Exegesis and Theology, 77 (Leuven: Peeters, 2015), 187–207.

Temple again. Then, finally, the sixth feast to be mentioned is the third and final Passover, which 'was near' (11:55), is 'six days' away (12:1), is the point 'before' which Jesus eats with his disciples, speaks with them and prays to the Father, knowing that 'his hour had come to depart out of this world to the Father' (13:1), and then, at 'the day of Preparation for the Passover, about the sixth hour', he is crucified (19:14, cf. 19:31). After these six temporal and festal indicators, there then comes, as seventh, the temporal markers of his appearance to Mary Magdalene 'on the first day of the week' (20:1), to the disciples, without Thomas, 'on the evening of that day' (20:19), and again 'eight days later' (20:26) to the disciples with Thomas. Six feasts, for four of which Jesus is in the Temple, culminating in his crucifixion on the day of Preparation, followed by a new beginning with the risen Christ on the first and eighth days—John has clearly arranged his presentation of Christ in a highly sophisticated manner.

Moreover, five of these six feasts are also connected with actions and words that identify Christ as the Temple and the fulfilment of the feasts celebrated therein. The first mention of Passover is the setting for Christ to speak about the Temple that he would raise up three days after its destruction, speaking of course about his own body (2:13–25). The second mention of Passover (6:4) leads into a discussion, on the following day, about the bread of life that descends from heaven and is in fact his flesh (6:22–71). On the last day of the Feast of Tabernacles, Christ identifies himself as the living water (7:37–8) and, early on the following morning, as 'the light of the world' (8:12), key themes for this feast. At the Feast of the Dedication, it is Christ, not the Temple, who is 'consecrated' by the Father (10:36). And at the Passion itself, Christ is, finally, presented as the Temple. Moreover, as Mary Coloe points out, the sequence from 5:1, when Jesus went to Jerusalem, to his final departure from the Temple in 10:40 (with the 'porticoes' mentioned in each place forming an *inclusio*) begins with the weekly Sabbath and then proceeds through the liturgical year: Passover in the first month, Tabernacles in the seventh, and Dedication in the ninth. There is no need to rearrange the material, as Bultmann and others since have suggested, in an attempt to smooth out Jesus' geographical itinerary; the sequence is that of the liturgy of the Temple.[4] What is announced in 2:13–25 is completed, through the course of the liturgical year, at the Passion, when he bestows the Spirit upon the mother and identifies himself with the disciple standing unashamed at the foot of the cross (19:26–7, 30) and then shows himself to his disciples on the first and eighth day, fulfilling his promise that he and his Father will make their 'home' in those who love him (14:23).

[4] Coloe, *God Dwells with Us*, 118–19. Bultmann, *John*, 209–10, suggested that the original order of the chapters was 4, 6, 5, 7, to account for the fact that in 4:54 Jesus is in Galilee, and in 6:1 he crosses over to the other side of the sea of Galilee, with no mention of a return trip from Jerusalem, where he is in 5.

JOHN 1:14

Intimations that Christ himself is the new and true Temple of God are already given in the Prologue to the Gospel.[5] The key verse here is John 1:14: 'And the Word became flesh and dwelt among us, full of grace and truth; we have beheld his glory, glory as of the only-begotten of the Father'. The word 'dwelt', *ἐσκήνωσεν*, is used in the New Testament only here and in Revelation, while the corresponding nouns, *σκῆνος* and *σκήνωμα*, 'tent', are used to describe the human body.[6] The word itself, having the same root consonants as the Hebrew term for 'tent' or 'tabernacle' (*skn*), and the connection with beholding the 'glory' of God evokes 'the tent of meeting' or 'the tent of witness' (regularly translated as *ἡ σκηνὴ τοῦ μαρτυρίου* in the LXX) in which the glory of God dwelt.[7] Although 'the glory of the Lord' had already appeared in the pillar of cloud and the pillar of fire guiding Israel towards the promised land (Exod. 13:21–2; 16:10), and Moses had a temporary 'tent of witness' which he would pitch 'outside the camp' and in which he would speak with God 'face to face' (Exod. 33:7–11), Exodus presents the elaborate construction of the 'tent of witness' and all its furnishings as being the culmination of God's desire to dwell in the midst of his people. When Moses and Joshua ('Jesus' in the LXX) ascended Mount Sinai, 'the glory of the Lord descended' upon the mountain, covering it for six days, before God called to Moses 'on the seventh day', who then entered into the cloud to be instructed, over forty days, about the construction of the tabernacle (Exod. 24:15–18). Finally, at the end of Exodus, when Moses 'had finished [*συνετέλεσε*] all the works, the cloud covered the tent of witness and the tent was filled with the glory of the Lord' such that Moses was unable to enter into it (Exod. 40:27–32[33–8]). Likewise, when Solomon had completed the Temple, and had placed in it the ark of the Lord, the tent of witness, and all the holy vessels, 'the glory of the Lord filled the house of the Lord'.[8] The glory of the Lord, however, departed from Solomon's Temple prior to it being destroyed with the fall of Jerusalem in 587 BCE (cf. Ezek. 10; 11:22–3), and although it was rebuilt, many held that, lacking the tent, the ark, and the altar, the Second Temple also lacked the presence of the glory of the Lord (cf. 2 Makk. 2:5–8).

[5] See esp. Hoskins, *Jesus as the Fulfillment*, 116–25.

[6] Apoc. 7:15; 12:12; 13:6; 21:3. The related verb *κατασκηνόω* is used in Mark 4:32; Matt. 13:32; Luke 13:19 (each being a quotation of Ps 103:12); Acts 2:26. For *σκῆνος* see 2 Cor. 5.1, 4, and for *σκήνωμα* 2 Pet. 1:13–14, both referring to our earthly body.

[7] For a survey of the various traditions regarding God's dwelling place in Israel, the Ark, the Tabernacle, and the Temple, and the place of the Temple in Apocalyptic literature and God's presence in the Targums, see Coloe, *God Dwells with Us*, 31–63; Hoskins, *Jesus as the Fulfillment*, 38–107; and, though older, Yves M.-J. Congar, *The Mystery of the Temple: Or, The Manner of God's Presence to His Creatures from Genesis to the Apocalypse* (Westminster, MD: Newman Press, 1962).

[8] 3 Kgdms. (1 Kings), 8:11; cf. 2 Suppl. (2 Chron.) 5:13–14; 7:1–3.

Yet in Ezekiel's vision of the restored Temple, God also promised that 'I will dwell [κατασκηνώσω] in their midst forever' (Ezek. 43:9), a promise reiterated by Zechariah: 'Behold, I am coming, and will dwell [κατασκηνώσω] in your midst, says the Lord' (Zech. 2:10). These words repeat God's promise to dwell in the consecrated Tabernacle (Exod. 25:7[8]; 29:45),[9] and are proclaimed by John as having been fulfilled in Christ, when the Word becomes flesh. Jesus is now the dwelling place of God among his people, and so replaces the Tabernacle and the Temple. But, as John 1:16, 'grace upon [ἀντί, lit. "instead of"] grace', suggests, Christ is not simply a repetition or renewal of that which went before, but rather, as Hoskins puts it, he 'brings a new and unexpected twist to the dwelling of God among his people. God makes himself accessible to people in an unprecedented form, a body'.[10]

JOHN 1:50–1

A further allusion to the theme of the dwelling place of God is given in the middle of the three-day triptych that follows 'the witness of John' regarding his own role, the baptism of Jesus and the descent of the Spirit (1:19–34).[11] On 'the next day', when John the Baptist again describes Jesus as 'the Lamb of God' (1:36; cf. 1:29), Andrew, one of the disciples of John who heard his words, reported to his brother Simon (Peter) that 'We have found the Messiah (which means Christ)' (1:41). On the following day, after Philip told Nathanael that they have found 'the one of whom Moses in the law and the prophets wrote, Jesus of Nazareth, the son of Joseph' (1:45), and Nathanael says to Christ, 'Rabbi, you are the Son of God! You are the King of Israel!' (1:49), Christ replies to him: '"Because I said to you, I saw you under the fig tree, do you believe? You will see [ὄψῃ, singular] greater things than these." And he said to him, "Truly, Truly, I say to you, you will see [ὑμῖν, ὄψεσθε, plural] heaven opened and the angels of God ascending and descending upon the Son of Man"' (1:50–1). This amazing crescendo of titles applied by the disciples to Christ, in the first two days of his ministry (and within only nine verses), is however insufficient. Christ, instead, identifies himself, although obliquely, as

[9] The LXX readings of these two verses differ from the Masoretic text, obscuring the connection (LXX: Exod. 25:7, 'I shall appear among you'; 29:45, 'I will be invoked among the sons of Israel and will be their God'), though there are variants that have the same reading as the Masoretic text.

[10] Hoskins, *Jesus as the Fulfillment*, 124. That the word ἀντί in John 1:16 should be read in its usual sense of 'in place of', rather than 'upon', is argued by Hoskins, ibid. 120–3.

[11] On the attempts to read this 'third day' as the 'seventh day', beginning with John 1:19, and so indicating a new creation, see Brown, *John*, 1.105–6; to do so requires introducing an unmentioned fourth day, and the Gospel itself only draws attention to 'the third day'.

the Son of Man, which given his words about 'seeing greater things' and the heavens being 'opened', must be taken in a fully apocalyptic manner.[12] What is affirmed at the final stages in the Synoptics, in the last Son of Man saying, when Christ says 'hereafter [ἀπ'ἄρτι] you will see the Son of Man seated at the right hand of Power', is here promised at the beginning of John's Gospel.[13]

The title 'Son of Man', together with the 'ascending and descending' motif, will be analysed in Chapter 4. For now, what is important is that, as is commonly recognized, the vision of the 'angels ascending and descending' harkens back to Jacob and his vision of a ladder, reaching from earth to heaven, with 'the angels of God ascending and descending upon it' (Gen. 28:12).[14] A further connection between this passage and Jacob/Israel in Genesis is the description of Nathanael as 'an Israelite in whom there is no deceit' (1:47), for whereas the name Jacob is associated with 'deceit' (Gen. 27:35), 'Israel', the name given to Jacob after he wrestles with God (Gen. 32:28; cf. 35:10), is associated with the Lord's blessing (Gen 32:26–9). Although there are Jewish exegetical traditions that play upon the ambiguity of the Hebrew to read the text as saying that the angels ascend and descend upon Jacob, which will be considered in Chapter 4, the LXX makes it clear that it is the ladder that is being referred to (with the feminine pronoun referring back to 'the ladder'), as also does John, through his implicit identification of Nathanael with Jacob: the climax to the series of messianic titles applied to Jesus by the disciples is Jesus' self-identification as the Son of Man, the true ladder (κλίμαξ), the only connection between heaven and earth, the way up and the way down. Jacob's reaction to his dream is to say: 'The Lord is in this place, yet I did not know it! . . . How awesome is this place! This is nothing other than the house of God and this is the gate of heaven' (Gen. 28:16–17). There is no such equivalent response by Nathanael. Instead, as Ashton notes, John switches from the singular to the plural: 'What Jacob concluded about a *place*, Bethel, is transferred by the evangelist to a *person* who, as Son of Man, is the locus of revelation. . . . by jumping from singular to plural in what looks like a grammatical solecism, the evangelist is deliberately extending the promise made to Nathanael (ὄψῃ) to a larger audience—not just the other disciples present at the scene, but the readers of the Gospel'.[15] Christ himself is not only the Tabernacle or Temple in which God dwells in his glory, but is also the true 'house of God', Bethel.

[12] Reynolds, *The Apocalyptic Son of Man*, 90–103.

[13] Matt. 26:64; cf. Mark 14:62; Luke 22:69. It is not the last mention of the 'Son of Man' in the Gospel of Luke (cf. 24:7), but it is the last saying from Jesus himself. As Reynolds, *Apocalyptic Son of Man*, 100, points out, the presence of ἀπ'ἄρτι in John 1:51 in some mss (*A Θ Ψ* $f^{1.13}$ 33 and the Syriac versions) suggests that 'at least some early Christians may have made the connection between the final Son of Man saying in Mark and Matthew and the first Son of Man saying in John'.

[14] Cf. Hoskins, *Jesus as the Fulfillment of the Temple*, 125–35.

[15] Ashton, *Fourth Gospel*, 251, italics original.

JOHN 2:1–12

The final scene of this triptych is the wedding in Cana, which takes place 'on the third day' (2:1), when, although Christ addresses his 'mother' with the words 'woman what have you to do with me, my hour has not yet come' (2:4–5), he nevertheless changes the water into 'the good wine' and so 'manifested his glory' as 'the first of his signs' (2:10–11). The 'third day' alludes backwards to the descent of the Lord upon Mount Sinai to give the Law to Moses and manifest his glory (Exod. 19:16–20; 24:16–17), and forward to the raising of Christ's body, the true temple, on the third day (2:19–21). The 'six' jars for the purification rites suggests the inadequacy of the Law, while the 'good wine', into which Jesus changes the water they contain, anticipates the abundance of wine promised for the eschatological banquet (cf. Isa. 25:6; Amos 9:13–14; *1 Enoch* 10.19; *2 Bar.* 29.5), realized in the meal that Christ had with his disciples when, finally, 'his hour had come' (13:1). Christ's unusual manner of addressing his 'mother' as 'woman' is repeated at the crucifixion, though now with an acknowledgement of their relationship: Christ 'said to his mother, "Woman, behold your son"'.[16] The connection between these scenes is already made by Irenaeus, who identifies the wine that his mother, symbolizing the Church, desired to partake of before the time, as 'the cup of recapitulation' (*haer.* 3.16.7), the cup that is filled with the blood that flowed, together with water, from Christ's side (19:34), and which alone 'cleanses us from all sin' (1 John 1:7). This opening three-day triptych to the Gospel—John's witness to 'the lamb of God' and the disciples' identification of Christ in messianic terms; the promise of the heavens being opened and the appearance of the Son of Man; and the changing of water into wine at the marriage feast—recapitulates the Gospel and connects Christ's position as the true 'house of God' to the Passion, an identification that will be made in the 'hour' that is yet to come.

JOHN 2:13–25

After these initial intimations, the first mention of Jesus going to Jerusalem for a feast is also the most explicit identification of Jesus and the Temple. Following the wedding in Cana, and after spending a few days in Capernaum with his mother, brothers, and disciples, 'Jesus went up to Jerusalem' for the Passover (2:12–13). What follows brings together the cleansing of the Temple

[16] John 19:26. Lying in the background here, of course, is the description of 'the woman' 'with child' in Apoc. 12. These connections between the Gospel and the Apocalypse will be treated in the last section of this Chapter, which treats John 19:17–42.

together with the saying about the Temple that in the Synoptics occurs separately and later (after Jesus' final entry into Jerusalem leading to the crucifixion) into this early period, so emphasizing the key in which the Gospel is to be read.[17] Between the introduction (2:13) and the conclusion (2:23–5), both of which mention the Passover, the account itself is structured as a diptych—the cleansing (2:14–17) and the Temple saying (2:18–22)—tied together in an intricate manner. Each part of the diptych begins with a mention of the 'Temple' and goes on to modify how it is described or what is in fact being spoken about. Each part also contains words spoken by Jesus in the imperative (2:16, 'take away'; 2:19, 'destroy'). And further, each part also concludes with a reference to the disciples remembering the Scriptures and his actions and words. The first part begins with Jesus driving those selling the animals, the animals, and the money-changers out of the Temple with 'a whip of cord'.[18] Jesus then speaks of the Temple as 'my Father's house', intimating that he understands the Temple to be something other than the 'house of trade' that it has become.[19]

The second part of the diptych opens with the Jews asking 'what sign have you to show us for doing this?'[20] Not having read the first chapters of the Gospel that describe Jesus' relationship to the Father (eg. 1:18) or the allusions to the Temple that we have already seen, the Jews do not pick up on his words about his 'Father's house', but instead focus on his actions, asking for a 'sign' to legitimate his action, thereby indicating that they had some understanding of what he was doing;[21] and when they do later fully grasp the import of Jesus' words about 'his Father', they seek to kill him for 'making himself equal with God' (5:18). Jesus' reply, 'Destroy this temple, and in three days I will raise it up' (2:19), is also not understood, and so, after a perplexed question about how this could be possible, the Evangelist explains, 'he spoke of the temple of his body' (2:21). Just as the vocabulary changed from 'Temple' to 'my Father's house' in the first part of the diptych, so here the point of reference changes from the 'Temple', which has become no more than a market place, to the

[17] The 'cleansing' in Matt. 21:12–13; Mark 11:15–19; Luke 19:45–6; the *logion* in Matt. 26:61; 27:40; Mark 14:58; 15:29. On the absence of the *logion* from Luke, see P. Walker, *Jesus and the Holy City: New Testament Perspectives on Jerusalem* (Grand Rapids, MI: Eerdmans, 1996), 60–4; Coloe, *God Dwells with Us*, 68.

[18] John 2:15. Margaret Barker, *King of the Jews*, 192, would see in this action an allusion to the cleansing of the Temple on the Day of Atonement, and especially the Passover envisioned by Ezekiel (45:18–25) as a springtime equivalent of the Day of Atonement.

[19] John 2:16, perhaps alluding to Zech. 14:21 (MT). Cf. Kerr, *Temple of Jesus' Body*, 79–81.

[20] John 2:18. On 'the Jews' in John, see John Ashton, 'The Identity and Function of the *Ioudaioi* in the Fourth Gospel', *NovT.* 27 (1985), 40–75.

[21] Although as Jacob Neusner ('Money-Changers in the Temple: The Mishnah's Explanation', *NTS* 35.2 (1989), 287–90, at 289) points out, to anyone aware of the sacrifical system of the Temple, Jesus' actions would have been 'incomprehensible and unintelligible', Coloe (*God Dwells with us*, 76) is right to note that they do not ask Jesus 'Why have you done this?', thus implying that 'they at least have some understanding of the meaning of Jesus' actions'.

body of Christ himself, the true Temple of God, the house of the Father. Finally, each part of the diptych ends with the disciples, who are not mentioned as having accompanied Jesus to Jerusalem and do not appear anywhere else in this scene, 'remembering' a scriptural verse and what he had said (2:17, 22), something that in the presentation of the Gospel only occurs after the resurrection. As Coloe puts it: the disciples' 'sole purpose is to remember the Scripture and the words of Jesus and to testify to their belief. In their remembrance they function as a proleptic presence of the post-resurrection community under the guidance of the Paraclete whose task is "to bring to your remembrance all that I have said to you" (14:26)'.[22] In the first part, 'the disciples remember that it was written, "Zeal for your house will consume me"', with the Evangelist changing the aorist of the Psalm verse into the future tense, so pointing forward to the consummation of this verse in the Passion, when Christ, the Lamb of God, is sacrificed and consumed.[23] This point is made clear in the conclusion to the second part, though now with reference to the Temple/body saying of 2:19: 'when therefore he was raised from the dead, his disciples remembered that he had said this, and they believed the Scripture and the word which Jesus had spoken' (2:22). Finally, in the conclusion to this scene, although 'many believed in his name when they saw the signs that he did', Jesus did not trust himself to them, knowing them and not needing their witness (2:23–5). The next scene opens with one of this group, Nicodemus, approaching Jesus as a 'Rabbi', a 'teacher come from God' because of the 'signs' that he had done (3:1–2). The Prologue had already asserted that 'those who believe in his name' are given the power to be 'born of God' (1:12–13), and so the discussion with Nicodemus that ensues returns to this birth 'from above'. In this context, Jesus speaks more directly about his Passion, but as he does so in terms of the figure of the Son of Man (3:13–16), consideration of this passage will be deferred until Chapter 4.

JOHN 4:1–42

Before Jesus returns to Jerusalem and the Temple for the second feast mentioned in the Gospel (5:1), his encounter with the Samaritan woman (4.1–42) also provides a number of images relating Jesus to the Temple as the place of

[22] Coloe, *God Dwells with Us*, 78–9. 'Remembering' in the Gospel of John is always connected in some way to the death and resurrection of Christ: cf. 2:22; 12:16; 15:20; 16:4, 21. John 14:26, the only other occasion of 'remember' in John, lacks an explicit connection to the Passion, the hour, persecution, or travail, but the context is the imminent departure of Jesus and the Spirit's role in bringing to the disciples' remembrance all that Christ said.

[23] John 2:17; Ps. 68:10. The connection between the verb 'consume' and the sacrifice and consumption of the Lamb of God is suggested by Kerr, *Temple of Jesus' Body*, 83–6.

worship.[24] It begins with Jesus sitting 'upon' Jacob's well.[25] Genesis has no mention of a well connected with Jacob, though it does appear in the Targums: the stones which Jacob had used as a pillow became one stone, which he then erected as a pillar, and which others tried, but failed, to roll away from the mouth of the well; Jacob however 'raised the stone from above the mouth of the well and the well overflowed and came up to its mouth and was overflowing for twenty years'.[26] In later rabbinic tradition, the well travelled with Jacob, just as the well given to the children of Israel in the desert (Num. 21:16–18) was also held to have travelled with them, as a 'gift' of God.[27] Jesus, however, sitting upon the well, is himself the 'gift of God' and gives 'living water' (4:10), and is therefore 'greater than Jacob' (4:12). While the image of water is often applied in Scripture to the Word of God (e.g. Isa. 55:10–11), and subsequently to Wisdom (e.g. Prov. 16:22, 'a fountain of life'; 18:4, 'a gushing stream') or to the Law (Sirach 24:23–5), or alternatively to the Spirit of God (e.g. Isa. 44:3–4; Ezek. 36:25–7), Coloe points out that, in the cultic context of John 4, the more important reference is to the description of the new Temple in Ezekiel, with the waters flowing up from under its foundations, just as the rivers had flowed from Eden to the whole of creation, providing life and fruitfulness to a new creation, which is now ready for harvest (cf. 4:35).[28] The image of 'the water of life' flowing from the throne of God, together with the tree of life, appears again in the Apocalypse (Apoc. 22.1–2), and is brought to realization at the crucifixion, when, from his body water flows (19:34) and the Spirit is handed over to the woman and her son, that is, those who have put on the identity of Christ (19:26–7, 30). As such, 'the hour is coming', Jesus tells the woman, 'when neither on this mountain nor in Jerusalem will you worship the Father' (4:21), but rather 'the hour is coming and now is, when true worshippers will worship the Father in spirit and truth' (4:23).

[24] For a full analysis of this highly structured section, see Coloe, *God Dwells with Us*, 84–113.

[25] John 4:6, ἐπί, not 'besides' παρά. Brown, *John*, 1.169, comments: 'literally "on the well"; the well was a vertical shaft covered by a stone'. He also notes that P^{66} has 'on the ground', which Boismard had argued may be the original reading (RB 64 [1957] 397), though as Coloe, *God Dwells with Us*, 95 n. 38, comments this may also be 'a correction, due to the strangeness of the image of Jesus resting "on" the well'.

[26] *Tg Neof.* Gen 28:10. Cf. J. H. Neyrey, 'Jacob Traditions and the Interpretation of John 4:10–26', *CBQ* 41 (1979), 419–37.

[27] Neyrey, 'Jacob Traditions', 422, citing the late rabbinic text, *Pirque R. El.* 35, and *Tg. Neof.* Num. 21:17–18.

[28] Ezek. 47:1–12; Gen. 2:10–14. According to Margaret Barker, *Gate of Heaven: The History and Symbolism of the Temple in Jerusalem* (London: SPCK, 1991), 18: 'The waters under the earth were all gathered together beneath the temple, they believed, and it was necessary to ensure that sufficient was released to ensure fertility, but not so much as to overwhelm the world with a flood'. Cf. Frédéric Manns, *L'Evangile de Jean à la lumière du Judaisme*, Studium Biblicum Franciscanum Analecta 33 (Jerusalem: Franciscan Printing Press, 1991), 135; Coloe, *God Dwells with Us*, 95.

The transition between the 'hour' lying in the future in 4:21 to v. 23, where it is both in the future and yet also in the present, is facilitated by 4:22: 'You worship what you do not know; we worship what we know, for salvation is from the Jews'. As Coloe points out, the 'we' here does not refer to 'the Jews', who in the narrative time of the Gospel 'never know correctly', but instead 'must therefore refer to the future Christian community' (just as did the disciples in John 2:13–25).[29] In 4:21, when Christ speaks of God as 'Father' for the first time in this passage, he identifies him neither as the God of the Jews nor as the God of the Samaritans, but rather as the one revealed by Jesus, most perfectly in the hour which is coming. The woman, in turn, first addresses Jesus as 'a Jew' (4:9), then, after the discussion about the well and its water, she calls him 'a prophet' (4:19; one 'like' Moses, Deut. 18:15, for the Samaritans did not accept the prophetic literature), and then, finally, when she uses the word 'Messiah',[30] Christ replies: 'I who speak to you am he', though the Greek, *ἐγώ εἰμὶ, ὁ λαλῶν σοι*, 'I AM, the one talking to you', alludes to the divine name in a way that is obscured in the usual English translation (cf. esp. Isa. 52:6, *ἐγώ εἰμι αὐτὸς ὁ λαλῶν*). Jesus is thus revealed to be more than a prophet, a messiah, and even Jacob: the original 'supplantor' (cf. Gen. 27:36) has been supplanted. Christ is, rather, the very presence of God himself, the one who revealed his name to Moses (Exod. 3:14), and as such, the salvation he brings is not for the Jews or Samaritans only, for he is, as the Samaritans from the city conclude, 'the Saviour of the world' (4:42). Whereas Jacob recognized the 'house of God' (Gen. 28:17), his descendants, the Samaritans, recognize Jesus as 'the Saviour of the world', and so are invited into the relationship with God as the Father of Jesus, in which ancestral sites of worship are replaced by the one greater than Jacob and his well, that is, by the one who sits upon, and offers, living waters.

JOHN 5:1–18

The second feast to be mentioned is much briefer and less detailed: it is simply 'a feast of the Jews' for which Jesus 'went up to Jerusalem' (5:1). While there, Jesus healed a man who had been ill for thirty-eight years (5:5). This unusual and specific time period perhaps refers to the length of time that the people of Israel wandered in the wilderness before crossing the brook Zered, a period

[29] Ibid. 103.

[30] John 4:25. The word 'Messiah' is used here without an article, as is 'Christ' in the explanatory clause. By the end of the scene, the woman hesitantly asks the other Samaritans, 'Can this be the Christ?' (4:29), leaving them to decide on their own rather than her word, cf. 4:42; Ibid. 106–7.

long enough to ensure that 'the entire generation, that is, the men of war, had perished from the camp', but measuring the length of time not from their exodus from Egypt, but from their departure from Kadesh (Deut. 2:14), the place where Miriam had died, after which 'there was no water for the congregation', apart from that which Moses was able to extract from the rock (Num. 20:1–2, 11). Likewise the five porticoes surrounding the pool of water that the sick man hoped could heal him, but which remain inaccessible to him while he has no 'human being' to immerse him into its waters (5:7), perhaps represents the five books of Moses, which are not salvific unless it is realized that they in fact speak of Christ (cf. 5:46–7).[31] Christ, however, the living water, heals the man by his word, directing him to 'rise' (5:8, ἔγειρε). Despite their exchange, the man 'did not know who it was' who had healed him, for Jesus had 'withdrawn' because of the crowd, until Jesus 'found him in the Temple' (5:13–14). It is Jesus' statement, in reply to the Jews' challenge about breaking the Sabbath, 'My Father is working still and I am working', that prompts the Jews to seek his death for 'making himself equal with God' (5:17–18).

In what follows, Christ expounds upon his brief reply in 5:17, making clearer two particular points: first, what it means that the Father is still working, as is Christ (5:19–29); and second, the witnesses to him and his work (5:30–47). The work of the Father is not judgement, for 'he has given all judgment to the Son' (5:22). Rather, that which the Father does, and the Son, seeing this, does likewise (5:19), is to 'raise [ἐγείρει] the dead and give them life' (5:21). This point is repeated emphatically in the following verses: the one who hears the word of Christ and believes in him who sent him, 'has eternal life; he does not come into judgment, but has passed from death to life' (5:24); 'the hour is coming and now is' (the same combination of future and present, with the latter alluding to the post-resurrection community, as we have seen previously) when even 'the dead shall hear the voice of the Son of God and those who hear will live' (5:25); and 'just as the Father has life in himself, so he has granted the Son to have life in himself' (5:26), as well as 'the authority to execute judgement because he is a Son of Man' (5:27), that is, the one whose voice will be heard, when the hour comes, by all in the tombs, leading them into the resurrection either of life or of judgement (5:28–9). The issue of the working on the Sabbath has, thus, increased in scope: if the work of the Father, and the Son likewise, is to bring life out of death, and the Father is 'still working' (5:17 ἕως ἄρτι ἐργάζεται), then the 'sixth day' when 'God finished his works [συνετέλεσεν . . . τὰ ἔργα] that he had made and left off on the seventh day from all his works [ἀπὸ πάντων τῶν ἔργων] that he had made' (Gen. 2:2) refers to the 'hour' that is yet to come, when Christ affirms that then, indeed, it is 'finished' (19:30), for through the cross life has come through death.

[31] Cf. Augustine, *Homilies on John, Hom.* 17.2.

Likewise, if Moses 'wrote of me' (5:46), then his having 'finished all the works' (συνετέλεσεν ... πάντα τὰ ἔργα) for constructing 'the tent of witness' (τὴν σκηνὴν τοῦ μαρτυρίου), so that it was filled with 'the glory of the Lord' (Exod. 40:27–9[33–5]), also speaks of Christ, the Temple of God, when he is seen upon the cross in glory. The true Sabbath is Christ's rest in the tomb, celebrated in the feast of Pascha.

JOHN 6

The third feast mentioned by John is 'the Passover, the feast of the Jews' (6:4), the second of the three Passovers in his Gospel: the first being the occasion for the most explicit identification of Christ and the Temple (2:13–25) and the third being Christ's own Passion (19:14–42). This time, however, Jesus does not go up to Jerusalem and the Temple, but is besides the Sea of Galilee. Nevertheless, the whole of John 6 is shot through with intertextual references to Passover themes found in Exodus and Numbers:[32] Jesus is 'on the mountain' (6:3), as was Moses on Mount Sinai; the Passover (6:4; cf. Exod. 12); the question about where to get food (6:5; cf. Num. 11:13); the fish (6:9; cf. Num. 11:22); crossing the sea (6:16ff.; cf. Exod. 13–14), with the identification by the divine name (6:20; cf. Exod. 3:14; 20:2); the murmuring (6:41, 43, the Jews; 6:61, the disciples; cf. Num. 11:1); the bread, Jesus' flesh, is to be eaten (6:51; Num. 11:13, 'meat'), and is from heaven (6:33; cf. Exod. 16:4). After the feeding of the five thousand (6:1–15), and the crossing of the sea with the reassurance of the divine name (6:16–21), 'the next day' the people also crossed the sea to Capernaum and an initial discussion ensues, turning into one of the richest theological reflections in the Gospel (6:22–71), mirroring the miraculous feeding (6:1–15), and so placing the crossing of the sea and the utterance of the divine name (6:16–21) as the chiastic centre of the chapter.[33]

[32] For the parallels that follow see Kerr, *Temple of Jesus' Body*, 214, slightly altered. For a fuller investigation see Peder Borgen, *Bread from Heaven: An Exegetical Study of the Concept of Manna in the Gospel of John and the Writings of Philo*, SupNovT 10 (Leiden: Brill, 1965); Kerr, *Temple of Jesus' Body*, 214–26. Bertil Gärtner, *John 6 and the Jewish Passover*, Coniectanea Neotestamentica, 17 (Lund: Gleerup, 1959) had earlier argued that John 6 was structured according to the three key parts of the Jewish Passover Haggadah (the form and content of meal, paralleled by the miraculous feeling in 6:1–14; then the four questions by the sons, and the interpretation by the father, paralleled by the four questions by the Jews and the interpretation by Jesus in 6:26–52). As intriguing as such parallels may be, it must be noted that not only are they, as Brown puts it, 'quite artificial and strained' (*John*, 1.267), but the dating of the Haggadah to the Maccabean period, as Gärtner, *John 6*, 15–16, has it, is unrealistic. Cf. Kulp, 'Origins of Seder and Haggadah', and the discussion in the second section of Chapter 1, above.

[33] Cf. Peter F. Ellis, *The Genius of John: A Composition-Critical Commentary on the Fourth Gospel* (Collegeville, MN: Liturgical Press, 1984), 14–15, who would place this event as the chiastic structure of the Gospel as a whole.

Peder Borgen has persuasively argued that this discourse follows a homiletic pattern found in Philo and Palestinian midrashim.[34] It begins with the Jews offering a text from the Law: 'Our fathers ate manna in the wilderness; as it is written: "He gave them bread from heaven to eat".'[35] Jesus then explains the text: the 'he' is not Moses but 'my Father', 'gave' becomes 'gives', and the bread is now 'true bread' (6:32). 'The bread of God', moreover, 'is that which [ὁ, or "he who"] comes down from heaven and gives life to the world' (6:33), and is indeed Jesus himself (6:35, 38). Moreover, those who come to him 'shall not hunger' and those who believe in him 'shall never thirst' (6:35). That thirst will also be quenched by this bread indicates that more is being spoken about than physical nourishment: those who see and believe (cf. 6:36), who come to Jesus, will not be rejected (cf. 6:37), but rather, as Jesus says three times, he will 'raise' them up 'at the last day' (6:39, 40, 44). It is this resurrection into life that is, Jesus says, again three times, the will of the Father, whose work he has come to do (cf. 6:38, 39, 40). When the Jews 'murmur' against him, seeing him as 'the son of Joseph' (6:42), but not believing his words, Jesus then, following the second element of the homiletic pattern, replies with a verse from the prophets: 'It is written in the prophets, "and they shall all be taught by God".'[36] This is the teaching that Jesus is now giving, for 'every one who has heard and learned from the Father comes to me' (6:45). But although only he who is 'from God' 'has seen the Father' (6:46; cf. 1:18), nevertheless 'he who believes has eternal life' (6:47), the life given by Jesus, 'the bread of life' (6:48). So, while those who ate the manna in the wilderness died, those who eat this bread will 'not die' (6:49–50).

In the verses that follow, Jesus' words become more striking: 'the bread which I shall give for the life of the world is my flesh' (6:51c). This 'hard saying' (6:60) provokes a 'dispute' among the Jews (6:52) and is a 'scandal' or 'stumbling-block' for the disciples (6:61; cf. 1 Cor. 1:23), and to both Jesus replies with a saying about the Son of Man. When the Jews ask how they are 'to eat' (φαγεῖν) 'the flesh' (6:52), Jesus replies: 'Truly, truly, I say to you, unless you eat [φάγητε] the flesh of the Son of Man and drink his blood, you have no life in you' (6:53). He then reiterates the point using stronger language,

[34] Following Borgen, *Bread from Heaven*, 28–83; J. D. G. Dunn, 'John VI—A Eucharistic Discourse?', *NTS* 17 (1970), 328–38; Kerr, *Temple of Jesus' Body*, 215–25; Charles Kingsley Barrett, '"The Flesh of the Son of Man": John 6.53', in Barrett, *Essays on John* (Philadelphia: Westminster Press, 1982), 36–49; and Maarten J. J. Menken, 'John 6:51c–58: Eucharist or Christology', in R. Alan Culpepper ed., *Critical Readings of John 6*, BIS 22 (Leiden: Brill, 1997), 183–204, I take John 6 as an integrated whole, rather than taking 6:51c–8 as a separate, more 'eucharistic' discourse, that either originally belonged to the Last Supper scene (as Brown, *John*, 1.287–91) or as an interpolation by an 'ecclesial redactor' (as Bultman, *John*, 218–20, 234–7).

[35] John 6:31; a paraphrase of Exod. 16:4, 15, and perhaps Ps. 77:24.

[36] John 6:45, and Isa. 54:13, which Barrett, *John*, 245, describes as 'a sufficiently exact paraphrase and is probably dependent on the LXX'.

'chewing' (τρώγων), three times: 'he who chews my flesh and drinks my blood has eternal life and I will raise him up at the last day' (6:54); 'he who chews me will live because of me' (6:57); and 'he who chews this bread will live for ever' (6:58). To the scandalized disciples, Jesus asserts: 'Do you take offence at this? What, therefore, if you were to see the Son of Man ascending to where he was before?' (6:61–2), a protasis without an apodosis, but with significant implications.

The Flesh to be Eaten

There are several elements at play in 6:51–8. Most striking is the change in vocabulary, from eating bread to chewing the flesh of Jesus and drinking his blood, a change that is accompanied by the specification that these words apply to Jesus as the Son of Man, a title which almost invariably in the Gospel of John applies to him as exalted and glorified, that is, upon the cross.[37] Starting with the term 'flesh': elsewhere in the Gospel of John it refers to the world of appearances (cf. 8:15) or human weakness (cf. 1:13, 3:6, 17:2), it is unable to give life (cf. 6:63), and so is dead. In 6:51–8, however, the bread from heaven debated earlier in John 6 is now identified by Jesus with himself and specifically with his flesh: 'I am the living bread which came down [καταβάς] from heaven; if anyone eats of this bread, he will live for ever; and the bread which I will give [δώσω] for the life of the world is my flesh' (6:51). When the Jews misunderstand and speak only about 'the flesh' (6:52), Jesus further specifies that it is the flesh and blood *of the Son of Man* that must be eaten and drunk (cf. 6:53), reiterating more forcefully that this means to 'chew my flesh and drink my blood' (6:54, 56), or more strikingly to 'chew me' (6:57).[38] The change in 6:51 from the past tense to the future indicates that, although Jesus stands among them now as the bread which has descended, it is only as given for the life of the world that the identification between his flesh and the bread is established: as Menken puts it 'Jesus is the bread from heaven, not just as a human being, but as a human being who dies on the cross'.[39] In terms of this episode's place in the narrative of the Gospel, this of course has yet to

[37] Cf. 3:13–14; 8:28; 12:23; 12:34; 13:31; these and other passages speaking of the Son of Man will be discussed in Chapter 4.

[38] Menken, 'John 6:51c–58', 200, notes how: 'In v.51c, Jesus says that he will give *his* flesh, the Jews misquote him in v.52 by omitting the possessive, and Jesus corrects the omission in v.53: they have to eat the flesh *of the Son of Man*'. Italics original.

[39] Menken, 'John 6:51c–58', 191; there he also makes the important observation that using 'flesh and blood' to 'refer to a human being who suffers a violent death is also found in the OT [Old Testament] and in the Jewish environment of Early Christianity. It should be distinguished from the standard expression "flesh and blood" used to indicate man as an earthly being'. He refers to Eph. 2:13–14 and Col. 1:20–22, and, as background Ps. 78:2–3 (and quoted in 1 Makk. 7:17), Ezek. 32:5–6; 4 Makk. 6:6.

happen; this is an example of John's 'merging of times' discussed in the Introduction when we considered John and his readers. The point at issue in these verses relate somehow to the Eucharist, as we will see, and are behind the question about 'the Son of Man ascending to where he was before' (6:62). The other important instance of 'flesh' in the Gospel of John is of course 1:14. Whether this verse refers, as it is usually taken, to Jesus becoming that which we are, to appear alongside others in the frailty of the flesh in this world, or whether it relates to Jesus' identification as the bread which descends from heaven and which is his flesh, the flesh of the Son of Man, that is, the crucified and glorified Christ, is something we will return to below and again in Chapter 5, when we examine the Prologue.

What, then, is the flesh and blood that Christ as the Son of Man gives as food and drink? Scholars have been divided on whether 6:51c–58 should be interpreted as speaking of the Eucharist or in terms of Christology.[40] There is no doubt that John is drawing upon eucharistic terminology, but, as Menken points out, that does not mean that the passage is primarily or directly about the Eucharist itself.[41] Although Jesus 'gave thanks' before distributing bread to the five thousand (6:11: *εὐχαριστήσας*, cf. 6:23; 1 Cor. 11:24; Luke 22:19), there is no mention of any 'breaking the bread', a common element, as Dunn points out, in all the Synoptic accounts, and neither, for that matter, is 'giving thanks' always a reference to the Eucharist.[42] Moreover, throughout the discourse expounding upon the bread from heaven, it is Christ himself who is the centre of attention, and emphasis is placed on the need to have faith in him (6:29, 35, 36, 40, 47), so that, as Dunn puts it, 'the manna and the bread of the miracle are contrasted with and are symbols of Jesus, not of the Lord's Supper'.[43]

[40] As shown in the title of Menken's essay, 'John 6:51c–58: Eucharist or Christology', with a review of previous scholarly work in its opening pages. A further review of literature can be found in Meredith J. C. Warren, *My Flesh is Meat Indeed: A Nonsacramental Reading of John 6:51–8* (Minneapolis: Fortress Press, 2015), 23–52, who suggest that the background of this passage also lies in the trope of the relationship between the extraordinary mortal and an antagonistic deity used from the Homeric epics to the Romances dating to a slightly later period than John. Warren (ibid. 45) also makes the point that it is in fact rather anachronistic to use the terms 'Christology' and 'Eucharist' to describe a text dating to the late first or early second century. More specifically, Petterson (*Tomb to Text*, 56–7) points out that 'in the patristic period, issues of Christology and Eucharist could not be separated but were in fact completely intertwined', a connection which seems to have fallen apart, she suggests, in the controversies over the Eucharist in the Reformation period.

[41] Menken, 'John 6:51c–58', 187–9 (where he draws the parallels with Mark 14:22–4, Matt. 26:26–8, Luke 22:19–20, 1 Cor. 11:24–5, and to Ignatius, who he supposes to be independent of John and thus using already established terminology), and 201.

[42] Dunn, 'John VI', 332. Matthew and Mark use 'giving thanks' for the feeding of the five thousand, but not for the Last Supper, while its use in John 11:41 has no possible reference to the Eucharist.

[43] Dunn, 'John VI', 333. Kerr, *Temple of Jesus' Body*, 222, n. 45, likewise: 'In so far as the Passover has finished and is "replaced" by the Eucharist, I think it is possible to read elements of

As the discourse turns in 6:51c–58 to the 'flesh' of Christ, it might seem that possible allusions to the Passover lamb (for the context of John 6 is the feast of Passover) provide more tangible connections to the Eucharist. But in the Jewish Passover only the flesh of the lamb was eaten (cf. Exod. 12:8), whereas Jesus specifies that not only is his flesh to be chewed, but his blood is also to be drunk (6:53–6), something that would have appalled the Jews (and not only them), for whom drinking blood was absolutely prohibited (cf. Lev. 17:10–14). Jesus is, therefore, not presented here as a straightforward substitute for the Passover lamb. As Kerr puts it, Jesus 'is not urging his hearers to eat his flesh and blood as though he were the Passover Lamb to be consumed; rather he is pointing towards *his death as the Passover Lamb* in which his flesh and blood would be offered for the life of the world (6:33, 57)'.[44] The Temple, its sacrifices, and its festivals find their fulfilment not in themselves, nor in the eating, then and there, of the flesh of Jesus (and thus *only* then and there), but in the death of Christ, which is, as the Apostle had already concluded, a festival to be celebrated (cf. 1 Cor. 5:7–8) and proclaimed by the eating of the bread and drinking of the cup (cf. 1 Cor. 11:23–6). His human flesh and blood are offered, therefore, not to be consumed simply as such, but as the flesh and blood *of the Son of Man*.[45] Moreover, as Jesus affirms to the Jews, this flesh and blood are 'true food' and 'true drink' (6:55, ἀληθής), and the word 'chew' (6:54, 56, 57, 58) would seem to reinforce the reality of the eating required.[46]

As such it is not really the case, as Dunn has it, that the substitution of 'flesh' for 'bread' in 6:51c–58 is 'a deliberate attempt to exclude doceticism by heavily, if somewhat crudely, underscoring the reality of the incarnation in all its offensiveness', the situation of John 6 being, according to Dunn, 'one where the Christology of docetism has made a strong challenge'.[47] The 'docetism' Dunn has in mind is one which would challenge the 'Incarnation', taking that as the entry point of the Word into this world, by holding that Jesus only appeared to be a human being as he walked around upon the earth. Thus, according to Dunn, John makes two fundamental points in this discourse. The first is 'the reality of the incarnation and the necessity of the Incarnate One's death if men are to receive eternal life which is emphasized

the Eucharist into Jn 6:51–58. However, it makes better sense to see the primary reference to the Passover'.

[44] Kerr, *Temple of Jesus' Body*, 219, italics original.

[45] Liturgically speaking, it is always as the 'body and blood of Christ' that the Eucharist is received, not 'of Jesus'.

[46] Udo Schnelle, *Antidocetic Christology in the Gospel of John: An Investigation of the Place of the Fourth Gospel in the Johannine School*, trans. Linda M. Maloney (Minneapolis: Fortress, 1992), 204–5, esp. n. 180: '*Τρώγειν* here can scarcely be a mere vulgar synonym for ἐσθίεν, as some exegetes think (referring to John 13:18: replacement of ὁ ἐσθίων in Ps. 40:10 LXX with τρώγειν). The strong word τρώγειν cannot be explained as a mere substitution for another word'.

[47] Dunn, 'John VI', 336–7.

throughout, and especially in vv. 51c–58'.[48] But, he continues, this does not mean 'that John attempts to meet the challenge of docetism by referring his readers to the Lord's supper, as Ignatius did some years later, insisting, in other words, that eternal life comes through the actual eating of the bread and drinking of the wine in the Lord's Supper on the part of those who believe'. This leads Dunn to his second point, 'that eternal life comes only through the Spirit given by the Son of Man in his exaltation', a claim based on 6:63, 'it is the Spirit that gives life, the flesh is to no avail'.[49]

The qualification that Dunn draws from 6:63 is certainly appropriate, though with a further nuance which we will give below, but it is a mistake, however, to apply it to 6:51c–58, for a clear demarcation is made in 6:59 between what was said to the Jews in the synagogue at Capernaum in the preceding verses (6:51–8) and what is said to the disciples thereafter (6:60–71).[50] Moreover, it is not clear at all that the 'Incarnation', as that term is usually taken, is at issue in 6.51c–58, where the word 'flesh' is used. Rather, as Menken argues, the striking language of these verses is directed against the Jewish refusal to accept that Jesus, a crucified human being, is to be identified with the 'bread from heaven', and so is part of a discussion with the Jews, extending throughout the Gospel, regarding the death of Jesus.[51] To which one must add, however, that this 'bread' is in fact his flesh (and blood), given to us from heaven by Jesus as Son of Man, and given, moreover, specifically to be consumed. In other words, it is not only a discussion about the death of Jesus, but about eating his flesh and drinking his blood thereafter; that is, it is opposed to a docetic understanding of the Eucharist, as it were, rather than a 'docetic Christology' (as that is usually understood).

The same also goes for Ignatius, who, while indeed describing the 'bread' (he never mentions 'wine') as 'the medicine of immortality' (*Eph.* 20.2), emphasizes that this 'bread' is in fact 'the flesh of Jesus Christ'.[52] It is a docetic approach to the Eucharist that troubles Ignatius: those who abstain from the Eucharist do so because 'they do not confess that the Eucharist is the flesh of our Saviour Jesus Christ who suffered for our sins and whom the Father raised up' (*Smyrn.* 7.1). The same point can be made regarding the First Epistle of John, when it asserts that 'every spirit which confesses that Jesus Christ has come in the flesh is of God' (1 John 4:2). As de Jonge points out, 'That Jesus

[48] Ibid. 335.

[49] Cf. Dunn, 'John VI', 334 and 336, following Dodd's comment that 6:63 'is the clue that the reader must hold fast in attempting to understand the discourse'. Dodd, *Interpretation*, 341.

[50] Cf. Barrett, 'The Flesh of the Son of Man', 40.

[51] Menken, 'John 6:51c–58', 199–201.

[52] *Rom.* 7.3, and his 'blood' is 'incorruptible love'; cf. *Trall.* 8.1: 'remake yourself in faith, which is the flesh of the Lord, and in love, which is the blood of Christ'. Cf. Frederick C. Klawiter, 'The Eucharist and Sacramental Realism in the Thought of St Ignatius of Antioch', *Studia Liturgica* 37 (2007), 129–63.

came "in the flesh" means that he died on the cross',[53] with the same addition we made to Menken's observation, that 'coming in the flesh' by dying on the cross points to the flesh that is, thereafter, to be consumed. One thus does not need to see a radical change between the thrust of John 6:51c–58 and Ignatius, positing a distinction between the focus on Jesus himself in the former and upon the eucharistic elements in themselves in the latter. Ignatius is at pains to uphold 'the unity of the flesh and spirit of Jesus Christ' (*Magn.* 1, 13; *Smyrn.* 3), a unity which is dissolved when one distinguishes, and thus separates, a 'spiritual' reception of the Son of Man and the 'chewing' of his flesh.

But this need not entail attributing an efficacy to the physical matter of the eucharistic elements in themselves, a fear which seems to lurk behind Dunn's argument, as if these physical elements themselves, without the Spirit and faith, suffice, or as Carson puts it: 'Submit to the rite and win eternal life!'[54] As Dunn notes, the Evangelist is 'making the point that the flesh whose eating gives life is not and cannot mean Jesus in his earthly life when he has entered the sphere of *τὰ κάτω* and shares the weakness of the *σάρξ*, but must be understood as the flesh given up for the life of the world (v. 51c), and so refer to Jesus as raised up on the cross and to heaven'. He thus continues, by reiterating his second point, made on the basis of 6:63: 'The "hard saying" finds its fulfillment, therefore, when Jesus has been lifted up in the upward sweep of the cross–resurrection–ascension, in the giving of the life-creating Spirit. Jesus in his humanity as flesh and blood is no help to them but life comes through the Spirit given by the incarnate Jesus in his ascension'.[55] However, nothing is in fact said in these verses about the giving of the Spirit. Rather, the point of 6:63 is that it is the Spirit indeed who gives life, not the flesh; but by implication it is the flesh which is vivified by the Spirit, making it the life-giving flesh (and blood) of the Son of Man that must not only be 'eaten' but 'chewed', as vividly emphasized in the verses that precede, in order to come to share in life. It is neither the eucharistic elements in themselves, nor a gift of the Spirit apart from them, that avails, but rather the receiving and consuming of the flesh and blood of the Son of Man, vivified by the Spirit, and as such life-giving, not in themselves, but, as we will see at the end of this section, through the recipients' sharing in the Passion of Christ.

Whereas in 6:53–8, Jesus emphasizes to the Jews the reality of the flesh and blood that will be given by the Son of Man, in 6:60–71 he takes a different tack. In response to the disciples' 'murmuring' at the 'hard saying' of Jesus in the synagogue in Capernaum—where in four verses he asserted the need to 'chew the flesh of the Son of Man and drink his blood' twice (6:54, 56), 'to chew me'

[53] Marinus de Jonge, *Jesus: Stranger from Heaven and Son of God: Jesus Christ and the Christians in Johannine Perspective*, ed. and trans. John E. Steely, SBL Sources for Biblical Study 11 (Missoula, MO: Scholars press, 1977), 205.

[54] Carson, *Gospel According to John*, 297.

[55] Dunn, 'John VI', 337.

(6:57), and 'to chew the bread' which 'descended from heaven' (6:58)—Jesus asks the question, 'If, therefore, you were to see the Son of Man ascending to where he was before?' (6:62), a question that increases the sense of offence, such that 'many of his disciples drew back and no longer accompanied him' (6:66) and Jesus told the twelve that one of them is a devil, knowing that Judas would betray him (6:70–1). The question in 6:62 is the only use of the verb 'to ascend' in John 6, following on from seven instances of 'descend'. The descent, however, is not directly that of the Son of Man, but the 'bread which descends from heaven' (6:33, 50, 58), Jesus as the 'bread which has descended from heaven' (6:41, 51), and Jesus himself as the one who has 'descended from heaven' (6:38, 42); 6:41 and 42 are spoken by the Jews, leaving 6:38 being the only occurrence where Jesus speaks of himself as descending without any explicit reference to his being 'bread', though the weight of the other instances and the character of the chapter as a whole certainly gives this to be understood here as well. The change of tense in 6:51, as we have seen, points forward to the identification of the bread descending from heaven and the flesh of the Son of Man, given for the life of the world, that is, in the Passion, so that the act of chewing his flesh is not cannibalism but the consumption of the life-giving flesh of the Son of Man. This is reinforced by the two other mentions of the 'Son of Man' in this chapter, for it is the Son of Man who 'will give' (δώσει) food for eternal life (6:27), that is, the flesh and blood of the Son of Man which must be consumed to have life (6:53). The 'ascending' posed to the disciples in 6:62 thus stands in contrast not to an earlier descent of the Son of Man at a moment of 'Incarnation' taken as an 'episode in the biography of the Word' (to reuse William's phrase, though the 'Word' is not in discussion in John 6), but rather to the descent of the life-giving flesh and blood which will be given through Jesus' ascent of the cross. But what, then, does it mean to ask about seeing 'the Son of Man ascending to where he was before'?

The disciples' further offence is provoked not just by this question, but also by the words which immediately follow: 'It is the Spirit that gives life, the flesh is of no avail; the words I have spoken to you are spirit and life' (6:63). Here, Dunn's second point, to the effect that this verse undermines any reliance on the eucharistic elements taken in themselves, is absolutely correct.[56] Flesh, in itself, is not life-giving; it is so only when vivified by the Spirit and received as the flesh (and blood) of the Son of Man. 'Ascending to where he was before' would thus mean receiving this life-giving flesh and blood not simply as a 'medicine of immortality' (to misuse Ignatius words!) but as *that which is*

[56] Cf. Dunn, 'John VI', 337, followed by this sharp observation: 'Nor can I believe it to be an accident that in John's account of Jesus' last meal with his disciples the only handling of the elements which John describes is Jesus' giving (δίδωσιν) of the bread to Judas; and far from the eating of the sop meaning a chewing of the Son of Man's "living (= life-giving) flesh", for Judas it is immediately followed by *Satan*'s entry into him (xiii.27)'. Italics original.

sacrificed, offered, 'for the life of the world' (6:51) and as that which brings recipients to share in the life-giving Passion so that they too will be 'raised up on the last day' (cf. 6:39, 40, 44, 54), that is, through their death in conformity with Christ. As de Boer comments, '6:53–56 has been written and rhetorically shaped to make that terrifying and very physical form of discipleship palatable'.[57] And, as we will see at the end of this section, this is in fact how the Eucharist was understood in the early centuries, in an immediate and dramatic manner. To receive it as such requires the Spirit and the teaching, the words, of Jesus, words which are themselves 'spirit and life' (6:63), so that, led by the Spirit, who will remind us of all that he said (cf. 14:26), a remembrance accomplished through the Scriptures (e.g. 12:16), we may 'chew' on the flesh of the Word.

Chewing the Flesh

Regarding the word 'chew' used in 6:53–9, switching from the earlier 'eating bread' to 'chewing flesh', discussion has tended to focus on whether there is a significant difference between 'chewing' and 'eating', and if so, whether this is connected to an anti-docetic emphasis on the Incarnation, or the need to really eat the flesh of Christ in the Eucharist. However, another possible background for this 'chewing' is the directive in Leviticus 11:3, that we should eat those animals that 'divide the hoof' and 'chew the cud', which very early on provided a description for how we are to read Scripture: chewing and ruminating upon its words to find in it a deeper sense. This interpretation is already found in Philo, who comments on Leviticus 11:3 (which in the LXX has 'bring-up the cud' rather than 'chew'), and draws out the implication of this in terms of 'memory':

> For just as a cud-chewing animal after biting through the food keeps it at rest in the gullet, again after a bit draws it up and masticates it and then passes it on to the belly, so also the pupil after receiving from the teacher through his ears the principles and lore of wisdom prolongs the process of learning, as he cannot at once apprehend and grasp them securely, till by using memory to call up each thing that he has heard by constant exercises which act as the cement of conceptions, he stamps a firm impression of them on his soul.[58]

[57] De Boer, *Johannine Perspectives*, 230; on 231 he paraphrases the question of 6:62 in this way: 'You find what I have said about eating my flesh and drinking my blood a stumbling block (6:60–61), but what if you should see the Son of Man (upon whom God has set his seal, 6:27, and who shall give his flesh for the life of the world, 6:51c) ascending to where he was before?' It is worth recalling the passage from the *Epistle of the Apostles* 15, the earliest evidence we have for the celebration of Pascha, as we saw in Chapter 1: 'And we said to him, "O Lord, is it perhaps necessary again that we take the cup and drink?" He said to us, "Yes, it is necessary until the day when I come with those who were killed for my sake"'.

[58] Philo, *Spec.* 4.107; cf. *Agr.* 131–5, 142.

It is tempting to see this combination of 'chewing' and 'remembering' as the background for John's emphasis on the 'remembering' facilitated by the Spirit and occurring through scriptural interpretation (cf. esp. 14:26 and 12:16).

Origen, the most notable exponent of such exegesis, is perhaps the first to take Christ's words about 'chewing' in John 6:51c–58 in this sense.[59] In his homily *On Pascha*, he interprets the words of Exod. 12:10 thus:

> Just as the mysteries of the Passover which are celebrated in the Old Testament are superseded by the truth of the New Testament, so too will the mysteries of the New Testament, which we must now celebrate in the same way, not be necessary in the resurrection, a time which is signified by the 'morning' in which 'nothing will be left, and what does remain of it will be burned with fire'.[60]

After a few missing lines, Origen comments on the following words from the same verse, 'You shall break no bone, of it', asserting that: 'we partake of the flesh of Christ, that is, of the divine Scriptures'. After a further missing ten lines, he continues:

> for the Apostle professes that the lamb of our Passover is Christ when he says 'For Christ our Paschal Lamb has been sacrificed' [1 Cor. 5:7]; his flesh and blood, as shown above, are the divine Scriptures, chewing [τρώγωμεν] which, we have Christ; the words becoming his bones, the flesh becoming the meaning from the text, following which meaning, as it were, 'we see in a mirror dimly' [1 Cor. 13:12] the things which are to come, and the blood being faith in the gospel of the 'new covenant' [cf. 1 Cor. 11:5; Luke 22:20], as the Apostle attests in the following words, 'And profaning the blood of the covenant' [Heb. 10:29]. (*Pasch.* 33)

There is no doubt that Origen takes the 'chewing' of John 6:51c–58 to imply rumination upon the Scriptures, by doing which 'we have Christ'. But there is also no ambiguity about his words regarding the necessity of celebrating 'the mysteries of the New Testament', which have superseded the Old Testament Passover and which will themselves cease only in the resurrection.

In his treatise *On Prayer*, 27, Origen is also perhaps the first to bring John 6 into his discussion of the meaning of the 'daily bread' requested in the Lord's Prayer. After quoting Christ's words extensively (6:26–9, 32–5, 51, 53–7), he

[59] See also Irenaeus, *haer.* 5.8.3: 'they meditate day and night upon the words of God that they may be adorned with good works: for this is the meaning of the ruminants'. That this is not only an 'Alexandrian' approach is noted by Schnackenburg, *John*, 2, 66, who points out that it can be found also in Theodore of Heraclea (died *c.*355), 'who had links with the Antiochian school'; cf. Frags. 37 and 38 on John 6:53, 54–5, in Joseph Reuss, *Johannes-Kommentare aus der griechischen Kirche*, TU 89 (Berlin: Akademie, 1966), 74–5. Changing interpretations of John 6 have more to do, as we will see presently, with changing patterns of eucharistic prayers over time.

[60] *Pasch.* 32. The homily *On Pascha* was only discovered in 1941; the top part of its leaves, however, are almost completely missing, but can be reconstructed from other sources. The passage quoted here is preserved in Latin by Victor of Capua. Cf. O. Guéraud and P. Nautin, *Origène: Sur la Pâque*, Christianisme Antique, 2 (Paris: Beauchesne, 1979), 216.

draws various words from these passages together with John 1:14, in an intriguing manner, and concludes with John 6:58:

> This is the 'true food', the 'flesh' of Christ, which being 'Word' has become 'flesh', in accordance with the statement, 'and the Word became flesh'. When we 'eat' and 'drink' him, he also 'dwelt in us', and when he is distributed, there is fulfilled the saying 'we beheld his glory'. 'This is the bread which came down from heaven, not like that which the ancestors ate, and died. Whoever eats this bread shall live for ever'.[61]

Christ's dwelling in us and our beholding his glory, the consequences, in John 1:14, of the Word becoming flesh, are here the result of our eating the flesh of Christ, the true food, the bread descending from heaven. This cannot mean, as we have seen above, and as Origen would certainly agree, an act of cannibalism, and so the 'becoming flesh' of John 1:14, as Origen reads it here, must refer to the Word's becoming flesh in the ascent of Jesus upon the cross as the Son of Man, resulting in the descent of his life-giving flesh, the bread descending from heaven. That Origen says that this bread is 'distributed' (with a word change from John 6:11, *διέδωκεν* to *ἀναδιδῶται*), again makes an allusion to the Eucharist likely.

Eucharist and Martyrdom

Much of the scholarly discussion on John 6, as we have seen, has been preoccupied with the question of to what extent the Eucharist is itself in view for John, and have operated with the assumption that the celebration of the Eucharist would have included some form of the words given in the so-called 'institution narratives' (1 Cor. 11:23–6; Matt. 26:26–9; Mark 14:22–5; Luke 22:14–20) that are otherwise so conspicuously lacking in John. But it is, in fact, only during the course of the fourth century that the institution narratives were introduced into the eucharistic prayers, making them more catechetical and didactic.[62] And this, in turn, was the occasion for John 6 to be interpreted *primarily* and more specifically in terms of the Eucharist.[63] In the earlier period, eucharistic prayers resembled the house table prayers found in

[61] Origen, *Or.* 27.4 (Koetschau 365.22–6): *αὔτη δέ ἐστιν ἡ «ἀληθὴς βρῶσις,» «σὰρξ» Χριστοῦ, ἥτις «λόγος» οὖσα γέγονε «σὰρξ» κατὰ τὸ εἰρημένον «καὶ ὁ λόγος σὰρξ ἐγένετο.» ὅτε δὲ <φάγοιμεν καὶ> πίοιμεν αὐτὸν, «καὶ ἐσκήνωσεν ἐν ἡμῖν»· ἐπὰν δὲ ἀναδιδῶται, πληροῦται το «ἐθεασάμεωα τὴν δόξαν αὐτοῦ.»* My translation.

[62] Cf. esp. Maxwell E. Johnson, 'Martyrs and the Mass: The Interpolation of the Narrative of Institution into the Anaphora', *Worship* 87.1 (2013), 2–22.

[63] See, especially, Cyril of Alexandria, *Commentary on John, ad loc.*, and Ezra Gebremedhin, *Life-Giving Blessing: An Inquiry into the eucharistic Doctrine of Cyril of Alexandria*, Acta Universitatis Upsaliensis, Studia Doctrinae Christianae Upsaliensia, 17 (Uppsala: Borgströms Tryckeri, 1977).

Didache 9 and 10.[64] It was, rather, the martyrs, in their public and often ritualized sacrifice in witness to Christ, who 'receive the cup of salvation and call upon the name of the Lord' (Ps. 115:4). Polycarp, for instance, before his martyrdom, prayed 'that I may share, among the number of the martyrs, in the cup of thy Christ, for resurrection to eternal life' (*MartPol* 14.2), and when his body was burnt, the smell was of 'bread being baked' (*MartPol* 15.2). The Christians of Smyrna then made sure that they were not deprived of his body, 'for they desired to commune with his holy flesh' (*MartPol* 17.1: *κοινωνῆσαι τῷ ἁγίῳ αὐτοῦ σαρκίῳ*), and they did so by gathering around his tomb to celebrate the Eucharist. As Horsting comments, 'They commune with his flesh even as they commune with the body and blood of the Lord. The conflation of the two sacrifices, of the two offerings of flesh, is complete'.[65] Likewise Ignatius, who, while speaking of the Eucharist as 'the medicine of immortality' (*Eph.* 20.2), saw his own impending death as a martyr as the occasion whereby he hopes to become 'the pure bread of Christ', and 'a word of God', and, indeed, 'a human being' (*Rom.* 4.1; 2; 6). Just as Ignatius affirms that 'the Eucharist is the flesh of our Saviour Jesus Christ who suffered for our sins' (*Smyrn.* 7.1), so he opposes any claim that Christ's suffering was only 'in appearance' (*Smyrn.* 2), and connects the reality of Christ's suffering to his own: if they say that 'he only appeared to suffer (it is they who are the appearance), why am I in bondage, and why also do I pray to fight the wild beasts? I am then dying in vain and am, even more, lying about the Lord' (*Trall.* 10; cf. *Smyrn.* 4). Christians in this period needed no reminding what it means to reply affirmatively to Christ's question: 'Are you able to drink the cup that I drink or to be baptized with the baptism with which I am baptized?' (Mark 10:38).

But, as Johnson puts it,

> in a later age it becomes necessary to underscore that the Eucharist is not simply Christ's body and blood for viaticum or nourishment, life, and immortality, but Christ's body and blood as *sacrificed*, as given and shed in his own martyrdom on the cross for the life of the world, an emphasis that the narrative of institution makes clear in a way that nothing else could. And if in an earlier time it was martyrdom itself that was the public and dramatic ritual of sacrifice and the

[64] For eucharistic prayers without an institution narrative, in addition to *Didache* 9–10, Johnson ('Martyrs and the Mass', 18), following Robert Taft ('Mass without Consecration? The Historic Agreement on the Eucharist between the Catholic Church and the Assyrian Church of the East Promulgated 26 October 2001', *Worship* 77 (2003), 482–509 at 490–3) lists *Apostolic Constitutions* 7, the *Strasbourg Papyrus*, the Acts of Thomas, the Ethiopian *Anaphora of the Apostles*, and the prayer in *The Martyrdom of Polycarp*.

[65] Albertus G. A. Horsting, 'Transfiguration of Flesh: Literary and Theological Connections Between Martyrdom Accounts and eucharistic Prayers', in Maxwell E. Johnson, ed., *Issues in Eucharistic Praying in East and West: Essays in Liturgical and Theological Analysis* (Collegeville, MN: Liturgical Press, 2010), 307–25, at 318.

> Eucharist was private and hidden, that becomes now no longer the case and the Eucharist itself, 'the bloodless service upon that sacrifice of propitiation,' in the words of Cyril (John) of Jerusalem, becomes *the* public cult and dramatic sacrifice of Christians.[66]

This new element in the eucharistic prayers invited an approach to John 6 that focused more specifically on the Eucharist itself, so that the manna and the bread are correlated directly to the eucharistic gifts rather than to Jesus himself, the central focus throughout John 6, who through offering his flesh for the life of the world by ascending the cross descends as the Son of Man offering his flesh and blood, the 'true food', the bread descending from heaven to be chewed by Christians on their way to their own eucharistic martyrdom, becoming the 'pure bread of Christ', born into life, and becoming a human being (themes we will look at in Chapter 4). As such, Jesus' replacement of the Temple and its sacrifices in his own martyrdom results not only in the possibility of feeding upon the heavenly and life-giving bread in the (initially at least) private celebration of the Eucharist and by ruminating upon Scripture, but also allows those who follow him in the public spectacle (and liturgy) of martyrdom to become, as Robin Darling Young puts it, 'the instantiation of the Temple's new presence among Christians, who saw themselves as true Israel and spiritual temples'.[67]

JOHN 7:1–10:21

The next feast, the fourth to be mentioned, is that of Tabernacles, the most popular feast of the Temple, which was, as Josephus puts it, 'a most holy and most eminent feast' and so observed 'with special care'.[68] After the dramatic assertion that Jesus remained in Galilee rather than going to Judea 'because the Jews sought to kill him', John says simply 'Now the feast of the Jews, the Tabernacles was at hand' (7:1–2). Thus begins a long account of the happenings during the week of this feast. Although Jesus was initially reluctant to join his brothers in going up to Jerusalem, for 'my time has not yet come but your time is always here' (7:6), after they left, Jesus also 'went up, not publicly but in private' (7:10), and then, 'about the middle of the Feast, Jesus went up into the temple and taught' (7:14). 'On the last day of the feast, the great day', Jesus stood up to proclaim that he is the source of living waters (7:37), resulting in 'a

[66] Johnson, 'Martyrs and the Mass', 19, referring to *Catech. Myst.* 4.8.

[67] Robin Darling Young, *In Procession Before the World: Martyrdom as Public Liturgy in the Early Church*, The Père Marquette Lecture in Theology 2001 (Milwaukee: Marquette University Press, 2001), 12.

[68] Josephus, *Ant.* 8.4.1 (100); 15.3.3 (50).

division among the people over him' (7:43). On the next day 'early in the morning he came again to the Temple' where he again taught the people (8:2). Having stopped the woman from being stoned for her sins (8:3–11), his claim to be 'the light of the world' (8:12) and the teaching that followed so provoked the Jews that 'they took up stones to throw at him', upon which 'Jesus hid himself and went out of the Temple' (8:59). John then continues immediately, 'And as he passed by, he saw a man blind from birth' (9:1). His healing of the blind man on a Sabbath day (9:14) provoked another 'division among them' (9:16). And third 'division among the Jews' (10:19) resulted after Christ identifies himself as the good shepherd, who gives his life for the world (10:11). Only after the shepherd discourse is another temporal indicator given, when it is announced three verses later, that 'It was the Feast of the Dedication at Jerusalem' (10:22), a feast celebrated three months later.[69]

The Feast of Tabernacles

The Feast of Tabernacles or Booths (Lev. 23:33–43; Deut. 16:13–15; 2 Esdras [Ezra] 3:4; Zech. 14:16–19), also known as 'the feast of ingathering' (Exod. 23:16; 34:22), 'the Feast of the LORD' (Lev. 23:39; Judg. 21:19), or simply 'the Feast' (3 Kgdm [1 Kings] 8:65; 2 Suppl. 7:8; Neh. 8:14; Ezek. 45:25), was probably originally an agricultural festival, celebrated at the time of the harvest (when the workers slept in booths), but came to recall Israel's sojourn in the wilderness and God's providential care (cf. Lev. 23:39, 43). In the period of the Second Temple, due to this feast being the preeminent feast of the Temple, it developed an eschatological dimension, looking forward to the end times when all nations would come to Jerusalem to worship there (Zech. 14:16–19).[70] According to the Mishnah, which although written much later, undoubtedly reflects in its legislation practices from the period when the Temple still stood, during this week, the pilgrims carried the *lulab*, made of

[69] That John 10:1–21 both looks back to the feast of Tabernacles and forward to the Dedication is argued by Brown, *John*, 1, 388–90. Aileen Guilding, *The Fourth Gospel and Jewish Worship: A Study of the Relation of St John's Gospel to the Ancient Jewish Lectionary System* (Oxford: Clarendon, 1960), 129–30, has shown that 'on the sabbath nearest to the Feast of the Dedication virtually all the *regular* lections for every year of the cycle contain the theme of sheep and shepherds and of God the Shepherd of Israel'.

[70] Cf. G. MacRae, 'The Meaning and Evolution of the Feast of Tabernacles', *CBQ* 22 (1960), 251–76; Thierry Maertens, *A Feast in Honor of Yahweh*, trans. Kathryn Sullivan (Notre Dame, IN: Fides Publishers, 1965), 62–97; Coloe, *God Dwells with Us*, 115–43. Jeffrey L. Rubenstein, 'Sukkot, Eschatology and Zechariah 14', *RB* 103.2 (1996), 161–95, rightly cautions against placing emphasis on the eschatological dimensions of this feast, for 'all in all, the festival had a thorough thisworldy focus' (195); yet while he notes that '*Sukkot, more than any other festival, was associated with the temple, not with eschatology*', he acknowledges that this does give the feast an eschatological dimension: 'the temple is the key eschatological concept, while Sukkot is associated with eschatology as a reflex of its association with the temple' (187, italics original).

palm, willow, and myrtle branches bound together, together with a citron, which would be held aloft and waved during specific Psalm verses (*m. Sukkah* 3:11; 4:1, 5; cf. Lev. 23:40). Each morning began with a water-libation ceremony, which involved a procession of priests descending from the Temple to the Pool of Siloam. When they reached the Water Gate, the *shofar* was sounded, and the priests filled a golden flagon with the water, which was then brought back to the Temple, where the priest carrying the flagon ascended the ramp to the altar, and placed the water in one bowel, and wine in another, each with holes in them, so that the liquids would flow down below the Temple. By the end of the first century CE, the 'Water Gate', believed to be so named because the flask for water used for libation was brought through it, was understood to intimate the future time when, as Ezekiel saw in his vision, water would flow from the threshold of the Temple.[71] Another key aspect of this feast occurred in the evenings, in the Court of the Women (*m. Sukkah* 5.2–3). Four great golden candlesticks, with four golden bowels on top of them and four ladders to each of them, with wicks made out of the worn-out drawers and girdles of the priests, were set alight, so that 'there was not a courtyard in Jerusalem that did not reflect the light of the Beth ha She'ubah', that is, the House of the Water Drawing. Finally, a third component of the feast was carried out at daybreak, when the priests, standing at the upper gate, would blow the *shofar* three times, then descend to the tenth step, where again they blew the *shofar* three times, and then three times again upon reaching the Court of the Women. They went on until they reached the gate that leads eastward, where they turned to face the West (and so with their backs to the sun but facing the Temple) and said: 'Our fathers when they were in this place turned "with their backs towards the Temple of the Lord and their faces towards the East, and they worshipped the sun towards the East"; but as for us, our eyes are turned towards the Lord' (*m. Sukkah* 5.4; Ezek. 8:16).

With this background, we can now see clearly how several passages in this section of the Gospel of John identify Christ with the Temple and this feast. 'About the middle of the feast' (7:14), when Jesus taught in the Temple, the discussion turns to Moses, the Lawgiver. As the feast lasted for a week, it must have included a Sabbath and it is possible that the reading for this would have been Deuteronomy 10, for according to Guilding, this would have been the reading for such a Sabbath on one of the three-year lectionary cycles.[72]

[71] Cf. Ezek. 47.1–2 and *Tosefta Sukkah* 3:3; Pierre Grelot, 'Jean VII, 38: Eau du rocher ou source du Temple?' *RB* 70 (1963), 43–51, at 46; Germain Bienaimé, *Moïse et le don de l'eau dans la tradition juive ancienne: Targum et Midrash*, Analecta Biblica 98 (Rome: Biblical Institute Press, 1984), 202; and Rubenstein, 'Sukkot', 189: 'Israelite myth viewed the temple as *axis mundi* and the foundation of cosmic order, as located above the subterranean waters and as the ultimate source of fertility. The cult actualized those powers through ritual, tapping the temple's resources and bringing blessing and fertility to the land'.

[72] Cf. Guilding, *The Fourth Gospel and Jewish Worship*, 96.

Whereas the Jewish teachers would have traced their teaching back through a line of teachers that claimed to derive from Moses himself, Jesus traces his authority back to the one who sent him, the Father (cf. 7:16–18), and, alluding back to his healing of the lame man on the Sabbath the last time he was in Jerusalem (7:21; cf. 5:1–18), he argues that if circumcision is permissible on the Sabbath, then they should not be angry with him when he heals 'the whole human being' (7:23: *ὅλον ἄνθρωπον*). Although the Jews say 'we know where this man comes from; and when the Christ appears, no one will know where he comes from' (7:27), Jesus' rhetorical question given in reply suggests otherwise: 'You know me and you know where I come from?' Moreover, 'the one who sent me is true, and him you do not know' (7:28), he asserts, despite the fact that when he was last in Jerusalem he had clearly spoken about how he had come from the Father and in the Father's name, whereas they prefer to 'receive glory from one another and do not seek the glory that comes from the only God' (5:44): as such, it is Moses himself who stands in accusation against them (cf. 5:36–47). As Coloe concludes: 'In the context of Tabernacles and its daily ritual and affirmation of faith in Israel's one true God, the Jerusalemites are blind to the identity of Jesus and so repeat the act of their fathers who rejected God and turned to the sun (*m. Sukk.* 5:4)'.[73]

The water-libation ritual is alluded to on the last day of the feast in arresting words.[74] The three key verses are:

> [7:37] On the last day of the feast, the great day, Jesus stood up and proclaimed, 'If anyone thirst, let him come to me and drink. [38] He who believes in me, as the Scripture has said, "Out of his belly shall flow living waters"'. [39] Now this he said about the Spirit, which those who believe in him were yet to receive, for as yet the Spirit was not, because Jesus was not yet glorified. (7:37–9)[75]

The punctuation as given here, with a full stop after 'drink' at the end of 7:37, is how it is found in the second-century manuscript P[66] and also modern critical editions (Nestle–Aland 28th revised edition, 2013; UBS 4th revised edition, 1993). This makes 7:38 begin with a participial phrase, a very common feature of the Gospel of John, occurring forty-one times on Brown's count, rather than tacking it on to the previous conditional sentence, a construction not found in John, and, as Brown further notes, 'making the participle the anticipated subject of the Scripture citation . . . has little support in Johannine style'.[76] The apparent obstacle to taking the text the way that P[66], NA, and UBS

[73] Coloe, *God Dwells with Us*, 125.

[74] For a full discussion see Coloe, *God Dwells with Us*, 125–34.

[75] [37] *Ἐν δὲ τῇ ἐσχάτῃ ἡμέρᾳ τῇ μεγάλῃ τῆς ἑορτῆς εἱστήκει ὁ Ἰησοῦς καὶ ἔκραξεν λέγων, Ἐάν τις διψᾷ ἐρχέσθω πρός με καὶ πινέτω.* [38] *ὁ πιστεύων εἰς ἐμέ, καθὼς εἶπεν ἡ γραφή, ποταμοὶ ἐκ τῆς κοιλίας αὐτοῦ ῥεύσουσιν ὕδατος ζῶντος.* [39] *τοῦτο δὲ εἶπεν περὶ τοῦ πνεύματος ὃ ἔμελλον λαμβάνειν οἱ πιστεύσαντες εἰς αὐτόν: οὔπω γὰρ ἦν πνεῦμα, ὅτι Ἰησοῦς οὐδέπω ἐδοξάσθη.*

[76] Cf. Brown, *John*, 1.321.

do is that it seems to imply that the believer becomes a source of water for others, for the waters flow 'out of' the believer (ἐκ τῆς κοιλίας αὐτοῦ), something not implied in the similar text of John 4:14, where the waters flow 'in' the believer (ἐν αὐτῷ). Thus, some commentators propose that the text should be punctuated differently and translated otherwise. Brown suggests:

> If anyone thirst, let him come to me;
> and let drink he who believes in me.
> As the Scripture says,
> 'From within him shall flow rivers of living water'.[77]

Although this 'Christological' reading preserves the emphasis on Christ as the *source* of the living water, it is nevertheless odd, for 7:39 makes clear that what preceded is spoken as a whole by Christ, with him citing a scriptural verse with a third-person pronoun referring to the speaker ('his belly'). The source of the scriptural quotation is equally perplexing, with commentators selecting different verses depending on the way in which they interpret this passage.[78] Yet if the scriptural citation were a later interpolation, as Bultmann has it, it would surely, as Fee argues, been given in a clear enough form to be identifiable.[79]

Cutting through the division among the scholars about Jesus' words, Coloe has rightly drawn attention to the significance of the phrases which precede and follow the contested sentences. First, the setting is 'the last day of the feast, the great day' (7:37). As Coloe notes, this might refer to either the seventh day of the feast or the eighth day when 'a holy convocation' was to be held (Lev. 23:34–6). If 'the last day' refers to the former, then the water imagery in 7:37–8 alludes to the seventh day procession around the altar with the water-libation, for the water and light rituals only lasted during the seven days (*m. Sukkah* 4:1). On the other hand, the eighth day, the 'last festival-day of the feast' on which the *Hallel* and the Rejoicing continued (*m. Sukkah* 4:8), would, as Coloe puts it, 'have provided the vacuum in which Jesus' offer of water and light would have been more keenly appreciated'.[80] A third alternative, proposed by Zane

[77] Brown, *John*, 1.319. Brown claims that such an interpretation goes back to the second century, the time of Justin, and is paralleled by the *Gospel of Thomas*, 13, as well as Hippolytus, Tertullian, Cyprian, Irenaeus, Aphraates, Ephrem; and among modern commentators, Boismard, Braun, Bultmann, Dodd, Hoskyns, Jeremias, Macgregor, Mollat, and Stanley, to which Coloe (*God Dwells with Us*, 127) adds Ashton, Burge, Beasely-Murray, Moloney, and Schnackenburg. Brown describes the construction of these verses as an 'excellent poetic parallelism', though this has been called into question, and John makes very little use of such parallelism anyway. Cf. Coloe (ibid. 126) lists as those commentators who support the traditional reading: Barrett, Haechen, Lightfoot, Leon-Dufour, Kysar, Lindars, Marsh, Morris, Pfitzner, and Schwank.

[78] According to Coloe, ibid., 130–1, those who take a 'Christological' reading of 7:37–8, suggest Isa. 12:3; Zech. 13:1; Ezek. 47:1; Exod. 17:5–6; Num. 20:7–16 and Ps. 77:15–16; while those who take the traditional interpretation, suggest Zech. 14:8; Prov. 4:23, 5:15; Sir. 24:30–3; to which she also adds Isa. 58:11 and Prov. 18:4.

[79] Gordon D. Fee, 'Once More—John 7:37–9', *ExpTim* 89 (1978), 116–18, at 117.

[80] Coloe, *God Dwells with Us*, 129.

Hodges and followed by Coloe, is that the expression looks beyond the immediate context of the feast towards the final 'hour' of Jesus.[81] 'The last day' has already been mentioned several times in the preceding chapter, as the day when Jesus will raise up to life those who believe in him (6:39, 40, 44, 54), and will be mentioned again in the following chapters (11:24, 12:48), and the next 'great' day is the Passover-Sabbath day following the crucifixion (19:31). That it was 'still dark' 'on the first day of the week' means that it was still on this same 'great day' that Mary Magdalene found the tomb empty (20:1). Thus, as Hodges puts it, 'in the theology of this Gospel "the last day" signifies the day of resurrection for believers—and hence the day of their glorification!'[82] As 7:38 looks forward to a promised time when the rivers of living water 'shall flow' (ῥεύσουσιν), so also does 7:39, 'the Spirit was not because Jesus was not yet glorified', for believers in Jesus are 'yet to receive' the Spirit, which they receive, in the resurrection, on the eighth day (20:19–22). The eschatological orientation of 7:37–9 is clearly there with the reference to 'the last day' and the reading of Zechariah 14 as one of the *haphtarah* readings for the feast. As Coloe concludes, 'the rituals of Tabernacles provide the liturgical context for the proleptic interruption of the Johannine "last day"'.[83]

Regarding the scriptural quotation which speaks of 'living waters' flowing 'from his belly', Coloe, following Grelot, holds that this is an Aramaic idiom deriving from a targumic reading. Following the rabbinic exegetical principle of combing a verse, usually from the Torah, with another from the prophets, Grelot suggests that in this case Numbers 21:16, recalling the time when God provided water in the desert from the rock that Moses was commanded to strike (cf. Exod. 17:6), was combined with the 'living waters' of Zechariah 14:8 (and see also Ps. 77:20).[84] In this case the rock is Jesus (cf. 1 Cor. 10:4), from whose side flow the living waters. However, as we have also seen, the Water Gate was understood in terms of the Temple, from the threshold of which would flow waters that are also 'living' in that they give life (Ezek. 47:9). Given that Ezekiel 47:1 explicitly names the Temple as the place from where the waters flow, whereas Zechariah 14:8 only names Jerusalem, it is much more likely that it is Ezekiel's vision of the Temple that is in the background of the description of the feast than the traditions about the rock.

Yet the problematic third-person pronoun in 7:38 remains: it is clear that, even taking a Christological reading of 7:37–8, the 'his' must refer to the believer. Can the image of the Temple then also be applied to the believer? To explain this, Coloe appeals to the difference between the time of the scene of the feast and that of the writing and reading of the Gospel, the merging of

[81] Zane C. Hodges, 'Rivers of Living Water—John 7:37–9', *Bibliotheca Sacra* 136 (1979), 239–48, at 247; Coloe, *God Dwells with Us*, 129.

[82] Hodges, 'Rivers of Living Water', at 247.

[83] Coloe, *God Dwells with Us*, 130.

[84] Grelot, 'Jean, VII, 38', 47–8.

times or melding of horizons that we discussed in the Introduction, 'the paradox of presence in absence', as Coloe describes it, which is present throughout John's Gospel.[85] This is a distinction within the text of 7:37–9, as it too looks forward to the promise that rivers of water 'shall flow' out of the believer's side and that the Spirit will also be given when Christ is glorified. Whereas a reader, given everything we have seen, especially John 2:13–22, would have been expecting an affirmation that the living water would come from the side of Jesus, the 'jarring note' of the third-person pronoun in 7:38 is 'not immediately comprehensible', waiting for 7:39 which 'confirms that the text cannot be deciphered accurately in the present time, as there is a "not yet" time and a future gift to which the text refers'.[86] If within the framework of the narrative itself, the eighth day is the most appropriate day for Jesus' words on 'the last day of the feast', as the day when the waters and light have apparently stopped, so that it becomes evident that he is a source of water for the thirsty (7:37) and a light for those in darkness (8:12), for John and his readers, after the Passion, and after the destruction of the Temple (if the Gospel is dated to a later period), Jesus himself is the Temple, providing water and light, given through the gift of the Spirit bestowed upon the disciples in the resurrection on the eighth day (20:19–23). What applies to Christ himself within the narrative is promised, in a future time, to the believer, so that through the gift of the Spirit, as Coloe puts it, 'such cultic images will also apply to the believer. The future, post-resurrection time, forcefully interrupts the narrative, bringing the eschatological "last day" into the present moment in Jesus' words'.[87] As we saw in the conclusion of our discussion of John 6, Temple imagery was applied to the martyrs, and indeed was earlier affirmed, by the Apostle, of all believers, whose bodies are 'temple[s] of the Holy Spirit' (1 Cor. 6:19).

After the episode with the woman caught in adultery (8:2–11)—a passage that, as we have earlier noted, is perhaps alluded to by Papias, but that has no record in the early textual witnesses, nor in commentaries during the first millennium, yet does form a counterpart to the Jews' attempt to stone Jesus at the end of John 8—Jesus again speaks of himself in terms drawn from the Feast of Tabernacles: 'I am the light of the world; he who follows me will not walk in darkness but will have the light of life' (8:12). In addition to the festival light celebrated in the feast, as we have seen above, the image of light also, of course, alludes back to the pillar of fire and cloud that accompanied Israel in the wilderness and the 'glory of God' that filled the Tabernacle and the Temple. The discussion between Jesus and the Jews then turns to his origins, naming the one who sent him as 'Father' (8:19, unlike the parallel in 7:28–9),

[85] Coloe, *God Dwells with Us*, 130. See also the theme of 'the bubbling spring' and the doubling between Christ and Thomas in the *Gospel of Thomas* 13, discussed in Stang, *Our Divine Double*, 97–9.

[86] Coloe, *God Dwells with Us*, 133.

[87] Ibid. 133.

and using 'I AM' three times (8:18, 24, 28). There is another possible association between the divine name and the Feast of Tabernacles, which is that as the pilgrims went around the altar, carrying their willow branches, they would call upon the Lord using the Psalm verse, 'Save now, we beseech you, O LORD! We beseech you, O LORD [*ana YHWH*], send now prosperity' (Ps. 118:25 MT); though as this would have involved pronouncing the divine name, R. Judah asserted that they say '*Ani waho!* save us we pray' (*m. Sukkah* 4:5). And finally, parallel to the relationship between Christ and Moses addressed at the middle of the feast, John 8 closes by discussing the relationship between Christ and Abraham. The Jews, though claiming to be children of Abraham, are accused by Jesus of not doing what Abraham did: 'Your father Abraham rejoiced that he was to see my day; he saw it and was glad' (8:56). As Coloe notes, according to Jubilees, Abraham was the first to celebrate the Feast of Tabernacles and emphasizes his joy in so doing.[88]

The Blind Man

The theme of light continues into John 9: 'As long as I am in the world, I am the light of the world' (9:5). And as the light, it is appropriate that he now gives sight to the man born blind. This miracle is said to have taken place on a Sabbath day (9:14), and there is no reason to see this episode as taking place at any other time than during the Feast of Tabernacles. Certainly at the end of John 8 Jesus 'went out of the Temple' (8:59); but John 9 gives no sense of temporal distance: 'And as he passed by . . . ' (9:1; the regular omission of the 'and' in translations is what gives the impression that this is an independent block, standing in some unspecified time). Moreover, there is no reason, as Peter Leithart points out, to separate John 10:1–21 as a separate, stand-alone, discourse on 'the Good Shepherd': 10:1 also continues directly from the preceding verse.[89] In addition, the 'division' that the healing of the man

[88] Coloe, *God Dwells with Us*, 138–9; cf. *Jubilees*, 16.20–7 (in Charlesworth, *Old Testament Pseudepigrapha*, 2). As Coloe also notes, this passage contains some of the harshest invective against the 'Jews', which, it must be remembered, 'is best understood as a struggle between adolescent siblings trying to establish their own self-identity in the aftermath of the destruction of Jerusalem', so that 'the *Ioudaioi* in the Johannine Gospel must be read as a narrative device rather than as a description of members of Second Temple Judaism. . . . "The Jews" in the gospel narrative are a caricature of the unbelieving world that rejects Jesus, and in their rejection show that they are not true *sperma Abram*'. For further exploration of this theme, see Boyarin, *Border Lines*.

[89] Peter Leithart, *Deep Exegesis: The Mystery of Reading Scripture* (Waco, TX: Baylor University Press, 2009), 162: 'there is no change of scene at the beginning of chapter 10. Worse, there is no change of speaker. Jesus begins a speech in 9:41, and editors of the New Testament, going back to Stephen Langland, have rudely interrupted him with a chapter break. In John's original Greek, of course, there is no white space between "your sins remain" and "truly, truly I say to you". The Good Shepherd Discourse . . . is a continuation of Jesus' sharp rebuke to the

born blind causes among the Jews (9:16) is picked up again, in the third mention of a 'division' during this long account of the Feast of the Tabernacle, in 10:19 (the first 'division' being 7:43), with some saying that Jesus is possessed by a demon, and others asking 'can a demon open the eyes of the blind?' (10:21), clearly indicating that the discussion in 10:1–21 is about the miraculous healing that just preceded it. Only then do we pass, and directly, to 'It was the Feast of the Dedication' (10:22). John 7:1–10.21 must be understood as a complete unit.

There is another aspect of the healing of the man born blind, as it is described in this very intricately written narrative, which ties back to the earlier healing of the lame man, where it is specifically stated that Jesus heals 'the whole human being' (7:23: *ὅλον ἄνθρωπον*). Jesus does not just simply heal the man born blind by his word, but in the most peculiar way imaginable, by spitting on the ground, making clay, and anointing the man's eyes with the mud (9:6). His disciples' question that prompted this whole event, 'who sinned, this man or his parents, that he was born blind?' (9:2), though often taken as a question of theodicy, is answered by Jesus quite differently: it is not a matter of human sins, 'but that the works of God might be made manifest in him' (9:3). Putting these together, Irenaeus notes that the action by which Jesus healed the man born blind (and therefore not as a result of human causes) parallels the action by which God created human beings at the beginning, taking clay from the earth and mixing his own power with it, so that, as this is done 'that the works of God might be made manifest in him', Irenaeus can conclude 'the work of God is fashioning the human being'.[90]

The narrative of the blind man is one of the most masterfully drawn ones in the whole of the Gospel. As George Beasley-Murray points out, there are seven scenes, each obeying the rule that no scene should have more than two characters.[91] Through the gradual development of the dialogue, the man born blind is led progressively into a full confession of faith. Initially he has

Pharisees, which actually begins with Jesus announcing judgment on those who see (v.39)'. See also Ulrich Busse, 'Open Questions on John 10', in Johannes Beutler and Robert Fortna, eds, *The Shepherd Discourse of John 10 and its Context: Studies by Members of the Johannine Writing Seminar*, SNTSMS 67 (Cambridge: Cambridge University Press, 1991), 6–17. As Coloe, *God Dwells with Us*, 146–51, shows, although picking up on imagery from 10:1–21, 10:22–42 is a carefully structured unity, in which Christ defines his role as the Messianic Shepherd King.

[90] Irenaeus, *haer.* 5.15.2: *opera autem Dei plasmatio est hominis.* Daniel Frayer-Griggs, 'Spittle, Clay, and Creation in John 9:6 and Some Dead Sea Scrolls', *JBL* 132.3 (2013): 659–70, points to a possible background for the action of Christ in John 9 and Irenaeus' interpretation, in the description of the human being as 'spat saliva, moulded clay' in some texts of the Dead Sea Scrolls (1QS 11.21–2; 1QH 20.24–27, 31–2; 4Q511 frags. 28, 29).

[91] George R. Beasley-Murray, *John, Word Biblical Commentary* (Waco, TX: Word, 1987), 152: (1) 9:1–7, the account of the miracle; (2) 9:8–12, neighbours question the man; (3) 9:13–17, Pharisees' interrogation of the man; (4) 9:18–23, Pharisees interrogate parents; (5) 9:24–34, Pharisees further interrogate man; (6) 9:35–8 Jesus leads man to confession of faith; (7) 9: 39–31, Jesus and Pharisees.

no idea who healed him, for Jesus is not named in 9:6–7, and once he washes himself in the pool, as directed by Jesus, and returns, Jesus is gone. In 9:11 the man refers to 'the man called Jesus', and John again mentions Jesus' name in 9:14, and then he is not named again until 9:35, when Jesus hears that the man was 'cast out' (cf. 9:22, 'cast out of the synagogue'). During this time, through interrogation both by his neighbours and the Pharisees, the man describes the one who healed him 'as a prophet' (9:17) and one 'from God' (9:33), and then, after being asked by Jesus, 'Do you believe in the Son of Man?' (9:35), and being told, after asking about the identity of the Son of Man, 'you have seen him and it is he who speaks to you' (9:37), the man's role culminates with his confession and worship: '"Lord, I believe" and he worshiped him' (9:38). As the man's faith grows, however, the Pharisees in turn increasingly lose their sight. They start off by asserting that Jesus is 'not from God', for he does not keep the Sabbath (9:16); they threaten to expel Jesus' disciples from the synagogue (9:22); they claim that Jesus is 'a sinner' (9:24); they do not know where Jesus has come from (9:29). As Leithart puts it, 'by the end of the story, their blindness is obvious. A blind man has been given sight, and they cannot see the implications'.[92] Moreover, throughout the whole course of this episode Jesus is named seven times, and this is not, Leithart argues, an accident.[93] The miraculous healing of the man born blind, which, as Irenaeus already noted, recapitulates and completes the creation of the human being described in Genesis, is the sixth of the signs performed by Jesus in John's Gospel. The Sabbath on which this happens is not the Sabbath of the Pharisees, on which no work is carried out, but, by a merging of the times or melding of horizons, the Sabbath of God himself, whose 'work is fashioning the human being' in the stature of Christ himself, who is indicated by the number seven, not six.

JOHN 10:22–42

The account of the Feast of the Dedication of the Temple, the fifth feast to be mentioned, is much briefer than that of Tabernacles. This feast was not one of the three original pilgrim feasts, but a celebration of the rededication of the Temple in 164 BCE by Judas Maccabeus, after its desecration by Antiochus IV. The rededication was celebrated for eight days and was modelled on the Feast of Tabernacles, recalling how, as in Israel's earlier history, they too had wandered homeless in the mountains (cf. 2 Makk. 10:6). One of the main aspects of this rededication was the positioning of the lamp-stand in the Temple and lighting it with the fire that had been miraculously preserved

[92] Leithart, *Deep Exegesis*, 164. [93] Ibid. 166.

from the destruction of the first Temple (cf. 2 Makk. 1:18–36), so that it illumined the whole shrine (cf. 1 Makk. 4:50). As such, the feast was also known, according to Josephus, as 'Lights' (*Ant.* 12.7.7 [325]).

At the feast, while Jesus 'was walking in the Temple, in the portico of Solomon' (10:23), the Jews gathered round him, asking him to say plainly whether he is the Christ (10:24). In his reply, Jesus again uses shepherding imagery, but this time in terms of the sheep whom the Father has given him, who know his voice, and, moreover, 'no one is able to snatch them out of my hand' just as 'no one is able to snatch them out of the Father's hand', so that 'I and the Father are one' (10:28–30). Not surprisingly this identification provokes outrage, with the Jews again taking up stones to stone him, with the accusation that 'you, being a human, make yourself God' (10:33). This is the final charge that is brought against Jesus, and repeated in the trial scene (19:7: 'he has made himself the Son of God'). It is in Jesus' reply to this charge that the particular theme of the present feast is brought to the fore:

> Jesus answered them: 'Is it not written in your law, "I said you are gods"? If he called them gods to whom the Word of God came (and Scripture cannot be broken) do you say of him whom the Father consecrated and sent into the world, "you are blaspheming," because I said I am the Son of God? If I am not doing the works of my Father, then do not believe me; but if I do them, even though you do not believe me, believe the works, that you may know and understand that the Father is in me and I am in the Father'. (10:34–8; Ps. 81:6)

At issue here, as Ashton points out, is the interpretation of Psalm 81, specifically the question of to whom is it addressed?[94]

> [1] God stood in the congregation of gods,
> in their midst he judges the gods
> . . .
>
> [6] I said, 'you are gods,
> all sons of the Most High,
> but you shall die like human beings

It cannot be, as Ashton rightly observes, that Jesus appeals to Psalm 81:6 simply to reassure his audience that the term 'god' can be used loosely, for it would never then have provoked the reaction that it did. The background for the reaction is found, rather, in the various ways in which this Psalm was being read. Some took the word 'gods' as 'angels', as it is rendered in the Peshitta version, as J. A. Emerton pointed out ('God stood in the congregation of God, he judges amongst the angels . . . "You are angels, . . ."'), and as

[94] Cf. Ashton, *Fourth Gospel*, 91–4.

is also done elsewhere in the Peshitta and targumim, as well as texts from Qumran.[95] On the other hand, in some of the texts from Qumran, such as the songs for the Sabbath sacrifice, there appear, alongside other heavenly beings, such as princes and angles, other beings called *elim* and *elohim*: Carol Newsom translates the second by 'god-like beings', while Geza Vermes, though properly translating both by 'god', puts scare quotes around the second, when it is used for beings other than God.[96] Moreover, in the Melchizedek text (11Q13), the 'God' who has taken his place in the divine council (Ps. 81:1) is taken as referring to Melchizedek himself, who had appeared on earth as a human being (Gen. 14:18–20). With this background of the ways in which Psalm 81 was being read, its use by Jesus becomes more striking. As Ashton concludes, however, 'the big difference is that in the Fourth Gospel the whole heavenly court is encapsulated in the person of Jesus; apart from the Father he alone is given the title'.[97] He alone is not simply one of the sons of the Most High, but 'the Son of God' and himself 'God' (cf. 1:1; 1:18, reading μονογενὴς θεός; 20:28). And he is so specifically as the one that the Father has 'consecrated and sent [ἡγίασεν καὶ ἀπέστειλεν] into the world' (10:36). The verb for 'consecrated' is the very same verb that is used for the consecration of the Temple courts (1 Makk. 4:48; cf. 3 Makk. 2:9, 16), and, before that, for the house built by Solomon but consecrated by the Lord for his name (2 Suppl. 7:20). This episode at the Feast of the Dedication of the Temple therefore makes clear, once again, that it is Christ himself who is the Temple, the one who is consecrated by the Father and sent into the world as the locus of the glory of God (cf. 1:14). It is, finally, these same verbs, 'consecrate' and 'send', that will be used by Jesus in his prayer to the Father with regard to his disciples (17:17–19), that they too may be brought into the unity that he has with his Father and might share in his glory (17:21–4).

When Jesus leaves the Temple, never to return, he does so by going 'away again across the Jordan to the place where John at first baptized' (10:40). This movement from the Temple, to the portico of Solomon, eastward across the Jordan, as Coloe points out, 'traces the path of God's glory when it left the Solomonic Temple prior to its destruction by the Babylonians'.[98] The parallel is ominous, and looks ahead to Jesus' final moment.

[95] J. A. Emerton, 'Some New Testament Notes, I. Interpretation of Psalm 82 and John 10', *JTS* ns 11 (1960), 329–32; and J. A. Emerton, 'Melchizedek and the Gods: Fresh Evidence for the Jewish Background of John 10:34–6', *JTS* ns 17 (1966), 399–401.

[96] Cf. esp. 4Q403 1, 1, 30–6; Carol Newsom, *Songs of the Sabbath Sacrifice: A Critical Edition*, HSS 27 (Atlanta, GA: Scholars Press, 1985), 211–13; Geza Vermes, *The Complete Dead Sea Scrolls in English* (New York: Penguin, 1997), 325–6.

[97] Ashton, *Fourth Gospel*, 93.

[98] Coloe, *God Dwells with Us*, 155.

JOHN 14:1–3

After the Feast of the Dedication, the path towards Jesus' final hour, at the third Passover mentioned in the Gospel of John, moves relentlessly forward with increasing immediacy and urgency: after the raising of Lazarus, 'the Passover of the Jews was at hand' (11:55); 'Six days before the Passover' Jesus went to Bethany, where Mary anointed his feet with precious ointment, which she kept for his burial (12:1–8); 'the next day' Jesus entered Jerusalem to the cry 'Hosanna! Blessed is he that comes in the name of the Lord, the King of Israel' (12:12–13); when the Gentiles want to see Jesus, he knows that 'the hour has come for the Son of Man to be glorified' (12:20–3). Then, 'before the Feast of the Passover, when Jesus knew that his hour had come to depart out of this world to the Father, having loved his own who were in the world, he loved them to the end' (13:1). What follows prepares the way for Jesus to allude to the Temple in new ways. As Alan Kerr argues, the foot-washing, which is necessary if his disciples are to have a 'part' in him (13:8), cleanses them for entry into the new Temple, the Temple which is Jesus himself, and so to be a part of the Temple and all that entails, including laying down one's life, as Peter eventually does even if he first denies him three times, 'for you shall follow afterward' (13:36–8).[99]

In the words that follow, Jesus alludes to the Temple with three different words:

> [14:1] 'Let not your hearts be troubled; believe in God, believe also in me. [2] In my Father's household [οἰκίᾳ] are many dwelling places [μοναὶ]; if it were not so, would I have told you that I go to prepare a place [τόπον] for you? [3] And when I go and prepare a place [τόπον] for you, I will come again and will take you to myself, that where I am you may be also. [4] And you know the way where I am going'.

Although it is tempting to think of Jesus as speaking about heaven, he is not.[100] In the Hebrew text of the Scriptures, the Temple was in fact far more frequently spoken of as 'the House of the Lord'.[101] In the first and most explicit identification of Christ as the Temple in the Gospel, in John 2:13–25, the terminology changes from the 'holy place' (2:14, ἱερῷ) to 'the house of the Father' (2:16, οἶκον) to 'temple of his body' (2:21, ναοῦ), moving

[99] Kerr, *The Temple of Jesus' Body*, 278–92; Cf. J. C. Thomas, *Footwashing in John 13 and the Johannine Community*, JSNTSup 61 (Sheffield: Sheffield Academic Press, 1991).

[100] As does Carson, *John*, 489: 'The simplest explanation is best: *my Father's house* refers to heaven, and in heaven there are many *rooms*, many dwelling-places'.

[101] Coloe, *God Dwells with Us*, 160, n. 5, calculates that 'the House of the Lord' appears 231 times, while 'Temple' only sixty times. With the attention given to the furnishings, this is not surprising. Cf. M. Haran, 'The Divine Presence in the Israelite Cult and the Cultic Institutions', *Biblica* 50 (1969), 251–67, at 255.

from the physical building, to the identification with Jesus himself, and then to the living flesh of Christ. In John 14, this movement, as Coloe observes, 'continues and extends beyond one person to a group of people in a household or a familiar relationship'.[102] Whereas the term 'house' (*οἶκος*) is only used elsewhere in the Gospel of John to refer to a physical building (2:16–17; 11:20), the word *οἰκία* has a wider range of meanings, including not only a physical building (11:31; 12:3) but also a 'household' (4:53; 8:35). As with Jesus' words to the Samaritan woman, true worship of God is not localized in space (cf. 4:23). When the risen Christ comes to his disciples, although the doors are 'shut', there is no mention of a 'house' (20:19), not even eight days later when 'his disciples were again within' (20:26, *ἔσω*; English translations regularly supply the words 'the house'). As Kerr argues, 'this relativizing of space with respect to the Johannine Jesus is deliberate', so that even if the 'metaphors' used in 14:1–3 are 'spatial', they should not be understood in spatial terms.[103] They express, rather, in terms that allude to the Temple, not a building but instead the relationship to the Father through Christ entered into by the believer. Or as Robert Gundry put it, 'The Father's house is no longer heaven, but God's household or family'.[104]

The term 'dwelling place' (*μονή*) likewise can be understood as a physical residence, and hence the regular translation of 14:2 as 'In my Father's house are many rooms'. But, as with the change from 'house' to 'household', the term *μονή* needs to be understood within the context of John 14–15, and its repeated emphasis on 'dwelling' (*μένω*): the Father 'dwells' in Jesus (14:10); the Spirit, another 'Counsellor' after Christ, 'dwells' in the disciples and 'will be in' them (14:17); Jesus 'dwells' with the disciples (14:25).[105] In the midst of all these affirmations about 'dwelling', when Christ says in 14:23 that he and the Father will come to those who love him and keep his word 'and make our dwelling-place [*μονὴν*] with him', the dwelling-place must be understood not spatially, but as the dwelling of the Father and the Son in the believer. Moreover, as Coloe points out, the subject of the verb *μένω* throughout John 14 'is not the *believer* but *God*. The action therefore is not the *believers* coming to dwell in God's heavenly abode, but the *Father*, the *Paraclete*, and *Jesus* coming to dwell with believers'.[106] The setting of the scene for Jesus' departing words to his disciples reinforces the point: Jesus gathers 'his own' (13:1, *τοὺς*

[102] Coloe, *God Dwells with Us*, 161. [103] Kerr, *Temple of Jesus' Body*, 294.

[104] Robert H. Gundry, '"In My Father's House There are Many *Μοναί*" (John 14:2)', *ZNW* 53 (1967), 68–72, at 70.

[105] The language continues in John 15, beginning with the image of the vine: 'dwell in me and I in you' as the branch in the vine (15:4); 'the one who dwells in' Christ will bear much fruit, whereas one who does not so 'dwell' will be cast off (15:5–6); 'if you dwell in me and my words dwell in you', what you ask will be done (15:7); 'dwell in my love', twice, as Christ 'dwells' in the Father's love (15:9–10).

[106] Coloe, *God Dwells with Us*, 163. Italics original.

ἰδίους), and once Judas departed, addresses them as his 'children' (13:33, τεκνία; cf. 1:11–12). It is the community of believers, with the Spirit of God dwelling in them so that they become the dwelling place of the Father and the Son, that is now the household of God.

The third phrase used in 14:1–3, that of a 'place' (τόπος) that has been specially prepared, also harkens back to the way Scripture speaks of the Tabernacle and the Temple. According to Coloe, with the exception of Exod. 23:20, any mention of a specially prepared place in the Masoretic text refers to the place prepared for the Ark.[107] David 'built houses for himself in the city of David, and he prepared a place for the Ark of God and made a tent for it' (1 Suppl. 15:1). Likewise with the Temple: it is in 'the place that David had prepared' that Solomon built the Lord's house in Jerusalem (2 Suppl. 3:1). And, as Solomon reports in his prayer for wisdom: 'You said that I should build a Temple on your holy mountain, an altar in the city of your encampment, a copy of the holy tent that you prepared beforehand from the beginning' (Wis. 9:8). From the beginning God has been preparing this holy 'place' for his encamping. The Temple, as a copy of Moses' tabernacle, and the tabernacle itself, constructed by Moses 'according to the pattern that had been shown [to him] on the mountain' (Exod. 25:40), are 'copies and shadows' of the heavenly reality (cf. Heb. 8:5), prepared from the beginning and now realized in Christ and the 'place' that he prepares for his disciples. Moreover, the preparation of this holy place is closely bound up with the preparation of a people. It is by preparing a people that God comes to dwell among them: 'You prepared your people Israel for yourself, a people forever and you, O Lord, have become their God' (2 Kgdms. 7:24). It is not David who will build a house for the Lord, but rather David who is made a house, when the Lord raises up his offspring, as his own son ('I will be his father and he shall be my son'), for he 'will build a house for my name' (2 Kgdms. 8:11–14).

Likewise the word 'place' itself has special significance in the Gospel of John and its scriptural background. We have already seen the allusion to Jacob in John 1:50–1, transferring what Jacob said about a 'place' (Gen. 28:16, 'the Lord is in this place') to the person of Christ as the Son of Man. It was also mentioned in the dialogue with the Samaritan woman, in her question about Jerusalem being the 'place' where God is to be worshipped (4:20). In John 11:48, after the raising of Lazarus, the Pharisees worry that if Jesus is allowed to continue everyone will believe in him and the Romans will come and 'destroy our place and our nation'. It is through their determination to have him put to death (cf. 11:53), of course, that the true holy place, Christ himself, is raised up upon the earth. Finally, it is to 'the place of the skull' that Jesus was taken, bearing his own cross (19:17). Bearing the wood upon

[107] Ibid. 164.

which he would be sacrificed, Jesus fulfils the aborted sacrifice of Isaac, the beloved son of his father (cf. Gen. 22:2, 12), who bore the wood upon which he was to be sacrificed to the 'place' specified by God (Gen. 22:3, 4, 9, 14) in the land of Moriah upon the mountain identified by God (Gen. 22:2 MT), which became identified as the very spot upon which the Temple in Jerusalem was built (2 Suppl. 3:1). The 'place', moreover, is the place for the people: as Nehemiah prays, 'Plant your people in your holy place, as Moses promised' (2 Makk. 1:29).

'House' or 'household', 'dwelling place', and 'place', these words of Christ open out onto a rich broadening of the Temple as it is now completed, finished, perfected. The interconnection between the Temple and the people, or the substitution by the latter for the former, is not new to John, but is already found elsewhere. One of the most striking places in which the interchangeability of Temple and people is a verse from Sirach:

> How are we to magnify Zorobabel?
> He too was like a signet on the right hand,
> so was Jesus, son of Iosedek,
> who in their days, built a house
> and lifted up [ἀνύψωσαν] a holy temple/people to the Lord
> prepared for everlasting glory. (Sir. 49:11–12)

While some manuscripts of the text have 'temple' others have 'people'. As Coloe notes, this passage is full of associations with the Gospel of John: 'Jesus', being 'lifted up', 'house', 'prepare', and 'glory'.[108]

Further parallels to the idea of the community as the Temple or house of God are found in the Qumran texts. Some of these texts, especially the *Community Rule* (1QS), make it clear that the community, having broken with the Temple and priesthood in Jerusalem, thought of itself, the *Yahad*, the community, as being in some sense a new Temple.[109] The *Community Rule*, however, does not speak of God dwelling in the community. The imagery deployed tends to be more functional: the community takes on the functions of the Temple, it is the space in which atonement is made (cf. 1 QS 8:5–10;

[108] Ibid. 168.

[109] Cf. Bertil Gärtner, *The Temple and the Community in Qumran and the New Testament: A Comparative Study in the Temple Symbolism of the Qumran Texts and the New Testament*, SNTSMS 1 (Cambridge: Cambridge University Press, 1965), 16–46. The repeated view in scholarly literature that the community saw itself as the Temple has been nuanced by Melissa P. Pula, 'Rethinking the Community as Temple: Discourse and Spatial Practices in the *Community Rule* (1QS)', PhD dissertation (University of Denver, 2015), who argues that during the period when the Jerusalem Temple was considered to be defiled, and the new Temple had yet to be built, 'the authors of 1QS transformed the spatiality of temple into a mobile place through discourse and practice. The *Yahad* is not a replacement temple. Rather, the *Yahad* engaged in a spatial response to the defilement of the Temple.... It organizes social relationships and addresses concerns for a community without a physical temple: stability, prosperity, and control. In turn, members of the *Yahad* experience temple' (ibid. 191).

9:1–5). Much closer are, of course, the various Pauline statements about the Temple: 'Do you not know that you are God's temple and that God's Spirit dwells in you?...God's temple is holy, and that temple you are' (1 Cor 3:16–17); 'Do you not know that your body is a temple of the Holy Sprit within you, which you have from God?' (1 Cor. 6:19); and, collectively, 'We are the temple of the living God, as God said: "I will live in them and move among them, and I will be their God and they shall be my people"' (2 Cor. 6:16; cf. Lev. 26:11–12; Ezek. 37:27). It is precisely, just as it is in John's Gospel, because of the presence of God within the believer and the community that individually and collectively they are the temple of the living God. While the Qumran community developed a related understanding in alienation from the Temple, and John wrote his Gospel after its destruction and in a context of an increasingly hostile parting of the ways, that the apostle already expressed this idea so clearly and forcefully while the Temple still stood shows that, within the Christian tradition, the transference of the imagery of the Temple to the believer and the community derives not from the loss of a physical building but from the Passion of Christ and its opening of Scriptures to be read thereafter in a new manner

JOHN 19:17–42

Throughout his Gospel, John has skilfully and subtly portrayed Jesus with imagery drawn from the feasts of the Temple and as the Temple. Each scene that we have considered also points forward to, and in various ways anticipates, the final event, the Passion, Pascha. At the first of his signs, manifesting his glory, in Cana, Jesus tells 'the woman' that 'my hour has not yet come' (2:4); and then, at the first of the three Passovers mentioned in the Gospel, the most explicit identification of the body of Jesus with the Temple given in the Gospel is made by alluding to the Passion: 'Destroy this temple and in three days I will raise it up' (2:19). Yet only now, at the crucifixion, is this saying completed and the temple of his body raised up. The Passion is not, therefore, as Käsemann would have it, 'a mere postscript which had to be included because John could not ignore this tradition nor yet could he fit it organically into his work'.[110] It is, rather, the climax of the whole work, towards which it has been looking from the beginning.

Not only is the Passion the climax of the work, but it has determined the Gospel from the beginning in a very particular way. It is the 'hour' towards which Jesus has been looking from the beginning, and it is also he who is in control of the movement to this hour and what happens at that hour: it might

[110] Käsemann, *Testament of Jesus*, 7.

appear that he is executed, but by his voluntary self-offering he turns the destruction of the temple of his body into the act of raising it up. Thus, unlike in the Synoptics where he prays that the cup might pass, but reconciles himself to the will of the Father (cf. Matt. 26:39; Mark 14:36; Luke 22:42), in John's Gospel Jesus says instead, 'What shall I say? "Father save me from this hour"? No, for this purpose I have come to this hour' (12:27). Although it was the arrival at the feast of 'some Greeks' seeking 'to see Jesus' that prompted him to say, 'The hour has come for the Son of Man to be glorified' (12:20–3), Jesus specifies that 'for this purpose I have come to this hour' (12:27). At the time of his arrest, Jesus with his disciples 'go out' to a garden across the Kidron valley (18:1), and when Judas, the band of soldiers, officers from the chief priests, and Pharisees arrive bearing lanterns and torches (18:3),[111] it is Jesus who again 'goes out' to meet them and it is he who interrogates them, 'who do you seek?' (18:4), and then, as Barrett puts it, 'fells them to the ground with a word', identifying himself three times with the affirmation 'I AM' (ἐγώ εἰμι, 18:5, 6, 8).[112] In all of this, John presents Jesus not as being put to death, but rather, as the good shepherd, laying down his life of his own accord for his sheep so that they may be one flock (10:14–16), for as Jesus says, 'when I am lifted up from the earth, I will draw all to myself' (12:32). It is, moreover, 'for this reason [that] the Father loves me because I lay down my life that I may take it again' (10:17).

The account of the Passion (19:17–42) is the central part of a triptych, preceded by the trial before Pilate (18:28–19:16) and followed by John's account of the resurrection (20:1–31). The trial concludes on 'the day of Preparation for the Passover, [at] about the sixth hour' (19:14), having begun 'early', presumably on the same day (18:28). And, on the other side of the triptych, although Mary Magdalene came to the tomb on the following day, 'the first day of the week', it is specifically noted that she did so 'while it was still dark' (20:1), so that this too is similarly tied to the same Sabbath, as also is the arrival of Simon Peter and 'the other disciple' to the empty tomb and Mary's encounter with the risen Lord, supposing him to be the gardener (20:3–19). The risen Lord's appearance to the other disciples in the sealed room occurs 'on the evening of that day, the first day of the week' (20:19), while Thomas' encounter is 'eight days later' (20:26).

The first and last parts of this triptych are further tied to the central scene in thematic ways. The trial scene, itself divided into seven parts (recapitulating the seven witnesses to Jesus called upon during his public ministry), concludes

[111] This rather unlikely group of characters clearly has a representative character; as Schnackenburg, *Gospel*, 3, 223, puts it: John has 'Jesus confront the whole unbelieving cosmos. His "report" becomes a theological representation'. It is also noteworthy that only Judas and his companions bear lights and torches; having departed from 'the Light of the world' (8:12) they are in the darkness of the night (cf. 13:30).

[112] Barrett, *John*, 431.

with Jesus, vested with the marks of a divine sovereignty—the crown of thorns and purple (blooded) robe—presented to the Jews by Pilate as their King, while the Jews, in particular the chief priests, affirm that they have no king but Caesar.[113] The abandonment of the God proclaimed by Isaiah and brought to focus by John in Christ, abandoned by both Jews and Gentiles, means that what appears to be the judgement of Jesus and his condemnation to death, turns out to be *the* judgement of this world, putting it in crisis and demanding a response. The cosmic trial, enacted throughout the narrative of John, culminates at this point; the case is closed: the world, both Jew and Gentile, have been shown to be hostile to God and to have abandoned his ways. There is nothing left to do but for Jesus to be handed over to be crucified. The ambiguity of the Greek in 19:13, καὶ ἐκάθισεν ἐπὶ βήματος, with no direct object, could be taken as Pilate sitting Jesus upon the throne rather than sitting upon it himself.[114] That John does not explicitly do this, however, is because the moment of judgement is in fact his elevation upon the cross, which in turn is the true judgement seat: his earlier words, 'Now is the judgment of this world, now shall the ruler of this world be cast out, and I, when I am lifted up from the earth will draw all to myself' were said, John makes clear, 'to show by what death he was to die' (12:31–3).

The tableau of the crucifixion is also replayed in the third part of the triptych, that is, the account of the empty tomb and the encounters with the risen Christ. Two angels this time sit at either end of the place where Jesus' body had lain (20:12), deploying once again the familiar Johannine theme of

[113] On the structure of the trial, see Lincoln, *Truth on Trial*, 123–38. During the course of his public ministry, Christ provides seven signs which manifest his glory (2:1–11; 4:46–54; 5:1–18; 6:1–15; 6:16–21; 9:1–41; 11:1–53); seven witnesses are called upon (the Baptist, 1:19, 32, 34; 3:26; Jesus himself, 8:14; cf. 3:11, 32, 33; 7:7; 8:18; Jesus' works, 5:36; cf. 10:25; God the Father, 8:18; cf. 5:32, 37; the Scriptures 5:39; cf. 2:17; 3:14; 6:31–3; the Samaritan woman, 4:39; the crowd who bore witness regarding the death of Lazarus, 12:17); and the trial itself takes place in seven scenes (18:28–32 in the outside court of the prefect's residence, where Pilate demands to know what 'the Jews' accusation is, but receives no clear answer; 18:33–38a inside the praetorium, dialogue between Pilate and Jesus about the fact and nature of Jesus' kingship; 18:38b–40 Pilate goes outside to announce that he finds Jesus innocent and appeals to the custom of releasing a prisoner at Passover; 19:1–3 moves back inside: Pilate has Jesus scourged and Roman soldiers mock Jesus by investing him with insignia of royalty; 19:4–7 outside: Pilate again says he finds Jesus innocent, and employs mockery of Jesus to mock the crowd; they demand his crucifixion on grounds he has made himself the son of God; 19:8–11 inside: Pilate now questions Jesus about his origins and engages him in dialogue about power and authority; 19:12–16 outside: 'the Jews' insinuate Pilate's treason against Caesar, the judge's seat is occupied, and the chief priests persuade Pilate to crucify Jesus by declaring their own loyalty to Caesar).

[114] As Lincoln (*Trial on Truth*, 134) concludes: 'The blatant irony of kingship and the mention of the judgment seat in the context of the mocking of Jesus as king tilts the balance toward seeing the irony of judging as blatant and therefore taking the verb as transitive'. Barrett, *John*, 453, takes Pilate himself to have sat on the judgement seat, but suggests that John was consciously playing upon the ambiguity: 'We may suppose then that John meant that Pilate did in fact sit on the βῆμα, but that for those with eyes to see behind this human scene appeared the Son of Man, to whom all judgement has been committed (5:22), seated upon his throne'.

presence-in-absence. Jesus is still 'ascending to my Father and your Father', so that Mary is directed not to 'hold' him.[115] On the first day itself, the disciples now 'receive' from the risen Christ the Spirit that he had 'handed down' from the cross (20:22; 19:30), with the power to forgive sins. And then eight days later, Thomas is invited to identify the Risen One with the Crucified One by placing his fingers in the wounds on Christ's hands and his hands in Christ's pierced side, which he does not actually do but instead confesses him to be 'my Lord and my God'.[116] The judgement scene and the resurrection scene are thus patterned upon the crucifixion, pointing forward and backwards to the climactic event. As Brown puts it, 'Jesus is lifted up on the cross; he is raised from the dead; and he goes up to the Father—all as part of one action and one "hour"'.[117] The unity of all aspects of the Passion, Pascha—the Crucifixion, Resurrection, Ascension, and also Pentecost—in 'the hour' of a single 'day' (and celebrated as such by those who followed John, as we have seen in Chapter 1) is thus emphasized by John, giving way to the first and eighth day in the presence of the risen Christ by the power of the Spirit now received.

That Jesus was 'handed over to be crucified' (19:16) on 'the day of Preparation of the Passover, [at] about the sixth hour' (19:14) is reiterated two more times in the central triptych (19:31, 42), with the further specification that the Sabbath was a 'great day' (19:31). This is, as we observed earlier, the sixth feast to be mentioned by John, and the third Passover, which is followed by a new beginning, on the first day of the week and the eighth day, in the company of the risen Lord (20:1, 19, 26). That Jesus was handed over to be crucified on the day of Preparation at the sixth hour is significant. Unlike the Synoptics, where Jesus eats the Passover meal with the disciples and is crucified on the following day, in John Jesus is crucified at the moment when the Passover lambs were being slain in the Temple. Exodus 12:6 specifies that the lambs were to be slain 'towards the evening' on the fourteenth day of that month, which, in the first century, because of the sheer number of lambs needing to be slaughtered, was interpreted as meaning after the midday hour, as the sun begins to decline.[118]

[115] John 20:17. See the perceptive comments by Brown, *John*, 2.1012–15 on the distinct use of the 'ascension' theme in Acts, where it functions as a terminus of Jesus' resurrectional appearances, and in John, where it is rather the terminus of 'the hour' in which Jesus departs from this world to go to the Father, and the point that John 'is fitting a theology of resurrection/ascension that by definition has no dimensions of time and space into a narrative that is necessarily sequential' (2:1014), though see also *John*, 1.146; as Martinus C. de Boer comments, for Brown 'The death is only "climactic" to the extent that it is part of the process of Jesus' resurrection-ascension, which is the true climax.' De Boer, 'Johannine History and Johannine Theology: The Death of Jesus as the Exaltation and Glorification of the Son of Man', in G. van Belle, ed., *The Death of Jesus in the Fourth Gospel*, 293–326, at 317.

[116] John 20:24–9. Cf. Herbert Kohler, *Kreuz und Menschwerdung*, 173–90, esp. 177, 181.

[117] Brown, *John*, 2.1014.

[118] Cf. D. Senior, *The Passion of Jesus in the Gospel of John* (Collegeville, MN: Liturgical Press, 1991), 96–7; Raymond E. Brown, *The Death of the Messiah: From Gethsemane to the Grave*, 2 vols (New York: Doubleday, 1994), 1.847.

So, although crucified on the day of Preparation, the timing of the event, 'in the evening', ties it, on the Jewish pattern of reckoning days, to the Sabbath, which as it was not only the Sabbath but 'a great day', required that the body be taken down on the day of Preparation (19:31).

The Crucifixion, Title, and Tunic

The central scene in this triptych is itself formed of three parts: first, the crucifixion, title, and Jesus' tunic (19:17–25a); second, Jesus' words from the cross (19:25b–30); and, third, Jesus' deposition from the cross, the treatment of his body, and the disciple's witness (19:31–42). Christ is crucified, or rather as we will see, enthroned, between 'two others' (19:18); John does not call them 'thieves' or 'criminals' as do the Synoptics (Matt. 27:38; Mark 15:27; Luke 23:32). In the Synoptics an 'inscription' (ἐπιγραφή, Mark 15:26; Luke 23:38) or a 'charge' (αἰτία, Matt. 27:37), is placed over him, reading 'This is Jesus, the King of the Jews' (Matt.) or 'This is the King of the Jews' (Luke) or more simply still 'The King of the Jews' (Mark). In John, it is Pilate himself who wrote the 'title' (τίτλος): 'Jesus the Nazorean, the King of the Jews' (19:19). The second part of the 'title' picks up on Pilate's earlier words, 'Behold your King!' (19:14), and alludes further to the fact that the Temple is not only the house of God, but his palace, in which he reigns and judges as King of Israel and the whole creation: 'The Lord reigns, let the people tremble! He sits upon the cherubim; let the earth quake!'[119] The ambiguous Greek of John 19:13 is now clarified: it is Jesus himself, identified by the 'title' as the King, who is the judge. So too now, raised up upon the cross between 'two others', Jesus is positioned as the Lord enthroned in the holy of holies, on the mercy seat above the ark and between the two cherubim. It is, moreover, here that the Lord makes himself known: 'I will be known [γνωσθήσομαι] to you from there, and I will speak to you from above the mercy seat in between the two cherubim that are on the ark of witness' (Exod. 25:21). This is the moment about which Jesus had already spoken: 'When you have lifted up the Son of Man, then you will know that I AM' (8:28, τότε γνώσεσθε ὅτι ἐγώ εἰμι).

The first part of Pilate's 'title' is intriguing. Although often translated as 'Jesus of Nazareth', it is more accurately rendered 'Jesus the Nazorean' (19:19, Ἰησοῦς ὁ Ναζωραῖος, so also 18:5, 7). The only place where John mentions 'Nazareth' is at the beginning of the Gospel (1:45–6, twice), where in the first instance the word order in fact connects the place name much closer to Joseph: 'Jesus, son of Joseph, the one from Nazareth' (1:45: Ἰησοῦν υἱὸν τοῦ Ἰωσὴφ τὸν ἀπὸ Ναζαρέτ). The background for the title 'Nazorean', on the

[119] Ps. 98:1; cf. Pss. 46; 47; 92; 97.

other hand, is usually traced to the Hebrew word for 'to watch' or 'to keep' (*ntzr*), so that a 'Nazorean' was 'a watcher' or 'an observant one'.[120] Coloe, however, makes a strong case that the background for the use of the term 'Nazorean' in John 18–19 lies instead in the prophecy of Zechariah as it was read at the time of Christ.[121] The word of the Lord that came to the prophet includes the instruction:

> Take from them silver and gold, and make a crown and set it upon the head of Joshua [i.e. Jesus in LXX], the son of Jehozadak, the high priest; and say to him, 'Thus says the Lord of hosts, "Behold the man whose name is Branch: for he shall grow up in his place and he shall build the Temple of the Lord. It is he who shall build the Temple of the Lord and shall bear royal honour, and shall sit and rule upon his throne. And there shall be a priest by his throne and peaceful understanding shall be between them both"'. (Zech. 6:11–13, MT)

There is evidence from the Qumran texts that the name 'Branch' (*tzmh*) mentioned by Zechariah had become synonymous with the 'branch' (*ntzr*) spoken of by Isaiah in messianic terms: 'There shall come forth a shoot from the stump of Jesse and from his roots a branch shall bear fruit' (Isa. 11:1).[122] As such, one of the tasks of the expected Messiah is that he would build the eschatological Temple. Moreover, although the Greek term does not make clear what lies behind its transliteration, archaeological evidence shows that the name 'Nazareth' is based upon the root *ntzr*, rather than *nzr*.[123] So, as Coloe concludes, in John the title 'is not a name derived from a place, but a title that leads to Jesus' death and is written as part of the formal charge, followed immediately with its synonym, "King of the Jews"'.[124] Thus Jesus' claim that if the Temple were to be destroyed he would raise it up in three days, speaking of the temple of his body (2:19, 21), is fulfilled when he, the 'Branch' (*tzmh/ntzr*) foretold by Zechariah, is raised up upon the cross, the 'throne', presumably still wearing the crown, and identified as 'the Nazorean', the temple builder.

After relating how the title was written and affixed to the cross (19:19–22), John turns his attention for several verses to Jesus' tunic. While the soldiers were happy to divide his garments (ἱμάτια) into four, because 'the tunic was without seam, woven from above throughout' (ἦν δὲ ὁ χιτὼν ἄραφος, ἐκ τῶν ἄνωθεν ὑφαντὸς δι' ὅλου), the soldiers said 'Let us not tear it [μὴ σχίσωμεν], but cast lots [λάχωμεν] for it to see whose it shall be, so that the Scripture might be fulfilled, "They parted my garments among them and for my clothing they

120 Cf. Lindars, *John*, 540–1; Barker, *King of the Jews*, 522–3.
121 Coloe, *God Dwells with Us*, 171–3.
122 Ibid. citing Qumran 4 QFlor col. 1:11; 4 QpGen col. 5:3–4; 4 Q161 (4QpIsa[a] line 11, 18).
123 Cf. Stephen Goranson, 'Nazarenes', in David Noel Freedman, ed., *Anchor Bible Dictionary*, 4.1049–50, and James F. Strange, 'Nazareth', in ibid., 4.1050–1.
124 Coloe, *God Dwells with Us*, 173.

casts lots"' (19:23–4; Ps. 21:19). This carefully worded description of the tunic and the soldiers' actions alludes to the robe of the high priest: 'You shall make a foot-length undergarment entirely [ὅλον] in blue. And its collar shall be in the middle, having a border around the collar, a woven work [ἔργον ὑφαντὸς], with the binding interwoven with it, lest it be torn'.[125] Although the MT text speaks of this being 'the robe of the ephod' (Exod. 28:31), that is, the mantle worn on top on feasts, the LXX speaks of the 'undergarment', the equivalent of Jesus' 'tunic'.[126] Both garments are 'woven', though Jesus' tunic is woven 'from above', just as the vestments of the high priest were designed from above, 'as the Lord instructed Moses' (Exod. 36:12, etc.), and alludes to Christ's own divine origin (cf. 3:31; 8:23), which, moreover, opens the way for others to also to be born 'from above' (3:7). Both garments are also woven 'as a whole', and care is taken lest it be torn. In John, however, these two points are given further resonance. 'It is expedient', as the high priest Caiaphas had said, 'that one man should die for the people and that the whole [ὅλον] nation should not perish' (11:50), and the soldiers who put Christ to death were concerned not to 'split' (μὴ σχίσωμεν) the tunic, as in fact the nation had been 'split' by Jesus' words and actions (cf. 7:43; 9:16; 10:19). Thus as John Paul Heil puts it, 'by not tearing his unified tunic, the soldiers unwittingly advance the goal of Jesus as the good shepherd-high priest to unify all sheep (people) into a believing community, so that there will be one flock and one shepherd'.[127] Finally, the word used for the soldiers' action of 'casting lots' (λαγχάνω) is more typically used to describe how the duties of the priests in the Temple were divided (cf. Luke 1:9).

In all these ways, then, Jesus is depicted not only in regal terms, but also in sacerdotal imagery. However, as Coloe notes, if this is so, it is not in terms of 'doing cultic actions'.[128] Not only did Jesus drive out from the Temple the animals needed for such practices (cf. 2:15), but his own action of sanctifying himself by laying down his life, as Coloe also notes, is expressed in very different terms.[129] While the animals were sacrificed in the Temple for the expiation of sin, as indeed the Baptist described Jesus as 'the lamb of God who takes away the sin of the world' (1:29), when it comes to describing Jesus' death, the Gospel of John presents it in other terms, as giving himself 'for the

[125] Exod. 28:27–8 [31–2]. Cf. John Paul Heil, 'Jesus as the Unique High Priest in the Gospel of John', *CBQ* 57.4 (1995), 729–45, at 741–3.

[126] When Ignace de la Potterie, as part of his argument that there is no theology of the priesthood of Jesus in John, denies that the 'tunic' of Jesus alludes back to the garment mentioned in Exodus, he overlooks the witness of the LXX. See Ignace de la Potterie, 'La tunique sans couture, symbole du Christ grand prêtre?', *Biblica* 60.2 (1979), 255–69, at 261–2, and, *The Hour of Jesus: The Passion and the Resurrection of Jesus according to John* (New York: Alba House, 1989), 99.

[127] Heil, 'Jesus as the Unique High Priest', 743.

[128] Coloe, *God Dwells with Us*, 205.

[129] Ibid. 195.

life of the world' (6:51), for the sheep (10:11), and for the benefit of the nation and all the children of God (11:50–2), and, especially, as an act of love: 'Greater love has no man than this, that a man lay down his life for his friends' (15:13), and in so doing, he turns servants into friends, those who do his commandments and know everything that he has heard from the Father (15:14–15). In his Passion, the true temple is raised up, and a new form of sacrifice, that of love, is brought about. It is this to which the Jerusalem Temple, and the tabernacle before that, point, making them preparatory sketches, copies of what God showed to Moses on the mountain. Although not directly called a priest, the abundance of sacerdotal imagery here, and elsewhere, certainly points, as Coloe argues, to the identification of Jesus as the priest of this new sacrifice.[130] However it is noteworthy that in the prophecy from Zechariah which lies behind Jesus' title of 'the Nazorean', the only 'priest' actually mentioned is not the one upon the throne, but the one standing beside it: 'there shall be a priest by his throne and peaceful understanding shall be between them both'.[131] In this tableau, the one standing beside the throne, the cross, is John, 'the disciple whom Jesus loved' (19:26), and who, as we saw in Chapter 1, was in fact spoken of by Polycrates, in the name of the tradition which claimed to follow John in their observance of Pascha, as the high priest. We have seen other instances where aspects of the Temple and its feasts are shared by the believer, most concretely in the living water that will flow out of his belly (cf. 7:38). So perhaps also here, Christ's priesthood is shared by the disciple who stands by the cross unashamed, ministering at the throne.

The Words from the Cross

In the central part of the crucifixion triptych—the scene with the women and the disciple whom Jesus loved standing near the cross and being addressed by Jesus—Jesus' final words reconfigure the relationship between his mother and his disciple, introducing the disciple into his own familial intimacy and identity, and so creating a space, the house(hold) of God, where the Spirit can dwell and Christ's body can be established upon earth. The identity of the beloved disciple has been considered sufficiently in Chapter 1. With regard to his mother, it is important to note that there is a subtle shift in vocabulary across 19:25–6. It begins with the narrator describing how 'standing by the cross of Jesus were his mother' (ἡ μήτηρ αὐτοῦ) and the others; but when adopting the perspective of Jesus, the narrator says 'when Jesus saw the mother' (τὴν μητέρα); and, finally, when she is addressed from the cross, it is as 'woman' (γύναι). The only other place she appears in the Gospel of John is

[130] Ibid. 205. [131] Zech. 6:13 MT; the LXX has 'the priest shall be on his right'.

at Cana, where she is also described twice as 'the mother of Jesus', but addressed by him as 'woman' (2:1, 3–4). She is not named in the Gospel of John, nor is there any suggestion, as there is in the Synoptics, that the term 'mother' can be extended to all those who believe as there is in the Synoptics (cf. Matt. 12:46–50; Mark 3:33–5; Luke 8:19–21). Nor, for that matter, despite being repeatedly called the Son, or Son of God, Son of Man, and, once, 'the only Son' (3:16), is Jesus ever referred to as the son of the, or his, mother. And, although the Gospel relates how the disciple took her to his home (εἰς τὰ ἴδια) from that hour (19:27), Jesus' words to the two are not simply the discharge of a filial duty. The two exhortations, 'Woman behold your son!' and to the disciple 'Behold your mother!' speak instead of the disciple's adopted identity in, *and as*, Jesus.[132] As Coloe puts it, 'this divine filiation is the ultimate revelation of the Hour and brings Jesus' mission to completion'.[133] As we hear in the Prologue, 'to all who received him, who believed in his name, he gave the power to become children of God' (1:12). The completeness of his work is emphasized three times in as many verses: knowing 'that all was now finished' (19:28, τετέλεσται), Jesus said 'I thirst', so that the Scripture might be fulfilled (19:28, τελειωθῇ), and then, having received the vinegar (cf. Ps. 68:22), uttered his final word, 'it is finished' (τετέλεσται), it is completed or brought to perfection, as he, again actively, inclined his head and 'handed over the Spirit' (19:30).[134]

Elevated above the earth, Jesus hands down the Spirit from above, to the woman and the disciple standing at the foot of the cross, his throne, enabling the disciple to put on the identity of a son of God, born by the Spirit 'from above' (cf. 3:5–8), and as a son of 'the woman'. 'The mother of Jesus', as Judith Lieu puts it, 'therefore, marks the ending of the earthly story of Jesus, as she had also marked its beginning'.[135] The connection between beginning and end is reinforced by the way in which the miracle at Cana was said to have been 'on the third day' (2:1); John, of course, does not refer to the resurrection as being 'on the third day' (he rather speaks of the first and the eighth day), but it is

[132] The identification is made explicit by Origen, as we have already seen, who is prepared to take Jesus' words more literally than almost all modern commentators: 'We might dare say, then, that the Gospels are the firstfruits of all Scriptures, but that the firstfruits of the Gospels is that according to John, whose meaning no one can understand who has not leaned on Jesus' breast nor received Mary from Jesus to be his mother also. But he who would be another John must also become such as John, to be shown to be Jesus, so to speak. For if Mary had no son except Jesus, in accordance with those who hold a sound opinion of her, and Jesus says to his mother, "Behold your son" [John 19:26] and not "Behold, this man also is your son," he has said equally, "Behold, this is Jesus whom you bore." For indeed everyone who has been perfected no longer lives, but Christ lives in him [cf. Gal. 2:20], and since Christ lives in him, it is said of him to Mary, "Behold your son," the Christ'. (*Comm. Jo.* 1.23).

[133] Coloe, *God Dwells with Us*, 188.

[134] See the comments on the phrases 'it is finished' and 'he handed over the Spirit' in the opening paragraphs to Part II above.

[135] Judith Lieu, 'The Mother of the Son in the Fourth Gospel', *JBL* 117.1 (1998), 61–77, at 69.

clearly implied in the Temple saying (2:19). Cana (the wedding), the cross, and the resurrection are thus bound tightly together: 'Jesus' hour must first come; but the resurrection provides the context for cross and establishes it as a means of manifesting his glory'.[136]

Who, then, is this 'woman'? She appears one other time in the Gospel of John, when Jesus speaks words of comfort to his disciples. Here he mentions her again, but as one who is giving birth:

> [16:20] Truly, truly, I say to you, you will weep and lament, but the world will rejoice; you will be sorrowful, but your sorrow will turn to joy. [21] When the woman [ἡ γυνὴ] is in travail she has sorrow [λύπην] because her hour has come; but when she is delivered of the child [τὸ παιδίον], she no longer remembers the tribulation [θλίψεως], for joy that a human being is born into the world [ἐγεννήθη ἄνθρωπος εἰς τὸν κόσμον]. [22] So you have sorrow now, but I will see you again and your hearts will rejoice, and no one will take your joy from you.

'The woman' whose 'hour has come' is the link between the 'mother', addressed as 'woman' in Cana, when the hour has not yet come, and 'the mother', again addressed as 'woman' at the foot of the cross, once the hour has come. This transition is combined with a changing description of the offspring and the verb used: from a child of whom the woman is delivered, to 'a human being born into the world'. We will return to the question of the birth of a human being in Chapter 4, but for now it should be mentioned that these words, as Lieu points out, recall the 'human being coming into the world' mentioned in the Prologue (1:9, ἄνθρωπον ἐρχόμενον εἰς τὸν κόσμον).[137] Moreover, although there is a parallel between the disciples' 'sorrow' at the departure of Christ and the woman's 'sorrow' during her travail, both being replaced in the end by 'joy', the woman's tribulation is not simply the disciples' period of anguish between the departure and return of Christ. As Christ concludes his words of comfort a few verses later: 'in the world you have tribulation [θλῖψιν]; but be of good cheer, I have overcome the world' (16:33). As Lieu further notes, the perfect in 16:28 ('I have come into the world') 'does not precede but is coterminous with the parallel perfect' in 16:33 ('I have overcome the world'), so that 'this woman too mediates a beginning that is also an ending/an ending that is also a beginning in the merging of times and experiences that characterize these chapters'.[138] This leads Lieu to ask: 'So is this a birthing or a dying?'[139] Unlike Matthew and Luke, there is no infancy narrative in John, but rather, as Lieu concludes, 'we meet birth here only when we encounter death. Indeed, the birth, which is not narrated in this Gospel, becomes through 16:21 a death, or is the death a birth?'[140] Or, perhaps, the term 'human being' has a special significance that brings together both birth and death, a birth through death, as we will see in Chapter 4.

[136] Ibid. 70. [137] Ibib. 72. [138] Ibid. [139] Ibid. 73. [140] Ibid.

A 'woman' in the process of giving birth appears again, of course, in chapter 12 of the Apocalypse of John:

> And a great portent appeared in heaven, a woman [γυνή] clothed with the sun, with the moon under her feet, and on her head a crown of twelve stars; she was with child and she cried out in her pangs of birth, in anguish for delivery. (Apoc. 12:1–2)

The passage continues by describing how a dragon appeared from the heaven, standing before the woman, ready to devour her child, 'but she brought forth a male child, one who is to rule all the nations with a rod of iron, but her child was caught up to God and to his throne', and she fled into the wilderness, a place prepared by God (Apoc. 12:3–6). Already in the second century, in a passage we briefly considered in the Introduction, Hippolytus identifies 'the woman' with the Church, who, he says, will never cease 'bearing from her heart the Word that is persecuted by the unbelieving in the world', while the male child she bears is Christ, God and human, announced by the prophets, and 'whom the Church continually bears as she teaches all nations'.[141] The background for this fertile and generative understanding of the Passion seems to be the connection, already made by Paul, between the hymn of the suffering servant in Isaiah 52:13–53:12, and the first verse of the following chapter: 'Rejoice O Barren One, who did not bear; break forth into singing and cry aloud, you who have not been in travail! For the children of the desolate one will be more than the children of her that is married, says the Lord' (Isa. 54:1). Already for Paul, before the destruction of the Temple, this Barren One is 'the Jerusalem above . . . our mother' (Gal. 4:26).

The imagery of the heavenly Jerusalem appears again later in the Apocalypse of John when the time has finally come to 'rejoice and exalt and give him glory, for the marriage of the Lamb has come and his Bride has made herself ready' (19:7). When all is ready and complete:

> I saw the holy city, the new Jerusalem, coming down from God, prepared as a bride adorned for her husband; and I heard a loud voice from the throne saying, 'Behold the tabernacle of God is with humans [σκηνή τοῦ θεοῦ μετὰ τῶν ἀνθρώπων]. He will tabernacle [σκηνώσει] with them and they shall be his people, and God himself will be with them'. (Apoc. 21:2–3)

While the third part of the crucifixion triptych is focused, as we will see, upon Jesus as the paschal lamb, modifying the Baptist's introduction of Jesus at the beginning of the Gospel (1:29), the Baptist also speaks of Jesus as 'the Bridegroom', 'the one who has the bride', and himself as the friend of the bridegroom (3:29). Although Jesus' first 'sign', manifesting 'his glory', was at a wedding feast (2:11), at which Jesus addresses his mother with the words

[141] Hippolytus, *Antichr.* 61, . . . ὃν ἀεὶ τίκουσα ἡ ἐκκλησία διδάσκει πάντα τὰ ἔθνη.

'Woman, what have you to do with me? My hour has not yet come' (2:4), the imagery of bridegroom and bride does not recur elsewhere in the Gospel, prior to the hour itself. As Peter Leithart points out, Jesus encounters many women who might have been taken as a bride—the Samaritan woman at the well, the woman caught in adultery, Mary and Martha, and Mary Magdalene, telling the last not to touch him because he is going to the Father (20:17)—so that 'when we arrive at the end of John's gospel, we have a Bridegroom who has given his life for the Bride, waiting for the wedding feast to begin'.[142] His conclusion, however, that 'He might as well be a jilted Groom, because there is no Bride' would perhaps be better phrased by saying that now that 'the hour' has come the wedding feast has begun, in which the divine filiation is extended from Jesus, through the Spirit, to the disciples. But this is not yet fully unveiled, nor are its conclusions drawn and already lived out, so that, as Leithart puts it, 'only when John and Revelation are read together do we have a complete Johannine royal romance'.[143] Complete, we should add, not in the sense of a first part followed by a second, but rather, as we explored in Chapter 2, the veiled account in the Gospel and the unveiled account in the Apocalypse.

Further scriptural background for the 'woman' was found by the early Fathers in Genesis 2. Noting how both Adam and Jesus were 'asleep' when a rib (πλευράν) was removed from the former, to be fashioned into a woman (Gen. 2:21–2), and blood and water came out from the latter's side (πλευράν) when it was piereced (19:34), Tertullian comments:

> As Adam was a figure of Christ, Adam's sleep sketched out the death of Christ, who was to sleep a mortal slumber, so that from the wound inflicted on his side might be figured the true Mother of the living, the Church.[144]

While 'the woman' (ἡ γυνή) in Genesis is promised 'sorrow' (λύπη) in childbirth (Gen 3:16), as was 'the woman' of John 16:21, she was called by Adam 'Eve' (or 'Life' in the LXX) 'because she is the mother of all the living' (Gen. 3:20); and when she does give birth, she exclaims: 'I have acquired a human being from God' (Gen. 4:1, ἐκτησάμην ἄνθρωπον διὰ τοῦ θεοῦ). However, all her children die; for which the word 'sorrow' is more appropriate, for, as Lieu notes, 'this term is not otherwise used of physical or birth pain but usually applies to mental anguish'.[145] As such, it is, as Tertullian points out, the Church which is really 'the mother of those living', for whereas all those born to Eve die, those, on the other hand, who are born, through death (by baptism or martyrdom) in the Church, are living.

[142] Peter Leithart, 'You Shall Judge Angels: A Response to Fr Behr', in Chad Raith II, ed., *The Gospel of John*, 192–201, at 197.

[143] Ibid. See also Leithart, *Revelation 1–11*, 22–3.

[144] Tertullian *An.* 43.10.

[145] Lieu, 'The Mother of the Son', 74.

The rabbinic tradition also would see Genesis 2 in terms of a wedding: God's building of the rib into a woman is taken as 'fixing her hair', and then, acting as a groomsman, '[God] adorned her like a bride and brought her to him', while the precious stones of Eden (cf. Ezek. 28:13) are taken as referring to the marriage canopy (*Gen. Rab.* 18.2–4). It might also be possible to see a further allusion to Genesis in Mary Magdalene's supposition that Jesus was 'the gardener' (20:15), for that is the role of Adam in Genesis (2:15),[146] and, further, in Adam's words upon seeing his bride, that 'for this reason shall a man (*ἄνθρωπος*) leave his father and mother and cleave to his wife (*γυναῖκα*), and they shall be one flesh' (Gen. 2:24). For John, in the 'royal romance' played out across the Gospel and the Apocalypse, Jesus is the human being who has left his Father's side to join himself to his bride to become 'one flesh'.

That through the marriage of the lamb and the bride, as 'one flesh', God has his 'tabernacle' (*σκηνή*) with human beings, so that he 'will tabernacle' (*σκηνώσει*) with them as his people (Apoc. 21:3) cannot but recall John 1:14, where the Word, Jesus, 'became flesh and tabernacled in us', so that 'we have seen his glory'. We have already looked at the word 'tabernacle' (*σκηνή*) earlier in this chapter, and will examine the Prologue itself further in Chapter 5 and, from a phenomenological perspective, 'flesh' in Chapter 6, but we have already seen that 'the flesh' that Jesus offers us to eat is 'the flesh' that he becomes through the Passion: 'the bread of life that I shall give for the life of the world is my flesh' (6:51), the 'bread which comes down from heaven' (6:50, 51, 58), 'the flesh of the Son of Man' (6:53). This flesh is offered to us to become one with him, so that he does not merely tabernacle 'among us', as John 1:14 is usually translated, but 'in us' (*ἐν ἡμῖν*), as he and his Father, together with the Spirit, come to dwell 'in us' (chapters 14–15). The plural witness of John 1:14, 'we have seen his glory', is paralleled by the plural witness to 'the disciple bearing witness to these things' in John 21:24, 'we know that his witness is true', and both derive from emphatic singular, though third-person, witness in 19:35: 'He who saw it has born witness, his witness is true, and he knows that he tells the truth, that you also may believe'. The witness of the one standing at the cross is thus the basis for the witness of the whole Gospel, from beginning to end.

In all these ways, then, the Temple that Christ raises through his Passion is not simply a new physical structure, but a household (*οἰκία*) of many dwellings (*μοναί*), where the believer is brought into a new relationship with God, who, through the Spirit, comes to dwell, together with the Son, in the believer. As Coloe puts it:

[146] Cf. Carlos Raúl Sosa Siliezar, *Creation Imagery in John*, LNTS 546 (London: Bloomsbury, 2015), 174–9.

> The community, participating in Jesus' divine filiation, is the house (household) of God.... Just as Jesus could be described as Temple and Son because of his intimate union with God, so too these images of Temple and divine filiation can be applied to the Christian believer. In his Hour, the familial imagery is given a new depth of reality as Jesus' words and gift of the Spirit constitute a new household of God which can be rightly depicted as the new Temple.[147]

This is certainly correct, but it is also necessary to be more specific. If this is achieved by Jesus ascending the cross, then the same is expected of those who follow him, as we saw when considering John 6. And so, the 'witness' that God himself is and calls his people to become (cf. Isa. 43:10, 'Be my witnesses; I too am a witness, says the Lord God, and the servant whom I have chosen') now takes on the dimension of martyrdom, following 'the faithful witness, the first-born of the dead' (Apoc. 1:5), 'the Amen, the faithful and true witness, the beginning of God's creation' (Apoc. 3:14).[148] Although the Woman gave birth to her Son, he was 'caught up to God and to his throne' in Apocalypse 12, while she flees into the wilderness until the marriage feast is ready and there are further witnesses ready to take their thrones in the heavenly court:

> Then I saw thrones, and seated on them were those to whom judgment was committed. Also I saw the souls of those who had been beheaded for their witness [μαρτυρίαν] to Jesus and for the Word of God... They came to life and reigned with Christ for a thousand years. (Apoc. 20:4)

The household of God which is erected by Christ ascending the cross is precisely the assembly of faithful witnesses, martyrs, who are also enthroned and reign with Christ.[149] The Apocalypse, as Leithard puts it, unveils 'the formation of a fully human church as it describes the cruciformization of witnesses... These witnesses become, like Jesus in his suffering, fully human as they bear witness to God's glory in the face of Christ'.[150] Christ is indeed, as the Apostle puts it, 'the first born of many brethren', and the whole of creation is groaning, awaiting the revelation—the apocalypse, the unveiling—of the sons of God (cf. Rom. 8:18–30). The bride, as we have seen, is already present at the crucifixion, and the tomb becomes the womb for those born into life as the brethren of 'the firstborn of the dead' (Apoc. 1:5).

The Deposition from the Cross

Turning, finally, to the concluding portion of the crucifixion triptych, although the identification of Jesus as the paschal lamb was intimated by the

[147] Coloe, *God Dwells with Us*, 190.
[148] For full exploration of this, see Minear, *John: The Martyr's Gospel*.
[149] Cf. Leithart, 'You Shall Judge Angels', 197–200. [150] Ibid. 199.

day and hour on which he is crucified, it is not until the third part of the triptych that this is made explicit. The hyssop branch upon which the sponge of water is given to Jesus (19:29) probably alludes to the hyssop used to smear the blood of the lamb on the lintel of the door of the Israelite houses (Exod. 12:22). That, once Jesus' body was taken down from the cross so as not to remain there on the Sabbath (19:31), the soldiers determined not to break his legs but instead to pierce his side, at which 'at once there came out blood and water' (19:34), was to fulfil two quotations from Scripture: 'Not a bone of his shall be broken' (*συντριβήσεται*), and 'They shall look on him whom they have pierced' (19:36–7).

The flowing of blood and water, often taken thereafter as symbolizing baptism and Eucharist, alludes backwards to the image we have seen several times before of Ezekiel's eschatological temple with the water flowing from its side (Ezek. 47:1–2). The 'blood and water' appear again in the First Epistle of John, and in an intriguing manner: 'this is he who comes [*ὁ ἐλθὼν*] by water and blood, Jesus Christ' (1 John 5:6). Although the identity of Jesus as the Christ is debated throughout the Gospel (cf. 4:25–9; 7:26–43; 9:22; 10:24; 12:34), John is very careful how he uses the title 'Christ' to designate Jesus. The end of the Prologue asserts that 'grace and truth came through Jesus Christ' (1:18); the Baptist denies that he is the Christ (1:20, 25; 3:28); Andrew tells Peter that 'we have found the Messiah (which means Christ)' (1:41), words which, as we have seen, open out onto a greater understanding; in the context of the raising of Lazarus, after hearing Jesus say 'I am the resurrection and the life', Martha confesses that Jesus is 'the Christ, the Son of God, coming [*ἐρχόμενος*] into the world' (11:25–7); and Jesus asserts that 'this is eternal life, that they may know you, the only true God, and Jesus Christ whom you have sent' (17:3); finally, the very purpose of the Gospel is to establish the identity of Jesus as the Christ: 'these things are written that you may believe that Jesus is the Christ, the Son of God, and that believing you may have life in his name' (20:31). It is through 'blood and water', the Passion as it opens out for others to put on the identity of Christ, that Jesus, *as the Christ*, comes into the world.

The second quotation from the deposition scene is commonly agreed to have come from Zechariah 12:10 MT, which concludes with speaking of how 'those who look at him whom they have pierced' come to weep bitterly over him, as one weeps over 'a first-born'. Several scriptural passages may lie behind the first quotation: Exod. 12:10 (and v. 46) 'you shall not break a bone of it', that is, the paschal lamb; Numb. 9:12, 'they shall not break a bone of it'; and Ps. 33:21, 'the Lord will keep all their bones, not one of them will be crushed' (*συντριβήσεται*). The identical word used in the Psalm and John certainly indicates the influence of the Psalm verse, though the earlier mention of hyssop and the very day itself point to the Pentateuchal passages as being the primary points of reference for identifying Christ as the lamb.[151] Further evidence that John has the Passover in mind, Coloe argues, is given in the double mention of Jesus being 'bound' (18:12, 24; not mentioned in Luke, and only once in Matt. 27:2 and Mark 15:1) and its allusion to Isaac in Genesis 22: as Abraham placed the wood upon Isaac (Gen. 22:6), Jesus carries for himself the wood upon which he will die (19:17).[152] Although, as Coloe further notes, it is unlikely that there was a pre-Christian tradition of the *Aqedah* which saw Isaac as voluntarily going to his sacrifice, the Book of Jubilees indicates that the sacrifice of Isaac was seen, at least by some, as the original basis for the feast of Passover, for it describes the sacrifice of Isaac as having taken place on the fourteenth of the first month (Jub. 17:15; 18:3), and mentions that it was thereafter celebrated annually, as a week-long festival known as 'the feast of the LORD' (Jub. 18:17–19).[153] As such, the place of the temple changes, from the Temple Mount to the place of the skull, the new Moriah.[154]

There is, then, no doubt that, with this abundance of imagery and timing, Jesus is being presented by John as the paschal lamb. But despite the Baptist's identification of Jesus as 'the Lamb of God who takes away the sin of the world' (1:29, though not in 1:36), the slaying of the paschal lamb was not a sacrifice for the purpose of atoning for sin or a sacrifice of expiation.[155] Numbers 28:22 and Ezekiel 45:23 speak of a second sacrifice, a young goat, as 'a sin offering'. But nothing of this is found in Exodus 12: there, as Ashton puts it, the purpose of the slaying of the paschal lamb 'was not sacrifical but apotropaic'.[156] The blood from the lambs, marking of the lintels of the doors of the Israelites houses, is the sign for the LORD 'to pass over the door and not allow the destroyer to enter your house to slay you' (Exod. 12:23). Moreover, in the

[151] Barrett, *John*, 464. [152] Coloe, *God Dwells with Us*, 191.

[153] The term *aqedah* refers to the binding of the lamb in the daily offering (*m. Tamid* 4.1). Cf. Coloe, *God Dwells with Us*, 191–2; P. R. Davis and D. B. Chilton, 'The Aqedah: A Revised Tradition History', *CBQ* 40 (1978), 514–46; J. D. Levenson, *The Death and Resurrection of the Beloved Son: The Transformation of Child Sacrifice in Judaism and Christianity* (New Haven: Yale University Press, 1993), 111–42.

[154] Although 2 Suppl. 3:1 associates Moriah, the place where the sacrifice of Isaac was to take place (Gen. 22:2), with the Temple Mount, Levenson, *Death and Resurrection of the Beloved Son*, 121, notes: 'The idea that Moriah was always another designation of the Temple Mount in Jerusalem is as rare among critical scholars as it is ubiquitous in Jewish tradition'.

[155] As noted in the first section of the Introduction, there are scholars who would want to draw out expiatory significance to the death of Christ in John, as suggested by the Baptist's words in John 1:29. Although the slaying of the Passover lamb had no sacrificial significance in the Old Testament, as Severino Pancaro (*The Law in the Fourth Gospel: The Torah and the Gospel, Moses and Jesus, Judaism and Christianity, according to John*, SupNovT 42 (Leiden: Brill, 1975), 348) notes, that it was slain and consumed in the sanctuary, and that its blood redeems the firstborn, does imply sacrificial dimensions; and the association had already been made by the Apostle (1 Cor. 5:7–8; 11:23–6). See also Forestell, *The Word of the Cross*, 157–66, who sees, in the combination of the paschal lamb and Isaiah's suffering servant (53: 4, 7, 11, 12), 'the brilliant intuition of an original thinker' (ibid. 165).

[156] Ashton, *Fourth Gospel*, 466; see also Weidemann, *Der Tod Jesu*, 423–44.

repetition of this act, when asked about its meaning, the answer to be given is: 'By the strength of hand the LORD brought us out of Egypt, from the house of bondage' (Exod. 13:14). Part of the celebration of this feast also included the eating of the 'flesh' of the lamb, which was to be consumed entirely, burning anything that was left.[157] This is exactly the imagery with which we have seen John describe the Passion of Christ. He does not speak of Christ laying down his life on account of sin, but rather 'for the life of the world' (6:51), so that we are given the heavenly bread, his flesh, to eat. He lays down his life for the sheep (10:11) and for the nation and all the children of God (11:50–2). And, most particularly, this laying down of his life is an act of love, for 'Greater love has no man than this, that a man lay down his life for his friends' (15:13) and it is for this act that he is loved by the Father, 'because I lay down my life that I may take it again' (10:17). It is, moreover, exactly in this way that God has shown his own love: 'For God loved the world in this way [οὕτως] that he gave his only Son, that whoever believes in him should not perish but have eternal life' (3:16). Christ's life-giving death on the cross, although understood by others as an atoning death for sin (cf. Rom. 4:25), is not understood by John as a response to sin but rather as principally deriving from the love that God himself is (cf. 1 John 4:8) and has for the world (3:14–16). It is precisely this love, shown in this way, that has liberated human beings from the condition of being slaves to that of being friends (15:15), members of the household of God, enthroned in the Temple as sons alongside the Son, and the commandment that Jesus gives as his own is simply 'that you love one another as I have loved you' (15:12). Now, however, we know what is involved in such love.

John thus gives us a very rich understanding of Jesus as the Temple and the fulfilment of its feasts, and does so, at least in part, by following the order of the feasts in the narrative of his Gospel. However, as Leithart notes, to get the full effect of what John has done, we must also recognize that he has presented Jesus 'as a new Moses assembling and furnishing the new tabernacle that he is', and doing so as a 'tour of the tabernacle' by 'moving from the outer courts to the holy place, so that, by the time we arrive at the crucifixion we are in the inner sanctuary, the most holy place'.[158] We are given a spring of living water (4:5–15; 7:37–9) resembling the bronze laver between the door of the tabernacle and the altar (Exod. 30:17–21); the heavenly bread (6:22–71), as the manna which was kept in a jar in the ark (Exod. 16:33) and the bread of Presence lying on the golden altar (Exod. 25:29[30]); the light of the world (8:12), as the golden lamp-stand (Exod. 25:30[31]); and Jesus himself, offering prayer for his disciples to the Father (17:1–26) as the priest before the altar. However, whereas we might have expected the cross to be presented as one of

[157] Exod. 12:8–10. The LXX uses the word κρέα rather than σάρξ, as it has been prepared, 'roasted'; Hebrew only has one word for both, *basar*.

[158] Leithart, 'You Shall Judge Angels', 195.

the butcher blocks where the animals were slaughtered, we are, at the end of this tour, instead at the most holy place itself. As Leithart puts it:

> When the tabernacle was completed, Yahweh's glory descended from the mountain to take the throne above the cherubim. At the end of John's gospel, the glory of God announced in the Prologue is finally revealed in all its radiance. Broken and bleeding, Jesus crucified is Yahweh enthroned on the ark, hanging between two criminals who serve as cherubic throne-guardians. Later, the empty tomb will replicate the tableau of the cross, with two angels sitting at either end of the stone where Jesus lay. Cross and tomb are shocking places for divine glory to be revealed, scandalous, macabre arks, the polar opposite of holy spaces. (Can Yahweh dwell in Sheol!?) For John, they constitute the inner sanctuary where the glory of God is most fully displayed: In the mangled flesh of the crucified Word, in the emptiness of the tomb of the Risen Lord, *that* is where glory shines. . . . The one hanging on this new ark is the Word *made flesh*. The cross reveals the glory of God because it elevates the *image* of God to Yahweh's throne above the cherubim. In Jesus, Israel finally enters behind the veil into the most holy place. God takes his throne when he shares it with the God-man.[159]

This is the one about whom Moses wrote (5:46), whose day Abraham saw and rejoiced (8:56), whose glory Isaiah saw in the Temple (12:41). Scripture is now indeed fulfilled.

[159] Ibid. 195–6, italics original.

4

'Behold the Human Being'

As we saw in Chapter 3, John has a very rich understanding of the construction of the Tabernacle/Temple, not the copy made by hands after the image of that shown on the mountain, but the temple of his body, prepared throughout the six feasts mentioned over the course of his Gospel and culminating in the sixth feast (and the third Passover), on 'the day of the Preparation of the Passover' after the sixth hour (this temporal indicator tying the day, as we have seen, to the following day), when Christ was raised upon the cross, opening a new beginning with the risen Christ, on the first and eighth day, when believers are incorporated to dwell in the house of God as his household. But if, as Peter Leithart suggests, John is describing Jesus 'as a new Moses, assembling and furnishing the new tabernacle that he is',[1] John is not only looking back to Exodus, but to 'the beginning' itself, as is immediately indicated from the first words of his Gospel, alluding to the opening words of Genesis, the very first words of Scripture, in a characteristically 'apocalyptic' mode of bringing together the beginning and the end.

John also makes extensive use of Isaiah, drawing from the Book of Consolation (Isa. 40–55), as Andrew Lincoln has shown, to structure and provide the vocabulary for the cosmic lawsuit enacted by Jesus throughout the course of his public ministry, during which seven witnesses are called upon, culminating in the trial before Pilate (18:28–19:16), which is itself composed of seven distinct scenes, and concluding with the words 'they handed him over to be crucified'.[2] Isaiah, however, does not simply foretell things which are to come, but also harkens back to things which have been spoken from of old: there is no other God besides the one who 'declares the last things first [*ἀναγγέλλων πρότερον τὰ ἔσχατα*], before they happen, and they were brought to completion together [*ἅμα συνετελέσθη*]', the one who said, 'My whole plan [*βουλή*, or "purpose"] shall stand, and I shall do all the things I have planned' (Isa. 46:10). And this divine purpose, spoken of old and reiterated by Isaiah, is shown when God says 'I have made the human being for ever [*ἐποίησα ἄνθρωπον εἰς τὸν*

[1] Liethart, 'You Shall Judge Angels', 195.

[2] Lincoln, *Truth on Trial*, 23, 124–38.

$\alpha i\hat{\omega}\nu\alpha$]' (Isa. 44:7) and calls those who believe in him to the task of witnessing: 'Be my witnesses [μάρτυρες]; I too am a witness, says the Lord God, and the servant whom I have chosen, so that you may know and believe that I AM' (Isa. 43:10). At stake in this cosmic trial, moreover, is the very glory of God. If God is moved to act, to redeem Israel, it is for the sake of his name and to vindicate his glory which 'I will not give to another' (Isa. 48:11). Yet, as it is by being 'lifted up' that the servant is 'glorified exceedingly' (52:13), then those who follow the Servant as witnesses/martyrs are also glorified by God and God is glorified in them.[3]

THE LIVING HUMAN BEING: THE MARTYR

Those whom Lightfoot describes as 'the school of John' were, as we saw in Chapter 2, the first to have an annual celebration of Pascha, and most likely the only ones to do so until the middle to the end of the second century. Moreover, as we saw when examining John 6 in Chapter 3, they also saw a very close connection between the Eucharist and martyrdom: to partake of the cup of salvation is to share in the Passion of Christ by martyrdom. In addition, this school also seems to have had a very distinctive understanding of what it is to be a living human being, that is, it is the martyr who is identified as a living human being, and, in fact, the very glory of God. In the Introduction, we considered the necessity of projecting a historical horizon, in Gadamer's terms, as a step in understanding a historical text. This step might not only open up other perhaps unfamiliar horizons, but also, in turn, in the 'melding of horizons' that takes place in the act of understanding, might further reveal a surplus of meaning in a text, for authentic historical understanding is not only reproductive but also productive. As such, we will begin this chapter by exploring how the school of John held together life, martyrdom, and being human, before turning to the Gospel itself, so that further facets of the Gospel, which might otherwise escape us, can appear.

The Apocalypse of John

The Apocalypse of John, as we saw in Chapter 3, describes, in Leithart's words, 'the formation of a fully human church as it describes the cruciformization of witnesses. . . . These witnesses become, like Jesus in his suffering, fully human as they bear witness to God's glory in the face of Christ'.[4] When these

[3] Cf. Isa. 44:23; 45:25; 49:3; 49:5; 55:5.

[4] Leithart, 'You Shall Judge Angels', 197–200.

witnesses/martyrs take their place upon the thrones alongside Christ, reigning with him, they do so as ones who have 'come to life' (Apoc. 20:4, *ἔζησαν*). They do so, because it is Christ himself who is 'the living one': when John sees him, and falls 'at his feet as one dead', for no one can see God and live (cf. Exod. 33:20), Christ introduces himself in these words: 'Fear not! I am the first and the last and the living one [*ἐγώ εἰμι ὁ πρῶτος καὶ ὁ ἔσχατος καὶ ὁ ζῶν*]; I became dead, and behold I am living unto the ages of ages and I have the keys of Death and Hades' (Apoc. 1:17–18). 'Fear not! I am' echoes Jesus' words to the disciple on the boat in the midst of the storm (6:20), while 'I am the first and the last' is repeatedly used by Isaiah in his Book of Consolation. 'The living one', while drawing upon the many scriptural references to 'the living God' (cf. Ps. 41:3 etc), also echoes Jesus' word in John 5:26, 'as the Father has life in himself, so he has granted the Son also to have life in himself', but now with the specification that this belongs to Christ as the one who has died and is alive again. The contrast between dead and living is reinforced by the contrasting verbs used: Jesus 'became dead' (*ἐγενόμην νεκρὸς*) but 'is living' (*ζῶν εἰμί*), so that, as Swete puts it, 'the risen life of Jesus Christ is henceforth coterminous with his divine life'.[5] A little later Christ speaks of himself as 'The Amen, the faithful and true witness/martyr, the beginning of the creation of God' (Apoc. 3:14). Christ is precisely the response, 'the Amen', to God, and as such he is 'the beginning of the creation of God' (*ἡ ἀρχὴ τῆς κτίσεως τοῦ θεοῦ*). Finally, the adjectives just used, 'faithful and true', are later used as the names of the one who sits upon the white horse (Apoc. 19:11), who is 'clad in a robe dipped in blood, and the name by which he is called is The Word of God' (Apoc. 19:13: *κέκληται τὸ ὄνομα αὐτοῦ ὁ λόγος τοῦ θεοῦ*). 'The Word of God' is specifically said to be a title of the one with the bloodied robe, that is the crucified Jesus.

Ignatius of Antioch

One of the most striking testimonies to the idea of becoming human through martyrdom is found soon after John wrote his Gospel. Ignatius of Antioch, journeying slowly but surely towards his impending martyrdom in Rome, nevertheless embraced his fate with joy, urging the Roman Christians not to try to impede his martyrdom:

> It is better for me to die in Christ Jesus than to be king over the ends of the earth. I seek him who died for our sake. I desire him who rose for us. Birth-pangs are upon me. Suffer me, my brethren; hinder me not from living, do not wish me to die . . . Suffer me to receive the pure light; when I shall have arrived there, I will be

[5] Swete, *Apocalypse*, 20.

a human being [ἄνθρωπος ἔσομαι], suffer me to follow the example of the passion of my God. (*Rom.* 6)

Only by being a witness, a martyr, will Ignatius be born into life, receive the pure light, and, strikingly, be a human being, in the stature of Christ, 'the perfect human being' (*Smyrn.* 4.2) or 'the new human being' (*Eph.* 20.1) as the martyr refers to him. Ignatius also has other images for speaking about his martyrdom in ways that clearly derive from John and give further depths to what we have seen. Writing to the Romans, again, he states that 'there is living water speaking within me, saying "come to the Father,"' and 'I desire the bread of God which is the flesh of Jesus Christ, of the seed of David, and I desire his blood for my drink, which is incorruptible love' (*Rom.* 7.2–3). Earlier in the same letter, he applies this eucharistic imagery to himself and his martyrdom: he is 'the wheat of God and through the teeth of the beasts I shall be found to be [the] pure bread of Christ' (*Rom.* 4.1).

Ignatius also describes Jesus Christ as 'the Word emerging from silence' (*Mag.* 8.2 ἀπὸ σιγῆς προελθών), which, rather than deriving from some kind of 'Gnostic' speculation about the derivation of 'aeons', would seem to have more in common with the 'apocalyptic' opening of Scripture that we considered in Chapter 2, so that the divine plan is now revealed and the Word finally heard.[6] Alternatively, though connected with the previous suggestion, the 'silence' might be that of the Father at the time of the crucifixion, for at other 'theophanic' moments, such as the baptism or Transfiguration, a voice comes from heaven; the title 'Word of God' is, after all, as we have seen, a title which is ascribed by the Apocalypse of John to the crucified one. This would then provide the background for another way in which Ignatius describes his impending martyrdom: if you are 'silent about me', he tells the Roman Christians, that is, if they let him go to his martyrdom without hindrance, then 'I [will be] a word of God' (ἐγὼ λόγος θεοῦ); but if they are concerned for his flesh, 'I will again be a voice' (*Rom.* 2.1).[7]

Ignatius prays that in his coming trials he will be found to be a Christian, 'for if I be found to be so, I shall be able both to speak and then to be faithful, when I no longer appear in the world' (κόσμῳ μὴ φαίνωμαι). But, he continues by pointing out that now Jesus Christ is with the Father he is in fact 'more apparent' (μᾶλλον φαίνεται) than he was before (*Rom.* 3.2–3). It is, after all, only after the Passion that the disciples really 'see' and know who Christ is. But

[6] So, William Schoedel, *Ignatius of Antioch: A Commentary on the Letters of Ignatius of Antioch*, Hermeneia (Philadelphia: Fortress, 1985), 120–2. See also Mark Edwards, 'Ignatius and the Second Century: An Answer to R. Hübner', *ZAC* 2 (1998), 214–26, at 222–6.

[7] This image can also be found later, for instance, in Athanasius, who, in explaining how the Word took upon himself the sufferings of the body, says that this was done 'so that we, no longer being merely human, but as the Word's own [ὡς ἴδιοι τοῦ Λόγου], may participate in eternal life . . . the flesh being no longer earthly but henceforth being made word [λογωθείσης] through God's Word who for our sake became flesh'. *C. Ar.* 3.33.

seeing and touching the risen Christ is not simply a continuation of how they saw and touched him before: according to Ignatius, when Christ said 'reach out, touch me, and see that I am no bodiless demon', the disciples 'straightaway touched him and they believed as they were intermixed [κραθέντες] with his flesh and his Spirit' (*Smyrn.* 3.2). As discussed in Chapter 3, when examining John 6, this is as much directed against a docetic understanding of the Eucharist as it is against a possible docetic understanding of Incarnation; the disciples are 'intermixed' with his flesh and Spirit by touching him.

Picking up on the 'birth-pangs' which are upon him, and reinforcing what we have seen in John about the relationship between Christ and believers in the birth which is mediated by death, and in Apocalypse 12, where the Woman is taken as the Church always giving birth to Christ, Ignatius affirms that: 'Through [the cross], in his Passion, he invites you to be parts of his body, as a head cannot be born with the body-parts, as God promises unity, which he is' (*Trall.* 11.2). And finally, as he affirms frequently throughout his letters, this unity is primarily a unity of flesh and Spirit (*Eph.* 7; *Mag.* 1, 13; *Trall.* 1; *Smyrn.* 3). Of all these now-familiar Johannine themes, echoed and redeployed by Ignatius, none are as striking as those of being, through martyrdom, a living human being and a word of God.

Irenaeus of Lyons

Ignatius hoped to write a second booklet in which he would write what he has already begun, that is, an account of 'the economy that leads to the new human being' (*Eph.* 20.1). As far as we know, Ignatius was not able to complete this. But this is the theme par excellence of Irenaeus of Lyons. In his writings Irenaeus expounds 'the economy' in terms of the work of God fashioning the human being with his Hands, the Son and the Spirit.[8] Irenaeus' understanding of the economy of God is thoroughly Christocentric; it is Christ himself who is 'coming throughout the whole economy' (*haer.* 3.16.6), 'the Beginning who appeared at the end' (*haer.* 1.10.3). It is a continuous and uninterrupted project, worked out through the long pedagogy of the economy, at the end of which Adam is finally made in the image and likeness of God:

> For never at any time did Adam escape the Hands of God, to whom the Father speaking, said, 'Let us make the human being in our image, after our likeness' [Gen. 1:26]. And for this reason at the end [*fine*], 'not by the will of the flesh, nor by the will of man' [John 1:13], but by the good pleasure of the Father, his Hands perfected a living human being [*vivum perfecerunt hominem*], in order that Adam might become in the image and likeness of God. (*haer.* 5.1.3)

[8] Cf. Behr, *Irenaeus*, 144–203.

According to Irenaeus, the reason for the whole, and single, economy of God, is found in the words of Christ about the glory he had with the Father 'before the world was', the same glory with which he asks to be glorified as he approaches the cross (John 17:5), and further asks that his disciples should be there with him to behold that glory (John 17:24). Following the words of Isaiah, which speak of the gathering of the posterity, that is, 'who is called by my name, whom I created for glory, whom I formed and made' (Isa. 43:6–7), the disciples gather around his body, as the eagles gather around the carcass (cf. Matt. 24:28), and so 'participate in the glory of the Lord who has both formed us and prepared us for this, that when we are with him, we may partake of his glory' (*haer*. 4.14.1). It is to share in the eternal glory of God, to be that glory, that the economy, which climaxes upon the cross, is initiated, just as for John, as we have seen, the cross is primarily the expression of the love that God is.

The glory of God is one of the resounding themes of Irenaeus' theology: the glory of God that dwelt in 'the tent of meeting' or 'witness' (regularly translated as ἡ σκηνή τοῦ μαρτυρίου in the LXX), and likewise in the Temple, now culminates in the specific handiwork of God itself, for, as Irenaeus puts it in one of his most beautiful statements, 'the glory of God is a living human being' (*haer*. 4.20.7), meaning by this, as we will see, the martyr. This statement comes in the midst of a long chapter replete with further Johannine themes, such as life and seeing and knowing God. Irenaeus begins by contrasting the greatness of God, on account of which it is not possible to know God, with his love, by which the Word leads us to God (*haer*. 4.20.1). Scripture asserts that there is one God, and so too does the Lord when he claims that 'all things have been delivered to me by my Father' (Matt. 11:27; *haer*. 4.20.2). Irenaeus then explains the scope of this 'all things' by way of the Apocalypse:

> But in 'all things' [it is implied that] nothing has been kept back, and for this reason the same one is 'the judge of the living and the dead' [Acts 10:42]; 'having the key of David, he shall open, and no one shall shut, he shall shut, and no one shall open' [Apoc. 3:7]. 'For no one was able, either in heaven or in earth, or under the earth, to open the book' of the Father, 'or to behold him' [Apoc. 5:3], with the exception of 'the Lamb who was slain' [Apoc. 5:12], and who redeemed us with his own blood, receiving power over all things from the same God who made all things by the Word [cf. John 1:3], and adorned them by [his] Wisdom, when 'the Word was made flesh' [John 1:14]; so that even as the Word of God had the sovereignty in the heavens, so also might he have the sovereignty in earth, inasmuch as [he was] a righteous human, 'who did no sin, neither was there found guile in his mouth' [1 Pet. 2:22]; and so that he might have the preeminence over those things which are under the earth, he himself being made 'the first-begotten of the dead' [Col. 1:18]; and so that all things, as I have already said, might behold their King; and so that the paternal light might meet with and rest upon the flesh of our Lord, and come to us from his resplendent flesh; and so

> that in this way the human being might attain to immortality, having been invested with the paternal light. (*haer.* 4.20.2)

Only the slain lamb has received all power, wealth, wisdom and, might (cf. Apoc. 5:12) and so he alone is able to open the book, and this, Irenaeus specifies, is 'the book of the Father'. The revelation of the content of the paternal book by the slain lamb is associated by Irenaeus with the Word becoming flesh, for it is the slain, enfleshed, Word who alone makes known or exegetes (*ἐξηγήσατο*) the Father, as the Prologue of John concludes. This action enables five things: (1) it grants the Word pre-eminence upon earth and also under the earth; (2) it brings all to behold their King; (3) and it enables in this way the paternal light to come to rest on the flesh of Christ; (4) and, through his resplendent flesh, to us; (5) so that we too, finally, robed in this paternal light, might attain immortality.

Irenaeus then begins the next section by showing that there is one Word, the Son, who is always with the Father, and that Wisdom, the Spirit, is always present with him. He then continues:

> Now this is his Word, our Lord Jesus Christ, who in the last times became a human being among humans, that he might join the end to the beginning, that is, the human being to God. Wherefore the prophets, receiving the prophetic gift from the same Word, announced his advent according to the flesh, by which the blending and communion of God and the human being took place according to the good pleasure of the Father, the Word of God foretelling from the beginning that God should be seen by human beings, and hold converse with them upon earth, should confer with them, and should be present with his own creation, saving it, and becoming capable of being perceived by it, and freeing us from the hands of all that hate us, that is, from every spirit of wickedness; and causing us to serve him in holiness and righteousness all our days, in order that the human being, having embraced the Spirit of God, might pass into the glory of the Father. (*haer.* 4.20.4)

That at least is how the Latin and Armenian versions of the text read, translating the now-lost Greek original independently. There is a Greek fragment which has instead, 'who in the last times became a God among humans'.[9] It is possible that this reading might be original, preserving as it does a chiasm in the text; and there are words in Ignatius which might be taken similarly.[10] But it is more likely to be a scribal error, or perhaps,

[9] Florilegium Achridense: Codex Ochrid, Mus. Nat. 84 (Inv. 86), 145; ed. in Marcel Richard et Bertrand Hemmerdinger, 'Trois nouveaus fragments grecs de l'*Adversus haereses de saint Irénée*', *ZNW* 53 (1962), 252–5, at 254: *Ἔστι δὲ οὗτος ὁ Λόγος αὐτοῦ ὁ Κύριος ἡμῶν Ἰησους Χριστός, ὁ ἐν ἐσχάτοις καιροῖς θεὸς ἐν ἀνθρώποις γενόμενος, ἵνα τὸ τέλος συνάψῃ τῇ ἀρχῇ, τουτέστιν ἄνθρωπον θεῷ. Καὶ διὰ τοῦτο προφῆται περὶ αὐτοῦ τοῦ Λόγου τὴν προφητείαν λαβόντες προεφήτευσαν αὐτοῦ τὴν ἔνσαρκον παρουσίαν.*

[10] Cf. Ignatius, *Eph.* 7.2: 'There is one Physician, fleshly and spiritual, begotten and unbegotten, in a human being becoming God (*ἐν ἀνθρώπῳ γενόμενος θεός*), in death true life, both from

perplexed at the idea of Jesus Christ (and not simply the Word) becoming 'a human being among human beings', a scribe thought it better to say that he was a God among humans. However, if the Latin and Armenian versions are indeed correct, and Jesus Christ became 'a human being among human beings', it falls within the same pattern of thought as we have been tracing: the 'human being' that Jesus becomes is the same as Ignatius hopes to be by following him in his Passion.

Irenaeus continues the chapter by claiming that this is what the prophets spoke about beforehand: they were not speaking of 'another' visible God, alongside the Father, as some assert, but rather were speaking prophetically. In this way they could indeed assert beforehand that God should be seen by human beings, for Christ himself has confirmed that 'blessed are the pure in heart for they shall see God' (Matt. 5:8). On this basis Irenaeus is then able to go from God's declaration to Moses that 'no one shall see me and live', to the conclusion that it is in fact by seeing God that human beings live!

> But in respect to his greatness and his wonderful glory, 'no one shall see God and live' [Exod. 33:20], for the Father is incomprehensible; but in regard to his love and kindness, and as to his infinite power, even this he grants to those who love him, that is, to see God, which thing the prophets did also predict. 'For those things that are impossible with human beings, are possible with God' [Luke 18:27]. For a human being does not see God by his own powers; but when he pleases he is seen by human beings, by whom he wills, and when he wills, and as he wills. For God is powerful in all things, having been seen at that time indeed prophetically through the Spirit, and also seen adoptively through the Son, and he shall also be seen paternally in the kingdom of heaven, the Spirit truly preparing the human being in the Son of God, and the Son leading him to the Father, while the Father, too, confers incorruption for eternal life, which comes to every one from the fact of his seeing God. For as those who see the light are within the light, and partake of its brilliancy, so also those who see God are in God, and receive of his splendor. But [his] splendor vivifies them; those, therefore, who see God, do receive life. And for this reason, he, [although] beyond comprehension and boundless and invisible, rendered himself visible and comprehensible and within the capacity of those who believe, so that he might vivify those who receive and behold him through faith. For as his greatness is past finding out, so also his goodness is beyond expression; by which having been seen, he bestows life upon those who see him. It is not possible to live apart from life, and the means of life is found in participation in God; but participation in God is to know God, and to enjoy his goodness. Human beings therefore shall see God that they may live, being made immortal by that sight, and attaining even unto God. (*haer.* 4.20.5–6)

Mary and from God, first suffering and then impassible, Jesus Christ our Lord'. Such is Lightfoot's reading; Ehrman and Stewart prefer the reading ἐν σαρκὶ and translate as 'God come in the flesh' or 'God in the flesh' respectively. Although the construction 'first... then' only occurs in one clause, it would seem to govern each pair.

He continues that as human beings live by seeing God, the Word both reveals the Father through many economies, so that they should not cease to exist, but at the same time preserves his invisibility, so that they might always have something towards which to advance (*haer.* 4.20.7). And then he concludes:

> For the glory of God is a living human being and the life of the human being consists in beholding God. For if the manifestation of God which is made by means of the creation affords life to all living in the earth, so much more does that revelation of the Father which comes through the Word give life to those who see God. (*haer.* 4.20.7)

The transition from the Word of God to Moses, that 'no one shall see me and live', to living by seeing God is *not*, as is often explained later on, made on the basis of 'the Incarnation', understanding by that term 'an episode in the biography of the Word', who was previously without flesh, and so invisible, but having taken flesh is now visible in this world, alongside other things that also 'appear' in the world. That would be a 'sight' only available to a handful of people present at the time, all of whom have died! It is rather 'the pure in heart' that are blessed 'to see God', as Christ says (Matt. 5:8), and while Philip clearly 'saw' the one standing in front of him, his request, 'Show us the Father and we shall be satisfied' (John 14:8), clearly indicates that he knows neither Christ nor the Father, as Jesus points out. To see Jesus 'in the flesh', and so to know the Father, and so to live, is for John, Ignatius, and Irenaeus, pivoted upon the cross and sharing in his flesh.[11] And as such, as Irenaeus makes clear later, 'the living human being' is the martyr:

> For it is testified by the Lord that as 'the flesh is weak', so 'the Spirit is ready' [Matt. 26:41], that is, is able to accomplish what it wills. If, therefore, anyone mixes the readiness of the Spirit as a stimulus to the weakness of the flesh, it necessarily follows that what is strong will prevail over what is weak, so that the weakness of the flesh will be absorbed by the strength of the Spirit, and such a one will no longer be carnal but spiritual because of the communion of the Spirit. In this way, therefore, the martyrs bear witness and despise death, not after the weakness of the flesh, but by the readiness of the Spirit. For when the weakness of the flesh is absorbed, it manifests the Spirit as powerful; and again, when the Spirit absorbs the weakness, it inherits the flesh for itself, and from both of these is made a living human being: living, indeed, because of the participation of the Spirit, and human because of the substance of the flesh.[12]

The 'Letter of the Christians of Vienne and Lyons to those in Asia and Phrygia', probably written by Irenaeus himself, describes exactly such a martyr, the young

[11] For John, see Saeed Hamid-Khani, *Revelation and Concealment of Christ: A Theological Inquiry into the Elusive Language of the Fourth Gospel*, WUNT 2.120 (Tübingen: Mohr Siebeck, 2000), 331–406, and Josaphat C. Tam, *Apprehension of Jesus in the Gospel of John*, WUNT 2.399 (Tübingen: Mohr Siebeck, 2015).

[12] *Haer.* 5.9.2. Cf. PO 12.5, 738–9 (frag. 6); TU 36.3, 14–19 (frag. 10).

slave girl Blandina. Affixed to 'the wood', 'hanging in the form of the cross', she appeared to the Christians in the arena alongside her as the embodiment of Christ: 'with their outward eyes they saw in the form of their sister him who was crucified for them, so that she persuaded those who believe in him that all who suffer for the glory of Christ have forever communion with the living God' (*h.e.* 5.1.41). Although it is said that it is by their 'outward eyes' that this is seen, it is however only seen by those alongside her in the arena, or, more accurately, by the author of the letter himself and those who now read the letter.

Irenaeus further explains this changing relationship between life and death by drawing together passages from Genesis, Isaiah, and Paul.[13] Citing two verses from Isaiah—the Lord 'gives breath [*πνοή*] to the people upon the earth and Spirit [*πνεῦμα*] to those who trample on it' (Isa. 42:5), and while 'the Spirit proceeds from me', God has, instead, 'made every breath'[14]—Irenaeus concludes that whereas the 'breath' is common to all creation and is created, the Spirit is 'particularly on the side of God' and bestowed upon the human race in the last times through the adoption of sons (*haer.* 5.12.2). Moreover, as 'the created is other than him who creates', the breath is temporal, while the Spirit is eternal; the breath increases in strength, flourishes, then expires, while the Spirit 'embraces the human being inside and out' and remains with him permanently. This distinction between breath and Spirit is one which the Apostle also makes, contrasting the 'animation' provided by 'the breath of life' to the first Adam (cf. Gen. 2:7), and the life-giving spirit that the last Adam became (cf. 1 Cor. 15:45). For Irenaeus, this movement from breath to Spirit, from animation to vivification, is the arc of the whole economy of God. The sentence we considered earlier (*haer.* 5.1.3) was preceded by this carefully coordinated sentence:

> just as, at the beginning [*ab initio*] of our formation in Adam, the breath of life from God, having been united to the handiwork, animated [*animavit*] the human being and showed him to be a rational being, so also, at the end [*in fine*], the Word of the Father and the Spirit of God, having become united with the ancient substance of the formation of Adam, rendered the human being living [*effecit . . . viventem*] and perfect, bearing the perfect Father, in order that just as in the animated we all die, so also in the spiritual we may all be vivified [*vivificemur*].
> (*haer.* 5.1.3)

It must be emphasized that Irenaeus is not proposing two different forms of life, a 'natural' life contrasted with a 'supernatural' life, or that somehow our flesh is not to be vivified by the life-giving Spirit. In another exegetical tour de force, Irenaeus argues against his opponents that while 'flesh and blood may not inherit the kingdom' as the Apostle put it (1 Cor. 15:50), they can certainly

[13] Cf. Behr, *Irenaeus*, 149–62.

[14] Isa. 57:16: *πνεῦμα γὰρ παρ' ἔμου ἐξελεύσεται, καὶ πνοὴν πᾶσαν ἐγὼ ἐποίησα.*

'be inherited' (*haer.* 5.9–14), in the way that the martyrs, as we saw, do not provide their witness by the strength of the flesh, but by the Spirit vivifying the flesh, just as it is the flesh that is vivified by the Spirit in John 6:63, as we argued in Chapter 3.

It is only because the flesh is capable of life even now, through the breath (as in *haer.* 5.1.3), or through the vision of God given by creation (as in *haer.* 4.20.7), that it is also capable of being vivified by the Spirit through seeing the Father. But, as Irenaeus points out, the two cannot co-exist together (*haer.* 5.12.2): the reception of the life-giving Spirit requires that the creature die, with Christ, to receive the life given in Christ, through the Spirit bestowed from the cross (John 19:30), and so become living human beings. The 'breath' is thus not simply replaced by the Spirit, for it is by using the breath that the natural mortality of the creature can be turned into a voluntary self-offering in witness to Christ. 'Whoever seeks to preserve his life [*ψυχὴν*, the 'animation'] will loose it', Christ says, 'but whoever looses it will gain it' (Luke 17:33, *ζωογονήσει*, literally 'will beget life'). This is the life that Christ offers (John 10:10 etc.), that he himself is (John 14:6), or that has come to be in Christ, as Irenaeus, together with most other early writers and manuscripts, reads John 1:3–4: 'what came to be in him was life and the life was the light of human beings'.[15] Again, light, life, and human beings form a tight thematic unity.

The life of the Spirit is something that begins with the pledge of the Spirit, given in baptism understood as sharing in the death of Christ (cf. Rom. 6:3–11; Eph. 1:14):

> If then now, having the pledge, we cry 'Abba, Father', what shall it be when rising again we behold him face to face, when all the members shall burst forth in an exuberant hymn of exultation, glorifying him who raised them from the dead and gave them eternal life? For if the pledge, gathering the human being together into himself, makes him now say 'Abba, Father', what shall the full grace of the Spirit, which shall be given to human beings by God, effect? It will render us like unto him, and perfect the will of the Father: for it shall make the human being in the image and likeness of God. (*haer.* 5.8.1)

Begun in baptism it finds completion in the Eucharist, which, as with Ignatius, is understood as being closely intertwined with the death and resurrection of those following Christ. He knows, and quotes, the passage from Ignatius that we saw earlier when discussing John 6 in Chapter 3, which speaks about how he hopes to become 'the pure bread of Christ' (*haer.* 5.28.4). However, he develops this imagery much more fully in a beautiful and complex passage (a single sentence!), which deserves to be quoted in full:

[15] John 1:3–4; cf. Irenaeus *haer.* 1.8.5, 3.11.1; Origen, *Comm. Jo.* 2.132; and Chapter 5 below.

> Just as the wood of the vine, planted in the earth, bore fruit in its own time, and the grain of wheat, falling into the earth and being decomposed, was raised up manifold by the Spirit of God who sustains all, then, by wisdom, they come to the use of human beings, and receiving the Word of God, become Eucharist, which is the Body and Blood of Christ; so also, our bodies, nourished by it, having been placed in the earth and decomposing in it, shall rise in their time, when the Word of God bestows on them the resurrection to the glory of God the Father, who secures immortality for the mortal and bountifully bestows incorruptibility on the corruptible [cf. 1 Cor. 15:53], because the power of God is made perfect in weakness [cf. 2 Cor. 12:9], in order that we may never become puffed up, as if we had life from ourselves, nor exalted against God, entertaining ungrateful thoughts, but learning by experience that it is from his excellence, and not from our own nature, that we have eternal continuance, so that we should neither undervalue the true glory of God nor be ignorant of our own nature, but should know what God can do and what benefits the human, and so that we should never mistake the true understanding of things as they are, that is, of God and the human being. (*haer.* 5.2.3)

The whole economy of God is thus structured in such a way that we might learn the truth about God and the human being, and, in the end, become a living human being, the glory of God.

Melito of Sardis

We have another instance of a similar usage of the term 'human being' in the work *On Pascha* by Melito of Sardis, which we already mentioned in Chapter 1 in the context of discussing the celebration of Pascha in the second century. Polycrates of Ephesus mentions 'Melito, the eunuch, who in all things lived in the Holy Spirit, who lies at Sardis, awaiting the visitation from heaven when he shall rise from the dead' (*h.e.* 5.24.5): that is, Melito belonged to those who looked back to the disciple of the Lord, John, as the originator of the paschal celebration, which they resolutely held, as did he, on the 14 Nissan.[16]

That Melito had written a work on Pascha was known from Eusebius (*h.e.* 4.26.2), but apart from a few words quoted by Anastasius of Sinai nothing more was known until the twentieth century.[17] In 1932, Frederic Kenyon brought to attention eight leaves of a fifth-century papyrus codex that contained some material from *1 Enoch* together with an unidentified homily.[18]

[16] See the discussion in the second section of Chapter 1, about the origin and development of the paschal celebrations and the 'Quartodeciman' controversy at the end of the second century.

[17] The words of Anastasius are given in Alistair C. Stewart, ed. and trans., *Melito of Sardis*, 90. We will be using Stewart's translation of Melito in what follows.

[18] Frederic G. Kenyon, 'The Chester Beatty Biblical Papyri', *Gnomon* 8 (1932), 46–9. He subsequently published a facsimile edition of this papyrus: *The Chester Beatty Biblical Papyri:*

By reference to Anastasius' words, Cambell Bonner, in 1940, identified this homily as belonging to Melito and located a further six papyri leaves in the University of Michigan that had also belonged to the same fifth-century codex, and on this basis was able to publish a more complete form of Melito's *On Pascha*.[19] A couple of decades later, an almost complete Greek version was found in Papyrus Bodmer 13, and then three decades later a Coptic version of the work was also discovered.[20] This remarkable series of discoveries is paralleled by an equally remarkable development in understanding the work: whereas Bonner described this work of Melito as 'what would today be called a Good Friday sermon',[21] it is today generally recognized, through the brilliant suggestion of Stuart Hall and the full development of his insight by Alistair Stewart-Sykes, that it is in fact a paschal haggadah, used during the course of the seder, dating to sometime between 160 and 170 CE.[22]

Because of the coherence of the work as a whole, and its movement from the simple beginning to the dramatic conclusion, we must give a brief outline of the structure, before turning to the passage which particularly concerns us here. The work begins by referring to the words of Exodus 12 which have just been read and setting out the scope of what is to follow:

> [1] The Scripture of the exodus of the Hebrews has been read,
> and the words of the mystery have been declared:
> how the sheep was slaughtered
> and how the people was saved,
> and how Pharaoh was flogged by the mystery

Descriptions and Texts of Twelve Manuscripts on Papyrus of the Greek Bible, Fasc. 8, *Enoch and Melito* (London: Emery Walker, 1941).

[19] Campbell Bonner, *The Homily on the Passion by Melito Bishop of Sardis and Some Fragments of the Apocryphal Ezekiel*, Studies and Documents, 12 (London: Christophers, 1940).

[20] M. Testuz, ed., *Papyrus Bodmer XIII: Méliton de Sardis Homélie sur la Pâque* (Geneva: Bodmer, 1960); James E. Goehring, *The Crosby Schøyen Codex: MS 193 in the Schøyen Collection* (Louvain: Peeters, 1990).

[21] Bonner, *Homily on the Passion*, 19; so too Kenyon, *Chester Beatty Biblical Papyri*, 9, 'a sermon on the Passover and the Passion, evidently preached on Good Friday'.

[22] Stuart George Hall, 'Melito in the Light of the Passover Haggadah', *JTS* ns 22 (1971), 29–46, at 36–37, where he suggests that the work divides between a homily on Exodus 12 and the Haggadah for the Passover table rite. The fullest analysis of this text is that given by Alistair Stewart-Sykes (= Alistair Stewart), *The Lamb's High Feast*, who argues persuasively that the work should be considered as a whole, and analyses both how it works and its place in the development of Passover/paschal celebrations during the course of the second century. See also John Hainsworth, 'The Force of the Mystery: Anamnesis and Exegesis in Melito's *Peri Pascha*', *SVTQ* 46.2 (2002), 107–46, for an account of the issues involved and the relationship between exegesis and liturgical anamnesis exemplified in Melito's *On Pascha*. Finally, see Bokser, *The Origins of the Seder*, 26–7, for the significance of Melito as providing 'specific information about the practices and the ideas of Passover' important for understanding the development of the Jewish seder following the destruction of the Temple in 70 CE.

[2] Therefore, well-beloved, understand,
how the mystery of the Pascha
is both new and old
eternal and provisional
perishable and imperishable
mortal and immortal.

After the initial laying out of the 'thesis' (1–10), Melito turns to what Stewart identifies as the διήγημα or *narratio*, that is, the exposition of the narrative, in this case with heighted drama and pathos, of the Exodus account (11–45). This section ends by Melito telling his hearers to 'listen to the meaning of the mystery [τὴν δύναμιν τοῦ μυστηρίου]', followed by a full account of how a type relates to that which it typifies (34–45). The next section (46–65), is the second part of a normal speech in the Greek world, the κατασκευή or *probatio*, the confirmation, which, as Stewart puts it, was 'intended to show the true meaning and veracity of the preceding narrative'.[23] It begins in this way:

[46] You have heard the narrative of the type and its correspondence:
hear now the confirmation of the mystery.
What is the Pascha?
It is called by its name because of what constitutes it:
from 'suffer' comes 'suffering'.
Therefore, learn who is the suffering one and who shares in the suffering one's suffering,
and why the Lord is present on earth to surround himself with the suffering one,
and take him to the heights of the heavens.

Having begun with the exodus from the slavery of Egypt, Melito now turns to the whole narrative of humankind, showing the slavery to sin and suffering in which all human beings have lived since the beginning, so as to show that all stand in need of salvation (47–56). Yet Melito then shows that during this time the Lord also made 'advance preparation for his own suffering' (57), giving many examples from the patriarchs through to the prophets:

[59] Thus, if you wish to see the mystery of the Lord
look at Abel who is likewise slain,
at Isaac who is likewise tied up
at Joseph who is likewise traded,
at Moses who is likewise exposed,
at David who is likewise hunted down,
and the prophets who likewise suffer for the sake of Christ.

The final section, the *peroratio*, again in Stewart's words, brings 'together all the themes of his discourse, praising God, and making the salvation worked by

[23] Stewart, *Melito*, 63, n. 16.

God a reality for his audience'.[24] And this is indeed done dramatically. As Melito comes to the end of his oration, he utters these words:

> [100] The Lord clothed himself with the human being,
> and with suffering on behalf of the suffering one,
> and bound on behalf of the one constrained,
> and judged on behalf of the one convicted,
> and buried on behalf of the one entombed,
> [101] he rose from the dead and cried aloud:
> 'Who takes issue with me? Let him stand before me.
> I set free the condemned.
> I gave life to the dead.
> I raised up the entombed.
> Who will contradict me?'
> [102] 'It is I', says the Christ
> 'I am he who destroys death
> and triumphs over the enemy
> and crushes Hades
> and binds the strong man,
> and bears of humanity to the heavenly heights'.
> 'It is I', says the Christ.
> [103] 'So come all families of people,
> adulterated with sin,
> and receive forgiveness of sins.
> For I am your freedom,
> I am the Pascha of salvation
> I am the lamb slaughtered for you,
> I am your ransom,
> I am your life,
> I am your light,
> I am your salvation,
> I am your resurrection,
> I am your King.
> I shall raise you up by my right hand,
> I will lead you to the heights of heaven,
> and there shall I show you the everlasting Father'.

On the night of Pascha, with Exodus having been read, expanded, and explained, and the people exhorted, Melito now bursts into what can only be described as prophetic speech (perhaps this, together with the repeated mentions of ascending to the heights of heaven, is why the work was bound together with *First Enoch*), so that he no longer speaks about God, but rather speaks *as* the risen Christ, present to the community in their paschal celebrations and promising to raise them to the heights of heaven.

[24] Ibid. 69, n. 26.

In this magnificent oration, of particular importance for our present purposes is the verse that opens the *peroratio*:

> [66] This is the one coming from heaven onto the earth by means of the suffering one,
> and robes himself in the suffering one by means of a virgin womb,
> and goes forth a human being;
> he accepted the suffering of the suffering one
> through suffering in a body which could suffer,
> and set free the flesh from suffering.
> Through the Spirit which cannot die
> he slew the manslayer death.

The first line is extremely intriguing: 'this is one coming [ἀφικόμενος] from heaven onto earth'. In a lecture delivered in the crypt of St Paul's Cathedral in London in 1966, David Daube recalled how three decades earlier 'a scholar—or shall I say madman? he was both', that is, Robert Eisler, had suggested that the ceremonial *aphikomen* piece of bread broken off at the beginning of the Jewish Passover meal, hidden, and then revealed and consumed at the end, resembled the Christian celebration of the liturgy, in which a piece of bread is also broken off, hidden, and revealed at the end, as the body of Christ to be consumed.[25] When Eisler first proposed this it caused outrage, with leading Jewish and Christian scholars denouncing him. Daube, accepting that Eisler included 'in his argumentation a good deal that was speculative or even wild', nevertheless suggested that it was time for a calmer look at the matter, 'for the usual explanations of the ritual are palpably forced'.[26] His further words are worth quoting in full:

> In the course of the Jewish Passover eve service, then, whether at the conclusion of the supper (the practice which has carried the day) or at its commencement (as according to some Talmudic practice at least), a piece of unleavened bread is taken as the Messiah by the company. The traditional designation of this fragment is *Aphiqoman*. The word is neither Hebrew nor Aramaic. Medieval Jewish commentators give fanciful etymologies. Modern scholars realize that the word is Greek, yet for once their etymologies are even more whimsical than those of the Rabbis. They do not even disdain made-up formulations for which there is no evidence whatever in the whole of Greek literature. Lietzmann, in his article putting down Eisler, improving upon an idea of Jastrow's, claims that the word stands for *epi komon*, in German *auf den Bummel!*, 'off to a crawl!'. Eisler, however, was right: *Aphiqoman* is the Greek *aphikomenos* or *ephikomenos*, 'The Coming One', 'He That Cometh', Hebrew *Habba'*, Aramaic *'athe*. But for the

[25] David Daube, *He That Cometh* (London: Diocese of London, 1966), 6; referring to Robert Eisler 'Das letzte Abendmahl', *ZNW* 24 (1925), 161–92 and 25.1 (1926), 5–38; Daube refers to pp. 166ff.

[26] Daube, *He That Cometh*, 6–7.

> theological and historical consequences that follow, it is hard to believe that this obvious, philologically easiest, *näheliegendste* derivation would have been overlooked in favour of the most far-fetched, tortuous ones.[27]

Rather than claiming that the Jewish Passover seder as it developed after the destruction of the Temple borrowed elements from the ritual that Christians were already celebrating, which might be suggested by the fact that *aphiqoman* is clearly a Greek loan-word, Daube saw the Christians as bringing out the messianic significance of what was already there: 'What was new was the application of the idea to the situation. Just so, the rite of eating a broken off fragment of unleavened bread as the Messiah was there, the novelty—a tremendous one—was the application to the situation, the identification of the bread with Jesus'.[28]

Daube's argument, more carefully expressed than Eisler's, was generally accepted, though its application to Melito was not noted for another decade. That the word ἀφικόμενος in Melito (whose work antedates the Jewish Haggadot that we have) is being used in this way was first suggested by Stuart Hall, in a footnote to his edition and translation of the work.[29] This recognition was then fully developed by Alistair Stewart-Sykes: 'What we are claiming is that Melito understood the messianic significance of the ἀφικόμενος and that this ritual was part of his paschal tradition'.[30] The *aphikomen*, he continues,

> is the bread of life, the messianic bread of which John 6 speaks; it is by virtue of the rite of *aphikomen* that the bread of life becomes the subject of pre-Passover teaching in the Johannine church. This ritual forms the first part of the μνημόσυνον, the summary of the haggadah and the commemorative intent of the seder. In this act, Christ is present.

The identification is reiterated through the following verses of *On Pascha*, each one beginning with 'This is the one who . . . ' (68–72). We should perhaps imagine Melito pointing dramatically at the portion of bread as he makes this repeated identification. And Christ is indeed present, as we have seen: having consumed the bread identified with Christ, Christ stands in their midst, promising to lead them on high to the Father in heaven.

If this is the ritual context in which the first line of verse 66 is said, the second and third lines have greater depths than we might have at first assumed (modifying the translation slightly):

> This is the one coming from heaven onto the earth by means of the suffering one,
> robing himself in that very one by means of a virgin womb,
> and goes forth a human being;

[27] Ibid. 8. [28] Ibid. 13.

[29] Stuart George Hall, *Melito of Sardis: On Pascha and Fragments*, OECT (Oxford: Clarendon, 1979), 35.

[30] Stewart-Sykes, *The Lamb's High Feast*, 198.

Οὗτος, ἀφικόμενος ἐξ οὐρανῶν ἐπὶ τὴν γῆν διὰ τὸν πάσχοντα,
αὐτὸν δὲ ἐκεῖνον ἐνδυσάμενος διὰ παρθένου μήτρας
καὶ προελθὼν ἄνθρωπος.

Although Christ clearly comes to save, redeem, and give life to the suffering ones upon earth, this verse speaks of this in a very particular and careful way. This Christ, who comes in the *aphikomenos* at the paschal celebrations, comes to earth 'through the suffering one',[31] in the singular; robing himself in that suffering one through the virgin womb;[32] and, in this way, 'goes forth [προελθὼν, not "comes" ἐλθὼν] a human being'. It is through the Passion that Jesus is born as a 'human being' who now comes to us in the *aphikomenos*, enabling Christians to become his body, to become themselves human, and to join him with the Father in the heavens.

The Gospel of John

Ignatius, Melito, and Irenaeus certainly have a very distinctive approach to what it is to be a living human being, that is, a martyr and the glory of God.[33] If John, as does Isaiah, looks back to the things that are spoken of from old but only revealed in the end, then, in addition to the true Tabernacle/Temple, not made by hands, that is established in Christ, we should look further back in Moses to the opening words of Scripture, echoed in the opening words of his Gospel. When we do so, we can now note a striking difference in the way that God's creative activity is described there. Scripture begins with God issuing commands: 'Let there be light . . . a firmament . . . let the earth bring forth living creatures' (Gen. 1:3–25). This divine 'fiat'—'let it be'—is sufficient to bring all

[31] Although Grammars often indicate that διά with an accusative means 'on account of, for the sake of', the primary meanings given by LSJ s.v. are in fact: I, of place, 'through'; II of time, 'during'; III casual, of persons, 'thanks to, by the aid of'.

[32] Cf. Hippolytus, *Antichr.* 4: 'For the Word of God, being fleshless, put on the holy flesh from the holy virgin, as a bridegroom a garment, having woven it for himself in the sufferings of the cross, so that having mixed our mortal body with his own power, and having mingled the corruptible into the incorruptible, and the weak with the strong, he might save the perishing human being'.

[33] Although the language of 'deification' would soon come to predominate to describe the state thus achieved in putting on the identity of Christ, one can find similar reflections on what it is to be, or rather become, human in the later tradition, such as Gregory of Nyssa, *De hominis opificio*, and Maximus the Confessor, *Ambig.* 41, and, right at the end of the Byzantine tradition, the insistence that this is first manifest in Christ himself by Nicholas Cabasilas: 'It was for the new human being that human nature was created at the beginning, and for him mind and desire were prepared. . . . It was not the old Adam who was the model for the new, but the new Adam for the old. . . . Because of its nature, the old Adam might be considered the archetype to those who see him first, but for him who has everything before his eyes, the older is the imitation of the second. . . . To sum it up: the Savior first and alone showed to us the true human being, who is perfect on account of both character and life and in all other respects'. *The Life in Christ* 6.91–4 (ET 6.12 modified).

these creatures into existence: 'and it was so . . . and it was good'. But, then, having declared all these things into existence by a word alone, setting the stage, as it were, God, not with an imperative but a subjunctive, announces: 'Let us make the human being [ποιήσωμεν ἄνθρωπον] in our image, after our likeness' (Gen. 1:26). This is the only thing about which God specifically deliberates; it is his divine purpose and resolve. With Scripture opening with this announcement of the particular project of God, we can now hear a further dimension to Christ's last word from the cross in the Gospel of John: τέτελεσται, it is finished, completed, perfected (19:30), confirmed, moreover, though unwittingly, by Pilate: 'Behold, the human being' (19:5, ἴδου ὁ ἄνθρωπος).[34] The particular project of God, to create a human being in his image and likeness, is not accomplished simply by a divine fiat, then and there; it depends, rather, upon the fiat of Christ, and those like Ignatius who also, in Christ, give their own 'let it be'.[35]

Discussion about the relation between the seven days of creation and John's presentation of Christ seems to go back to the earliest days, beginning perhaps even with John himself. Irenaeus and Victorinus of Pettau independently

[34] These words of Pilate also harken back to the prophecy of Zechariah (6:12 MT) that we considered in Chapter 3: 'Behold the man, whose name is Branch . . . It is he who shall build the Temple of the Lord and shall bear royal honour and shall sit and rule upon his throne'. The LXX has Ἰδοὺ ἀνήρ. Cf. Wayne Meeks, *The Prophet-King: Moses Traditions and Johannine Christology*, SupNovT 14 (Leiden: Brill, 1967), 71–2, and Michael Azar, 'The Scriptural King', *SVTQ* 50.3 (2006), 255–75. Charles Panackel, *ΙΔΟΥ Ο ΑΝΘΡΩΠΟΣ (Jn 19, 35): An Exegetico-Theological Study of the Text in the Light of the Use of the Term ΑΝΘΡΩΠΟΣ Designating Jesus in the Fourth Gospel*, Analecta Gregoriana 251 (Rome: Pontifica Università Gregoriana, 1988), 312–22, surveying of the range of scholarly opinions about the meaning of 'the human being' in 19:5, mentions as taking the word in the sense of the human being par excellence, foretold by the prophets: F. M. Braun, G. Segalla, L. Morris, G. H. C. Macgregor, W. H. Brownlee. A more specific connection to Genesis is made, though only in passing, by: Edwin A. Abbot, *Johannine Grammar* (London: A & C Black, 1906), 53, '"Behold *the* man!" i.e. the Man according to God's Image, the ideal Man'; and Alan Richardson, *The Gospel According to St John: Introduction and Commentary* (London: SCM 1959), 197, 'Adam . . . . was created by God to be a king over the whole created world; all creation was to be ruled by a son of man. . . . In Christ, the Son of Man, God's original intention in the creation is fulfilled. He is the new Adam, the Messianic King'; W. Krusche, 'Jesus Christus als der neue Mensch', *Theologische Versuche* 8 (1977), 201–12, at 203 and John Charles Fenton, *The Passion According to John: With an Introduction, Notes, and Meditations* (London: SPCK 1961), 44, both refer to the new man, the second Adam. Panackel (*ΙΔΟΥ Ο ΑΝΘΡΩΠΟΣ*, 336–7, italics original) concludes that by Pilate's words, '*the evangelist intends above all to lay emphasis on the humanity of Jesus. . . . The evangelist, however, wishes that his readers see in the battered and bloody figure of the Ecce-homo-scene not only a very human Jesus, but at the same time also the Son of God*'. The link between 'human being' as used in 19:5 and 'Son of Man' will be treated in the next section of this chapter.

[35] Cf. Maximus, *Ambig.* 41, describing the culmination of Christ's work of reconciling the differences within creation through the cross: 'And finally, after all these things, according to the concept of humanity, he goes to God himself, having "appeared on our behalf", clearly, as it is written, "in the presence of the God" and Father [Heb. 9:24], as human—the one who as Word cannot be separated in any way at all from the Father—fulfilling as human, in deed and truth, with unchangeable obedience, everything that he, as God, has predetermined to take place, and accomplishing the whole will of the God and Father on our behalf'.

record a tradition, which goes back to Papias and the elders in Asia who knew John, about the seven ages of Christ's life, affirming even that John informed them that Christ had reached the age of a teacher, that is, between forty and fifty years old (*haer.* 2.22.4–5). According to Victorinus, in words which most likely go back to Papias, Christ 'consummates his humanity [*humanitatem ... consummat*] in the number seven: birth, infancy, boyhood, youth, young-manhood, maturity, death'.[36] In modern times, attempts at correlation have focused on the structure of John's narrative, seeing the seven days of creation played out over specific parts, such as 1:19–2:12, or chapters 1–5, or with the Gospel as a whole, or as correlated to the seven 'signs' worked by Jesus. However, none of these modern suggestions have met with much approval, nor do they help in making the point argued here.[37] It would of course be satisfying to see the days of creation plotted out along the course of John's Gospel, such that they culminate with Christ saying 'it is finished', and to have these marked out as clearly as the liturgical markers we noted in Chapter 3, charting the course of the narrative. However, there are three points prior to the Passion which indicate an understanding of 'human being' that not only laid the basis for the way in which it is used by his 'school' but that it was used in this way by John himself. These have already been discussed in Chapter 3, but are here brought into particular focus.

The first of these occurs during the healing of the lame man in John 5, where it states that the healing waters were inaccessible to him because he has no 'human being' to immerse him in them (5:7). Christ directs him to 'rise' (5:8, ἔγειρε), and in the ensuing exchange about working on the Sabbath, Christ asserts that 'my Father is working still [ἕως ἄρτι ἐργάζεται] and I am working' (5:17), leading the Jews to seek to kill him for making himself equal to God (5:18). As Jesus further expounds what this work is, he specifies that what the Father does, and the Son seeing this does likewise, is to 'raise [ἐγείρει] the dead and give them life' (5:21), so that one who hears the word of Christ and believes in him who sent him, 'has eternal life; he does not come into judgment, but has passed from death to life' (5:24), and this is so because 'just as the Father has life in himself, so he has granted the Son to have life in himself' (5:26). In these ways, then, the question about working on the Sabbath has been significantly increased in scope: the work in question is to bring life out of death, and so the 'sixth day' when 'God finished his works [συνετέλεσεν ... τὰ ἔργα] that he had made and left off on the seventh day from all his works [ἀπὸ πάντων τῶν ἔργων] that he had made' (Gen. 2:2) refers

[36] *De fabrica mundi*, 9. The best analysis of this material remains that of Chapman, 'Papias on the Ages of the Lord'. According to Anastasius of Sinai (*Haex.* 1.6.1; 7b.5.5), Papias was the first of the long line of Fathers to concern themselves with the seven days of creation, referring it to Christ and his Church.

[37] For a full critical review of the suggestions see Sosa Siliezar, *Creation Imagery in John*, 123–49.

to the 'hour' that is yet to come, when the work is 'finished' (19:30), and life comes about through death. Although crucified on the day of Preparation, the timing of the event, after the sixth hour (cf. 19:14), which, as we saw, because of the multitude of lambs that needed to be slain, was reckoned to be 'towards the evening' as specified by Exodus 12:6, ties that day, on the Jewish pattern of reckoning days, to the Sabbath, which was not only the Sabbath but 'a great day' (19:31). The true Sabbath is Christ's rest in the tomb, celebrated in the feast of Pascha: God ceases from his work, for his project is now completed.[38]

The second instance occurs during the Feast of Tabernacles, when Jesus, referring back to the healing of the lame man last time he was in Jerusalem (cf. 7:21), argues that if circumcision is permissible on the Sabbath, they should not be angry because 'on the Sabbath I made the whole human being sound' (7.23: ὅλον ἄνθρωπον ὑγιῆ ἐποίησα). This theme is continued, during the period of the same feast, but on the Sabbath (9:14), when Jesus heals the man born blind by spitting on the ground and smearing the mud where his eyes should have been. The whole lengthy account is, as we saw, skilfully divided into seven scenes, during the course of which Jesus is mentioned by name seven times. The question of his disciples that prompted this whole event, 'who sinned, this man or his parents, that he was born blind?' (9:2), though later taken in terms of theodicy, is answered by Jesus quite differently: he was born blind 'so that the works of God might be made manifest in him' (9:3). In the first interpretation of this passage we have, this answer, together with the peculiar manner by which Jesus heals the blind man, paralleling as it does the way in which God creates human beings as described by Genesis, leads Irenaeus to conclude, 'the works of God is fashioning the human being' (*haer.* 5.15.2: *opera autem Dei plasmatio est hominis*). Thus, the Sabbath on which this happens is once again not simply the Sabbath of the Pharisees, on which no human work is carried out, but the Sabbath of God himself, whose 'work' is 'fashioning the human being' in the stature of Christ himself, who is indicated by the number seven, not six, and is completed in the Passion when Christ is crucified after the sixth hour on the day of Preparation, that is, 'towards the evening', and then rests in the tomb on the Sabbath.

The third and most substantive indicator for the interpretation of John 19:5 and 30 we have suggested above, and one which brings together the beginning,

[38] This is echoed in the Byzantine hymn for Holy Saturday: 'Moses the great mystically prefigured this present day, saying: "And God blessed the seventh day". For this is the blessed Sabbath, this is the day of rest, on which the only-begotten Son of God rested from all his works, through the economy of death he kept the Sabbath in the flesh, and returning again through the resurrection he has granted us eternal life, for he alone is good and loves humankind [lit: loves *anthropos*]'. Doxasikon at the Praises for Holy Saturday Mattins. Greek text in *Τριώδιον Κατανυκτικόν* (Rome, 1879), 374; ET *The Lenten Triodion*, translated from the original Greek by Mother Mary and Kallistos Ware (South Canaan, PA: St. Tikhon's Seminary Press, 1999), 652–3, modified.

middle, and end of the Gospel, is the figure of the 'woman'. Appearing at Cana, when Jesus' 'hour' was not yet (2:4), and, when the 'hour' had come, at the foot of the cross, where she is addressed by Jesus as 'woman' (19:26) and described as 'his mother' by the Evangelist (19:25) but as 'the mother' when seen from the perspective of Jesus himself (19:26), she also appears in the words of consolation given by Christ to his disciples as his departure approaches:

> Truly, truly, I say to you, you will weep and lament, but the world will rejoice; you will be sorrowful, but your sorrow will turn to joy. When the woman [ἡ γυνὴ] is in travail she has sorrow [λύπην] because her hour has come; but when she is delivered of the child [ὅταν δὲ γεννήσῃ τὸ παιδίον], she no longer remembers the tribulation [θλίψεως], for joy that a human being is born into the world [ἐγεννήθη ἄνθρωπος εἰς τὸν κόσμον]. So you have sorrow now, but I will see you again and your hearts will rejoice, and no one will take your joy from you.
> (16:20–2)

'The woman' whose 'hour has come' is the link between Cana and the Passion. This passage also contains a transition from the birth of a 'child' to that of a 'human being into the world', words which, as Judith Lieu points out, recall the 'human being coming into the world' mentioned in the Prologue (1:9, ἄνθρωπος ἐρχόμενον εἰς τὸν κόσμον).[39] Although the disciples' 'sorrow' at the departure of Christ is paralleled by the woman's 'sorrow' during her travail, with both also being turned into 'joy', the 'tribulation' of the woman is not simply paralleled by the disciples' anguish between the departure and return of Christ. In the world, they certainly have 'tribulation' (θλῖψιν), but Christ comforts them: 'be of good cheer, I have overcome the world' (16:33). As Lieu further notes, the perfect in 16:28 ('I have come into the world') 'does not precede but is coterminous with the parallel perfect' in 16:33 ('I have overcome the world'), so that 'this woman too mediates a beginning that is also an ending/an ending that is also a beginning in the merging of times and experiences that characterize these chapters'.[40] So, as Lieu asks: 'So is this a birthing or a dying? . . . we meet birth here only when we encounter death. Indeed, the birth, which is not narrated in this Gospel, becomes through 16:21 a death, or is the death a birth?'[41] There are further parallels with Genesis at play in these words of comfort and the crucifixion scene. As Tertullian points out, with Adam being a figure of Christ, Adam's sleep foreshadows Christ's death, and so as Eve came forth from the side of the sleeping Adam, so too the Church, in the form of blood and water, comes forth from the side of Christ in mortal slumber.[42] Furthermore, 'the woman' (ἡ γυνή) in Genesis 3 is promised 'sorrow' (λύπη) in childbirth (Gen. 3:16), just as is 'the woman' of John 16:20–1, and when Eve does give birth, it is a 'human being' that she acquires

[39] Judith Lieu, 'The Mother of the Son in the Fourth Gospel', 72. [40] Ibid.
[41] Ibid. 73. [42] Tertullian, *An.*, 43.10; quoted in Chapter 3.

'from God' (Gen. 4:1, *ἐκτησάμην ἄνθρωπον διὰ τοῦ θεοῦ*), as it is also a 'human being' that is born in 16:21. However, although Adam calls 'the woman' 'Eve' (or 'Life' in the LXX), 'because she is the mother of the living' (Gen. 3:20), all her children in fact die; for which the word 'sorrow' (Gen. 3:16), rather than 'travail', is the appropriate term, applying as it does to mental anguish rather than physical or birth pain as Lieu points out.[43]

The Church thus turns out to be the true 'mother of the living', 'our mother' (Gal. 4:26; re. Isa. 54:1), as Christ is the true human (and Adam but a type, a preliminary sketch, cf. Rom. 5:14), acquiring as living human beings those who, following Christ, are born through martyric death, anticipated by baptism (cf. Rom. 6:3–11) and in partaking of the eucharistic cup, as we saw when discussing John 6 in Chapter 3. This combination of Pauline and Johannine themes, seeing Genesis as speaking about Christ and his Church, seems to have originated, according to Anastasius of Sinai, in Asia Minor in the circle of the elders who knew John and whose traditions Papias recorded.[44] God's purpose, spoken of old and reiterated by Isaiah, 'to make the human being for ever' (Isa. 44:7) is thus completed when the creatures give their own fiat to God's purpose, by following Christ, as Ignatius did, becoming witnesses, martyrs, no longer trying to secure one's own lives, but rather taking up the cross and living by dying: 'as dying, behold we live' (2 Cor. 6:9). 'Be my witnesses/martyrs: I too am a witness/martyr, says the Lord God, and the Servant whom I have chosen' (Isa. 43:10). The Gospel of the Theologian, thus, encompasses the beginning and end of all the work of God, as Christ's 'it is finished' brings to completion God's own purpose, the living human being, the glory of God. The unity of flesh and Spirit in the living human being, when the Spirit adorns the flesh with its own properties, so that it is not 'one flesh' but, united to the Lord, 'one spirit' (1 Cor. 6:16–17), is the final marriage celebrated in the paschal feast.

The Gospel of John moreover already has the martyrdom of believers in sight, as we saw when examining John 6 in Chapter 3. In his farewell discourse, Christ tells his disciples that they will be persecuted, just as he has been persecuted (15:20). This refers back to the only other place in which the word 'persecute' is used, in 5:16, where the Jews persecuted Jesus because he healed the lame man on the Sabbath. When Jesus asserts that 'the Father is still working and I am working', making himself equal to God, 'the Jews sought all the more to kill him' (5:17–18). That the predicted persecution of the disciples in 15:20 likewise has the weight of 'killing', is made explicit a few verses later in the farewell discourse: 'I have said all this to keep you from falling away. They will put you out of the synagogues; indeed, an hour is coming when whoever kills you will think he is offering worship to God. . . . I have said these things to

43 Lieu, 'The Mother of the Son in the Fourth Gospel', 74.

44 Anastasius of Sinai, *Haex.* 1.6.1; 7b.5.5.

you, that when their hour comes you may remember that I told you of them' (16:1–2, 4). Although this 'hour' lacks a definite article, which in John is reserved for 'the hour' of Christ's own Passion and 'the hour' of true worship (4:21, 23), the martyrdom of believers is nevertheless embraced by the same term and movement, the same glorification. That such martyrdom, sharing in the Passion of Christ, was already known by the time of the writing of the Gospel is clear from Christ's words to Peter, that he 'will stretch out his hands . . . to show by what death he was to glorify God' (21:18–19; cf. 12:33, 18:32).

Building upon Martyn, de Boer argues strongly that the second 'trauma' of 16:2, that of martyrdom, provides the background and context for the full development of the high Christology characteristic of the last stages of the composition of the Gospel of John (*c*.90 CE).[45] It is possible, and has been extensively debated, whether these reconstructions place too much weight on the term ἀποσυναγώγος, and its connection to the twelfth of the Eighteen Benedictions, directed against the Nazarenes and heretics, and its conjectured history.[46] Minear points out that Christians were persecuted by Jews from the earliest days (e.g. Paul, Gal. 1:13; Phil. 3:6), and were no doubt cast out of local synagogues before any kind of official excommunication, and that, moreover, this resulted in the deaths of Christians within a few decades, such as Stephen, Peter, James, and Paul, to name but those recorded.[47] Whether we place the writing of the Gospel earlier or later, Minear's characterization of it as 'the martyr's Gospel' is surely appropriate.

John has, in this way, given us a Christological reading of Genesis: Moses 'wrote of me', as Christ himself asserts in this Gospel (5:46). But whereas everything else is created immediately by a divine fiat, spoken into existence, what is shown ('behold') at the Passion is not spoken into existence by God, but is the very Word of God himself. As we have already seen, and will see again when examining the Prologue in Chapter 5, the title 'Word' is one that is ascribed to the crucified one, and is one that Ignatius too hopes to attain through his martyrdom, as he becomes a 'human being' (*Rom.* 2.1; 6). As Bultmann comments, regarding Pilate's words 'Behold the human being': 'The declaration ὁ λόγος σὰρξ ἐγέντο has become visible in its extremest consequence'.[48]

[45] De Boer, *Johannine Perspectives* (see 67–71 for summary and a table showing how Brown, Martyn, and de Boer would plot the history of the Johannine community and the composition of the Gospel); see also de Boer, 'Johannine History and Johannine Theology'. Martyn, *History and Theology*, takes the first 'trauma', that of being expelled from the synagogue, together with the second as both belonging to the 'middle period' of the Johannine community, *c*.85 CE.

[46] Cf. de Boer, *Johannine Perspectives*, 69, for a survey of the literature.

[47] Minear, *John: The Martyr's Gospel*, 55, concluding: 'This is why, in my judgment, texts like 16:1-3 are better mirrors of the situation in Judea before A.D. 66 than of a more generalized situation in Galilee or Syria after A.D. 80'.

[48] Bultmann, *John*, 659.

THE ASCENDING AND DESCENDING SON OF MAN

If, as we have argued, Pilate's statement 'Behold the human being' refers back to the purpose of God stated in Gen. 1:26, and is completed in Christ's Passion, and in those following him in martyrdom, so that the term 'human' means more than it does in common parlance, it is possible that we have here an insight that can be profitably brought to bear on the perplexing figure of the ascending and descending Son of Man in the Gospel of John. Already in the nineteenth century Westcott suggested that 'the human being' in Pilate's statement was a reference to the Son of Man, and he was followed by Dodd and Blank.[49] Barrett further speculates that 'by *ὁ ἄνθρωπος* John may however have meant something much more precise. *ὁ ἄνθρωπος* calls to mind those Jewish and Hellenistic myths of the heavenly or primal Man which lie behind John's use of the phrase *ὁ υἱὸς τοῦ ἀνθρώπου*'.[50] Much of recent scholarship on the Son of Man in John, such as Ashton as we will see, has seen John's use of this title as deriving from apocalyptic texts referring to such an otherwordly figure, though others have emphasized a continuity with the figure of the suffering Jesus in the Synoptic Gospels.[51] It is possible, however, given what we have seen of the distinctive use of 'human being' by the school of John, that these two positions are not diametrically opposed. As Moloney puts it: 'Throughout the Gospel the reader has been directed to look forward; in 13, 31 he has been told: "Now is the Son of man glorified" and finally, in the ironic coronation and investiture of Jesus, it is Pilate who announces: "Here he is—the Son of Man!" The absurd glorification through humiliation has reached its high point'.[52] The way up and the way down, that of glorification and

[49] Westcott, *St John*, 269, referring back to Jesus' words in 1:51, but including the words *ἀπ'ἄρτι*, found in some manuscripts, 'hereafter you will see the Son of Man'; Dodd, *Interpretation*, 437; Josef Blank, *Krisis*, 289 n. 60, and Josef Blank, 'Die Verhandlung vor Pilatus Joh 18,28–19,16, im Lichte johanneischer Theologie', *BZ* 3 (1959), 60–81, at 75 n. 38. Margaret Pamment, 'The Son of Man in the Fourth Gospel', *JTS* ns 36.1 (1985), 55–66, at 65, n. 28, suggests that 'Perhaps the Semitic expression is changed into its Greek equivalent for the lips of a Gentile'.

[50] Barrett, *John*, 450. Meeks, *Prophet-King*, 70–2, points to Zech. 6:12 ('Behold the man [*ἰδοῦ ἀνήρ*], whose name is Branch'), as well as Num. 24:17, as verses which lent themselves to eschatological interpretation.

[51] Most importantly, Francis J. Moloney, *The Johannine Son of Man*, 2nd edn, Biblioteca di Scienze Religiose, 14 (Rome: LAS, 1978). Revisiting his argument three decades later, Moloney concedes that this is a 'minority position', yet one that 'also starts from Daniel 7, but claims that already in that context, the "one like a son of man" in 7, 13 is to be identified with the holy ones of the Most High of vv.21–25.... With this understanding, the tradition did not begin with an otherworldly eschatological "Son of Man", and develop in the tradition until it was applied to the suffering Son of Man. It developed in the other direction. It began with the suffering Son of Man (Dn 7 and Jesus) and was shaped—in both the Christian preaching and the Jewish apocalyptic material—into a heavenly, eschatological figure'. Moloney, 'The Johannine Son of Man Revisited', in Gilbert van Belle, et al., *Theology and Christology in the Fourth Gospel*, 177–202, at 181.

[52] Moloney, *Johannine Son of Man*, 207.

humiliation upon the cross, are, to borrow a saying from Heraclitus, one and the same.[53] But now we can add that this is not simply the appearance in this world of an otherworldly figure, but the completion or perfecting, the appearance or unveiling, of God's project announced from the beginning.

The term 'son of man' is, in itself, simply a Semitic idiom, *barnasha*, used to refer to a human being, and can, in certain contexts, be used in an oblique manner to refer to the speaker himself.[54] This is true also of many of the 'son of man' sayings in the Synoptics. But through association with the enigmatic figure of one 'as a son of man' in Daniel (7:13, ὡς υἱὸς ἀνθρώπου), the figure denoted by the expression (now capitalized) 'Son of Man' comes to have apocalyptic associations. The words in Daniel are the root source of all subsequent utilization of the theme of the Son of Man:

> I kept watching, until thrones were set, and an Ancient of Days sat, and his clothing was white like snow, and the hair of his head was like pure wool; his throne was a flame of fire; its wheels were burning fire.... I was watching in the night visions, and behold, [one] as a Son of Man coming with the clouds of heaven. And he came as far as the Ancient of Days and was presented to him. And to him was given the dominion and the honor and the kingship and all peoples, tribes, languages, and all honour was serving him. And his authority is an everlasting authority, which shall never be moved—and his kingship, which will never perish. (Daniel 7:9, 13–14 OG)

Aspects of this description are already evident in the Synoptics, in the predictions which speak of the Son of Man as 'sitting on his glorious throne' (Matt. 19:28), 'coming in clouds with great power and glory' (Mark 13:26), 'seated at the right hand of the power of God' (Luke 22:69; cf. Mark 14:62), and all the tribulations that will occur at his fearful coming (Matt. 24:27–51; Luke 17:24–30).[55] However, as we noted earlier, what is affirmed in the last mention of 'the Son of Man' from Christ's own lips in the Synoptics—that 'hereafter, you will see the Son of Man seated at the right hand of power' (Matt. 26:64)—is promised at the beginning of the Gospel of John, in Jesus' enigmatic reply to Nathanael: after a string of titles applied to Christ (the 'Lamb who takes away the sin of the world', 'Messiah/Christ', 'Son of God', and 'King of Israel') the title 'Son of Man' is introduced in an apocalyptic fashion: '[Hereafter] You will see the heaven opened and the angels of God ascending and descending upon the Son of Man' (1:35–51).[56]

[53] Heraclitus, 61 [F38]: ὁδὸς ἄνω κάτω μία καὶ ὡυτή.

[54] Geza Vermes, 'The Use of *Barnash/bar nasha* in Jewish Aramaic', Appendix E in Matthew Black, *Aramaic Approach to the Gospels and Acts*, 3rd edn (Oxford: Clarendon, 1967), 310–28; Matthew Black, 'Aramaic *Barnasha and the "Son of Man"*', *ExpTim* 95 (1983), 200–6.

[55] For a full survey of the utilization of Daniel by the Synoptics and Acts, see Reynolds, *Apocalyptic Son of Man*, 65–81.

[56] As we noted earlier, Reynolds, *Apocalyptic Son of Man*, 100, points out the presence of ἀπ'ἄρτι in John 1:51 in some mss (*A Θ Ψ f* [1.13] 33 and the Syriac versions) and suggests that 'at

Not only does the apocalyptic Son of Man step on to the pages of the Gospel of John in this most dramatic manner, but there are features associated with the Son of Man in John that are specific to John, and striking. In particular, the Son of Man is said, in John 3:13, to ascend and descend (or is it descend and ascend?), and to act upon earth in the present, offering his flesh for consumption (6:51–3) and asking the man given sight if he believes in the Son of Man (9:35). With the narrative of the Gospel prefaced by the Prologue, and many centuries of theological reflection thereafter, we are tempted, if not conditioned, to read John's language of descending and ascending in terms of the Word, a heavenly figure, becoming incarnate on earth and then returning to the Father, an account of a descending and ascending Saviour which Bultmann claimed was drawn from various Gnostic redeemer myths.[57] But this is *not* what we are presented with in the Gospel. As Ashton points out, 'in the body of the Gospel when John combines the notions of descent and ascent it is in relation to the Son of Man, not the Logos'.[58] Indeed the Logos, as a heavenly figure, does not appear in the rest of the Gospel nor is Jesus identified there by this title. There are of course numerous other ways in which Jesus' heavenly origin is made clear without using either the title 'Son of Man' or the language of ascending and descending: he is 'from above' (3:31; 8:23), 'sent' from the Father (5:36–7), coming from and going to the Father, into the world and leaving it (16:28), and so on. Regarding the title 'Son of Man', with whom the language of ascending and descending is associated, however, Ashton also points out that far from what we might expect, that 'Son of Man' would refer to Christ as human and 'Son of God' to Christ as divine, the identification is paradoxically the reverse: '"Son of God", originally at any rate, indicates a human being, the Messiah; whereas "Son of Man" points to a figure whose true home is in heaven'.[59] In common with many other scholars, Ashton leaves the Prologue to one side while investigating the figure of the ascending/descending Son of Man, both to be more focused on what the Gospel of John actually says about the Son of Man, and also because, as he puts it, 'John's Gospel is

least some early Christians may have made the connection between the final Son of Man saying in Mark and Matthew and the first Son of Man saying in John'.

[57] Cf. Rudolf Bultmann, 'Die Bedeutung der neuerschlossen mandäischen und manichäischen Quellen für das Verständis des Johannesevangeliums', *ZNW* 24 (1925), 100–46, repr. in Bultmann, *Exegetica*, 55–104; Rudolf Bultmann, 'The History of Religions Background of the Prologue to the Gospel of John', in John Ashton, *Interpretation of John*, 27–46 (originally appeared as 'Der religionsgeschichtliche Hintergrund des Prologs zum Johannesevangelium', *ΕΥΧΑΡΙΣΤΗΡΙΟΝ: Festschrift für H. Gunkel*, 2 vols (Göttingen, 1925), 2.3–26). For critique see the now classic articles, by Wayne A. Meeks, 'The Man from Heaven in Johannine Sectarianism', *JBL* 91 (1972), 44–72, repr. in Ashton, *Interpretation of John*, 169–205, and Charles H. Talbert, 'The Myth of a Descending-Ascending Redeemer in Mediterranean Antiquity', *NTS* 22.4 (1976), 418–43.

[58] John Ashton, 'The Johannine Son of Man: A New Proposal', *NTS* 57 (2011), 508–29, at 512.

[59] Ashton, *Fourth Gospel*, 240.

better understood if one's understanding also relates to the making of it', holding, as do many others, that the Prologue was a later addition in the stages of the composition of the Gospel.[60] Ashton's argument, as we will see, is that John 3:11–13 refers back to an earlier episode in which 'Jesus received a new revelation, so much more than a new law, in the course of a visit to heaven of an apocalyptic seer', adding that 'some may find it easier to believe than the Prologue's mythic account of a divine being taking flesh'.[61] Whether the Prologue should be understood this way is the subject of Chapter 5, after we have explored the mysterious figure of the ascending/descending Son of Man in this.

There are eight passages in which the term 'Son of Man' occurs in the Gospel of John: (1) 1:51; (2) 3:13, 14; (3) 5:26–7; (4) 6:27, 53, 62; (5) 8:28; (6) 9:35; (7) 12:23, 34 twice; and (8) 13:31. Five of these are relatively straightforward. Two pertain to judgement, which has been given to the Son 'because he is a Son of Man' (5:26–7, the only anarthrous use of the title in John), and similarly 9:35 (cf. 9:39, 'for judgement I came into the world'), where Jesus asks the man with his sight restored if he believes in the Son of Man, and then obliquely identifies himself as such, though, importantly (as we will see) not as an object of sight but of hearing (9:37). Three passages pertain to the Passion: 'when you have lifted up the Son of Man, then you will know that I AM' (8:28); 'The hour has come for the Son of Man to be glorified' (12:23), provoking a dialogue in which the crowd then ask Jesus: 'How can you say that the Son of Man must be lifted up? Who is the Son of Man?' (12:34); and 'Now is the Son of Man glorified and in him God is glorified' (13:31). John 3:14 also refers to the Passion in speaking of the Son of Man being 'lifted up', but as it is tied together with the ascending and descending from heaven in 3:13, it is more complex and will be considered in detail below.[62] It should be noted that the three passages which speak of the Son of Man being 'lifted up' do not use the verb ἀναβαίνω, 'to ascend' (as in 1:51; 3:13; 6:62), but ὑψόω (3:14; 8:28; 12:34), which is undoubtedly derived from Isaiah 52:13 ('my servant shall understand and he shall be exalted [ὑψωθήσεται] and glorified [δοξασθήσεται] exceedingly'), so that, although it has the basic meaning of 'to lift up', it is regularly translated as 'to exalt' because of its association with glorification. That the 'lifting up' in 12:32 is said to be 'from the earth' (ἐκ τῆς γῆς), thereby showing by what death he was to die (12:33), further ties John's

[60] John Ashton, 'The Johannine Son of Man', 529. This point is one he makes forcefully throughout his *Fourth Gospel*, see especially pp. 14–19 of the second edition.

[61] Ashton, 'Johannine Son of Man', 527.

[62] It should be noted that the terms ascending/descending are also used in other contexts than speaking of the Son of Man: the Spirit descends upon Jesus (1:32, 33), whom the Baptist testifies that 'this is the Son of God' (1:34); and Jesus speaks of himself as 'ascending to my Father and your Father, my God and your God' (20:17), and so as Son of God, but a sonship shared with others.

use of 'lifting up' with the text of Isaiah (cf. 53:8: 'his life was taken from the earth', *ἀπὸ τῆς γῆς*).[63] Similarly, the glorification spoken of in 13:31, without any reference to 'lifting up', no doubt derives also from Isaiah 52:13.[64] In John 6, Jesus' question mentions the 'Son of Man ascending to where he was before' (6:62), but, although there is no mention of the Son of Man 'descending', there are plenty of references in that chapter to the bread which 'descends' from the heavens (6:33, 50, 58), to Jesus as the one who has himself 'descended from heaven' (6:38, 42), and to Jesus as the 'bread which descended from heaven' (6:41, 51)—seven mentions of 'descending' before the single description of the Son of Man ascending. John 6, however, has sufficiently been treated in Chapter 3, where we explored the identification of Jesus as the Son of Man in and through the Passion and the call to martyrdom that his invitation to 'chew' his flesh entails. Thus only two of the Son of Man passages, both which also speak of his ascending and descending, need further investigation, that is 1:51 and 3:13, along with John 9 and the particular use that John Ashton makes of this chapter.

John 1:51

When we examined John 1:51 in Chapter 3, we did so looking for intimations of the Temple, or in this case, the house of God, through its allusions to Jacob's vision. John, as we saw, subtly changes the locus of Jacob's vision of the ladder, with angels ascending and descending upon it (or him), from a place, Bethel—'truly this is the house of God and this is the gate of heaven' (Gen. 28:17)—to a person, the Son of Man, as the sole locus of revelation. But there are two other aspects of the odd description of angels ascending and descending upon the Son of Man that need investigating. The first is that contrary to what we might expect—that angels would descend from heaven before ascending—here the ascending comes first. The second aspect is that the angels move up and down not upon a ladder but upon a person.

The idea that the angels ascend and descend upon a person is facilitated by the ambiguity of the Hebrew, where the pronoun can be taken as referring to Jacob, unlike the LXX where the feminine pronoun must refer back to the ladder (Gen. 28:12). Following the lead of Burney and Odeberg, Ashton draws on the rabbinic discussion about this point to find the parallels for John 1:51.[65] For example, two rabbis had this to say about Genesis 28:12:

[63] Cf. van Belle, 'The Death of Jesus and the Literary Unity of the Fourth Gospel', 21.

[64] Cf. de Boer, 'Johannine History and Johannine Theology', at 308–9, 311; he provides an excellent summary of the interpretations given to the exaltation and glorification language in John and the issues involved.

[65] Burney, *Aramaic Origins*, 116–17; Hugo Odeberg, *The Fourth Gospel Interpreted in its Relation to Contemporaneous Religious Currents in Palestine and the Hellenistic-Oriental World*

R. Hiyya the Elder and R. Yannai: One of them said, '"They were going up and coming down" on the ladder'. The other said, '"They were going up and coming down" on Jacob'. The one who says, '"They were going up and coming down" on the ladder' has no problems. As to the one who says, '"They were going up and coming down" on Jacob', the meaning is that they were raising him up and dragging him down, dancing on him, leaping on him, abusing him. For it is said, 'Israel, in whom I will be glorified' [Isa. 49:3]. [So said the angels] 'Are you the one whose image is engraved above?' They would then go up and look at his features and go down and examine him sleeping. The matter may be compared to the case of a king who was in session and judging cases in a judgment chamber. So people go up to the basilica and find him asleep. They go down to the judgment chamber and find him judging cases.[66]

Jacob is, in a sense, in two places at once, asleep on earth while his image is fixed in the heavens; it is to the heavens that the angels ascend to see his features, before they descend to earth to see him sleeping. And, on the following verse:

'And behold, the Lord stood on him' [Gen. 28:13]: R. Hiyya and R. Yannai: One said, '"On him" means "on it, namely, on the ladder"'. The other said, '"On him" means "on Jacob"'. The one who said, '"On him" means "on it, namely the ladder"', has no problems. But as to the one who said, '"On him" means "on Jacob"', the sense is that he stood over him. Said R. Yohannan, 'The wicked stand over their gods [to protect them]: "And Pharaoh dreamed, and behold, he stood over the river" [Gen. 41:1]. But as to the righteous, their God stands over them: "And behold, the Lord stood on him"'. Said R. Simeon b. Laqish: 'The patriarchs are themselves the chariot [of God]: "God went up from Abraham" [Gen. 17:22]. "And God went up from upon him" [Gen. 35:13]. "And behold the Lord stood upon him" [Gen. 28:13]'. [*Gen. Rab.* 69.3.2–3]

The later Palestinian Targums also mention the divine chariot, the Merkavah, in their retelling of this episode, and also provide a reason for why the angels ascend first, before descending:

The angels that had accompanied him from the house of his father ascended to bear good tidings to the angels on high, saying: 'Come and see the pious man whose image is engraved in the throne of Glory, who you desired to see'. And behold, the angels from before the Lord ascended and descended and observed him.[67]

(Uppsala: Almquist & Wiksell, 1929), 33–47; Ashton, *Fourth Gospel*, 245–51. See also Neyrey, 'The Jacob Allusions in John 1:51', *CBQ* 44 (1982), 586–605.

[66] *Gen. Rab.* 68.12.6. Jacob Neusner, *Genesis Rabbah: The Judaic Commentary to the Book of Genesis: A New American Translation* (Atlanta, GA: Scholars Press, 1985), 3.13, translates as 'Are you the one whose visage is incised above?' I have modified this to read 'image' (for the word is a transliteration of *εἰκών*) and 'engraved' for conformity with the passage from the Targums translated below. Cf. Burney, *Aramaic Origins*, 116–17.

[67] *Tg. Neof.* Gen. 28:12; see also *Tg. Ps.-J.* Gen.28:12. The dating of this material is of course an extremely complex affair; there seem to have been written Targums already in the second

Again we have a duplication of the figure of Jacob, on earth and portrayed in the throne of Glory, simultaneously. The angels, on the other hand, must ascend and descend to see him in heaven and on earth: they cannot be in both places simultaneously.

Ashton calls upon a third piece of evidence, not used by earlier commentators, but brought to attention by Jonathan Z. Smith, that is, a fragment from a text known as 'The Prayer of Joseph', preserved by Origen.

> [Jacob, at least, says,] 'For I who speak to you am Jacob and Israel, an angel of God and a primal spirit, and Abraham and Isaac were created before any work. But I am Jacob, he who was called Jacob by men, but my name is Israel, he who was called Israel by God, a man who sees God because I am the firstborn of every living being which is given life by God'. [And he adds,] 'And when I was coming from Mesopotamia of Syria, Uriel, the angel of God came out and said that I descended to the earth and dwelt among men, and that I was called Jacob by name. He was jealous, and fought with me, and wrestled with me, saying that his name preceded my name and that of every angel. And I mentioned his name to him and how great he is among the sons of God: "Are you not Uriel, my eighth, and I Israel, an archangel of the power of the Lord and chief of the captains of thousands among the sons of God? Am I not Israel, the first minister in the presence of God, and did I not invoke my God by his unquenchable name?"'[68]

Once again, we have a similar duplication of a single figure, called 'Jacob' by men on earth, but 'Israel' by God in heaven. What is new in this text is that it is this figure himself, not the angels, who descends: Israel descends to earth, where he is known as Jacob, forgetful of his true origin until reminded by Uriel and after a struggle with this angel. Although it is not explicit in this fragment, it is likely that, although Israel/Jacob is described as 'an angel of God', he is, unlike the angels that ascend and descend to see him, able to remain in both heaven and earth simultaneously, for there is no indication that Israel/Jacob departs from earth once wakened to a knowledge of his heavenly status by Uriel's words and the ensuing struggle.

In analysing this passage, under the subtitle of 'The Descent Myth', Smith quotes M. R. James' words that 'the leading idea of the principal fragment is that angels can become incarnate in human bodies, live on earth in the likeness of men, and be unconscious of their original state. Israel does so apparently in

century BCE, fragments of which were found in Qumran and rabbinic sources also indicate the existence of written Targums in the late third to early fourth century, but the texts that we now have date from the end of the first millennium. Cf. Martin McNamara, introduction to *Targum Neofiti 1: Genesis*, The Aramaic Bible, 1A (Collegeville, MN: Liturgical Press, 1992), 43–5.

[68] Origen, *Comm. Jo.* 2.189–90. Cf. Jonathan Z. Smith, 'The Prayer of Joseph', in J. Neusner, ed., *Religions in Antiquity: Essays in Memory of Erwin Ramsdell Goodenough* (Leiden: Brill, 1968), 253–94, repr. in Jonathan Z. Smith, *Map is Not Territory: Studies in the History of Religions* (Chicago: University of Chicago Press, 1993), 24–66.

order that he may become the father of the chosen people'.[69] Smith further notes that the words of Uriel to Jacob allude to Sirach 24:8, and that it is 'the Jewish Wisdom-Shekinah theology that has been the preoccupation of many students of the Prologue to the Fourth Gospel since the pioneering work of J. Rendel Harris'.[70] Whether this is so or not, John himself, as Ashton points out, makes no mention of, or allusion to, the theme of the tabernacling of Wisdom upon the earth in the portrait he sketches in 1:51 of the Son of Man, nor, for that matter, as we have already noted, is it the Son of Man who descends in this scene.[71]

One further text should be brought into consideration, which puts Israel/Jacob and Christ in a heavenly and earthly realm mirroring each other. This is Origen's conclusion, in his *On First Principles*, about how the narrative of Scripture should be read. Noting that 'stumbling blocks' and 'obstacles and impossibilities' (cf. Rom. 9:33; 14:13) have been placed in the narratives of Scripture so that we do not remain only at a purely superficial understanding of the text (*Princ.* 4.2.9), and similarly for the Gospel (*Princ.* 4.3.3), Origen proposes a deeper reading of these narratives. Paul's statements, 'Behold, Israel according to the flesh' (1 Cor. 10:18) implies, Origen says, that 'there is an Israel according to the Spirit' (*Princ.* 4.3.6), a distinction that Origen also finds in Paul's words that 'For it is not the children of the flesh that are the children of God, for not all who are descended from Israel belong to Israel' (Rom 9:8, 6), and in the Apostle's contrast between one who is 'a Jew openly' and one who is 'a Jew in secret' (Rom 2:28–9). As such, Origen proposes that we should read Scripture in this double fashion:

> Jacob was the father of the twelve patriarchs, and they of the rulers of the people, and these again of the rest of the Israelites. So, then, the bodily Israelites have reference to the rulers of the people, and the rulers of the people to the patriarchs, and the patriarchs to Jacob and those still higher up; the spiritual Israelites, on the other hand, of whom the bodily were a type [*οἱ δὲ νοητοὶ Ἰσραηλῖται, ὧν τύπος ἦσαν οἱ σωματικοί*], are they not from the clans, the clans having come from the tribes, and the tribes from some one individual [i.e. Jacob] having a birth not of a bodily kind but of the better kind, he too being born from Isaac, and he being descended from Abraham, all referring back up to Adam, whom the Apostle says is Christ? For the beginning of every lineage as [referring] to the God of all began lower down from Christ, who is next to the God and Father of all, being thus the father of every soul, as Adam is the father of all human beings. And if Eve is touched on by Paul as referring to the Church, it is not surprising—Cain being born of Eve and all after him having reference to Eve—to have here types of the Church, they all being born from the Church in a preeminent sense.[72]

[69] Smith, 'Prayer', 54; M. R. James, *The Testament of Abraham: The Greek Text Now First Edited with an Introduction and Notes*, Text and Studies, 2.2 (Cambridge, 1892), 30.

[70] Smith, 'Prayer', 55.

[71] Ashton, *Fourth Gospel*, 248.

[72] *Princ.* 4.3.7. This passage is only preserved in the Greek passages from the *Philokalia.*

Not only is there a correspondence between the lineage in the flesh and in the spirit, but, as he continues, there is also a corresponding topography; while the mother city of all the cites in Judah is Jerusalem (*Princ.* 4.3.6), Origen points out (*Princ.* 4.3.8) that Paul describes 'our mother' as 'the Jerusalem above' (Gal. 4:26), 'the city of the living God, the heavenly Jerusalem, . . . the church of the firstborn who are enrolled in the heavens' (Heb. 12:22–3). And likewise, he speculates, 'If there are spiritual Israelites, it follows that there are also spiritual Egyptians and Babylonians' for, after all, what Ezekiel says about Pharaoh or the Prince of Tyre cannot possibly be taken as referring to a human being ruling over Egypt or Tyre (*Princ.* 4.3.9; cf. Ezek. 29:1–9; 28).

For Origen these are not two independent realms. Rather they correspond to each other, and in fact the lower is a projection of the higher. The term Origen uses to describe this derivation is the scriptural term *καταβολή*, usually translated as 'foundation', but which he makes clear has more the sense of a 'casting downwards'.[73] Especially important for him is Ephesians 1:4, which speaks of how God 'has chosen us before the foundation of the world'. As the saints, in the end, will inhabit those worlds which are 'not seen' and 'eternal' (2 Cor. 4:18), that end, he argues, must always have been: we are 'called' into existence 'before the foundation of the world'.[74] As such our beginning in this world can only be thought of as a 'descent' or a 'falling away'. The cause of this is not, however, simply sin, for although some did fall away because of their own diversifying movements, others descended in order to serve the whole world, to work for 'the sons of God to be revealed [*ἀποκαλυφθῆναι*, to be unveiled]', for which 'the whole creation has been groaning in travail until now' (Rom. 8:19, 22). Rather, as I have argued elsewhere, the cause of the descent was 'the lamb slain from the foundation of the world' (Apoc. 13:8).[75] Seen from below, it is 'from', and not before, 'the foundation of the world', that the lamb is 'slain', and done so for our sins, but seen from above, as in the Gospel of John, as we have seen, Christ voluntarily gives his life as the expression of the life, love, and being of God. This is indeed a scandal and folly (cf. 1 Cor. 1:23). The cross causes all the rational beings to fall away, as the disciples did in the Synoptics at the time of the crucifixion, but not John in his Gospel. The same cross, however, is also the means of entering the life of God.

[73] See especially *Princ.* 3.5.4, and my comments in *Origen: On First Principles*, vol. 1, lxii–lxv.

[74] Origen seems to propose a hierarchy of the verbs used to describe creation: to call, to create (*κτίζειν*), to make (*ποιεῖν*), to mould (*πλάσσειν*), all of which are different ways of speaking about the same reality, rather than a mythological account of different actions; although 'to create' would seem to come first, it is in fact only completed at the end, for Christ is 'the Amen, the beginning of God's creation' (Apoc. 3:14: *ἡ ἀρχὴ τῆς κτίσεως τοῦ θεοῦ*). Cf. Behr, *Origen: On First Principles*, vol. 1, lxi–lxii.

[75] Cf. Behr, *Origen: On First Principles*, vol. 1, lxxxii–lxxxiii.

In Origen's schema of correspondence, Jacob is the head of the 'bodily Israelites' and is descended from those further back. On the spiritual level, Jacob, by means of a spiritual birth, traces his lineage back through Isaac and Abraham to Adam, whom, Origen says, is Christ.[76] The background for this double lineage is perhaps the contrast between the genealogies of Matthew (1:1–17), where 'the birth [γένεσις] of Jesus' (Matt. 1:1, 18) is described in a descending line from Abraham, and that of Luke (3:23–38), given after Jesus' baptism, which traces the genealogy backwards or upwards to Adam the son of God; the first genealogy describes the descent of Israel according to the flesh, the second the descent (or rather ascent) of the spiritual Israel. Following Paul, Adam and Eve, the heads of all those descended from them, are paralleled by Christ and the Church, the heads of all those who live in God. Origen's picture also differs from that of the rabbis in that for them it is Jacob's 'image' that is in heaven, whereas for Origen the earthly figures are 'types' of their spiritual counterparts. With a different end in view, and the heavens now opened, 'our citizenship', as the Apostle says, 'is in the heavens and from it we await a Saviour, the Lord Jesus Christ, who will change our lowly body to be like his glorious body' (Phil. 3:20–1).

These forays into the strange worlds of rabbinic and early Christian reading and interpretation of Scripture, especially the idea of correspondences between heaven and earth, remind us of the 'two-level' drama that we encountered when looking, in Chapter 2, at the theme of 'apocalyptic'. It is worthwhile repeating the words of Ashton cited there:

> For Enoch, and for apocalyptic writers generally, there are not two worlds but one: or rather the whole of reality is split into matching pairs (rather like the biological theory of DNA) in which one half, the lower, is the mirror-image (albeit in this case a distorting mirror) of the higher. That is why a revelation of what is above is not just relevant or related to what happens or is about to happen on earth: rather what happens on earth is a re-enactment in earthly terms of what has happened in heaven: a correspondence![77]

While the use of this 'two-level' drama by Ashton, and before him by Martyn, to correlate John's account of Christ with the life of the Johannine community has been called into question, there is no doubt that it provides an appropriate framework for understanding the enigmatic figure of the Johannine Son of Man. In the light of what we have seen, the dramatic words of Jesus in John 1:51 are not so out of place as it might have first seemed.

[76] Origen makes similar assertion in *Comm. Jo.* 1.108: 'And perhaps for this reason, he is not only the *firstborn of all creation* [Col 1:15], but also Adam, [which] means "human being". And because he is Adam, Paul says, *The last Adam has become a life-giving spirit* [1 Cor. 15:45]'. See also *Cels.* 4.40.

[77] Ashton, *Fourth Gospel*, 327.

From the rabbinic texts, then, we can see parallels to the idea of angels ascending and descending upon a person, although, as these texts are later than John, it may well be John 1:51 that suggested to the rabbis that the ambiguous pronoun of Genesis 28:12 could be taken as referring to Jacob rather than the ladder. That this might be the case is suggested by those texts which speak of the one who takes the pronoun as referring to the 'ladder' as having 'no problems', while the one (that is, R. Yannai) who takes it as referring to Jacob is forced to come up with ingenious exegetical explanations. And from Origen we have a wholesale picture in which all rational beings have descended in the foundation of the world as we know it, the world that labours in travail towards the unveiling of the sons of God, much like 'the woman' of John 16:20–2, as we saw earlier, who is the link between Cana and the crucifixion, and between Eve and the Church, suffering tribulation 'in this world' (cf. 16:33), until that tribulation is changed into joy when 'a human being is born into the world' (16:21).

Ashton suggests that in the rabbinic texts which speak of Jacob being asleep on earth and his image engraved on the heavenly throne there is no concern to establish which is the 'real' Jacob: 'to put the question in this way may be to presuppose a dichotomy not envisaged by the writer, who is more concerned to establish the identity between the two figures than to arbitrate between them'.[78] The gist of this is certainly correct, but there remains the fact that the angels nevertheless have to ascend to see him above and descend to see him below. The Son of Man figure in John 1:51, on the other hand, although only appearing when the heavens are opened, is not some kind of divine man standing in the heavens now accessible to sight, or ready to be sent on a mission, to descend to earth. The language of mission is nowhere used by John to describe the Son of Man and his activities. The Son of Man, at least in 1:51, is not a divine emissary sent from above, but rather an intermediary, a figure who embraces both heaven and earth, in himself, the place, or rather the person, where heaven and earth meet together. If the angels ascend and descend upon him, it is because the way up and the way down is one and the same.

Two questions regarding John 1:51 remain. First, why does John describe the figure who appears when the heavens are opened as 'the Son of Man', and, second, when is this promised vision seen? Regarding the first, that the title is introduced as the climax of an ascending series of titles across 1:35–49 (the Lamb of God, Messiah/Christ, Son of God, King of Israel), indicates that something more is yet to be seen; as noted earlier, four of the instances of the use of 'Son of Man' in John refer to the Passion (3:14; 8:28; 12:23, 34; 13:31). That the other titles used in 1:35–49 are deployed across the Synoptics,

[78] Ibid. 247.

in which the last mention of the 'Son of Man' from Christ's own lips is the promise that 'hereafter you will see the Son of Man seated at the right hand of Power', seems to indicate that John is picking up where the Synoptics left off (reinforced, as Reynolds argues, by the use of ἀπ'ἄρτι in 1:51 in some variants), and providing an account of Jesus permeated from the beginning and thereafter with this high vision.[79] The other text in which 'the Son of Man' figures greatly, of course, is the 'Book of Parables' in *1 Enoch*, where Enoch ascends to heaven and is identified as 'the son of man born for righteousness' (71:14). We have left this aside for now as it does not add to our investigation of John 1:51, but will take it up again when examining 3:13–14 and 9:35.

As to when the promised vision is seen, it is important to note that the promise to Nathanael alone in 1:50, 'you will see [ὄψῃ, singular] greater things than these', morphs into a promise made to many in 1:51, 'you will see [ὄψεσθε, plural] the heavens opened and the angels of God ascending and descending upon the Son of Man', which must, as Ashton asserts, be taken to include not only other disciples present at the scene, but all readers and hearers of the Gospel thereafter.[80] After the promise of 1:51, the next words are 'on the third day' (2:1; following the 'days' of 1:35 and 43). Although John does not use the terminology of 'the third day' in describing the resurrection of Christ (he is encountered, rather, on the first and eighth days, 20:1, 19, 26), anyone with a broader knowledge of the Christian Gospel would have made this connection. It is moreover in the following scene at Cana that Jesus performs 'the first of his signs' and 'manifested his glory' (2:11). However, it would be wrong to take the promise as being fulfilled only here. As we have abundantly seen, the whole of the Gospel of John is a carefully framed account of Jesus' construction of the true Temple of God, which he himself is and which climaxes when he is crucified. So, in a sense, Reynolds is right to conclude that the vision of the apocalyptic Son of Man 'encompasses all of Jesus' work, his revelation and glorification of the Father, which is ultimately fulfilled in the death, resurrection, and return to the Father in glory'.[81]

However, perhaps one can be more specific. If we are promised 'to see' the Son of Man, this is specifically fulfilled with Pilate's injunction, given unwittingly and with a typical Johannine double meaning, *to see*: 'Behold the human being' (19:5). What it means to see Christ in this way was seen by John, standing at the foot of the cross while the woman gives birth to a human being (cf. 16:21, 19:26, discussed above). It is, moreover, a vision not limited to that specific occasion but also seen by those of John's 'school' in those who undergo martyrdom: when Blandina, for instance, was 'hung on a stake [ἐπὶ ξύλου]' her fellow Christians alongside her in the amphitheatre, 'seeing her hanging in the form of a cross . . . beheld with their outward eyes, through the sister, him who

[79] Reynolds, *Apocalyptic Son of Man*, 100. [80] Ashton, *Fourth Gospel*, 251.
[81] Reynolds, *Apocalyptic Son of Man*, 103.

was crucified for them', providing encouragement to those who had lapsed, so that 'there was great joy for the Virgin Mother in receiving back alive those who she had miscarried as dead'.[82] The glory of God revealed in the Passion of Christ is beheld in the martyr, 'the living human being' who is, as Irenaeus puts it, the very 'glory of God' (*haer.* 4.20.7), and, indeed, the embodiment of Christ.

John 3:13

We can now come to the most perplexing verse in the Gospel of John, that is, 3:13. This verse follows on from Jesus' discussion with Nicodemus about the need to be born again or from above (ἄνωθεν) to see the Kingdom of God (3:3, 7), a birth which is 'of water and the Spirit' enabling entry into the Kingdom (3:5), for while flesh is born of flesh, 'that which is born of the Spirit is spirit' (3:6). When Nicodemus, 'a teacher of Israel' no less (3:10), still doesn't understand, Jesus then says:

> [3:11] Truly, truly, I say to you, we speak of what we know and bear witness to what we have seen [ἑωράκαμεν]; but you do not receive our testimony. [12] If I have told you earthly things and you do not believe, how can you believe if I tell you heavenly things? [13] And no one has ascended into heaven except he who descended from heaven, the Son of Man [*καὶ οὐδεὶς ἀναβέβηκεν εἰς τὸν οὐρανὸν εἰ μὴ ὁ ἐκ τοῦ οὐρανοῦ καταβάς, ὁ υἱὸς τοῦ ἀνθρώπου*]. [14] And as Moses lifted up [ὕψωσεν] the serpent in the wilderness, so must the Son of Man be lifted up [ὑψωθῆναι], [15] so that whoever believes in him may have eternal life.

The passage continues by describing the love of God, shown in this way, by giving his Son so that those who believe may have eternal life (3:16), and sending him not for the condemnation of the world but so that it might be saved (3:17), with the result that the one who believes is not condemned, while the one who does not believe is 'already' condemned (3:18).

The perplexity caused by this passage is due to the fact that Jesus says that what 'we speak', in the present, bears witness to what 'we have seen', in the past. Yet the subject of discussion to this point has been the birth 'from above' and 'of the Spirit'. But the Spirit, as John says later, 'was not yet, because Jesus was not yet glorified' (7:39), even though the Baptist saw the Spirit descending from heaven and remaining upon Jesus (1:32). Who, then, are the 'we' and what have they 'seen' (3:11)? If these words refer back to Jesus' baptism, then the 'heavenly things' that are now being spoken about are not events in heaven seen by the Son of Man prior to his descent. But why is there such an emphatic

[82] 'The Letter of the Churches of Vienne and Lyons to Asia and Phrygria', probably written by Irenaeus, and preserved by Eusebius (*h.e.* 5.1.4–63, at 41, 45).

beginning to 3.13: 'And no one has ascended'? What is the relationship between the perfect tense 'has ascended' (ἀναβέβηκεν) and the aorist participle 'descended' (καταβάς, the same as in 6:51)? Although the 'has ascended', in the order of the words, comes first, is the 'descent' assumed to have preceded it? And, finally, what is the force of the phrase εἰ μή? Is it to be taken as 'except', so that indeed the Son of Man has ascended into heaven (before descending?), or should it be translated, as is often done, as 'but'?[83] Such a knot of questions from a handful of words!

'Armed, or blinkered, by our knowledge of the rest of the Gospel', Ashton asserts, 'we can easily miss the natural reading of vs. 11–13'.[84] The perfect tense of 'has ascended' naturally implies that by the time of his discussion with Nicodemus, Jesus has already ascended into heaven and also descended from there as the Son of Man—*in that order*. Following the lead of Hugo Odeberg, who noted that the opening verse must be understood as a polemic against other claimants to have ascended to heaven, and, more recently, Jan-Adolf Bühner, who suggested that behind 3:13 lay an inherited tradition that Jesus had been transformed into the Son of Man, John Ashton has revised his previous analysis of this verse and taken up this reading wholeheartedly.[85] John, in this reading, is reacting against other claimants to have ascended to heaven, in particular Moses, but also Enoch and Elijah, to insist that it is Jesus alone who has ascended into the heavens, where he was transformed into the Son of Man, perhaps at the Transfiguration, an event which, although not mentioned in John, 'the united testimony of the synoptic gospels is strong evidence for [such] an episode in Jesus' life'.[86] After this heavenly metamorphosis, Ashton claims, Jesus then descended to earth as the Son of Man with the ability to judge on earth, just as Daniel's Son of Man had been given authority

[83] For a summary the various options taken by scholars in their interpretation of 3:13, and a full grammatical analysis of this sentence, utilizing recent developments of the understanding of Greek grammar, see Madison N. Pierce and Benjamin E. Reynolds, 'The Perfect Tense-Form and the Son of Man in John 3:13: Developments in Greek Grammar as a Viable Solution to the Timing of the Ascent and Descent', *NTS* 60 (2014), 149–55; they conclude that: 'When the verbal aspect of ἀναβέβηκεν is considered primary (and not the time value), the "problem" of the perfect is removed. The grammatical arguments of verbal aspect and the relative time value of the participle καταβάς make it reasonable to translate ἀναβέβηκεν with a present time value and thus conclude that Jesus, the Son of Man, did not ascend prior to his descent nor must ἀναβέβηκεν indicate a past event'. More fundamental, as we will suggest in what follows, is the blending of times characteristic of John.

[84] John Ashton, 'The Johannine Son of Man: A New Proposal', *NTS* 57 (2011), 508–29, at 513–14.

[85] Cf. Odeberg, *The Fourth Gospel*, 72–98; and Jan-Adolf Bühner, *Der Gesandte und sein Weg im vierten Evangelium: Die kultur- und religionsgeschichtlichen Grundlagen der johanneischen Sendungschristologie sowie ihre traditionsgeschichtliche Entwicklung* (Tübingen: Mohr Siebeck, 1977). For Ashton's earlier reading, see *Fourth Gospel*, 251–9. See also Ashton's further reflections, 'Intimations of Apocalyptic: Looking Backwards and Looking Forward', in Catrin H. Rowland and Christopher Williams, eds, *Intimations of Apocalyptic*, 3–36, esp. 31–2.

[86] Ashton, 'Johannine Son of Man, 519.

to judge in heaven, and charging the disciples 'to tell no one what they had seen until the Son of Man should have risen from the dead' (Mark 9:9). Most commentators, however, have not taken this route. We will turn to see what leads Ashton to do so when considering John 9 next, where Ashton finds the explanation for why John chose the term 'Son of Man'.

Rather than speculating about events which are not mentioned, the apparently confusing nature of 3:11–13 is best explained by reference to the merging of times or melding of horizons that we discussed in the Introduction and that we observed at various points in Chapter 3. That such a fusion of temporal horizons is at work here is made abundantly clear from the change from 'I say' to 'we say' within v. 11: the 'we' clearly includes John and his readers, engaged in dialogue with the teachers of Israel.[87] Regarding the ascent/descent in v. 13, Martyn comments: 'The Son of Man ascends to heaven on the cross, but in some sense he returns to earth in the person of the Paraclete and can therefore enter into conversation with "Nicodemus" as he who *has ascended* to heaven (3:13). The Paraclete makes Jesus present on earth as the Son of Man who binds together heaven and earth'.[88] Just as in John 6, where Jesus as the Son of Man offers us his flesh and blood to consume, so too here, Jesus is present in this discussion with Nicodemus as the one who has ascended to heaven through the cross. Moreover, 3:13 is so intimately tied to vv. 14–16 that it cannot be taken separately: v. 13, as does v. 14, begins with a modest 'and' (which is almost invariably left out of translation and consideration), and both end with 'the Son of Man'; and the step from Moses to the Son of Man is then connected, through the repeated 'in this way', to God's love:

> [13] Both no one has ascended into heaven except he who has descended, the Son of Man,
>
> [14] and, as Moses lifted up [ὕψωσεν] the snake in the wilderness, in this way [οὕτως] must be lifted up [ὑψωθῆναι δεῖ] the Son of Man,
>
> [15] that whoever believes in him may have eternal life.
>
> [16] In this way [οὕτως] God loved the world: that he gave the unique Son that whoever believes in him should not perish but have everlasting life.

John 3:13 and 14 are set in parallel, with the purpose given in v. 15 and traced back to God himself in v. 16. Although Jesus had already spoken of destroying and raising the Temple in three days (2:19), it was only after the resurrection that the disciples understood what he had spoken about (2:22). John 3:13–16, then, is the first time within the narrative of the Gospel that Jesus speaks

[87] Cf. Frey, *Die johanneische Eschatologie*, 2.252–7; Barrett, *John*, 176: 'The perspective . . . is not that of the historical ministry (cf. 7:39—the work of the Spirit was not at that time knowable), but that of the Church. The community of those who have been born of water and Spirit addresses the Synagogue'.

[88] Martyn, *History and Theology*, 138.

directly about his Passion (as having happened but, narratively, yet to happen), and as with the Passion predictions in the Synoptics it is done so with respect to 'the Son of Man'. But, while the Synoptics speak about how the Son of Man will be killed (Matt. 17:22–3; Mark 9:31; Luke 9:22), delivered to be crucified (Matt. 26:2; Mark 10:33), and suffer (Mark 8:31; Luke 9:22), John, on the other hand, uses a word with a very different meaning, which he also substitutes in v. 14 for the nondescript words used in Numbers (21:8–9, 'place', *θὲς*, and 'stood', *ἔστησεν*), and that is 'lift up' or 'exalt' (*ὑψόω*). This word, as we have seen, is undoubtedly derived from the 'exalt and highly glorify' of Isaiah 52:13, the verse which is also behind the other references to the Passion of the Son of Man in John: 'exalt' in 8:28 and 12:34, and 'glorified' in 12:23 and 13:31. The verb *ὑψόω* is not the same as that used for 'ascend' (*ἀναβαίνω*) in 3:13 (and 1:51 and 6:62), but its primary meaning is nevertheless 'to lift high', 'to raise up' (translating it as 'exalt' is done on the basis of the second verb in Isaiah 52:13, 'glorify'). There is no reason, then, not to see 3:13 and 14, conjoined in parallel as they are, as speaking of the same event, that is, the raising up to heaven of Jesus upon the cross.

The only other passage in John in which both 'ascend' and 'descend' are used of the Son of Man is John 6, where Jesus' question about seeing the Son of Man 'ascending to where he was before' (6:62) follows on from seven instances of 'descend', not applied to the Son of Man directly, but certainly implied: the 'bread which descends from heaven' (6:33, 50, 58), Jesus as 'the bread which has descended from heaven' (6:41, 51) and Jesus himself (6:38, 42). It is this bread, which he 'will give for the life of the world' (narratively in the future), that is, in the present, his flesh (6:51), so that those who 'eat the flesh and drink the blood of the Son of Man' have life (6:53) and abide in him as he does in them (6:56). The descent of the life-giving flesh and blood of the Son of Man, as we argued in Chapter 3, is given through the ascent of Jesus upon the cross and received by those who share in his Passion. Likewise in John 3:13–16, if the 'ascent' of v. 13 is the 'exaltation' through the cross, and given everything we have seen in the previous chapters about the unity of the paschal event and its celebration by the followers of John, then the descent of the Son of Man exalted in this way, the entry of the exalted Son of Man into the world (in the present) occurs in the same way, through the cross and the taking up of the cross, the path of martyrdom, by those who follow him, in whom he now abides. The way up is, once again, the way down.

John 9 and Seeing the Voice

What is it then that leads John to bring together the 'setting' and 'standing' of Numbers 21:8–9 with the 'exalting and highly glorifying' of Isaiah 52:13, in 3:14, and associate these words of Isaiah with the title 'Son of Man' (in 3:14

and also 8:28, 12:23, 34; 13:3)? Ashton, in a 'new proposal', suggests that the turning point in the development of John's thought is found in 9:35, which also thereby indicates a reason for the polemical note in 3:13, both of these passages having a Sitz-im-Leben (following Martyn) after the parting of the ways of two groups within the synagogue, but before the composition of the Prologue.[89] Ashton, whose work has, more than any other, helped unveil the 'apocalyptic' dimensions of the Fourth Gospel, and who has inspired much of this present work, presents his 'new proposal' with a speculative but fascinating train of thought; although the conclusions he reaches are not ones that we would follow, they do nevertheless also point towards another solution, and as such, his essay will be quoted extensively in what follows.

The polemical tone of 3:13 might best be explained, Ashton argues, by reference to rival claimants to have ascended into heaven. Such claims are, in fact, found on behalf of Moses in rabbinic texts. For instance, Wayne Meeks, in exploring the various traditions of Moses' ascent, cites a midrash on Psalm 106:2 which asserts that 'Not even Moses who went up into heaven to receive the Torah from God's hand into his own could fathom heaven's depth'.[90] That Moses not only ascended Sinai but also into the very heavens themselves, even if he could not fully understand their depths, is simply assumed. Another midrash given by Meeks speaks of how when the angel of death, Sammael, comes to claims Moses' soul, Moses defiantly claims superiority over all the angels, because, as he says, 'I ascended to heaven . . . spoke face to face with the Lord of the world, conquered the heavenly household, received the Torah'.[91] Similarly the *Exagoge* of Ezekiel the Tragedian, relates how Moses describes to his father-in-law a dream he had had:

> On Sinai's peak I saw what seemed a throne, so great in size it touched the clouds of heaven. Upon it sat a man of noble mien, crowned and with a sceptre in one hand while with the other he did beckon me. I made approach and stood before the throne. He handed over the sceptre and he bade me mount the throne and gave to me the crown. (*Exagoge* 68–75)

In interpreting this dream, his father-in-law predicts that Moses, sitting upon the throne, will be able to see 'things below and things above God's realm: things present, past, and future you shall see' (*Exagoge* 88–9). If the rabbinic texts and their traditions are difficult to date, the *Exagoge* of Ezekiel seems to date firmly to a period before the first century BCE, and so could possibly stand

[89] Ashton, 'The Johannine Son of Man'; see also Ashton's further reflections, 'Intimations of Apocalyptic: Looking Backwards and Looking Forward'.

[90] *The Midrash on Psalms*, trans. William G. Braude, Yale Judaica Series 13, 2 vols (New Haven: Yale University Press, 1959), 2, 188; quoted in Meeks, *The Prophet-King*, 205.

[91] *Mekilta de-Rabbi Ishmael*, ed. and trans. Jacob Z. Lauterbach, 3 vols (Philadelphia: Jewish Publication Society of America, 1949), 2, 224; quoted in Meeks, *Prophet-King*, 205.

behind the polemic of 3:13: Jesus alone, not Moses, has ascended into the heavens to tell us of heavenly things.[92]

But these texts do not explain how Jesus presents himself, even if obliquely, as the Son of Man in 3:13 and 9:35, for none of the rabbinic texts use that title of Moses or present us with such a figure. We do find such a figure, however, in the 'Book of Parables' in *1 Enoch*. The Son of Man is first introduced in chapter 46, where Enoch reports what he had seen in a heavenly vision:

> There I saw one who had a head of days, and his head was like white wool. And with him was another, whose face was like the appearance of man; and his face was full of graciousness like one of the holy angels. And I asked the angel of peace, who went with me and showed me all the hidden things, about that Son of Man—who he was and whence he was (and) why he went with the Head of Days. And he answered me and said to me, 'This is the Son of Man who has righteousness and righteousness dwells with him. And all the treasuries of what is hidden he will reveal; for the Lord of Spirits has chosen him, and his lot has prevailed through truth in the presence of the Lord of Spirits forever'.[93]

The background for this description is, of course, Daniel 7:13. After further heavenly visions, the 'Book of Parables' concludes with this surprising identification:

> And that Head of Days came with Michael and Raphael and Gabriel and Phanuel, and thousands and tens of thousands of angels without number. And that angel came to me and greeting me with his voice and said to me: 'You are that son of man who was born for righteousness, and righteousness dwells on you, and the righteousness of the Head of Days will not forsake you'. (*I Enoch* 71.12–14)

The Book of Parables, however, is extremely difficult to date, and could fall anywhere from the middle of the first century BCE to the end of the first century CE.[94] A similar figure also appears in *Fourth Ezra* (*Second Esdras*) 13, which is clearly dated after the destruction of the Temple. Here Ezra, in a dream, sees a figure who, in the Latin translation, is simply called 'a man' or 'that man', but is sketched with all the attributes of an apocalyptic Son of Man:

[92] For the dating see the introduction to the *Exagoge* provided by R. G. Robertson, in Charlesworth, *Old Testament Pseudepigrapha*, 2.803–4.

[93] *First Enoch* 46:1–3; translated by George W. E. Nickelsburg and James C. VanderKam, *1 Enoch: A New Translation: Based on the Hermeneia Commentary* (Minneapolis: Fortress, 2004).

[94] It is noteworthy that no material from the Book of Parables is to be found among the fragments of *First Enoch* discovered in Qumran, but as Black, 'Aramaic Barnasha', 201, points out, 'this argument is less impressive when it is realized that these fragments constitute only about 5 per cent of the total Book'. It must also be remembered that the only complete text of *First Enoch* that we have is the Ethiopic version. For a full assessment of the various textual traditions, see Michael A. Knibb, with the assistance of Edward Ullendorff, *The Ethiopic Book of Enoch: A New Edition in the Light of the Aramaic Dead Sea Fragments*, 2 vols (Oxford: Clarendon Press, 1978), 2.1–46.

> And I looked, and behold, this wind made something like a figure of a man come up out of the heart of the sea. And I looked, and behold, that man flew with the clouds of heaven; and wherever he turned his face to look, everything under his gaze trembled, and whenever his voice issued from his mouth, all who heard his voice melted as wax melts when it feels the fire. (*4 Ezra* 13.1–4)

In the interpretation of the dream then given by the Most High, he is told the identity of this man:

> This is he whom the Most High has been keeping for many ages, who will himself deliver his creation and he will direct those who are left. . . . He will stand on top of Mount Zion. And Zion will come and be made manifest to all people, prepared and built, as you saw the mountain carved out without hands. And he, my Son, will reprove the assembled for their ungodliness. . . . Just as no one can explore or know what is in the depths of the sea, so no one on earth can see my Son or those who are with him, except in the time of his day. (*4 Ezra* 13.26, 36–7, 52)

Two other texts which use the imagery from Daniel 7 are *2 Baruch* (*Syriac Baruch*) and the fragment from Qumran identified as 4Q246, variously known as the Apocalypse of the Son of God or 'the Son of God text', or more simply an Aramaic Apocalypse.[95] *2 Baruch* is also to be dated after the destruction of the Temple. It draws upon imagery from Daniel in its description of the Messiah and many new revelations are given through visions, although the figure of the Son of Man does not appear and neither is there an ascent into the heavens.[96] Finally, 4Q246, measuring only 14.1 × 8.8 cm, with two columns of text, provides very little detail. The 'Son of God' is mentioned, and also called the 'Son of the Most High', and apocalyptic imagery from Daniel does occur. In Cross' reconstruction of the text, he would insert 'a son of man', but this is speculative and has not been adopted by others.[97]

Ashton concedes that 'it is impossible to be sure that the fourth evangelist was influenced, consciously or not, by any of these different strands of tradition'. 'But', he continues,

> he may well have been, and if he was then he will have been much less bothered than his later readers are likely to be by the ambiguity of 'No one has ascended'. He would wish to insist upon the exclusive claim of his own hero, and deny outright that any other Jewish seer, above all Moses, but also Enoch and Elijah,

[95] Cf. Frank M. Cross, 'The Structure of the Apocalypse of "Son of God" (4Q246)', in S. M. Paul et al., eds, *Emanuel: Studies in Hebrew Bible, Septuagint, and Dead Sea Scrolls in Honor of Emanuel Tov* (Leiden: Brill, 2003), 151–8; in Geza Vermes, *The Complete Dead Sea Scrolls in English* (New York: Penguin, 1997) it has the simple heading 'An Aramaic Apocalypse'.

[96] Cf. Reynolds, *Apocalyptic Son of Man*, 56–60.

[97] In Cross' translation ('Structure', 157–8): '[And there shall arise a son of man.] He shall be a great [king] over the [whole] earth [and all mankind] shall serve [him], and he shall minister [to him]. [The Holy One of the g]reat [God] shall he be called, and by his name he shall be surnamed. Son of God he shall be called, and by his name shall he be surnamed'. For influences from Daniel see Reynolds, *Apocalyptic Son of Man*, 61–4.

> had either mounted up to heaven as an apocalyptic visionary or had been translated there at the end of his life.[98]

Ashton then argues that if these claims were being advanced by some on behalf of Jesus, as John 3:13 implies, this must have been at a period when this new understanding of Jesus' heavenly origin and identity, Käsemann's characterization of John's Jesus as a 'God striding over the earth', had not yet replaced the memory of the human Jesus:

> it must have been made before the evangelist and his community had become convinced that Jesus' sojourn on earth followed a long period in heaven—at a time when the Jesus group in the synagogue had not yet come to think of him as divine, but saw him simply as the Messiah and a great prophet, a remarkable, but still recognizably human, human being: before, that is to say, the Prologue was added to form a new introduction to the Gospel.[99]

Although not mentioning any ascent to heaven, it is nevertheless in conflict with the disciples of Moses (cf. 9:28) that Jesus identifies himself as the Son of Man (9:35), and then says that it is to enact judgement that he has come, condemning for spiritual blindness those who had 'reviled' and 'cast out' (9:28, 35) the man with sight now restored (9:39–41). What is being claimed here is far more than simply the ability to heal or work miracles. It is rather, as Ashton puts it, a claim that:

> precisely *as Son of Man* Jesus was entitled to exercise *on earth* the authority to judge that in Daniel's vision had been bestowed upon the Son of Man *in heaven*. This means that *the evangelist himself had concluded that the heavenly figure of the Son of Man had come down to earth in the person of Jesus.*[100]

It was only 'at a relatively late stage in the history of the Jesus group within the synagogue' that Ashton sees 'the evangelist adopting this ancient tradition', that is, regarding Jesus' transformation into Son of Man at an earlier event,

[98] Ashton, 'Johannine Son of Man', 518. In an essay presented to a colloquium devoted to Ashton's *Fourth Gospel*, held in 2010, that is, a year before the 'new proposal' was printed (although by the time of the publication of the proceedings of the colloquium in 2013 he can refer to the 'new proposal'), Ashton is more confident: 'The John who composed the Fourth Gospel has one belief that he shares with the John who composed the book of Revelation: the belief in a new revelation that completely supersedes the old. The second John made use of the abundant material he found in what we now call the Old Testament. The first John, I believe, had a model for his own powerful conviction that the revelation that Jesus had come to bring was "the truth", something that could no longer be claimed for the message of Moses. This model was Enoch. He, alone among the apocalyptic writers of the Second Temple, believed that his own revelations were superior to the Mosaic Law. He, not Moses, was the one who ascended to heaven and saw God. He, not Moses, was the true recipient of heavenly secrets, frequently summed up as wisdom, and wrote them down in a book to be read by his descendants. If, as I think likely, the fourth evangelist read this book, then Enoch's sheer effrontery may well have inspired him to make similar claims on behalf of his own hero'. 'Intimations of Apocalyptic', 31–2.

[99] Ashton, 'Johannine Son of Man', 519.

[100] Ibid. 521, italics original.

most likely the Transfiguration.[101] The 'definitive breakup of the two parties in the synagogue', indicated in John 9, was thus the occasion for 'the first full awareness on the part of the Johannine community that Jesus was something more than an exceptional human being: that he was in fact a heavenly or angelic being who had descended to earth with divine authority'.[102] And this, as we saw above, is for Ashton 'the original meaning, I think, of this lapidary text', that is, 3:13, 'that Jesus received a new revelation, so much more than a new Law, in the course of a visit to heaven as an apocalyptic seer'.[103]

As such, John's picture of an ascending and descending Son of Man is not derived from some Gnostic myth, as has captivated imagination since Bultmann, nor even from the Wisdom-Shekinah theology, though he clearly deploys this. Rather, Ashton argues, it 'must be seen as arising from the confluence of two originally distinct developments, first the tradition of Jesus as a visionary seer, and secondly the outcome of a long debate with "the disciples of Moses" that originated within the synagogue'.[104] This developing awareness of who Jesus truly is led, at a later stage, to the prefacing of the Gospel by the Prologue. And this, with its powerful movement from above to below, from the Word with God and as God to 'the Incarnation' (understood as 'an episode in the biography of the Word', to come back to William's phrase), then came to overshadow, but not eradicate, traces of how Jesus originally came to be thought of primarily in terms of an emissary from heaven to earth. Aware of the surprise that such a claim will cause, Ashton finishes his essay by saying that 'readers with this great hymn before their eyes, perhaps picturing Jesus as watching and listening to God in some pre-existent state, are likely to pay no heed to what was probably the apocalyptic, visionary source of the real Jesus' knowledge of God'. However, he concludes, 'John's Gospel is better understood if one's understanding also relates to the making of it'.[105] And indeed, as he commented earlier, 'some may find it easier to believe than the Prologue's mythical account of a divine being taking flesh'.[106]

But what was it in the developing conflict in the synagogue that provoked the separation itself and what was it that enabled John to identify Jesus as the apocalyptic Son of Man? Was it claims about Moses' ascent to heaven, as we have seen in the *Exagoge*, which definitely predated John by more than a century, even though its description of Moses' ascent does not include the figure of the Son of Man nor Moses' identification as the Son of Man? Was it the 'Parables' of *1 Enoch*, which does include an apocalyptic ascent to heaven to see the Ancient of Days and the Son of Man, and Enoch's installation as the son of man, even though it is impossible to know if it predated John or whether it was inspired by John? Or was it the Synoptics, not only in their Passion predictions regarding the Son of Man, which John undoubtedly did

[101] Ibid. 520. [102] Ibid. 523. [103] Ibid. 527. [104] Ibid. 527–8.
[105] Ibid. 529. [106] Ibid. 527.

pick up and transformed in his own particular fashion, but also, perhaps, their description of the Transfiguration (even though John does not include this event nor recount an alternative event of ascent and transformation) which John now implicitly adopts, as Ashton would have it, assuming it to have been an ascent into heaven to be identified there with the Son of Man before descending to earth to talk with Nicodemus?

In regard to John's utilization of Isaiah's words (52:13), about the servant being 'exalted and highly glorified', to describe the crucifixion itself, Ashton takes a different explanatory route. 'This extraordinary conceit', he says, 'is surely his own invention'; and even if it belongs to a prior exegetical tradition, how this application came about would still require explanation.[107] Ashton then continues:

> Our familiarity with this well-known trope can blind us to the extraordinary transmutation of a barbaric punishment into a vision of exaltation. *Someone* must have been the first to have had this visionary gleam, and why should that someone not have been the evangelist himself? Meeks speaks of this saying as an 'ironic pun' and a 'jarring bit of gallows-humor', but it is surely more than that. We should ask ourselves then how John *imagined* the crucifixion. If he had ever actually witnessed a man dying in agony on the cross, one might suppose that a memory of this appalling torture would lead him to picture a scene something like, to take a well-known example, the terrifying portrayal of the crucifixion by Mathias Grünewald. If he had done so this tormented figure would surely have blocked out altogether any awareness of a man raised up, exalted, ascending to heaven. The deliberate choice of a word meaning exalted (reinforced by an avoidance of the words cross and crucifixion, suffering, death, and dying) is surely something other than a clever verbal device.[108]

This determination to see the crucifixion as a glorious event is even stronger, Ashton notes, in 12:23, when Jesus declares, 'the hour has come for the Son of Man to be glorified'. He then asserts:

> Accordingly the evangelist is inviting his readers to *see past* their own memory or knowledge of Jesus' agonizing death to his triumph over the forces of evil: 'Now is the judgment of this world, now shall the ruler of this world be cast out' (12:31), words spoken in the context of the third and last passion prediction. This invitation can best be accounted for if we suppose that John himself had a vision overwhelming enough to eliminate the painful and humiliating aspects of Jesus' passion and to replace them with signs of exaltation and glory.[109]

[107] Ibid. 524–5, continuing: 'Many commentators believe that John is adopting and adapting the expression "exalted and greatly glorified" he found in LXX Isa. 52:13. They may well be right, but authors borrow for a reason and the reason is never to be found in the text that is borrowed'.

[108] Ibid. 525, italics original, referring to Meeks, *Prophet-King*, 181 and 185.

[109] Ashton, 'Johannine Son of Man', 525–6, italics original.

Ashton continues by citing C. H. Dodd's assertion that 'the thought of this gospel is so original and creative that a search for its "sources", or even for the "influences" by which it may have been affected, may easily lead us astray'.[110] Yet, he argues, the solution is not to be found in what Dodd in the next sentence calls the Evangelist's 'powerful and independent mind', for John's insight is not attained, Ashton rightly maintains, simply by 'an especially brilliant collocation of two series of Jewish texts, one concerning the descent of angels to earth on a redemptive mission, the other concerning the ascent to heaven of apocalyptic visionaries'. Rather, he concludes: 'The explanation must lie rather in some sort of mystical experience that allowed the evangelist to see the hoisting-up of Jesus onto the cross as an exaltation'.[111]

Two points must be made regarding Ashton's train of thought. First, that John, in fact, is the only evangelist to claim to be an eyewitness of the crucifixion: there is no need for us to imagine him imagining it. Second, we have to hand just such an account of a 'mystical experience', indeed of an apocalyptic seer ascending to heaven and seeing the Son of Man, and *it is not Jesus who has this experience*! It is, moreover, given as a personal testimony, under the seer's own name, and in the present, rather than an account ascribed to a pseudonymous figure from an ancient past such as 'Enoch'.[112] This account is, of course, that given in the opening chapter of the Apocalypse. It is a familiar passage, but, as it seems to have been forgotten, it is worth quoting:

> I was in the Spirit on the Lord's day, and I heard behind me a loud voice like a trumpet saying, 'Write what you see in a book and send it to the seven churches, to Ephesus and to Smyrna and to Pergamum and to Thyatira and to Sardis and to Philadelphia and to Laodicea'. Then I turned to see the voice that was speaking to me, and on turning I saw seven golden lampstands, and in the midst of the lampstands one like a Son of Man, clothed with a long robe and with a golden girdle round his breast; his head and his hair were white as white wool, white as snow; his eyes were like a flame of fire, his feet were like burnished bronze, refined as in a furnace, and his voice was like the sound of many waters; in his right hand he held seven stars, from his mouth issued a sharp two-edged sword, and his face was like the sun shining in full strength. When I saw him, I fell at his feet as though dead. But he laid his right hand upon me, saying, 'Fear not, I am the first and the last, and the living one; I died, and behold I am alive for evermore, and I have the keys of Death and Hades'. (Apoc. 1:10–18)

[110] Dodd, *Interpretation*, 6. [111] Ashton, 'Johannine Son of Man', 526.

[112] The other testimony to such a visionary ascent is of course Paul: 'I will go on to visions and apocalypses of the Lord. I know a man in Christ who fourteen years ago was caught up to the third heaven... I know this man was caught up into Paradise... on behalf of this man I will boast, but on my own behalf I will not boast except of my weakness' (2 Cor. 12:1–5).

As we noted in Chapter 2, most contemporary scholars do not hold the Apocalypse to be written by John the Evangelist, even though the unanimous tradition from the second century is certain that it was. Yet even of those who dispute the common authorship, most are prepared to accept that it belongs to the same 'school'. Moreover, as we also noted in Chapter 2, a number of scholars have advanced serious arguments that it should be dated before the destruction of the Temple, and, therefore, probably before the Gospel was written or at least achieved its final form.[113]

The passage quoted is introduced by what is in effect a quotation from Daniel 7:13: 'Behold, he is coming with the clouds' (Apoc. 1:7, *ἰδοὺ ἔρχεται μετὰ τῶν νεφελῶν*; Dan. 7:13 *ἰδοὺ μετὰ τῶν νεφελῶν . . . ἐρχόμενος*). And the one John sees is said to be 'one like a Son of Man' (1:13, *ὅμοιον υἱὸν ἀνθρώπου*, also 14:14) which is much closer to Daniel 7:13 (*ὡς υἱὸν ἀνθρώπου*, OG and *Θ*), than the title 'the Son of Man' used in the Synoptic Passion predictions and its final promise, 'you will see the Son of Man seated at the right hand of Power and coming on the clouds of heaven' (Mark 14:62; Matt. 26:64), and throughout John (except for 5:27, where it lacks the definite article). This similarity strongly suggests that the Apocalypse has a closer connection to Daniel than does the Gospel, and therefore played a role in the development of the author's understanding of Jesus and what had happened in the Passion.

A further, and much more specific, instance of this development is in the verse preceding the one mentioning 'one like a Son of Man': 'I turned to see the voice that was speaking to me' (Apoc. 1:12). That he should turn 'to see the voice' provides a plausible background for John's otherwise unexplained words of Jesus, playing on a difference between present and past tenses, to the man who has just been given sight and asked by Jesus if he believes in the Son of Man: 'You have seen him and it is he who speaks to you' (9:37). Sight belongs to the past; being addressed vocally by the Son of Man is in the present. It is, after all, only after the crucifixion, and as the crucified one, that Jesus is called the Word of God: it is the one who sits on the white horse (Apoc. 19:11), who is 'clad in a robe dipped in blood, and the name by which he is called is The Word of God' (Apoc. 19:13: *κέκληται τὸ ὄνομα αὐτοῦ ὁ λόγος τοῦ θεοῦ*).[114] Similarly, as we have also seen, Ignatius too hopes to become

[113] Robinson, *Redating*, 227, points out that 'there is good reason to suppose that the Apocalypse too presupposes a time when the final separation of Christians and Jews had not yet taken place. For is it credible that the references in Apoc. 2.9 and 3.9 to those who "claim to be Jews but are not" could have been made in that form after 70?'.

[114] Cf. James H. Charlesworth, 'The Jewish Roots of Christology: The Discovery of the Hypostatic Voice', *SJT* 29 (1986), 19–41, at 20: 'I have slowly become convinced that the author of the Apocalypse of John intended 1:12 to be understood literally: "And I turned to see the Voice who spoke with me . . . " Verse 10 also seems to refer to the same concept, namely a divine being who is "the Voice"'. See also M. Eugene Boring, 'The Voice of Jesus in the Apocalypse of John', *NovT* 34.4 (1992), 334–59.

'a word of God' by his following Christ in martyrdom (*Rom.* 2.1). Although Jesus is presented in the Gospel as the Son of Man speaking to us, he is not called 'the Word', nor is 'the Word' mentioned in the stated aim of the Gospel, that we 'should believe that Jesus is the Christ, the Son of God' (20:31). Whether the Prologue, understood as describing a heavenly being called the Word waiting to become incarnate, reflects a development yet to be achieved by the author of the Gospel or another, as Ashton and others would have it, or whether we should hear the term 'Word' as used in the Prologue with other resonances besides that of the name of a divine being, we leave for Chapter 5.

Given everything we saw in our analysis of John 6 in Chapter 3, about how Jesus is the bread of life which descends from heaven, the bread that is his flesh, the flesh of the Son of Man, and also what we saw of the celebration of Pascha as declaimed by Melito, it is also important to note that this vision of John occurs 'in the Spirit on the Lord's day' (Apoc. 1:10 *ἐν πνεύματι ἐν τῇ κυριακῇ ἡμέρᾳ*). Given what we also saw of the development of the celebration of Pascha and Sunday in Chapter 1, it is virtually impossible to determine whether this 'Lord's day' is Pascha or a weekly Sunday, or, more specifically, whether the themes of the death and resurrection celebrated annually in Pascha by the disciples of John, had come to predominate in the weekly celebrations of the Lord's day. Either way, Irenaeus makes a fascinating connection between this vision and the Lord's supper as described in John. In connection with the very passage we have given above, Irenaeus comments:

> But when John could not endure the sight—for he says, 'I fell at his feet as dead' [Apoc. 1:17], that what was written might come to pass: 'No man sees God and lives' [Exod. 33:20]—the Word, reviving him and reminding him that it was he upon whose bosom he had leaned at supper [cf. John 13:23, 25], when he put the question as to who should betray him, declared: 'I am the first and the last, and he who lives and was dead, and behold, I am alive for evermore, and have the keys of Death and of Hades' [Apoc. 1:18]. (*haer.* 4.20.11)

This connection between the vision of the Son of Man and the one upon whose breast he leant at supper is reflected much later in the Venetian version of the *Life of St Brendan*, dated between 1270 and 1350, where Elijah in paradise says:

> He [the Antichrist] will win the world for himself by many means; many prophets have spoken of him, and so did Saint John the Evangelist in the Apocalypse, which was a vision which appeared to him when he was in anguish at the Last Supper, grief-stricken on hearing that Judas would betray the Lord.[115]

Who knows by what conjecture or tradition the author of this text came to this conclusion! What is important, however, is not any claim to historical

[115] W. R. J. Barron and Glyn S. Burgess, *The Voyage of St. Brendan* (Exeter: University of Exeter Press, 2002), 221.

reliability, but the insight that there is a deep connection, already seen by Irenaeus, between the Lord's day, upon which John, in the Spirit, saw the vision of the Son of Man and the meal at which John reclined upon the Lord's breast.[116]

Origen, in a passage we have already used in a different context, also points to the significance of leaning on the breast of the Lord at the supper to understand John's Gospel, 'whose meaning no one can understand who has not leaned on Jesus' breast nor received Mary from Jesus to be his mother also. But he who would be another John must also become such as John, to be shown to be Jesus, so to speak', meaning, adapting Paul's words, that he 'no longer lives, but Christ lives in him' (*Com. Jo.* 1.23; cf. Gal. 2:20). To understand John, one must lie, as he did, upon the Lord's breast (13:23, ἐν τῷ κόλπῳ τοῦ Ἰησοῦ), just as it is 'the only begotten Son/God who is in the breast of the Father' who alone can make him known or expound him (1:18, ὁ ὢν εἰς τὸν κόλπον τοῦ πατρὸς ἐκεῖνος ἐξηγήσατο). Should, then, the image of leaning upon the breast perhaps be taken as a designation of an apocalyptic vision, unveiling the appearance of the crucified Christ and the Scriptures, to get, as it were, at the heart of the matter?

Ashton's contrast between 'imagining' the suffering Jesus upon the cross and seeing him exalted in glory, with the first needing to be overlooked, forgotten, or reimagined, is a false one, at least from John's perspective. As we saw in Chapter 1, the celebration of Pascha—which began with John and remained particular to 'the school of John' until the latter part of the second century—was initially celebrated as a unitary event, holding together both the crucifixion and the resurrection. Only subsequently was it 'refracted' into a spectrum of colours, as a full liturgical cycle developed. But even then, each element was held together in the pure white light of Pascha: it is by his death that Christ conquers death and gives life through the cross. This is true even of the Isenheim altarpiece painted by Grünewald, for, as Ashton notes, on the reverse side there is a depiction of Christ rising in glory—both have to be held together.[117] This unity is also something we have seen in John's descriptions of the ascending/descending Son of Man: the way up *is* the way down. We

[116] On the liturgical background and context for the Apocalypse, see Otto A. Piper, 'The Apocalypse of John and the Liturgy of the Church', *CH* 20.1 (1951), 10–22; and José Adriano Filho, 'The Apocalypse of John as an Account of a Visionary Experience: Notes on the Book's Structure', *JSNT* 25.2 (2002), 213–34.

[117] Ashton, 'Johannine Son', 525, n. 49: 'Such in fact is the scene portrayed on the reverse side of the Isenheim altarpiece, a glorious Christ rising upwards out of the tomb; with modern technology the transformation might be conveyed by fading one side of Grünewald's painting into the other'. It is in fact the reverse side of the right-hand wing which, when opened, portrays, on the left the Nativity and on the right the risen Christ. These three scenes, together with the image of the dead Christ taken down from the cross at the bottom of the altarpiece (which remains constantly in view), are further tied together by the tunic of Christ on the cross, the swaddling-cloth for the new-born infant, and the cloth trailing from the risen Christ, which

have also repeatedly seen how John stands in a dialectical relationship with the Synoptics, a relationship which is captured in the words from the Anaphora of Chrysostom: 'in the night in which he was given up, or rather gave himself up for the life of the world'.[118] John's Gospel was never thought of as replacing the others, but rather, as we saw in Chapter 1, as completing or finishing their accounts. If it seems that John has emphasized the glory to such an extent that it overshadows all else, this is simply because, among the four Gospels, John's is the paschal gospel.

The Temple and the living human being, the glory of God, are thus brought to perfection with Jesus' own word from the cross, 'it is finished'.[119] Yet our account of the Gospel is not yet finished. We must now turn to look at the Prologue. Is it the case, as Ashton suggests, following Bultmann, Käsemann, Meeks, and others, that the Prologue presents a mythological account of a descending divine being, the Word, that now overshadows all other aspects of the Gospel? Or does the Prologue too share in the paschal nature of the Gospel so that it also proclaims the theological theme that Käsemann asserted, rightly, to be the one that is carried on from generation to generation, preserving the continuity of the history of theology, rather than any theological system, and that is, 'the hope of the manifestation of the Son of Man on his way to enthronement . . . which sprang from the Easter experience and determined the Easter faith'?[120]

appear to be identical. The reverse side of the left-hand wing portrays the Annunciation on the left and the Virgin in a chapel on the right.

118 Text and translation by Ephrem Lash, *Ἡ Θεία Λειτουργία τοῦ ἐν Ἁγίοις Πατρός ἡμῶν Ἰωάννου τοῦ Χρηυστοστόμου/The Divine Liturgy of our Father among the Saints John Chrysostom* (London: Greek Orthodox Archdiocese of Thyateira and Great Britain, 2011), 45.

119 See Maximus the Confessor, *Amb.* 41 (PG 91, 1309cd), describing the recapitulating work of Christ, which culminates in this way: 'And finally, after all these things, he, according to the aspect of humanity, comes to God himself [*πρὸς αὐτὸν γίνεται*], "appearing" as a human being, as it is written, "before the face of the God" and Father [Heb. 9:24]—he, who as Word cannot be separated in any way at all from the Father, fulfilling as a human being, in deed and truth, with unchangeable obedience, everything that he, as God, has predetermined to take place and accomplishing the whole will of the God and Father on our behalf'. And in so doing, Maximus continues, he shows that 'the whole creation exists as one, like another human being', *καθάπερ ἄνθρωπον ἄλλον*.

120 Käsemann, 'Beginnings', 107.

5

The Prologue as a Paschal Hymn

We have seen that the Gospel of John is a paschal gospel, proclaiming the fulfilment, in the Pascha of Christ, of the construction of the Temple and the manifestation of the glory of God in, or rather *as*, the living human being, the completion of God's project. Yet what of the Prologue? What are the first eighteen verses of the Gospel of John, what do they say, and how are they related to the Gospel that is thereafter narrated?

Over the last century or more, there have been two main approaches to the Prologue, the first (the 'H camp', as designated by Ashton) which follows Harnack in holding that the Prologue was based upon a pre-existing hymn to the Logos, taken over and modified in various ways by John, and the second (the 'B camp', after Barrett) which holds that the Prologue was an original composition by John for the express purpose of introducing the Gospel.[1] Each of these positions has difficult issues with which they must grapple. For the 'H camp', there are the questions of the source of this Logos hymn (though here Bultmann's claims for a pre-Christian Mandaean origin have rightly been abandoned),[2] what verses constitute the original hymn, and what are John's additions, attempting to tie this hymn to the rest of the Gospel, and at what stage in the composition of the Gospel was it added and did it affect any later layers of the text of the Gospel? For the 'B camp', the question is primarily

[1] See John Ashton, 'Really a Prologue?', in Jan G. van der Watt, R. Alan Culpepper, and Udo Schnelle, *The Prologue of the Gospel of John: Its Literary, Theological, and Philosophical Contexts. Papers Read at the Colloquium Ioanneum 2013*, WUNT 359 (Tübingen: Mohr Siebeck, 2016), 27–44, at 27. Ashton notes a third, smaller group, which accepts that the Prologue was adopted from some prior source, but was nevertheless used by John as the introduction to the Gospel, which he then wrote on its basis. Cf. A. Harnack, 'The History of Religions Background of the Prologue to the Gospel of John'; 'Über das Verhältniß des Prologs des vierten Evangeliums zum ganzen Werk', *ZKT* 2 (1892), 189–231; Charles Kingsley Barrett, *The Prologue of St John's Gospel: The Ethel M. Wood Lecture Delivered before the University of London on 19 February 1970* (London: Athlone, 1971); Barrett, *John*.

[2] Rudolf Bultmann, 'The History of Religions Background of the Prologue to the Gospel of John', first published in *Eucharisterion: Festschrift für H. Gunkel* (Göttingen: Vandenhoeck & Rpurecht, 1923), 2, 3–26; translated in John Ashton, ed., *The Interpretation of John*, Studies in New Testament Interpretation, 2nd edn (Edinburgh: T & T Clark, 1997), 18–35, see esp. 32–3.

what is the relationship of the Prologue to the rest of the Gospel: how does it introduce the Gospel, when so many of the key themes of the Prologue are not present in the Gospel and *vice versa*? Although many key themes from the Prologue do reappear in the Gospel (life, light, knowledge, truth, glory), others do not appear; most strikingly, the Incarnation of the Word is not even alluded to, not even in the stated aim of the Gospel itself: 'these things are written that you may believe that Jesus is the Christ, the Son of God' (20:31). It is not sufficient to claim to find the Incarnation in the repeated affirmations that the Son is sent from God and the ascending/descending of the Son of Man, for in neither case are these said of the Word, and in any case the language of sending and ascending/descending is not used in the Prologue. And, in reverse, key themes from the Gospel, such as the words and actions of Jesus that it narrates, seem not to be alluded to at all in the Prologue, not even, most strikingly, the Passion. The difficulties that each camp faces, having set out on their path, are huge, for the 'B camp' probably insurmountable, and for the 'H camp' ultimately indeterminable.[3]

However, despite having two distinct approaches to explaining the Prologue, what unites both 'camps' is the conviction that at the heart of the Prologue and the Gospel (simply as such for the 'B camp' and in its final form for the 'H camp', as a strong indicator that the Gospel underwent various redactions and remains even in its final form in an uneasy tension) is the assertion that 'the Word became flesh', taken in the sense of the incarnation of a pre-existent, pre-incarnate divine being, called the Word, taking a body so that the invisible God now becomes visible in the flesh as Jesus Christ, the Incarnate Word. Undoubtedly, as has frequently been observed from the time of Harnack and Rendel Harris,[4] and as we saw in Chapter 3 when looking at Temple imagery, the next phrase of 1:14 draws from Sirach 24:8 where Wisdom (later the Law, 24:23) is directed to 'tabernacle in Jacob'. Yet Wisdom and the Law are never said to have become flesh; 'the Word became flesh' is a new and dramatic claim. But does it say quite what, without further reflection, we think it does? Does seeing Jesus, physically, enable us to see the Word of God and so see the Father? Apart from John, who witnessed the crucifixion, and Isaiah, who saw Jesus' glory (12:41), the inability of the disciples, let alone others, to do so, at least until after the Passion, should cause us to pause for further thought.[5] Likewise, does the word 'flesh' simply designate a physical body, visible in the horizon of the world, or is something more involved? We will examine both of these aspects from the point of view of contemporary

[3] Theobald, *Die Fleischwerdung des Logos*, 71, 85, 95, 134 charts out 39 different suggested reconstructions of the original form of the Prologue.

[4] J. Rendel Harris, 'The Origin of the Prologue of John's Gospel', *Expositer* 12 (1916), 147–70; 314–20; 388–400; 415–26.

[5] Cf. Catrin H. Williams, '(Not) Seeing God in the Prologue and Body of John's Gospel', in Jan G. van Der Watt, et al., eds, *Prologue*, 79–98.

phenomenology in Part III; here we will remain with scriptural exegesis. If we have held back in examining the Prologue to this point, it is not so much because of a conviction with regard to any theory concerning how the Gospel came to be written. A strong case can indeed be made for seeing various stages in its development, and, as Ashton insistently reminds us, our understanding of the Gospel is deepened when attention is paid to the making of it. If we have reserved treatment of the Prologue until now, it is because we want to establish, by historical investigation and exegesis of its text, the character of the Gospel—that it is not an 'incarnational' Gospel, as that it usually taken, but a paschal gospel—before we take the further step of examining the Prologue.

But before we turn to the Prologue itself, it is worth recalling some of the observations made in the Introduction, especially Quentin Skinner's caution about the fallacy of 'the mythology of doctrines' and the change in subject from Jesus to the Word. Regarding the first, it has become an unquestioned assumption of modern theology that Christian theology is dominated by two great themes, Trinity and Incarnation, where the latter is understood as, to revisit Rowan Williams' phrase, 'an episode in the biography of the Word'. So much is this the case that it is simply presumed by both the 'H group' and the 'B group'. Yet, as Skinner reminds us, ideas are not eternal hypostatized entities, for which an account always has to be given. Rather, we should examine each historical text on its own terms to see how it works out its own framework, vocabulary, and points of reference, in itself and in its historical context. It should also be borne in mind that John was not writing in a context that included a full Christian liturgical cycle: the celebration of Pascha, as a single event, was held to have originated with John; its refraction into different elements (crucifixion, burial, resurrection, ascension, Pentecost) was a later development, and so too was the feast of the nativity of Christ, the celebration of which makes clear that it too is refracted from the Paschal light.[6]

What gave rise to the assumption with which the Prologue is approached is perhaps the fact that, as Herbert McCabe claims, the idea of the 'pre-existent Christ', or, we should say more accurately (as we suggested in the Introduction), the 'pre-incarnate Word' was 'invented' in the nineteenth century, 'as a way of distinguishing the eternal procession of the Son from the incarnation of

[6] See especially Raymond Brown, *The Birth of the Messiah: A Commentary on the Infancy Narratives in the Gospels of Matthew and Luke* (New York: Doubleday, 1993), and much more briefly, *An Adult Christ at Christmas: Essays on Three Biblical Christmas Stories* (Collegeville, MN: Liturgical Press, 1978); and Behr, *Mystery of Christ*, 134–8. The connection is made in the hymnography for the feast and most explicitly in the iconography, where Christ is depicted, with a cross in his halo, not in a house or stable (as a historicizing depiction of the infancy narratives would require), but wrapped in swaddling cloths as a corpse, laid in a manger as food (for those who eat the body of Christ; with Bethlehem meaning the house of bread), placed in a cave embracing in its shape the Virgin, just as the crucified Christ was placed in a new tomb, in which no one had ever yet been laid (Luke 23:53, i.e. 'virginal'), belonging to (the other) Joseph (Matt. 27:60).

the Son'.[7] This is combined, as we noted, with a historical or historicizing approach to reading Scripture, rather than an 'apocalyptic' or 'unveiling' reading (which we further explored in Chapter 2). This led to the idea, the assumption with which the Prologue is unquestioningly approached but which McCabe totally, and rightly, rejects, 'that God has a life-story, a divine story, other than the story of the incarnation... *First* the Son of God pre-existed as just the Son of God and *then* later he was the Son of God made man'; or in terms of the Prologue, the question becomes: at which point does the Word become Jesus? To think in such terms, he points out, is incoherent and 'incompatible at least with the traditional doctrine of God', for 'there can be no succession in the eternal God, no change. Eternity is not, of course, a very long time; it is not time at all.... it totally transcends time'.[8] Another way of putting the matter would be to note that in the traditional phrase, 'Jesus Christ is God become man', the 'is' points to an ontological priority not a chronological period prior to 'becoming', though, of course, the 'becoming' in fact has epistemological priority, for it is on the basis of what Jesus has done, the economy, that we make claims about who *he* is, theology. Or, alternatively, in a statement such as 'Jesus Christ is begotten from the Father outside of time and from the mother inside of time', the begetting from the Father does not happen before, chronologically, the birth from the mother (if it did, one would have to ask: How long before? How old was the Word when he was born from Mary as Jesus?). When the language of the 'eternal begetting' of the Word, Jesus, begins to be used, it is, on the basis of Proverbs 8:25 ('before the hills he begets me'), in the present tense.[9] Eternity and temporality do not intersect as parallel durations of time, and likewise the distinction made between theology and economy corresponds to two different questions (regarding who Christ is, and what he has done), where only the latter is played out within time.[10] To do otherwise is to speak of 'Incarnation' in purely mythical terms.

Now, of course, these theological subtitles cannot simply be attributed to John or whomever one might hold to be the author of the Prologue. But perhaps more important is that, as we argued in the Introduction, such mythologizing of God and the Incarnation has led to the change in subject, from Jesus to the Word: one begins with the pre-incarnate Word, in an eternal

[7] McCabe, 'Involvement', 49. [8] Ibid., italics original.

[9] Cf. Origen, *Princ.* 1.2.1 and 4. This is moreover an 'eternal begetting' in which creatures can also participate. For instance, Origen *Hom. Jer.* 9:4: 'The Savior is eternally begotten by the Father, so also, if you possess the "Spirit of adoption" [Rom 8:15] God eternally begets you in him according to each of your works, each of your thoughts. And being begotten you thereby become an eternally begotten son of God in Christ Jesus'. *καὶ ἀεὶ γεννᾶται ὁ σωτὴρ ὑπὸ τοῦ πατρός, οὕτως καὶ σὺ ἐὰν ἔχῃς 'τὸ τῆς υἱοθεσίας,' ἀεὶ γεννᾷ σε ἐν αὐτῷ ὁ θεὸς καθ' ἕκαστον ἔργον, καθ' ἕκαστον διανόημα, καὶ γεννώμενος οὕτως γίνῃ ἀεὶ γεννώμενος υἱὸς θεοῦ ἐν Χριστῷ Ἰησοῦ·.*

[10] As Young, *Biblical Exegesis*, 143, notes: 'There is no possibility of "narrative" in *theologia*, but narrative constitutes *oikonomia*; one is in time, the other beyond time'.

state, waiting with God, and then moves on, later, to the Incarnation, the enfleshed Word, Jesus—though accounting for 'when' in the Prologue this happens is a source of perplexity: for Jesus seems to be present in the world in 1:8–13, before the Word becomes flesh, and perhaps also in 1:3–5. But this is not, in the main and certainly in the most important examples, how early Christian theology speaks, despite it being assumed and repeated endlessly. As we noted, the first work called *On the Incarnation*, written by Athanasius, the great defender of Nicene theology, barely mentions the birth of Jesus, and never the name Mary, focused as it is on two accounts of what is accomplished in the death of Jesus; and it is in fact this, the Passion, that, in the first part of the work, *Against the Gentiles*, he specifies to be the subject of his treatise: he will show why Christians confess 'that he who ascended the cross is the Word of God and Saviour of the universe'; the *order* of predication is important.[11] Likewise the Creeds of Nicaea and Constantinople, taking their lead from Paul ('One God the Father... and one Lord Jesus Christ', 1 Cor. 8:6) do not even use the title 'Word'; and, when the definition of Chalcedon does use it, it is as one of the many titles of 'the one Lord Jesus Christ'. Finally, the great defender of the unity of the one Jesus Christ, Cyril of Alexandria, specifies how different titles, 'the Word' among them, are attributed to Jesus Christ: 'We say that there is one and the same Jesus Christ, from the God, the Father, on the one hand, as the God Word, and, on the other hand, from the seed of the godly David according to the flesh'.[12] There is one subject, Jesus Christ, who, as from the God and Father is the Word of God. So much is this the case that Cyril can state, rather jarringly to our modern ears: 'One is the Son, one Lord, Jesus Christ, both before the incarnation and after the incarnation'.[13] It is none other than Jesus Christ who is the one subject, both before and after the Incarnation! If this is the predominant idiom of Christian antiquity, whether or not John was consciously aware of the difficulties of speaking about the intersection of eternity and temporality, one would hesitate to presume for him the idiom of much modern theology instead. And, in fact, the order of predication (that it is to Jesus Christ, 'the one who ascended the cross', that the title 'Word' is attributed) is, as we saw in Chapter 4, followed in the only instance of the title 'Word' (this time 'the Word of God') actually being applied to Jesus Christ in the New Testament, and that is in the other Johannine writing (or at least from the same 'school'), the Apocalypse, where it is of the

[11] *C. Gent.* 1: *ὁμολογεῖν Θεοῦ Λόγον καὶ Σωτῆρα εἶναι τοῦ παντὸς τὸν ἐπὶ τοῦ σταυροῦ ἀναβάντα.*

[12] Cyril of Alexandria, *That Christ is One* (ed. Pusey, 371.12–14): *ἕνα καὶ τὸν αὐτὸν εἶναί φαμεν Χριστὸν Ἰησοῦν, ἐκ Θεοῦ μὲν Πατρὸς ὡς Θεὸν Λόγον, ἐκ σπέρματος δὲ κατὰ σάρκα τοῦ θεσπεσίου Δαυείδ.*

[13] Cyril of Alexandria, *First Letter to Succensus*, 4: *εἷς οὖν ἐστιν υἱός, εἷς κύριος, Ἰησοῦς Χριστὸς καὶ πρὸ τῆς σαρκώσεως καὶ μετὰ τὴν σάρκωσιν.*

rider on the white horse, 'clad in a robe dipped in blood', that it is said that 'the name by which he is called is the Word of God' (Apoc. 19:13).

That it is in fact Jesus Christ who is the one subject spoken about throughout the Prologue is, moreover, asserted in the first full comment we have on the text, which comes from Irenaeus of Lyons, whom, as we saw in Chapter 1, is linked directly to John by way of Polycarp of Smyrna. Irenaeus' comments come in response to an interpretation of the Prologue by Ptolemy and cited by Irenaeus. As Irenaeus quotes Ptolemy:

> John the disciple of the Lord, wishing to narrate the origin of all things, according to which the Father emitted all things, proposes a kind of beginning [ἀρχήν τινα], the first thing begotten by the Father, whom he called Son and Only-begotten God, by whom the Father emitted all things as through a 'seed'. They say that Word was emitted by this Only-begotten and in him was emitted the whole substance of the Aeons, whom the Word himself formed later.
>
> (*haer.* 1.8.5; Greek from Epiphanius)

Ptolemy, as it were, reified or hypostatized the different nouns in the Prologue—Word, Life, Light, etc.—to present the Prologue as an account of the derivations of the aeons within the pleroma. The first of these is not, intriguingly, the Word, but rather the beginning, whom he identifies as the Son, for it is *in* the beginning that the Word is before being emitted. After pointing out that this derivation of Aeons does not follow the order of the words in the Prologue and introduces figures not mention therein, such as Church (*haer.* 1.9.1), Irenaeus responds with his own understanding of the words of the Prologue:

> Manifest, then, is the false fabrication of their exegesis. For John, proclaiming one God, the Almighty, and one Jesus Christ, the Only-begotten, 'by whom all things were made' [1:3], declares that this is 'the Word of God' [1:1], this 'the Only-begotten' [1:18], this the Maker of all things, this 'the true Light who enlightens every human being' [1:9], this 'the Maker of the world' [1:10], this the one who 'came to his own' [1:11], this the one who 'became flesh and dwelt among us' [1:14], they, speciously distorting the exegesis, hold that the Only-begotten, by emission, is another, whom they call the Beginning, and they hold that another became the Saviour, and another the Logos, the son of the Only-begotten, and another the Christ, emitted for the reestablishment of the Fullness.... But that the apostle did not speak concerning their conjunctions, but concerning our Lord Jesus Christ, whom he knew to be the Word of God, he himself has made evident. For, summing up what he said above in the beginning about the Word [Ἀνακεφαλαιούμενος γὰρ περὶ τοῦ εἰρημένου αὐτῷ ἄνω ἐν ἀρχῇ λόγου], he adds [ἐπεξηγεῖται], 'And the Word was made flesh, and dwelt among us' [1:14].
>
> (*haer.* 1.9.2)

Irenaeus clearly and emphatically reads the whole of the Prologue as being about Jesus Christ: he is the Word in the beginning with God, and everything thereafter speaks of him. The Word becoming flesh, moreover, is taken as a recapitulation and an epexegetical gloss on what had been said by John in the beginning.

None of the proposed backgrounds for the Prologue really hold, whether Bultmann's Mandaean or Gnostic myth of a descending Saviour, or the many variations thereof proposed since, or even Sirach 24, the vocabulary of which has clearly been deployed in 1:14, yet which never affirms that Wisdom or the Law became flesh. It is possible, as some have suggested, that the original hymn was developed within the Johannine community and subsequently added to the Gospel as its preface, but such suggestions still assume that the hymn speaks of the becoming flesh of a pre-incarnate Word in the way that we have discussed, and questioned, above. Very few modern theologians have taken seriously what was obvious for Irenaeus, that is, that the Prologue does in fact speak, throughout, of Jesus, the most notable being of course Karl Barth:

> In Jn. 1[1] the reference is very clear: ὁ λόγος is unmistakably substituted for Jesus. His is the place which the predicates attributed to the Logos are meant at once to mark off, to clear and to reserve. It is He, Jesus, who is in the beginning with God. It is He who by nature is God. This is what is guaranteed in Jn. 1[1].[14]

Several modern scriptural scholars have argued that 1:5–13 speaks of Jesus Christ, and his saving activity.[15] Others would take this back further to include 1:3–5; as Paul Lamarche comments regarding v. 4: 'taking the words at their face value with no preconceived ideas one might well see in the formulation of v.4a not just the incarnation but everything that happened to Christ, his whole earthly life and above all his death, resurrection and glorification'.[16] Serafin de Ausejo went further to argue, on the basis of other hymns to Christ in the New

[14] Barth, *Church Dogmatics* 2.2, *The Doctrine of God*, 96.

[15] Cf. Ernst Käsemann, 'Structure and Purpose of the Prologue to John's Gospel', in Käsemann, *New Testament Questions for Today*, 138–67, at 150: 'There is absolutely no convincing argument for the view that vv. 5–13 ever referred to anything save the historical manifestation of the Revealer'. Brown, *John*, 1.28–9 argues that vv. 10–12b refers to the earthly ministry of Jesus, noting that so too do Büschel, Bauer, and Harnack.

[16] Paul Lamarche, 'The Prologue of John', in John Ashton, *Interpretation of John*, 47–65 (originally appeared as 'Le Prologue de Jean', *RSR* 52 [1964], 407–537), at 54; see also his comment on 53: 'Legitimate though it may be to use the first verses of the Prologue to "get back to" the Trinity, it is plain that the perspective here is not purely and simply Trinitarian but above all "economic" [in the sense of the economy of salvation]. We have to do with the "foundation" of the world, and the title of Logos designates not only the *Word*, as we now call him, but Christ the Saviour'. In his endnote to this sentence he adds (63, n. 19): 'Perhaps we should pay more attention to the precise meaning of the Johannine Logos both in the study of Patristic Christology and in current developments in theology'. See also T. Evan Pollard, 'Cosmology and the Prologue of the Fourth Gospel', *VC* 12 (1958): 147–53; Ignace de la Potterie, *La Verité dans Saint Jean*, Analecta Biblica 73, 2 vols (Rome: Biblical Institute, 1977), 1.161–5; Theobald, *Fleischwerdung*, 224–7. McHugh, *John 1–4*, 11–20, and Martinus C. de Boer, 'The Original Prologue to the Gospel of John', *NTS* 61 (2015), 448–67, both take similar positions, and

Testament—which consistently speak of Jesus Christ as the one who pre-exists, followed by a kenotic sojourn upon the earth, and then his exaltation—that the whole Prologue, from v. 1 onwards, refers to Jesus Christ, though he would restrict the earthly sojourn to 1:13–14b.[17] Most pertinent, however, is the point made by Matthijs de Jong, asking why it is that Jesus Christ is only named at the end of the Prologue: 'Is it a literary procedure, intended to hold it in tension? That is not likely. As if the readers are holding their breath until verse 17 (or at least verse 14) wondering: "Who could this *Logos* be?" No, the text wants, from v. 1, to underline the eternal pre-history and the divine origin of Jesus Christ'.[18] Rather than a narrative beginning with a figure called the Word who later on becomes Jesus Christ, the Prologue—whether taken over in whole or in part, composed by John himself or within his community, modified and redacted in various ways—is, as we have it (and we don't have it in any other form), in some sense at least, a hymn about Jesus Christ, speaking about him and his work in various ways.

All scholars agree that it is necessary to understand the Prologue, and the Gospel, in the milieu in which they were written. But this means that, besides looking for parallels in other first-century literature such as the Palestinian Jewish apocalypses and rabbinic traditions (to which we paid considerable attention in Chapter 4), we should also attempt to understand the Prologue in the light of the Gospel, and vice versa, and both in terms of the Christian theological tradition to which they gave rise in figures such as Irenaeus, without falling into the fallacy of the 'mythology of doctrines' regarding both the Gospel and its Prologue and also the early Christian theologians and exegetes.[19] As such, the question before us now is what the hymn looks

both provide a full, clear, and concise summary of the issues involved and the various positions taken.

[17] Serafin de Ausejo, '¿Es un himno a Cristo el prólogo de San Juan? Los himnos christologicos de la iglesia primitiva y el prologo del IV evangelo: Fil. 2, 6–11; Col. 1, 15–20; 1 Tim. 3, 16; Hebr. 1, 2–4; Jn. 1, 1–18', *Estudios Biblicos* 15 (1956): 223–77, 381–427; 395 for the restriction to 1:13–14ab.

[18] Matthijs de Jong, 'De proloog van Johannes', in de *Bijbel in Gewone Taal*', *Met Andere Worden* 31.4 (2012), 27–41, at 31, continuing on 32: 'In this way, the Prologue makes it clear that it concerns God's whole plan for the world, from beginning to end. Jesus Christ is not, as saviour of the world, a part of God's comprehensive plan, but he is, *as the Logos*, the sole divine executor of God's whole plan, from before the creation until eternity'. If, as we argued in Chapter 4, the divine purpose and plan, to make a human being in his image, is in fact only first completed or perfected in the crucified and exalted Christ, then de Jong's qualification (that Christ as saviour is not part of the plan) is not needed; indeed, Irenaeus would put it the other way round: 'since he who saves pre-exists, it was necessary that he who would be saved should come into existence, so that the Saviour does not exist in vain' (*haer.* 3.22.3); creation and salvation are part of one single economy.

[19] The effect of the 'mythology of doctrines' is clearly seen in Brown's comments (*John* 1.23) on de Ausejo's 'novel theory': Brown notes that de Ausejo 'correctly insists that the Pauline hymns tend to refer to Jesus Christ throughout', but then claims that: 'This way of speaking is strange to Christian theology in the aftermath of Nicaea; for before the Incarnation one speaks of

like when read this way, as speaking throughout of Jesus, and whether, when this is done, it coheres with what we have seen of the Gospel of John as a paschal gospel.

A few more preliminary comments need to be made regarding the Prologue, concerning the demarcation, structure, and character of these verses as a 'prologue'. P. J. Williams has pointed out that the demarcation of 1:1–18 as a separate block of text is only given graphical form with Griesbach's edition of the New Testament in 1777.[20] The earliest papyrus of the text, P^{66}, dated around 200 CE, demarcates 1:1–5 as a separate block by leaving a blank space following the punctuation mark at the end of v. 5, so beginning v. 6 on a new line, a demarcation that seems to have been regularly followed in later manuscripts.[21] This division is also followed, Williams argues, by early exegetes, though whether they do so to the exclusion of 1:6–18 is not clear; Irenaeus, in the passage quoted above (*haer.* 1.9.2), extends his treatment at least as far as v. 14.[22] Some scriptural scholars, as already noted, have seen in 1:3–5 a description of Christ's saving work and have argued on this basis that 1:1–5 is indeed a complete unit, whose tight textual connection is reinforced by its 'staircase parallelism', in which an important word or concept at or near the end of a line is picked up again at the beginning of the next.[23]

Verse 1:6, introducing 'a human being sent from God whose name was John', clearly begins a new section. As vv. 1:6–8 and 15 (and perhaps, as we will argue, 16–18) speak of John the Baptist, while 1:9–14 speak of Christ, the material pertaining to the Baptist has (by Ashton's 'H camp') been taken as interpolations into an original Logos/Christ hymn. Alternatively, 1:6 could be taken as beginning of the narrative of Gospel (cf. 1 Kgdms. 1:1 LXX: 'There was a human being... and his name was Elkana'), or, as we will suggest, 1:6–18 is another integrated block, with 1:19 ('And this is the witness of John') beginning the narrative that continues thereafter.

Finally, although often described as a hymn, and certain verses are indeed poetic (though it is not easy to differentiate clearly between poetry and prose), the placement of these verses, whether 1:1–5 or 1–18, at the beginning of the work means that they are read as a 'prologue'. According to Aristotle (*Rhet.* 5.14.1), an

the Second Person of the Trinity and it is insisted that Jesus Christ came into being at the moment of the Incarnation. But the NT [New Testament] made no such precise distinction in its terminology, and de Ausejo may well be right'. Given what we have seen earlier in this chapter and in the Introduction (especially in the comment of Cyril of Alexandria: 'One is the Son, one Lord, Jesus Christ both before the incarnation and after the incarnation'), Brown is simply wrong here, though his concession that de Ausejo may be right that the Prologue speaks throughout of Jesus is welcome (even if I would not follow de Ausejo in his analysis of the Prologue).

20 Cf. P. J. Williams, 'Not the Prologue of John', *JSNT* 33.4 (2011), 375–86, at 381.

21 Ibid. 376–8.

22 Ibid. 378–9; Irenaeus (*haer.* 3.11.1; Williams cites according to Harvey's numeration as 3.11.7) does indeed cite John 1:1–5 as a block, but he continues by also citing 1:14.

23 Cf. De Boer, 'The Original Prologue', 449–50.

exordium in the case of a speech, a prologue for poetry, and a prelude for flute playing, 'are all beginnings and as it were pave the way for what follows'; they should include the keynote and attach the main subject, so giving enough information as to enable readers or hearers to understand the theme and its development. This means, as Jean Zumstein puts it, that: 'This opening word does not place itself on the same level as the following narrative; rather, it assumes a prior reflection about that narrative. The meta-reflective nature of the Prologue marks its intratextual relationship with the narrative, which properly begins in 1:19'.[24] The question for us here is whether or not this 'meta-reflective' character of the Prologue is such that it includes a reference to the Passion, which is clearly the central theme of the Gospel.

JOHN 1:1

There are three particular verses that with greater investigation may open up a better and more satisfactory way of reading the Prologue. First, of course, is 1:1:

> Ἐν ἀρχῇ ἦν ὁ λόγος, καὶ ὁ λόγος ἦν πρὸς τὸν θεόν, καὶ θεὸς ἦν ὁ λόγος.
>
> (RSV) In the beginning was the Word, and the Word was with God, and the Word was God.

There are three key words here that need closer examination: 'beginning', 'Word', and 'with'. While the term ἀρχή may certainly be translated as 'beginning', its range of meanings is much wider: origin, first principle, source, first place, sovereignty, authority. Reading the term simply as a temporal starting point obscures all these other resonances. In his *Homily on the Passover*, explaining the verse 'This month is for you the beginning [ἀρχή] of months; it is the first [πρῶτος] month of the year for you' (Exod. 12:2), Origen explains the difference between the words 'beginning' and 'first' as used by Scripture: 'properly speaking, "first" applies only when nothing comes before, and "beginning" applies to those which are beginning, even if they come last. What is "first" is always "beginning", but "beginning" is not always "first."'[25] To show that this isn't simply his assertion, Origen calls as a witness the words of the Saviour in the Apocalypse, where he identifies himself as both

[24] Jean Zumstein, 'Intratextuality and Intertextuality in the Gospel of John', in Tom Thatcher and Stephen D. Moore, eds, *Anatomies of Narrative Criticism: The Past, Present, and Futures of the Fourth Gospel as Literature* (Atlanta, GA: SBL, 2008), 121–36, at 123.

[25] Origen, *Pasch.* 8.24–32: τ[ὸ μὲν] [γ]ὰρ πρῶ[τον μό]νον μη[δένος] προάγο[ντος κυρίω]ς λέγ[εται], ἡ δὲ ἀρχὴ ἐπὶ τ[ῶν ἀρ]χεμέ[νων] κἂν τελευταῖ[α γέ]νηται, συμαίνεται. Κ[αὶ ὅ τι] μὲν πρῶτόν ἐστιν, τοῦ[τ]ο κ[αὶ] ἀρχή ἐστιν, οὐχ ὅ τι δὲ ἀρχή, ἤδη καὶ πρῶτον.

'the beginning' and 'the first', thereby showing that there is also a difference between them: 'I am the Alpha and Omega, the first and the last, the beginning and the end' (Apoc. 22:13). Christ is therefore both, Origen maintains, the 'first' as 'the first-born of all creation' (Col. 1:25), and the 'beginning' as Wisdom, for Wisdom says of herself, 'The Lord created me the beginning of his ways' (Prov. 8:22). And then he concludes:

> And this is probably what John had in mind when he began his Gospel with the words: 'In the beginning was the Word, and the Word was with God, and the Word was God. He was in the beginning with God' [1:1–2]. He takes the 'beginning' to signify Wisdom, and says that the Word is not 'beginning' but 'in the beginning'. For when the Son is with the Father in his own proper glory [cf. 17:5], he is not said to be 'first', for this belongs to the Father alone, for God alone is unbegotten. The Son is not 'first'... [break in text] [but inasmuch as he] rules all things with wisdom he is the 'beginning'. That is why, when he comes into the world, John does not say 'First was the Word', but 'In the beginning was the Word'. (*Pasch* 10.4–11.31)

As is clearer in his work *On First Principles* (1.2), Origen is trying to work out the hierarchy of the titles of Christ (rather than a hierarchy of Aeons as Ptolemy attempted). The primary title of Christ is 'Wisdom', while 'the Word' is '*in* the beginning', that is, it is a title ascribed to Christ on the basis of his already being the Wisdom of God, 'the beginning of his ways' (Prov. 8:22). And as it is *in* Wisdom that God creates (cf. Ps. 103:24), Christ is the 'first' as 'the firstborn of all creation' (Col. 1:15) and 'the firstborn of the dead' (Col. 1:18), and also the 'beginning' of the ways of God, and, in fact, 'the beginning of the creation of God' (Apoc. 3:14), or, more simply and absolutely, 'he is the ἀρχή' (Col. 1:18). And so, as Origen puts it, 'when he comes into the world' John doesn't start with 'First was the Word', but rather 'In the beginning was the Word'. Likewise, when Origen asks, in the opening lines of his *Homilies on Genesis*, what is 'the beginning' in which God made heaven and earth? He answers, who else can it be 'except our Lord and "Saviour of all", Jesus Christ, "the firstborn of every creature"?'[26] He continues by citing John 1:1–3 and concludes that 'Scripture is not talking here about any temporal beginning, but it says that the heaven and the earth and all things which were made were made "in the beginning", that is, in the Saviour'.[27] Likewise Cyril of Alexandria: 'No beginning that is the least bit temporal can be applied to the Only-Begotten because he is before all time and has his existence before the ages'.[28]

Irenaeus, taking a different scriptural verse, gives a further insight into how 'beginning' can be used. The messianic verse Isaiah 9:6[5], 'Unto us a Son is

[26] Cf. Origen, *Hom. Gen.* 1.1, citing 1 Tim 4:10 and Col. 1:15.
[27] Ibid. *Non ergo hic temporale aliquod principium dicit.*
[28] Cyril of Alexandria, *Com. Jo.* 1.1 (ed. Pusey, vol. 1, 18.2–4).

given and the government [ἀρχή] will be upon his shoulder', refers, according to Irenaeus 'to the cross, upon which his shoulders were nailed, for that which was and is a reproach for him and, through him, for us, the cross, that, he says is his government, which is a sign of his reign'.[29] It is through the cross that Christ reigns and it is by reigning upon this throne that he is indeed the ἀρχή. Origen likewise connects the cross to Christ's lordship and, indeed, to the whole of his creative activity: 'The Son became king through suffering the cross'.[30] Whatever 'beginning' means in all this, it is clearly not understood as a point in time; it is rather something like 'source', 'origin', 'head'—*in principium*, as the Latin translation has it, not *in initium*. In first place, in headship, as the source of all things was and is the Word, the crucified Lord and Saviour, Jesus Christ.

With regard to the term 'Word' it should now be evident that there is more going on with its meaning than simply the name of a divine being. It is possible, as Dodd and others have suggested, that John's adoption of this term here is an apologetic outreach 'to a public nurtured in the higher religion of Hellenism'.[31] In 1:14 it is clear that John has adopted imagery from Sirach 24, and so it is possible that John has simply substituted the term 'Word' for 'Wisdom', perhaps on the basis of the way in which the Word (*dabar*) of God appears in the later Targums, as the *Memra*, 'Word', a quasi-personalized entity introduced as a way of avoiding the anthropomorphisms found in Scripture. Much closer to hand is the fact that, as Edwyn Hoskyns points out, by the time John was writing, the term 'Word' had already become synonymous for the Gospel itself.[32] For instance, in Mark 8:32, having just told the disciples for the first time that the Son of Man must suffer and be killed, Jesus, it says, 'spoke the Word openly'. Luke's Gospel opens by referring to what has been handed down to his generation 'by those who from the beginning were eyewitnesses and ministers of the Word' (Luke 1:2). The Gospel that Paul preaches is Christ crucified (cf. 1 Cor. 1:23; Gal. 3:1) and that this Jesus Christ is Lord (cf. 2 Cor. 4:6); and Paul says that his task, in preaching this gospel, is 'to make the Word of God fully known, the mystery hidden from all ages and generations but now made manifest to the saints' (Col. 1:25–6). The 'gospel', 'the Word of God' (2 Cor. 2:17; 4:2), 'the Word of Christ' (Col. 3:16), or simply 'the Word' (Gal. 6:6; Col. 4:3) are all ways of speaking about the apostolic preaching. With this abundance of usage and with themes that we have seen throughout our examination of John, especially

[29] Irenaeus, *Dem.* 56; so too Cyril of Alexandria, *Com. Jo.* 1.1 (ed. Pusey vol. 1, 22.4–5): 'Therefore the Word "was" in the "beginning", that is, in the dominion that is over everything'.

[30] *Comm. Jo.* 1.278: ἐβασίλευσε γὰρ διὰ τοῦ πεπονθέναι τὸν σταυρόν. For the connection between the cross and creation in Origen, see Behr, *Origen: On First Principles*, vol. 1, lvi–lxv.

[31] Dodd, *Interpretation*, 296.

[32] Cf. Hoskyns, *Fourth Gospel*, 159–63.

that of a hidden mystery now being revealed (rather than another episode in an ongoing biography), there really is no need to look elsewhere apart from these early Christian reflections to see where the background from which John draws a term pregnant with meaning. As such, in using the term 'the Word' the Prologue already contains a reference to the death and resurrection of Jesus; the Gospel has become identified with the content of the Gospel, Jesus Christ.

We must, moreover, take this 'identification' fully. As we saw in the Introduction, Origen asserts that 'the high exaltation of the Son of Man which occurred when he glorified God in his own death consisted in the fact that he was no longer different from the Word but was the same with him'.[33] Likewise, for Gregory of Nyssa, the identification of Jesus as the Right Hand of God is wrought through the Passion. This is not, we suggested, some form of adoptionism in which a human being becomes adopted as God, but rather that, as we paraphrased it earlier, through the Passion, Jesus Christ, *as human*, becomes that which, *as God,* he always is. As Heraclitus put it, the way up and the way down are one and the same, pivoted, we would add, upon the cross. The 'two-level drama' of apocalyptic vision, heaven and earth, touch, as it were, on the cross.

Through the Passion we can no longer differentiate, except conceptually (and narratively, though in John the horizons are always blurred), between a set of human properties and a set of divine properties; as iron in the fire, it remains the same entity but is now known only by the properties of fire, while the fire in turn *is now embodied.* As such, the title 'Word' is, as we have seen in the Apocalypse and Athanasius, only predicated upon 'the one who ascended the cross'. If, then, the title 'Word' is not used for Jesus during the course of the narrative of the Gospel this is only to be expected, for he has not yet ascended the cross. That the stated aim of the Gospel is to identify Jesus as 'the Christ, the Son of God' (20:31) rather than the Word, may indeed suggest that the Prologue has reached a higher stage of reflection than the Gospel. Yet having, as human, become identified with the Word of God through the Passion, he is, eternally, the Word of God, and in turn the eternal Word of God is only known as the crucified and risen Christ. And as such, throughout the Gospel, as we have seen, this is how Jesus appears even if not called such. He is, as Käsemann puts it, a 'God striding over the earth', whose hour is not yet, but always anticipated and even realized in the blending of times and melding of horizons characteristic of John's Gospel.

Finally, the term 'with'. While it is true that πρὸς can be used with the meaning 'with', with an accusative its primary meaning conveys the sense of

[33] *Comm. Jo.* 32.325. ἡ δὲ ὑπερύψωσις τοῦ υἱοῦ τοῦ ἀνθρώπου, γενομένη αὐτῷ δοξάσαντι τὸν θεὸν ἐν τῷ ἑαυτοῦ θανάτῳ, αὕτη ἦν, τὸ μηκέτι ἕτερον αὐτὸν εἶναι τοῦ λόγου ἀλλὰ τὸν αὐτὸν αὐτῷ.

'motion or direction towards an object'.[34] As Stanley Porter observes of 1:1, 'the translation which has been institutionalized, "with", does not do full justice to this use of the preposition to mean face-to-face presence'.[35] Yet even 'face-to-face presence' doesn't quite do justice to the sense of movement-towards implied in the preposition, even when it is used of speaking 'to' someone. With the term being capable of meaning both 'towards' and 'with', exegetes have varied between these meanings. Some have argued for a more dynamic sense of 'towards' so as to provide an inclusio with 1:18, the only-begotten God who is 'in [εἰς] the bosom of the Father'.[36] Others have argued that in Hellenistic Greek there was a general weakening of the distinction between prepositions of motion and localization, so that a simple 'with' is sufficient.[37] A third approach, noted by Jan G. van der Watt, is that of comparative linguistics, either assuming the influence of Aramaic on John,[38] or through calculating the usage of the word on a broader canvas, though, as van der Watt notes, this 'raises the question as to what the influence of the broader context is on the meaning of the word', in particular in 1:1.[39] A more immediate context for understanding the semantic import of the preposition is of course the Gospel of John, of which this text is, in some sense at least, a Prologue. As McHugh notes, 'no other text of John uses πρὸς with the accusative to denote proximity'; he could easily have used παρά and μετά, as do the Wisdom texts, to convey that meaning (as does John in 8:38 παρὰ τῷ πατρί), and, moreover, '1 John uses πρὸς with the accusative to denote orientation towards'.[40] If we hear 1:1b not simply as a statement about a 'pre-incarnate' Word waiting with God, but as speaking of Jesus Christ, the Word of God, the import of the directionality of the preposition becomes evident. At least from the second chapter of the Gospel, Jesus is on the move, drawing ever closer to his final hour in Jerusalem. More specifically, during his farewell discourse to his disciples, after opening with the words 'I am the way and the truth and the life; no one comes to the Father [πρὸς τὸν πατέρα] but by

[34] LSJ s.v.

[35] Stanley Porter, *Idioms of the Greek New Testament*, 2nd edn (Sheffield: Sheffield Academic Press, 1995), 173. See also Jan G. van der Watt, 'John 1:1—A "Riddle"? Grammar and Syntax Considered', in Van Der Watt, et al., eds, *Prologue*, 57–78, esp. 63 n.31, detailing the overwhelming use in John of the preposition in the sense of towards somebody (59×), saying something to someone (20×), against the nine other usages, among which he includes 1:1 and 2.

[36] Cf. Ignace de la Potterie, 'L'emploi dynamic de εἰς dans saint Jean et ses incidences théologiques', *Bibl.* 43 (1962), 366–87.

[37] Cf. Brown, *John*, 2, 4–5.

[38] As Barrett, *John*, 129–30.

[39] Cf. van der Watt, 'John 1:1', 67, who notes the study of Caragounis examining the 400,000 uses of the preposition from the beginning to the sixteenth century. The study referred to is in J. G. van der Watt and C. Caragounis, 'The Grammar of John 1:1', *Filologia Neotestamentaria* 22 (2009), 1–52 (this is an online journal, in which it appears as 21 (2008), 91–138: <https://www.bsw.org/filologia-neotestamentaria/vol-21-2008/a-grammatical-analysis-of-john-1-1/525/> accessed 13 February 2017).

[40] McHugh, *John 1–4*, 9.

me' (14:6), Jesus says of himself four times that he is going 'to the Father' (πρὸς 14:12, 28; 16:10, 28), once that he is going 'to' the one that sent him (16:5), and the phrase 'to the Father' is repeated one more time by the perplexed disciples (16:17). This haunting refrain characterizes Jesus on the way to the cross and to the Father, but is not understood by the disciples; Jesus will depart from this world and go to the Father, but the disciples' sorrow at their apparent loss will turn to joy, when 'a human being is born into this world' (16:21). If readers of the Prologue, admittedly ones who know the Gospel, are to hear any further resonances in the 'towards' of 1:1, it is surely this; this, at least, is the dominant way in which the preposition is used by John with respect to Jesus being 'towards God'. That in the farewell discourse he speaks not of God but his Father befits the narrative, with the Son addressing his Father, rather than the abstract noun Word which is more closely allied with God.

The lack of an article in the third clause has been sufficiently commented on by others; a predicative noun placed before the verb generally lacks the article, yet still carries the full force of a definite noun.[41] The affirmation of the last clause anticipates the confession, made by Thomas, at the end of the Gospel: 'My Lord and my God' (20:28, ὁ θεός μου). This is the most emphatic scriptural statement attributing to Jesus the full sense of the word 'God', explicitly with an article.

John 1:1 thus consists of three short affirmations, which also affirm, as noted since the time of Chrysostom, existence, relationship, and predication.[42] They are coordinated by a simple 'and', and each use the same verb, the imperfect of 'to be', ἦν. The verb, 'to be' and its tense contrasts with the verb, 'to become', and with the aorist tense of 1:3 and 6, which refers to that which has happened, and finished, in the past. The imperfect conveys a sense of continuity, and in this case it continues into the present, and indeed is an eternal affirmation.[43] As Chrysostom puts it, 'this first "was" applied to "the Word" is only indicative of his eternal existence', or as Brown suggests, '"The Word was" is akin to the "I AM" statements of Jesus in the Gospel proper'.[44] The identification manifest on the cross, that Jesus is the Word of God, reigning with authority from his throne, although *in time* it began in the past, it yet holds eternally: it is this one whom Moses and all the prophets spoke about and whom Isaiah saw.[45] The 'was' in 1:1a does not refer to a prior

[41] See van der Watt, 'John 1:1', 68–77 for full discussion.

[42] Cf. John Chrysostom, *Hom. Jo.* 3 (PG 59.40).

[43] In terms of verbal aspect, as Porter, *Idioms*, 21, puts it: the '*imperfective aspect is the meaning of the present tense, including the so-called imperfect form* (augmented present form with secondary endings): *the action is conceived of by the language user as being in progress*'. Italics original.

[44] Chrysostom, *Hom. Jo.* 3 (PG 59.40; see also 42); Brown, *John*, 1.4.

[45] See the comments of McCabe ('Involvement', 50), quoted fully and discussed above in the Introduction: 'Moses could certainly have said, "It is true now that the Son of God exists",

temporal period in which the Word was waiting, as it were, for an unspecified length of time before becoming incarnate. Although in the imperfect tense, the full force of 1:1 can only be captured by including the present, if not simply translating it as a present.[46] Given all we have seen, then, the first verse of the Prologue is best rendered thus:

In first place was [and is the crucified Jesus,] the Word,
and the Word was [and is going] towards God,
and the Word was [and is] God.

As such, this verse is nothing other than a summary of the whole Gospel: that Jesus is in first place on the cross, as the head of the body, as the king in authority upon his throne, and as the source and fulfilment of all things; he is going, through the cross, to the God and Father; and, as the crucified and ascended one, he is confessed as God. What better summary of the whole Gospel could one have? It fulfils the most basic theme of Christian theology that, as Käsemann puts it, is 'the hope of the manifestation of the Son of Man on his way to enthronement . . . which sprang from the Easter experience and determined the Easter faith'.[47]

JOHN 1:2–5

The next verse, or cluster of verses, to consider is 1:2–5, but especially 1:3. This section begins with an emphatic resumptive pronoun, making clear about whom it is that is being spoken of—that is, the one described in 1:1—in what follows:

[2] οὗτος ἦν ἐν ἀρχῇ πρὸς τὸν θεόν.
[3] πάντα δι' αὐτοῦ ἐγένετο, καὶ χωρὶς αὐτοῦ ἐγένετο οὐδὲ ἕν.
ὃ γέγονεν [4] ἐν αὐτῷ ζωὴ ἦν, καὶ ἡ ζωὴ ἦν τὸ φῶς τῶν ἀνθρώπων:
[5] καὶ τὸ φῶς ἐν τῇ σκοτίᾳ φαίνει, καὶ ἡ σκοτία αὐτὸ οὐ κατέλαβεν.

(RSV)

but he could not have truly said "The Son of God exists now". *That* proposition, which attributes *temporal* existence ("now") to the Son of God, is the one which became true when Jesus was conceived in the womb of Mary. The simple truth is that apart from the Incarnation the Son of God exists in no time at all, at now "now", but in eternity, in which he acts upon all time but is not himself "measured by it", as Aquinas would say. "Before Abraham was, I am"'. Italics original.

46 That John can use the imperfect with a present sense is shown by 11:8, νῦν ἐζήτουν σε λιθάσαι οἱ Ἰουδαῖοι, translated by the RSV as 'the Jews were but now seeking to stone you'. As Porter points out (*Idioms*, 35), 'the adverb is to be taken seriously', and so he translates as, 'the Jews are now seeking to stone you'.

47 Käsemann, 'Beginnings', 107.

[2] He was in the beginning with God;
[3] all things were made through him and without him was not anything made. That which has been made [4] in him was life, and the life was the light of human beings.
[5] The light shines in the darkness and the darkness has not overcome it.

That the last two words of 1:3 are to be taken with the following sentence is the reading of the overwhelming majority of early witnesses, and is the reading adopted by the UBS and NA; it is given as an alternative in the RSV.[48] These verses begin with a reaffirmation of 1:1, 'This one' (not merely 'he') is in the beginning towards God, with all that we have seen this entail.[49]

Of most interest is 1:3. That Christ was active in the creation of the universe at the beginning is asserted elsewhere in the New Testament, most clearly in what is sometimes called 'the Christ hymn' of Colossians (1:13–20), about the one who 'has delivered us from the dominion of darkness' and 'reconciled to himself all things, whether on earth or in heaven, making peace by the blood of his cross'.[50] Of this one it is said that 'in him all things were created... all things were created through him and for him' (Col. 1:16, *ἐν αὐτῷ ἐκτίσθη τὰ πάντα ... τὰ πάντα δι'αὐτοῦ καὶ εἰς αὐτὸν ἔκτισται*), such that he is 'the head of the body, the church; he is the beginning' and is so as 'the firstborn of the dead' (Col. 1:18: *αὐτος ἐστιν ἡ κεφαλή τοῦ σώματος τῆς ἐκκλησίας· ὅς ἐστιν ἀρχή, πρωτότοκος ἐκ τῶν νεκρῶν*).[51] In John 1:3, however, the verb used is not *κτίζω* (to 'create') but *γίνομαι* ('to come to pass', 'to happen'). Moreover, John does not use the word *πάντα* with an article, as does Col. 1:16, which would be the standard way of speaking about the universe, but rather without an article, meaning more simply 'everything'. Picking up on these observations as made by T. Evan Pollard, then further developed by Paul Lamarche, Ashton has made a strong case that 1:3 is not about the creation of the universe as we tend to think, but is rather speaking in another key or register.[52]

[48] Cf. Kurt Aland, 'Eine Untersuchung zu Joh. 1.3–4: Über die Bedeutung eines Punktes', *ZNW* 59 (1968): 174–209; Hartwig Thyen, ''O *γέγονεν*: Satzende von 1,3 oder Satzeröffnung von 1,4?', in Thyen, *Studien zum Corpus Johanneum*, WUNT 214 (Tübingen: Mohr Siebeck, 2007), 411–17.

[49] Tom Thatcher, 'The Riddle of John the Baptist and the Genesis of the Prologue: John 1.1–18 in Oral/Aural Media Culture', in A. Le Donne and T. Thatcher, eds, *The Fourth Gospel in the First-Century Media Culture*, LNTS 426 (London: T & T Clark, 2011), 29–48, at 32, would take the *οὗτος* as harkening back to *ὁ λόγος* at the end of v. 1, so continuing the 'stair-case' parallelism of the first verse, and making 1:1–5 a single block.

[50] Cf. Behr, 'Colossians 1:13–20: A Chiastic Reading', *SVTQ* 40.4 (1996), 247–65.

[51] C.F. Burney, 'Christ as the *APXH* of Creation', *JTS* 27 (1925), 160–77 suggests that the various prepositions used in Col. 1:16, (in, by, for), followed by the various affirmations made in Col. 1:17–18 (Christ is the beginning, sum-total, head, firstborn) are based upon a Rabbinic exegesis of the first two words of Genesis (*b-re'shit*) through the prism of Prov. 8:22.

[52] Pollard, 'Cosmology and the Prologue'; Lamarche, 'Prologue'; and John Ashton, 'The Transformation of Wisdom', *NTS* 32 (1986), 161–86, reprinted in Ashton, *Studying John:*

Ashton notes that whereas the Latin translation, captivated by the allusion to Genesis two verses earlier, rendered 1:3 inaccurately as *omnia per ipsum facta sunt*, 'everything was made by him' (followed by our English translations), the old Syriac translation renders the verse: 'everything came to pass in him and apart from him not even one thing came to pass'.[53] In fact, as McHugh points out, this is how John uses the verb γίνεσθαι not only in the three instances in this verse, but whenever the verb is used in the Gospel with an indeterminate and neuter subject: 'Whenever this construction is found elsewhere in John, γίνεσθαι always applies to an historical *event*, which either *happened, took place* (1:28; 3:9; 13:19 [x2]; 14:22, 29 [x2]; 19:36) or which *will come to pass* (15:7)'.[54] As Ashton further notes, Latin, not having a definite article, cannot differentiate between the two uses of the term πάντα, and, moreover, when Ptolemy wanted to read the text cosmologically, he inserted a definite article into his quotation of the verse.[55] Following the lead of Pollard and Lamarche, Ashton points to a passage from 'The Community Rule' from Qumran, as an important parallel:

> All things came to pass by his knowledge;
> He establishes all things by his design
> And without him nothing is done.[56]

The parallel is clear, and, as Pollard pointed out, the context of this verse 'has no reference to creation, but rather to the doctrine prominent in the Scrolls, that God is in control of everything, and particularly of human destiny'.[57] Lamarche adds a further text to illumine the meaning of 1:3, and that is a passage from the Gospel of Truth, which itself is 'a paraphrase of the Prologue': 'Nothing happens without him nor does anything happen without the will of the Father' (*Gospel of Truth*, 37.21). On the basis of these texts (together with Apoc. 1:19 and Judith 9:5–6), Lamarche concludes, 'v.3 is essentially concerned with the realization of the divine plan'.[58] Building upon these insights, Ashton draws in another text:

Approaches to the Fourth Gospel (Oxford: Oxford University Press, 1994), 18–21; Ashton, *The Gospel of John and Christian Origins*, 145–55; and Ashton, 'Really a Prologue?', 41–2. Ashton's first essay on the topic was treated briefly and critically by Peter M. Phillips, *The Prologue of the Fourth Gospel: A Sequential Reading*, LNTS 294 (London: T & T Clark, 2006), and responded to by Ashton in his subsequent essays. See also E. L. Miller, *Salvation History in the Prologue of John: The Significance of John 1:3/4*, SupNovT 60 (Leiden: Brill, 1989).

[53] *Evangelion da-Mepharreshe: The Curetonian Version of the Four Gospels, with the Readings of the Sinai Palimpsest and the Early Syriac Patristic Evidence*, ed. Francis Crawford Burkitt (Cambridge: Cambridge University Press, 1904), 1:423. See, more recently, George Anton Kiraz and Andreas Juckel, eds, *Comparative Edition of the Syriac Gospels Aligning the Old Syriac (Sinaiticus, Curetonianus), Peshitta and Harklean Versions*, vol. 4, *John*, 2nd edn (Piscataway, NJ: Gorgias Press, 2002).

[54] McHugh, *John 1–4*, 13, italics original.

[55] Ashton, 'Really a Prologue?', 41; Ptolemy, *Letter to Flora*, in Epiphanius, *Pan.* 33.3.6.

[56] 1QS 11:11, translated by Vermes, *Dead Sea Scrolls*, 116.

[57] Pollard, 'Cosmology', 152.

[58] Lamarche, 'Prologue', 52.

> From the God of knowledge comes all that is and shall be. Before ever they existed he established their whole design, and when, as ordained for them, they come into being, it is in accord with his glorious design and they accomplish their task without change.[59]

It is this 'glorious design' belonging to 'the God of knowledge of all that is and shall be' that, says Ashton, '*is precisely the concern of the author of the Logos hymn—not creation, but the plan of God*'.[60] And he continues: 'What astounded the author of the hymn was his vision of wisdom in the flesh, whereas what preoccupied the evangelist was such an overwhelming sense of the divine glory of the man whose story he was telling that it led him to play down the purely human traits found in abundance in the other three gospels'.

Whether this really is the right characterization of the relationship between John and the Synoptics is open to question, for after all, it is only in John that Jesus has 'friends' and 'cries', two of the most human of traits. Might, however, the insights gained so far, that 1:3 is not about creation and that the verb should be translated as does the old Syriac—everything came to pass (or happened) through him and apart from him not one thing came to pass (or happened)—point to a difference between John and the Synoptics that we have had occasion to observe at various points throughout this study? That is, a difference we have characterized earlier in terms of the line from the Anaphora of John Chrysostom: 'in the night in which he was given up, no, rather, gave himself up for the life of the world'. In the Synoptics, it seems to the unenlightened disciples that Christ is forcibly put to death, so that they abandon and deny the crucified one. It is not even enough to see the risen Christ, for in each encounter it is only after a turning point that they recognize him. This is most clear in Luke 24: only after he opens the Scriptures to show that Moses and all the prophets spoke about how the Son of Man must suffer to enter into his glory, are their eyes are opened in the breaking of bread so that they recognize him, only to have him immediately disappear from sight (we will discuss the issue of phenomenality in Part III). In contrast, in the Gospel of John—where the disciples already from the beginning of the narrative identify Jesus as the one spoken of by Moses and the prophets (cf. 1:45), though still do not understand the full import of this and, apart from John, abandon Christ at the crucifixion—there is no doubt that Christ is always in control: the hour comes when he is ready and it is he who lays down his life in an act of love. As 1:3 says, of 'this one', everything that happened came to pass through him, and nothing happened without him.[61]

[59] 1QS 3.15–17; Vermes, *Dead Sea Scrolls*, 101. Cf. Ashton, *Gospel of John and Christian Origins*, 150–2, drawing upon Carol A. Newsom, *The Self as Symbolic Space: Constructing Identity and Community at Qumran*, Studies on the Texts of the Desert of Judah 52 (Leiden: Brill, 2004), 84–6.

[60] Ashton, 'Really a Prologue?', 42; italics original.

[61] Cf. McHugh, *John 1–4*, 13: 'Verse 3, so interpreted, would then mean that *every single event* in the story of salvation which is about to unfold *takes place* only *through* the Logos, and that *not one thing happens independently of* him'. Italics original.

The remaining two words of 1:3 and 1:4, read together, follow on by explaining what it was that came to pass: 'What came to pass in him was [and is] life'.[62] The life that Christ offers, as we saw in Chapter 4, is the life that comes through death, the life lived by the risen Christ and, following him, by the martyrs, 'living human beings, the glory of God'. And as we also suggested in Chapter 4, this is indeed the glorious plan, and project, of God: 'Let us make a human being in our image' (Gen. 1:26), completed upon the cross with Christ's words, 'it is finished', brought to perfection (19:30). This life is the light of human beings; it is, as we have seen, when he attains to the light that Ignatius will become a living human being (*Rom.* 6). It is this light, that of the life preached in the gospel, which shines in darkness but is not overcome by it. 1:2–5 is also, just as 1:1 is, a summary of the whole Gospel.[63]

JOHN 1:6–18

The next block of text opens with John, the human being sent from God to bear witness/martyrdom (1:6). The most important verse here, which shapes how we read this block and so with which we will begin, is of course 1:14:

> *Καὶ ὁ λόγος σὰρξ ἐγένετο καὶ ἐσκήνωσεν ἐν ἡμῖν, καὶ ἐθεασάμεθα τὴν δόξαν αὐτοῦ, δόξαν ὡς μονογενοῦς παρὰ πατρός, πλήρης χάριτος καὶ ἀληθείας.*
>
> (RSV) And the Word became flesh and dwelt among us, full of grace and truth; we have beheld his glory, glory as of the only Son[64] from the Father.

This is, of course, along with 1:1, the verse that has reverberated most profoundly and forcefully across all later theological reflection and, indeed, one might say, the whole of Western culture. It is the verse that is seen as the 'pivot' of the Prologue, the moment at which the pre-incarnate eternal Word

[62] That this verse, taken with this punctuation, must be translated this way, see McHugh, *John 1–4*, 14–15, 104–7.

[63] De Boer, 'Original Prologue', 466, on 1:3–4: 'The language of creation from Genesis is being used to present the salvific work of Christ as a new creation'. Whether the language of 'new creation' is appropriate for John is debatable: we have argued that Christ's words from the cross, 'it is finished', refer back to the announcement of God's 'project' given in the opening verses of Scripture: 'Let us make a human being in our image', a 'completion' also aimed at by Ignatius in the passage referred to above; it is, in fact, the exalted Christ who is 'the *ἀρχή* of the creation of God' (Apoc. 3:14).

[64] Although I have retained the rendering of most modern translations (as the burden of my analysis is not on this point), it should be noted that *μονογενοῦς* simply means 'unique one'; while 'Son' is not explicitly here, a link and contrast is being made with the 'children of God' in the 1:12. For full review, see the comments of McHugh, *John 1–4*, 45–6, 58–9, 97–103, though his conclusion (103)—that in 1:14 the term only means '*quite unique, in a class of his own*. This is the starting-point of the revelation in the Fourth Gospel, from which the nature of the Father and of Jesus' Sonship is gradually disclosed'—would need to be modified if my reading of 1:14 is upheld.

becomes flesh as Jesus Christ, enabling us to see his glory. However, in the light of what we have argued above, what does it mean if we read it as saying: Jesus became flesh?

Commentators typically take the word 'flesh' as referring to 'the whole man',[65] arguing that the word 'flesh', rather than 'human', is used so as to emphasize weakness, frailty, 'that which is earth-bound (3:6), transient and perishable (6:63), the typically human mode of being, as it were, in contrast to all that is divine and spiritual'.[66] However, as the Prologue is clearly meant to relate, in some way at least, to the Gospel, we should consider more carefully how the term 'flesh' is used in the Gospel. In 3:6 ('that which is born of flesh is flesh', see also 1:13), 8:15 ('you judge according to the flesh'), 17:2 (the Father gave the Son 'power over all flesh'), and 6:63 ('the Spirit gives life, the flesh is of no avail'), the word 'flesh' is indeed used in a way that connotes the world, that which appears, that which is weak. However, there is another and startling way in which the term is used, and that is in John 6, the latter half of which is in fact nothing short of a meditation on the flesh of Jesus by Jesus himself, and which we examined fully in Chapter 3. Most striking are the following verses:

> I am the living bread which descended [καταβάς] from heaven; if anyone eats of this bread, he will live for ever; and the bread which I shall give [δώσω] for the life of the world is my flesh. . . . Truly, truly I say to you, unless you eat the flesh of the Son of Man and drink his blood, you have no life in you; he who eats my flesh and drinks my blood has eternal life and I will raise him up at the last day. For my flesh is true food and my blood is true drink. He who eats my flesh and drinks my blood dwells in me and I in him. (6:51–6)

The change, in 6:51, from the aorist participle used to describe the descent of the living bread (referring back to bread from heaven given in the miraculous feeding earlier in John 6) to the *future* tense for the bread which Jesus *will give as his flesh* indicates that this 'flesh' is something that Jesus must *become*. Jesus is not inviting his hearers to eat his flesh and drink his blood simply as such (an act of cannibalism only available to those then and there), but that which he will give, through the Passion, as the living bread which descends from heaven, the flesh and blood of the Son of Man, whom he already (and always) is in the blending of time and merging of horizons. His ascent of the cross to become this flesh is paralleled by the descent of the living bread, the Son of Man descending from heaven to offer us his flesh and blood. As we saw in Chapter 3, the word 'flesh' continues to be used in this way by Ignatius in his opposition to docetism, not so much an 'incarnational' doceticism, but rather that of those who 'do not confess that the Eucharist is the flesh of our Saviour Jesus Christ who suffered for our sins and whom the Father raised up' (*Smyrn.* 7.1). And, as we also saw, Origen brings John 1:14 together with

[65] Brown, *John*, 1, 13. [66] Schnackenburg, *John*, 1, 267.

John 6 in exactly this way. After quoting Christ's words extensively (6:26–9, 32–5, 51, 53–7), he draws various words from these passages together with John 1:14 and concludes with John 6:58:

> This is the 'true food', the 'flesh' of Christ, which being 'Word' has become 'flesh', in accordance with the statement, 'and the Word became flesh'. When we 'eat' and 'drink' him, he also 'dwelt in us', and when he is distributed, there is fulfilled the saying 'we beheld his glory'. 'This is the bread which came down from heaven, not like that which the ancestors ate, and died. Whoever eats this bread shall live for ever'.[67]

If 'the Spirit gives life, the flesh is of no avail' (6:63), it is nevertheless the flesh that is in fact vivified by the Spirit, to become, and be given as, the life-giving flesh of Christ. This is a theme that resounds throughout the later tradition, perhaps nowhere more clearly and emphatically than Cyril of Alexandria: 'Whoever does not acknowledge the Lord's flesh to be vitalizing and to belong to the very Word of God the Father, but says it belongs to somebody different joined to him by way of rank or merely possessing divine indwelling, instead of being vitalizing, as we said, because it has come to belong to the Word who has power to vivify everything, shall be anathema'.[68] Cyril also brings together John 1:14 and chapter 6. Commenting on 6:54, he says: 'Here too we should especially admire the holy Evangelist for crying out explicitly, "And the Word became flesh." He did not hesitate to say, not that he became "in flesh" but that he became "flesh", in order to show the unity.... Therefore whoever eats of the holy flesh of Christ has eternal life because the flesh has in itself the Word, who is life by nature. For this reason he says, "I will raise them up on the last day"'.[69]

It is through the Passion that Jesus becomes the flesh (and blood) that he offers to us as food and drink so that the one partaking of them 'dwells in me and I in him' (6:56). This consequence is, of course, the next clause in 1:14, though phrased in the language of tabernacling drawn from Sirach 24 and the texts pertaining to 'the tent of meeting' (or 'tent of witness', *ἡ σκηνὴ τοῦ μαρτυρίου*, as it is regularly translated in the LXX) in which the glory of the Lord dwells: 'the Word became flesh and tabernacled in us' (*ἐν ἡμῖν*, 'in' not 'among'). The consequence of this is that 'we have seen his glory', which, in the Gospel of John, is again pivoted upon the cross. And finally, the word 'and' at

[67] Origen, *Or.* 27.4 (Koetschau 365.22–6): *αὕτη δέ ἐστιν ἡ «ἀληθὴς βρῶσις,» «σὰρξ» Χριστοῦ, ἥτις «λόγος» οὖσα γέγονε «σὰρξ» κατὰ τὸ εἰρημένον «καὶ ὁ λόγος σὰρξ ἐγένετο.» ὅτε δὲ <φάγοιμεν καὶ> πίοιμεν αὐτὸν, «καὶ ἐσκήνωσεν ἐν ἡμῖν»· ἐπὰν δὲ ἀναδιδῶται, πληροῦται το «ἐθεασάμεωα τὴν δόξαν αὐτοῦ.»* My translation.

[68] Cyril of Alexandria, 'Third Letter to Nestorius', 12.11 (eleventh anathema). See Henry Chadwick, 'Eucharist and Christology in the Nestorian Controversy', *JTS* ns 2 (1951), 145–64, and Gebremedhin, *Life-Giving Blessing.*

[69] Cyril of Alexandria, *Com. Jo.* 4.2 (ed. Pusey, vol. 1, 532.18–21, 533.1–4).

the beginning of 1:14 ties this verse back to the preceding sentence, which spoke about how those who receive him are born of God to become children of God.[70] Unless there is good reason not to, the most obvious way of taking 1:12–13 and 14 are as a reference to baptism and Eucharist, both of which are predicated upon the crucifixion, with the blood and water flowing from the side of Christ (19:34), and are lived out in martyrdom, taking up the cross to become living human beings, who are, as Irenaeus put it, 'the glory of God' (*haer.* 4.20.7). Jesus Christ is 'the one coming [ὁ ἐλθὼν] by water and blood' (1 John 5:6), tabernacling in those who receive him, such that they put on his identity and become his body.[71]

A final ambiguity in this block of text upon which we might be able to offer new light is 1:9, 'The true light that enlightens every human being was coming into the world' (RSV), and specifically the question of whether the participial phrase, 'coming into the world' (ἐρχόμενον εἰς τὸν κόσμον), should apply to the light or the human being. As Brown notes, the early versions, the Greek Fathers, and many modern scholars take the phrase as referring to human beings. However, he argues, 'it creates a redundancy, for in rabbinic literature "they who come into the world" is an expression for men'. On the other hand, he points out, the Sahidic version, the Latin Fathers, and 'most modern commentators' take the phrase to refer to the light, as fitting the context better, where the stress is on the Word, the light, and as paralleling 3:19, 'the light has come into the world'.[72] However, given what else we have seen about what it means to be a human being and, especially, regarding the whole movement of the Gospel from Cana to the cross, connected by Jesus' words about the suffering woman whose travail is turned into joy when 'a human being is born into the world' (16:21), it would seem better to stay with the early versions and the Greek Fathers, but with the clarification that this is not just an enlightening of every male and female born into the world, but rather the enlightening of those who follow Christ to become a human being. 'When I shall have reached the light, then I will be a human being', as Ignatius put it, speaking about his impending martyrdom (*Rom.* 6).

The following verse, 'He was in the world, and the world came to be through him, yet the world knew him not' (1:10) is striking in its threefold use of the term 'world', each accompanied by a different verb. The word κόσμος primarily means 'order' or 'adornment', but came to be extended to the inhabited world and to universe as a whole.[73] In the New Testament, outside of John, it tends to mean simply 'the world', while in John, who uses the term far more

[70] On the singular of 'was born' of 1:12, which is found in many early Fathers, but in no manuscripts, see McHugh, *John 1:1–4*, 107–10; it may be, as Brown, *John*, 12, suggests an adaptation of John to the Virgin birth found in Matthew and Luke.

[71] Cf. de Jonge, *Jesus: Stranger from Heaven and Son of God*, 205: 'That Jesus came "in the flesh" means that he died on the cross'.

[72] Brown, *John*, 1.9–10.

[73] For the history of its usage, see McHugh, *John 1–4*, 34–40.

extensively than any other, it is more subtle and fluid: though made by him, it did not know him (1:10); although it hates Christ and his disciples (15:18), the world is nevertheless the object of God's love and the salvific activity of Christ (3:16–17; 12:47), a salvation which is effected by passing over from the world to the Father (13:1). The emphasis in 1:10–11 is that although Christ was in the world, which had come into being by him, and had come to 'his own', nevertheless the world and 'his own' resolutely refused to know him or receive him. John is clearly sketching out here the rejection of Christ in the broadest possible scope, so as to draw out the universal scope of Christ's work of salvation.[74] As John McHugh comments:

> When the central human figure in the story is a God crucified by those whom he created, the κόσμος (in the threefold sense of the Empire, the Earth, and the Universe) is the only theatre large enough to accomodate the tragedy, and the audience must be men and women of all races, of every place and of every time. The κόσμος did not know him, and the κόσμος did not welcome him.[75]

The abandonment of God by the entire world, as we saw in Chapter 3, in the cosmic trial that is narrated throughout the Gospel of John and which climaxes in the trial scene before Pilate when Jesus is condemned to death (18:28–19:16), nevertheless turns out to be the judgement of the world as Christ is lifted up upon the cross (cf. 12:31–3). In turn, the only suitable conclusion to the dramatic assertion in 1:10–11, is what is given, in 1:12–14, to those who instead receive him, and that is not an 'incarnation' eclipsing the Passion, or even as the starting point for the movement to the cross, but rather an 'incarnation', as we have argued, effected through baptism and Eucharist, with all that this entails as we have seen in previous chapters when examining John 6 and martyrdom, that is, becoming an enlightened human being (echoing 1:9), or, as Irenaeus puts it, 'the glory of God' that is 'a living human being' (*haer.* 4.20.7).

The final block of text begins with 1:15 which, returning to John the Baptist, is almost invariably seen as an insertion into an original hymn, breaking up

[74] It should be noted that the assertion that the world 'came to be' (ἐγένετο) through Christ occurs in the context of its rejection of him. It is similarly in the context of an 'apology for the cross' that Athanasius (*Gent.* 41) develops, for the first really clear time, the idea of creation *ex nihilo*. Cf. Behr, *Nicene Faith*, 1.179–83. In a very different context, Simone Pétrement makes the interesting suggestion that it is, in fact, the cross that provides the stimulus for this teaching about creation: 'In the Old Testament the world was so narrowly and directly dependent upon God that God himself... was in turn almost tied up with and chained to the world.... The image of the cross is an image that liberates.... *The cross separates God from the world.* If it does not separate him absolutely, at least it puts him at a very great distance. It puts him much further away than the distinction between Creator and creature could do.... It is indeed, as Paul sees, something that is profoundly new, "a scandal to the Jews and folly to the Greeks"'. *A Separate God: The Christian Origins of Gnosticism*, trans. C. Harrison (New York: HarperCollins, 1990), 37, italics original.

[75] McHugh, *John 1–4*, 39.

the perceived continuity between 1:14 and 1:16. But, again, the idea that these verses (1:14, 16) are continuous are based on the assumption about what the 'Logos hymn' is saying. The first comment we have on 1:15–18, from Origen, takes it as all being spoken by John the Baptist himself, against those who think that 1:16–18 are from John the apostle.[76] By taking 1:15–18 as a complete unit, spoken by the Baptist, we have an *inclusio* with 1:6–7, which spoke about the human being, John the Baptist, sent to bear witness; indeed 1:15–18 is his witness. The narrative of the Gospel proper begins, in the following verse, with this witness: 'And this is the witness of John' (1:19). As such, in 1:6–18 we now have a third summary of the Gospel, structured this time as a chiasm, with the world's rejection of Christ at the crucifixion as its centre and climax, followed by the baptism and the Eucharist now offered to those who receive him and follow him on his path of *martyria*, so becoming a human being enlightened by the light that is Christ.

In the light of this investigation, then, it would seem that what we have in the Prologue are three summaries of the Gospel, starting in the most lapidary, concise, and poetic or hymnic form, in three strophes of one verse, and then becoming ever fuller in the following two summaries. As proposed, the Prologue looks like this:

[1] In first place was [and is the crucified Jesus,] the Word,
and the Word was [and is going] towards God,
and the Word was [and is] God.

[2] This one was [and is] in first place towards God;
[3] all things came to pass through him, and without him nothing came to pass.
What came to pass [4] in him was life, and the life was the light of human beings.
[5] The light shines in the darkness and the darkness has not overcome it.

a [6] There was a human being sent from God, whose name was John. [7] He came for testimony [martyrdom], to bear witness to the light, that all might believe through him. [8] That one was not the light, but came to bear witness to the light.

b [9] That was the true light that enlightens every human being coming into the world.

c [10] He was in the world, and the world came to be through him, yet the world knew him not. [11] He came to his own, and his own received him not.

b′ [12] But to all who received him, who believed in his name, he gave power to become children of God; [13] who were born, not of blood

[76] Origen, *Comm. Jo.* 2.213; Origen makes the same point in *Comm. Jo.* 6.13–14, though there it is only 1:17–18 that is in view, as having been asserted by Heracleon to have come from the Baptist.

nor of the will of the flesh nor of the will of man, but of God. [14] And the Word [Jesus] became flesh and tabernacled in us, full of grace and truth; we have beheld his glory, glory as of the only Son from the Father.

a′ [15] John bore witness to him, and cried, 'This was he of whom I said, "He who comes after me ranks before me, for he was before me". [16] And from his fullness have we all received, grace upon grace. [17] For the law was given through Moses; grace and truth came through Jesus Christ. [18] No one has ever seen God; the only-begotten God, who is in the bosom of the Father, he has made him known'.

As three summaries of the paschal gospel, the Prologue is best designated as a paschal hymn, as indeed it is still heard in the paschal liturgy as celebrated by Eastern Orthodox Christians, followed by the continuous reading of the Gospel of John throughout Pascha-tide, the only season in which it is regularly read.[77]

[77] It should be noted that the lectionary specifies 1:1–17. This is already the case in the Armenian lectionary translated from a Greek text reflecting the practice in Jerusalem at the beginning of the fifth century. See Athanase Renoux, *Le codex arménien Jérusalem 121*, PO 35.1 (Introduction), 36.1 (text and translation) (Turnout: Brepols, 1969, 1971); for the rubric see PO 36.1, p. 87. Williams, 'Not the Prologue of John', 379, suggests that the division of the text at 1:17, which Origen attributes to Heracleon (see note 76 above), reflects a more widespread view, 'a fact which may explain why second-century sources such as Tatian's *Diatessaron* and then the subsequent Greek lectionary tradition put a major division between 1, 17 and 1, 18 not between 1, 18 and 19' and affected the Greek exegetical tradition thereafter.

Part III

The Phenomenology of Life in Flesh

6

Johannine Arch-Intelligibility

Reading the Gospel of John in company with Ignatius and those whom Lightfoot calls his 'later school', that is, Melito, Irenaeus, and Polycrates, in the context of the paschal tradition that the latter traces back uniquely to John, the high priest of the paschal mystery, and adding Origen to their ranks, has led to profound insights regarding the glory of God, that is, the martyr, born into life through sharing in the *pathos* of Christ to emerge as a living human being, a word of God. These themes are strikingly echoed in one of the most stimulating and provocative readings of John in modern times, one that comes not from a scriptural scholar or a historical theologian, but a French philosopher of the phenomenological tradition, Michel Henry. Having begun our study in a systematic key—problematizing the usual understanding of 'Incarnation' (as 'an episode in the biography of the Word', putting on the flesh/a body to appear in the world as a human being), by the issues raised by McCabe concerning the notion of 'pre-existence' and the intersection of time and eternity, and heeding the caution given by Skinner regarding 'the mythology of doctrines'—we now turn, after our historical and exegetical explorations, to a philosophical key, with Henry's analysis of the phenomenological structure of Christianity, as unveiled most explicitly in the Gospel of John. Because of the very different nature of Henry's discourse and mode of thinking, this chapter will be given over to expounding his thought, leaving to Chapter 7 an attempt to put this contemporary reader of John in dialogue with the other readers of John we have heard in Parts I and II. In the conclusion, we will then offer some final reflections on the nature and task of theology, so that this work, as a whole, can be considered as a prologue to the practice of theology.

It was only in the last decade of his life that Michel Henry (1922–2002) directed his attention explicitly to Christianity, writing three books that explore Christian phenomenology: first, *I Am the Truth: Towards a Philosophy of Christianity*, then several years later, during which time he read Tertullian and most importantly Irenaeus, *Incarnation: A Philosophy of Flesh*, and finally, appearing in print posthumously, *Words of Christ.*[1] Although sometimes

[1] Michel Henry, *C'est moi la vérité: Pour une philosophie du christianisme* (Paris: Seuil, 1996), ET Susan Emanuel, *I Am the Truth: Towards a Philosophy of Christianity*, Cultural Memory in

characterized as being part of a 'theological turn' in French Phenomenology, it is rather the case that Henry found in Christianity, especially as expressed by John, the paradigmatic structure of phenomenology that he had been investigating from his initial magnum opus, *The Essence of Manifestation*, through numerous other studies, on the body, Marx, psychoanalysis, Kandinsky, and in his devastating indictment of our contemporary scientific and technological culture, *Barbarism*.[2] As the title of his first work, *The Essence of Manifestation*, indicates, what is of interest to him is 'manifestation', not the various phenomena themselves and their content, which are the proper study of the appropriate sciences (chemical phenomena for chemistry, historical for history, etc.), but that which these sciences never take into account, that is, 'what makes each of them a phenomenon: the appearing in which they show themselves to us—this appearing as such'.[3] Modern phenomenology as practised rigorously by Husserl, and even as carried out by Heidegger, remained, for Henry, too captivated by phenomena, as objects that appear in the world to a subject who observes them, to have considered the fact of 'appearing' itself, that is, that which enables the phenomena to appear. As such, Henry understood his work as a radicalization or reversal of phenomenology, rather than a turn towards Christianity or the mystical. Yet, that this radicalized phenomenology should have led him to the study of Christianity is not surprising for, as he notes, the key terms of phenomenology—'givenness; showing; phenomenalization; unveiling; uncovering; appearance; manifestation; and revelation'—are also central for religion and theology.[4] As such, Henry does not present us with an account of the doctrines of Christian theology

the Present (Stanford: Stanford University Press, 2003); *Incarnation: Une philosophie de la chair* (Paris: Seuil, 2000), trans. Karl Hefty, *Incarnation: A Philosophy of Flesh*, Northwestern University Studies in Phenomenology and Existential Philosophy (Evanston IL: Northwestern University Press, 2015); *Paroles du Christ* (Paris: Seuil, 2002), trans. Christina M. Gschwandtner, *Words of Christ*, Interventions (Grand Rapids, MI: Eerdmans, 2012). I will refer to the English translations given, but occasionally note a particular French expression or turn of phrase significant for Henry. Henry uses italics and capitals frequently; in what follows I have occasionally reproduced his italicization, without specifically noting it, and generally followed his use of capitalization when discussing his work.

[2] Michel Henry, *L'essence de la manifestation* (Paris: Presses Universitaires de France, 1963; 2nd edn 1990); trans. Girard Etzkorn, *The Essence of Manifestation* (The Hague: Martinus Nijhoff, 1973); *La Barbarie* (Paris: Grasset & Fasquelle, 1987); trans. Scott Davidson, *Barbarism*, Continuum Impacts (London: Continuum, 2012). For the 'theological turn', see Dominique Janicaud, *Phenomenology and the 'Theological Turn': The French Debate*, trans. Bernard Prusak (New York: Fordham University Press, 2000), 70–103, although this was in fact written before any of Henry's trilogy appeared. See also Peter Jonkers and Ruud Welten, *God in France: Eight Contemporary French Thinkers on God*, Studies in Philosophical Theology (Leuven: Peeters, 2005), which includes a useful summary essay on Henry by Welten, 'God is Life: On Michel Henry's Arch-Christianity', ibid. 119–42, as does Christina M. Gschwandtner, *Postmodern Apologetics: Arguments for God in Contemporary Philosophy*, Perspectives in Continental Philosophy (New York: Fordham University Press, 2013), 125–42.

[3] Henry, *Incarnation*, 22. [4] *Incarnation*, 23. Cf. *I Am the Truth*, 13, 23.

or a reading of Scripture such as we might expect. Instead Henry opens up the phenomenological structure of Christianity, as given to us especially by John, manifesting Truth in the generation of Life in the Living One, incarnate in or as flesh, and the call to Life given by Christ's own words.

THE *PATHOS* OF LIFE

The title of the first book in Henry's trilogy, *I Am the Truth*, his fullest account of Christianity and its phenomenological structure, is drawn from Christ's self-description in the Gospel of John: 'I am the way and the truth and the life' (14:6). He opens this work by casting his earlier phenomenological investigations, which had been developed largely in dialogue with Husserl and Heidegger,[5] into a truly Johannine contrast between the world and its truth, on the one hand, and, on the other, the Truth that is Christ himself, in whom alone is found Life. His chief criticism of phenomenology, and in fact philosophy more generally from the ancient Greeks onwards, is that it has been exclusively focused on things that appear, phenomena, 'the totality of what lies in the light of day or can be brought to light', as Heidegger famously etymologized the word.[6] Whether an empirical event, such as the darkening sky or the smile of a child, or an a priori geometrical principle, such as all the radii of a circle being equal, these are all phenomena that appear to us and whose truth we can ascertain 'in the light of day'. Whether we naively hold (as we usually do unthinkingly) that we have direct access to the things of the world as they are in themselves, or whether in a more sophisticated fashion we recognize that they are known to us only as representations given through the intentional structure of our consciousness (which is always 'consciousness of something'), they stand before us, in the light of the world, as phenomena. The 'world' is not simply the totality of what appears, the realm of being, but rather the prior horizon of visibility, the 'outside', in which things appear.

Radically different to such phenomena, and the phenomenality by which they appear, are phenomena such as joy and pain. In this case, although we can clearly see, and empathize with, people in pain, the suffering and the pain they undergo does not itself actually 'appear' in the world; they are invisible to the world. Moreover, in such cases there is a strict identity between the

[5] For Henry's engagement with Husserl's own phenomenological texts, see especially his *Phénoménologie matérielle* (Paris: Presses Universitaires de France, 1990), ET Scott Davidson, *Material Phenomenology*, Perspectives in Continental Philosophy (New York: Fordham University Press, 2008), and also *Incarnation*, 22–92.

[6] Martin Heidegger, *Being and Time*, ET Joan Stambaugh (Albany: State University of New York Press, 2010), 27.

suffering, the *pathos*, of pain and the pain itself: suffering of pain *is* the pain.[7] It is, moreover, only through suffering pain ourselves that we know what pain is, for the pain cannot be 'seen' elsewhere; it exists nowhere else than in the *pathos* itself. Thus, invisible though it is in the world, suffering, *pathos*, possesses an identity between itself, as it is in itself, and how it appears to us, directly and immediately, not via 'the world'; it does not appear as something else, or speak to us of something other than the suffering that it is. 'Suffering experiences itself' (*La souffrance s'éprouve elle-même*), as Henry puts it, adding that: 'It is only in this way that suffering speaks to us; it speaks to us in its suffering. And what it says to us, by speaking to us in this way, is that it suffers, that it is suffering'.[8]

A phenomenon that we see in the world, however, appears in that which is external to itself. In the very act of appearing, then, it is cast outside itself into a world that is other than it and indifferent to it, for 'the fact of self-showing is as indifferent to what shows itself as is the light to what it illuminates'.[9] What it is that appears cannot be accounted for by the world or by its mode of appearing in the world: it could as well be a blue sky rather than a threatening one, the homicidal rage of a murderer rather than an innocent child, or any other geometrical principle. Everything that appears in the world is subject, in its appearing as a phenomenon, to the world and to its truth, and thus shows itself, in the world, 'as other than itself, as forsaken by it, uncovered as a this or a that, but a "that" which might be different from what is shown, a content that is contingent, abandoned to itself, lost. What is true in the world's truth in no way depends on this truth: it is not supported by it, guarded by it, loved by it, saved by it'.[10] Appearing as other than itself, the only language known in the play of appearances that constitutes the world is the lie, a word that speaks of content external to it and other than it; a word, moreover, that, unlike

[7] As Susan Emanuel observes in her 'Notes on Terminology' prefacing *I Am the Truth*, 'Michel Henry uses French *pathos* and *pathétique* in what amounts to the sense of these words' Greek roots. For *pathos*, that semantic domain extends from 'anything that befalls one' through 'what one has suffered, one's experience' (including its negative inflection in something like English 'suffering'), to 'any passive state or condition'. For this reason, she renders the word as 'pathētik'. I have instead followed Christina M. Gschwandtner (*Words of Christ*, xxx–xxxi) in rendering it '*pathos*' or '*pathos*-filled' as appropriate.

[8] *Words of Christ*, 74. The expression '*s'éprouver*', here used of suffering but frequently, as we will see, used for life, is a significant term for Henry. As Karly Hefty notes in his introduction to *Incarnation*, xvi: 'the verb *éprouver* means "to feel" or "to experience", but also "to suffer", "to sustain", "to test", "to put to the test", and even "to afflict" or "to distress". The dynamic tension between active and passive meanings is not accidental, and in Henry's construction the term is not merely reflexive, but exceedingly so, and no single English verb can do justice to the richness of the original French. Henry does not exactly mean that life is the "experience of oneself", as if a substantial self were there prior to it that it would then experience. The sense is something more like what experiencing *it*self undergoes'.

[9] *I Am the Truth*, 13. [10] Ibid. 16.

the word of suffering, is powerless to establish the reality of that about which it speaks.[11]

The production of the 'world', as the horizon of visibility, is moreover intrinsically related to time, so much so that Henry can simply identify the two: 'Time and the world are identical: they designate a single process in which the "outside" is constantly self-externalized'.[12] Time 'is' not, in the manner of phenomena appearing to us in the world, it is, rather, as a projection of a horizon in front of us, an imagined future, which arrives in a present in which we think we exist, and flows into a past into which everything that is present immediately passes away—the three intentionalities of Husserl, the temporal ek-stases analysed by Heidegger, or 'expanses of externality' as Henry calls them, that constitute the flux of this world.[13] It is, as Henry puts it, 'in the continuous passage of these three ek-stases into one another . . . that the horizon of visibility is formed, of which the world's appearing is composed'.[14] But as Henry points out, '*In time there is no present, there never has been one, and there never will be one*. In time, things come into appearance, but since this coming-into-appearance consists in coming-outside, things do not arise into the light of this "outside" except as torn from themselves, emptied of their being, already dead'.[15]

That the phenomena of the world are dead is connected to the fact that life does not and cannot appear at all in the world: 'life never shows itself in it . . . *we see living beings but never their life*'.[16] If we try to examine the phenomenon of life, we end up scrutinizing phenomena that do appear: amino acids, chains of neurons, physical particles, and so on. And so, as François Jacob, the French biologist frequently quoted by Henry, put it, 'Biologists no longer study life today'.[17] It is not that biologists do not know what life is. As Henry colourfully remarks: 'they know it like everyone else, since they, too, live and love life, wine, and the opposite sex; they get jobs, have careers, and themselves experience the joy of new departures, chance encounters, the boredom of administrative tasks, the anguish of death'.[18] But as with life itself, all these modalities of the *pathos* of

[11] *Words of Christ*, 75; see also, *I Am the Truth*, 218–20; *Incarnation*, 39–41.

[12] *I Am the Truth*, 17.

[13] Ibid. 17–18; see also *Incarnation*, 37–9, 51–5.

[14] Ibid. 38.

[15] *I Am the Truth*, 19.

[16] Ibid. 40. For a short essay on 'life', originally delivered as a lecture in 2000, encapsulating, Henry thought, the essence of his philosophical project, see 'Phénoménologie de la vie', in Michel Henry, *Phénoménologie de la vie*, vol. 1, *De la phénoménologie* (Paris: Presses Universitaires de France, 2003), 59–76; 'Phenomenology of Life', trans. Nick Hanlon, *Angelaki: Journal of the Theoretical Humanities*, 8.2 (2003), 97–110.

[17] *I Am the Truth*, 38; this quotation is repeated frequently in Henry.

[18] Ibid. 38. It should be noted that in his phenomenological analysis of life, Henry resolutely leaves living beings other than human beings out of consideration: 'A decision like this is not arbitrary. It is justified by a methodological choice to speak of what we know rather than of what we do not'. *Incarnation*, 3. Or as he asks in *I Am the Truth*, 47: 'Is it not paradoxical for someone who wants to know what life is to go and ask protozoa, or, at best, honeybees? It is as if we had a

life, the very 'stuff' or 'flesh' of life, also do not appear in the world, and so the world, in turn, as the outside horizon in which things appear in the light, is truly lifeless, dead.

In contrast to the world and its phenomenality, Christ, as most clearly presented in the Gospel of John, unveils, according to Henry, another mode of phenomenality altogether. In John, there is no equivocation: 'I am not of the world' Christ asserts dramatically (8:23); 'I am', rather, 'the Way and the Life and the Truth' (14:6). This particularly Johannine identification of Life and Truth, and the Way that leads to them, for Henry, is grounded in the fact that Christ does not speak of a truth and a life other than that which he himself is: there is no equivocation, as there always is in the phenomenality of the world. The revelation of God is not the revelation of something else, a phenomenon alongside other phenomena appearing outside themselves in the exteriority of the world and known by its light: 'God is that pure Revelation that reveals nothing other than itself: God reveals himself'.[19] The Truth of Christianity thus 'concerns not what shows itself, but the fact of self-showing, not what appears but the way of its appearing, not what is manifest, but the pure manifestation, in itself and as such . . . not the phenomenon but phenomenality'.[20] God is not 'seen', either with the physical senses or those of the intellect, in the light of the world, as an object thrown before us in the outside that is the world, but is apprehended in, by, and as, his own light—'in your light we see light' (Ps. 35:10)—the Light that God is and in which there is no darkness (cf. 1 John 1:5).

Invisible to the world, in the darkness of its night, God reveals himself in a phenomenality that is other than that by which things appear as phenomena in the outside of the world, one that is pure revelation, because (like suffering, as noted above) it is self-revelation. This phenomenality is not that which operates in the light of the world, but instead in life, revealing itself to, and in, living ones, yet never itself seen in the world. Life is not seen, as an object in the world, but is that in which and by which those who live see. Life itself is perceived only in the act or the experience of living, in the *pathos* of life, in suffering in all its modalities—pain and joy, desires and fears, wonder and boredom, brokenness and exhilaration. Invisible to and in the world, life is never sundered from itself in the play of appearances that constitutes the world. Life is only experienced and known in the act of living, and there it is not known as something other than itself: '*what Life reveals is itself*'.[21] Or as Henry puts it elsewhere: 'Revealing itself to itself, life speaks to us of itself'.[22] And in so doing, revealing itself in life as Life, Life is, by its complete self-identity, the Truth, and is, as revelation, a word, not the *logos* of the Greeks,

relation with life that was every bit as totally external and fragile as the one we have with beings about which we know nothing—or very little. As if we were not ourselves living'.

[19] *I Am the Truth*, 25. [20] Ibid. 23, 25. [21] Ibid. 29. [22] *Words of Christ*, 74.

but 'the Word of Life' (1 John 1:1). Even the words of the Word, as he appears, not in the world but in the Gospel of John, 'are Spirit and are Life' (John 6:63).

Life reveals itself in such a way that it is not externalized as a phenomenon within the world. It is itself what is revealed in this revelation, ignoring the 'outside' of the world. And so, strictly speaking, '*Living is not possible in the world.* Living is possible only outside the world, where another Truth reigns, another way of revealing, that of Life. Life does not cast outside itself what it reveals but holds it inside itself, retains it in so close an embrace that what it holds and reveals is itself'.[23] Living beings are lost to the world and its history, in which even those few beings who have lived in the world and about whom we know something are only known as historical records; as living, however, even if invisible (lost) to the world, as is life itself, they can never be lost to Life. Life reveals itself, takes place, in the 'experiencing of oneself' (*s'éprouver soi-même*), as *pathos*, and, as we will see further in the next section, 'in the affective flesh of pathos'.[24] This is the first form of any conceivable phenomenality: before we come to observe the phenomena of the world, we are already in life, in its embrace and given to ourselves.[25] Life also precedes any form of thinking, for it is only because life comes into itself that vision and thought are possible.[26] 'To experience oneself', explains Henry, means 'to experience what is, in its flesh, nothing other than that which experiences it'. And so 'this identity between experiencing and what is experienced is the original essence of Ipseity' or 'self', a 'living one'.[27] The generation of Ipseity, the self, is intrinsic to the revelation of Life, as that in which life is realized, effectuated, known. There is, in Henry's phenomenology, no 'self' who exists before living; it is in the *pathos* of living that the 'self' is.

The Gospel of John, especially in its Prologue and Christ's prayers as he approaches his Passion, unveils, for Henry, both the identity of Christ as Life and how, in his relationship to the Father, this life is generated or engendered, as well as how it is engendered in us, such that: 'there is only one Life, that of Christ, which is also that of God and human beings'.[28] 'I am the First and the

[23] *I Am the Truth*, 29–30. [24] Ibid. 56.

[25] Henry finds this radical phenomenology already intimated in the 'Second Meditation' of Descartes, who, when imagining an evil genie who deceives him in all that he sees, concludes, *at certe videre videor*, 'at least it seems to me that I see': '*Videre* denotes the appearing of the world. *Videor* designates the semblance, the appearing in which seeing is revealed to itself. *Only because the appearing in which seeing is revealed to itself differs in principle from the appearing in which seeing sees all that it sees can the former be certain when the latter is doubtful*'. *Incarnation*, 70. The implication of this insight was 'immediately lost in the work of the great Cartesians (Malebranche, Spinoza, and Leibniz)', and was subject to a 'massive misunderstanding' by Husserl, 'an extraordinary reversal . . . the complete denaturing of the Cartesian cogito'. Ibid. 65, 71.

[26] Cf. *Incarnation*, 93. [27] *I Am the Truth*, 56.

[28] Ibid. 36; repeated slightly differently on p. 101, 'Life has the same meaning for God, for Christ, and for the human being'.

Last, I am the Living One, I was dead and behold I am Living' (Apoc. 1:17–18).[29] That Christ is 'the Living One' is because it is in him that the life of God is revealed, effectuated, generated. Life lives, as noted above, in such a manner that it generates Ipseity; there is 'no Life without a Living One' and 'no Living One without Life'.[30] In this generative process of Life, 'Life generates within itself he whose birth is the self-accomplishment of this Life . . . The Father . . . eternally engenders the Son within himself . . . the First Living One in whose original and essential Ipseity the Father experiences himself'.[31] The God who is Life is thus necessarily the Father of a Son, and so Christ is the First Living One not simply as the first who happened to come along, as is the case in a human family, but as 'the one who inhabits the Origin, the very Beginning—the one who is engendered in the very process whereby the Father engenders himself'.[32] In this way, Christ is given by the Father to have life in himself as does the Father himself (cf. John 5:26). Christ is, in Henry's idiom, 'the Arch-Son', who as 'the beginning [*arche*], the firstborn of the dead' (Col. 1:18) is 'the firstborn of many brethren' (Rom. 8:29). Christ's sonship, his status as 'the Arch-Son', is the prior, or transcendental, condition for the sonship of all other sons.

The engendering of the Arch-Son from the Father is, in turn, an 'Arch-birth', meaning 'a birth that does not take place in a pre-existing life but that belongs as a constituent element to the upsurge of this life itself'—the birth of life that strictly speaking belongs only to the Son.[33] This birth of the Son in life and as Life, is the prior, or transcendental, condition for any other possible birth. But such birth, as understood by the phenomenology of life, has a very different meaning than its customary usage in the world. In the world, 'birth' signifies coming into existence or more precisely coming into the world by appearing in it. But the birth of Christ is the birth of Life itself, life that, as we have seen, does not appear in the world. Thus, Henry asserts, 'in the world, according to Christianity, no birth is possible. . . . To be born is not to come into the world. To be born is to come into life. . . . To come into life means to

[29] The Greek here for 'the living one' is simply the participle (ζῶν); Henry also uses the participle, 'vivant', which has been variously rendered by different translators, as 'the living' or 'living beings', with the note of caution given by Scott Davidson (introduction to *Material Phenomenology*, xv–xvi), that 'Henry seeks to distinguish "the living" from "beings" in the sense of external objects, and so the emphasis should remain on the fact that "living beings" are alive and not that they are beings'. However, to speak of 'the living' is awkward and usually denotes a plural, so I have opted for supplying 'one' or 'ones'.

[30] *I Am the Truth*, 60. [31] Ibid. 56. [32] Ibid. 57.

[33] Ibid. 58. See also, Henry, 'Phénoménologie de la naissance', in Henry, *Phénoménologie de la vie*, vol. 1, *De la phénoménologie* (Paris: Presses Universitaires de France, 2003), 123–42; trans. Andrew Sackin-Poll, 'The Phenemenology of Birth', *Pli: The Warwick Journal of Philosophy* 28 (2017), 119–39.

come from life, starting from it, in such a way that life is not birth's point of arrival, as it were, but its point of departure'.[34]

It is this 'genuine birth' that Henry sees 'expounded in John's stunning prologue', which presents a 'dazzling summary' of the whole Gospel as well as its 'conclusion'.[35] John does not know of any human generation, neither that of Christ, nor those to whom he addresses his work, for they are 'born not of blood nor of the will of the flesh nor of the will of man, but of God' (John 1:13). Instead John speaks of the One in the beginning, with God, and as God. In so doing, John 'explodes the very concept of birth, which always assumes a "before" . . . [and] the concept of son, which, in the language of the world, always presupposes a father who came before him'.[36] John does not know of any before or after in the relationship between Father and Son, but only of the phenomenological reciprocity between them, for 'Life is not cast into itself except in the Ipseity of the First Living One in such a way that the former carries the latter within it and vice versa'.[37] For this reason, as Henry sees it, 'the Johannine texts give voice decisively to an endless movement in which the Father and the Son embrace each other', and so the works that Christ does are indeed those of the Father who sent him, transmitting life through him.[38]

For this reason, throughout the Gospel of John, Henry contends, we see 'a phenomenology whose phenomenality is Life and no longer the world, [and which] is contained in the words that give access to the content of Christianity, to God, albeit at the price of a complete overturning of the presuppositions guiding the course of Western thought since its origins with the Greeks: "Before long the world will not see me anymore, *but you will see me because I live and because you also will live.*"'[39] 'Seeing' Christ, for John, does not mean to 'see' him as the world looked upon Jesus before his Passion, but rather to live as Christ lives, to share in the *pathos* of his life, the *pathos* of Life that he is. The revelation of Life in life and as life is not known in the world of appearances, where duplicity and mendacity reign, but is known only by and in those who are living. Engendered in Life's own self-generation, belonging to God himself, Christ speaks words, 'especially in John', that belong to

[34] *I Am the Truth*, 59–60. [35] Ibid. 77; *Words of Christ*, 81. [36] *I Am the Truth*, 79.

[37] Ibid. 78. Cf. *Words of Christ*, 85: 'Thus the Father (Life all-powerful which self-engenders itself) remains in his Son (the Word in which this Life engenders itself in experiencing itself and in revealing itself in this way to itself), just as the Son (this Son in whom Life experiences itself and loves itself infinitely) remains in this life (which experiences itself in him in such a way that it experiences itself in it). Thus one is in the other in this way, the Father in his Son, the Son in his Father according to a reciprocal inwardness (each experiencing, living, loving one in the other), which is an interiority of love, which is their common love, their Spirit'.

[38] *I Am the Truth*, 88.

[39] Ibid. 85; John 14:19 (*ὑμεῖς δὲ θεωρεῖτέ με, ὅτι ἐγὼ ζῶ καὶ ὑμεῖς ζήσετε*) as rendered and italicized by Henry. Although Henry does not explicitly put it this way, these words of Christ as he approaches his Passion, indicate that the phenomenology of life pivots around the cross.

God himself, words which spoken in this lifeless world bring about his condemnation to death.[40]

This radical reversal of phenomenality is continued in the First Epistle of John, which appears to begin with a worldly manifestation ('what we have heard . . . seen with our eyes'), but abruptly breaks with the phenomenality of the world, for what has been heard and seen is 'the Word of Life', so that what is 'proclaimed' is 'the eternal Life that was with the Father and manifest to us' (1 John 1:1–5). In this self-revelation of Life we attain to Life and thus the Word, but 'certainly not', Henry adds, 'through its appearance as a man visible in a world'. And, he adds, 'this is what the Johannine problematic and all of Christianity will establish'.[41] The irreducibility of these two kinds of phenomenality—that of Life in its self-revelation as the Word of Life, on the one hand, an identity that establishes it as Truth, and, on the other, that given in the light of the world, externalizing the phenomena as other than what they are, and thus duplicitous—lies, Henry adds later on, 'at the origin of John's problematic and of the Christian drama in general'.[42] In the light of the world, Christ appears as a man, sometimes strange and enigmatic, saying and doing wonderful and disturbing things, but no more; that he is the Word of God does not, and cannot, appear as a phenomenon in the world. There is no access to him, as the very Word of God, as God's revelation, within the world and its truth; 'there is no way of reaching the Son other than in the course of Life's self-embrace, in the same way as there is no other way for life to embrace itself except in this essential Ipseity of the First Living One—no other way for it to reveal itself except in the Word'.[43] 'In your light', not elsewhere by another light, 'we see light'.

Before we turn to Henry's understanding of 'flesh' and 'Incarnation', a further word should be said about how, within this phenomenology of life, human beings are understood. Human beings, we unthinkingly hold, are beings within the world and of the world. We live alongside inanimate things and living animals, but are distinct from the latter in that we possess *logos*, that is, reason and language. However, our prizing of *logos* over life, as that which characterizes us as human in distinction from the irrational animals, means, in turn, that the life we think we have is less than human, shared as it is with protozoa and bees.[44] The modern scientific outlook is even more reductive, reducing the human being to a part of the material universe, ultimately no more than a particular configuration of physical and chemical elements, 'brother to the automata that can be constructed according to the same laws',[45] and in which 'the kiss lovers exchange is only a bombardment of microphysical particles'.[46] The turn of philosophy to the phenomenology of consciousness over recent centuries has opened up a way of thinking about

[40] *I Am the Truth*, 63–4. [41] Ibid. 83. [42] Ibid. 86. [43] Ibid. 88.
[44] Cf. Ibid. 50–1. [45] Ibid. 103–4. [46] *Incarnation*, 101.

human beings that distinguishes them from other beings in the world, as uniquely open to and engaged with the world, as 'transcendental subjects' capable of 'having' a world, of experiencing the world in a way that is particular to their humanity. Yet even this transcendental subjectivity remains (perhaps the more so) intrinsically and essentially tied to the world, whether in Husserl's analysis of the intentionality of consciousness (that it is always 'conscious of something') or Heidegger's analysis of the being-in-the-world of *Dasein*.[47] In each of these approaches, the human being is fundamentally a being of the world.

In stark contrast to common sense, science, and philosophy, Christianity holds that humans are not beings of the world: 'they are not of the world, even as I am not of the world' says Christ (John 17:14). As living ones they are, rather, sons of life, and so sons of God: 'You are gods, sons of the Most High', says the Psalmist (81:6), the first words of which are quoted by Christ in the Gospel of John and applied to all those to whom the Word came (John 10:34).[48] Isaiah likewise opens with the assertion of the Lord: 'I have begotten sons and exalted them' (Isa. 1:2). Before being seen in the light of the world, a light which ultimately obscures their true identity, and even before the exteriority of the world appears, humans are already sons of Life. And life, as we have seen, is foreign to the world, for the mode in which life phenomenalizes itself, in the *pathos* of life as a living one, does not open up a world, nor does it show itself in the outside that is the world. Thus, in contrast to all other ways of conceiving the human being, 'Christianity opposes a radically different human being, the Son of God, the Son of Life, the new transcendental human being born within absolute phenomenological Life, engendered within this Life's self-engendering and drawing his essence from it alone—the human being resembling Christ, the human being in the image of God'.[49] It is the Prologue of John, with its insights into the generation of life, that enables this reading of Genesis, Henry says, showing it to be 'the first true and rigorous analysis of the human condition'.[50]

Although, as we will see, there is an important distinction to be made between Christ as the Son of God, and human beings as sons in the Son, the

[47] For this reason Henry sees in the mode of revelation disclosed in Heidegger's analysis of Dasein 'the murder of life—not accidentally but rather in principle'. Ibid. 46.

[48] See also Ashton's comments, noted above in Chapter 4, that in contrast to the way in which the titles 'Son of God' and 'son of man' tend to be used in Christological discussion, as referring to Christ as divine and as human respectively, '"Son of God", originally at any rate, indicates a human being, the Messiah; whereas "Son of Man" points to a figure whose true home is in heaven' (*Fourth Gospel*, 107).

[49] *I Am the Truth*, 100, modified by rendering 'l'homme' as 'human being' rather than 'man' (done hereafter).

[50] *Words of Christ*, 85. Cf. *Incarnation*, 222–37 (§ 45, 'The Degrees of Passivity: From Genesis to the Prologue of John'), esp. 229: it is 'the initiatory propositions of the Prologue of John that allow us to understand *the unity and transcendental aim of Scripture*'.

life they live is nevertheless one and the same. As Henry puts it, 'Inasmuch as, in the self-movement by which Life ceaselessly comes into itself and experiences itself, is erected an Ipseity and thus a Self (because to experience oneself [*s'éprouve soi-même*] is effectively the same as that self, is necessarily that self), then the Self engendered in this self-movement of Life is effectively the same as that Self, too, and is necessarily this one or that one, a singular Self, in essence different from any other. I am myself this singular Self engendered in the self-engendering of absolute Life, and only that. *Life self-engenders itself as me*'.[51] Or as Meister Eckhart puts it, in words to which Henry frequently returns, 'God engenders me as himself'.[52] In this way, Henry can even say that human beings are '*not* created', if by creation we mean the creation of the world, the 'outside' where the visible reigns.[53] The world is created; life is engendered. 'Like God, the human being is nothing of the world, and nothing in him can ultimately be explained by the world. . . . No one has ever seen God, but no one has ever seen a human being—a human being in his actual reality, a transcendental living Self. . . . It is because he is Life that God is invisible. And for this reason the human being is too. The human being has never been created, he has never come [*venu*] in the world. He has come in Life. And it is in this sense that he is in the likeness of God, cut from the same cloth as Him, as every life and all the living are. From the cloth that is the pure phenomenological substance of life itself'.[54] Or as Christ himself instructs us: 'Call no-one on earth your father, for you have one Father who is in heaven'.[55]

[51] *I Am the Truth*, 104.

[52] Quoted in ibid. 104, modified; Eckhart immediately turns the saying around (see below), and Henry quotes it in both ways in different places. The French at this point in *I Am the Truth* has the first form ('Dieu m'engendre comme lui-même'); the translation gives the second form ('God engenders himself as me'). The saying is from Meister Eckhart's German Sermon 6 (ed. Quint) or 65 (ed. Pfeiffer); the full context is as follows: 'The Father bears his Son in eternity like himself. "The Word was with God and God was the Word": the same in the same nature. I say more: he has borne him in my soul. Not only is she with him and he equally with her, but he is in her: the Father gives birth to his Son in the soul in the very same way as he gives birth to him in eternity and no differently. He must do it whether he likes it or not. The Father begets his Son unceasingly, and furthermore, I say, he begets me as his Son and the same Son. I say even more: not only does he beget me as his Son but he begets me as himself and himself as me, and me as his being and his nature. In the inmost spring, I well up in the Holy Ghost, where there is one life, one being, and one work'. *The Complete Mystical Works of Meister Eckhart*, trans. Maurice O'C. Walshe, revised by Bernard McGinn (New York: Crossroad, 2009), 331. Henry's earliest, and fullest, engagement with the writings of Eckhart is in *Essence of Manifestation*, § 39–40, pp. 309–35.

[53] *I Am the Truth*, 103.

[54] *Incarnation*, 229. Cf. *Words of Christ*, 4: 'Engendering human beings as living ones, giving them a life which exists in himself, God has in this way given them the same nature as his own: that of life. It is in this way that God has made humanity in his own image and likeness'.

[55] Matt. 23:9; quoted in *Words of Christ*, 40, with the further comment: '"In heaven" obviously does not mean: in interstellar space, in the astro-physical universe explored by cosmonauts . . . "In heaven" means: in this invisible life in which all living ones live, in which they are themselves invisible, just like this life'. *Words of Christ*, 41. Cf. *I Am the Truth*, 73–4: 'the

The 'self-affection'—that is, the identity of that which affects and that which is affected that constitutes the essence of life in both God and the human being—nevertheless has a different modality in each case. In a strong sense, it applies only to God, where it is Life's generation of itself, in the Ipseity of the Son who is coeternal with the engendering Father and given by the Father to have life in himself. In our own case, however, this self-affection is of a different, weaker, order, for 'I have not brought myself into this condition of experiencing myself. I am myself, but I have no part in this "being myself" . . . I am given to myself without this givenness arising from me in any way. . . . I do not affect myself absolutely, but, precisely put, I am and I find myself self-affected'.[56] My condition of life is essentially and always passive, so that the self I find myself to be is put in the accusative case, 'a "me" and not an "I"'.[57] It is Christ's Ipseity as the Arch-Son that is the prior or transcendental condition of all other sons; he precedes all other sons, as 'the firstborn of many brethren' (Rom 8:29), not in the anteriority of the temporality of the world, but in the generation of Life: 'Before Abraham was, I AM' (John 8:58).

Despite being 'self-affected' in this weaker sense, human beings, as living ones, have the ground of their being, their phenomenological birth into life, in the eternity of God, a birth that is, phenomenologically speaking, prior to the creation of the world and its temporality. When speaking of the world and its creation, Henry does not do so in the register in which history or science speaks, but in a phenomenological key: 'the creation of the world . . . consists in the opening of this horizon of exteriority, of this "Outside" where any thing becomes visible in showing itself to us outside of us—hence as external, as different, as other'.[58] Life on the other hand is foreign to all this, to exteriority, to being separated from itself in its self-affectivity, otherwise it would stop being life. As such, 'Life is uncreated. Stranger to creation, stranger to the world, any process imparting Life is a process of generation'.[59] The phenomenological priority of Life to appearance means that creation is essentially secondary or subsequent to begetting, though not, of course, referring to a sequence within the temporality and causality belonging to the world of appearance. Christianity, asserts Henry, 'obliges us to find . . . an entirely new and unusual conception of temporality—one that is the essence of Life's own temporality'. Such 'temporality' would not be distanced from itself in the horizon of exteriority, relegated to the ek-stasy of the past, but is a 'radically immanent, inek-static, and pathos-filled [*pathètique*] temporality', in which 'there is neither before nor after in the sense we understand them, but rather eternal movement, an eternal flux in which life continuously experiences itself

connection that Christ's discourse constantly establishes between the Father and Heaven gives the latter the value of a rigorous concept: *that of a Life which does not appear in any world and is revealed only in itself*'.

[56] *I Am the Truth*, 107. [57] Ibid. 107. [58] *Words of Christ*, 84. [59] Ibid. 84.

in the Self that life eternally generates, and which is never separated from itself'.[60] And so, before the appearance of the world, with its laws of space, time, and causality, 'the singular Self that I am experiences itself only within the movement by which Life is cast into itself and enjoys itself in the eternal process of its absolute self-affecting'.[61] Human beings, as living ones, have their identity in the Living One, in Christ but hidden from the world—for 'your life is hid with Christ in God' (Col. 3:3)—'chosen in him before the foundation of the world' (Eph. 1:4).

'I have begotten sons and exalted them', says the Lord through Isaiah. Then he adds: 'but they have rejected me' (Isa. 1:2). This rejection is understood by Henry in terms of a 'forgetting', but not that of a prior event within the time of the world resulting in a forgetting of what went, temporally, before. It is rather a radical 'Forgetting' of the immediacy of life in which we live. Coming into life as a self in the experience of life, a life which is given to 'me', the self enters into possession of itself and each of its powers, is able to exercise them, so that it is no longer a 'me' but asserts itself as an 'I', able to say 'I can': 'There is an incontestable experience that leads the "I" to say, specifically, *I* take, *I* walk, *I* feel. . . .'.[62] The very fact of coming into life is the occasion for succumbing to a false egoism, in which the Ego considers itself to be the ground of its own life, as the Self simultaneously directs its attention away from the source of life, Life itself, towards that which it can see, do, or perceive in the world that opens up. As Henry puts it, 'the occultation of the condition of the Son coincides apparently paradoxically with the very genesis of this condition'.[63] In this way, the self is 'doubled', between, on the one hand, the 'me' that lives at the heart of Life, hidden in Christ, but which has forgotten itself, absorbed by the world, and, on the other hand, my appearance as an 'I' in the world.[64] This duplicity of appearing means that, for Christianity, everything is doubled: '*Because the way of appearing is double*, what appears, *even if it is the same, nevertheless appears in two different ways, in a dual aspect*'.[65] Our body, most immediately, appears to us in two ways: as the living body whose life I experience as my own, and, on the other hand, as an object body, that the 'I can' touches externally, as skin, not the self-affecting *pathos*-filled flesh. As doubled, one is an image of the other; one the reality, the other a shadow or projection. Christ unveils the truth, by revealing the truth of Life and exposing the phenomenality of the world for what it is, an appearance.[66] Likewise, the falsity of the Ego's delusion is shown, phenomenologically, by the fact that each

[60] *I Am the Truth*, 158, 159–60. [61] Ibid. 107. [62] Ibid. 137. [63] Ibid. 135.

[64] Ibid. 165. Cf. *Words of Christ*, 16: '[the] radical division between the two realms of the visible and of the invisible concerns us, who belong to the world as much as to life. On the one hand, the human being shows itself in the world as an objective body similar to that of things. . . . Yet we know that the body is only the visible appearance of a living flesh, experiencing itself in life and invisible as such'.

[65] *I Am the Truth*, 195. [66] Cf. Ibid. 194–8.

of the powers at the disposal of the 'I can', the I who can indeed exercise them when and as it wants, is nevertheless given to it: 'This is something over which the "I" has no power whatsoever, which is allocated to it quite apart from the will'.[67] As Christ, in John, reminds us: 'Apart from me you can do nothing'.[68]

It is to this 'forgotten' condition of being a son that Christ calls us, and is able to do so on the basis of the fact that, although 'forgotten', our innermost identity or essence, the only way in which the self is—as a 'me' before (in a non-temporal sense) an 'I'—is as born into life. As such, and only because of this, is it always able to be reborn. It is to regain his condition, as a son of the Father, that the prodigal son returns home and is welcomed back. 'To come back to Life, to be reborn, is given as a possibility always present to the one who is born of Life. A rebirth is thus implied in any birth, because the new life to be reached, the second life, is just the first one, the oldest Life, the one that lived at the Beginning and that was given in its transcendental birth to all living ones: because, outside it and without it, no living one nor any life would be possible'.[69] But this return and rebirth requires that the 'Forgetting' be defeated, and this is nothing less than 'the decisive mutation thanks to which the very life of the ego is changed into the Life of the absolute'.[70] As rebirth of and in Life, it is 'the Christian ethic', a transformation of life itself, manifest most fully in the work of mercy: 'Only the work of mercy practices the forgetting of the self in which, all interest for the Self (right down to the idea of what we call a self or a me) now removed, no obstacle is now posed to the unfurling of Life in this Self extended to its original essence'.[71] This ethic, as well as the astonishing affirmations given by Christ about himself and his relationship to the Father, 'blazes out of the extreme limit of paradox, where one must lose one's life in order to keep it'.[72] In a revealing turn of phrase towards the end of *Incarnation*, Henry writes of the conclusion towards which this ethic leads: 'Thus, finally, this flux, this seemingly absurd parade of modest pleasures and oppressive thoughts, is secretly oriented toward an agony, toward the ultimate transition from the ultimate suffering of despair to the eruption of an unlimited joy, as evidenced by the Parousia concealed on the wood of the cross'.[73]

INCARNATION

The Life that is God, revealed in and as Christ, is communicated to us through the Incarnation. For Henry, however, 'Incarnation' is not about the Word

[67] Ibid. 137. [68] John 15:5; cf. *Words of Christ*, 96; *Incarnation*, 174–7.
[69] *I Am the Truth*, 164. [70] Ibid. 165. [71] Ibid. 170.
[72] *Words of Christ*, 48. Cf. Luke 17:33. [73] *Incarnation*, 250.

coming into the world by taking a body, to appear alongside other phenomena in the outside horizon of the world, as, in Rowan Williams' turn of phrase, 'an episode in the biography of the Word'. 'Incarnation', rather, refers to the state of being enfleshed that is proper to living beings. Building upon his earlier work, and in dialogue with Irenaeus especially, Henry devotes his penultimate work, *Incarnation*, to elucidating what is meant generally by 'flesh' and specifically the Christian theme of 'Incarnation', becoming flesh.

Henry opens *Incarnation* by providing a preliminary phenomenological distinction between flesh and body. Building upon Heidegger's comment that a table does not 'touch' the wall against which it is placed, Henry points out that 'what is proper to a body such as ours . . . is that it senses every object that is close to it: it perceives each of its qualities, it sees its colours, hears its sounds, breathes in a scent, determines the hardness of the soil with a foot, and the smoothness of a fabric with a hand'.[74] An incarnate being, such as we are, senses the world in which we live 'only because it feels its own feeling first, in the effort it exerts to ascend the lane and in the impression of pleasure that sums up the cool of the water or wind'.[75] This is something that, in principle, differentiates a body that is properly ours, 'which feels itself at the same time it senses what surrounds it', and the inert bodies that make up the universe in which we live, whether stones on the path or the microphysical particles we suppose constitute it. It is the former alone that is properly, or phenomenologically, called flesh: 'our flesh is nothing other than what *feels itself, suffers itself, undergoes itself and bears itself, and thus enjoys itself according to impressions that are always reborn*'.[76] There is no flesh without a body, and, indeed, the exhaustion we feel in the flesh, as we ascend the lane, is directly related to the heaviness of the body. Yet 'body' and 'flesh' are diametrically opposed to each other, as distinct 'as sensing and un-sensing—that which enjoys itself on the one hand; blind, opaque, inert matter, on the other'.[77] This distinction, Henry suggests, may even be impossible to think through fully, for one pole, the inert matter of material nature, always escapes us: our knowledge of it is only mediated through the impression that it creates upon our flesh.[78] To be 'incarnate', then, is not simply a matter of having a body, being corporeal, a material body within

[74] Ibid. 3–4. [75] Ibid. 4. [76] Ibid. [77] Ibid. 4.

[78] Ibid. 5: 'A metaphysical aporia bars our way, because the ultimate physical element must still reach us somehow and there is no way around this final order of things. A flash on a screen . . . arrives in our flesh nowhere else but where this flesh impresses upon itself. Outside this inevitable reference, it remains unknown and unknowable what the object of physics, the "thing in itself", or what Kant called the "noumena", would be. *The analysis of the body can never become an analysis of our flesh, or eventually its explanatory principle; rather the contrary is true: Our flesh alone allows us to know, within the limits prescribed by this inescapable presupposition, something like a "body"*'.

the world. Rather, 'to be incarnate is to have flesh, and, perhaps more precisely, to be flesh'.[79]

This distinction between body and flesh corresponds to the different modes of phenomenality, that of the world and that of life, with which we began our exposition of Henry. The body that appears in the light of the world, 'owes to that mode of appearing certain phenomenological characteristics, all of which derive from exteriority—but *never its existence*'.[80] It exists before being uncovered in the horizon of the world, and thus independently of it, but is only seen in the world in this exteriority, in its skin or as bodily organs. Flesh, on the other hand, is always and only encountered in the self-affectivity, the *pathos*, of life, and so flesh is coextensive with the coming of life itself. Flesh, as encountered phenomenologically, is always 'an impressional and affective flesh, whose impressional character and affectivity never results from anything other than the impressional character and affectivity of life itself'.[81] It is life, not the matter drawn from the earth, that gives the flesh, as a pure phenomenological substance, its impressional and affective character. And in turn, life, as the *pathos* of self-affectivity, does not live anywhere else but in the flesh. 'The flesh is precisely the manner in which life is made Life', as Henry puts it, so that there is 'no Life without flesh, but no flesh without Life'.[82] The arrival of Life in the First Living One, the Arch-Son, examined in the previous section of this chapter, thus creates, or better engenders, flesh, considered in its pure phenomenological substance: 'this originary connection and this reciprocity (this reciprocal interiority of Flesh and Life) concerns a life like ours only because, before time, before every conceivable world, it is established in absolute Life as the phenomenological mode according to which this Life arrives eternally in itself in the Arch-Pathos of its Arch-Flesh'.[83] It is the flesh of the First Living One, Christ himself, the Word become flesh, that is the prior, transcendental, condition for our own flesh, our existence as incarnate living beings.[84] Just as to be born, for Henry, does not mean to come into the world of appearances, but rather to come from life into life, so too 'to be born means to come in a flesh where every flesh comes in itself, in the Arch-Flesh of Life'.[85] And so, the phenomenology of flesh, as unfolded by Henry, leads ineluctably to the phenomenology of Incarnation.

[79] Ibid. 4. [80] Ibid. 121. [81] Ibid. 121. [82] Ibid. 121. [83] Ibid. 121.

[84] Cf. *I Am the Truth*, 116: 'No self is possible that does not have as its phenomenological substance, as its flesh, the phenomenological substance and flesh of the Arch-Son.... This growth of the self in any possible me, this self-affection in which the self touches itself at every point of its being, is its flesh, its phenomenological flesh, its living flesh. In my living flesh I am given to myself and thus I am a me—I am myself. But it is not me who has given me to myself; it is not me who joins me to myself. I am not the gate, the gate that opens me to myself, nor am I the grass, the grass that allows my flesh to grow. In my flesh I am given to myself, but I am not my own flesh. My flesh, my living flesh, is Christ's'.

[85] *Incarnation*, 124.

Turning to the specifically Christian sense of the word 'Incarnation', John's stunning assertion that 'the Word became flesh' entails, for Henry, rethinking what it means to be human, the relation between God and human beings, and what is meant by the revelation of God in the Word's becoming flesh. Regarding the first point, 'the Incarnation of the Word' is consistently understood by the Christian tradition as the way in which the Word became human. But this means, as Henry notes, that 'the human being is defined as flesh'.[86] John, and those thereafter commenting on him, do not say that the Word became human and for this reason took on flesh along with other attributes. It is, rather, the reverse: by becoming flesh, the Word becomes human. For Henry, this is nothing short of a complete overturning of the Greek conception of the human being, and, indeed, our usual understanding of ourselves, in which 'flesh' defines only our animality, that which we have in common with the animals, from whom we are distinct by the possession of other capacities, such as the ability to think and form ideas, the possession of *logos* lacking in animals. In that framework, the relation between God and the human being would be relatively easy to comprehend, for it would be located on a spiritual plane, the mind or the spirit of the human being relating to a God who is himself mind and spirit. But if this were the case, to 'become flesh' would not mean to become human but instead the opposite, 'to get rid of its own essence, to close off the human condition, to be nothing more than animal'.[87] If instead the Word becoming flesh is in fact how the Word becomes human, then, in turn, our relationship with God must also take place in and through the flesh itself. The flesh is not the obstacle, hindering the supposedly better part of ourselves from knowing that to which it is, again supposedly, akin, but is the locus of our identity with God. 'It is by identifying himself with the Word's flesh (with the body of Christ, *corpus Christi*) that the Christian human being may identify himself with God'.[88]

The becoming flesh of the Word is also consistently understood, by the Christian tradition, in terms of revelation, for by it 'we have seen his glory' (John 1:14). But how is the becoming flesh of the Word understood as a revelation? This is most often taken in terms of the Word becoming flesh in order to reveal itself to us, the invisible Word showing itself to human beings by taking an objective body like their own, so that 'becoming-visible in a visible-body would be the principle of the Word's revelation'.[89] However, as Henry points out, there are two massive difficulties with this line of interpretation. The first is that if this is the case, then 'what would show itself to them in this appearance would really still be only a body like theirs, about which nothing would allow them to know that it is precisely not the body of an ordinary man but of the Word'. This would be nothing short of a 'banalization

[86] Ibid. 11. [87] Ibid. 11. [88] Ibid. 14. [89] Ibid. 16.

of Christ'.[90] The second difficulty is that, quite simply, this is not what John says: 'For John does not say that the Word took on a body, or assumed the appearance of one. He says that it "was made flesh"'.[91] John speaks neither of a body, but of flesh, nor of appearance, but of becoming flesh. 'Incarnation', then, does not speak of the addition of an heterogeneous element to the Word, to appear in the world, but of the Word itself becoming flesh.[92] 'It is of itself, in itself, and by itself, that [the Word] was made flesh'.[93] For John, then, as Henry reads him, flesh is not the means of a revelation understood as appearance in the world, but flesh is itself the revelation.

Henry further expounds the nature of the flesh that lies at the heart of the Incarnation spoken by John by contrasting its treatment in Tertullian and Irenaeus. In his work *On the Flesh of Christ*, Tertullian staunchly defends the reality, specifically the material reality, of the flesh of Christ against Marcion and the Valentinians. For Tertullian, flesh, birth, and death, are intrinsically bound up together: 'there is no birth without flesh, and no flesh without birth', and as there is no dispute, Tertullian acknowledges, between himself and his opponents regarding the spiritual substance of Christ, 'it is his flesh that is under investigation ... whence it came and of what sort it was'.[94] Moreover, 'Christ, being sent to die, had of necessity also to be born, so that he might die. For customarily nothing dies except what is born. Birth and death have a debt they owe to the other; the project of dying is the reason for being born'.[95] But, as Henry points out, in this investigation, despite connecting the flesh of Christ to his Passion, to his suffering in the flesh, 'the phenomenological and ontological horizon that presides over [Tertullian's] conception of flesh, its birth, and its reality, is the appearing in the world'.[96] The flesh exposed to view by Tertullian (who 'still thinks Greek')[97] is, in his words, that which is 'suffused with blood, scaffolded of bones, threaded through with sinews, intertwined with veins',[98] and its birth in the womb is described by Tertullian in as graphic a manner as possible to invite the disgust of Marcion.[99] 'What is

[90] Ibid. 17. [91] *Incarnation*, 17.

[92] Cf. *I Am the Truth*, 98–101 on the difficulties of a 'two-nature Christology', when each term, the divine and the human, are understood or defined independently.

[93] *Incarnation*, 18. [94] Tertullian, *Carn. Chr.* 1 (Evans trans., occasionally modified).

[95] *Carn. Chr.* 6. [96] *Incarnation*, 129. [97] Ibid. 14.

[98] Tertullian, *Carn. Chr.* 5.

[99] Cf. *Carn. Chr.* 4: 'Beginning then with that birth you strongly object to, orate, attack now, the nastiness of genital elements in the womb, the filthy curdling of moisture and blood, and of the flesh to be for nine months nourished on that same mire. Draw a picture of the womb getting daily more unmanageable, heavy, self-concerned, safe not even in sleep, uncertain in the whims of dislike and appetites. Next go all out against the modesty of the travailing woman, a modesty which at least because of danger ought to be respected and because of its nature is sacred. You shudder, of course, as the child passed out along with his afterbirth, and of course bedaubed with it. You think it shameful that he is straightened out with bandages, that he is licked into shape with applications of oil, that he is beguiled by coddling. This natural object of reverence, you Marcion, spit upon: yet how were you born?'

flesh', Tertullian asks, 'but earth transformed into shapes still its own?' And he continues: 'Consider its attributes one by one: the muscles as clods of earth, the bones as rocks, even a sort of pebbles around nipples'.[100] The flesh, that of Christ and that of our own, is defined for Tertullian by its material reality and appearance in the exteriority of the world. He knows, as we have seen, of the connection between the flesh of Christ and his Passion, the suffering and death upon the cross; indeed he can even affirm that 'the sufferings proved that there was [in Christ] the flesh of a human being'.[101] But this briefly glimpsed intuition is never followed through. 'It is', Henry comments, 'without philosophical transition and without any conceptual justification that to this conception of the objective body (whose reality is the world's matter) the presupposition of a radically different flesh (of an other order) is juxtaposed—*a suffering flesh that draws the reality of its suffering from the pathos-filled phenomenalization in life*'.[102] This *pathos*-filled flesh is of a different phenomenological order than the material elements drawn from the earth that comprise, in Tertullian's account, the flesh of Christ. As Henry emphatically puts it:

> In the silt of the earth, there are only bodies, but no flesh. Something like flesh can happen and come to us only from the Word. All the characteristics of flesh come from the Word, and are explained by it and it alone. First of all, the fact, the little fact, that flesh is always the flesh of someone, my own for example, so that it bears a 'self', which is immersed in it, and from which it does not have the leisure to separate itself any more than it can be separated from itself; that this flesh is not divisible or breakable, since it is composed neither of particles nor atoms, but of pleasures and sufferings, hunger and thirst, desire and fatigue, strength and joy—a wealth of lived impressions, none of which have ever been found by rummaging through the soil of the earth or by digging through its layers of clay.[103]

The impressional and affective, *pathos*-filled, flesh does not draw its reality from the earth but from the Word itself. It is this flesh that is spoken of by the word 'Incarnation', the becoming flesh of the Word, as the Arch-Flesh of the Arch-Son, the First Living One. 'The incarnation of Christ, and in an exemplary way his passion, now have their reality and truth from a flesh that is defined by its suffering'.[104]

At the heart of Irenaeus' own battle with his opponents (largely the same ones as Tertullian), especially in book five of his *Against the Heresies*, is also the reality of the flesh. Irenaeus, like Tertullian, notes that everyone accepts that we are 'a body pulled from the earth and a soul receiving the Spirit of God'.[105] Christ, moreover, recapitulating in himself the ancient formation, preserved the analogy with Adam: as Adam was taken from 'untilled and

[100] *Carn. Chr.* 9. [101] *Carn. Chr.* 5. [102] *Incarnation*, 130. [103] Ibid. 18.
[104] Ibid. 130. [105] Irenaeus, *haer.* 3.22.1.

virgin soil' and formed by the Word of God, so the Word took his body from the virgin, so that it is our own handiwork (*plasma*) that is saved, rather than another handiwork altogether.[106] However, when it comes to speaking of the flesh of Christ, Irenaeus does not focus on its exterior appearance in the world but rather points, emphatically and consistently, to its fundamental characteristic, that it, the flesh, is that which is able to be vivified by God. The body derives from the earth, but as flesh it derives from God: 'when the body is transformed into flesh by the operation of Life, it draws its fleshly condition only from Life, which gives to it to undergo experiencing itself in it and to become flesh in this way—which is in no way like a material body that in itself has no power to feel or experience anything at all, that is forever incapable of being flesh'.[107] Henry summarizes Irenaeus' argument against his opponents in two fundamental propositions: 'far from being incapable of taking on flesh, life is its condition of possibility. Far from being incapable of receiving life, the flesh is its phenomenological effectuation'.[108] Against his opponents' reading of Paul's words that 'flesh and blood shall not inherit the Kingdom' (1 Cor. 15:50), Irenaeus insists that flesh and blood *can be inherited* in the Kingdom, for it is, he repeatedly says, the flesh that God vivifies, and that alone, and so, in turn, flesh is that which is vivified by God. If God did not vivify what is mortal, that is the flesh, he would not be powerful.[109] That the flesh can be vivified by God is because it is 'fit for and capable of receiving the power of God', for 'those things which partake of the skill and wisdom of God, do also partake of his power'.[110] And this being the case, Irenaeus delivers his coup de grâce against his opponents:

> But if the power of him who is the Giver of life is made perfect in weakness—that is, in the flesh—let them inform us, when they maintain the incapacity of flesh to receive the life granted by God, whether they say these things as being living at the present and partakers of life, or acknowledge that, having no part in life whatever, they are at the present moment dead. But if they really are dead, how is it that they move about and speak . . . But if they are now alive, and if their whole body partakes of life, how can they venture the assertion that the flesh is not qualified to be a partaker of life, when they confess that they have life at the present moment.[111]

This is, as Henry calls it, 'Irenaeus' Christian cogito', the 'cogito of the flesh' that is 'implied in John's Word': 'Nothing that is living fails to attest in its life that it is living. Nothing that is flesh fails to attest in its flesh that it is flesh'.[112] This is not a movement of thought, reflecting back upon itself and its activities, as with Descartes' 'cogito', but is rather a movement of flesh in

[106] Ibid. 3.21.10. [107] *Incarnation*, 133. [108] Ibid. 133.
[109] Cf. Irenaeus, *haer.* 5.3.2, 7.1. [110] Ibid. 5.3.2. [111] Ibid. 5.3.3.
[112] *Incarnation*, 135.

life: 'it formulates it in its flesh, in a Speech that is the Speech of flesh, more precisely of Life'.[113] This is, he says, 'one of the most astonishing theses formulated by human thought', that is, '*the interpretation of flesh as ineluctably bearing an Arch-intelligibility within itself*, Life's own, in which it is given to itself, and in which it is made flesh'.[114]

Irenaeus' understanding of the flesh derives, according to Henry, from 'the Johannine rereading of Genesis', which taught him to think of creation 'not as the positing of a worldly thing outside itself but as the generation of flesh through the insufflation of life in a body of mud—by the breath of life that is the Spirit'.[115] The apostasy of sin of course has meant that, in Irenaeus' words, we who 'are of God by nature' have become alienated from God, 'alienated contrary to nature', resulting in our forgetting of our original condition.[116] It is this proper belonging of our flesh in the Word of Life that the Incarnation, the arrival of this Word in the flesh, re-establishes. 'By becoming incarnate in a flesh like ours, the Word really comes into what he himself generated in his Life in the beginning, into that which he made not only possible but real'.[117] Yet insofar as the flesh, our flesh, is generated by the Word of Life, 'outside of which no flesh is possible and within which every flesh abides, the Word was never absent from its creation', for as Irenaeus affirms, 'He was always present with the human race, united to and mingled with his own handiwork'.[118] Through the apostasy, enticed by the deceptive appearance of beauty, having fallen prey to sin and death, the flesh assumed by the Word is 'a finite flesh like ours'.[119] As Henry summarizes Irenaeus' account of Christ's salvific work, 'by incarnating himself, the Word thus took upon himself the sin and death inscribed in our finite flesh, and himself destroyed them by dying on the cross', so that 'what is restored then is the original human condition, his transcendental birth in divine life outside of which no life occurs to life'.[120]

It is only in his last work, *Words of Christ*, that Henry turns to John's fullest account of the flesh of Christ in John 6. The words spoken here are so strong that they scandalize even his disciples (6:60). At issue is Christ's identification of himself: 'I am the living bread which comes down from heaven; if anyone eats of this bread he will live for ever; and the bread which I shall give for the life of the world is my flesh'; this is 'the flesh of the Son of Man', which, unless we eat of it, 'you have no life in you' (6:51–3). Unlike our own words, which, as we have seen, operate in the duplicity of the world and are powerless to effect that about which they speak, 'the omnipotence of the divine Word is that of absolute Life'. Henry continues:

113 Ibid. 135. 114 Ibid. 134. 115 Ibid. 232. 116 Irenaeus, *haer.* 5.1.1.
117 *Incarnation*, 232. 118 Ibid. 232; Irenaeus, *haer.* 3.16.6. 119 *Incarnation*, 234.
120 Ibid. 234.

> The institution of the Eucharist which the Synoptic Gospels report exhibits this power: 'This is my body'. During the unbroken memorial of this institution across the centuries, Christ's sovereign word, repeated by the priest, consecrates the offering. The economy of salvation is shown in all clarity in Capernaum. The omnipotence of the Word is the invincible coming into itself of absolute Life, revealing itself in its Word. Because the Word has become incarnate in Christ's flesh, the identification with this flesh is the identification with the Word—to eternal Life. 'Those who eat my flesh and drink my blood have eternal life, and I will raise them up on the last day'.[121]

By sharing in the flesh of Christ, we are given to ourselves in our flesh, as a living flesh which is ultimately that of Christ himself: 'In my flesh I am given to myself, but I am not my own flesh. My flesh, my living flesh, is Christ's'.[122]

Henry's careful, phenomenological, analysis of the Johannine themes of flesh and incarnation, inspired by Irenaeus, thus forces us to reconsider our all too ready identification of flesh and body. These are, in a phenomenological perspective, distinct realities: there is no flesh without a body, but the flesh is what it is precisely as that which is vivified by God. The 'doubling' which results from our forgetfulness (in a temporality which is not of this world) of our originary condition, between the 'I' that appears in the world and the 'me' that lives, or is given to live, at the heart of Life, is seen in the distinction between our body and our flesh, which are distinguished, not as separate objects or realities, but rather as situated on different phenomenological planes. 'Reduced to its objective aspect, our body is only one representation among others, a sort of reflection like that seen in a mirror. It also has the lightness, the transparency, the lack of reality, and the powerlessness of this image'.[123] As solid as it appears to us, it is only a reflection or a projection of our true reality. Henry continues: 'This represented body, the object offered to the gaze, draws its reality, its stunning, dynamic, and pathos-filled depths which makes of our incarnate condition what it is, from our invisible flesh. . . . it is in our invisible subjectivity where our actual reality is found'. The transcendental condition of this flesh is the effectuation of the Life that is God in the First Living One, the *pathos* of Life which is also effectuated as flesh, the Arch-Flesh engendered by the Arch-Pathos. Forgetful of our own true nature, absorbed in the appearances of the world, the Word of God, by his Incarnation, his becoming flesh, unveils for us, and so calls us back to, our proper condition as sons of God, born into life as living ones in the Living One, enfleshed in his flesh, through a birth which now has the aspect of a rebirth. The manifestation of the flesh, which is not governed by the world's phenomenality, is found only within the flesh; the flesh is not the means of the Word's revelation within the world, but, when the Word becomes flesh, the flesh is itself what is

[121] *Words of Christ*, 124. [122] *I Am the Truth*, 116. [123] *Words of Christ*, 17–18.

revealed. On the final page of *Incarnation*, in perhaps his most enigmatic, and certainly most provocative statement, Henry concludes: 'In its pathos-filled auto-impressionality, in its very flesh, given to itself in the Arch-passibility of absolute Life, it reveals this, which reveals it to itself, and it is in its pathos Life's Arch-revelation, the Parousia of the absolute. In the depth of its Night, our flesh is God'.[124]

JOHANNINE ARCH-INTELLIGIBILITY

Throughout this chapter I have been referring to Henry's 'reading of John'. But if it is such it is quite unlike anything to which we have become accustomed in scriptural scholarship or theology more generally. When he turns to examine 'The Word of God, Scripture', in the twelfth and penultimate chapter of *I Am the Truth*, he admits that 'text, here Scriptural text, has never been the object of our study'.[125] He continues: 'This is because any text aims at an object, or (as they say) has a referent. So it is not the text that gives us access to the object to which it refers. Because the object shows itself to us, the text can refer to it, and more generally, the word can speak of it'. Henry's way of 'reading', if we can use that word, Scripture, *as Scripture*, that is, as the Word of God addressed to us, is bound up with his phenomenality of Life and its difference to the phenomenality of the world.

That he is going to be doing something quite different is stated at the outset and unequivocally in the opening pages of his first volume of his Christian trilogy, where he is concerned with what or who Christianity considers as Truth: 'the truth of Christianity has precisely no relation whatsoever to the truth that arises from the analysis of texts or their historical study'.[126] The historical study of texts either considers the events reported in the texts or examines the texts themselves. With regard to the former option, the criterion of truth with which history operates is, in Henry's terms, that 'an event is historically true if it appeared in the world as a visible phenomenon of an objective sort'.[127] But, as already noted, most events throughout history, especially those concerning particular individuals, are lost to history; history is incapable of grasping the reality it defines as truth. As such, historical study turns instead to the texts themselves, so that 'from the perspective of history and its concept of truth as appearance in the world, the corpus of writings composing the New Testament suddenly acquires a decisive importance, *becoming the sole mode of access to what it is these texts are about, to Christ*

[124] *Incarnation*, 262; see also Henry, 'Phenomenology of Life', 108.

[125] *I Am the Truth*, 229.

[126] Ibid. 3. Cf. *Incarnation*, 226, on Genesis.

[127] *I Am the Truth*, 3.

and to God'.[128] But this again results in a quandary, for, apart from questions of the internal economy of a text (about which there are many possibilities), 'the reference of this text to reality, indeed, to a state of things foreign to the text itself is what constitutes its truth in the eyes of a historian'.[129] But is it indeed the case that to establish the historical truth about a text—the date at which it was written, its particular social and economic context, and so on—is to establish the truth of the events about which the text speaks?

More fundamentally, can the truth of Christianity be reduced to that of history, when the latter is understood as objectively visible phenomena appearing in the world? The truth of Christianity, Henry points out, is not that a certain Jesus wandered around from village to village, followed by disciples, until his arrest and crucifixion. Nor is it that this Jesus claimed, as a visible event in the world, to be the Messiah, the Son of God, which then led to his death. Even if this could be proved according to rigorously historical criteria, it could still be the ravings of a lunatic! 'Rather', as Henry continues, 'the truth of Christianity is that the One who called himself the Messiah was truly that Messiah, the Christ, the Son of God, born before Abraham and before time, the bearer in himself of Eternal Life, which he communicated to whomever he wanted, making that which is be no longer, or else that which is dead come alive'.[130] This is not a truth that can be established by dating the documents as near to the event as possible, for it would be no less true even if they were written centuries later. Neither is it possible to establish this truth through human language. Human speech, the speech of this world, is a manner of showing in this world, but a showing that is unreal and powerless, presenting nothing more than an image yet never making present, by its word, the reality about which it speaks.[131] My saying that I have a hundred thalers in my pocket does not make me any the richer!

In contrast to the phenomenality of the world and its language, as we have seen, the phenomenality of Life speaks another word, the Word of Life, a word that speaks directly and immediately, without any distance or duplicity. It speaks in the *pathos* of life that is the condition of every living one. 'Everywhere that Life's self-generation (and thus its self-revelation, and thus its Logos) is implicated, there too speaks the Word of Life. The Word of Life does not speak only at the beginning: it speaks in all living ones. What the Word of Life says within any living one is his Living'.[132] Speaking directly in the very condition of living, the Word of Life itself provides the ability for hearing its word:

> Moreover, engendering the one to whom it is addressed and doing so by making him a living one, the Word of Life has conferred on him in his very generation (somehow even before he lives, in the very process by which he came to life, in his

[128] Ibid. 5. [129] Ibid. 5. [130] Ibid. 6. [131] Ibid. 218–19. [132] Ibid. 223.

> transcendental birth) the possibility of hearing it—the word he heard in the first spasm of his own life, when he experienced himself for the first time, the life whose embrace of self, whose Word, had joined him to himself in the very surge of its Self and for ever after.[133]

In this immediacy, the Word of Life does not use human words, words which operate in the play of appearances in the world, the gap between the signifier and the signified, the unreal image and reality. Moreover, unlike human dialogue, this Word is not addressed to someone who pre-exists the Word, waiting to be addressed: 'Nobody is there before the Word, before it speaks. But the Word engenders the one to whom it is destined'.[134]

What then of Scripture, composed as it is of human words? Is it too not caught in the powerlessness of human language, recording a history to which we no longer have access, lost as it is to history, or having a referent to which we have no mode of other access? Henry, of course, recognizes that Scripture does indeed speak in human language. But in revealing to us the Word of God, the Word of Life, it directs us not to a lost past, to something that appears in the world, or even beyond the world, nor does it, of itself, create that about which it speaks. Rather:

> Scripture says that we are Sons of God. Saying this, it speaks in the manner of the world's word.... Relative to its worldly word, this referent—the condition of Sons of God—is exterior to them. Scripture does not have the ontological power to bring it into being, to make it exist, any more than does any other human word. It says but cannot prove that we are the Sons of God. But this referent, which is exterior to it and which it cannot bring into existence, *this is where we are, we the living ones*—living in Life, generated in absolute Life's self-generation, self-revealed in our transcendental Self in the self-revelation of this absolute Life, in the Word of God. By saying, 'You are Sons', the worldly word of Scripture turns away from itself and indicates the site where another word speaks.[135]

Scripture, as the Word of God addressed to us, in human words, breaks through our forgetfulness of our originary condition; it calls us back, as prodigals, to our primal condition as sons of the Father. This is not the remembering of a piece of information, in the way that for Plato knowledge is always a re-cognition of what was always already known by the subject himself. 'In Christianity, primitive knowledge—notably that which allows us to recognize the truth of Scripture—is the condition of Son. Therefore, it is not

[133] Ibid. 226.

[134] Ibid. 226. Cf. Ibid. 217: 'The other Word . . . differs in nature from any human speech. It understands neither words nor meanings, neither signifier nor signified, it has no referent, it does not come from an actual speaker, nor is it addressed to some interlocutor, *to anyone at all who might have existed before it—before it spoke.* It is this other Word that allows us to understand Scriptural speech and, in addition, to understand that this speech is of divine origin'.

[135] Ibid. 229–30.

me, the ego, who is capable as ego, through my thought or my will of re-cognizing that Scripture is true. It is not me who decides that this voice is the voice of an angel or of Christ: it is only the Word of life in me'.[136] As with Irenaeus' 'Christian cogito', it is because we are always already living, the life that is ultimately the life of God himself, that we are able to hear and recognize the Word of Life. And the locus for this is, once again, the flesh: 'Only God can make us believe in him, but he inhabits our own flesh'.[137]

When Henry stated, as we saw at the beginning of this section, that the scriptural text has never been his object of study, it was for the reason, as he put it, that it is only because something shows itself to us that a text can refer to it. The objects of history—past people and events showing themselves in the world—are never accessible to us, and so, as we saw, scriptural study, in the mode of history, turns to the text (which is before us) and its history, as if it were our only way to access that about which these texts speak, that is Christ and God. However, as God and his Christ are only revealed in their own light, not in the light of the world, they are present to us, in us, in the *pathos* of living. As such, regarding the texts of the New Testament, Henry asserts: 'It is not the corpus of the New Testament texts that can offer us access to the Truth, to that absolute Truth of which the corpus speaks. On the contrary, it is Truth and Truth alone that can offer us access to itself and by the same token to that corpus, allowing us to understand the text in which Truth is deposited and to recognize it there'.[138] It is only when read in this way, in the light of the Truth that is Christ, that these texts, one might say, are being read *as Scripture*, as the Word of God addressed to us, recalling us to Life. The Truth with which they are concerned is self-validating, known to us in the Christian 'cogito', that is, in the flesh, in living flesh. It cannot be attested by any other means or through any other form of phenomenality: 'Only Truth can attest to itself—reveal itself in and through itself'.[139]

Henry's final work, *Words of Christ*, examines how it is possible 'for humans to hear in their own language a word [*parole*] which would speak in another language, namely that of God or more exactly of his Word [*Verbe*]'.[140] He does this by tracing, not the narrative of the life of Christ presented in the Gospels, but how Christ's words address human beings about their own condition. Christ's words begin by disintegrating the world, reversing all of its standards and ideas about justice, resulting in an upheaval of the human condition itself. Then, in their own language, he addresses human beings about himself and his divine status, offering them the Word of Life, while also tackling the difficulty that humans have in hearing his word. His words culminate, on Henry's telling, with the passage quoted above, the words spoken in Capernaum regarding himself and his flesh.

[136] Ibid. 231. [137] Ibid. 233. [138] Ibid. 9. [139] Ibid. 10.
[140] *Words of Christ*, 8.

It is in John that we have the most profound and elevated words regarding Christ's own divine status, as the Son of the Father, life, and flesh. Henry's explanation of how John is able to speak these words are strikingly reminiscent of Origen's comments on John that we saw in an earlier chapter:

> It is in John . . . that the question of Christ's legitimation of his divine status gives rise to more intricate developments until finally it is given a reply of unfathomable depths.
>
> For John is not content with reproducing the confrontations which will lead to Jesus' condemnation and torment in all their tragic tension. His plan, at first glance unrealizable, is to validate Christ's affirmation of his status as Son by placing himself as it were at the interior of this affirmation and in being coextensive with its movement. More radically: by placing himself at the interior of the very condition of Christ and in identifying with it.[141]

John can speak as he does because he has become identified with Christ. Speaking from this position, identified with Christ, John unveils, in Henry's terms, an 'Arch-intelligibility', meaning an intelligibility which is other than, prior to, and the transcendental condition for, any other form of intelligibility. With this 'Arch-intelligibility', already given in the Prologue, 'a mode of revelation comes into play that is different from the one by which the world becomes visible; and that, for this reason, what it reveals is made up of realities that are invisible in this world and unnoticed by thought': that is, the Word, Life, and Flesh.[142] As we have seen when examining what is meant by 'becoming flesh', 'an entirely new definition of humanity is formulated, which is as unknown to Greece as it is to modernity: *The definition of an invisible, and at the same time carnal, human being—and invisible in so far as it is carnal*'.[143]

The final chapter of *Incarnation* is devoted to this theme of the 'Johannine Arch-intelligibility'. The Word, Life, and Flesh form an 'Arch-intelligibility' as it is not thought which gives access to them, but rather they which gives access to thought, inasmuch as thought is a mode of life and is revealed to itself only in Life lived in flesh. From the beginnings of Greek philosophy, Henry contends, 'thought, the distancing of the ek-static horizon where it moves—nature as the primitive "outside itself", contemplation of Ideas, representation, the subject–object relation, intentionality, being-in-the-world—has been . . . the phenomenological basis for, and thus the essence of, intelligibility'.[144] But before the world opens up and thought moves within it, the *pathos* of life is already there as the only truly originary, though invisible, beginning. Thus:

> Only absolute Life carries out this self-revelation of the Beginning. It is here that the pretension of human thought to attain Truth *by the force of its own thinking*

[141] Ibid. 62 modified (*Paroles*, 80). [142] *Incarnation*, 18. [143] Ibid. 19.
[144] Ibid. 254–5.

> goes up in smoke. It is here that the phenomenological intuitions of Life join together with those of Christian theology—*recognizing a common presupposition that is no longer that of thought.* Before thought, thus before phenomenology and theology alike (before philosophy or any other theoretical discipline), a Revelation is at work, which owes them nothing but which they all equally assume. Before thought, before the opening of the world and the unfolding of its intelligibility, absolute Life's Arch-intelligibility fulgurates, the Parousia of the Word in which it is embraced.
>
> We are thus presented with Life's paradox: Only its Arch-intelligibility allows us to understand what in us is the most simple, most elementary, most banal, and most humble, and which, as an effect of this Arch-intelligibility whence we originate, reaches us in the heart of our being. In the heart of our 'being': where all the living come to life, where Life gives it to itself in the Arch-intelligibility of its absolute self-givenness—in our transcendental birth, and where we are Sons.[145]

This revelation of life is, as we have seen, equally the revelation of flesh. This is not a revelation made by means of a body visible in the horizon of the world, 'the coming of an intelligible Logos in a material putrescible body', an understanding of Incarnation that 'dissipates like a mirage in the Johannine Arch-intelligibility'.[146] It is, rather, 'the extraordinary concept of flesh unveiled in Christianity. A flesh that is sensible only in the secret of its affective tonalities and its invisible, *pathos*-filled determinations'.[147] Whereas the Greek *logos* denotes both reason and the possibility of human language, words signifying an empty presence, the Word of Life is manifest in and as flesh, a flesh which is incapable of lying: 'Flesh does not lie because it cannot lie, because at bottom where it is gripped by Life, it is Life that speaks, Life's Logos, the Johannine Arch-intelligibility'.[148]

The Arch-intelligibility of Word, Life, and Flesh are given, as we have seen, in 'the event without measure that is the Christian Incarnation', that which 'since it occurred . . . has always been lived by Christians as the revelation of God himself'.[149] In the final pages of *Incarnation*, Henry turns once more to the question of how the revelation that is proper to the Incarnation of the Word, taken in terms of John's Arch-intelligibility, is to be understood. As long as the flesh is confused with the body, this revelation will be confused with an appearing in the world. But, as Henry reminds us, 'Is it not enough to recall a final time that the Incarnation of the Word is not its coming in a body, but in flesh?' As he then raises this question one final time, he rephrases it, with a twist:

> Or, to say it in a more rigorous way, that its coming in this body that some have seen was not dissociable from the coming of absolute, invisible Life in its Word.

145 Ibid. 255. 146 Ibid. 256. 147 Ibid. 256. 148 Ibid. 257.
149 Ibid. 257–8.

> And that it is this Word in its Arch-passibility that was made flesh, not dissociable from this flesh itself, and like our own, destined to suffer and also to die. Its hidden reality now takes place in the Coming of the Word in its visible body, the eternal generation of the Only Son, first born in absolute Life's self-generation.[150]

Here, for the first time, Henry connects the Word becoming flesh with the coming of the Word in a (physically) visible body, even if only by the repeated negative assertion that it is 'not dissociable' from the flesh and its invisible life in its Word.

But he does so to subvert, once again, our deeply engrained suppositions. For Philip, as he points out, is still unable to see and understand what Christ says to him, that he is in the Father and the Father in him. 'But what are we ourselves?' Henry asks; and answers: '*Are we not a flesh that in its reality is like the one the uncertain gaze of Philip questions?*', that is, 'an invisible flesh generated in absolute Life's self-generation in its Word, in the Arch-passibility from which every conceivable flesh draws its pure phenomenological material, its pathos-filled auto-impressionality?'[151] This generation takes place when God breathed the breath of life into the clay, making it living flesh, and it is to this transcendental birth that the Incarnation recalls us, tearing away the illusion that we are worldly beings and revealing to us that our proper condition, as human beings, is filial. The connection between John and Genesis—of such importance to Irenaeus, and following him Henry as well—holds together the insufflation of life into the clay with the Johannine generation of flesh in the Word. Although the Word, as Irenaeus says, 'was already in the world and invisibly sustained all created things', it was in the last days that he was made man, so that, as Henry comments, 'from then on, the historical Incarnation of the Word in a visible body has the goal of reminding human beings that it is in this Word that he had been made in the beginning, in the image and likeness of God: in the invisible'.[152] It had only been 'said', Irenaeus notes, that human beings were made in the image of God, but it was not 'shown', for the Word was as yet invisible, and so human beings easily lost the condition of manifesting 'likeness' to the Word. 'But', Irenaeus continues, 'when the Word of God became flesh, he confirmed both of these, showing forth the image truly, since he became himself what was his image, and he re-established the likeness in a sure manner, by assimilating the human being to the invisible Father through means of the visible Word'.[153] Henry comments on this: 'What the Incarnation of the Word in the human condition spoke, therefore, was ultimately the transcendental generation of every living, carnal Self in this Word; it was the transcendental truth of the human being'.[154]

[150] Ibid. 258. [151] Ibid. 258. [152] Ibid. 259. [153] Irenaeus, *haer.* 5.16.2.
[154] *Incarnation*, 259.

Yet Philip, standing bodily before Christ, remains hesitant. So, Henry asks, 'How can we overcome the paradox that entrusts to the visible the revelation of the Invisible?' And in reply: 'In order for the Word that has become visible in its Incarnation to allow us to see in this Incarnation the Word in whose likeness we have been made, must we not presuppose that the One that we see, or rather that they have seen, and also testify that they have seen, is precisely the Word? Must we not already believe in him? *Then what does it mean to believe when believing means believing in the Christ?*'[155] Again, it is not a matter of establishing the form of an appearance within the world, but reflecting on what it means to believe. Belief, for Henry, is not an act of thought, representing for itself in thought that which it thinks, so that it can claim to have evidence for its belief, to give it the status of knowledge, but always an inferior form of knowledge to that of the world for which the objects of its knowledge appear in the light of day. As the content of belief does not appear in the horizon of the world, we are drawn back to the phenomenological foundation of Life's self-revelation in its Word, which, as we have seen, is 'foreign to the world, to every sight and every thought, where belief and faith are possible, where everything is given without separation'.[156] To say, 'I believe in Christ', means then, as Henry rephrases it, 'I am certain of the truth which is in Him', or rather, 'which is in You'. Yet this is a truth, as we have seen, that is also in us. So, Henry continues:

> But how can I be certain of the truth which is in the One to whom I say 'You', unless it is because His own Truth is in me? This presupposes in the first place that since the truth that is in me—my own certainty—is the truth that is in Him, *it is homogeneous with him, and is indeed neither thought, nor the certainty of a thought, but the truth proper to the Word, the Truth of Life, the Arch-intelligibility we're talking about.* . . . 'I am certain of the truth which is in You' now means: I draw my certainty, my truth from the truth that is in You, I draw my life from yours, 'it is no longer I who live, it is you who live in me'. Because 'God engenders himself as myself', and because 'God engenders me as himself', then, truly, because it is his life that has become my own, my life is nothing other than his own: I am deified, according to the Christian conception of salvation.[157]

While Philip still does not understand the One he sees, and what this One standing before him says of himself and his relation to the Father, John, standing at the foot of the cross and putting on the identity of Christ, does, and does so precisely by putting himself at the interior of the condition of Christ. It is John's testimony to what he has seen that witnesses to us the fact of the Incarnation of the Word: it is in his words that we 'see', or perhaps better 'hear', the Incarnate Word speaking to us from his flesh and recalling us to that flesh which we also share.

[155] Ibid. 259. [156] Ibid. 260. [157] Ibid. 260.

In the final instance, then, the Johannine Arch-intelligibility, 'in which every Self experiences itself in the one firstborn Son in whom absolute life undergoes its own trial and enjoys itself', is an 'Arch-gnosis', 'arch' in the sense that it 'comes before the world's "outside itself", before every intelligibility that sees in it, before every form of knowledge and science, before what we have always called a "knowing", a "gnosis"'.[158] It is not a 'gnosis' akin to the 'gnosis falsely so-called' opposed by Irenaeus, which, ignoring the truth, was 'only able to develop dangerous, imaginary, extravagant, speculative constructions, the product of mere fantasies'.[159] But it is nevertheless an initiation into a truth hidden from the world and which will abide even when the world passes away. It is, Henry says, 'the secret hidden since the origin of the world, into this great secret that we are. This secret is the Johannine Arch-intelligibility in which we are initiated into what we are in our transcendental generation in Life'.[160] He then continues:

> But because Arch-intelligibility is an Arch-passibility—the Arch-passibility in which God eternally loves himself in the infinite love of his Word—because it is also in this Arch-passibility that this Word has taken on flesh and that every flesh is possible (ours as well as his own), then it truly inhabits all flesh shattering the idea that we have of this.[161]

We come back to the fact, a scandal to the disciples at Capernaum, that the revelation, effectuated by and in the Word, is itself this flesh.

Never before has so much been placed at stake on the flesh, that it should be the locus of knowledge, life, and God himself. 'In the depths of its Night, our flesh is God', writes Henry, and continues:

> We had never before asked flesh to hold the principle of knowledge within it, and supreme knowledge, which is even more. That is why it disconcerts and defies the wisdom of the wise and the science of the scholars, and every form of knowledge that arises from the world, which thinks, measures, and calculates from it every thing that we have to think, to do, and to believe. We had never before asked flesh to hold the principle of our knowledge and our action, but it itself has never asked anything of anyone—or anything other than to enlighten it, to enlighten it about itself and to tell us what it is. When in its innocence each modality of our flesh undergoes experiencing itself, being nothing other than itself, when suffering says suffering and joy joy, it is actually flesh that speaks, and nothing has power against its word.[162]

This is the word, the Word of Life, which does not lie and cannot be spoken against. Irenaeus' 'Christian cogito' is not a belief that is an inferior form of knowledge, but the originary form of all knowledge, an 'Arch-gnosis'. It is in

[158] Ibid. 261. [159] Ibid. 261. [160] Ibid. 261. [161] Ibid. 261.
[162] Ibid. 262.

the flesh that we live, and knowing life know Christ, needing to be recalled, by his Incarnation, to our own proper existence as flesh, the flesh of life.

We will leave our exposition of Henry, with the closing paragraph of *Incarnation*:

> Thus John's Arch-intelligibility is implicated everywhere there is life, it extends even to these beings of flesh that we are, taking into its incandescent Parousia our paltry wants and our hidden scars, as it did for the wounds of Christ on the Cross. The more each of our sufferings happens in us in a way that is pure, simple, stripped of everything, and reduced to itself and to its phenomenological body of flesh, the more strongly the unlimited power that gives it to itself is felt in us. And when this suffering reaches its limit point in despair, the Eye of God looks upon us. It is the unlimited intoxication of life, the Arch-pleasure of its eternal love in its Word, its Spirit, that submerges us. All who are brought low will be raised. 'Blessed are those who suffer', who perhaps have nothing left but their flesh. Arch-gnosis is the gnosis of the simple.[163]

[163] Ibid. 262, modified; the statement 'Blessed are those who suffer' ('Heureux ceux qui souffrent', translated as 'Happy are those who suffer'), is given in *Essence of Manifestation*, 671, with the reference Matt. 5:10 ('Blessed are those who are persecuted for righteousness sake'); it is repeated also at the end of Henry's essay, 'Phenomenology of Life', 108 ('Happy are those who suffer. In the Depths of its Night, our flesh is God. The Archignosis is the gnosis of the simple').

7

History, Phenomenology, and Theology

Michel Henry's phenomenological analysis of the Christian revelation unveiled in particular by John is radically different, in its idiom and movement of thought, to the historical and scriptural analyses offered in the first parts of this work. As we noted in the Introduction, most modern readers of John have tended to work within the historical horizon projected as the domain for their scholarship: John's text is read either as reflecting or responding to that projected historical context (such as persecution, the parting of the ways between Christianity and Judaism, or tensions within the Johannine community), seeing this as the background for a developing understanding of the person of Christ, or else as framing its account of Christ in the narrative of the Gospel by deploying the literary forms (such as biographies) and frameworks or modes of thinking available in that context (such as Platonism, Gnosticism, or more recently and fruitfully apocalyptic), or a combination of both. Such accounts, as illuminating as they are, however, are only the first step in the hermeneutic of understanding, needing to be melded together, as Gadamer put it, with our own horizons. The other readers of John we have listened to in this study, such as Ignatius, Melito, and especially Irenaeus—when read with a similar historical discipline to avoid Skinner's 'mythology of doctrines'—read John with just such a melding of horizons in their own time (yet one that we have argued is in continuity, historically and theologically, with John himself), reading the Gospel in a paschal and martyric light and elaborating, on the basis of the poetics of his text (and those of others, especially Paul), what is best described as a theo-anthropological domain of reflection. Henry, on the other hand, rejects in principle the historical and exegetical project undertaken by modern scholars, and instead, stimulated by the poetics and logic of John's text (and Irenaeus and others), hears the Word addressed to us through Scripture as he reflects phenomenologically upon life, how it appears, and what it is to live in the *pathos* of the flesh, a horizon which is inescapably and insistently in the present. Yet as different as Henry's domain of thought is to other ways of reading John, he clearly attains insights similar to those we have found through the historical and exegetical disciplines, especially pertaining to what it is to be born into life as a living human being sharing in the *pathos* of Christ.

Can, then, these different domains of thought be brought into dialogue with each other, even if not directly? Common to these three discourses is a concern for revelation, or more specifically *apocalypsis*: indeed, this vocabulary ('unveiling', 'manifestation', 'appearance', 'revelation') is, as Henry notes, common to both phenomenology and theology,[1] and also, as we saw in Chapter 2, scriptural exegesis as practised by the apostles and evangelists themselves. The 'apocalypse of the mystery' that is 'the preaching of Jesus Christ' is 'made manifest and made known through the prophetic writings' (Rom. 16:25–7), when Christ takes away the veil that lies upon Moses so that we, with unveiled face, can turn to the Lord to see his glory, and be changed into his likeness from one degree of glory to another (cf. 2 Cor. 3.14–18). Similarly in the Synoptic presentation of Christ, it is only through the opening of the Scripture that the disciples are able to recognize Christ in the breaking of the bread (Luke 24), to know, that is, that his Passion—by which he offers us, in the present, to share in his living flesh—is not a defeat, as it appears to the world, but a victory and the source of life. And likewise for John: although that Jesus is the one spoken of by Moses and the prophets is known to the disciples at the outset (1:45), it is only once Christ has been glorified that the disciples are able to 'remember' what had been written of him (12:16), and, by the guidance of the other Paraclete, the Spirit, be taught all things and remember all that he had said (14:26), and so chew the flesh that he now offers as the exalted Son of Man (6:35–66). Continuing in this vein, Irenaeus also speaks of the cross as unveiling the treasure, Christ himself, hidden in the Scriptures, which are otherwise read only as 'myths' or narratives about the past (*haer.* 4.26.1), and which makes possible a participation in the Eucharist that transforms our own death into a eucharistic offering 'so that we should never mistake the true understanding of things as they are, that is, of God and the human being' (*haer.* 5.2.3).

For Henry, on the other hand, it is the rigorous application of phenomenology that pierces the veil of the world that lies over our minds, enabling us to see through the lies of the world and so come to know truth and life, God as Life and ourselves as living ones in his life and sharing in the *pathos* of his flesh. Henry's phenomenological analysis of the Arch-intelligibility of the Christian revelation does not proceed by analysing texts, for, as he argues, it is only because texts speak of a referent which *also* shows itself to us that texts can even speak of it, whether this is a showing in the appearance of the world, where even past historical events can 'show' themselves to us in the unreal content of our thought, or whether it is Christ showing himself to us in the immediacy of our own *pathos* of life, which is ultimately his originary *pathos*, and calling us into life as enfleshed beings. Yet, for Henry, it is nevertheless

[1] *Incarnation*, 23. Cf. *I Am the Truth*, 13, 23.

by *reading* Scripture that we can be recalled, because of our originary identity with Christ as living ones in the Living One, from our absorption in the appearances of this world, to encounter Christ in the *pathos* of life: Henry's phenomenology is therefore also a reading of Scripture.[2]

Through our historical and exegetical explorations in Parts One and Two, we have seen how the apostles and evangelists read Scripture (the Old Testament) in the light of the Passion to encounter the Living One, the Word of God made flesh, and how those following them continued to read Scripture (now both Old and New Testaments) in the paschal light and a context of martyrdom and eucharistic celebration, being born into life and receiving the life-giving flesh of the Word. Similarly, through his phenomenological reading of Scripture (now primarily if not exclusively the New Testament) Henry finds life in the *pathos* of the flesh deriving from the Arch-*Pathos* of Christ himself, the First Living One, and his flesh.[3] The question of how the *pathos* explored by Henry relates to the *pathos* that is the Passion of Christ is one that will be addressed shortly below. But for now, it is important to have established that Henry's phenomenological reading of Scripture rests upon its unveiling just as much as does the apostolic and early Christian practice of reading Scripture, as discerned through a historically oriented reading of their texts. And Henry does this while also addressing head-on the need to lift the other veil, that lying over our own minds (cf. 2 Cor. 3:15), as also does the early Christian tradition, especially in the ascetic realm, so that we can turn to the Lord and see his glory, in the immediacy of the *pathos* of life, before the horizon, or veil, of the world spreads itself across our perception.[4] By attending, then, through historical discipline, to how Scripture was read *as Scripture*, a space has opened up in which exegetes, theologians, *and* phenomenologists can together read Scripture *as Scripture*, chewing its cud, as Origen puts it, to be nourished by the Word.

[2] For an examination of the way in which Scripture is used (surprising frequently) in French phenomenology, and calling for a greater attentiveness to hermeneutics, as exemplified by Paul Ricœur, see Christina M. Gschwandtner, 'Phenomenology, Hermeneutics, and Scripture: Marion, Henry, and Falque on the Person of Christ', *Journal for Cultural and Religious Theory* 17.2 (2018), 281–97.

[3] The question naturally arises whether Henry's reading of Scripture resembles that of the Valentinians, whom Irenaeus (*haer.* 2.13.3) accused of projecting their own inner states onto the heavens, a conclusion reiterated by David Dawson, commenting that Valentinus turns the drama of Scripture into a 'psychodrama', so that 'In the end, this state of being [wrought by the *Gospel of Truth*] is the speaker's own; as a visionary, Valentinus's ultimate concern is neither for textuality nor language in general, but for the personal subject or self'. David Dawson, *Allegorical Readers and Cultural Revision in Ancient Alexandria* (Berkley: University of California Press, 1992), 171, 165. This, however, is beyond the scope of this study; suffice it to say that Henry is reading Scripture as a phenomenologist, not a visionary, and is doing so in company with Irenaeus (as are we).

[4] Cf. Douglas Burton-Christie, *The Word in the Desert: Scripture and the Quest for Holiness in Early Christian Monasticism* (Oxford: Oxford University Press, 1993).

Unveiling necessarily results in a 'doubling', contrasting how things appear in this world and the reality that is revealed when the appearances are unveiled.[5] As this unveiling pivots upon the cross, the originary doubling is that of the proclamation of Christ crucified, the gospel: a stumbling block and foolishness, on the one hand, but on the other the power and wisdom of God (cf. 1 Cor. 1:23–4). And in the wake of this proclamation a series of other doublings follow: the text of Scripture, which had been read as narratives of the past turn out to be speaking of Christ and his cross; Christ, who had been known as the son of Joseph and Mary, turns out to be the eternal Word of God, the Son of the Father; the Eucharist, which appears in this world to be bread, is his living flesh; Jerusalem, an earthly city, is our heavenly mother (cf. Gal. 4:26); and regarding ourselves, though we have 'an earthly tent', we also 'have a building from God, a house not made by hands, eternal in the heavens' (2 Cor. 5:1), with a name 'written before the foundation of the world in the book of life of the lamb who was slain' (Apoc. 13:8), a contrast, in Henry's terms, between being bodily sons and daughters of human parents yet, as living flesh, sons and daughters of God.[6]

John Ashton, as we noted when exploring in Chapter 2 how the Gospel of John might be described as an 'apocalyptic gospel', asserts that 'for Enoch, and for apocalyptic writers generally, there are not two worlds but one: or rather the whole of reality is split into matching pairs (rather like the biological theory of DNA) in which one half, the lower, is the mirror image (albeit in this case a distorting mirror) of the higher'.[7] In a similar manner, Martyn describes John as having a 'stereoptic vision', holding together, in the blending of times that characterizes John's Gospel, the Christ who had been present with his followers and who is also now, having ascended to heaven through the cross, still present with his community, testifying, with them, to others: 'we bear witness to what we have seen' (John 3:11). This stereoptic vision can also be seen between the presentation of Christ in the Synoptics and that in John, which, we suggested, follows the movement of thought in the line from the Anaphora of John Chrysostom, 'in the night in which he was given up or rather gave himself up': in the Synoptics Jesus is put to death and abandoned by his disciples, in John he voluntarily goes to the cross and the Evangelist stands unashamed at its foot. Both are held together in the stereoptic vision of the fourfold gospel. A stereoptic vision, we further suggested, might also well describe the relationship between the Gospel and the Apocalypse, written

[5] For a broader examination of the theme of 'doubling' from Plato to Plotinus, via Thomas, Gnoticism, and Mani, see Charles Stang, *Our Divine Double* (Cambridge, MA: Harvard University Press, 2016).

[6] For a full exposition of this doubling, see Origen's exposition of how Scripture should be read in *Princ.* 4.3.6–15, treated above in Chapter 4.

[7] Ashton, *Fourth Gospel*, 327.

(if we take John to be the author of both) by one who stood at the foot of the cross and at the throne in heaven, at the same time, for the cross is the throne from which Christ reigns: the Gospel, as a narrative climaxing in the apparent defeat of the cross, as it seems to the world, veils the victory of Christ under irony, double meaning, and the blending of times, while the Apocalypse in turn unveils the eternal and universal dimensions of the gospel.

Doubling is also a prominent feature of Henry's presentation of the Christian revelation. The 'duplicity of appearing' that occurs on the world's stage, means that 'in Christianity everything is doubled':[8] appearance and truth; body and flesh; the 'me' given to myself in the *pathos* of life and the 'I' that I project in this world. He continues a little later: 'Everything is doubled, but if what is double—what is offered to us in a double aspect—is in itself one and the same reality, then one of its aspects must be merely an appearance, an image, a copy of reality, but not that reality itself—precisely its double'.[9] In exegetical terms, when the Scriptures are read as speaking of Christ, the lamb slain at Passover, for instance, is seen to be a 'type' of Christ, bearing his imprint or stamp, such that the reality in fact precedes the type (for the seal precedes the imprint in the wax upon which it is stamped), even though the type appears first in the time of the world.[10] For Henry, however, the image of reality is not simply a mirror image, or a even distorting mirror, but, in a harsher (Johannine) manner, a 'trap' and a 'lie', unfolding 'a universe whose principle is hypocrisy'.[11] Does Henry, then, have a 'stereoptic vision'? He clearly sees two different realms of appearance: that of life and that of the world. Identity, for Henry, is found in life: it is in the *pathos* of life, which is identical with itself in its self-affectivity, that we find our true identity, and indeed an identity, though derivatively, with God. In the world, all we have is the duplicitous doubling of this identity, the appearance of a body rather than the flesh. Is there, then, no reality to the body, to what appears in the world and the world itself? Is Henry's phenomenological presentation of Christianity some kind of resurgence of Gnosticism, as has been claimed?[12] Alternatively, is the Christ on the cross, appearing in the world and its history, a deceptive

[8] Henry, *I am the Truth*, 194. [9] Ibid. 195.

[10] Recall the words of Nicholas Cabasilas, quoted earlier: 'It was not the old Adam who was the model for the new, but the new Adam for the old.... Because of its nature, the old Adam might be considered the archetype to those who see him first, but for him who has everything before his eyes, the older is the imitation of the second.... To sum it up: the Savior first and alone showed to us the true human being, who is perfect on account of both character and life and in all other respects'. *The Life in Christ* 6.92–4 (ET 6.12 modified).

[11] *I am the Truth*, 195.

[12] Most forcefully by Jad Hatem, *Le sauveur et les viscère de l'être: Sur le gnosticisme et Michel Henry* (Paris: L'Harmattan, 2004); see also Joseph Rivera, *The Contemplative Self After Michel Henry: A Phenomenological Theology*, Thresholds in Philosophy and Theology (Notre Dame, IN: Notre Dame University Press, 2015), 153–66.

illusion, resulting in some kind of monism?[13] Or, to put the question as we raised it earlier: what is the relationship between the *pathos* that is the Passion of Christ, Pascha, and the *pathos*, or the Arch-*Pathos*, of which Henry speaks?

It is striking that Henry almost never speaks of the Passion—meaning the single event that encompasses the crucifixion, resurrection, and ascension—nor the cross. In part this is no doubt because he is not reading the Gospels as narratives or biographies, dramas unfolding on the stage of the world and its history and leading towards their climax on the cross. In this, his work is akin to Origen's *On First Principles*, which also expounds the 'principles' of Christian theology, including two full chapters on how the one Christ is spoken of as divine and human, without any mention there, or elsewhere in the work, of the Passion, apart from an allusive passage, if my reading of this is accepted.[14] Henry's phenomenological analyses in his Christian trilogy culminate, rather, in the last paragraphs of *Words of Christ*, with Christ's words in Capernaum and the institution of the Eucharist celebrated across the centuries. Moreover, that Henry focuses primarily on Christ as 'the Living One' (not surprising perhaps given his lifelong fascination with life and its own proper phenomenality) indicates that the Christ he presents us with, throughout his trilogy, is not, as he puts it, the Jesus who wandered from village to village, the proper subject for history, but is rather, although he never quotes from this book, the one who speaks in the Apocalypse: 'I am the First and the Last, I am the Living One, I was dead and behold I am Living' (Apoc. 1:17–18).

So, far from there being no place for the cross in Henry's reflection, it is rather that, while rarely speaking of it, the one whom he is concerned to present as the Arch-Intelligibility of Christianity is always and only the one who is known through the Passion, the paschal Christ.[15] Like Paul, Henry is

[13] Rivera, *The Contemplative Self After Michel Henry*, 162, would see in Henry not so much a Gnostic dualism, but a '*qualified monism* in the particular sense that it prioritizes the interior non-temporal world at the utter expense of the exterior temporal field of the world' (italics original). See also Emmanuel Falque, 'Is There a Flesh Without Body? A Debate with Michel Henry', *Journal of French and Francophone Philosophy*, 24.1 (2016), 139–66; and Emmanuel Falque, 'Michel Henry théologien (à propos de *C'est moi la vérité*', *Laval théologique et philosophique* 57.3 (2001), 525–36. Falque would see in Henry a monism akin to Spinoza, developing from a 'monism of life' in *I am the Truth* to a 'carnal monism' in *Incarnation.*

[14] Origen, *Princ.* 2.6.3, for comment on this passage, see Behr, ed. and trans., *Origen: On First Principles*, lxvi–lxxvii, and for *On First Principles* as an 'apocalyptic work', ibid., lxxx–lxxxviii.

[15] Kevin Hart, '"Without World": Eschatology in Michel Henry', in Neal DeRoo and John Panteleimon Manoussakis, eds, *Phenomenology and Eschatology: Not Yet in the Now*, Ashgate New Critical Thinking in Religion, Theology, and Biblical Studies (Farnham, UK: Ashgate, 2009), 167–92, at 179, notes that: 'Henry's philosophy of Christianity is eschatological through and through', though for Hart this results in a Christology that 'inclines sharply to monophysitism' (ibid. 177), a 'philosophy [that] is at heart Neoplatonic' (ibid. 177), and which 'disassociates history and eschatology, including the *historia salutis* and the *ordo salutis*, so completely as to risk becoming Marcionite. That the incarnation takes place in Jewish flesh is overlooked completely' (ibid. 178), differing from Balthasar 'in his bypassing of the Passion as central to eschatology, and in the soteriological significance of the Passion'. Henry no doubt appears so

focused on Christ and him crucified (cf. 1 Cor. 2:2); and as with Paul he does not dwell on the way that the crucified one appeared in the world and to the world, but rather focuses on the one proclaimed (thus heard, not seen) as the wisdom and the power of God (cf. 1 Cor. 1:24). Indeed, so much is this the case, that in *Barbarism* Henry can contrast the truth of arithmetic with the truth that is, simply, 'the Christ on the cross'.[16] Likewise, in words which echo Athanasius, he can write, towards the end of *Incarnation*, of 'the Parousia concealed on the wood of the cross'.[17] Finally, though more allusively, there is the passage, given in full and analysed in Chapter 6, which describes how the coming of the Word in a visible body is 'not dissociable' from the coming of invisible Life in its Word. He writes there that: 'Its hidden reality now takes place in the Coming of the Word in its visible body, the eternal generation of the Only Son, first born in absolute Life's self-generation'.[18] This Coming of the Word in its visible body would seem to be nothing other than the Parousia of the Word upon the cross, visible indeed to the world, but only as dead, while invisibly alive in the flesh generated as the very substance of life. The Passion is, to borrow de Boer's phrase, 'the Apocalypse of God',[19] the manifestation of the invisible reality that takes place in the heart of God himself, the self-generation of absolute Life in the eternal generation, through the Arch-*Pathos*, of the Arch-Son, the First Living One and Living Flesh. Upon the cross, the body of Christ is exposed to the world for all to see, or rather hear (in the proclamation); however, 'seeing' living and life-giving flesh, not a dead body, is only done in the field of life not the world (heard not seen), and so requires being called back to the life in which we already live before the world appears: 'the world will not see me, but you will see me because I live and you also will live', as Henry quotes John.[20]

For Henry, then, there is no stereoptic vision looking simultaneously to heaven and earth, above and below, as two distinct places, as there is in the Targums on Genesis, as we saw in Chapter 4, with the angels ascending and

when labouring under Skinner's 'mythology of doctrines' and a corresponding presupposition about how Scripture is read; however when read in the light of the historical and exegetical explorations carried out the first two parts of this study, it can be seen that Henry's approach, as different as it is in its phenomenological approach, yet has much in common with early Christian theology.

[16] *Barbarism*, 125.

[17] *Incarnation*, 250; cf. Athanasius, *Inc.* 19: while the disciples fled at the time of the crucifixion, 'what is most wonderful, even at his death, or rather at the very trophy over death, I mean the cross, all creation confessed that he who was made known and suffered in the body was not simply a human being but Son of God and Savior of all. For the sun turned back and the earth shook and the mountains were rent, and all were awed. These things showed the Christ on the cross to be God and the whole of creation to be his servant, witnessing in fear the advent [*parousia*] of the Master'.

[18] *Incarnation*, 258.

[19] De Boer, 'Apocalyptic as God's Eschatological Activity', 51.

[20] *I Am the Truth*, 85; John 14:19, . . . ὑμεῖς δὲ θεωρεῖτέ με, ὅτι ἐγὼ ζῶ καὶ ὑμεῖς ζήσετε, usually translated as 'you will see me; because I live you will also live'.

descending to compare Jacob on earth with his figure inscribed on the throne in heaven, an image that John transposes to the Son of Man as the one who bridges heaven and earth so that the angels ascend and descend upon him (1:51). In the unity of the paschal event as understood by John, as we have explored it in various ways throughout this work—whose Gospel does not narrate how Christ was put to death, nor present his Passion in terms of an atonement for sin, but rather affirms that he offers himself for the life of the world, a self-offering which is the paradigmatic expression of love—there is not simply a correspondence between heaven and earth, but a coincidence or identity: heaven and earth touch upon the cross; as clay is lifted up from the earth into heaven, heavenly bread, Christ's life-giving flesh, is brought down from heaven. Heaven, however, is clearly not, as Henry puts it, 'interstellar space, in the astro-physical universe explored by cosmonauts' but is rather the Life that is invisible to the world, the Arch-*Pathos* of the First Living One, whose life pulsates at the heart of all living ones.[21] And so rather than saying that heaven and earth touch upon the cross, it would be better to say that the apocalypse of the cross reveals heaven as the realm of life inhabited by all those who live, though invisible to the world.

To adapt the image used by Origen (*Princ.* 2.6.6, itself borrowed from the Stoics and which we already used in the Introduction), when a piece of iron, known by its particular properties (cold and hard), is placed in a fire, while remaining the iron it is, it is no longer known by the properties of iron but only by those of the fire (burning hot and fluid). So too, before the Passion Jesus Christ is known by certain observable properties and by them identified in various ways deriving from human perception (the carpenter from Nazareth, a teacher, and so on), yet ascending through the cross into the heavens and to God, a 'consuming fire' (Deut. 9:3; Heb. 12:29), he is known as the Word of God and his body, remaining what it is by nature, is now only known by the properties of God, beyond space and time, and the fire that is God in turn is now embodied, though a body not measured by the space and time of our world. Pascha is both *pathos* (as with Melito) and *passage* (as with Origen), the hour in which Christ departs from this world to the Father (John 13:1), no longer present in a body seen by the world but instead received as the flesh which gives life to the world, though in the world this remains veiled as bread. This is indeed a 'monism', for in the end God will be 'all in all'.[22] And so doubling in Henry is not that of a correspondence between two different and self-subsisting realms, seen by a stereoptic vision that looks to two different places at once, but is rather that resulting from an unveiling effected by 'the Apocalypse of God', or, as Richard Hays puts it, 'the eschatological *apokalypsis* of the cross'.[23] And the stereoptic vision that this eschatological unveiling

[21] Henry, *Words of Christ*, 41.

[22] 1 Cor. 15:28; cf. Origen, *Princ.* 3.6.2–3.

[23] Hays, *Echoes of Scripture*, 169.

facilitates is to see in 'the sufferings of this present time' (and not elsewhere) the groaning of creation, its labouring in travail, awaiting 'the *apokalypsis* of the sons of God', who are foreknown by God and predestined by him 'to be conformed to the image of his Son so that he might be the first-born of many brethren'.[24]

Until the consummation, then, 'the sufferings of this present time', the time of the world and the world itself, are real, as is the heaviness of the body.[25] But 'this present time' is only transitory, the birth-pangs necessary for life to be born, but not remembered when the woman finally gives birth to a human being (cf. John 16:21, and our comments in Chapters 3 and 4). In the light of the eschatological *apocalypsis* of the cross, these sufferings are seen as preceded by and embraced in the *pathos* of life found in Christ, just as the Passover lamb is preceded by and embraced in the paschal Christ.[26] As Henry puts it in the sentence concluding in the phrase we have previously cited: 'Thus, finally, this flux, this seemingly absurd parade of modest pleasures and oppressive thoughts, is secretly oriented toward an agony, toward the ultimate transition from the ultimate suffering of despair to the eruption of an unlimited joy, as evidenced by the Parousia concealed on the wood of the cross'.[27] When the veil of the world is finally and fully lifted, and the sufferings of the present time give way to unlimited joy in the birth into life, we find that our true identity is, and always has been, as living enfleshed sons and daughters of God, living ones in the Living One. For now, however, although 'our citizenship is in the heavens', we still await from it our Saviour (Phil. 3:20); if we have died to the world, born into and from the life that does not appear in the world, then 'our life is hidden with Christ in God', and so when he appears,

[24] Rom. 8:18–19, 29. For discussion and critique of the eschatological dimensions of Henry's phenomenology, see Kevin Hart, '"Without World": Eschatology in Michel Henry', and Jeffrey Hanson, 'Phenomenology and Eschatology in Michel Henry', in DeRoo and Manoussakis, eds, *Phenomenology and Eschatology*, 153–66.

[25] As Falque ('Is There a Flesh Without Body?' 157) points out: 'it does not suffice to recognize "the pain that is produced by climbing this sloping road" [the *pathos* in which Henry sees the flesh]; it is also necessary to recognize the weight of our own body (with its kilos, we dare to say!) without which this pain would never be experienced and which is necessary to climb to the summit of this town or countryside'. But Flaque presses too hard the distinction he wishes to make; as we have seen Henry assert, 'what is doubled—what is offered to us in a double aspect—is in itself one and the same reality' (*I am the Truth*, 195). In the world the weight of the body is real, as is the hardness of the iron, but not when seen in God, the consuming fire.

[26] As Origen points out regarding the Transfiguration: when the disciples saw Moses and Elijah speaking with Christ about his exodus they fell on their faces, knowing that one cannot see the face of the one who speaks with Moses on the mountain and live (cf. Exod. 33:20), but 'after the touch of the Word, lifting up their eyes they saw Jesus only and no other. Moses, the Law, and Elijah, the prophetic element, became one only with the Gospel of Jesus; and they did not remain three as they formerly were, but the three became one'. *Comm. Matt.* 12:43. Cf. Behr, *Way to Nicaea*, 171–2. See also Melito, *Pasch.* 35–45, the first full exposition of 'typology'.

[27] *Incarnation*, 250.

we too 'will appear with him', not in the world or a different spatio-temporal place called heaven, but 'in glory' (Col. 3:3–4).

It is in this context, exploring our life in Christ, that Henry comes to some of his most provocative statements. Perhaps the most dramatic, and seeming to imply a radical monism, is when he says that 'Life self-engenders itself as me',[28] or, in the saying of Meister Eckhart, of which he is so fond: 'God engenders me as himself'. To be born into life, however, 'is not to come into the world. To be born is to come into life.... To come into life means to come from life, starting from it, in such a way that life is not birth's point of arrival, as it were, but its point of departure'.[29] So much is this the case for Henry, that he can also say that, as living, human beings are '*not* created'![30] Henry is not speaking, as we tend to, in a historical or scientific register, but in a phenomenological one, in which 'the creation of the world... consists in the opening of this horizon of exteriority', in which something appears as other than it is in the self-affectivity of life, life which is nevertheless always prior to the appearance of the world.[31] As such, creation is essentially secondary or subsequent to begetting, though (as with scriptural types of Christ) they appear first in the sequence of temporality and causality belonging to the world of appearance. As such, as we saw, Henry claims that what is revealed in Christ 'obliges us to find... an entirely new and unusual conception of temporality—one that is the essence of Life's own temporality'.[32] Such 'temporality' would not be a distancing from itself, in the horizon of exteriority that is the temporality of the world, but, a 'radically immanent, inek-static, and pathos-filled [*pathètique*] temporality', in which 'there is neither before nor after in the sense we understand them, but rather eternal movement, an eternal flux in which life continuously experiences itself in the Self that life eternally generates, and which is never separated from itself'.[33]

Henry's assertions seem to be very much at odds with traditional theology, in which the fundamental distinction would be between God and everything else, created *ex nihilo*, and which would rather start by narrating the eternal generation of the second person of the Trinity, before turning to creation with its narration of creation and the fall, followed by a long history of salvation culminating with Incarnation and the Passion, which opens up the possibility for human beings to become, at the end (rather than the beginning), sons and daughters of God through baptism. Yet we must once again heed Skinner's cautions about the 'mythology of doctrines', to consider whether the ways in which we are used to hearing various doctrines are in fact the best or even appropriate. As we have seen at various points, Ignatius is insistent that it is only by sharing in the Passion of Christ that he will be born into life as a human being (*Rom.* 6), to 'be found to be the pure bread of Christ' (*Rom.* 4),

[28] *I Am the Truth*, 104. [29] Ibid. 59–60. [30] Ibid. 103.
[31] *Words of Christ*, 84. [32] *I Am the Truth*, 158. [33] Ibid. 159–60.

and indeed 'a word of God' (*Rom.* 2). His birth into life is founded upon the Passion of Christ and sharing in it. And as such, when, with Origen, the language of the 'eternal begetting' from the Father is used, it is so with respect to the Saviour and is an eternal begetting extended to the believer as well: they too are eternally begotten from the Father.[34] Even more striking is the affirmation of Maximus the Confessor, as paraphrased by Gregory Palamas: 'the saints clearly state that this adoption and deifying gift, actualized by faith, is real.... The divine Maximus has not only taught that it is real, but also that it is unoriginate (and not only uncreated), uncircumscribed and supra-temporal, so that those attaining it are thereby perfected as uncreated, unoriginate, and uncircumscribed, although in their own nature they derive from nothing'.[35] To understand this startling claim, it is helpful to return to the image of iron and fire, which we had used above in a Christological context: we ourselves, though coming into existence in the space and time of this world, have our end in the consuming fire that is God, in which the earthy matter that we are, while remaining what it is, will only be known by the properties of the fire, as 'uncreated, unoriginate, and uncircumscribed' by space or time. To enter into the eternity of God is not to enter at some moment of time, to be there thereafter, for there is no before or after in his eternity; we have to say that we are already there, and always have been, in what Henry describes as the 'radically immanent, inek-static, and pathos-filled temporality', in which there is neither before nor after, but an 'eternal flux in which life continuously experiences itself in the Self that life eternally generates', the Apocalypse of God at the cross, revealing Christ himself, as the First Living One, and us as living ones in him.

It might be the case that it was the 'Arian' controversy that resulted in the uncreated/created distinction becoming the primary distinction for theology. However, even when writing later in the fourth century against Eunomius, Gregory of Nyssa would put the matter somewhat differently, and more akin to what we have seen earlier in this chapter. Following the Apostle Paul's distinction between things that are seen and transient and those that are unseen and eternal (2 Cor. 4:18), Gregory asserts:

> Now, the ultimate division of all being is into the intellectual and the perceptible [*Πάντων τῶν ὄντων ἡ ἀνωτάτω διαίρεσις εἴς τε τὸ νοητὸν καὶ τὸ αἰσθητὸν τὴν τομὴν ἔχει*]; the perceptible nature is called by the Apostle 'that which is seen'. For

[34] Origen, *Hom. Jer.* 9:4: 'The Savior is eternally begotten by the Father, so also, if you possess the "Spirit of adoption" [Rom 8:15] God eternally begets you in him according to each of your works, each of your thoughts. And being begotten you thereby become an eternally begotten son of God in Christ Jesus' (*καῖ ἀεὶ γεννᾶται ὁ σωτὴρ ὑπὸ τοῦ πατρός, οὕτως καὶ σὺ ἐὰν ἔχῃς 'τὸ τῆς υἱοθεσίας,' ἀεὶ γεννᾷ σε ἐν αὐτῷ ὁ θεὸς καθ' ἕκαστον ἔργον, καθ' ἕκαστον διανόημα, καὶ γεννώμενος οὕτως γίνῃ ἀεὶ γεννώμενος υἱὸς θεοῦ ἐν Χριστῷ Ἰησοῦ·*).

[35] Gregory Palamas, *Triad* 3.1.31:... *ὡς καὶ τοὺς αὐτῆς εὐμοιρηκότας δι'αὐτὴν ἀκτίστους, ἀνάρχους, καὶ ἀπεριγράπτους τελέσαι, καὶτοι διὰ τὴ οἰκείαν φύσιν ἐξ οὐκ ὄντων γεγονότας.*

> as all body has colour, and the sight apprehends this, he calls this world by the rough and ready name of 'that which is seen'... The common term, again for the intellectual world, is with the apostle, 'that which is not seen': by withdrawing all idea of comprehension by the senses he leads the mind [διάνοιαν] on to the immaterial and intellectual. Reason [ὁ λόγος] again divides this 'which is not seen' into the uncreated and the created, inferentially comprehending it: the uncreated being that which effects the creation, the creation that which owes its origin and its force to the uncreated. In the sensible world, then, is found everything that we comprehend by our organs of bodily sense, and in which the differences of qualities involve the idea of more or less... But in the intelligible world—that part of it, I mean, which is created—the idea of such differences as are perceived in the perceptible cannot find a place; another method, then, is devised for discovering the degrees of greater and less.[36]

The distinction between the uncreated and the created finds its place within the overarching apostolic distinction between the seen and transient, on the one hand, and the unseen and eternal, on the other. The Apocalypse of God reveals the fundamental distinction between what is seen and unseen, within which we are led by reason to distinguish between uncreated and created.[37] And the vision of God this opens up—unseen by the world, but running throughout Scripture—is not that of a later philosophical deism, with God considered in or by himself (or as three), prior to and independent of everything else, but rather a vision of God as presiding over the heavenly court, in the celebration of the heavenly liturgy: 'God is in the congregation of gods' (Ps. 81:1). This vision pervades the Scriptures, and increases in the literature of Second Temple Judaism and apocalyptic works, to the New Testament proclamation that the crucified and risen Christ has been exalted to sit at the right hand of the Majesty on high (Heb. 1:3), in the throne room beheld by John in his Apocalypse, in which the One who sits on the throne and the slain lamb are offered 'blessing and honour and glory and might unto the ages of ages' (Rev. 5:13).[38] It was not only in the opening of Scriptures that

[36] Gregory of Nyssa, *Eun.* 1.270–3.

[37] Recall the words of Simone Pétrement quoted in Chapter 6: 'In the Old Testament the world was so narrowly and directly dependent upon God that God himself... was in turn almost tied up with and chained to the world.... The image of the cross is an image that liberates.... *The cross separates God from the world.* If it does not separate him absolutely, at least it puts him at a very great distance. It puts him much further away than the distinction between Creator and creature could do.... It is indeed, as Paul sees, something that is profoundly new, "a scandal to the Jews and folly to the Greeks"'. *A Separate God*, 37, italics original.

[38] The literature on this is vast, some of which has already been referred to in our discussion of apocalyptic. A full and excellent survey of the primary literature, from ancient Canaan to the New Testament and apocalyptic literature, together with many further references to modern studies, can be found in Paul B. Sumner, 'Visions of the Divine Council in the Hebrew Bible', PhD thesis (Malibu CA: Pepperdine University, 1991), several revised chapters of which can be found online at <http://www.hebrew-streams.org/works/hebrew/council.html> (accessed 19 December 2015).

the apostles encountered Christ, but in the breaking of bread, and similarly for those who followed them, and so also for Henry, as he concludes his trilogy by turning to the words of Christ in Capernaum and 'the unbroken memorial of this institution [of the Eucharist] across the centuries'.[39] As Bryan Spinks says of this dimension of Christian worship:

> In Christ the space of heaven and the region of earth are united. In the Eucharist the worshipper enters heaven through Christ, and is represented by the High Priest. Here time and eternity intersect and become one, and this world and the world to come elide.[40]

It is, perhaps, only when the liturgical context of the opening of the Scriptures is neglected that the distinction between created and uncreated becomes the primary marker for speaking about God and his creation.

The 'doubling' that we have been exploring, resulting from the unveiling effected by the Apocalypse of God through the cross, simultaneously reveals that what we had thought to be real and our real condition is in fact a veil, occluding the truth about ourselves. But it is also a veil, as we have seen, that is not only not dissociable from ourselves, but rather is oriented towards the final unveiling of our true condition as sons and daughters of God. As the Psalmist says, in the person of God: 'I say "You are gods, sons of the Most High; yet all of you shall die like human beings"' (Ps 81:6–7). It is by sharing in the *pathos* of Christ that we not only die like human beings, but in fact become living human beings, sons of God. Likewise Isaiah: 'I have begotten sons and exalted them', then adding, 'but they have rejected me' (Isa. 1:2). This rejection is not an episode in the history of the world—a 'Fall' preceded by a time in paradise and followed by a long history of salvation culminating in the Incarnation (a Plan A followed by a Plan B, as it were)—but is again inseparable from the act of unveiling, for there is no unveiling unless there is a veil, so that the veil becomes the medium in and through which the unveiling occurs. In exegetical terms, when the Scripture is unveiled, we don't see something else, but rather the Christ who has always been there, as treasure hidden in the types and prophecies it contains, which could not be understood prior to cross (cf. Irenaeus, *haer.* 4.26.1) As such the veil of the world is intrinsic to our arrival in life, the life which is itself, as Henry noted, always the point of departure.

As such, as Henry puts it, 'the occultation of the condition of the Son coincides apparently paradoxically with the very genesis of this condition'.[41] Coming into life is itself the very occasion for an egoism, in which I consider myself to be the ground of my own life, directing my attention away from the

[39] Henry, *Words of Christ*, 124.

[40] Bryan D. Spinks, *The Sanctus in the Eucharistic Prayer* (Cambridge: Cambridge University Press, 1991), 206.

[41] *I Am the Truth*, 135.

source of life towards that which I can see, do, or perceive in the world that opens up before me, resulting in a doubling between, on the one hand, the 'me' that is given to itself in life and that lives in the heart of Life, hidden in Christ, but which, on the other hand, forgetting itself by being absorbed in the world, appears as an 'I' in the world. Yet the appearances of the world are a flux that Henry sees as being oriented towards the final unveiling of unlimited joy in the Parousia of the Word on the cross. Similarly, Maximus the Confessor: 'Together with coming-into-being, the first human being gave this power—I mean the natural desire of the mind for God—by use of the faculty of perception to perceptible things, activating, in the very first movement, an unnatural pleasure through the medium of the senses'.[42] From the very first moment we open our eyes, as living beings, our perception is caught by what appears and life in turn disappears from such sight. Yet as Maximus goes on to explain, by the cycle of pleasure and pain in which we are then immersed, the cycle of genesis (coming-into-being) and corruption (death), we are brought back to ourselves in the life that Christ offers, as, by his Passion, he 'converted the use of death' so that we too might be able to 'use death' as the means which 'mystically leads to divine and unending life'.[43] It is only when the solution is unveiled on the cross that the problem is seen for what it is, but the problem is thereby turned inside out and becomes, instead, the means of sharing in the solution, so resulting, as we saw in Chapter 4, in the living human being, the glory of God, the martyr following Christ in his Passion, and thereby bringing to completion God's project announced in the opening verses of Scripture.

In all these ways, then, for Henry it is the Gospel of John and especially its Prologue that enables us 'to understand *the unity and transcendental aim of Scripture*', enabling a reading of Genesis as '*the first true and rigorous analysis of the human condition*'.[44] Flying in the face of science and philosophy, and indeed common sense, and despite all appearances, Christianity asserts that human beings are not beings of the world: 'they are not of the world, even as I am not of the world', says Christ (John 17:14). As living ones, they are, instead, sons and daughters of life and so sons and daughters of God. 'You are gods, sons of the Most High', says David (Ps. 81:6), the first words of which are quoted by Christ and applied to all those to whom the Word came (John 10:34). Thus, unlike every other way of understanding ourselves, 'Christianity opposes a radically different human being, the Son of God, the Son of Life, the new transcendental human being born within absolute phenomenological Life, engendered within this Life's self-engendering and drawing his essence

[42] Maximus the Confessor, *Ad Thal.* 61 (ed. Laga and Steel, 85): *Ταύτην δὲ τὴν δύναμιν—λέγω δὲ τὴν κατὰ φύσιν τοῦ νοῦ πρὸς τὸν Θεὸν ἔφεσιν—ἅμα τῷ γενέσθαι τῇ αἰσθήσει δοὺς ὁ πρῶτος ἄνθρωπος πρὸς τὰ αἰσθητὰ κατ' αὐτὴν τὴν πρώτην κίνησιν διὰ μέσης τῆς αἰσθήσεως ἔσχε παρὰ φύσιν ἐνεργουμένην τὴν ἡδονήν·.*

[43] *Ad. Thal.*, 61 (ed. Laga and Steel, 95, 99).

[44] *Incarnation*, 229; *Words of Christ*, 85.

from it alone—the human being resembling Christ, the human being in the image of God!'[45] It is only because being sons and daughters of God, living ones in the Living One, is, from the first, our true condition, that we can be recalled to it, just as it is only because he has always been a son that the prodigal can return to the father's house, his proper dwelling.

Following the Prologue, the Christian tradition has consistently understood the becoming flesh, the Incarnation, of the Word as *the* moment of revelation par excellence, for by it 'we have seen his glory' (1:14). But this is not as straightforward a statement as it is often assumed. Henry points out that there are three ways in which this assertion can be taken.[46] Either, first, it can be taken as saying that 'the Word has taken flesh *in order to reveal itself to human beings*', in which case the revelation is a work of the flesh, or, second, the revelation is a work of the Word, leaving unanswered why the Word needs flesh for this revelation. The first line of interpretation is, indeed, the way in which the verse has been understood by many theologians and scriptural scholars: it is 'an episode in the biography of the Word', to return to Rowan Williams' phrase, in which the Word, by becoming flesh becomes human, as a being physically visible in the world. Or, as Henry puts it, 'the coming of the Word in human flesh is interpreted as the way in which the invisible Word of God shows itself to men and women by making itself visible to them in the form of an objective body. Becoming-visible in a visible-body would [then] be the principle of the Word's revelation'.[47] But, as Henry comments, there are two overwhelming difficulties to this line of interpretation. First, if this were so, then 'what would show itself to them in this appearance would really still be only a body like theirs, about which nothing would allow them to know that it is precisely not the body of an ordinary man but of the Word'. It is not enough to see, physically, Jesus, living in first-century Judea (or now in our historical reconstructions), to see the Word of God.[48] This is, as Henry puts it, a 'banalization of Christ'.[49] This is indeed a position sketched out by Athanasius in *On the Incarnation*, as Henry notes, but it is taken only to be transcended. As part of his account of the rationale, the *logos*, of the Passion,

[45] *I Am the Truth*, 100. [46] *Incarnation*, 16. [47] Ibid.

[48] As for instance Bauckham (*Jesus and the Eyewitnesses*, 404, italics original): 'Those who deny that "we" in "we have seen his glory" (1:14) are the eyewitnesses correctly point out that to "see his glory" cannot refer merely to the sight of Jesus with the physical eyes that all who came into contact with Jesus had. However, this does not mean that it has no relationship to such empirical contact with Jesus. The preceding context of this statement reads: "The Word became flesh and lived among us..." Whether the "us" in this case are humanity in general or the eyewitnesses in particular, there is undoubted reference here to the physical presence of the Word in the midst of physical humanity. In this context, to "see his glory" must surely be to recognize his divine glory *in his physical presence*'. Likewise for John 2:11: 'The glory was revealed—and therefore seen—then and there, in a named place where something happened'. (Ibid. 405).

[49] Ibid. 17.

Athanasius suggests that as our minds were caught by things of sense perception the Word had to take a body to catch our attention, as it were. Yet it is only by what he does (not how he appears) that we learn 'that he is not a man only but God and the Word and the Wisdom of the true God', primarily and paradigmatically upon the cross, such that he is thereafter no longer an object of physical sight.[50]

The second difficulty raised by Henry is that, quite simply, this is not what John says: 'For John does not say that the Word took on a body, or assumed the appearance of one. He says that it "was made flesh"'.[51] John does not speak of a body, but flesh, and not of appearance, but becoming that flesh. Moreover, John does not say that the Word became human, and therefore took on flesh along with other attributes (such as a soul, reason, and so on). John in fact overturns our understanding of what it is to be human. In our usual understanding, 'flesh' is that which refers only to our materiality and animality, that which we have in common with animals, from which we are distinct by having other faculties, such as the ability to think and form ideas, the possession of *logos* lacking in animals, and which thus characterizes us as human, rational animals. In this case, however, 'becoming flesh' would be to become less than human! Rather, as Henry puts it, if the Christian tradition takes the 'becoming flesh' as the way in which the Word became human, then, 'the human being is defined as flesh'.[52]

'Incarnation', then, does not speak of the addition of a heterogeneous element to the Word, enabling the Word to appear in the world, but rather of the Word itself becoming flesh, and in so doing redefining what it is to be human. Thus, the third alternative offered by Henry for understanding the connection between revelation and becoming flesh is that the flesh is not the means of a revelation understood as an appearance in the world, but is itself the revelation: 'It is of itself, in itself, and by itself, that [the Word] was made flesh'.[53] If the Word reveals God to us through the flesh, then in turn our relationship with God must also take place through the flesh. 'It is by identifying himself with the Word's flesh (with the body of Christ, *corpus Christi*) that the Christian human being may identify himself with God'.[54] As we argued in our interpretation of John 6 in Chapter 3 and of the Prologue in Chapter 5, the 'flesh' that the Word, Jesus, becomes through the Passion, is the life-giving flesh of Christ offered in the Eucharist, which to be received as life-giving requires sharing in his Passion, to be born into life as a living human

[50] Athanasius *Inc.* 15–16; Behr, *Nicene Faith*, 1.198–200; Henry, *Incarnation*, 17, 258. It should be noted that when he comes to deal with the resurrection, Athanasius does not even mention the resurrectional appearances as related in the Gospels, but rather focuses on those who, taking up the faith of the cross, are his body.

[51] *Incarnation*, 17. [52] Ibid. 11. [53] Ibid. 18. [54] Ibid. 14.

being, the glory of God. The Incarnate Word of God is heard, not seen, and received as life-giving flesh in those who live in his *pathos*.

Finally, if John is able to unveil what it is to be human, connecting God's announcement of his project in the opening verses of Scripture to the final word of Christ on the cross, it is, as both Henry and Origen assert, because he has placed himself at the very heart of the mystery. As Henry puts it, John's 'plan, at first glance unrealizable, is to validate Christ's affirmation of his status as Son by placing himself as it were at the interior of this affirmation and in being coextensive with its movement. More radically: by placing himself at the interior of the very condition of Christ and in identifying with it'.[55] It is as the disciple who alone stands at the foot of the cross (and at the throne in heaven) that John speaks, having become identified with Christ. As Origen put it, to understand the firstfruits of the Gospels which is John, one must also have leant on his breast and received Mary to be his mother also, and so 'be shown to be Jesus', standing at the foot of the cross and hearing the words 'Behold your Son': 'for indeed everyone who has been perfect "no longer lives but Christ lives in him" and since "Christ lives in him" it is said of him to Mary, "Behold your son," the Christ'.[56] For his early followers and readers, John is, as we have seen, the high priest of the paschal mystery, and for Henry he is the one who initiates us into the Arch-gnosis, the gnosis of the simple, that is, the Arch-intelligibility of Life itself. If, in addition, he is also *the* theologian, as he has been recognized from the early centuries onwards, then perhaps we are, finally, in a position to draw this study together by reflecting on the shape of Christian theology.

[55] *Words of Christ*, 62 modified (*Paroles* 80).

[56] Origen, *Comm. Jo.* 1.23.

Conclusion

A Prologue to Theology

In this work we have explored the figure of John and readings of his Gospel through historical investigation, scriptural exegesis, and philosophical reflection. We have seen that John was regarded, by those who in the following two generations traced their lineage back to him, as being the high priest of the paschal mystery, and then explored how his Gospel reads as a paschal gospel and its Prologue as a paschal hymn. As we have seen, the lifting up of Christ on the cross at the Passion puts the world in judgement, *krisis*, by lifting the veil of Scripture and that of the world and its phenomenality, revealing the *pathos* of life, so that we can see, in Christ laying down his life in an act of love to offer us his life-giving flesh, how the construction of the Temple is completed and the project of God, to make a human being in his image, is brought to perfection. Through the different readings of John that we have explored, the problematics we sketched out in the Introduction—concerning the relationship between scriptural exegesis and theological reflection, the 'mythology of doctrines', and the idea of 'Incarnation' that it has produced, that is, as 'an episode of the biography of the Word' now in the past—can now be seen in a new light. The 'Incarnation' is not a past event, reconstructed by a historicizing reading of Scripture, but a participation in the life-giving flesh of Christ, incorporated as his body in the life of witness or *matyria*. 'The Apocalypse of God' at the cross, to borrow de Boer's expression once again, is a call to take up the same cross: 'Be my witnesses [μάρτυρες]; I too am a witness, says the Lord God, and the servant whom I have chosen, so that you may know and believe that I AM' (Isa. 43:10). In the words of Irenaeus, whose work has informed so much of this study, the apocalyptic opening of Scripture by the slain lamb enables us to see the Lord, with the paternal light resting upon his flesh and coming to us through his resplendent flesh, so that we too might be invested with the paternal light and become living human beings, the glory of God (*haer*. 4.20.2, 7).

What lessons can we learn from these explorations, so that we might bring together the historical, scriptural, and philosophical threads spun in this work, as a prologue to the task of theology? It is perhaps useful to begin by recalling that alone among the evangelists and apostles, only John is called 'the theologian'. And yet, as we noted in Chapter 1, John Ashton, whose studies have greatly inspired this present work, concluded that 'the fourth evangelist was not a theologian', if by that one means someone who works out 'a consistent and satisfactory Christology'.[1] In his classic study of the principles of early doctrinal development, Maurice Wiles presents two key soteriological axioms that he sees as having driven the development of just such a Christology. In their interpretation of Scripture, nourished by their worship, Wiles discerns two convictions regarding the salvific work of Christ that led to the key Christian doctrines of the Trinity, in the controversies and councils of the fourth century, and Christology and Incarnation, in those of the fifth: 'On the one hand was the conviction that a saviour must be fully divine; on the other hand was the conviction that what is not assumed is not healed. Or, to put the matter in other words, the source of salvation must be God; the locus of salvation must be man'.[2] These two principles, Wiles notes, 'often pulled in opposite directions', but the 'the Council of Chalcedon was the Church's attempt to resolve, or perhaps rather to agree to live with, that tension', though he himself would question their necessity.[3] This might indeed seem to be the obvious way to characterize the developments from Nicaea to Chalcedon, that is, as the elaboration of Trinitarian theology and Christology, and if this is how we think of theology, Ashton is right that John is not a theologian. But this approach seems to be labouring under the 'mythology of doctrines' in holding that the doctrine of the Trinity (Nicaea) and the Incarnation (Chalcedon), as we now understand them, are givens of the Christian faith, towards which all earlier writers were working. However, if we start with John as *the* theologian, and bring the explorations that we have given to bear upon this, the matter looks rather different. There are, I would suggest, three principles involved.

The first principle is that the one Lord Jesus Christ with whom theology is concerned is always the crucified and risen one as proclaimed by the apostles in accordance with the unveiled Scriptures, enfleshed in the broken bread and those who partake of his life-giving flesh, with all that we have seen that this

[1] Ashton, *The Gospel of John and Christian Origins*, 201.

[2] Maurice Wiles, *The Making of Christian Doctrine: A Study in the Principles of Early Doctrinal Development* (Cambridge: Cambridge University Press, 1967), 106.

[3] Ibid. 106–7: 'Are they necessary presuppositions for all theological reasoning? Certainly they can be stated in a form which makes them appear to be self-evident propositions.... But when stated in this bare form the axioms are of little value for determining the true expression of Christian doctrine. We may still ask whether it would not be possible for God to be the ultimate author of salvation and man the recipient without the agent or mediator of that salvation being himself necessarily of a fully divine or fully human nature—let alone both'.

entails. The 'Apocalypse of God' occurs on the cross, unveiling the Scriptures and providing the life-giving flesh of Christ to those who follow him in his *pathos*. The starting point for theological reflection is the Passion, which, as we have seen, was initially understood as a single event, and certainly was so by John and those who followed him in their annual celebration of this feast. As a pure white light, it can be refracted into a spectrum of colours, both within the narratives of the Gospels and the development of the annual liturgical cycle and iconographic depiction of these feasts. But it must be borne in mind that these are all aspects of the Passion. This is most evident, as we have noted, in the development of iconography, which began by depicting Christ on the cross as the Living One, as we see it in earliest depictions of the crucifixion: on the doors of the St Sabina Church in Rome, perhaps dating to the early fifth century, and the sixth-century Rabbula Gospels and the images on the reliquary box in the Lateran Palace. When, perhaps in the ninth century, images of the resurrection become more prevalent, images of the dead Christ upon the cross also begin to appear: the unitary character of the feast has been refracted (or doubled), as it were, into two distinct *figurae*. But even then, the images of the resurrection do not depict Christ rising from his tomb (which appear later still), but rather Christ, with his arms outstretched, in the figure of the cross, standing on the gates of Hades, likewise placed crosswise, raising up Adam and Eve, the human race. Similarly, the development of the feast and iconography for the nativity also draws out further colours from the white light of Pascha.

This in turn has implications for how the Gospels are read *as Scripture*, and specifically as *gospel*. Only with Diodore of Tarsus and Theodore of Mopsuestia are the Scriptures (now decisively the '*Old* Testament') no longer read in the previously ubiquitous manner, as unveiled by the cross to speak of Christ and his Passion, but as its own narrative or *historia* distinct to and other than that of the New Testament, which in turn is no longer read as a recapitulation or epitome of the Scriptures. The starting point for understanding Christ is no longer the types revealed in the unveiling of Scripture (the 'Old Testament'), but the narratives of the New Testament themselves, beginning with what happens in the womb of Mary before, and independently of, the Passion.[4] Christ is no longer revealed in the play between veiling and unveiling effected by the Apocalypse of God opening the Scriptures, which always remain the Scriptures even when unveiled, for it is there (not elsewhere) that, in the types and prophecies, we see Christ. Reading the Old Testament and the New Testament as two distinct narratives is, lamentably, the way in which the Gospels are still read by many theologians and much popular piety. But, as we have learned from scriptural scholarship and historical investigation of early

[4] Cf. Behr, *The Case against Diodore and Theodore*, 66–83.

exegesis, the Gospels are, rather, scripturally mediated memories in the light of the Passion, which to be read, or rather heard, *as gospel* must be 'translated', as Origen put it, from the form of a biographical narrative to become a proclamation, 'the eternal gospel', or, as Henry would insist, the Word of God addressing us through these texts, not by projecting a past history, but by shattering the world of appearances to recall us back to life.

The second principle is that in and through the Passion, the one Lord Jesus Christ becomes, as human, that which he, as God, always is. We already discussed this idea in the Introduction, when considering ways in which 'incarnation' might be understood other than as an 'episode in the biography of the Word', specifically with reference to texts from Origen, Gregory of Nyssa, and Cyril of Alexandria. Although it might sound rather adoptionistic (a man becomes God), it is not. The Passion is a transformative event, both *pathos* (as Melito) and *passage* (as Origen), as a result of which we no longer know Jesus through the properties by which we might have identified him before the Passion (height, shape of body, etc.), but now only know him as the Word of God. The analogy of iron and fire is, once again, helpful: the properties by which we identify a piece of iron (cold and hard) no longer identify that piece of iron when it is placed in the fire; it is instead only known by the properties of the fire (hot and fluid), even while remaining the same matter that it is. Our God, Scripture tells us, is a 'consuming fire' (Deut. 9:3; Heb. 12:29), one not measured by space and time, for these are the dimensions of that which he has created. And so, ascending into heaven and to God through the Passion, while remaining that which he is, he nevertheless, *as human*, becomes that which he (the same one), *as God*, always is, the eternal Word of God: he, while remaining all that he is as human, is only known, as the iron in the fire is, by the properties of God, and God, in turn, while remaining unchanged, as does the fire when it receives the iron, is now, nevertheless, embodied, though the body is no longer measured by the space and time of our world to be seen in the world.

In exegetical terms, it is not through the historical reconstruction of the life of Jesus, on the basis of New Testament texts, that we encounter the Word of God, but through the unveiled Scriptures (the Old Testament), and their distillation in the scripturally mediated writings of the Gospels. Or to put it in Henryan terms, his body, which was measured by space and time in this world, in the past, is now available to all, throughout space and time, though taking us out of space and time, as life-giving flesh, for those who receive this by following the path of Christ, so that they too become as Maximus, as paraphrased by Gregory Palamas, put it, 'uncreated, unoriginate, and uncircumscribed, although in their own nature they derive from nothing'.[5] This

[5] Gregory Palamas, *Triads*, 3.1.31.

means, moreover, that theology does not start with the Word of God who then becomes incarnate as Jesus Christ, to ascend the cross later on; to do so would necessarily result in a 'dyoprosopic' Christology, in which the particularizing properties of the Word are distinct from (because identified apart from) those of Jesus Christ. Rather, theology does not know the Word of God in any other way than as the crucified and risen Christ: he is the eternal Word of God, or, to put the matter another way, 'Word of God' is a title applied to this one (cf. Apoc. 19:13) and a title, though without the article, that is also shared by those, such as Ignatius, who follow him (cf. *Rom.* 2). 'One is the Son, one Lord, Jesus Christ', as Cyril puts it, 'both before the incarnation and after the incarnation'.[6]

The third principle is that this one Lord Jesus Christ shows us what it is to be God in the way he dies as human, simultaneously showing us what it is to be human. This is in fact the thrust of the creeds and definitions of the Councils: this one, the one Lord Jesus Christ, the subject of the second article of the creeds, is truly God, consubstantial with the Father, and truly human, consubstantial with us, in one *prosōpon*, one 'face', and one *hypostasis*, one concrete being, who is the *eikōn*, 'the image of the invisible God' (Col. 1:15). But rather than hearing this as an attempt to bring together divinity and humanity into one composite being, where each term is already defined by us independently of each other and on our own terms (for we think we know what it is to be human, after all, and have some idea about who or what God is or should be), we should, rather, take our starting point, once again, from him: he defines for us what it is to be God and what it is to be human, in one, at the same time. In the *way* in which he dies as a human being—not simply by dying, but rather as his voluntary Passion has been understood by the unveiling of the Scriptures revealed most clearly in the Gospel of John—he shows us *what* it is to be God, not, that is, yet another divine action of a humanly conceived God, but the very being of God, consubstantial with his Father; yet at the same time he shows us what it is to be human, as the fullness of this is now also revealed, thereby showing that Adam and those following him were and are but a type or a preliminary sketch of the one to come (cf. Rom. 5:14), needing to give their own 'fiat'—'Let it be'—to complete the project of God himself. The mystery of God and the mystery of the human being, though as distinct as fire and iron, are only known together, as one and the same, the *theanthropos*, the God-man.

Put this way, these principles do justice to the impulses of both Antioch and Alexandria (though the use of these terms to denote two different 'schools' of Christology is problematic, both in historical terms and as suffering from the 'mythology of doctrine'). Because our focus is now on the transformative

[6] Cyril of Alexandria, *First Letter to Succensus*, 4: *εἷς οὖν ἐστιν υἱός, εἷς κύριος, Ἰησοῦς Χριστὸς καὶ πρὸ τῆς σαρκώσεως καὶ μετὰ τὴν σάρκωσιν.*

event of the Passion, and only looks back to the 'life of Jesus' prior to the Passion through the unveiling of Scripture (rather than taking the New Testament as a distinct narrative from that of the Old), we can see both the human contribution and yet not lose sight of the one Lord, the paschal Christ. It is by giving, as human, his own 'fiat', that he is one with the Word, as both Theodore of Mopsuestia and Origen assert;[7] yet this 'fiat' is only seen in theoretical reflection (*ἐν θεωρίᾳ μόνῃ*), as Cyril insists, as we contemplate the divinity and humanity, the fire and the iron, inseparably held together in the one Lord Jesus Christ. Or as Maximus puts it when describing the culmination of Christ's work of reconciling the differences within creation through the cross: 'And finally, after all these things, according to the concept of humanity, he goes to God himself, having "appeared on our behalf", clearly, as it is written, "in the presence of the God" and Father as human—the one who as Word cannot be separated in any way at all from the Father—fulfilling as human, in deed and truth, with unchangeable obedience, everything that he, as God, has predetermined to take place, and accomplishing the whole will of the God and Father on our behalf'.[8]

Moreover, as it is by giving the same 'fiat' that we too, in Christ, complete the project of God spoken in the opening words of Genesis, the 'us' addressed when God says, 'Let us make a human being in our image' (Gen. 1:26) includes, indeed, us! In this way, the work accomplished in this volume also aligns itself with some of the deep and keenly felt impulses of twentieth-century theology, as seen especially in Karl Barth and Karl Rahner, as different as they are.[9] In his 1956 lecture 'The Humanity of God', Barth revised his earlier emphasis on 'the infinite qualitative distinction' between God and the human being, with its insistence that 'there is in the Bible only *one* theological interest, namely, that in God; that only *one way* appears, namely, that from above downwards'.[10] His earlier rejection of the '*religionistic, anthropocentric*, and in this sense *humanistic*' tendencies of earlier theology, he now realized, needed to be balanced by a second revision, 'from the Christological perspective

[7] Cf. Origen, *Comm. Jo.* 32.324–6, and Leontius LT 2–6 (Behr, *Case against Diodore and Theodore*, 42–7); see also the comments in the Introduction above.

[8] Maximus the Confessor, *Ambig.* 41, citing Heb. 9:24.

[9] To which one should of course add the strain of nineteenth- and twentieth-century Russian religious philosophy/theology, exemplified in: Vladimir Solovyov, *Lectures on Divine Humanity*, ET Boris Jakim (Hudson, NY: Lindisfarne Press, 1995 [1878–81]); Sergius Bulgakov, *The Lamb of God*, ET Boris Jakim (Grand Rapids, MI: Eerdmans, 2008 [1933]); and, in a different manner, Nicolas Berdyaev, *The Beginning and the End*, ET R. M. French (London: Geoffrey Bles, 1952 [1941]).

[10] Karl Barth, 'The Humanity of God', in Barth, *The Humanity of God* (London: Collins, 1967), 33–64, at 39, italics original here and in subsequent quotations; the lecture was first published as 'Die Menschlichkeit Gottes', in *Theologische Studien* 48 (Zürich: Evangelischer Verlag, 1956), 3–35. I have modified the translation slightly, rendering 'Mensch' as 'human' or 'human being' as appropriate.

and thus from the superior and more exact standpoint of the central and entire witness of Holy Scripture' that 'in *Jesus Christ*, as he is attested by Holy Scripture, we are not dealing with the human being in the abstract, . . . but neither are we dealing with *God* in the abstract: nor with one who in his divinity exists only separated from the human being, distant and strange and thus a non-human if not indeed an inhuman God'.[11] Rather, as he puts it, 'it is precisely God's *divinity* which, rightly understood, includes his *humanity*'.[12] He continues a little later on:

> God requires no exclusion of humanity, no non-humanity, not to speak of inhumanity, in order to be truly God. But we may and must, however, look further and recognize the fact that actually his divinity *encloses humanity in itself*. . . . It would be the false divinity of a false God if in his divinity his humanity did not also immediately encounter us. Such false deities are by Jesus Christ once for all made a laughingstock. In him the fact is once for all established that God does not exist without man.[13]

And then, more strikingly: 'In this divinely free volition and election, in this sovereign decision (the ancients said, in his decree), God is *human*'.[14] That God is indeed human is shown for Barth by the way in which he is depicted in Scripture: the father caring for his lost son, the king for the insolvent debtor, the Samaritan who takes pity on the one who fell among the robbers, concluding: 'The very One who speaks in these parables takes to his heart the weakness and the perversity, the helplessness and the misery, of the human race surrounding him. . . . In the mirror of this humanity of *Jesus Christ* the humanity of *God* enclosed in his divinity reveals itself'.[15]

Similarly, though through a quite different process of reasoning, Rahner, in his essay 'On the Theology of the Incarnation', determines that:

> We could now define the human being, within the framework of his supreme and darkest mystery, as that which ensues when God's self utterance, his Word, is given out lovingly into the void of god-less nothing. Indeed, the Logos made man has been called the abbreviated Word of God. This abbreviation, this code-word for God is the human being, that is, the Son of Man and human beings, who exist ultimately because the Son of Man was to exist. If God wills to become non-God, the human being comes to be, that and nothing else, we might say.[16]

He then continues, connecting theology directly to anthropology:

> And if God himself is human and remains so for ever, if all theology is therefore eternally an anthropology; if the human being is forbidden to belittle himself,

[11] Ibid. 35, 43. [12] Ibid. 42. [13] Ibid. 47. [14] Ibid. 48. [15] Ibid. 49.

[16] Karl Rahner, 'The Theology of the Incarnation', in Rahner, *Theological Investigations*, vol. 4, *More Recent Writings* (London: DLT, 1966), 105–20, at 116, rendering 'Mensch' as 'human' or 'human being' as appropriate. Original in Karl Rahner, *Schriften zur Theologie, vol. 4, Neuere Schriften* (Zürich: Benziger, 1960), 137–55.

> because to do so would be to belittle God; and if this God remains the insoluble mystery, the human being is for ever the articulate mystery of God.[17]

And, as with Barth, and all that we have seen in this volume, the connection of theology and anthropology is, of course, Christology:

> Christology is the end and beginning of anthropology. And this anthropology, when most thoroughly realized in Christology, is eternally theology. It is the theology which God himself has taught, by speaking out his Word, as our flesh, into the void of the non-divine and sinful. It is also the theology which we pursue in faith, unless we think that we could find God without the human Christ, and so without the human being at all.[18]

Thus the conclusions of some of the great theologians of the twentieth century, coming from very different backgrounds and reflecting in very different modalities, concur with the historical, exegetical, and phenomenological explorations carried out in this volume. But through the work that we have done, we are now also in a better position to understand how it is that we speak in theology and of what it is that we are speaking, that is, the Incarnation, not, one final time, an 'episode in the biography of the Word' in the past, but God becoming human and our becoming gods, or better *the becoming human of both*, the divine fire becoming, without change, embodied in bodies, earth becoming living flesh, aflame with the divine fire, the glory of God.

Finally, with the paschal focus of the three principles articulated above, we can return to the rhetorical questions asked by Käsemann with which we began Chapter 2: 'has there ever been a theological system which has not collapsed? Have we been promised that we should know ourselves to be in possession of a *theologia perennis*?'[19] Clearly not, is the answer demanded. Theology does not aim at providing a definitive system, or synthesis of what has gone before, establishing a basis in terms of which everything can then be explained. To do so is especially problematic, as we noted in the Introduction, when the 'system' so constructed is oblivious to the exegetical practices in which were carried out the theological reflections that such a 'system' aims to synthesize or incorporate and is combined instead with a very different way of reading Scripture, as historical narratives rather than the play between veiling and unveiling effected by the Apocalypse of God upon the cross in which revelation occurs, both historically and, in the present, exegetically and phenomenologically.

As Käsemann further suggests, it is 'only certain theological themes in the proclamation [that] are carried on from one generation to the next and thus preserve the continuity of the history of theology', chief among which is 'the hope of the manifestation of the Son of Man on his way to enthronement; and

17 Rahner, 'The Theology of the Incarnation', 116.
18 Ibid. 117.
19 Käsemann, 'Beginnings', 107.

we have to ask ourselves whether Christian theology can ever survive in any legitimate form without this theme, which sprang from the Easter experience and determined the Easter faith'.[20] With this we fully concur. Rather than thinking of theological reflection, and the history of this, as providing us with dogmas for our own synthesis, it would be better, I would suggest, adapting an image of Irenaeus, to think in terms of a symphony: the coming together of many distinct voices, each heard only when attended to with all due historical discipline (rather than labouring under Skinner's 'mythology of doctrines'), resulting in a symphony that is polyphonous, both diachronically and synchronically.[21] Speaking theologically, it is the continuity of the paschal experience and faith that enables the diversity of voices to be heard as a symphony, rather than a cacophony, and, moreover, shows that the symphony is not constructed by any individual voice, or all the voices together, but is governed by its own rhythms and rules, under the one conductor, so that, as Irenaeus puts it, it is God who 'harmonizes the human race to the symphony of salvation' (*haer.* 4.14.2). The purpose of attending to the history of theology, then, is to harmonize us to this symphony, attuning us to the melody that is theology. Yet theology proper only begins when, having read attentively through the score of earlier movements, we take our own part in the ongoing symphony, to sing in new voices that don't simply repeat what went before but continue the symphony in the present, in always new and surprising ways, melding the horizons, in Gadamer's terms, to result in a reading that is not merely reproductive but productive, creative.

The site of the theologian, then, is undoubtedly historical, but also inescapably exegetical and phenomenological: standing, as John the theologian, at the foot of the cross—the definitive Apocalypse of God, unveiling the Scriptures and ourselves—patiently and dialogically or symphonically learning to hear the Word of God addressed in the present to us, so as to encounter Christ both in the opening of the Scriptures, by chewing its cud, and in the reception of the life-giving flesh of Christ as our flesh, by sharing in his *pathos*, and also in, or even *as*, ourselves (just as John puts on the identity of Christ), so taking our part in a history of witnesses to this encounter and a tradition of such theology, which makes claims *about* creation, human beings, and the work of God, or rather the particular work of God that is the human being, and also makes claims *upon* its hearers, so bringing all under the sign of the cross and oriented by the vision of the glory of God that it offers, that is, the living human being.

[20] Ibid.

[21] Cf. Behr, 'Reading the Fathers Today', in Justin A. Mihoc and Leonard Aldea, eds, *A Celebration of Living Theology: A Festschrift in Honor of Andrew Louth* (London: T & T Clark, 2002), 7–19.

Bibliography

Scripture

The Apocalypse of St John in a Syriac Version hitherto Unknown, ed. J. Gwynn (Dublin, 1897).

Comparative Edition of the Syriac Gospels Aligning the Old Syriac (Sinaiticus, Curetonianus), Peshitta and Harklean Versions, vol. 4, *John*, 2nd edn, George Anton Kiraz and Andreas Juckel, eds (Piscataway, NJ: Gorgias Press, 2002).

Evangelion da-Mepharreshe: The Curetonian Version of the Four Gospels, with the Readings of the Sinai Palimpsest and the Early Syriac Patristic Evidence, ed. Francis Crawford Burkitt (Cambridge: Cambridge University Press, 1904).

The Gospel According to John in the Byzantine Tradition, ed. Roderic L. Mullen with Simon Crisp and D. C. Parker (Stuttgart: Deutsche Bibelgesellschaft, 2007).

The Greek New Testament, 5th rev. edn, ed. Barbara Aland, Kurt Aland, Carlo M. Martini, and Bruce M. Metzger (Stuttgart: Deutsche Bibelgesellschaft, American Bible Society, United Bible Societies, 2014).

A New English Translation of the Septuagint, ed. Albert Pietersma and Benjamin G. Wright (New York: Oxford University Press, 2007).

The New Oxford Annotated Bible with the Apocrypha, Revised Standard Version, ed. Herbert G. May and Bruce M. Metzger (New York: Oxford University Press, 1977).

Novum Testamentum Graece, 28th rev. edn, ed. Eberhard and Erwin Nestle, Barbara and Kurt Aland, Johannes Karavidopoulos, Carlo M. Martini, and Bruce Metzger (Stuttgart: Deutsche Bibelgesellschaft, 2012).

Novum Testamentum Latine, John Wordsworth and Henry J. White, 3 vols (Oxford: Oxford University Press, 1889–91).

Septuaginta: Id est Vetus Testamentum graece iuxta LXX interpretes, ed. Alfred Rahlfs, rev. by Robert Hanhart (Stuttgart: Deutsche Bibelgesellschaft, 2006).

Septuaginta: Vetus Testamentum Graecum, Academiae Scientiarum Gottingensis editum (Göttingen: Vanderhoeck & Ruprecht, 1974–), 23 vols to date.

Apocrypha/Pseudoepigrapha

Charlesworth, James H. *The Old Testament Pseudepigrapha*, 2 vols (Garden City, NY: Doubleday, 1985).

Elliott, J. K. *The Apocryphal New Testament* (Oxford: Clarendon Press, 1993).

Gurtner, Daniel M. *Second Baruch: A Critical Edition of the Syriac Text with Greek and Latin Fragments, English Translation, Introduction and Concordances*, Jewish and Christian Texts Series, 5 (London: T&T Clark, 2009).

James, M. R. *The Testament of Abraham: The Greek Text Now First Edited with an Introduction and Notes*, Text and Studies, 2.2 (Cambridge: Cambridge University Press, 1892).

Knibb, Michael A., with the assistance of Edward Ullendorff, *The Ethiopic Book of Enoch: A New Edition in the Light of the Aramaic Dead Sea Fragments*, 2 vols (Oxford: Clarendon Press, 1978).

Nickelsburg, George W. E., and James C. VanderKam, *1 Enoch: A New Translation: Based on the Hermeneia Commentary* (Minneapolis: Fortress, 2004).

Sparks, H. F. D. *Apocryphal Old Testament* (Oxford: Clarendon Press, 1984).

Wright, W. ed., *Apocryphal Acts of the Apostles* (London: Williams and Norgate, 1871).

Classical, Rabbinic, and Patristic Texts and Translations

Anastasius of Sinai, *Hexaemeron*. Ed. and ET Clement A. Kuehn and John D. Baggarly, OCA 278 (Rome: Pontificio Isituto Orientale, 2007).

Athanasius, *Against the Gentiles*. Ed. and ET R. W. Thomson, *Athanasius: Contra Gentes and De Incarnatione*, OECT (Oxford: Clarendon Press, 1971).

Athanasius, *On the Incarnation*. Ed. and ET John Behr, *St Athanasius: On the Incarnation*, PPS 44a (Crestwood, NY: St Vladimir's Seminary Press, 2011).

Athanasius, *Orations against the Arians*. *Orations* 1 and 2 in K. Metzler and K. Savvidis eds, *Athanasius Werke*, vol. 1, pt 1, fasc. 2 (Berlin: De Gruyter, 1998). *Oration* 3 in K. Metzler and K. Savvidis eds, *Athanasius Werke* vol. 1, pt 1, fasc. 3 (Berlin: De Gruyter, 2000). ET in NPNF series 2, 4.

Augustine, *Homilies on John*. ET Edmund Hill, *Homilies on the Gospel of John 1–40*, The Works of Augustine: A Translation for the 21st Century, 3.12 (Hyde Park, NY: New City Press, 2009).

Barnabas, *The Epistle of Barnabas*. Ed. and trans. K. Lake, LCL Apostolic Fathers, 1 (Cambridge, MA: Harvard University Press, 1985).

Cabasilas, Nicholas. *Life in Christ*. Ed. and French trans. M.-H. Congourdeau, SC 355, 361 (Paris: Cerf, 1989, 1990); ET C. J. deCatanzaro (Crestwood, NY: St Vladimir's Seminary Press, 1974).

Clement of Alexandria, *Stromata*. *Clemens Alexandrinus II: Stromata I–VI*. Ed. O. Stählin, 3rd edn, rev. L. Früchtel, GCS 52 (Berlin: Akademie Verlag, 1972); trans. in ANF 2; *Clemens Alexandrinus III: Stromata VII, VIII, Excerpta ex Theodoto, Eclogae Propheticae, Quis Dives Salvetur, Fragmenta*, ed. O. Stählin, 2nd edn, rev. L. Früchtel and U. Treu, GCS 17 (Berlin: Akademie Verlag, 1970); trans. in ANF 2.

Clement of Alexandria, 'Who is the Rich Man Being Saved?', in *Clemens Alexandrinus III*. ET in ANF 2.

Clement of Alexandria, Fragments. In *Clemens Alexandrinus III*. ET in ANF 2.

Le codex arménien Jérusalem 121. Ed. and French translation Athanase Renoux PO 35.1 (Introduction), 36.1 (text and translation) (Turnout: Brepols, 1969, 1971).

Cyprian, *Ad Fortunatum*. Ed. G. Hartel, CSEL 3 (Vienna, 1871).

Cyril of Alexandria, *Commentary on John*. P.E. Pusey ed., *Sancti Patri Nostri Cyrilli Archiepiscopi Alexandrini, in D. Ioannis Evangelium* 3 vols (Oxford: James Parker, 1872; rep. Brussels: Culture et Civilisation, 1965); ET David R. Maxwell, Ancient Christian Texts (Downers Grove, IL: IVP Academic, 2013).

Cyril of Alexandria, *That Christ is One*. P.E. Pusey, ed., *Sancti Patri Nostri Cyrilli Archiepiscopi Alexandrini, ... Quod unus Christus dialogus* (Oxford: James Parker, 1877; rep. Brussels: Culture et Civilisation, 1965); ET J. A. McGuckin, *St Cyril of*

Alexandria: On the Unity of Christ, PPS (Crestwood, NY: St Vladimir's Seminary Press, 1995).

Cyril of Alexandria, 'First Letter to Succensus'. Ed. and ET Lionel R. Wickham, *Cyril of Alexandria, Select Letters*, OECT (Oxford: Clarendon Press, 1983).

Cyril of Alexandria, 'Third Letter to Nestorius'. Wickham, *Cyril of Alexandria*.

Dead Sea Scrolls. Vermes, Geza, *The Complete Dead Sea Scrolls in English* (New York: Penguin, 1997).

Didache. Ed. and ET Bart D. Ehrman, *The Apostolic Fathers*, vol. 1, LCL 24 (Cambridge, MA: Harvard University Press, 2003), 416–43.

Didascalia Apostolorum. *The Didascalia Apostolorum in Syriac*. Ed. and trans. Arthur Vööbus, CSCO 402, 408, scrip. syr. 176, 180 (Louvain: Peeters, 1979).

Dionysius bar Salibi, *In Apocalypsim*. Ed. and Latin trans. I. Sedlack, *Dionysius bar Salibi in Apocalypsim, Actus et Epistulas catholicas*, CSCO 101, scrip. syr. 2 (1909, text; 1910, Latin version, 2–3).

Ephrem the Syrian, *Hymns on Virginity*. ET Kathleen E. McVey, *Ephrem the Syrian: Hymns*, Classics of Western Spirituality (Mahwah, NY: Paulist Press, 1989).

Epiphanius, *Panarion*. Ed. K. Holl: Epiphanius I, *Ancoratus, Panarion* (heresies 1–33), GCS 25 (Leipzig: Hinrichs Verlag, 1915); Epiphanius II, *Panarion* (heresies 34–64), rev. J. Dummer, GCS 31 (Berlin: Akademie Verlag, 1980); Epiphanius III, *Panarion* (heresics 65–80), rev. J. Dummer, GCS 37 (Berlin: Akademie Verlag, 1985). Selective ET P. R. Amidon, *The Panarion of Epiphanius of Salamis: Selected Passages* (Oxford: Oxford University Press, 1990).

Eusebius of Caesarea, *Historial ecclesiastica*. Ed. and ET K. Lake, LCL, 2 vols (Cambridge, MA: Harvard University Press, 1989); ET H. J. Lawlor and J. E. L. Oulton, *Eusebius Bishop of Caesarea: The Ecclesiastical History and the Martyrs of Palestine*, 2 vols (London: SPCK, 1927).

Eusebius of Caesarea, *Oration in Praise of Constantine*. PG 20; ET NPNF series 2, 1.

Genesis Rabbah. Jacob Neusner, *Genesis Rabbah: The Judaic Commentary to the Book of Genesis: A New American Translation*, 3 vols, BJS 104, 105, 106 (Atlanta, GA: Scholars Press, 1985).

Gospel of Truth. Harold W. Attridge and George W. MacRae, ed. and trans. 'The Gospel of Truth', in Harold W. Attridge ed., *Nag Hammadi Codex I (The Jung Codex): Introductions, Texts, Translations, Indices*, The Coptic Gnostic Library (Leiden: Brill, 1985).

Gregory of Nazianzus Oration 40. *Orations* 42–43, ed. and French trans. J. Bernardi, *Grégoire de Nazianze: Discours 42–43*, SC 384 (Paris: Cerf, 1992). ET in NPNF series 2, 7.

Gregory of Nyssa, *Against Eunomius 1*. Ed. W. Jaeger, *Contra Eunomium libri*, GNO 1 (Leiden: Brill, 2002 [1921, 1960]); trans. Stuart Hall in L. F. Mateo-Seco and J. I. Bastero, *El 'Contra Eunomium I'* (Pamplona: Universidad de Navarra, 1988); trans. also in NPNF 5.

Gregory of Nyssa, *Against Eunomius 3*. Ed. W. Jaeger, *Contra Eunomium libri*, GNO 2 (Leiden: Brill, 2002 [1921, 1960]); ET Stuart Hall available at <http://theo.kuleuven.be/page/translations> (accessed 23 December 2015); ET also in NPNF series 2, 5 (where *Eun*. 3.3 is counted as *Eun*. 5, and only divided by chapters, not sections).

Gregory of Nyssa, *Antirrheticus against Apollinarius*. Ed. F. Müller, in W. Jaeger, ed., *Opera dogmatica minora*, GNO 3.1 (Leiden: Brill, 1958), 131–233. ET Robin Orton, FC 131 (Washington, DC: Catholic University of America, 2015).

Gregory of Nyssa, *Epistle to Peter* (= Basil *Ep.* 38). Ed. and ET in R. J. Deferrari, *St Basil: The Letters*, vol. 1. LCL (Cambridge, MA: Harvard University Press, 1926–34).

Gregory of Nyssa, *Homilies on the Song of Songs*. Ed. H. Langerbeck, *In Canticum canticorum*, GNO 6 (Leiden: Brill, 1986); Greek text and ET Richard H. Norris, *Gregory of Nyssa: Homilies on the Song of Songs*, WGRW 13 (Atlanta, GA: SBL, 2012).

Gregory of Nyssa, *On the Making of Man*. PG 44.125–256; ET in NPNF series 2, 5.

Gregory of Nyssa, *To the Greeks, On Common Notions*. Ed. F. Müller, in W. Jaeger ed., *Opera dogmatica minora*, GNO 3.1 (Leiden: Brill, 1958), 19–33. ET in D. F. Stramara, 'Gregory of Nyssa, *Ad Graceos "How it is that we Say There Are Three Persons in the Divinity But Do Not Say There Are Three Gods"* (To The Greeks: Concerning The Commonality Of Concepts)', *GOTR* 41.4 (1996): 375–91, at 381–91.

Gregory Palamas, *Triads*. Ed. Παναγιώτης Κ. Χρήστου, *Ὁ Γρηγόριος Παλαμᾶς: Συγγράμματα*, 1, 2nd edn (Thessalonika: [publisher not identified], 1988), 362–694.

Heraclitus, Fragments. *The Texts of Early Greek Philosophy: The Complete Fragments and Selected Testimonies of the Major Presocratics*, trans. and ed. Daniel W. Graham, 2 vols (Cambridge: Cambridge University Press, 2012), 1.135–96.

Hippolytus, *Contra Noetum*. Ed. and ET R. Butterworth (London: Heythrop Monographs, 1977).

Hippolytus, *On the Christ and the Antichrist*. Ed. H. Achelis, GCS 1.2 (Leipzig: Heinrichs Verlag, 1897), 1–47; ET in ANF 5.

Ignatius of Antioch, *Letters*. Ed. and ET Alistair Stewart, PPS (Crestwood, NY: St. Vladimir's Seminary Press, 2013).

Irenaeus of Lyons, *Against the Heresies*. *Haer.* 1–3 ed. and French trans. A. Rousseau and L. Doutreleau, SC 263–4, 293–4, 210–11 (Paris: Cerf, 1979, 1982, 1974); *Haer.* 4 ed. and French trans. A. Rousseau, B. Hemmerdinger, L. Doutreleau and C. Mercier, SC 100 (Paris: Cerf, 1965); *Haer.* 5 ed. and French trans. A. Rousseau, L. Doutreleau and C. Mercier SC 152–3 (Paris: Cerf, 1969); ET ANF 1; *Haer. 1*, D. J. Unger, rev. J. J. Dillon, ACW 55 (New York: Paulist Press, 1992); *Haer.* 2, ACW 65 (New York: Paulist Press, 2012); *Haer.* 3, D. J. Unger, rev. Irenaeus M. C. Steenberg, ACW 64 (New York: Newman Press, 2012).

Irenaeus of Lyons, *Demonstration of the Apostolic Preaching*. K. Ter-Mekerttschian, and S. G. Wilson, with Prince Maxe of Saxony, eds and ET, French trans. J. Barthoulot, PO 12.5 (Paris, 1917; repr. Turnhout: Brepols, 1989); ed. and French trans. A. Rousseau, SC 406 (Paris: Cerf, 1995); ET J. Behr, *Irenaeus of Lyons: On the Apostolic Preaching* PPS 17 (New York: Saint Vladimir's Seminary Press, 1997).

Jerome, *Comm. Matt.* Ed. D. Hurst and M. Adriaen, CCSL 77 (Turnhout, 1969); ET FC 117.

Jerome, *On Famous Men*. PL 33.601–720; ET in NPNF series 2, 3.

Jerome, *Against Jovinianus*. PL 23; ET in NPNF series 2, 6.

Johannes-Kommentare aus der griechischen Kirche. Ed. Joseph Reuss, TU 89 (Berlin: Akademie, 1966).

John Chrysostom, *Homilies on John* PG 59; ET in NPNF series 1, 14.

John Chrysostom, *The Divine Liturgy*. Text and translation by Ephrem Lash, *Ἡ Θεία Λειτουργία τοῦ ἐν Ἁγίοις Πατρός ἡμῶν Ἰωάννου τοῦ Χρηυστοστόμου/The Divine Liturgy of our Father among the Saints John Chrysostom* (London: Greek Orthodox Archdiocese of Thyateira and Great Britain, 2011).

Josephus, *Jewish Antiquities*. ET William Whiston, with introduction and commentaries by Paul L. Maier, *The Complete Works of Josephus*, revised and expanded edition (Grand Rapids, MI: Kregel Publications, 1999).

Justin Martyr, *Dialogue with Trypho*. Ed. M. Marcovich, *Iustini martyris dialogus cum Tryphone*, PTS 47 (Berlin: De Gruyter, 1997); ET in ANF 1.

Justin Martyr, *First and Second Apologies*. Ed. and ET Denis Minns and Paul Parvis, *Justin, Philosopher and Martyr: Apologies*, OECT (Oxford: Oxford University Press, 2009).

The Lenten Triodion. Τριώδιον Κατανυκτικόν (Rome, 1879); ET Mother Mary and Kallistos Ware (South Canaan, PA: St. Tikhon's Seminary Press, 1999).

Martyrdom of Polycarp. Ed. and ET Bart D. Ehrman, *The Apostolic Fathers*, vol. 1, LCL 24 (Cambridge, MA: Harvard University Press, 2003).

Maximus the Confessor, *Ad Thalassium*. Ed. Carl Laga and Carlos Steel, *Maximi Confessoris Quaestiones ad Thalassium*, CCSG 7, 22 (Turnhout: Brepols. 1980, 90); select ET in Paul M. Blowers and Robert Louis Wilken, *On the Cosmic Mystery of Christ: Selected Writings from St Maximus the Confessor*, PPS 25 (Crestwood, NY: St Vladimir's Seminary Press, 2003); complete ET in Maximus Constas, *On Difficulties in Sacred Scripture: The Responses to Thalassios*, FC 136 (Washington, DC: CUA Press, 2018).

Maximus the Confessor, *Ambigua*. Ed. and ET Nicholas Constas, *On Difficulties in the Church Fathers: The Ambigua*, Dumbarton Oaks Medieval Library, 2 vols (Cambridge, MA: Harvard University Press, 2014).

Melito of Sardis, *On Pascha*. Campbell Bonner, *The Homily on the Passion by Melito Bishop of Sardis and Some Fragments of the Apocryphal Ezekiel*, Studies and Documents, 12 (London: Christophers, 1940).

Melito of Sardis, *On Pascha*. Frederic G. Kenyon, *The Chester Beatty Biblical Papyri: Descriptions and Texts of Twelve Manuscripts on Papyrus of the Greek Bible*, Fasc. 8, *Enoch and Melito* (London: Emery Walker, 1941).

Melito of Sardis, *On Pascha*. ed. M. Testuz, *Papyrus Bodmer XIII: Méliton de Sardis Homélie dur la Pâque* (Geneva: Bodmer, 1960).

Melito of Sardis, *On Pascha*. ed. and ET Stuart George Hall, *Melito of Sardis: On Pascha and Fragments*, OECT (Oxford: Clarendon Press, 1979).

Melito of Sardis, *On Pascha*. Alistair C. Stewart, ed. and ET, *Melito of Sardis, On Pascha, with the Fragments of Melito and Other Material Related to the Quartodecimans*, 2nd edn, PPS 55 (Crestwood, NY: St Vladimir's Seminary Press, 2016).

Mekilta de-Rabbi Ishmael. Ed. and trans. Jacob Z. Lauterbach, 3 vols (Philadelphia: Jewish Publication Society of America, 1949).

The Midrash on Psalms. ET William G. Braude, Yale Judaica Series 13, 2 vols (New Haven: Yale University Press, 1959).

The Mishnah. The Mishnah: Translated from the Hebrew with Introduction and Brief Explanatory Notes, by Herbert Danby (Oxford: Oxford University Press, 1989).

Muratorian Canon. Ed. and ET Samuel Prideaux Tregelles, *Canon Muratorianus: The Earliest Catalogue of the Books of the New Testament* (Oxford: Clarendon Press, 1867).

Muratorian Canon. Ed. and trans. in Daniel J. Theron, *Evidence of Tradition* (Grand Rapids, MI: Baker Book House, 1958), 106–9.

Origen, *Against Celsus*. Ed. Paul Koetschau, GCS 2 and 3, Origenes Werke 1 and 2 (Leipzig, Hinrichs, 1899); ed. and French trans. M. Borret, SC 132, 136, 147, 150, 227 (Paris: Cerf, 1967, 1968, 1969, 1976); ET H. Chadwick (Cambridge: Cambridge University Press, 1953).

Origen, *On Prayer*. Ed. Paul Koetschau, GCS 3, Origenes Werke 2 (Leipzig, Hinrichs, 1899); ET Alistair Stewart-Sykes, *Tertullian, Cyprian, Origen: On the Lord's Prayer*, PPS (Crestwood, NY: St Vladimir's Seminary Press, 2004).

Origen, *Commentary on John*. Ed. Erwin Preuschen, GCS 10, Origenes Werke 4, (Leipzig, Hinrichs, 1903); ed. and French trans. C. Blanc, SC 120, 157, 222, 290, 385 (Paris: Cerf, 1966, 1970, 1975, 1982, 1992); ET R. E. Heine, FC 80, 89 (Washington, DC: Catholic University of America, 1989, 1993).

Origen, *Homilies on Genesis*. Ed. W. A. Baehrens, GCS 29, Origenes Werke 6 (Leipzig: Hinrichs, 1920); ed. and French trans., L. Doutreleau, SC 7 (Paris: Cerf, 1976); ET Ronald E. Heine, FC 71 (Washington, DC: Catholic University of America, 1981).

Origen, *Commentary on Matthew*. Ed. Erich Klostermann and Ernst Benz, GCS 40, Origenes Werke, 10, two parts (Leipzig: Hinrichs Verlag, 1935, 1937); ed. and French trans. of books 10–11, R. Girod, SC 162 (Paris: Cerf, 1970); partial ET in ANF 10.

Origen, *Homilies on Luke*. Ed. M. Rauer, GCS 49, Origenes Werke 9, rev. edn (Berlin: Akademie, 1959); ed. and French trans. H. Crouzel et al., SC 87 (Paris: Cerf, 1962); ET Joseph T. Lienhard FC 94 (Washington, DC: Catholic University of America, 1996).

Origen, *Homilies on Jeremiah*. Ed. Erich Klostermann, rev. P. Nautin, GCS 6, Origenes Werke 3, 2nd edn (Berlin, 1983); ed. and French trans. P. Nautin et al., SC 232, 238 (Paris: Cerf, 1976, 1977); ET John Clark Smith, FC 97 (Washington, DC: Catholic University of America Press, 1998).

Origen, *Philocalia*. Ed. Marguerite Harl, *Origène: Philocalie 1–20: Sur les Écritures*; together with Nicholas de Lange, ed. and trans. *La Lettre à Africanus sur l'histoire de Suzanne*, SC 302 (Paris: Cerf, 1983); ET Lewis, George, *The Philocalia of Origen* (Edinburgh: T & T Clark, 1911).

Origen, *On First Principles*. Ed. and ET John Behr, *Origen: On First Principles*, OECT (Oxford: Oxford University Press, 2017).

Papias, Fragments. Ed. C. de Boor, *Neue Fragmente des Papias, Hegesippus und Pierius: In bisher unbekannten Excerpten aus der Kirchengeschichte des Philippus Sidetes* TU 5.2b (Leipzig: Hinrich's, 1888).

Papias, Fragments. J. Kürzinger, *Papias von Hierapolis und die Evangelien des Neuen Testaments* (Regensburg: Pustet, 1983).

Paschal Chronicle. Ed. L. Dindorf, CSHB 17–18 (Bonn: Weber, 1832).

Philo, *On Agriculture*. Ed and ET F. H. Colson, LCL, Philo 3 (Cambridge MA: Harvard University Press, 1954).

Philo, *On the Special Laws*. Ed. and ET F. H. Colson, LCL, Philo 8 (Cambridge MA: Harvard University Press, 1954).

Targum Neofiti I: Genesis. ET Martin McNamara, The Aramaic Bible, The Targums, 1A (Collegeville, MN: Liturgical Press, 1992).

Targum Pseudo-Jonathan: Genesis. ET Michael Maher, The Aramaic Bible, The Targums, 1B (Collegeville, MN: Liturgical Press, 1992).

Tertullian, *Prescription against the Heresies*. Ed. R. F. Refoulé, SC 46 (Paris: Cerf, 1957); ET ANF 3.

Tertullian, *On the Incarnation of Christ (Carne Christi)*. Ed. and ET E. Evans (London: SPCK, 1956).

Tertullian, *On the Soul*. Ed. J. H. Waszink (Amsterdam: Mülenhoff, 1947); ET ANF 3.

Tertullian, *On Fasting*. ET ANF 4.

Theodore of Mopsuestia, *Commentary on the Gospel of John*. ET George Kalantzis, Early Christian Studies, 7 (Strathfield, NSW: St Paul's Publications, 2004).

Theodore of Mopsuestia, Fragments. Ed. and ET in John Behr, *The Case Against Diodore and Theodore: Texts and Their Contexts*, OECT (Oxford: Oxford University Press, 2011).

Theodoret of Cyrrhus, *Remedy for the Greek Illnesses*. PG 83.

Tosefta. ET Jacob Neusner, *The Tosefta: Translated from the Hebrew with a New Introduction* (Peabody, MA: Hendrickson, 2014).

Victorinus, *Commentary on the Apocalypse*. Ed. and French trans. M. Dulaey, SC 423 (Paris: Cerf, 1997).

Victorinus, *On the Making of the World*. Ed. and French trans. M. Dulaey, SC 423 (Paris: Cerf, 1997).

Modern and Contemporary Works

Abbot, Edwin A., *Johannine Grammar* (London: A & C Black, 1906).

Adams, Samuel V., *The Reality of God and Historical Method: Apocalyptic Conversations in Conversation with N.T. Wright* (Downers Grove, IL: IVP Academic, 2015).

Aland, Kurt, 'Eine Untersuchung zu Joh. 1.3–4: Über die Bedeutung eines Punktes', *ZNW* 59 (1968), 174–209.

Anatolios, Khaled, *Athanasius: The Coherence of His Thought* (London and New York: Routledge, 1998).

Anderson, Paul N., *The Christology of the Fourth Gospel: Its Unity and Disunity in the Light of John 6* (Valley Forge, PA: Trinity Press International, 1997).

Anderson, Paul N., 'The *Sitz im Leben* of the Johannine Bread of Life Discourse and Its Evolving Context', in Culpepper, ed., *Critical Readings of John 6*, 1–59.

Ashton, John, 'The Identity and Function of the *Ioudaioi* in the Fourth Gospel', *NovT* 27 (1985), 40–75.

Ashton, John, 'The Transformation of Wisdom', *NTS* 32 (1986), 161–86, reprinted in idem, *Studying John*, 5–35.

Ashton, John, *Studying John: Approaches to the Fourth Gospel* (Oxford: Oxford University Press, 1994).

Ashton, John, ed. *The Interpretation of John*, Studies in New Testament Interpretation, 2nd edn (Edinburgh: T&T Clark, 1997).

Ashton, John, *Understanding the Fourth Gospel*, new edn (Oxford: Oxford University Press, 2007 [1991]).

Ashton, John, 'The Johannine Son of Man: A New Proposal', *NTS* 57 (2011), 508–29.

Ashton, John, *The Gospel of John and Christian Origins* (Minneapolis, MN: Fortress, 2014).

Ashton, John, 'Intimations of Apocalyptic: Looking Back and Looking Forward', in Catrin H. Williams and Christopher Rowland, eds, *John's Gospel and Intimations of Apocalyptic*, 3–35.

Ashton, John, 'Really a Prologue?', in Jan G. van der Watt, et al., eds, *The Prologue of the Gospel of John*, 27–44.

Ashton, John, 'Riddles and Mysteries: The Way, the Truth, and the Life', in Robert T. Fortna and Tom Thatcher, eds, *Jesus in Johannine Tradition*, 333–42.

Ashton, John, 'Second Thoughts on the Fourth Gospel', in Tom Thatcher, ed., *What We have Heard from the Beginning*, 1–21.

Asiedu-Peprah, Martin, *Johannine Sabbath Conflicts as Juridical Controversy*, WUNT 132 (Tübingen: Mohr Siebeck, 2001).

Attridge, Harold W., 'Philo and John: Two Riffs on one Logos', *The Studia Philonica Annual* 17 (2005), 103–17.

Aune, David E., 'The Apocalypse of John and the Problem of Genre', *Semeia* 36 (1986), 65–96.

Aune, David E., 'The Apocalypse of John and Palestinian Jewish Apocalyptic', *Neotestamentica* 40.1 (2006), 1–33.

Ausejo, Serafin de, '¿Es un himno a Cristo el prólogo de San Juan? Los himnos christologicos de la iglesia primitiva y el prologo del IV evangelo: Fil. 2, 6–11; Col. 1, 15–20; 1 Tim. 3, 16; Hebr. 1, 2–4; Jn. 1, 1–18', *Estudios Biblicos* 15 (1956): 223–77, 381–427.

Azar, Michael, 'The Scriptural King', *SVTQ* 50.3 (2006), 255–75.

Baarda, Tjitze, 'John 3:13: "The Son of Man Who is in Heaven": A Plea for the Longer Text', in Jan Krans, ed., *Paul, John, and Apocalyptic Eschatology*, 256–73.

Bakhtin, Mikhail M., 'Response to a Question from the *Novy Mir* Editorial Staff, in Bakhtin, *Speech Genres and Other Late Essays*, translated by Vern W. McGee (Austin: University of Texas Press, 2013), 1–9.

Bakhtin, Mikhail M., 'Toward a Methodology for the Human Sciences', in Bakhtin, *Speech Genres*, 159–72.

Barclay, John, 'Foreword', in Blackwell, *Christosis*.

Barker, Margaret, *Gate of Heaven: The History and Symbolism of the Temple in Jerusalem* (London: SPCK, 1991).

Barker, Margaret, *King of the Jews: Temple Theology in John's Gospel* (London: SPCK, 2014).

Barr, James, *Holy Scripture: Canon, Authority, Criticism* (Philadelphia: Westminster Press, 1983).

Barrett, Charles Kingsley, *The Gospel According to St John: An Introduction with Commentary and Notes on the Greek Text* (London: SPCK, 1967).

Barrett, Charles Kingsley, *The Prologue of St John's Gospel: The Ethel M. Wood Lecture Delivered before the University of London on 19 February 1970* (London: Athlone Press, 1971).

Barrett, Charles Kingsley, '"The Flesh of the Son of Man": John 6.53', in Barrett, *Essays on John* (Philadelphia: Westminster Press, 1982), 36–49.

Barron, W. R. J., and Glyn S. Burgess, *The Voyage of St. Brendan* (Exeter: University of Exeter Press, 2002).

Barth, Karl, *Church Dogmatics* 2.2, *The Doctrine of God* (Edinburgh: T & T Clark, 1957).

Barth, Karl, 'The Humanity of God', in Barth, *The Humanity of God* (London: Collins, 1967), 33–64; first published as 'Die Menschlichkeit Gottes', in *Theologische Studien* 48 (Zürich: Evangelischer Verlag, 1956), 3–35.

Bartlet, Vernon, 'Papias' "Exposition": Its Date and Contents', in Herbert George Wood, ed., *Amicitiae Corolla: A Volume of Essays Presented to James Rendel Harris, D. Litt. on the Occasion of His Eightieth Birthday* (London: University of London Press, 1933), 15–44.

Bauckham, Richard, 'Papias and Polycrates on the Origin of the Fourth Gospel', *JTS* ns 44 (1993), 24–69.

Bauckham, Richard, *The Climax of Prophecy: Studies on the Book of Revelation* (London: T & T Clark, 1993).

Bauckham, Richard, *The Theology of the Book of Revelation*, New Testament Theology (Cambridge: Cambridge University Press, 1993).

Bauckham, Richard, *Jesus and the Eyewitnesses: The Gospels as Eyewitness Testimony* (Grand Rapids, MI: Eerdmans, 2006).

Bauckham, Richard, *Jesus and the God of Israel: God Crucified and Other Studies on the New Testament's Christology of Divine Identity* (Grand Rapids, MI: Eerdmans, 2008).

Bauckham, Richard, 'The Fourth Gospel as the Testimony of the Beloved Disciple', in Richard Bauckham and Carl Mosser, eds, *The Gospel of John and Christian Theology*, 120–41.

Bauckham, Richard, and Carl Mosser, eds, *The Gospel of John and Christian Theology* (Grand Rapids, MI: Eerdmans, 2008).

Beale, G. K., and Benjamin L. Gladd, *Hidden but Now Revealed: A Biblical Theology of Divine Mystery* (Downers Grove, IL: IVP Academic, 2014).

Beasley-Murray, George R., *John*, Word Biblical Commentary (Waco, TX: Word, 1987).

Becker, Jürgen, *Das Evangelium des Johannes*, 2 vols (Gütersloh: Mohn, 1979, 1981).

Behr, John, 'Colossians 1:13–20: A Chiastic Reading', *SVTQ* 40.4 (1996), 247–64.

Behr, John, 'Severus of Antioch: Eastern and Oriental Orthodox Perspectives', *St Nersess Theological Review*, 3.1–2 (1998), 23–35.

Behr, John, *The Way to Nicaea*, Formation of Christian Theology, vol. 1 (Crestwood, NY: St Vladimir's Seminary Press, 2001).

Behr, John, 'Reading the Fathers Today', in Justin A. Mihoc and Leonard Aldea, eds, *A Celebration of Living Theology: A Festschrift in Honor of Andrew Louth* (London: T & T Clark, 2002), 7–19.

Behr, John, *The Nicene Faith*, Formation of Christian Theology, vol. 2 (Crestwood, NY: St Vladimir's Seminary Press, 2004).

Behr, John, *The Mystery of Christ: Life in Death* (Crestwood, NY: St. Vladimir's Seminary Press, 2006).

Behr, John, ed., trans. and introduction, *The Case Against Diodore and Theodore: Texts and Their Contexts*, OECT (Oxford: Oxford University Press, 2011).

Behr, John, *Irenaeus of Lyons: Identifying Christianity* (Oxford: Oxford University Press, 2013).

Behr, John, ed., trans. and introduction, *Origen: On First Principles*, OECT (Oxford: Oxford University Press, 2017).

Behr, John, 'John 18:28–19:16: Witnessing Truth', in Chad Raith II, ed., *The Gospel of John*, 178–91.

Beker, J. Christiaan, *Paul the Apostle: The Triumph of God in Life and Thought* (Philadelphia: Fortress, 1980).

Belle, Gilbert van, ed., *The Death of Jesus in the Fourth Gospel*, BETL 200 (Leuven: University Press, 2007).

Belle, Gilbert van, ed., 'The Death of Jesus and the Literary Unity of the Fourth Gospel', in Belle, ed., *Death of Jesus in the Fourth Gospel*, 3–64.

Belle, Gilbert van, J. G. Van der Watt, and P. Maritz, eds, *Theology and Christology in the Fourth Gospel*, BETL 184 (Leuven: University Press-Peeters, 2005).

Benoît, Pierre, 'Préexistence et Incarnation', *RB* 77.1 (1970), 5–29.

Berdyaev, Nicolas, *The Beginning and the End*; ET R. M. French (London: Geoffrey Bles, 1952 [1941]).

Beutler, Johannes and Robert T. Fortna, eds, *The Shepherd Discourse of John 10 and its Context: Studies by Members of the Johannine Writings Seminar*, SNTSMS 67 (Cambridge: Cambridge University Press, 1991).

Bienaimé, Germain, *Moïse et le don de l'eau dans la tradition juive ancienne: Targum et Midrash*, Analecta Biblica 98 (Rome: Biblical Institute Press, 1984).

Bingham, D. Jeffrey, 'Christianizing Divine Aseity: Irenaeus Reads John', in Richard Bauckham and Carl Mosser, eds, *The Gospel of John and Christian Theology*, 53–67.

Black, Matthew, 'Aramaic *Barnasha* and the "Son of Man"', *ExpTim* 95 (1984), 200–6.

Blackwell, Ben C., *Christosis: Engaging Paul's Soteriology with His Patristic Interpreters* (Grand Rapids, MI: Eerdmans, 2016).

Blackwell, Ben C., 'Paul and the Apocalyptic Imagination', in Ben C. Blackwell et al., eds, *Paul and the Apocalyptic Imagination*, 3–21.

Blackwell, Ben C., John K. Goodrich, and Jason Maston, eds, *Paul and the Apocalyptic Imagination* (Minneapolis: Fortress, 2016).

Blackwell, Ben C., John K. Goodrich, and Jason Maston, 'Paul and the Apocalyptic Imagination', in Ben C. Blackwell et al., eds, *Paul and the Apocalyptic Imagination*, 3–21.

Blank, Josef, 'Die Verhandlung vor Pilatus Joh 18,28–19,16, im Lichte johanneischer Theologie', *BZ* 3 (1959), 60–81.

Blank, Josef, *Krisis: Untersuchungen zur johanneischen Christologie und Eschatologie* (Freiburg: Lambertus, 1964).

Bockmuehl, Marcus, *Revelation and Mystery in Ancient Judaism and Pauline Christianity*, WUNT 2.36 (Tübingen: Mohr Siebeck, 1990).

Bockmuehl, Marcus, *Seeing the Word: Refocusing New Testament Study*, STI (Grand Rapids, MI: Baker Academic, 2006).

Boer, Martinus C. de, *The Defeat of Death: Apocalyptic Eschatology in 1 Corinthians 15 and Romans 5*, JSNTSup 22 (Sheffield: Sheffield Academic Press, 1988).

Boer, Martinus C. de, *Johannine Perspectives on the Death of Jesus*, BET 17 (Kampen: Pharos, 1996).

Boer, Martinus C. de, 'Paul and Apocalyptic Eschatology', in John J. Collins, ed., *The Encyclopedia of Apocalypticism* (New York/London: Continuum, 1998), 345–83.

Boer, Martinus C. de, 'Paul, Theologian of God's Apocalypse', *Interpretation* 56.1 (2002), 21–33.

Boer, Martinus C. de, *Galatians: A Commentary*, New Testament Library (Louisville, KY: Westminster John Knox Press, 2011).

Boer, Martinus C. de, 'The Original Prologue to the Gospel of John', *NTS* 61 (2015), 448–67.

Boer, Martinus C. de, 'Apocalyptic as God's Eschatological Activity in Paul's Theology', in Ben C. Blackwell et al., eds, *Paul and the Apocalyptic Imagination*, 45–63.

Boer, Martinus C. de, 'Johannine History and Johannine Theology: The Death of Jesus as the Exaltation and Glorification of the Son of Man', in Gilbert van Belle, ed., *The Death of Jesus in the Fourth Gospel*, 293–326.

Boer, Martinus C. de, 'Jesus' Departure to the Father in John: Death or Resurrection?', in Gilbert van Belle, et al., eds, *Theology and Christology in the Fourth Gospel*, 1–19.

Boer, Martinus C. de, 'Paul and Jewish Apocalyptic Eschatology', in Joel Marcus and Marion L. Soards, eds, *Apocalyptic and the New Testament*, 169–90.

Boismard, M. E. *St John's Prologue* (Westminster, MD: Newman Press, 1957).

Bokser, Baruch M., *The Origins of the Seder: The Passover Rite and Early Rabbinic Judaism* (Berkeley: University of California Press, 1984).

Boomershine, Thomas E., 'Epistemology at the Turn of the Ages in Paul, Jesus, and Mark: Rhetoric and Dialectic in Apocalyptic and the New Testament', in Joel Marcus and Marion L. Soards, eds, *Apocalyptic and the New Testament*, 147–67.

Borgen, Peder, *Bread from Heaven: An Exegetical Study of the Concept of Manna in the Gospel of John and the Writings of Philo*, SupNovT 10 (Leiden: Brill, 1965).

Borgen, Peder, 'Observations on the Targumic Character of the Prologue of John', *NTS* 16.3 (1970), 288–95.

Borgen, Peder, 'Some Jewish Exegetical Techniques as Background for the Son of Man Sayings in John's Gospel (John 3:13–14 and Context', in Marinus de Jonge, ed., *L'Évangile de Jean: Sources, redaction, théologie* (Leuven: Peeters, 1977), 243–58.

Borgen, Peder, 'John 6: Tradition, Interpretation and Composition', in Culpepper, ed., *Critical Readings of John 6*, 95–114.

Boring, M. Eugene, 'The Voice of Jesus in the Apocalypse of John', *NovT* 34:4 (1992), 334–59.

Bornkamm, Günther, 'Towards the Interpretation of John's Gospel: A Discussion of *The Testament of Jesus* by Ernst Käsemann', in John Ashton ed., *The Interpretation of John*, 97–119.

Borsch, Frederick Houk, *The Son of Man in Myth and History* (Philadelphia: Westminster Press, 1967).

Bowker, J., '"The Son of Man"', *JTS* ns 28.1 (1977), 19–48.

Bowker, J., *The Religious Imagination and the Sense of God* (Oxford: Oxford University Press, 1978).

Boxall, Ian, 'From the Apocalypse of John to the Johannine "Apocalypse in Reverse": Intimations of Apocalyptic and the Quest for a Relationship', in Catrin H. Williams and Christopher Rowland, eds, *John's Gospel and Intimations of Apocalyptic*, 58–78.

Boyarin, Daniel, *Dying for God: Martyrdom and the Making of Christianity and Judaism*, Figurae: Reading Medieval Culture (Stanford, CA: Stanford University, 1999).

Boyarin, Daniel, 'The Gospel of the *Memra*: Jewish Binitarianism and the Prologue to John', *HTR* 94.3 (2001), 243–84.

Boyarin, Daniel, 'The Ioudaioi in John and the Prehistory of "Judaism"', in J. C. Anderson et al., eds, *Pauline Conversations in Contexts: Essays in Honor of Calvin J. Roetzel* (Sheffield: Sheffield Academic Press, 2002), 216–39.

Boyarin, Daniel, *Border Lines: The Partition of Judaeo-Christianity* (Philadelphia: University of Pennsylvania, 2004).

Bradshaw, Paul F., and Maxwell E. Johnson, *The Origins of Feasts, Fasts, and Seasons in Early Christianity*, Alcuin Club Collections 86 (Collegeville, MN: SPCK/Liturgical Press, 2011).

Bradshaw, Paul F. and Lawrence A. Hoffman, eds, *Passover and Easter: Origin and History to Modern Times* (Minneapolis, MN: Fortress Press, 2016).

Braun, F.-M., *Jean le Théologien et son évangile dans l'église ancienne*, 3 vols (Paris: Gabalda, 1959, 1964, 1972).

Brown, Raymond E., *The Gospel According to John*, The Anchor Bible 29, 29A (New York: Doubleday, 1966, 1970).

Brown, Raymond E., *An Adult Christ at Christmas: Essays on Three Biblical Christmas Stories* (Collegeville, MN: Liturgical Press, 1978).

Brown, Raymond E., *The Birth of the Messiah: A Commentary on the Infancy Narratives in the Gospels of Matthew and Luke* (New York: Doubleday, 1993).

Brown, Raymond E., *The Death of the Messiah: From Gethsemane to the Grave*, 2 vols (New York: Doubleday, 1994).

Bruce, F. F., 'St John at Ephesus', *Bulletin of the John Rylands Library* 60.2 (1978), 339–6.

Bühner, Jan-Adolf, *Der Gesandte und sein Weg im vierten Evangelium: Die kultur- und religionsgeschichtlichen Grundlagen der johanneischen Sendungschristologie sowie ihre traditionsgeschichtliche Entwicklung* (Tübingen: Mohr Siebeck, 1977).

Bulgakov, Sergius, *The Lamb of God*; ET Boris Jakim (Grand Rapids, MI: Eerdmans, 2008 [1933]).

Bultmann, Rudolf, 'Die Bedeutung der neuerschlossen mandäischen und manichäischen Quellen für das Verständis des Johannesevangeliums', *ZNW* 24 (1925), 100–46, repr. in Bultmann, *Exegetica* 55–104.

Bultmann, Rudolf, 'The History of Religions Background of the Prologue to the Gospel of John', in John Ashton, *Interpretation of John*, 27–46 (originally appeared as 'Der religionsgeschichtliche Hintergrund des Prologs zum Johannesevangelium', *ΕΥΧΑΡΙΣΤΗΡΙΟΝ*: *Festschrift für H. Gunkel*, 2 vols [Göttingen, 1925], 2.3–26).

Bultmann, Rudolf, *The Gospel of John: A Commentary*, trans. George R. Beasley-Murray et al. (Philadelphia: Westminster Press, 1971 [1964]).

Bultmann, Rudolf, 'The Primitive Christian Kerygma and the Historical Jesus', in Carl E. Braaten and Roy A. Harrisville, eds, *The Historical Jesus and the Kerygmatic Christ* (Nashville, TN: [publisher not identified] 1964), 15–42 [= *Exegetica* 445–69).

Bultmann, Rudolf, *Jesus Christ and Mythology* (London: SCM, 1966).

Bultmann, Rudolf, *Exegetica*, ed. E. Dinkler (Tübingen: Mohr <Siebeck>, 1967).

Bultmann, Rudolf, *Faith and Understanding: Collected Essays*, (Philadelphia: Fortress Press, 1969).

Bultmann, Rudolf, *Theology of the New Testament*, 2 vols printed in 1, trans. Kendrick Grobel (Waco, TX: Baylor University Press, 2007 [1951]).

Burkett, Delbert, *The Son of Man Debate: A History and Evaluation*, Society for New Testament Studies, Monograph Series, 107 (Cambridge: Cambridge University Press, 2007).

Burney, C. F., *The Aramaic Origin of the Fourth Gospel* (Oxford: Clarendon Press, 1922).

Burney, C. F., 'Christ as the *APXH* of Creation', *JTS* ns 27 (1925), 160–77.

Burridge, Richard A., *What are the Gospels: A Comparison with Graeco-Roman Biography*, SNTSMS 70 (Cambridge, Cambridge University Press, 1992).

Burridge, Richard A., 'Gospel Genre, Christological Controversy, and the Absence of Rabbinic Biography: Some Implications of the Biographical Hypothesis', in David G. Horrell and Christopher Tuckett, eds, *Christology, Controversy, and Community: New Testament Essays in Honour of David R. Catchpole* (Leidon: Brill, 2000), 137–56.

Burton-Christie, Douglas, *The Word in the Desert: Scripture and the Quest for Holiness in Early Christian Monasticism* (Oxford: Oxford University Press, 1993).

Busse, Ulrich, 'Open Questions on John 10', in Johannes Beutler and Robert T. Fortna, eds, *The Shepherd Discourse*, 6–17.

Busse, Ulrich, 'Theologie oder Christologie im Johannesprolog?', in Joseph Verheyden et al., eds, *Studies in the Gospel of John and its Christology*, 1–36.

Camilleri, Sylvain, 'Phenomenology and Soteriology in the "Christian Trilogy" of Michel Henry', in Jeffrey Hanson and Michael R. Kelly, eds, *Michel Henry: Affects of Thought*, 111–34.

Capelle, Philippe, and Michel Henry, *Phénoménologie et christianisme chez Michel Henry: Les derniers écrits de Michel Henry en débat*, Philosophie et théologie (Paris: Cerf, 2004).

Caragounis, Chrys C., *The Son of Man: Vision and Interpretation*, WUNT 38 (Tübingen: Mohr Siebeck, 1986).

Carson, Donald A., *The Gospel According to John* (Leicester: Inter-Varsity Press, 1991).

Casey, Maurice, *The Son of Man: The Interpretation and Influence of Daniel 7* (London: SPCK, 1979).

Casey, Maurice, *The Solution to the 'Son of Man' Problem* (London: Continuum, 2009).

Cave, Terence, *Recognitions: A Study in Poetics* (Oxford: Clarendon Press, 1990).

Cerrato, J. A., *Hippolytus between East and West: The Commentaries and the Provenance of the Corpus*, Oxford Theological Monographs (Oxford: Oxford University Press, 2002).

Chadwick, Henry, 'Eucharist and Christology in the Nestorian Controversy', *JTS* ns 2 (1951), 145–64.

Chapman, John, 'Papias on the Age of Our Lord', *JTS* 9 (1907), 42–61.

Chapman, John, *John the Presbyter and the Fourth Gospel* (Oxford: Clarendon Press, 1911).

Charlesworth, James H., 'The Jewish Roots of Christology: The Discovery of the Hypostatic Voice', *SJT* 29 (1986), 19–41.

Charlesworth, James H., *The Beloved Disciple: Whose Witness Validates the Gospel of John?* (Valley Forge, PA: Trinity Press International, 1995).

Clark, Elizabeth A., *History, Theory, Text: Historians and the Linguistic Turn* (Cambridge, MA: Harvard University Press, 2004).

Collins, John J., 'Introduction: Towards the Morphology of a Genre', in Collins, ed., *Apocalypse: The Morphology of a Genre* (*Semeia* 14: Missoula, MT: Scholars Press, 1979), 1–20.

Collins, John J., *The Apocalyptic Imagination: An Introduction to Jewish Apocalyptic Literature*, 2nd edn (Grand Rapids, MI: Eerdmans, 1998 [1987]).

Coloe, Mary L., *God Dwells with Us: Temple Symbolism in the Fourth Gospel* (Collegeville, MN: Liturgical Press, 2001).

Colson, F. H., '*Τάξει* in Papias (The Gospels and the Rhetorical Schools)', *JTS* 14 (1912), 62–9.

Congar, Yves M.-J., *The Mystery of the Temple: Or, The Manner of God's Presence to His Creatures from Genesis to the Apocalypse* (Westminster, MD: Newman Press, 1962).

Coutsoumpos, Panayotis, 'The Origin of the Johannine "Son of Man" Sayings', in Stanley Porter and Hughson Ong, eds, *The Origins of John's Gospel*, 285–300.

Cross, Frank M., 'The Structure of the Apocalypse of "Son of God" (4Q246)', in S. M. Paul, et al., eds, *Emanuel. Studies in Hebrew Bible, Septuagint, and Dead Sea Scrolls in Honor of Emanuel Tov* (Leiden: Brill, 2003), 151–8.

Culpepper, R. Alan, *The Johannine School: An Evaluation of the Johannine-School Hypothesis Based on an Investigation of the Nature of Ancient Schools*, SBL Dissertation Series, 26 (Missoula, MO: Scholars Press, 1975).

Culpepper, R. Alan, 'The Pivot of John's Prologue', *NTS* 27 (1979), 1–31.

Culpepper, R. Alan, *Anatomy of the Fourth Gospel: A Study in Literary Design*, New Testament: Foundations and Facets (Philadelphia: Fortress, 1983).

Culpepper, R. Alan, *John, the Son of Zebedee: The Life of a Legend* (Columbia, SC: University of South Carolina, 1994).

Culpepper, R. Alan, ed., *Critical Readings of John 6*, BIS 22 (Leiden: Brill, 1997).

Culpepper, R. Alan, 'The Prologue as Theological Prolegomenon to the Gospel of John', in Jan G. van der Watt, et al., eds, *The Prologue of the Gospel of John*, 3–26.

Culpepper, R. Alan and C. Clifton Black, eds, *Exploring the Gospel of John: In Honor of D. Moody Smith* (Louisville: Westminster John Knox, 1996).

Czachesz, István, 'The *Gospel of the Acts of John:* Its relation to the Fourth Gospel', in Tuomas Rasimus, ed., *The Legacy of John*, 49–72.

Dahls, Nils A. 'Christ, Creation and the Church', in W. D. Davies and D. Daube, eds, *The Background of the New Testament and Its Eschatology: Studies in Honour of C. H. Dodd* (Cambridge: Cambridge University Press, 1954), 422–43.

Daise, Michael A., *Feasts in John: Jewish Festivals and Jesus' 'Hour' in the Fourth Gospel*, WUNT 2.229 (Tübingen: Mohr Siebeck, 2007).

Daley, Brian E., '"Faithful and True": Early Christian Apocalypic and the Person of Christ', in Robert J. Daly, ed., *Apocalyptic Thought in Early Christianity*, 106–26.

Daley, Brian E., ed. and trans. and introduction, *Leontius of Byzantium: Complete Works*, OECT (Oxford: Oxford University Press, 2017).

Daly, Robert J., ed., *Apocalyptic Thought in Early Christianity* (Grand Rapids, MI: Baker Academic, 2009), 106–26.

Daube, David, *He That Cometh* (London: Diocese of London, 1966).

Davies, P. R., and B. D. Chilton, 'The Aqedah: A Revised Tradition History', *CBQ* 40 (1978), 514–46.

Davis, Joshua B., and Douglas Harink, eds, *Apocalyptic and the Future of Theology: With and Beyond J. Louis Martyn* (Eugene, OR: Cascade, 2012).

Dawson, David, *Allegorical Readers and Cultural Revision in Ancient Alexandria* (Berkley: University of California Press, 1992).

Delff, Hugo, *Geschichte des Rabbi Jesu von Nazareth* (Leipzig: Wilhelm Friedrich, 1889).

Delff, Hugo, *Das vierte Evangelium, ein authentischer Bericht über Jesus von Nazareth, wiederhergestellt, übersetzt und erklärt* (Husum: C. F. Delff, 1890).

DeRoo, Neal, and John Panteleimon Manoussakis, eds, *Phenomenology and Eschatology: Not Yet in the Now*, Ashgate New Critical Thinking in Religion, Theology, and Biblical Studies (Farnham: Ashgate, 2009).

Dodd, C. H., *The Interpretation of the Fourth Gospel* (Cambridge: Cambridge University Press, 1953).

Donahue, J. R., 'Recent Studies on the Origin of "Son of Man" in the Gospels', *CBQ* 48 (1986), 484–98.

Dunn, James D. G., 'John VI—A Eucharistic Discourse?', *NTS* 17.3 (1971), 328–38.

Dunn, James D. G., 'Let John be John: A Gospel for its Time', in Peter Stuhlmacher, ed., *The Gospel and the Gospels* (Grand Rapids, MI: Eerdmans, 1991), 293–322.

Eckhart (Meister), *The Complete Mystical Works of Meister Eckhart*, trans. Maurice O'C. Walshe, revised by Bernard McGinn (New York: Crossroad, 2009).

Edwards, Mark, 'Ignatius and the Second Century: An Answer to R. Hübner', *ZAC* 2 (1998), 214–26.

Edwards, Mark, *John*, Blackwell Bible Commentaries (Oxford: Blackwell, 2004).

Ehrman, Bart D., *How Jesus Became God: The Exaltation of a Jewish Preacher from Galilee* (San Francisco: HarperCollins, 2014).

Eisler, Robert, 'Das letzte Abendmahl', *ZNW* 24 (1925), 161–92 and 25.1 (1926), 5–38.

Eisler, Robert, *The Enigma of the Fourth Gospel: Its Author and Its Writer* (London: Methuen, 1938).

Ellis, Peter F., *The Genius of John: A Composition-Critical Commentary on the Fourth Gospel* (Collegeville, MN: Liturgical Press, 1984).

Emerton, J. A., 'Some New Testament Notes I: The Interpretation of Psalm lxxxii in John x', *JTS* ns 11 (1960), 329–32.

Emerton, J. A., 'Melchizedek and the Gods: Fresh Evidence for the Jewish Background of John X.34–36', *JTS* ns 17.2 (1966), 399–401.

Estes, Douglas, *The Temporal Mechanics of the Fourth Gospel: A Theory of Hermeneutic Relativity in the Gospel of John*, Biblical Interpretation Series, 92 (Leiden: Brill, 2008).

Evans, Craig A., *To See and Perceive: Isaiah 6:9–10 in Early Jewish and Christian Interpretation*, JSOTSup 64 (Sheffield: Sheffield Academic Press, 1989).

Evans, Craig A., *Word and Glory: On the Exegetical and Theological Background of John's Prologue* (London: T & T Clark, 1993).

Evans, C. Stephen, 'The Historical Reliability of John's Gospel: From What Perspective Should It Be Assessed', in Richard Bauckham and Carl Mosser, eds, *The Gospel of John and Christian Theology*, 91–119.

Falque, Emmanuel, 'Michel Henry théologien (à propos de *C'est moi la vérité*)', *Laval théologique et philosophique* 57.3 (2001), 525–36.

Falque, Emmanuel, 'Is There a Flesh Without Body? A Debate with Michel Henry', *Journal of French and Francophone Philosophy*, 24.1 (2016), 139–66.

Fee, Gordon D., 'Once More–John 7:37–39', *ExpTim* 89.4 (1978), 116–18.

Fenton, John Charles, *The Passion According to John: With an Introduction, Notes, and Meditations* (London: SPCK, 1961).

Filho, José Adriano, 'The Apocalypse of John as an Account of a Visionary Experience: Notes on the Book's Structure', *JSNT* 25:2 (2002), 213–34.

Forestell, J. Terence, *The Word of the Cross: Salvation as Revelation in the Fourth Gospel*, Analecta Biblica, 57 (Rome: Biblical Institute Press, 1974).

Fortna, Robert T., and Tom Thatcher, eds, *Jesus in Johannine Tradition* (Louisville: Westminster John Knox, 2001).

Fossum, Jarl E., 'The New *Religionsgeschichtliche Schule*: The Quest for Jewish Christology', SBLSP 1991, ed. E. Lovering (Atlanta: Scholars, 1991), 638–46.

Fossum, Jarl E., *The Image of the Invisible God: Essays on the Influence of Jewish Mysticism on Early Christology* (Freiburg: Universitätsverlag Freiburg; Göttingen: Vandenhoeck & Ruprecht, 1995).

Fowl, Stephen E., *Engaging Scripture: A Model For Theological Interpretation* (Eugene, OR: Wipf & Stock, 1998).

Frayer-Griggs, Daniel, 'Spittle, Clay, and Creation in John 9:6 and Some Dead Sea Scrolls', *JBL* 132.3 (2013), 659–70.

Freed, E. D., *Old Testament Quotations in the Gospel of John*, SupNovT 11 (Leiden: Brill, 1965).

Freed, E. D., 'The Son of Man in the Fourth Gospel', *JBL* 86 (1967), 402–9.

Freedman, David Noel, ed., *Anchor Bible Dictionary* (New York: Doubleday, 1992).

Frey, Jörg, *Die johanneische Eschatologie*, 3 vols WUNT 96, 110, 117 (Tübingen: Mohr Siebeck, 1997, 1998, 2000).

Frey, Jörg, 'Die "theologia crucifixi" des Johannesevangelium', in Andreas Dettwiler and Jean Zumstein, eds, *Kreuzestheologie im Neuen Testament*, WUNT 151 (Tübingen: Mohr Siebeck, 2002), 169–238.

Frey, Jörg, 'Das Corpus Johanneum und die Apokalypse des Johannes: Die Johanneslegende, die Probleme der johanneischen Verfasserschaft, und die Frage der Pseudonymität der Apokalypse', in Stefan Alkier, Thomas Hieke, and Tobias Nicklas, *Poetik und Intertextualität der Johannesapokalypse*, WUNT 346 (Tübingen: Mohr Siebeck, 2015), 71–134.

Frey, Jörg, 'Eschatology in the Johannine Circle', in Gilbert van Belle, et al., eds, *Theology and Christology in the Fourth Gospel*, 47–82.

Frey, Jörg, 'Erwägungen zum Verhältnis der Johannesapokalypse zu den übrigen Schriften des Corpus Johanneum', in Martin Hengel, *Die johanneische Frage*, 326–429.

Frey, Jörg, 'God's Dwelling on Earth: "*Shekhina*-Theology" in Revelation 21 and the Gospel of John', in Catrin H. Williams and Christopher Rowland, eds, *John's Gospel and Intimations of Apocalyptic*, 79–103.

Furlong, Dean, 'John the Evangelist: Revision and Reinterpretation in Early Christian Sources', PhD (Amsterdam: Vrije Universiteit, 2017).

Gadamer, Hans-Georg, *Wahrheit und Methode: Grundzüge einer philosophischen Hermeneutik*, 6th edn (Tübingen: Mohr Siebeck, 1990); *Truth and Method*, 2nd rev. edn, with revised ET Joel Weinsheimer and Donald G. Marshall (London: Continuum, 2004).

Gärtner, Bertil, *John 6 and the Jewish Passover*, Coniectanea Neotestamentica, 17 (Lund: Gleerup, 1959).

Gärtner, Bertil, *The Temple and the Community in Qumran and the New Testament: A Comparative Study in the Temple Symbolism of the Qumran Texts and the New Testament*, SNTSMS 1 (Cambridge: Cambridge University Press, 1965).

Gebremedhin, Ezra, *Life-Giving Blessing: An Inquiry into the Eucharistic Doctrine of Cyril of Alexandria*, Acta Universitatis Upsaliensis, Studia Doctrinae Christianae Upsaliensia, 17 (Uppsala: Borgströms Tryckeri, 1977).

Gerlach, Karl, *The Antenicene Pascha: A Rhetorical History*, Liturgia condenda 7 (Louvain: Peeters, 1998).

Giulea, Dragos-Andrei, 'Seeing Christ through the Scriptures at the Paschal Celebration: Exegesis as Mystery Performance in the Paschal Writings of Melito, Pseudo-Hippolytus, and Origen', *OCP* 74 (2008), 27–47.

Giulea, Dragos-Andrei, 'Melito, That New Enoch, the Divine Scribe: Typological Interpretation as Revelation of the Divine Mysteries in *Peri Pascha*', in Vahan S. Hovhanessian, ed., *Exegesis and Hermeneutics in the Churches of the East*, Select Papers from the SBL Meeting in San Diego, 2007 (New York: Peter Lang, 2009), 107–19, 157–62 (end notes).

Giulea, Dragos-Andrei, *Pre-Nicene Christology in Paschal Contexts: The Case of the Divine Noetic Anthropos*, SupVC 123 (Leiden: Brill, 2014).

Gladd, Benjamin L., *Revealing the Mysterion: The Use of Mystery in Daniel and Second Temple Judaism with its Bearing on First Corinthians*, BZNW 160 (Berlin: De Gruyter, 2008).

Goehring, James E., *The Crosby Schøyen Codex: MS 193 in the Schøyen Collection* (Louvain: Peeters, 1990).

Goranson, Stephen, 'Nazarenes', in David Noel Freedman, ed., *Anchor Bible Dictionary*, 4.1049–50.

Grant, Robert M., *Second-Century Christianity: A Collection of Fragments* (London: SPCK, 1946).

Grelot, Pierre, 'Jean VII, 38: Eau du rocher ou source du Temple?', *RB* 70 (1963), 43–51.

Griffith-Jones, Robin, 'Apocalyptic Mystagogy: Rebirth-from-Above in the Reception of John's Gospel', in Williams and Rowland, eds, *John's Gospel and Intimations of Apocalyptic*, 274–99.

Gschwandtner, Christina M., *Postmodern Apologetics: Arguments for God in Contemporary Philosophy*, Perspectives in Continental Philosophy (New York: Fordham University Press, 2013).

Gschwandtner, Christina M., 'The Truth of Christianity? Michel Henry's *Words of Christ*', *Journal of Scriptural Reasoning* 13.1 (2014), online at: <http://jsr.shanti.virginia.edu/back-issues/vol-13-no-1-june-2014-phenomenology-and-scripture/the-truth-of-christianity-michel-henrys-words-of-christ/> (accessed 25 March 2018).

Gschwandtner, Christina M., 'Phenomenology, Hermeneutics, and Scripture: Marion, Henry, and Falque on the Person of Christ', *Journal for Cultural and Religious Theory* 17.2 (2018), 281–97.

Guéraud, O., and P. Nautin, *Origène: Sur la Pâque*, Christianisme Antique, 2 (Paris: Beauchesne, 1979).

Guilding, Aileen, *The Fourth Gospel and Jewish Worship: A Study of the Relation of St John's Gospel to the Ancient Jewish Lectionary System* (Oxford: Clarendon, 1960).

Gundry, Robert H., '"In My Father's House There are Many *Μοναί*" (John 14:2)', *ZNW* 53 (1967), 68–72.

Gundry, Robert H., *Jesus the Word according to John the Sectarian* (Grand Rapids: Eerdmans, 2001).

Gunther, John J., 'The Elder John, Author of Revelation', *JSNT* 11.1 (1981), 3–20.

Hägerland, Tobias, 'John's Gospel: A Two-Level Drama?', *JSNT* 25.3 (2003), 309–22.

Hahneman, Geoffrey Martin, *The Muratorian Fragment and the Development of the Canon*, Oxford Theological Monographs (Oxford: Clarendon, 1992).

Hahneman, Geoffrey Martin, 'The Muratorian Fragment and the Origins of the New Testament Canon', in Lee Martin McDonald and James A. Sanders, eds, *The Canon Debate* (Peabody, MA: Hendrickson, 2002), 405–15.

Hainsworth, John, 'The Force of the Mystery: Anamnesis and Exegesis in Melito's *Peri Pascha*', *SVTQ* 46.2 (2002), 107–46.

Hakola, Raimo, 'The Reception and Development of the Johannine Tradition in 1, 2, and 3 John', in Tuomo Rasimus, ed., *The Legacy of John*, 17–47.

Hall, Stuart George, 'Melito in the Light of the Passover Haggadah', *JTS* ns 22 (1971), 29–46.

Hamburger, Jeffrey F., *St. John the Divine: The Deified Evangelist in Medieval Art and Theology* (Berkeley, CA: University of California Press, 2002).

Hamid-Khani, Saeed, *Revelation and Concealment of Christ: A Theological Inquiry into the Elusive Language of the Fourth Gospel*, WUNT 2.120 (Tübingen: Mohr Siebeck, 2000).

Hannah, Darrell D., 'Isaiah's Vision in the *Ascension of Isaiah* and the Early Church', *JTS* ns 50 (1999), 80–101.

Hanson, Jeffrey, 'Phenomenology and Eschatology in Michel Henry', in Neal DeRoo and John Panteleimon Manoussakis, eds, *Phenomenology and Eschatology: Not Yet in the Now*, 153–66.

Hanson, Jeffrey, and Michael R. Kelly, eds, *Michel Henry: The Affects of Thought*, Continuum Studies in Continental Philosophy (London: Bloomsbury, 2013).

Hanson, Paul D., 'Apocalypse, Genre' and 'Apocalypticism', in Keith R. Crim ed., *The Interpreter's Dictionary of the Bible: Supplementary Volume* (Nashville: Abingdon, 1976), 27–34.

Hanson, Paul D. 'Apocalypses and Apocalypticism (Genre, Introductory Overview)', in David Noel Freedman ed., *Anchor Bible Dictionary*, 1.279–82.

Hanson, Richard P. C., *The Search for the Christian Doctrine of God: The Arian Controversy, 318–81* (Edinburgh: T & T Clark, 1988).

Hanson, Richard P. C., 'The Achievement of Orthodoxy in the Fourth Century AD', in R. Williams, ed., *The Making of Orthodoxy: Essays in Honour of Henry Chadwick* (Cambridge: Cambridge University Press, 1989), 142–56.

Haran, M., 'The Divine Presence in the Israelite Cult and the Cultic Institutions', *Biblica* 50 (1969), 251–67.

Hare, Douglas R. A., *The Son of Man Tradition* (Minneapolis: Fortress, 1990).

Harnack, Adolf von, 'Über das Verhältniß des Prologs des vierten Evangeliums zum ganzen Werk', *ZKT* 2 (1892), 189–231.

Harnack, Adolf von, *Lehrbuch der Dogmengeschichte, Erster Band, Die Entstehung des kirchlichen Dogmas*, 4th edn (Darmstadt: Wissenschaftliche Buchgesellschaft, 1964 [Tübingen 1909]).

Harris, Elizabeth, *Prologue and Gospel: The Theology of the Fourth Gospel*, JSNTSup 107 (Sheffield: Sheffield Academic Press, 1994).

Harris, J. Rendel, 'The Origen of the Prologue to St. John's Gospel', *Expositor*, 12 (1916), 147–70, 314–20, 388–400, 415–26.

Hart, James G., 'Michel Henry's Phenomenological Theology of Life: A Husserlian Reading of *C'est moi, la vérité*', *Husserl Studies* 15 (1999), 183–230.

Hart, Kevin, 'Inward Life', in Jeffrey Hanson and Michael R. Kelly, eds, *Michel Henry: Affects of Thought*, 87–109.

Hart, Kevin, '"Without World": Eschatology in Michel Henry', in Neal DeRoo and John Panteleimon Manoussakis, eds, *Phenomenology and Eschatology: Not Yet in the Now*, 167–92.

Hatem, Jad, *Le sauveur et les viscères de l'être: Sur le gnosticisme et Michel Henry* (Paris: L'Harmattan, 2004).

Hays, Richard B., *Echoes of Scripture in the Letters of Paul* (New Haven and London: Yale University Press, 1989).

Hays, Richard B., 'Apocalyptic *Poesis* in Galatians: Paternity, Passion, and Participation', in Mark W. Elliott et al., eds, *Galatians and Christian Theology: Justification, the Gospel and Ethics in Paul's Letters* (Grand Rapids: Baker, 2004), 200–19.

Heidegger, Martin, *Being and Time*, translated by Joan Stambaugh (Albany: State University of New York Press, 2010).

Heil, John Paul, 'Jesus as the Unique High Priest in the Gospel of John', *CBQ* 57 (1995), 729–45.

Hengel, Martin, *The Johannine Question* (London: SCM, 1989).

Hengel, Martin, *Die johanneische Frage: Ein Lösungsversuch*, with a contribution on the Apocalypse by Jörg Frey, WUNT 67 (Tübingen: Mohr Siebeck, 1993).

Hengel, Martin, *The Four Gospels and the One Gospel of Jesus Christ*, trans. John Bowden (Harrisburg, PA: Trinity Press International, 2000).

Hengel, Martin, 'The Four Gospels and the One Gospel of Jesus Christ', in C. Horton, ed., *The Earliest Gospels: The Origins and Transmission of the Earliest Christian Gospels: The Contribution of the Chester Beatty Codex P45* (London: T & T Clark, 2004), 13–26.

Hengel, Martin, 'The Prologue of the Gospel of John as the Gateway to Christological Truth', in Richard Bauckham and Carl Mosser, eds, *The Gospel of John and Christian Theology*, 265–94.

Henry, Michel, *L'essence de la manifestation* (Paris: Presses Universitaires de France, 1963; second edition 1990); ET Girard Etzkorn, *The Essence of Manifestation* (The Hague: Martinus Nijhoff, 1973).

Henry, Michel, *La Barbarie* (Paris: Grasset & Fasquelle, 1987); ET Scott Davidson, *Barbarism*, Continuum Impacts (London: Continuum, 2012).

Henry, Michel, *Phénoménologie matérielle* (Paris: Presses Universitaires de France, 1990); *Material Phenomenology*, translated by Scott Davidson, Perspectives in Continental Philosophy (New York: Fordham University Press, 2008).

Henry, Michel, *C'est moi la vérité: Pour une philosophie du christianisme* (Paris: Seuil, 1996); ET Susan Emanuel, *I Am the Truth: Towards a Philosophy of Christianity*, Cultural Memory in the Present (Stanford: Stanford University Press, 2003).

Henry, Michel, *Incarnation: Une philosophie de la chair* (Paris: Seuil, 2000); ET Karl Hefty, *Incarnation: A Philosophy of Flesh*, Northwestern University Studies in Phenomenology and Existential Philosophy (Evanston, Ill.: Northwestern University Press, 2015).

Henry, Michel, *Paroles du Christ* (Paris: Seuil, 2002); ET Christina M. Gschwandtner, *Words of Christ*, Interventions (Grand Rapids, MI: Eerdmans, 2012).

Henry, Michel, 'Phénoménologie de la vie', in Michel Henry, *Phénoménologie de la via*, vol. 1, *De la phénoménologie* (Paris: Presses Universitaires de France, 2003), 59–76; 'Phenomenology of Life', trans. Nick Hanlon, *Angelaki: Journal of the Theoretical Humanities*, 8.2 (2003), 97–110.

Henry, Michel, 'Phénoménologie de la naissance', in Henry, *Phénoménologie de la vie*, vol. 1, *De la phénoménologie* (Paris: Presses Universitaires de France, 2003), 123–42; trans. Andrew Sackin-Poll, 'The Phenemenology of Birth', *Pli: The Warwick Journal of Philosophy*, 20 (2011[illegible]), 119–39.

Henry, Michel, 'Phénoménologie de la chair: Philosophie, théologie, exégèse: Réponses', in Philippe Capelle and Michel Henry, eds, *Phénoménologie et christianisme*, 143–90.

Henze, Matthias, *Jewish Apocalyptism in Late First Century Israel: Reading Second Baruch in Context*, Texts and Studies in Ancient Judaim, 142 (Tübingen: Mohr Siebeck, 2011).

Hernandez-Dispaux, Joaquin, 'Michel Henry lecteur de Claude Tresmontant: création, révélation, écritures', *Revue internationale Michel Henry* 4 (2013), 57–75.

Hill, Charles E., 'What Papias Said About John (And Luke): A "New" Papian Fragment', *JTS* ns 49.2 (1998), 582–629.

Hill, Charles E., 'The *Epistula Apostolorum*: An Asian Tract from the Time of Polycarp', *JECS* 7 (1999), 1–53.

Hill, Charles E., *The Johannine Corpus in the Early Church* (Oxford: Oxford University Press, 2004).

Hill, Charles E., *From the Lost Teaching of Polycarp*, WUNT 186 (Tübingen: Mohr Siebeck, 2006).

Hill, Charles E., *Who Chose the Gospels? Probing the Great Gospel Conspiracy* (Oxford: Oxford University Press, 2010).

Hill, Charles E., '"The Orthodox Gospel": The Reception of John in the Great Church Prior to Irenaeus', in Tuomas Rasimus, ed., *The Legacy of John*, 233–300.

Himmelfarb, Martha, *Ascent to Heaven in Jewish and Christian Apocalypses* (Oxford: Oxford University Press, 1993).

Hock, Ronald F., and Edward N. O'Neil, *The Chreia in Ancient Rhetoric*, vol. 1, *The Progymnasmata*, Graeco-Roman Religion Series 9, Texts and Translations 27 (Atlanta: Scholars Press, 1986).

Hock, Ronald F., and Edward N. O'Neil, *The Chreia and Ancient Rhetoric: Classroom Exercises*, WGRW 2 (Atlanta, GA: SBL, 2002).

Hock, Ronald F., *The Chreia and Ancient Rhetoric: Commentaries on Aphthonius's Progymnasmata*, WGRW 31 (Atlanta, GA: SBL, 2012).

Hodges, Zane C., 'Rivers of Living Water—John 7:37–39', *Bibliotheca Sacra* 136 (1979), 239–48.

Hooker, M., 'The Johannine Prologue and the Messianic Secret', *NTS* 21.1 (1974), 40–58.

Horbury, William, 'The Wisdom of Solomon in the Muratorian Fragment', *JTS* ns 45 (1994), 149–59.

Horsting, Albertus G. A., 'Transfiguration of Flesh: Literary and Theological Connections between Martyrdom Accounts and Eucharistic Prayers', in Maxwell E. Johnson, ed., *Issues in eucharistic Praying in East and West*, 307–25.

Hort, Fenton John Anthony, *The Apocalypse of St John I–III* (London: Macmillan, 1908).

Hoskins, Paul M., *Jesus as the Fulfillment of the Temple in the Gospel of John*, Paternoster Biblical Monographs (Eugene, OR: Wipf and Stock, 2006).

Hoskyns, Edwyn C., *The Fourth Gospel*, 2nd rev. edn, ed. Francis Noel Davey (London: Faber and Faber, 1947).

Howard, Wilbert Francis, *The Fourth Gospel in Recent Criticism and Interpretation*, revised by C. K. Barrett (London: Epworth Press, 1955).

Hurtado, Larry, *Lord Jesus Christ: Devotion to Jesus in Earliest Christianity* (Grand Rapids, MI: Eerdmans, 2003).

Hurtado, Larry, *Ancient Jewish Monotheism and Early Christian Jesus-Devotion: The Context and Character of Christological Faith*, Library of Early Christianity (Waco, TX: Baylor University Press, 2017).

Janicaud, Dominique, *Phenomenology and the 'Theological Turn': The French Debate*; ET Bernard Prusak (New York: Fordham University Press, 2000).

Johnson, Luke Timothy, *The Real Jesus: The Misguided Quest for the Historical Jesus and the Truth of the Traditional Gospels* (San Francisco: Harper Collins, 1997).

Johnson, Maxwell E. ed., *Issues in Eucharistic Praying in East and West: Essays in Liturgical and Theological Analysis* (Collegeville, MN: Liturgical Press, 2010).

Johnson, Maxwell E., 'Martyrs and the Mass: The Interpolation of the Narrative of Institution into the Anaphora', *Worship* 87.1 (2013), 2–22.

Jong, Matthijs de, 'De proloog van Johannes', in de *Bijbel in Gewone Taal*', *Met Andere Worden* 31.4 (2012), 27–41.

Jonge, Marinus de, *Jesus: Stranger from Heaven and Son of God: Jesus Christ and the Christians in Johannine Perspective*, ed. and trans. John E. Steely, SBL Sources for Biblical Study 11 (Missoula, MO: Scholars press, 1977).

Jonkers, Peter, and Ruud Welten, *God in France: Eight Contemporary French Thinkers on God*, Studies in Philosophical Theology (Leuven: Peeters, 2005).

Judge, Peter J. 'Come and See: The First Disciples and Christology in the Fourth Gospel', in Joseph Verheyden et al., eds, *Studies in the Gospel of John and its Christology*, 61–9.

Juel, Donald, *Messiah and Temple: The Trial of Jesus in the Gospel of Mark*, SBL Dissertation Series, 31 (Missoula, MO: Scholars Press, 1977).

Kartsonis, Anna D., *Anastasis: The Making of an Image* (Princeton: Princeton University Press, 1986).

Käsemann, Ernst, *Exegetische Versuche und Besinnungen: Erster und zweiter Band* (Göttingen: Vandenhoeck and Ruprecht, 1964).

Käsemann, Ernst, *The Testament of Jesus: A Study of the Gospel of John in the Light of Chapter 17*, trans. Gerhard Krodel (Philadelphia: Fortress, 1968 [German 1966]).

Käsemann, Ernst, *New Testament Questions for Today* (Philadelphia: Fortress, 1979).

Käsemann, Ernst, 'The Beginnings of Christian Theology', in Käsemann, *New Testament Questions for Today*, 82–107 (first published in *ZKT* 57 [1960], 162–85).

Käsemann, Ernst, 'Blind Alleys and the "Jesus of History" Controversy', in Käsemann, *New Testament Questions for Today*, 23–65.

Käsemann, Ernst, 'On the Subject of Primitive Christian Apocalyptic', in Käsemann, *New Testament Questions*, 108–37 (first published in *ZKT* 59 [1962], 257–84).

Käsemann, Ernst, 'The Structure and Purpose of the Prologue to John's Gospel', in Käsemann, *New Testament Questions for Today*, 138–67 (first published as 'Aufbau und Anliegen des johanneischen Prolog', in *Libertas Christiana: Friedrich Delekat zum 65. Geburtstag*, ed. Walter Matthias and Ernest Wolf, Beiträge zur evangelischen Theologie 26 [Munich: Kaiser, 1957], 75–99).

Kelly, J. N. D., *Early Christian Doctrines*, 5th edn (San Francisco: Harper, 1978 [1958]).

Kenny, Anthony, *A Stylometric Study of the New Testament* (Oxford: Clarendon Press, 1986).

Kenyon, Frederic G., 'The Chester Beatty Biblical Papyri', *Gnomon* 8 (1932), 46–9.

Kerr, Alan R., *The Temple of Jesus' Body: The Temple Theme in the Gospel of John*, JSNTSup 220 (London: Sheffield Academic Press, 2002).

Klauck, Hans-Joseph, 'Do They Never Come Back? *Nero Redivivus* and the Apocalypse of John', *CBQ* 63 (2001), 683–98.

Klawiter, Frederick C., 'The Eucharist and Sacramental Realism in the Thought of St. Ignatius of Antioch', *Studia Liturgica* 37 (2007), 129–63.

Knöppler, Thomas, *Die theologia crucis des Johannesevangeliums: Das Verständnis des Todes Jesu im Rahmen der johanneischen Inkarnations- und Erhöhungschristologie*, WMANT 69 (Neukirchen: Neukirchener, 1994).

Koester, Craig R., *Symbolism in the Fourth Gospel: Meaning, Mystery, Community*, 2nd edn (Minneapolis: Fortress, 2003).

Kohler, Herbert, *Kreuz und Menschwerdung im Johannesevangelium: Ein exegetisch-hermeneutischer Versuch zur johanneischen Kreuzestheologie*, ATANT 72 (Zürich: TVZ, 1987).

Körtner, U. H. J., *Papias von Hierapolis: Ein Beitrag zur Geschichte des frühen Christentum*, FRLANT 133 (Göttingen, 1983).

Köstenberger, Andreas J., and Stephen O. Stout, '"The Disciple Jesus Loved": Witness, Author, Apostle—A Response to Richard Bauckham's *Jesus and the Eyewitnesses*', *Bulletin for Biblical Research* 18.2 (2008), 209–31.

Kovacs, Judith L., '"Now Shall the Ruler of This World be Driven Out": Jesus' Death as Cosmic Battle in John 12:20–36', *JBL* 114.2 (1995), 227–47.

Kovacs, Judith, and Christopher Rowland, *Revelation*, Blackwell Biblical Commentaries (Oxford: Blackwell, 2004).

Krans, Jan, et al. ed., *John, Paul, and Apocalyptic Eschatology: Essays in Honour of Martinus C. de Boer*, SupNovT 149 (Leiden: Brill, 2013).

Krusche, W., 'Jesus Christus als der neue Mensch', *Theologische Versuche* 8 (1977), 201–12.

Kugel, James L., *Traditions of the Bible: A Guide to the Bible as it was at the Start of the Common Era* (Cambridge, MA: Harvard University Press, 1998).

Kulp, Joshua, 'The Origins of the Seder and Haggadah', *CBR* 4.1 (2005), 109–34.

Kühn, Rolf, 'Archi-intelligibilité johannique dans la phénoménologie de Michel Henry', *Revue international Michel Henry* 4 (2013), 77–98.

Kürzinger, J., *Papias von Hierapolis und die Evangelien des Neuen Testaments* (Regensburg: Pustet, 1983).

Kuschel, Karl-Josef, *Born Before All Time? The Dispute over Christ's Origin* (New York: Crossroad, 1992).

L'Huillier, Peter, *The Church of the Ancient Councils: The Disciplinary Work of the First Four Ecumenical Councils* (Crestwood: SVS Press, 1996).

Lacomara, A., 'Deuteronomy and the Farewell Discourse (Jn 13: 31–16:13)', *CBQ* 36 (1974), 65–84.

Lalleman, Pieter, *The Acts of John: A Two-Stage Initiation into Johannine Gnosticism*, Studies on the Apocryphal Acts of the Apostles, 4 (Leuven: Peeters, 1998).

Lamarche, Paul, 'The Prologue of John', in John Ashton, ed., *The Interpretation of John*, 47–65 (originally appeared as 'Le Prologue de Jean', *RSR* 52 [1964], 407–537).

Lawlor, H. J., *Eusebiana* (Oxford: Clarendon Press, 1912).

Ledgeway, Adam, *From Latin to Romance: Morphosyntactic Typology and Change*, Oxford Studies in Diachronic and Historical Linguistics (Oxford: Oxford University Press, 2012).

Leithart, Peter, *Deep Exegesis: The Mystery of Reading Scripture* (Waco, TX: Baylor University Press, 2009).

Leithart, Peter, *Revelation 1–11*, The International Theological Commentary on the Holy Scriptures of the Old and New Testaments (London: Bloomsbury T & T Clark, 2018).

Leithart, Peter, *Revelation 12–22*, The International Theological Commentary on the Holy Scriptures of the Old and New Testaments (London: Bloomsbury T & T Clark, 2018).

Leithart, Peter, '"You Shall Judge Angels": A Response to Fr. Behr', in Chad Raith II, ed., *The Gospel of John*, 192–201.

Leivestad, Ragner, 'Exit the Apocalyptic Son of Man', *NTS* 18 (1971–2), 243–67.

Leonhard, Clemens, *The Jewish Pesach and the Origins of the Christian Easter* (Berlin: de Gruyter, 2006).

Lett, Jonathan, 'The Divine Identity of Jesus as the Reason for Israel's Unbelief in John 12:36–43', *JBL* 135.1 (2016), 159–73.

Levenson, J. D., *The Death and Resurrection of the Beloved Son: The Transformation of Child Sacrifice in Judaism and Christianity* (New Haven: Yale University Press, 1993).

Liddell, Henry George, and Robert Scott, revised by Henry Stuart Jones, *A Greek-English Lexicon* (Oxford: Clarendon Press, 1996).

Lietaert Peerbolte, Bert Jan, 'How Antichrist Defeated Death: The Development of Christian Apocalyptic Eschatology in the Early Church', in Jan Krans, ed., *Paul, John, and Apocalyptic Eschatology*, 238–55.

Lieu, Judith, 'The Mother of the Son in the Fourth Gospel', *JBL* 117.1 (1998), 61–77.

Lieu, Judith, *I, II, and III John: A Commentary* (Louisville: Westminster John Knox, 2008).

Lieu, Judith, 'Anti-Judaism, the Jews, and the Worlds of the Fourth Gospel', in Richard Bauckham and Carl Mosser, eds, *The Gospel of John and Christian Theology*, 168–82.

Lieu, Judith, 'Text and Authority in John and Apocalyptic', in Catrin H. Williams and Christopher Rowland, eds, *John's Gospel and Intimations of Apocalyptic*, 235–53.

Lightfoot, J. B., *Essays on the Work Entitled Supernatural Religion* (London: Macmillan, 1889).

Lincoln, Andrew T., *Truth on Trial: The Lawsuit Motif in the Fourth Gospel* (Peabody, MA: Hendrickson, 2000).

Lindars, Barnabas, *Jesus, Son of Man: A Fresh Examination of the Son of Man Sayings in the Gospels in the Light of Recent Research* (London: SPCK, 1983).

Lindars, Barnabas, *The Gospel of John*, New Century Bible Commentary (Grand Rapids, MI: Eerdmans, 1987 [1972]).

Loader, William R. G., 'Christ at the Right Hand—Ps. CX.1 in the New Testament', *NTS* 24 (1977), 199–217.

Loader, William R. G., *The Christology of the Fourth Gospel: Structure and Issues*, 2nd rev. edn, BBET 23 (Frankfurt am Main: Peter Lang, 1992).

Loader, William R. G., 'What is "Finished"? Revisiting Tensions in the Structure of Johannine Christology', in Gilbert van Belle, ed., *The Death of Jesus in the Fourth Gospel*, 457–67.

Loader, William R. G., 'The Significance of the Prologue for Understanding John's Soteriology', in Jan G. van der Watt, et al., eds, *The Prologue of the Gospel of John*, 45–55.

Loke, Andrew Ter Ern, *The Origin of Divine Christology*, SNTSMS 169 (Cambridge: Cambridge University Press, 2017).

Louth, Andrew, *Discerning the Mystery: An Essay on the Nature of Theology* (Oxford: Clarendon Press, 1983).

Luttikhuizen, Gerard P., 'The Thought Pattern of Gnostic Mythologizers and their Use of Biblical Traditions', in J. D. Turner and A. McGuire, eds, *The Nag Hammadi Library after Fifty Years: Proceedings of the 1995 Society of Biblical Literature Commemoration*, Nag Hammadi and Manichaean Studies, 44 (Leiden: Brill, 1997), 89–101.

MacRae, George W., 'The Meaning and Evolution of the Feast of Tabernacles', *CBQ* 22 (1960), 251–76.

Maertens, Thierry, *A Feast in Honor of Yahweh*, trans. Kathryn Sullivan (Notre Dame, IN: Fides Publishers, 1965).

Manns, Frédéric, *L'Evangile de Jean à la lumière du Judaisme*, Studium Biblicum Franciscanum Analecta 33 (Jerusalem: Franciscan Printing Press, 1991).

Marcus, Joel, *The Way of the Lord: Christological Exegesis of the Old Testament in the Gospel of Mark* (London: T & T Clark, 1992).

Marcus, Joel and Marion L. Soards, eds, *Apocalyptic and the New Testament*, JSNTSup 24 (Sheffield: Sheffield Academic Press, 1989).

Marion, Jean-Luc, 'They Recognized Him And He Became Invisible To Them', *Modern Theology* 18.2 (2002), 145–52.

Martyn, J. Louis, *The Gospel of John in Christian History: Essays for Interpreters* (New York: Paulist Press, 1979).

Martyn, J. Louis, *Galatians: A New Translation with Introduction and Commentary*, The Anchor Bible, 33A (New York: Doubleday, 1997).

Martyn, J. Louis, *Theological Issues in the Letters of Paul*, Studies of the New Testament and its World (Edinburgh: T & T Clark, 1997).

Martyn, J. Louis, *History and Theology in the Fourth Gospel*, The New Testament Library, 3rd edn (Louisville: Westminster John Knox, 2003 [1968]).

Martyn, J. Louis, 'Apocalyptic Antinomies', in Martyn, *Theological Issues*, 111–23.

Martyn, J. Louis, 'Christ and the Elements of the Cosmos', in Martyn, *Theological Issues*, 125–40.

Martyn, J. Louis, 'Epistemology at the Turn of the Ages', in Martyn, *Theological Issues*, 89–110.

Martyn, J. Louis, 'John and Paul on the Subject of Gospel and Scripture', in Martyn, *Theological Issues*, 209–30.

Marxsen, Willi, *Mark the Evangelist: Studies on the Redaction History of the Gospel* (Nashville: Abingdon Press, 1969).

Mason, Steve, 'Jews, Judaeans, Judaizing, Judaism: Problems of Categorization in Ancient History', *JSJ* 38 (2007), 457–512.

McCabe, Herbert, 'The Involvement of God', in McCabe, *God Matters* (London: Continuum, 2012), 39–51 (originally appeared in *New Blackfriars*, November 1985).

McGinn, Bernard, 'Turning Points in Early Christian Apocalypse Exegesis', in Robert J. Daly, ed., *Apocalyptic Thought in Early Christianity*, 81–105.

McHugh, John F., *John 1—4: A Critical and Exegetical Commentary*, International Critical Commentary (London: Bloomsbury, 2014).

Meeks, Wayne, 'Galilee and Judea in the Fourth Gospel', *JBL* 85 (1966), 159–69.

Meeks, Wayne, *The Prophet-King: Moses Traditions and Johannine Christology*, SupNovT 14 (Leiden: Brill, 1967).

Meeks, Wayne, 'The Man from Heaven in Johannine Sectarianism', *JBL* 91 (1972), 44–72; repr. in John Ashton, ed., *The Interpretation of John*, 169–205.

Menken, Maarten J. J., *Numerical Literary Techniques in John: The Fourth Evangelist's Use of Numbers of Words and Syllables*, SupNovT 55 (Leiden: Brill, 1985).

Menken, Maarten J. J., *Old Testament Quotations in the Fourth Gospel: Studies in Textual Form* (Kampen: Kok Pharos, 1996).

Menken, Maarten J. J., *Studies in John's Gospel and Epistles: Collected Essays*, Contributions to Biblical Exegesis and Theology, 77 (Leuven, Peeters, 2015).

Menken, Maarten J. J., 'Genesis in John's Gospel', in Menken, *Studies in John's Gospel*, 131–45.

Menken, Maarten J. J., 'Jewish Feasts in the Gospel of John', in Menken, *Studies in John's Gospel*, 187–207.

Menken, Maarten J. J., 'John 51c–58: Eucharist or Christology?', in Culpepper, ed., *Critical Readings*, 183–204.

Menken, Maarten J. J., 'Observations on the Significance of the Old Testament in the Fourth Gospel', in Gilbert van Belle et al., eds, *Theology and Christology in the Fourth Gospel*, 155–75.

Menken, Maarten J. J., 'What Authority does the Fourth Evangelist Claim for his Book?', in Jan Krans et al., ed., *John, Paul, and Apocalyptic Eschatology*, 186–202.

Metzger, Bruce M., *A Textual Commentary on the Greek New Testament*, 2nd edn (Peabody, MA: Hendrickson, 2005).

Meyendorff, John, *Christ in Eastern Christian Thought* (Crestwood, NY: St Vladimir's Seminary Press, 1975).

Meyer, Marvin, 'Whom Did Jesus Love Most? Beloved Disciples in John and Other Gospels', in Tuomas Rasimus, ed., *The Legacy of John*, 73–91.

Michaelis, Wilhelm, '*σκηνή*', in *TDNT* 7.368–94.

Miller, E. L., *Salvation History in the Prologue of John: The Significance of John 1:3/4*, SupNovT 60 (Leiden: Brill, 1989).

Miller, Ed. L., 'The Johannine Origins of the Johannine Logos', *JBL* 112.3 (1993), 445–57.

Minear, Paul S., *John: The Martyr's Gospel* (Eugene, OR: Wipf and Stock, 1984).

Mitchell, Margaret M., *Paul, the Corinthians, and the Birth of Christian Hermeneutics* (Cambridge: Cambridge University Press, 2010).

Moberly, Robert B., 'When was Revelation Conceived?', *Biblica* 73:1 (1992), 376–93.

Moloney, Francis. J. *The Johannine Son of Man*, Biblioteca di Scienze Religiose, 14, 2nd edn (Rome: Libreria Ateneo Salesiano, 1976).

Moloney, Francis. J. *The Gospel of John*, Sacra Pagina Series, 4 (Collegeville MN: Liturgical Press, 1998).

Moloney, Francis. J. 'The Function of Prolepsis in the Interpretation of John 6', in G. Culpepper ed., *Critical Readings of John 6*, 129–48.

Moloney, Francis. J. 'The Johannine Son of Man Revisited', in Gilert van Belle et al., eds, *Theology and Christology in the Fourth Gospel*, 177–202.

Moody Smith, D., *The Theology of the Gospel of John*, New Testament Theology (Cambridge: Cambridge University Press, 1995).

Morgan-Wynne, John, *The Cross in the Johannine Writings* (Eugene, OR: Pickwick Publications, 2011).

Mosshammer, Alden A., *The Easter Computus and the Origins of the Christian Era*, OECS (Oxford: Oxford University Press, 2008).

Müller, U. B., 'Die Bedeutung des Kreuzestodes Jesu im Johannesevangelium: Erwägung der Kreuzestheologie im NT', *Kerygma und Dogma* 21 (1975), 31–78.

Mussner, Franz, *ΖΩΗ: Die Anschauung vom 'Leben' im vierten Evangelium unter Berücksichtigung des Johannesbrief* (Munich: Zink, 1952).

Mussner, Franz, *The Historical Jesus in the Gospel of St John* (London: Burns and Oats, 1967).

Mutschler, Bernard, *Irenäus als johanneischer Theologe: Studien zur Schriftauslegung bei Irenäus von Lyon*, Studien und Texte zu Antike und Christentum 21 (Tübingen: Mohr Siebeck, 2004).

Mutschler, Bernard, 'Was weiß Irenäus vom Johannesevangelium? Der historische Kontext des Johannesevangeliums aus der Perspektive seiner Rezeption bei Irenäus von Lyon', in J. Frey and U. Schnelle, eds, *Das vierte Evangelium in religions- und traditionsgeschichtlicher Perspektive*, WUNT 175 (Tübingen: Mohr Siebeck, 2004), 695–742.

Mutschler, Bernard, 'John and His Gospel in the Mirror of Irenaeus of Lyons: Perspectives of Recent Research', in Tuomas Rasimus, ed., *Legacy of John*, 319–43.

Nagel, Titus, *Die Rezeption des Johannesevangeliums im 2. Jahrhundert: Studien zur vorirenäischen Aneignung und Auslegung des vierten Evangeliums in christlicher und christlicher-gnostischer Literatur*, Arbeiten zur Bibel und ihrer Geschichte, 2 (Leipzig: Evangelische Verlagsanstalt, 2000).

Neusner, Jacob, 'Money-Changers in the Temple: The Mishnah's Explanation', *NTS* 35.2 (1989), 287–90.

Newman, Carey C., *Paul's Glory-Christology: Tradition and Rhetoric*, SupNovT 69 (Leiden: Brill, 1992).

Newsom, Carol, *Songs of the Sabbath Sacrifice: A Critical Edition*, HSS (Atlanta, GA: Scholars Press, 1985).

Newsom, Carol, *The Self as Symbolic Space: Constructing Identity and Community at Qumran*, Studies on the Texts of the Desert of Judah 52 (Leiden: Brill, 2004).

Neyrey, Jerome H., 'Jacob Traditions and the Interpretation of John 4:10–26', *CBQ* 41 (1979), 419–37.

Neyrey, Jerome H., 'The Jacob Allusions in John 1:51', *CBQ* 44 (1982), 586–605.

Neyrey, Jerome H., *The Gospel of John*, The New Cambridge Bible Commentary (Cambridge: Cambridge University Press, 2007).

Nicholson, Godfrey C., *Death as Departure: The Johannine Descent-Ascent Schema*, SBLDS 63 (Chico, CA: Scholars Press, 1983).

O'Day, Gail M., *Revelation in the Fourth Gospel* (Philadelphia: Fortress Press, 1986).

O'Grady, John F., 'The Prologue and Chapter 17 of the Gospel of John', in Tom Thatcher, ed., *What We Have Heard from the Beginning*, 215–28.

O'Neill, J. C., 'Son of Man, Stone of Blood (John 1:51)', *NovT* 45.4 (2003), 374–81.

O'Sullivan, Michael, *Michel Henry: Incarnation, Barbarism and Belief: An Introduction to the Work of Michel Henry* (Bern: Peter Lang, 2006).

Odeberg, Hugo, *The Fourth Gospel: Interpreted in its Relation to Contemporaneous Religious Currents in Palestine and the Hellenistic-Oriental World* (Uppsala: Almquist & Wiksell, 1929).

Olsson, Birger, *Structure and Meaning in the Fourth Gospel: A Text-Linguistic Analysis of John 2:1–11 and 4:1–42*, Coniectanea Biblica, New Testament Studies 6 (Lund: Gleerup, 1974).

Owen, Paul, and David Shepherd, 'Speaking Up for Qumran, Dalman, and the Son of Man: Was *Bar Enasha* a Common Term for "Man" in the Time of Jesus?', *JSNT* 81 (2001), 81–122.

Pagels, Elaine, 'Exegesis of Genesis 1 in the Gospels of Thomas and John', *JBL* 118.3 (1999), 477–96.

Paget, James Carleton, *The Epistle of Barnabas: Outlook and Background* (Tübingen: Mohr, 1994).

Painter, John, 'The Death of Jesus in John: A Discussion of the Tradition, History, and Theology of John', in Gilbert van Belle, ed., *The Death of Jesus in the Fourth Gospel*, 327–61.

Painter, John, 'The Prologue as an Hermeneutical Key to Reading the Fourth Gospel', in Joseph Verheyden et al., eds, *Studies in the Gospel of John and its Christology*, 37–60.

Pamment, Margaret, 'The Meaning of *Doxa* in the Fourth Gospel', *ZNW* 74 (1983), 12–16.

Pamment, Margaret, 'The Son of Man in the Fourth Gospel', *JTS* ns 36.1 (1985), 56–66.

Panackel, Charles, *ΙΔΟΥ Ο ΑΝΘΡΩΠΟΣ (Jn 19, 35): An Exegetico-Theological Study of the Text in the Light of the Use of the Term ΑΝΘΡΩΠΟΣ Designating Jesus in the Fourth Gospel*, Analecta Gregoriana 251 (Rome: Pontifica Università Gregoriana, 1988).

Pancaro, Severino, *The Law in the Fourth Gospel: The Torah and the Gospel, Moses and Jesus, Judaism and Christianity, according to John*, SupNovT 42 (Leiden: Brill, 1975).

Parsenios, George, '"No Longer in the World" (John 17:11): The Transformation of the Tragic in the Fourth Gospel', *HTR* 98.1 (2005), 1–21.

Parsenios, George, *Rhetoric and Drama in the Johannine Lawsuit Motif*, WUNT 258 (Tübingen: Mohr Siebeck, 2010).

Parsenios, George, 'A Sententious Silence: First Thoughts on the Fourth Gospel and the *Ardens* Style', in Susan E. Myers, ed., *Portraits of Jesus: Studies in Christology* (Tübingen: Mohr Siebeck, 2012), 13–26.

Patrick, James, *Andrew of Bethsaida and the Johannine Circle: The Muratorian Tradition and the Gospel Text*, Studies in Biblical Literature, 152 (New York: Peter Lang, 2013).

Patten, P., 'The Form and Function of Parable in Select Apocalyptic Literature and their Significance for Parables in the Gospel of Mark', *NTS* 29 (1983), 246–58.

Peppard, Michael, *The Son of God in the Roman World: Divine Sonship and its Social and Political Context* (New York: Oxford University Press, 2011).

Peppard, Michael, 'Adopted and Begotten Sons of God: Paul and John on Divine Sonship', *CBQ* 73 (2011), 92–110.

Petersen, W. L., 'Eusebius and the Paschal Controversy', in Harold W. Attridge and Gohei Hata, eds, *Eusebius, Christianity and Judaism* (Leiden: Brill, 1992), 311–25.

Pétrement, Simone, *A Separate God: The Christian Origins of Gnosticism*, trans. C. Harrison (New York: HarperCollins, 1990).

Petterson, Christina, *From Tomb to Text: The Body of Jesus in the Book of John* (London: Bloomsbury T & T Clark, 2017).

Phillips, Peter M., *The Prologue of the Fourth Gospel: A Sequential Reading*, LNTS 294 (London: T & T Clark, 2006).

Pierce, Madison N., and Benjamin E. Reynolds, 'The Perfect Tense-Form and the Son of Man in John 3:13: Developments in Greek Grammar as a Viable Solution to the Timing of the Ascent and Descent', *NTS* 60 (2014), 149–55.

Piper, Otto A., 'The Apocalypse of John and the Liturgy of the Ancient Church', *CH* 20.1 (1951), 10–22.

Poirier, Paul-Hubert, 'The Trimorphic Protennoia (NHC XIII,1) and the Johannine Prologue: A Reconsideration', in Tuomas Rasimus, ed., *The Legacy of John*, 93–103.

Pollard, T. Evan, 'Cosmology and the Prologue of the Fourth Gospel', *VC* 12 (1958), 147–53.

Porter, Stanley E., *Idioms of the Greek New Testament*, 2nd edn (Sheffield: Sheffield Academic Press, 1995).
Porter, Stanley E., *John, His Gospel, and Jesus: In Pursuit of the Johannine Voice* (Grand Rapids, MI: Eerdmans, 2015).
Porter, Stanley E., and Hughson T. Ong, eds, *The Origins of John's Gospel*, Johannine Studies 2 (Leiden: Brill, 2016).
Porter, Stanley E., 'The Date of John's Gospel and its Origins', in Stanley Porter and Hughson Ong, eds, *The Origins of John's Gospel*, 11–29.
Potterie, Ignace de la, 'Jesus King and Judge According to John 19:13', *Scripture (The Quarterly of the Catholic Biblical Association)*, 13 (1961), 97–111.
Potterie, Ignace de la, 'L'emploi dynamic de εἰς dans saint Jean et ses incidences théologiques', *Biblica* 43 (1962), 366–87.
Potterie, Ignace de la, *La Verité dans Saint Jean*, Analecta Biblica 73, 2 vols (Rome: Biblical Institute, 1977).
Potterie, Ignace de la, 'La tunique sans couture, symbole du Christ grand prêtre?', *Biblica* 60.2 (1979), 255–69.
Potterie, Ignace de la, *The Hour of Jesus: The Passion and Resurrection of Jesus According to John* (New York: Alba House, 1989).
Pryor, John W., 'The Johannine Son of Man and the Descent-Ascent Motif', *JETS* 34.3 (1991), 341–51.
Pula, Melissa P., 'Rethinking the Community as Temple: Discourse and Spatial Practices in the *Community Rule* (1QS)', PhD dissertation (University of Denver, 2015).
Rae, Murray, 'The Testimony of Works in the Christology of John's Gospel', in Richard Bauckham and Carl Mosser, eds, *The Gospel of John and Christian Theology*, 295–310.
Rahner, Karl, 'The Theology of the Incarnation', in Rahner, *Theological Investigations* vol. 4, *More Recent Writings* (London: DLT, 1966), 105–20. Original in Rahner, *Schriften zur Theologie*, vol. 4, *Neuere Schriften* (Zürich: Benziger, 1960), 137–55.
Rahner, Karl, *The Trinity* (Tunbridge Wells, UK: Burns and Oates, 1970 [German edn 1967]).
Rainbow, Paul A., *Johannine Theology: The Gospel, The Epistles, and The Apocalypse* (Downers Grove, IL: IVP Academic, 2014).
Räisänen, H., *The 'Messianic Secret' in Mark's Gospel*, trans. C. Tuckett (Edinburgh, T & T Clark, 1990).
Raith II, Chad, ed., *The Gospel of John: Theological-Ecumenical Readings* (Eugene, OR: Cascade, 2017).
Ramelli, Ilaria, and David Konstan, *Terms for Eternity: Aiônios and Aïdios in Classical and Christian Texts* (Piscataway, NJ: Gorgias Press, 2011).
Rand, Jan A. du, 'The Creation Motif in the Fourth Gospel: Perspectives on its Narratological Function within a Judaistic Background', in Gilbert van Belle et al., eds, *Theology and Christology in the Fourth Gospel*, 21–46.
Rasimus, Tuomas, *The Legacy of John: Second-Century Reception of the Fourth Gospel*, SupNovT 132 (Leiden: Brill, 2010).
Rasimus, Tuomas, 'Ptolemaeus and the Valentian Exegesis of John's Prologue', in Rasimus, ed., *The Legacy of John*, 145–71.

Reinhartz, Adele, *The Word in the World: The Cosmological Tale in the Fourth Gospel*, SBLMS 45 (Atlanta, GA: Scholars Press, 1992).

Reynolds, Benjamin E., *The Apocalyptic Son of Man in the Gospel of John*, WUNT 2.249 (Tübingen: Mohr Siebeck, 2008).

Reynolds, Benjamin E., 'John and the Jewish Apocalypses: Rethinking the Genre of John's Gospel', in Catrin H. Williams and Christopher Rowland, eds, *John's Gospel and Intimations of Apocalyptic*, 36–57.

Richard, Marcel and Bertrand Hemmerdinger, 'Trois nouveaux fragments grecs de l'*Adversus haereses de saint Irénée*', *ZNW* 53 (1962), 252–5.

Richardson, Alan, *The Gospel According to St John: Introduction and Commentary* (London: SCM 1959).

Richter, Georg, *Studien zum Johannesevangelium*, ed. Joseph Hainz (Regensburg: Pustet, 1977).

Ricœur, Paul, *Essays on Biblical Interpretation* (Philadelphia: Fortress Press, 1980).

Riesenfeld, Harald, 'The Sabbath and the Lord's Day in Judaism, the Preaching of Jesus and Early Christianity', in Riesenfeld, *The Gospel Tradition* (Oxford: Blackwell, 1970), 111–37.

Rigato, Maria-Luisa, 'L' "apostolo ed evangelista Giovanni", "sacerdoto" levitico', *RevistB* 38 (1990), 451–83.

Rigby, B. H., 'The Cross as an Expiatory Sacrifice in the Fourth Gospel', *JSNT* 15 (1982), 51–80.

Rivera, Joseph, *The Contemplative Self after Michel Henry: A Phenomenological Theology*, Thresholds in Philosophy and Theology (Notre Dame, IN: University of Notre Dame Press, 2015).

Roberts, C. H., J. W. B. Barns, and H. Zilliacus, *The Antinoopolis Papyri* (London, 1950–67).

Robinson, James M., 'Gnosticism and the New Testament', in B. Aland, ed., *Gnosis: Festschrift für Hans Jonas, in Verbindung mit U. Bianchi* et al. (Göttingen, 1978), 125–42.

Robinson, James M., 'Logoi Sophon: On the Gattung of Mark (and John)', in Robinson, *The Future of our Religious Past: Essays in Honour of Rudolf Bultmann* (London: SCM, 1971), 84–130.

Robinson, John A. T., 'The Relation of the Prologue to the Gospel of St John', *NTS* 9.2 (1963), 120–9.

Robinson, John A. T., *Redating the New Testament* (Philadelphia: Westminster Press, 1976).

Robinson, John A. T., *The Priority of John*, ed. J. F. Coakley (London: SCM, 1985).

Rojas-Flores, Gonzalo, 'The *Book of Revelation* and the First Years of Nero's Reign', *Biblica* 85 (2004), 375–92.

Romanowsky, John W., '"When the Son of Man is Lifted Up": The Redemptive Power of the Crucifixion in the Gospel of John', *Horizons* 32.1 (2005), 100–16.

Rouwhorst, Gerard, 'The Quartodeciman Passover and the Jewish Pesach', *Questions Liturgiques*, 77 (1996), 152–73.

Rowland, Christopher, *The Open Heaven: A Study of Apocalyptic in Judaism and Early Christianity* (London, 1982).

Rowland, Christopher, '"Intimations of Apocalyptic": The Perspective of the History of Interpretation', in Catrin H. Williams and Christopher Rowland, eds, *John's Gospel and Intimations of Apocalyptic*, 128–43.

Rowland, Christopher, and Christopher R. A. Morray-Jones, *The Mystery of God: Early Jewish Mysticism and the New Testament*, CRINT 12 (Leiden, Brill 2009).

Rubenstein, Jeffrey L., 'Sukkot, Eschatology, and Zechariah 14', *RB* 103.2 (1996), 161–95.

Russell, D. S., *The Method and Message of Jewish Apocalyptic: 200 BC–AD 100* (Philadelphia: Westminster Press, 1964).

Russell, D. S., *Divine Disclosure: An Introduction to Jewish Apocalyptic* (Minneapolis: Fortress Press, 1992).

Sanday, William, *The Criticism of the Fourth Gospel* (Oxford: Clarendon Press, 1916).

Sanders, E. P., *Paul and Palestinian Judaism: A Comparison of Patterns of Religion* (Philadelphia: Fortress Press, 1977).

Schnackenburg, Rudolf, *The Gospel according to St. John*; vol. 1 ET Kevin Smyth (London: Burns and Oats, 1968), vol. 2 ET Cecily Hastings et al. (London: Burns and Oats, 1980), vol. 3 ET D. Smith and G. A. Korn (New York: Crossroad, 1982).

Schnelle, Udo, *Antidocetic Christology in the Gospel of John: An Investigation of the Place of the Fourth Gospel in the Johannine School*, trans. Linda M. Maloney (Minneapolis: Fortress, 1992).

Schoedel, William, *The Apostolic Fathers*, vol. 5, *Polycarp, Martyrdom of Polycarp, Fragments of Papias* (New York: Nelson, 1967).

Schoedel, William R., *Ignatius of Antioch: A Commentary on the Letters of Ignatius of Antioch*, Hermeneia (Philadelphia: Fortress Press, 1985).

Schwartz, Eduard, 'Aporien in vierten Evangelium', *Nachrichten von der königlichen Gesellschaft der Wissenschaft zu Göttingen: Philologisch-historische Klasse* (1907), 342–72; (1908), 115–88, 497–650.

Segal, Alan F., *Two Powers in Heaven: Early Rabbinic Reports about Christianity and Gnosticism* (Leiden, 1977).

Segal, Alan F., *Paul the Convert: The Apostolate and Apostasy of Saul the Pharisee* (New Haven: Yale University Press, 1990).

Segal, J. B. *The Hebrew Passover: From the Earliest Times to A.D. 70*, London Oriental Series, 13 (London: Oxford University Press, 1963).

Senior, Donald, *The Passion of Jesus in the Gospel of John* (Collegeville, MN: Liturgical Press, 1991).

Shults, F. LeRon, 'A Dubious Christological Formula: From Leontius of Byzantium to Karl Barth', *Theological Studies* 57 (1996), 431–46.

Siegert, F., 'Unbeachtete Papiaszitate bei armenischen Schriftstellern', *NTS* 27 (1981), 605–14.

Skinner, Quentin, 'Meaning and Understanding in the History of Ideas', *History and Theory* 8 (1969), 3–53; reprinted in a much abbreviated and extensively revised version in Quentin Skinner, *Visions of Politics*, vol. 1, *Regarding Method* (Cambridge: Cambridge University Press, 2002), 57–89.

Skinner, Quentin, 'A Reply to My Critics', in James Tully, ed., *Meaning and Context: Quentin Skinner and His Critics* (Cambridge: Cambridge University Press, 1988), 231–88.

Slater, Thomas B., 'Dating the Apocalypse to John', *Biblica* 84 (2003), 252–8.

Smit, Peter-Ben, 'The Gift of the Spirit in John 19:30? A Reconsideration of *παρέδωκεν τὸ πνεῦμα*', *CBQ* 78.3 (2016), 447–62.

Smith, Jonathan Z., 'The Prayer of Joseph', in Jacob Neusner, ed., *Religions in Antiquity: Essays in Memory of Erwin Ramsdell Goodenough* (Leiden: Brill, 1968), 253–84; reprinted in Jonathan Z. Smith, *Map is not Territory*, 24–66.

Smith, Jonathan Z., 'Good News is No News: Aretalogy and Gospel', in Jacob Neusner, ed., *Christianity, Judaism and Other Greco-Roman Cults: Studies for Morton Smith at Sixty* (Leiden: Brill, 1975), Part One, New Testament, 67–90; reprinted in Jonathan Z. Smith *Map is Not Territory*, 190–207.

Smith, Jonathan Z., *Map is Not Territory: Studies in the History of Religions* (Chicago: University of Chicago Press, 1978).

Solovyov, Vladimir, *Lectures on Divine Humanity*; ET Boris Jakim (Hudson, NY: Lindisfarne Press, 1995 [1878–81]).

Sosa Siliezar, Carlos Raúl, *Creation Imagery in the Gospel of John*, LNTS 546 (London: Bloomsbury, 2015).

Souletie, Jean-Louis, 'Incarnation et théologie', in Philippe Capelle and Michel Henry, eds, *Phénoménologie et christianisme*, 135–94.

Spinks, Bryan D., *The Sanctus in the Eucharistic Prayer* (Cambridge: Cambridge University Press, 1991).

Sproston North, Wendy E., '"Is Not This Jesus, the Son of Joseph . . . ?" (John 6.42): Johannine Christology as a Challenge to Faith', *JSNT* 24 (1985), 77–97.

Sproston North, Wendy E., 'John for Readers of Mark? A Response to Richard Bauckham's Proposal', *JSNT* 25.4 (2003), 449–68.

Staley, Jeff, 'The Structure of John's Prologue: Its Implications for the Gospel's Narrative Structure', *CBQ* 48 (1986), 241–64.

Stang, Charles, *Our Divine Double* (Cambridge, MA: Harvard University Press, 2016).

Steegen, Martijn, 'To Worship the Johannine "Son of Man": John 9:38 as Refocusing on the Father', *Biblica* 91 (2010), 534–54.

Steegen, Martijn, 'Finding the "True Place" of God: Comments on the Temple Scene in the Gospel of John', in Joseph Verheyden et al., eds, *Studies in the Gospel of John and its Christology*, 71–87.

Steinbock, Anthony J., 'The Problem of Forgetfulness in Michel Henry', *Continental Philosophy Review*, 32 (1999), 271–302.

Stendahl, Krister, 'The Apocalypse of John and the Epistles of Paul in the Muratorian Fragment', in William Klassen and Graydon F. Snyder, eds, *Current Issues in New Testament Interpretation* (New York: Harper, 1962), 239–45.

Stewart-Sykes, Alistair, 'The Asian Context of the New Prophecy and of *Epistula Apostolorum*', *VC* 51 (1997), 416–38.

Stewart-Sykes, Alistair, *The Lamb's High Feast: Melito, Peri Pascha, and the Quarto-deciman Paschal Liturgy at Sardis*, SupVC 42 (Leiden: Brill, 1998).

Stewart, Alistair, *Original Bishops: Office and Order in the First Christian Communities* (Grand Rapids, MI: Baker Academic, 2014).

Stibbe, Mark W. G., *John as Storyteller: Narrative Criticism and the Fourth Gospel*, Society for New Testament Studies, Monograph Series, 73 (Cambridge: Cambridge University Press, 1992).

Stone, Michael E., 'Lists of Revealed Things in Apocalyptic Literature', in Frank M. Cross, Werner E. Lemke, and Patrick D. Miller Jr, eds, *Magnalia Dei: The Mighty Acts of God: Essays on the Bible and Archaeology in Memory of G. Ernest Wright* (Garden City, NY: Doubleday, 1976), 414–52.

Strange, James F., 'Nazareth', in David Noel Freedman, ed., *Anchor Bible Dictionary*, 4.1050–1.

Studer, Basil, *Trinity and Incarnation: The Faith of the Early Church*, trans. Matthias Westerhoff, ed. Andrew Louth (Collegeville MN: Liturgical Press, 1993).

Sumner, Paul B. 'Visions of the Divine Council in the Hebrew Bible', PhD dissertation (Malibu, CA: Pepperdine University, 1991).

Sundberg, A. C., 'Towards a Revised History of the New Testament Canon', *Studia Evangelica*, 4.1 (1968), 42–61.

Sundberg, A. C., 'Canon Muratori: A Fourth-Century List', *HTR* 66 (1973), 1–41.

Suter, David Winston, 'Masal in the Similitudes of Enoch', *JBL* 100.2 (1981), 193–212.

Swete, Henry Barclay, *The Apocalypse of St John: The Greek Text with Introduction, Notes, and Indices* (London: Macmillan, 1906).

Tabory, Joseph, 'Towards a History of the Paschal Meal', in Bradshaw and Hoffman, eds, *Passover and Easter*, 62–80.

Taft, Robert, 'Mass without Consecration? The Historic Agreement on the Eucharist between the Catholic Church and the Assyrian Church of the East Promulgated 26 October 2001', *Worship* 77 (2003), 482–509.

Talbert, Charles H., 'The Myth of a Descending-Ascending Redeemer in Mediterranean Antiquity', *NTS* 22.4 (1976), 418–40.

Talmon, S., 'The Emergence of Jewish Sectarianism in the Early Second Temple Period', in P. D. Miller et al., eds, *Ancient Israelite Religion: Essays in Honor of Frank Moore Cross* (Philadelphia: Fortress, 1987), 587–616.

Tam, Josaphat C., *Apprehension of Jesus in the Gospel of John*, WUNT 2.399 (Tübingen: Mohr Siebeck, 2015).

Thatcher, Tom, ed., *What We have Heard from the Beginning: The Past, Present, and Future of Johannine Studies* (Waco, TX: Baylor University Press, 2007).

Thatcher, Tom, 'The Riddle of John the Baptist and the Genesis of the Prologue: John 1.1–18 in Oral/Aural Media Culture', in A. Le Donne and Tom Thatcher, eds, *The Fourth Gospel in the First-Century Media Culture*, LNTS 426 (London: T & T Clark, 2011), 29–48.

Theobald, Michael, *Die Fleischwerdung des Logos: Studien zum Verhältnis des Johannesprolog zum Corpus des Evangeliums und zu 1 Joh*, Neutestamentliche Abhandlungen, NF 20 (Münster: Aschendorff, 1988).

Theron, Daniel J., *Evidence of Tradition: Selected Source Material for the Study of the History of the Early Church, the New Testament Books, the New Testament Canon* (Grand Rapids, MI: Baker Books, 1958).

Thomas, J. C., *Footwashing in John 13 and the Johannine Community*, JSNTSup 61 (Sheffield: Sheffield Academic Press, 1991).

Thomassen, Einar, 'Heracleon', in Tuomas Rasimus, ed., *The Legacy of John*, 173–210.

Thompson, Marianne Meye, *The Humanity of Jesus in the Fourth Gospel* (Philadelphia: Fortress, 1988).

Thüsing, Wilhelm, *Die Erhöhung und Verherrlichung Jesu im Johannesevangelium*, 3rd edn (Münster: Aschendorff, 1979 [1960]).

Thyen, Hartwig, '*Ὃ γέγονεν*: Satzende von 1,3 oder Satzeröffnung von 1,4?', in Thyen, *Studien zum Corpus Johanneum*, WUNT 214 (Tübingen: Mohr Siebeck, 2007), 411–17.

Thyen, Hartwig, 'Über die Versuche, eine Vorlage des Johannesprologs zu rekonstruieren', in Thyen, *Studien zum Corpus Johanneum*, 372–410.

Tobin, Thomas H., 'The Prologue of John and Hellenistic Jewish Speculation', *CBQ* 52 (1990), 252–69.

Torjesen, Karen Jo, *Hermeneutical Procedure and Theological Method in Origen's Exegesis*, PTS 28 (Berlin: De Gruyter, 1986).

Tovey, Derek, *Narrative Art and Act in the Fourth Gospel*, JSNTSup 151 (Sheffield: Sheffield University Press, 1977).

Trebilco, Paul, *The Early Christians in Ephesus from Paul to Ignatius* (Grand Rapids: Eerdmans, 2007).

Tuckett, Christopher. ed., *The Messianic Secret* (Philadelphia: Fortress Press, 1983).

Tuckett, Christopher, 'Seeing and Believing in John 20', in Jan Krans, ed., *Paul, John, and Apocalyptic Eschatology*, 169–85.

Turner, Max B., 'Atonement and the Death of Jesus in John—Some Questions to Bultmann and Forestell', *Evangelical Quarterly* 62 (1990), 99–122.

VanderKam, James C., *From Joshua to Caiaphas: High Priests after the Exile* (Minneapolis: Fortress, 2004).

VanderKam, James C., and William Adler, *The Jewish Apocalyptic Heritage in Early Christianity*, CRINT 4 (Assen: Van Gorcum, 1996).

Verheyden, Joseph, Geert van Oyen, Michael Labahin, and Reimund Bieringer, *Studies in the Gospel of John and its Christology: Festschrift Gilbert van Belle*, Biblitheca Ephemeridum Theologicarum Lovaniensium 265 (Leuven: Peeters, 2014).

Vermes, Geza, 'The Use of *Barnash/bar nasha* in Jewish Aramaic', Appendix E in Matthew Black, *Aramaic Approach to the Gospels and Acts*, 3rd edn (Oxford: Clarendon, 1967), 310–28.

Vinzent, Markus, *Christ's Resurrection in Early Christianity and the Making of the New Testament* (Farnham: Ashgate, 2011).

Voorwinde, S. 'John's Prologue: Beyond Some Impasses of Twentieth-Century Scholarship', *WTJ* 63 (2002), 15–44.

Walker, P., *Jesus and the Holy City: New Testament Perspectives on Jerusalem* (Grand Rapids, MI: Eerdmans, 1996).

Walker, William O. 'John 1.43–51 and "The Son of Man" in the Fourth Gospel', *JSNT* 56 (1994), 31–42.

Warren, Meredith J. C., *My Flesh is Meat Indeed: A Nonsacramental Reading of John 6:51–58* (Minneapolis: Fortress Press, 2015).

Watt, Jan G. van der, 'The Composition of the Prologue of John's Gospel: The Historical Jesus Introducing Divine Grace', *WTJ* 57 (1995), 311–32.

Watt, Jan G. van der, and C. Caragounis, 'The Grammar of John 1:1', *Filologia Neotestamentaria*, 21 (2008), 91–138, online at <https://www.bsw.org/filologia-neotestamentaria/vol-21-2008/a-grammatical-analysis-of-john-1-1/525/> (accessed 13 February 2017).

Watt, Jan G. van der, 'John 1:1—A "Riddle"? Grammar and Syntax Considered', in Jan G. van der Watt et al., eds, *The Prologue of the Gospel of John*, 57–78.

Watt, Jan G. van der, R. Alan Culpepper, and Udo Schnelle, *The Prologue of the Gospel of John: It's Literary, Theological, and Philosophical Contexts. Papers Read at the Colloquium Ioanneum 2013*, WUNT 359 (Tübingen: Mohr Siebeck, 2016).

Weder, Hans, '*Deus Incarnatus*: On the Hermeneutics of Christology in the Johannine Writings', in R. Alan Culpepper and C. Clifton Black, eds, *Exploring the Gospel of John*, 325–45.

Weidemann, Hans-Ulrich, *Der Tod Jesu im Johannesevangelium: Die erste Abschiedsrede als Schlüsseltext für den Passions- und Osterbericht*, BZNW 122 (Berlin: de Gruyter, 2004).

Welten, Ruud, 'God is Life. On Michel Henry's Arch-Christianity', in Peter Jonkers and Ruud Welten, eds, *God in France*, 119–42.

Westcott, B. F. *The Gospel According to St John* (London: John Murray, 1882).

Wiles, Maurice, *The Making of Christian Doctrine: A Study in the Principles of Early Doctrinal Development* (Cambridge: Cambridge University Press, 1967).

Wilkens, Wilhelm, *Die Entstehungsgeschichte des vierten Evangeliums* (Zollikon: EVZ, 1958).

Wilkens, Wilhelm, *Zeichen und Werke: Ein Beitrag zur Theologie des vierten Evangeliums in Erzählungs- und Redestoff*, AThANT 55 (ZürichL TVZ, 1969).

Williams, Catrin H., '(Not) Seeing God in the Prologue and the Body of John's Gospel', in Jan G. van der Watt et al., eds, *The Prologue of the Gospel of John*, 79–98.

Williams, Catrin H., 'Unveiling Revelation: The Spirit-Paraclete and Apocalyptic Disclosure in the Gospel of John', in Catrin H. Williams and Christopher Rowland, eds, *John's Gospel and Intimations of Apocalyptic*, 104–27.

Williams, Catrin H., and Christopher Rowland, eds, *John's Gospel and Intimations of Apocalyptic* (London: Bloomsbury, 2013).

Williams, P. J., 'Not the Prologue of John', *JSNT* 33.4 (2011), 375–86.

Williams, Rowan, *Arius: Heresy and Tradition*, 2nd edn (London: SCM Press, 2001 [1987]).

Wills, M., *The Quest of the Historical Gospel: Mark, John, and the Origins of the Gospel Genre* (London: Routledge, 1997).

Wilson, J. Christian, 'The Problem of the Domitianic Dating of Revelation', *NTS* 39 (1993), 587–605.

Wilson, Stephen G., *Related Strangers: Jews and Christians, 70–170 C.E.* (Minneapolis: Fortress Press, 1995).

Wilson, Mark, 'The Early Christians in Ephesus and the Date of Revelation, Again', *Neotestamentica* 39.1 (2005), 163–93.

Wrede, W., *Charakter und Tendenz des Johannesevangelium* (Tübingen, 1903).

Wrede, W., *The Messianic Secret*, trans. J. C. G. Greig (Cambridge and London: James Clarke, 1971 [German 1901]).

Wright, N. T., *The New Testament and the People of God* (Minneapolis: Fortress, 1992).

Wright, N. T., *Paul and His Recent Interpreters* (Minneapolis: Fortress, 2015).

Wright, N. T., 'Apocalyptic and the Sudden Fulfillment of Divine Promise', in Ben C. Blackwell et al., eds, *Paul and the Apocalyptic Imagination*, 111–34.

Yarbro Collins, Adela, 'Introduction: Early Christian Apocalypticism', *Semeia* 36 (1986), 1–11.

Yarbro Collins, Adela, *Cosmology and Eschatology in Jewish and Christian Apocalypticism*, supplements to the Journal for the Study of Judaism, 50 (Leiden: Brill, 1996).

Yarbrough, R. W., 'The Date of Papias: A Reassessment', *JTS* ns 26 (1983), 181–91.

Yee, Gale A., *Jewish Feasts and the Gospel of John* (Wilmington, DE: Michael Glazier, 1989).

Young, Frances M., *Biblical Exegesis and the Formation of Christian Culture* (Cambridge: Cambridge University Press, 1997).

Young, Franklin W., 'A Study of the Relation of Isaiah to the Fourth Gospel', *ZNW* 46 (1955), 215–33.

Young, Robin Darling, *In Procession Before the World: Martyrdom as Public Liturgy in the Early Church*, The Pére Marquette Lecture in Theology 2001 (Milwaukee: Marquette University Press, 2001).

Yuval, Israel J. 'Easter and Passover As Early Jewish-Christian Dialogue', in Paul F. Bradshaw and Lawrence A. Hoffman, eds, *Passover and Easter*, 98–124.

Zelyck, Lorne, 'Irenaeus and the Authorship of the Fourth Gospel', in Stanley Porter and Hughson Ong, eds, *Origins of John's Gospel*, 239–58.

Zumstein, Jean, 'Intratextuality and Intertextuality in the Gospel of John', in Tom Thatcher and Stephen D. Moore, eds, *Anatomies of Narrative Criticism: The Past, Present, and Futures of the Fourth Gospel as Literature* (Atlanta, GA: SBL, 2008), 121–36.

Index of Ancient Sources

Where texts are not divided into books and chapters, reference is given to the page number of the edition cited in the bibliography

I: Scripture

Index of Authors